Within The Portal

*A Near-Death Experience Memoir
and Guide to Spiritual Awakening*

(A Triumph Over Tragedy)

Krishnanand aka Scott A Spackey

WITHIN THE PORTAL

A Near-Death Experience Memoir

and Guide to Spiritual Awakening

Within The Portal cover art yantra (outside-in):

Concept by Krishnanand. Created by Christine Michelle Spackey

◊ **White light radiance**

◊ **12 Lotus petals of the *anahata* heart chakra**

◊ **Ochre ring of protection (Guru)**

◊ **Violet radiance for higher conscience, *sahasrara* chakra**

◊ **Ochre star banishing perimeter**

◊ **Violet hendecagram as saw in vision**

◊ **Ouroboros: "infinity & eternality" image, serpent swallowing its tail**

◊ **Light radiance from Within**

◊ **Center: "bindi", focal point**

Dedications

For my beloved Kripalu

Eternally yours, Krishnanand

And for you . . .

I hope you enjoy this paradox of the human experience. The few that read this entire text will have a catharsis of growth and expansion of mind and spirit. And hopefully a good time too!

I am not the true author of this book. Whilst I am the composer of its words, celestial and spiritual forces are the true architects and engineers of the events. See for yourself . . .

But if some people still find difficulty in understanding this doctrine, it will be due to my deficient knowledge and awkward style, for the doctrine itself is good and necessary. But I am inclined to believe that even if it were presented with greater accuracy and polish, only a few would find profit in it, because we are not writing on pleasing and delightful themes addressed to the kind of spiritual people who like to approach God along sweet and satisfying paths. We are presenting a substantial and solid doctrine for all those who desire to reach this nakedness of spirit.

—St John of the Cross, "Dark Night of the Soul"

Viscera Within the Portal
(Table of Contents)

ACT I: In My Time of Dying

0. Dead and alive   2
1. Dead   6
2. Resurrection   11
3. It Could Be Worse   20
4. Endure   32
5. Props to Props
   (Respect to Supporters)   40
6. Home Again, Home Again   50
7. The Deep End of the Pool
   (Glossary and Reference)   63
8. Dialogue With
   The Other Side   70
9. The Portal   85
10. Die Bandit   93
11. The Wayback Machine   100
12. Happy Accidents   106
13. Happy Pilgrims   127
14. Get to Work On Time   150
15. The Underground Stream   159
16. Déjà vu: Reincarnation 101
17. Astral Travel   183
18. Shappy Anniversary   196
19. Isle of Denial   203
20. Second Home Sanctuary   207
21. Shopping at the
    Akashic Records Store   216
22. Indigo Children
    & Soulmates   227
23. Retreat   238
24. Despedida Ciudad Los Angeles:
    (Farewell City of Angels)   248

ACT II: Exile to the Garden

00. Alive and Dead   263
25. Guardian Angel   266
26. Chow Chow Bang   289
27. Sanitarium   301
28. Puget Sound Purgatory   319
29. First and Lasts   328
30. NDE Goes International   339
31. Agony in the Garden   349

ACT III: Almost Home

000. Out Of Exile   363
32. Yogmaya   365
33. To Live and Die in LA   372
34. Karma and Kundalini
35. Life's a Beach   404
36. Bhakti Shakti Pat
    & Disposable Items   421
37. Outgoing Calls   434
38. Game Changer   442

ACT IV: Anand (Bliss)

39. Videshi in Kripalu's Court   454
40. String of Pearls,
    Crown of Thorns   475
41. Out of Retirement   485
42. Curse of the Kitty   492
43. Texodus   504
44. Blissed Out: Sadhana Purge   513
45. Not Living on Bread Alone   528
46. Full Circle   539
47. PROPHECY   550

ACT I

In My Time of Dying

0.

DEAD AND ALIVE

Only when you drink from the river of silence shall you indeed sing.
And when you have reached the mountain top, then you shall begin to climb.
—Khalil Gibran

O death, where is your victory? O death, where is your sting?
—Corinthians 15:55

Well, well, well . . . So, I can die easy.
—Led Zeppelin and Blind Willie Johnson ("In My Time of Dying")

Even dead, *I am alive.*

A thunderous hum surrounds me.

It is an atmosphere. Comforting and soothing because it is familiar within this strange and unknown dimension. I do not know within which cell, atom, or nuclei of my body or brain the hum resides—or how, when, or where I know of it, but its familiarity reminds me that I am AWARE.

I am alive. I live. I exist.

Even dead . . . *I am alive.*

I am primordial. I am soul.

The hum, the harmony of the spheres, is comforting, like a sweet, omnipresent flute.

There is no "where," no "place," no "when," no "I."

I've no identity, *only awareness*. I exist within a mesh of celestial awareness, stretched across a fabric of empty space.

The thunderous hum surrounding me causes emotions. It drifts closer through this primordial, celestial space . . .

A presence is with me; *I am not alone.*

She is ochre, a smoldering orange, deep and rich in texture. She is gentle, smart, soothing, caring. It is wisdom. It is love. It is my origin. My source. My protection. *She is Divinity.*

My soul has left my body.

My body lies on pavement, swathed in motor oil and body oil—hot motor oil pours over me and crimson body oil flows from my nostrils, mouth, ears, and eyes. A pastor recites the last rites as I lie dead in the street. "*May the Lord in his love and mercy help you with the grace of the Holy Spirit. May the Lord who frees you from sin save you and raise you up.*"

But who is he praying over? I am not there: *the spirit has left the body*. It teleported upon impact; journeying in an instant to *the other side*. The three elements of my being have been separated:

- My physical body of flesh and bones lies on the pavement of an accident scene.
- My energy body made of wheels of light remains and hovers above.
- My causal body and consciousness are in another dimension altogether.

At the moment of impact, my spirit catapults through light years and constellations, landing softly in a dark that is not dark, in a place that has no place, in light that is not light. No time, location, or identity. In the darkness of light, in the light of darkness, there is peace, comfort, and sublimity.

The spiritual presence of ochre-saffron assures me all is well.

> *I have no doubt.*

> *All I feel is well. Peace. Comfort.*

***

She was love, knowledge, wisdom, and safety. There was no concern. I was content. I had no needs, no wants. Her presence *was* peace and contentment.

I knew I was dead, *but I was not afraid.* I asked the saffron presence, "Will I return as I was? Where are the angels? The loved ones who passed on before me? I do not feel alone, yet I am alone."

She guided me, *"You shall return. Rest. You will need the rest for what you will endure upon return. I will always be with you. Even when you do not believe or are aware of me, I will always be with you. As I've always been, I always will be. I am yours. You are mine."*

I had no doubt.

She is *eternal. We have* been together always.

Death was not scary. It was not worrisome. It was not blissful nor joyful. It was . . . *temporary.*

A silly delay, like a road detour on your way home. Nothing to get worked up about. Within The Portal that lay between death and life, I had no need for a body or possessions.

My mind was clear. My spirit was intact. I was in clear contact with my essence, *my soul.* No body, ego, or desires existed between us; *my mind was aligned with my soul.*

Not confined by space or time, I was able to know and be aware—without witnessing or being told—that the body known as Scott was being resuscitated by paramedics in an intersection.

"I'm not ready. Can I remain here awhile?"

"Your soul is the life force that animates your body. Without it, your body cannot live. Your soul must be returned to your body; your time of death has not come."

It was arranged that my soul would be rejoined with my physical body to sustain it. Much of my spirit and my mind would remain . . . *here.*

I had no need to understand nor to plan or review. It was all known—like an instant download—within my mind: The meaning of life, the meaning of death, perfect clarity of the human condition. Who I truly am (a Divine soul), who I have been (infinite lives and incarnations), and who I could become (pure Divine consciousness).

The cosmic upload revealed the body of flesh is disposable; it is merely dense matter. Beneath it is the energy body providing a base for form; it is subtle matter. Beyond both is my *causal* body: all my thoughts, knowledge, perceptions, emotions, destinies, and karmas from many lifetimes are stored within a causal frame; it is consciousness. All of them are made of worldly matter, some ethereal, formless, and subtle, some dense and physical. Underlying all of them is my true essence: *my soul*. It is ever-pure and never-changing, perfect and divine.

I understood that only my soul is Divine. The rest of me is ordinary. Identity and body are ephemeral, ever-changing, and of dense matter. Mind and consciousness are ethereal, ever-changing, but ever the same and of subtle energy. I understood there are just two phenomena: spiritual and material. The soul is spiritual, God is spiritual, and the rest is material.

***

"It's time to return."

I have no thoughts about this. I have no preference. I only want to please Her. Return, stay, suffer, exalt . . . whatever She wants. I belong to Her.

And She belongs to me.

"Will I remember here? What I know? What I truly am?"

"It will all reside within you. You can remember anytime you truly wish from your heart and with good intention. I am always with you. I am all there is to remember. I am all there is to know."

1.

DEAD

The god of **death** bows his head before those who chant and listen to the names of God.
—Kripalu Maharaj

Don't ever say die/Never, never, never say die —**Black Sabbath ("Never Say Die")**

On June 19, 2013, I was killed . . .

Dead in the street.

Mangled, bloody, shattered, and . . .

DEAD.

Life can go from light to dark in an instant.

***

"Sorry, I can't," my love-of-life girlfriend tells me when I call and ask her to take a walk with me in the park. "I got too much to do before I clock in at work."

"It's cool, just thought I'd ask. Too nice a day to waste."

"Well, I know you'll enjoy the walk on your own. It *is* a nice day."

"Can't," I add. "I confess: I don't have shoes to walk in and part of my reason for inviting you to join me was so that you'd bring over my shoes and some shorts."

"Ahh . . . the truth is revealed!" she says with a giggle that makes me miss her even more.

"I'll skip the walk and scoot over to the clinic for my overdue physical. It's better than sitting here counting ceiling tiles to pass the time."

A harmony of "Okays" and "I love yous" and our conversation ends.

I'm blessed: The private counseling practice I started from nothing now had grown to the point where I could afford a sweet corner office in a building overlooking a park in a peaceful, suburban, LA neighborhood. I'm booked pretty much back-to-back every day, all day, serving a middle-class community as a specialist in crisis, addiction, and behavioral disorders. I advocate strictly cognitive strategies as I wage a quiet, backend war against the over-prescribing medical empire.

Blessed: Mid-forties; fit; a single father who is close with his son, a recent high school graduate; and a partner with whom I have a magically romantic connection. We'd just celebrated our tenth anniversary with a trip to India and Nepal. In nine days, we would celebrate my forty-eighth birthday, probably with a simple meal out or a sexy evening in—or both.

I live an unconventional life: My partner and I live a block apart, having chosen to reject the blended family option to avoid subjecting my only son and her son and daughter to the dysfunction of blending a family during the critical teen years. Her name is said as Jeanette, but spelled uniquely: *Janete*. We will both be empty nesters in a few years. My counseling career had begun eight years ago after I awoke one day and found I could no longer stomach my job in commercial contracting. So I did a one-eighty, risked it all, and started saving people from dysfunction as a private counselor.

Life can go from light to dark in an instant. . .

***

I expect a client or two to reschedule here and there, but never once have I had three clients rescheduled on the same day. All three appointments were back-to-back, and my clients all texted me to say they couldn't make their appointment within the span of ten minutes. Suddenly, I realized I had over four hours to kill. I had no backup work with me since I was booked solid all day, and I'd ridden my motorbike to work, so I had no change of shoes for a hike up the hill in the lovely park my corner office overlooked.

If only one or two clients rescheduled, I would have remained in my office for the day.

Most days, I drive my car to the office. Once or twice a week, I ride my MP3 motorbike, an unusual, 500cc scooter from Italy.

To avoid wrinkling my office clothes, I change into track pants and a t-shirt and don my riding gear over them to ride up the boulevard to the local clinic for an overdue physical.

I'm healthy as a bull, but the research I was doing for my next book had some risks, so I thought it best to check the stats.

I exit my parking garage on my motorcycle and turn right instead of my usual left. In the several years I've worked in that office I had <u>never</u> exited by turning right instead of left. The right turn leads to a road with traffic and stoplights, while the left turn leads to a quiet side street into town. To this day I do not and never will know why I turned right instead of left on that particular day, *but I did.*

Two blocks away, I pause at a stoplight to turn left. I am alone in the left-turn lane, no one is behind or in front of me. A green arrow lights up, giving me exclusive right of way to turn. I ease out to turn, and an oncoming driver in a full-size SUV barrels through the red light and hits me in the face, killing me instantly.

Killed.

Dead in the street.

Mangled, bloody, shattered, and . . .

> *DEAD.*

Life had gone from light to dark in an instant. . .

On the SE corner, there was a man on his cell phone. He was waiting outside a tire shop for his daughter's car to be completed. He had rearranged his plans for the day to help her at the last minute.

He ran to the accident scene as onlookers shouted at him, *"Leave him alone! Don't touch him! Help is on the way!"*

Pastor Tom ignored their pleas. He felt certain God had put him in that place at that time for a reason. He crouched to the ground, put his hands under the accident victim's arms, and dragged him from the undercarriage of the vehicle.

The body was bleeding from his head, nose, mouth, and eyes. His cycle helmet strap was stretched across his throat, causing deep red grooves.

Pastor Tom undid the strap and released the helmet.

It was too late.

The body was not breathing. There was no heartbeat. Pastor Tom began to administer the last rites to the man's soul. *"Go forth from this world in the name of God the almighty Father, who created you . . ."*

Fifty yards away (45 meters), two paramedics are in *front* of a fast-food drive-thru, waiting on their burgers. The two emergency medical responders see the accident occur and are on the scene in moments, bringing my body back to life.

- If they had wanted tacos instead of burgers that day . . . *I would not be here.*
- If they had been in the <u>back</u> of that drive-thru line . . . *I would not be here.*

They bring my body back to life, but my condition is critical. I am now in a stage 3 coma, defined as "deep coma or death." Stage 3 is the lowest scale of living, virtually synonymous with death. I am rushed to the ICU.

- Had the accident happened near my home, just three miles away, I would've been too far to make it to the ICU in time, and *I would not be here.*

At the moment of the accident, my son's close friend was passing through that particular intersection, even though . . .

- He lives nowhere near there.
- He is rarely in that area.
- He had a rare errand at the DMV at that exact time at that exact corner.

He phoned my son. "*Brandon, your dad's been in an accident. They're pushing him into an ambulance.*"

"*How do you know it's my dad?*"

"*His bike. No one has a bike like that. It's him.*"

This is how my family was alerted to the emergency.

- Paramedics had no way to alert anyone or identify me. My phone and ID had been lost in the crash.

My loved ones converged at the hospital and were met by two doctors *and a priest.*

They are told it is unlikely I will ever wake up, and that if I do, my brain trauma is so severe that I will probably be bedridden for life and need care for as long as I continue to breathe.

- My girlfriend fainted and collapsed.

They were told that my face had been so damaged that, even with extensive plastic surgery, I will remain scarred and misshapen.

I awoke nine days later.

On my birthday.

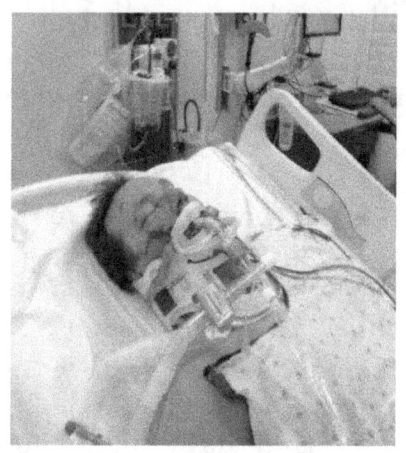

- I did not know who I was.
- I did not know how to talk.
- I did not know how to walk.

I did not know what a hospital was, what a motorcycle accident was, or even what life and death were. I did not know who the young man sitting at my bedside was: *my twenty-year-old-son.*

I did not know who the worrying woman in my room was: *my girlfriend of eleven years.*

_____ **2.**

RESURRECTION

From what is not, lead me to what is; from darkness, lead me to light; from death, lead me to what is undying.

—Brhadaranyaka Upanisad (I.3.28)

I'll get a new start/Live the life I should/I'll get up and fly away

—Grateful Dead ("Wharf Rat")

Upon impact, my soul left my body.

I do not *suspect* this; I *know* it. I *know* my soul did not reenter my body until after I awoke from my coma nine days later. How do I know this?

I know it the same way you know there is a China and a solar system, even though you've never been to China or toured the solar system. It is a crystal-clear, intuitive awareness. It is a component of your base of knowledge: It's just part of the collection of stuff you know about yourself, like knowing you were once a child and went to school. Even without documented evidence, your personal experiences are self-verified. Like when you're hungry or tired: *self-verified*.

I do not need tangible, scientific proof or historical evidence Antarctica is real and will be there tomorrow nor do I require it to know my soul was in a dormant state and not inhabiting my body for nine days.

My soul was in a transitional state, in between physical form and spiritual form.

It was . . .

pending.

My soul didn't just *leave* my body. *It catapulted.* It did not *arise, float,* or *ascend.* I was hit in the face by a truck and instantly killed, and my life force bolted the fuck outta there. I teleported from the material realm of planet Earth to an obscure dimension.

It wasn't dark. It wasn't light. It was formless, timeless, and matterless . . . and I was not alone.

There was a comforting presence. I was not "here" nor "there," as there was no spatial reference. This presence was not a "she" or a "he." The presence was care. Concern. *Love.*

Communication was telepathic. I had no mouth with which to speak nor ears with which to hear, but I was able to receive what I needed to know through my thoughts and emotions.

I was not alone.

I was not surrounded by others, nor did I see or contact anyone. But there was a *presence,* a presence of intelligence and comfort. Angels? Spirits? God? I was made aware, in a telepathic manner, that the presences surrounding me were *spiritual administrators.* Gentle and kind, concerned and loving, these "beings" uploaded things into my awareness.

I was not afraid.

I was not anxious.

I wasn't at peace or "okay" with everything either. I just wasn't opposed to it.

I felt a *perfection* in all things, that what I thought or felt about things was irrelevant and *imperfect.* I had complete and perfect *trust* that everything, everywhere, all the time is exactly the way it should be: *perfect.*

***

My consciousness was aware and understanding. The presence was ochre. Warm and soothing. As I wondered and desired answers to the mystery I experienced, this presence uploaded my situation to me.

"You are in a celestial dimension between life and death. All souls come here for a period of reflection between lifetimes. It is a place of rest and insight."

My curiosities are thought: "Is this the Akashic dimension? Where all things past, present, and future and all true knowledge is stored?"

"That is another name for this, yes. Any names and explanations you receive here will be in terms you are familiar with."

"If I were Christian, would it be heaven?"

"Something like that. Heaven is a final celestial abode. Your Western religions know this temporary space as purgatory, Buddhists know it as the Bardo, and the Eastern spiritual path you follow knows it as Akashic. I am providing you with knowledge in terms you can understand. This is temporary. You have life to live. Your final destiny in this life is not complete."

"Can I choose not to return?"

"No, you've not completed your soul's full journey. You have great knowledge of this already. You have full acceptance that souls live life after life until they complete the journey of the soul to a Divine state of being. You have made great progress but must complete the final stages of complete and humble surrender to the Divine to break free of the material realm forever."

"I have lived infinite lifetimes and have been close countless times. Yet, I have never attained Divine and permanent illumination. Every lifetime I start anew without knowledge or memory of prior progress. I do not want to live on as a human in the material world. I want to become pure spirit. Please, help me."

"You will receive insights here that will serve you well. You must make the most of your time here. See where you've been, where you could have gone, and how to progress. The past is bygone, the future obscure, only the present is in your hands."

"Will I remember and retain what I am shown here to help me once I return?"

"Some will be lost; some will remain foggy. Transferring from this Akashic space back to matter will compromise some of what is gained here. You will gain much clarity in the knowledge you already have. You will learn much from the Life-Review and the Life-Preview you will experience."

"Life-Review? The life-passing-before-my-eyes experience?"

"Life-Review and Preview are provided to all who undergo the Transmigration of the soul. It is provided so you can learn from experience: to see—in truth, our life's choices to learn and strengthen our choices, commitments, and decisions in the future. Life-Review reveals what we have done wrong and right, and Life-Preview gives us perspective by seeing the results of our upcoming destinies and fates."

"I see. Review gives me insights into my past that were spiritual or material, selfish, or selfless. Preview shows me upcoming consequences to learn from them." Apparently, Dickens was a sage as he storied about old Ebenezer Scrooge's ghosts of past and future.

***

It was made known to me that if I wished, I could witness past lives that are significant to my spiritual journey.

"Life-Review is a standard feature of the death-to-life experience: your-whole-life-passing-before-your-eyes phenomena. You are being offered a rare supplement to your Life-Review: instead of reviewing just this lifetime, you are being offered a review of multiple lifetimes."

And I accepted the offer. "Why are You offering this multiple Life-Review to me?"

"Seeing many past lives will bring you a more complete perspective of your Soul's Journey and help accelerate your progress."

"Yes. Bring it. Bring it all on. Whatever will help my soul's ultimate journey.

"I'm not interested in the mundane lives of material ambitions. I'd like to see where I went wrong on my spiritual ambitions to learn how to get it right."

I am cautioned: *"Many of these lifetimes may be traumatic. Many may collapse some of your systems of belief. Many may be hard to accept and will dismantle much of what you think you know to be true in the world, true of existence, true of God. Few souls receive a Review of multiple lifetimes."*

My mind was present in this spiritual space of dark-light, matterless- matter, timeless-time, spaceless-space. My spirit was immersed in diaphanous light. With a sensation of motion, my spirit separated from the nothingness I inhabited and connected with a flowing current, like a river of beautiful energy, flowing past time, contacting a life . . . a being . . . a person . . . a me . . . in another lifetime, another era, another body, and identity. . .

A collection of Life-Reviews began. It spanned over ten-thousand years and was infused with truths to many mysteries. Like a sequence of dreams, entire lifetimes were condensed and displayed before me. The Life-Review was a cinema of past lives over hundreds and even thousands of years, a collection of dozens, even hundreds, of lifetimes that chronicled my soul's spiritual journey, the lifetimes in which I got closer to spiritual perfection and the ones in which I went in the other direction.

I was given a clear Review of *past* lifetimes involved with many of the most significant events in human history and revelations of *future* lifetimes.

Then I am shown my own personal future Life-Previews, which are potential realities, not *hard* destinies, revealing outcomes based on choices I can make, such as what may result if I return and live a life of material pursuits and what could manifest if I return to spiritual pursuits. A simple equation: Will I choose to pursue the material happiness related to romantic love, family, and success in the world, or will I dedicate myself even more strongly toward spiritual life and practice?

Material actions yield mundane results. If I focus on money, prestige, and material comforts, I will perpetuate more of the same, a *loop* of lives repeating the same things: romantic love and family with beauty and heartache, health and wealth that fluctuate. All these material lives never yield a perfect happiness, only temporary ones that can always be better. Such is the nature of the world. The spiritual life paths lead closer to Divine love, and it was revealed that it is possible to become One with this love for eternity: *game over, I win.*

I witnessed the Reviews and Previews as an observer, watching my own lives as a cosmic cinema.

Grand mysteries were uploaded into my consciousness. Someday soon, after my soul reenters my form and my mind settles back into grey-matter tissue, I will be able to draw from all I received while on *the other side.*

Soon, I am to return to the material realm of being to continue my journey of the soul in this lifetime and endure these tragedies, using them as fuel to reach my soul's journey's end.

"I can't go back."

"That's not an option."

"I don't mean I don't want to. I don't mean 'can't' in a metaphorical way. I mean *can't.* I'm breaking. Broken. Fed up. No room, capacity, ability. . . . I'm afraid I'll only get worse, *not better.*"

"You are going back. That's the way. You've not completed your Soul's Journey."

"Yeah, no. I'm not doing anything else either. Aren't you supposed to be, like, *comforting* me? Consoling me? Reassuring me? All these souls come here and say they were told they had "work to do," that they had a mission to fulfill, a purpose to complete, that they *chose to go back.*"

"*All souls that come here go back. It's not optional. It is presented as optional to motivate them to want to return and be more spiritually aware.*"

"Are you real or just an extension of my consciousness? You seem to be rather informal. Instead of, like . . . *angelic.*"

The angel presence gives a soft chuckle. "*Yes, I'm real. We're all real here. This is not an extension or a projection of your own consciousness. This telepathic conveyance is not a projection of your own mind, but the style and language are an extraction of your mind. All that you receive here is presented in a manner that you can best understand and accept. In that sense, it is an extension of your consciousness. You don't speak Hebrew or Sanskrit, so we speak to you in a language you can accept. We're not really using language at all. These are just thoughts uploaded into your mind, which interprets it as dialogue.*"

This *conversation* is occurring telepathically with a spiritual presence. I am in a dualistic reality: *two places at once.*

My *physical* body is lying in a coma in a Los Angeles suburb, and my spirit is in an ethereal dimension of space

My life force, a.k.a. *soul, ansh, jeev, ruh, spirit,* has bolted from my body, and it took my mind with it. This is not a metaphor meaning I've *lost my mind* due to dying! My mind—the thinking and feeling apparatus of my *being* that thinks, reasons, feels, and *knows*, is a separate thing. A thing that is attached to the thing we call soul. The soul is the *essence of being,* the mind is its material appendage through which the soul experiences life. My Spirit has *left the proverbial building.*

Departed, left, arose, ascended . . . these do not accurately describe my condition. My soul and mind *bolted!* The accident occurred, my body died, and my spirit teleported the hell out of there!

I did not have the classic O.B.E.—out-of-body experience. I did not float above, hang around to witness them resuscitating me, my motorbike lying on its side, traffic stopped, people coming out of shops and offices to see the commotion, the driver who hit me weeping and pleading, "*I didn't see him! It was an accident! Oh, my gawd!*" My body was killed, and "*I*" catapulted the fuck out of there.

I instantly teleported to a timeless and spaceless dimension, an ethereal, subtle place. I have no body or form here, and there is nothing to "see" and I *do not* "see." I am merely consciousness. I am *aware*—of being, of existing. Of peace. Of beauty. Of life. *And death.*

The Presence explains, *"Souls that come here do have work to do and return to, but it's not a choice. They must fulfill their destinies."*

"I don't want to go back. The world may be a nice place to visit, but I don't wanna *live* there."

"Ha . . . you're funny . . . You're not going back this instant. Your body is not prepared yet, and there are things for you to know of before you depart this space."

"Is She here? Can I see Her? Can I have Her darshan? Her vision?"

"She is as close to you as you are now. Ever-present and within you. You will have Her darshan the instant you fully surrender."

"I don't know how. It is not faith that I lack nor the belief that I need. I *know* She is the Lord of all creation and love. Why do I not see Her? I know I am not worthy, but . . ."

"Feeling unworthy means you do not trust Her. Let go. . . ."

"I think you're getting away from the point: *I can't go back.* I'm not saying I want to stay here either. This is pretty austere and shadowy, peaceful and worriless and beautiful, but still not . . . uh . . . *final?* It feels, *temporary*, like you said. Like I'm not 'home.'"

"Ha-ha . . . no! It's not final! This is the stopover! The place all souls come to in between lifetimes. This is the dimension you know as the Akashic Library, where all events of time are stored, where all knowledge and truth are preserved. You're not going back empty- handed, Krishnanand! You're going back with tremendous insight to proceed and progress to your ultimate aim to never go back!"

It is comforting the angelic-presence calls me by my spiritual name, Krishnanand.

"No, no . . . I been here an infinite number of times. I been *there* infinite times. Here leads to there, there leads to here. I need to get off this wheel. I only want Him. Nothing else. I don't want heaven, I don't want nirvana, no 'self-realization' or 'oneness with the universe' . . . no, no. I don't just want *out.* I want Him. I want to be with divine love. Don't you get it? I'm *never* gonna *qualify.* I am never, ever—never have and never will— qualify or be worthy of Him. No matter how far I come, I'm a still a wretch. A sinner. A defect. *A human.* A desire machine, shrouded in ego and illusions of power, knowledge, and obscure clarities. She has to take me as I am. Eventually, She'll have to take me with my faults, defects, ignorance, pride . . . and the whole collection of imperfections. He has to take me as I am. I may get better, but I may get worse. I can't keep doing the same thing expecting a different result. I give up. I quit."

"Now you're getting it. THAT . . . is the attitude you've been missing through infinite lives. Stop trying. Stop doing. You need to give up. Quit. Let go. Surrender.

"Those tears you're weeping are tears of your soul. They are the only ones that matter. That anguish is the anguish of your soul. Let go of mind. No . . . you can't go back: but you're going. Finish what needs to be done. Accept with grace. Do your best. We will help you. We will serve you. Go back, live out your destinies and don't lose your hope and faith that you will join Him. Don't lose your confidence and trust Him to lead you closer to Him. You've never been alone. She has always been with you in your darkest hours. She will be your source of light. Though you may not see Her light, it always surrounds you. Never forget that. He is giving you what you need to come Home. Forever. Never doubt that."

"Okay. . . ." My awareness of ultimate divinity was not quite genderless. God's projection of power and creation is male. God's persona of pure love and grace is female. Together They are One.

I react to the Life-Preview: the upload of witnessing what is to come . . .

"I can see all I am to endure, and I am terrified. Broken, injury, sorrow, tragedy, suffering, loss . . . how can I be strong enough through that to never doubt? I will never doubt *Him*! I doubt *myself*! I'm a stupid fucking human! I'm a collection of desires and needs! I'm not worthy and have no such capacity to ever be worthy! I am not the worst, but I'll never be the best. This may be the best I can be! Please . . . please . . . take me! I don't care when; I don't care how. . . . I will endure a thousand lives of pain! I will suffer eons of suffering! Just to be with Him once!"

"She will never leave you. She never has. You can do this. These circumstances are extraordinary. You're receiving a very special Grace. Your infinite collection of past-life events, decisions, actions, and attitudes have been arranged to give you the biggest chance you've ever had before! We know you will not waste it! You've been graced with such supernatural events and undeniable occurrences.

"You've provided this spiritual administration with such a rare set of raw, past-life and current-lifetime material that We have arranged them in such a way to bring you closure: Ultimate, eternal closure.

"You are witnessing a mosaic of events from your current life, and your past lives, significant to your journey's end. Also, a preview of what is to come once you return. You are not starting from scratch! Your memory will be deleted: That's a set law. It can't be changed. But . . . the body and brain you're returning to is the same one you just left. You're reincarnating as yourself! This is extremely rare!

"In time . . . with effort and determination, you will be capable of accessing what you received here. You will still have all the spiritual progress you've made along with this Akashic Library visit. Stay on the Path. Remain true to Him. And you may never return here again."

"Thank you. I will endure the fates still destined for this lifetime. I will try. I will do my best to give up. To fully surrender my useless, futile Will. I am nothing. I have nothing. He will need to take me as I am. It's all I have to give: nothing."

***

It would soon be time for my soul to reenter my body back in the dimension of matter.

My death experience was just beginning, though.

I was destined to return without memory: As my soul condensed to reenter my body, my memory would be virtually deleted. One's identity is the sum total collection of their past thoughts, feelings, and experiences; no memory—no identity. It would be some time after my soul reentered my body before I would remember and access the visions and communications I received while there. Someday . . . it will all be recalled. Someday it will all become accessible.

_____3.

IT COULD BE WORSE

> A man with outward courage dares to die;
>
> a man with inner courage dares to live.
>
> —Lao Tzu (<u>Tao Te Ching</u>)

> Darkness, imprisoning me/All that I see, Absolute horror
>
> I cannot live, I cannot die/Trapped in myself
>
> —Metallica ("One")

It really sucks when the best thing you can say about your life is that it could be worse.

Things can ALWAYS be worse! And for someone, somewhere, they certainly are, and we should all definitely keep our perspective about that in our darkest hours. But each person hearing my story, which was doled out multiple times a day, such as when someone noticed my inability to get up, hold a spoon to eat, or saw me tear up at the thought of being confined to a perpetual state of suffering in a hospital for as long as I lived, gave the generic, classless, thoughtless response: "OMG! You were lucky!" Referring to the proximity of paramedics at my moment of impact, the proximity of a hospital, and that I had survived.

My life was OVER, and I did not consider getting hit in the face by a truck to be "lucky."

Lucky is when you discard four cards in five-card stud and get a flush or a straight. Lucky is when you hit every green light on your commute to work.

Lucky is when you almost get hit by a truck in the face, not when you get killed in the street!

Indeed, it could've been worse. . . .

So to summarize:

- I turned right out of my office instead of left for the first time ever.
- A pastor[1] was on the corner who pulled me from the wreck and read me my last rites.
- Two paramedics were 40 yards away at the front of a drive-thru.
- The hospital was a life-saving distance from my impact.
- My son's best friend was at that intersection at the time of the collision.
- I was wearing a Museum of Death t-shirt under my riding gear.

When I changed into street clothes to leave my office, the randomly selected t-shirt I had with me was from Hollywood's Museum of Death. It was sheared off of me by paramedics when they attempted to revive me. I've got dozens of collectible t-shirts from landmark places, but the one I grabbed that day had a darkly hilarious cartoon caricature of a dismembered cat with Museum of Death scrolled across the chest.

Top: the shirt cut off my body by paramedics.

Bottom: the original shirt

My injuries were:

- Stage 3 Glasgow coma
- Ten broken ribs

---

[1] I had no knowledge of Pastor Tom until Brandon's mother casually mentioned him six years later. I located him, we spoke by phone and he gave me details.

- Punctured lung
- Life-threatening lacerations on my face and head
- A spinal complication that would not be realized for seven months, resulting in fourteen hours of spinal fusion surgery
- Severe structural damage to the face and skull
- Left leg injured
- Traumatic brain injury (TBI)
  - Diffuse axonal injury (DAI)
- Death

Lucky, huh?

One hundred percent of Stage 3 Glasgow coma BFDP (bilateral fixed dilated pupils) patients die. I was an RP—Reactive Pupil—patient, and only 42 percent of them die! My head was swollen to the size of my actual bike helmet. My ten broken ribs punctured my lungs. I could not breathe on my own, so a tube was inserted into my mouth, down into my throat, and into my lungs, and oxygen was fed into me by a machine. I could not breathe, swallow, or . . . well . . . anything. There were multiple contusions on my face and head. My third vertebrae was damaged, and my left leg was so twisted and misshapen that it required an ankle-to-hip brace just to keep it "straight."

When my son and girlfriend arrived at the hospital, they could not see me as I was in emergency ICU care. They were met by two doctors and a priest. They were asked to sign consent forms relating to death arrangements.

When they first laid eyes on me, my girlfriend of eleven years, Janete, fainted. My son, Brandon, took it in and tried to process this person, his father and close confidante and very good and trusted friend and mentor, potentially dead.

My traumatic brain injury (TBI) was a DAI (diffuse axonal injury). This is one of the most severe forms of TBI and occurs when the white and grey layers of the brain shear (rip) due to the force of an impact. Over 90 percent of DAI sufferers never regain consciousness, and those who do remain significantly impaired.

While I was comatose, I had dozens of procedures performed to sustain my life and repair me. I do not remember anything that took place. I was in a coma for nine days and awoke on my birthday.

Yeah . . . as if it wasn't supernatural enough, I awoke from my coma on my actual birthday. Being resurrected on my actual birthday let me keep my astrological sign and numerology data. That might come in handy when and if I could comprehend such things again.

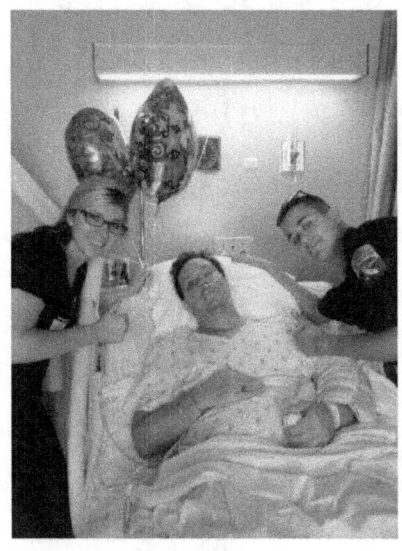

June 28, 2013,
Happy 47th!

Brandon and Janete's daughter, Morgan.

My loved ones were told there was less than a 30 percent chance I would wake from my coma, and there was no way to anticipate what my condition would be: they were advised I was going to be severely impaired, and IF I ever woke up, I would likely need constant care as long as I lived, such as feeding and machines to move my bowels and bladder.

They were also told my face was so damaged that even with extensive plastic surgery, I would be visibly and grotesquely scarred for life.

My girlfriend and life partner for over a decade, entered into a denial state, replying, "Oh . . . okay. So he'll be getting up soon, and we'll take him home. That's good."

That's when my son and her daughter looked at her in disbelief and cried out, "OH MY GOD! DID YOU NOT HEAR WHAT THE DOCTOR JUST SAID?"

Her denial was a psychological protective mechanism to prevent her from going into a state of shock until able to accept the realities: the closest person in her life was effectively gone.

***

When I awoke, Janete fainted. Since I was alive, her denial shock evaporated, reality washed in, and she finally reacted to what had been taking place.

I had no memory and did not know who she was or who I was. I didn't know what a hospital was or life or death or anything.

My first words to my family were, "Why are you in London?"

I did *not* ask them what *I* was doing in London. I did not even ask *where* I was. I *knew* where I was: *London*. This was not a suspicion any more than being aware at this moment I am currently upstairs, at my desk, working on my laptop.

The odd thing about my delusions was not the delusions themselves. Yes, it's strange I thought I was in London, but what was even stranger was the fact I was more curious as to why my loved ones were in London than *who* they actually were.

"What're you guys doing in London?"

My loved ones nodded politely at what they assumed were brain-injury delusions. What they *didn't* know was that my soul and mind were not yet secured and settled within my body, so I was experiencing dual dimensions. I was indeed confused, but not in the way the doctors thought.

I was visiting past lives throughout my coma and afterward. Among the lives I'd reviewed was a very recent one in which I lived in London. Janete and I were together in that life too. So was Brandon.

***

I remained in the ICU for twelve days.

When the circumstances were explained to me, I nodded my head politely as if someone told me about the weather. I was unable to comprehend these concepts but had an intuitive sense to calmly say the right things, such as mumbling, "Oh, okay. That sucks. I hope everything turns out all right. Thank you."

My damaged brain struggled to respond as I was just learning how to articulate: I would have a thought and want to speak it but couldn't yet connect the dots between thought and speech.

Since it was my birthday when I awoke from my coma, my little family brought cupcakes with candles and balloons and sang me "Happy Birthday" and took pictures and a video. I nearly look like I know what is going on in the pictures and video, but in truth, I had no idea what was happening. I didn't know what a birthday was or who these people were but instinctively knew to smile and say thank you.

I felt like an alien who had woken up on a strange planet.

On my third night, I turned to this girlfriend person and said to her, very privately, "Don't leave me here at night! These nurses and hospital people do very strange things to me when I'm here alone! Please, don't let them!"

In my barely conscious state, I am sure I was delusional and felt the surgeries and other procedures performed on me at night, like changing my catheter, were really alien-abduction probing.

About ten days out of my coma, my son, Brandon, was encouraged by the physical therapist to get me to squeeze a ball or even try to toss one to me from a foot or two away. I agreed to the request to play catch and felt a bit insulted they were treating me like a child, asking me to play catch like a good boy. But when my son tossed this soft round thing to me from two feet away, I watched it bounce into my head, unable to gauge the timing to even raise my hand to catch it.

Brandon asked me, "Dad, do you remember home?"

"Of course . . ."

"Describe it. Tell me what the front of the house looks like."

I could not.

"Describe your bedroom, the door, the walls, your bed . . . you know . . ."

I could not.

I could get a sense of what home was, and I knew I had one, but all the details were inaccessible to me. All the things I couldn't remember had no sensation of being forgotten. Instead, they were simply not there, as if they never were. It wasn't like I could not remember things. It was like they never existed to me at all.

This accentuated the feelings of isolation and fear, fear that I could be trapped this way. Even though I felt like I didn't know how to do anything to begin with, there was the simultaneous and contradictory feeling that I'd lost the ability to do things.

And there were other simultaneous sensations as well: an inner sense of encouragement and achievement at being able to do something, yet at the same time, an equal sense of despair and sorrow that came with the unavoidable awareness my limitations were not something I'd ever encountered before! I lived in a paradoxical condition: I could not remember anything, but I had a feeling of loss at their absence. I could not remember how to walk or function, yet I felt like a loser for not being able to.

Other people came to see me in the hospital too. Men I played tennis with every week came to see me. I was embarrassed. I didn't know them or me or what tennis was.

Many of my clients came to see me, and many cried and prayed and said such kind and wonderful things to me, "Please, Scott, stay strong. You saved my life and gave me hope when I thought my life was over. I would never have made it through my (divorce /addiction/grief) without you. Don't leave us. We need you."

These pleadings and prayers became sustenance to my body and mind as I felt a powerful need to not let my friends and clients down. They all saw me as an inspiration of strength and perseverance, and I could NOT let them down and deprive them of triumph and hope (whoever these strangers were)!

I wasn't too sad over my own circumstances, but when it brought others pain, it became empathetically intolerable!

I didn't know who this Scott guy was they lamented over, but it was tragic and made me cry each time. It felt like someone had died, never to return, like this person abandoned these people who seemed to, like, love and rely on him. They were all so . . . grateful. Whatever I had been or done had made quite an impact on everyone, and I felt like a colossal failure for being unable to remember such important things and people. I felt severe guilt for abandoning them and being less than who they wanted.

***

I was not in pain. I had very little body awareness. I was not hungry or sleepy or thirsty or really aware of any bodily needs. I was virtually numb, aware of my physical form and discomfort from lying down or sitting up too long, but nothing severe. I now know that my prior self was annoyingly energetic and restless, yet here I was, confined to a bed constantly, and I did not feel the need to stretch or expand. My bodily needs were all mechanized: my food came through one IV tube and my waste was taken away by another!

I could not really identify as a body yet. I was mostly aware of only spirit and consciousness. This disconnect between consciousness and body made me virtually immune to physical reality: pain, hunger, discomfort. . . .

I wanted to stand and walk because I saw these other humans doing this walking thing, and it looked easy and good. But when I tried to stand, I fell. My motivation was two-fold: I wanted to be self-reliant and independent, and I felt ashamed of being a burden. I began to feel urgency to improve to simply not be a source of pain, fear, and worry to these kind people, though I could not remember who they were. I felt love for them, sort of like a muscle memory—a reflex—that was simply present. Being mostly in a spiritual state, I loved them and all living things; it was automatic. Loving them was the only thing I could feel emotionally, and I felt empathy for their worry and concern and self-loathing for being the source of it.

When I would fall asleep in the hospital, I would wake up in the dark and my conscious, aware brain could not help but remember where I was and why I was there. And it would be paralyzing. And you work so hard to "shut off" the dark, hopeless thoughts, to think of other things, fantasize about recovery and a future of being restored to yourself as if it were all just a bad, bad, horrible dream. And if fortunate, you drift back to sleep.

Thoughts of Janete, Morgan, Brandon, Cody, sister, clients, associates, healthy and normal . . . it is simultaneously comforting and lonely as you become painfully aware that if you were gone tomorrow, they would live on and eventually be productive and happy without you. They would eventually adjust to a world they live in where you had died, and you feel insignificant and abandoned and then . . . lonely—so, so lonely. Not "alone." That'd be easy . . . but "lonely."

Since this tragedy, I feel alone ALL the time, even when Brandon or Janete are right next to me. I feel like we are not together because I am in a different place. Our bodies are near to each other, and we might even be talking or sharing a movie or meal together, but they are nowhere near where I am; we are so many millions of miles apart. I am on a different planet and in a whole other galaxy. . . . And I love them. My God . . . it's not even love. . . . It's so much more and total than "love." I need them to feel safe and loved. The only thing I am truly concerned about is their safety and happiness. I only care about my own life as far as it affects them.

I am willing to surrender my life, here and now, for them to feel safe. If they could see they are spirit, not human, they would feel safe. As humans, we experience love in very fundamental octaves. But as spirits we experience love in expansive octaves, and I am experiencing love on spiritual octaves now rather than human ones.

At night, when visiting hours were over and I was alone in this sterile room with one window, I contemplated my reality. I made rational, sensible conclusions that if I was to be a source of worry and fear to those I loved, I was going to . . . exit.

I was not emotional or upset or hysterical. I was calm and private. I was reasonable and practical. My girlfriend and son were young, and I refused to limit their lives with having to care for me, never being able to fully live because of me. I decided, calmly and rationally, to . . . exit.

It was the right thing to do.

Sure . . . they'd hurt over it for a while, but over time, they would move on and be free, and I would become merely a tragic memory. She would find a man to live and travel and make love with, and my son would continue his life and get married and have children and a career someday, and I would be this dark "episode" in their lives, a collection of photos and objects reminding people of you. What you're reduced to when you're dead is memorabilia. Death is a part of life, and the world keeps spinning around, and the sun comes up and goes down whether I, or anyone in particular, is here, or not. They will move on. It is best to let them go so they can repair and live again. The sooner the better. . . .

And I imagined their futures—without me: Birthdays I'd never attend, anniversaries I'd never make romantic and grand, adventures I'd never have with my amazing grown son, grandkids and a beautiful daughter- in-law I'd never meet. And they would all grow older and occasionally come across some memorabilia that brings me to mind and cause a tear or two as they wonder for a moment . . . *what if.* . . .

And in my head, I heard someone argue back.

"Yes, they will move on, and you will become that great, inspiring man who met a sad and tragic end. They will remember you with fondness. But who in this world will love and care for them as well as you? Do you want to abandon them to mediocrity? The only alternative is if you somehow miraculously rise from these ashes and resurrect yourself. That'd be quite an amazing feat. Then you wouldn't be remembered for what you were but would continue this lifelong legacy of representing strength, perseverance, and triumph."

And that was the moment.

That was the moment I decided to fight to live and become a medical miracle if I had to and show, by example, that life is a choice, and you do NOT have to play the cards you are dealt!

I decided to press on: If this thing's gonna beat me, it's gonna have to KILL me to do it. I will make this tragedy EARN and WORK its ass off to take me! I will exhaust it! I will make it work so hard it'll just give up, confessing that it has met its match. I will make killing me <u>so not worth it</u>!

I truly did NOT feel strong or that I had a fraction of a chance of ever being even remotely self-reliant again. I was not brave nor strong nor positive. I was *spiteful!*

I was determined to make this criminal of my life have to work nonstop to keep me enslaved, and if it got drowsy, I would bludgeon it in its sleep! I was going to KILL death.

I was terrified of living confined to a bed, unable to think and feel. I began to sense the cornerstone of my identity had been my near-superhuman ability to think and feel, that the only thing making people different from animals was our wide-ranging ability to think and to feel.

I was not motivated to live on because of bravery or fearlessness or even hope—no. I was determined because I was in absolute terror of continuing the way I was. I would try till my death merely to avoid a life of suffering.

See, I did not and do not accept suicide as an option. I had seriously considered it when I was twenty-eight and kicking dope after twelve years of hard-core IV meth addiction, but it crossed my mind I might try it and, with my luck, screw it up, crippling me and leaving me a bedridden vegetable with no way to end it all—trapped and imprisoned by this selfish act of suicide gone wrong!

Nuh-uh! No way!

Suicide is not an option for me because I know death is not an ending. I know that you live on in some form or manner, and that no matter how bad something seems, it could indeed be worse!

It is often said death is the worst, but no, it's not. Suffering is far worse than death, and I was terrified of living on in an even worse state than I was. There seemed no option but to try.

I wished and prayed for another option, as trying seemed to be a causeless, useless notion, but since I seemed to be living on, breathing in and out, for an undetermined amount of time, I decided I'd better get on with it and try to get the fuck out of this mess.

I had to try to make it . . . *better*. And if I could make it to *better*, then I could go farther. I decided to see where the end was. Where was the limit to my restoration? The point of no return? Where was the wall? I wanted to get there and see what was on the other side.

This made me try. . .

***

In about twelve days, I was able to form and express thoughts and told my partner-in-love, "I do not know if it is humanly possible to ever get beyond this. I only know that if it is, *I will*. I do not know if I will ever walk again, but I know that if I can take a single step, it will be truthful evidence that I can take two. I do not know how far I can go, *but I'm going to find out*."

This may sound motivational-speaker inspiring, but this is NOT how I felt.

I was NOT positive. I was NOT encouraged, inspired, or hopeful. I figured I was delusional, but since I kept waking up and breathing, whether or not I wanted to, I had nothing else to do but to try and *get the fuck out of bed*.

The days were becoming longer, as I was now only unconscious twenty hours a day instead of twenty-four. Then I was able to stay awake for five or six hours each day, and these stretches of time seemed eternal.

I was alone much of the time, as loved ones could not ignore work and other responsibilities to sit at the bedside of a man who could not even play checkers or converse.

I was getting bored as the only thing to occupy my time was this TV thing in my room that showed these really stupid people doing really stupid things. The only other distractions I had were hospital staff trying to get me to take drugs, which I refused, and my worrying loved ones who came for hours when they could. I begged them to stay more but was racked with guilt over it as I imprisoned them out of their sense of duty to me.

The rest of each waking moment was spent in an anguishing awareness that I had once been this living, vibrant thing and was now just taking up space . . . *forever!*

The hospital staff discovered I was depressed and tried persuading me to take antidepressants. "Why?" I asked. "Will they make me forget I was hit in the face by a truck and I'm in a hospital, maimed for life? If not, then no thanks, I'll pass on the drugs. But I tell you what, the moment I STOP being depressed about my circumstances, please drug the hell out of me because THEN something is seriously wrong!"

The staff thought I was . . . uh . . . *difficult.*

I was in the hospital for one month, twenty-eight days to be exact, one lunar cycle. When I was released, I was nowhere near capable of caring for myself. But since my insurance had been maxed out on in-patient care, it was time to go home.

_4._

ENDURE

> Though he slay me, I will hope in Him.
> —Job 13:15

> Changes come/Life will have its way/With your pride, son
> Take it like a man
> —Puscifer ("Momma Sed")

I lived in a sterile room for twenty-eight days. One full lunar cycle. After painful menstruation, it was time to be discharged.

I was unable to take care of myself and knew nothing beyond the hospital.

The world was a large and scary place, and while the hospital room was confining and sterile, it was safe. I hated it but was more terrified of a world I could not relate to at all.

I imagine this is how infants and animals feel. I was this small mass of vulnerability in a huge mass of machinery and the chaos of cars and automated doors. My so-called suburb of LA has a population of 150,000, and each and every one of those people could walk and talk and do things. But I couldn't! I didn't understand things like ordering food at a counter and menus and parking spaces. Even as a passenger, I was overwhelmed.

My existence was reduced to _"being."_ It took every ounce of thought and effort just to "be."

When I was awake, I was in a dream, or fugue, state, my mind cloudy and thoughts unclear. I can only imagine how painfully boring it was for my loved ones to spend time with me in the small hospital room with nothing but windows and a TV. They were all well and capable people with responsibilities and interests interrupted daily to console the quasi-dead guy. I wasn't much of a conversationalist, which is contrary to my ultra-pedantic nature!

Nor did I yet have the ability to form full thoughts. My thinking capacity was reduced to that of a household pet.

Actually, this was only the case with *practical* thought: I couldn't relate or understand things like my surroundings, how to eat and use the toilet, and the goings-on of things in the world. . . . But the abstract things: life, death, spirit, consciousness . . . were not beyond my capacity to understand. Those existential thoughts played in a never-ending loop in my mind.

I could only see and relate to the world and humanity around me through a spiritual lens.

Prior to NDE, I was already concerned with humanity's lack of passion for the spiritual in favor of the pursuit of the material. I want to save the world and wake them to benefits of spiritual beauty over material pleasures. But who am I to sit in judgment of humanity? So I keep my concern quiet.

Here's a summary of the procedures I received (endured) in those twenty-eight days:

- Multiple brain procedures to relieve the pressure and fluids within my hemorrhaging brain
- Surgery to repair my punctured lung
- Procedures to repair my broken ribs
- Procedures to repair my fractured facial bones
- IV feed of Demerol and Fentanyl, the two most potent and addictive opiate pain killers on the planet
- Physical therapies (daily):
  - Walks through the hallways and stairwells, a few feet at a time only and with support of wheelchairs, crutches, and personal assistants
  - Elementary grade-level word puzzles

o Various fundamental motions (standing on one foot, leaning, . . .)

There were many more procedures documented in my encyclopedia-thick file, which I do not look at to avoid retraumatizing myself.

I did everything the staff prescribed, plus a little more: If they wanted me to walk down one hallway, I walked down one and a half. If they wanted me to do a word puzzle, I did two (badly!). I followed their directions and advice with some exceptions: I refused to take behavioral drugs like antidepressants and very quickly upon waking from my coma refused to take pain narcotics too. This decision was intuitive: I had not yet remembered I was an internationally accomplished drug addiction counselor, specialist, and author opposed to gratuitous medications, nor had I remembered I was once an IV drug addict. My motivation to be drug-free was from a different conclusion altogether.

I refused to take anything that compromised my ability to think clearly and to feel. The pain meds made me feel more unlike myself than I already was, which I could not tolerate. Trying to become a functioning person was the only thing I could grasp that had purpose, and I refused to compromise that goal for physical comfort. What truly separates us from being primitive animals is our ability to think and to feel. Medications, especially pain meds, numbed what I soon referred to as *my thinking and feeling apparatus*.

This tearful realization came while lying prone in a bed, alone in the dark, feeling the world passing me by and seeing people who could walk and function, taking for granted their ability to be mobile and to act at will. I had no memory of what it was like to walk or be well. This broken state was all I knew; the same way a baby only knows how to be a baby and a dog, a dog. They've no insight or any reference to anything else.

I vowed to never forget the miracle of being able to move and be self-reliant if I were ever able to achieve them. I vowed to always honor the ability to think and feel because for twenty-eight days, and almost forever more, I was unable to.

The hospital drugs numbed and anesthetized the very things that made me human and alive. I did not want to sleep—*ever again*! I wanted to remain conscious and aware and not lose a moment. I preferred to feel the physical discomfort and pain because they were joyous reminders I was alive.

Many people say they do not fear death.

Most say it.

It is common that people are not preoccupied with death. People feel that fearing death prevents them from actually living, so they do not consider it much. I was once like this too. But I can tell you this: Everyone—and I do mean everyone—fears death once confronted with it. *Everyone.*

Extreme sports competitors, doctors, firefighters, policemen, soldiers . . . when, or if, they are within an actual life-threatening circumstance in which their death seems inevitable and certain, they realize how precious the life they have is and want to preserve it. Be conscious every moment of your life! Respect it! Honor *death* and you will honor *life.*

I'm not referring to suicidal people who have severe emotional, psychological dysfunction, which anyone committing suicide has to a degree. I'm referring to emotionally stable, mentally adjusted people who are not in perpetual states of suffering. And even those who are impaired certainly would choose the *good-life / feeling-better* option over death. I knew my despair was a *healthy* reaction to the circumstances, the same way physical pain is a warning sign from your body meant to get your attention and make you *do something!*

***

I became suspicious the hospital staff was more motivated to drug me to make me more docile and compliant. A drugged and sleepy patient is a low-maintenance! I do not recall being obstreperous or uncooperative, but my memory is far from intact, and rebellion is part of the fabric of my character, so I probably was a PIA (*pain-in-the-ass)* patient.

For years to come, driving past a hospital can trigger a PTSD event. While in the hospital, I was helpless. I had no power or ability. In the very beginning, I could not perform the most basic functions, and even twenty-eight days in, I was 80 percent reliant on staff or machinery for everything.

In summary, I will define my hospital care as . . . *adequate.*

The college-degreed professionals and their staff *did their jobs.*

Not much more or less.

Even in hindsight, my opinion has not changed. They did what was required to preserve my life, but I am not of the opinion anyone went the so-called extra mile and thought outside the box or beyond their academic training. I am also confident if someone *had*, other than myself and my supportive team of family, I would have not only recovered quicker but would have had less to recover from. There were opportunities to anticipate forthcoming issues, minimize them, and even avoid several that became threatening. There were treatments and procedures that could've been done differently—or not at all—that caused domino effects worse than the problem they were designed to fix.

It was my girlfriend's daughter who earns them the *adequate* rating. If she'd not been my hospital advocate, the hospital staff would have received a grading of C-minus.

If you, or someone you care about, is forced to require hospital care, please use this unsolicited advice! No one will care about you or your care as much as you or your loved ones will. You better pay attention, get second and third opinions, and know what the hell is going on while it is happening or there will be costs well beyond a mortgage-sized bill! It takes a wide-angle view to be effective when treating ailments. If a procedure or treatment works on one issue but the fallout from it causes another more severe issue, it may be best to leave well enough alone. We can't spend a dollar to earn a dime.

From a medical perspective, this is the difference between *allopathic* and *homeopathic* treatments. Allopathy is conventional medicine designed to treat the *symptoms* of an illness while homeopathic medicine treats the *source* of the illness. On the other hand, holistic medicine is designed to treat the entire living organism as a whole.

For example, while I was given frequent high doses of powerful, addictive opiates, I was given nothing for the withdrawal symptoms I suffered when they were discontinued, nor was I given supplements to compensate for the damage these toxic detonators were doing to my entire body. What? You think you can IV fentanyl and your liver/kidney/spleen and all your other organs are just gonna walk it off like it never happened? Allopathy robs Peter to pay Paul.

My physical therapies and other allopathic procedures effectively treated the symptoms they were supposed to, but allowed, and even caused, other avoidable issues down the line, issues worse than what had been treated! Conventional allopathic doctors have no *vision*.

I can accept many potential issues were not evident, but as you explore this experience with me, I think you will often agree above-average common sense with PhD education should qualify professionals who command strong six-figure salaries to go above the call of duty. You will also hear of a couple of instances where some did. My *personal* support team, however, has never gotten the credit it deserves, and I would like to raise awareness about their efforts and the work they did for me. Whatever I write here cannot make up for the fact that could not acknowledge or thank them for their actions while they occurred.

The actions they encouraged, supported, and assisted with were game-changers. And their devotion to me is the wellspring source of my motivation, strength, and courage. I wish I could give them a pill—a dose—of the will they gave me. If they had a tiny dose of it, they'd never be afraid again and would conquer Everest in their sleep!

<u>LESSON</u>

If you suffer from a TBI or any severe crisis, you are NOT qualified to assess whether your loved ones are helping you. Be grateful as best you can because the crushing regret of not appreciating them can make permanent tears in your relationships.

It is not your fault, but it needs mentioning. When suffering is your entire experience, the mind manufactures blame as a protective survival mechanism. We cannot psychologically accept nothing can be done. It is too grand and impossible to accept a no-solution scenario. This inability to accept such a magnitude of suffering gets expressed passive aggressively as we look for a scapegoat: In order to cope, we manufacture the view there is indeed a solution, and if people truly loved you, were smarter, doctors did their jobs, God didn't hate you, you weren't evil, etc., then you would get saved from this. Don't blame others, but also don't blame yourself for this wrongful loathing!

You are immersed in circumstances beyond your comprehension and are truly not responsible for your fear, sorrow, anger, denial, and the myriad spectrum of emotions and perspectives seeming oh-so-accurate as you endure.

Please hold on to that keyword: ENDURE.

You must ENDURE.

There may not ever be anything you can do to make this better, but there are droves of things you can do (or not do) to make it worse!

However, on that same note, if your loved ones cannot accept you're not quite yourself, then maybe their capacity for love is not what it should be.

<u>Loved ones</u>: Be tolerant and forgiving of your sufferer's attitudes. When this smoke clears, they will see things entirely differently, but they do not have the luxury of being tolerant, grateful, and forgiving yet. THEY . . . are dealing with a dramatic and terrifying shift in their life. Count your blessings and forget ALL the stupid crap they say and feel for what may be several years until they recover at least 70 percent and begin to see the truth. Do not hold them accountable!

<u>Sufferers</u>: Back off! Remember this axiom with every thought, opinion, and feeling you have during this ever-ongoing tragedy: Less is more! Say only a third of what you think (or less), and whenever you feel anxious, upset, or angry— don't trust it! It may be authentic and accurate, but you have a massive brain trauma, so you're not too qualified to hold the deciding vote on these conclusions yet!

As heroic as I thought and felt my loved ones were for me, it was a mere fraction of what they truly were. And by the way . . . THEY were going through some crap too! My shift from normalcy to defective was without notice, and in a moment, my life was tragically different! SO WAS THEIRS!

My son was at work, thinking of the Dodger standings and his potential career as a firefighter and trying to deal with picky customers as usual, and my girlfriend was doing some yard work and random chores during her one day off from a job that underpaid her when their lives dramatically altered with a call from the hospital!

In an instant, they went from having a reliable man who loved contributing to their lives to the broken-hearted fear they were on their own.

We are all having our own personal tragedy, and while it varies in magnitude, each has a right to their own manner of coping with this tragedy. You do not hold the patent on what is the correct or incorrect way of coping. Judge not lest ye be judged!

5.

PROPS to PROPS: (Respect to Supporters)

> When you are dead Dharma is your best friend.
> —The Vedas

> You're my sunshine and I want you to know/That my feelings are true/I really love you/Oh, you're my best friend
> —Queen ("You're My Best Friend")

I was raised by not being raised.

My parents had a very hands-off approach to parenting, for which I am fortunate and grateful. Mom was motherly and affectionate, and Dad was generically not. Mom had been raised in an upper-middle-class family, and Dad was from the wrong side of the tracks, literally (there were railroad tracks dividing the Ohio town they grew up in and one side was the ghetto side), and he raised himself. The reason I consider myself fortunate for this hands-off parenting approach is it crystallized my self-reliance from a young age.

I did chores as a child and had to be responsible for my own progress. No chores meant no allowance, and as tiny as allowance was in our poor household, $5 for several hours of lawn-mowing and housecleaning was better than nothing.

When I or my four siblings (two biological, two foster) whined about being hungry, Mom said, "You know where the kitchen is ..." Even though she prepared dinners on most nights, morning through evening, we were on our own. And we all knew what we could have and what we couldn't, and no one cheated: We had enough to get by, but nothing extra. By the time I was ten, I was quite capable in the kitchen, among other things.

This self-reliance had been so hardwired into my character that I was and am grossly uncomfortable with any outside contributions, support, or assistance—*for anything*. I'm not a control freak; I just don't want to wait around for anyone else to take care of my business: *I know where the kitchen is*. And by the time I can explain what I want and how I want it, it is typically faster and simpler to make it, get it, build it, take it, leave it, *ad infinitum, myself*.

I may not be able to remember my name most mornings at this early stage of my recovery, but my soft- and hardware programming only understands self-reliance. Besides ... *nothing* is free. Anyone who assists will expect and eventually feel obligated to ask for some form of compensation, which I'm fine with *so long as I know the terms beforehand*.

I don't want *anything* for free. Free is synonymous with *on loan*. If you don't *own* it, then someone can take it. Free is obligatory. As Bob Dylan said, *You're gonna have to serve somebody!*

These features of life not only made me self-reliant but efficient. It is rumored it was Bonaparte that said if you want something done right, you best do it yourself. I subscribe whole-heartedly. Unless it's something I *can't* do.

There were a host of things I couldn't do now. I saw those "human" things: walking, standing, opening doors, crossing rooms ... I heard people do things like drive machines called cars from place to place too. Those things were beyond me. When I saw them being done, it looked simple. No one I saw walking seemed to struggle to do it, yet if *I* tried, it took laser focus and a massive effort to not get my two feet things tangled up and end up needing someone to catch me.

The paradox was that even though I had no memory recall and was more than excused from doing anything well, I was drowning in a sense of shame, thinking, *I can't do the simplest things*. This made me feel like a failure. I was learning there were many innate perceptions and feelings that don't need to be learned, and shame is one of them.

I suspected happiness is one too, but I couldn't identify it. I was not just unhappy because of my wicked circumstances; I was unhappy because my traumatized brain couldn't produce the endorphins serotonin and dopamine. My thinking and feeling apparatus was all fucked up.

***

What follows here is partly a guide to those suffering from brain traumas such as mine and others. I'm a stupid human and stupid humans learn best by trial and error. I hope my trials and errors can save you from making the same mistakes. I wouldn't say that would make my suffering *worth it,* but since I learned some things the hard way, why not use my knowledge to prevent the same errors from being made by others?

What is here are not only descriptions of things I did to recover but also my for-better-or-worse attitudes and perspectives, offered so you can learn from my mistakes. The only mistakes I truly regret were the emotional ones, *not* the clinical ones. I easily forgive myself for rejecting some good ideas offered to me. I struggle with the *way* I rejected them. Eventually, I took good advice that healed me. The pain I caused others with my resistance will haunt me as long as I live.

Walks on Wheels

When I was still in the hospital, my girlfriend escorted me to the hospital cafeteria most mornings and afternoons. I did not want to go. I was ashamed and embarrassed at being *un-whole.* I felt sorry for her that she had to be with such an incompetent and broken man, and this shame made me resistant instead of grateful.

She helped me into the wheelchair and wheeled me to the cafeteria or around the walkway outside of the ward. She encouraged and often insisted that I steer and rotate the wheels on my own. She insisted I get into and out of the chair on my own and encouraged me to stand or walk a few steps when outdoors. What she got in exchange for her devotion was attitude and ingratitude. Even up to a year later, I was incapable of remembering or realizing what she and others had tried to do for me. I am shamefully aware now, but my ingratitude has left scars that may always be present in them, and for that I am sorry.

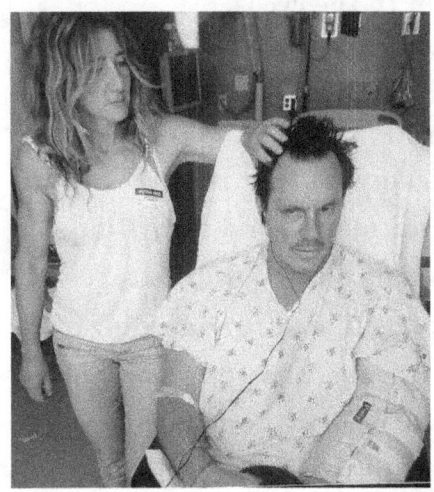

I lost 38 pounds during 9 day coma. You'd think I'd be smiling.

Playing Ball in the House

My son assisted me daily by playing catch with a ball, getting me up from bed, and walking the halls and eventually the stairwells. Once I was home from the hospital, he became my physical therapy coach, teaching me how to catch a ball. He watched Dodger games with me, explained the news stories on TV, and took care of our house all on his own. He went from being a son to being a parent in an instant, and I struggle to forgive myself for being the source of his pain and fear. There isn't much about him in these pages, but his role in my long-term recovery and after is beyond expression, but I will attempt to express it later!

I don't recall ever giving him attitude when he coached me in PT (physical therapy) or taught me how to drive or do a myriad of other things. And as painful as it was, I loved the irony of my son, whom I had once taught how to walk and drive, was now teaching me.

But I often rejected his instructions out of fatherly pride. Then I'd do whatever it was when I was alone and show him later what I could do. I gave him all the credit, but it was always delayed. *Pride kills*. It has no place in trauma recovery. Humility is *not* weakness: it is true strength and power.

Paying the Bills

During my hospital stay, my girlfriend and her family assisted by managing my affairs. When this began, they had to figure out how to access my bank accounts, my monthly bills, and other financial responsibilities, like my mortgage, the rent on my office, and my auto and health insurance. Once a few clients showed up for their counseling appointments with no idea where I was, my girlfriend called dozens of my clients and my family too to alert them to the crisis.

I was (and am again) an entirely self-sufficient person and not one area of my life was delegated to anyone else, so trying to manage it while I was incapable of having any input was miraculous. In addition to this, my partner is NOT a multi-tasker! She is often overwhelmed by deadlines, commitments, and things outside of her somewhat small comfort zone. I . . . was the manager of our lives together. She was never required nor asked to care for my responsibilities, or our joint ones, and she was suddenly thrust into them while simultaneously worrying and being terrified that she would end up alone and permanently lose the person she had been intimately linked to for over ten years. Many people would've walked away. And she not only stayed the course, but it was a full year before I was capable of self-managing and nearly three years before I was capable of seeing what she had done and being grateful for it.

I was clueless about these efforts by her and her family. They intervened when I was hospitalized in a coma, and they never even mentioned anything about managing my home, bills, and obligations. I never asked because I literally had no sense of these matters. I didn't even know what a house was, let alone a mortgage. I don't remember ever acknowledging gratitude for this.

I will bear that cross until the day I die (again).

Emotional Support and Company

My girlfriend's daughter spent more time in my hospital room than anyone else. She kept me company and quietly micromanaged my care in the hospital. As a super-smart young woman with early-stage medical training, she knew how to ask the right questions and subtly influence the hospital staff to do more than they would've done on their own.

By asking the right questions, she was able to get the staff to think from more angles without questioning their authority and maintaining a delicate rapport. Having a smart, qualified person looking out for me made the staff more aware of their performance and thereby raise their game. She was carefully diplomatic, restraining herself from blatantly calling them out on their underperformance, but sometimes she lost her shit and got downright blatant too!

I cannot imagine how much worse off I'd have been then—and now—if it weren't for her presence and intervention.

She also became the liaison between the doctors, hospital staff, and my other loved ones. She made herself understand the procedures and language the staff used and put it into layman's terms so that everyone could understand what to expect and take a role in making it better.

I will always be in her debt for this.

To *this,* I will say, *I was lucky!*

It wasn't *luck* that I had supportive loved ones:

My partner, her children, and parents and my own family and friends had bonded over the years through good times and bad. I am so grateful they rose to the occasion to help me, not out of obligation but out of mutual affection. They were grateful for whom I had always tried to be in their lives and rallied to my aid. It wasn't *luck.*

But the *luck* of having a nursing student who is smart, competent, and takes initiative at my bedside was a godsend!

I cannot praise her enough and was told I used to beg her not to leave me, that I wanted everyone to stay, but she, in particular, was someone I would plead to stay. Again, this is completely contrary to my character, as I am not someone who is comfortable asking for favors in any situation.

If you're well and capable, then make your investments: when you can help or assist someone within your inner circle without enabling them, *do it.*

Don't do it so that they *owe* you when your own chips are down; do it because being a part of someone's progress and improvement is a glorious feature of the human condition. I have lived a life of service out of selfishness: *I enjoy it.* It gives me purpose and makes me feel satisfied and good. I'm not a saint! I'm a greedy man in pursuit of pleasure, and helping others is a selfish way to feel good about myself!

Hospital Delusions

"Please don't leave me here alone. They do stuff to me when no one's around. Secret experiments they don't want you guys to know about."

This was a plea to my partner on several occasions. I whispered this to her in fear the "alien" hospital people would hear me.

I was convinced the hospital was taking me to some sort of underground laboratory at night to perform experiments on me. I can now assume the surgeries and other procedures I underwent made me paranoid. I was unconscious, or only quasi-conscious, and saturated with highly potent narcotics most of the time. I didn't have the ability to make sense of what was happening to me. Ya see . . . I didn't know what a hospital was. I thought I'd been abducted by either ghosts or aliens, even though I had no idea what ghosts or aliens were!

My personal team had no indication that paranoia was going to be temporary. Even as a professional serving delusional clients it can get tiresome. If you are in trauma, trust me, the weird shit you're going on about doesn't make any sense to others, and their indulgence of you is a gift!

Past-Life Regression or Delusion?

I seemed satisfied when hospital staff told me *who* these family people were, even though none of it seemed right. I intuitively accepted labels for them like *"son,"* *"girlfriend," "Dad,"* etc., but none of this matched my experience. I was like, *"Okay . . . sure. My "son." My "dad." My "girlfriend." Whatever. I assume these labels have significance and these are good things to have, so I can go along with this . . . sure.*

A nurse stood next to Janete and spoke to me in baby talk like I was a child, "Do you know who *this* is?" It was offensive, and I was determined to deprive this self-righteous nurse of any satisfaction of me being impaired, so I replied, "Sure. She's the queen."

It is unclear whether I meant the Queen of England, since I thought I was in London, or was just grasping at a pet name I thought was appropriate since it was inferred this was someone I was close to and should know well.

After ten years of being together, my girlfriend and I never had *pet* names, like dear, darling, or sweetie, and certainly nothing like king or queen. We have always referred to each other by name, personally finding pet names juvenile and *beneath* us! (We're such snobs!)

I was also viewing a life she and I shared in the 1400s, and in *that* life she and I were actually royalty: We were not king and queen, but we were of nobility in the Salisbury region near Stonehenge. In that lifetime, we performed a magical ceremony within the old temple of Stonehenge that ended quite tragically. I wasn't seeing her just as my current partner but as the priestess I'd married in the 1400s and several other eras. The locals we served in Salisbury referred to her as the queen out of their loving devotion for her.

I saw my loved ones, and everyone actually, as spirit souls, each with a string of past-life identities as well as their current one. It was such an obvious feature of life that I assumed everyone saw this way. My most recent prior life was spent in London, so my mind was confused about the time and place I was in currently. Kinda like I hear how rock stars lose track of what city they're in when they tour, shouting out, *"How ya all doin', Detroit!"* when they're really in Des Moines.

I now know the memory deletion of prior lives is standard operating procedure within The Portal: you're not supposed to carry one life's memories into the next life. It can be overwhelming! I was caught in a Portal matrix glitch: I was experiencing multiple lives and identities simultaneously, like a collage.

That, or I was simply whacked out from trauma, meds, and nine days of being in a coma, which will give you the mental fuzzies like you can't imagine. I needed a triple espresso, *stat!*

Hell, I can't function after waking from *seven* hours of sleep without my morning joe, so *nine days?* Fuggedabout it!

***

The conclusion of my hospital stay and care is comparatively insignificant, so I will conclude it with a summary to avoid those nagging comments about leaving out the basics.

First 12 days:

- Unconscious in coma for nine

- I was confined to the bed and received nourishment intravenously
- I had a catheter and wore some form of diaper for waste removal
- Upon waking, I was only conscious one to three hours each day total, twenty to sixty minutes at a time.

Days 12-20:

- Catheter and IV feeding tube removed
- Awake three to four hours per day (not in a row)
- Spent one to two hours per day in physical therapy rooms, learning to:
    - Stand, walk, grasp, and perform other fundamental tasks
    - Speak and think (speech therapy and brain puzzles like word searches, connect-the-dots, and first-grade-level logic and memory problems

Days 20-28:

- More of the same therapies but more advanced
- Awake four to five hours each day
- Able to perform basic functions like eating and holding brief conversations
- Became more aware of my circumstances and condition
- Still felt no pain, mostly due to a total absence of physical sensations

When the staff told me I'd be going home within a few days, I was terrified. I felt certain that my insurance company was limiting my care and wanted to slow the financial bleeding they were being subjected to.

I *hated* being in a hospital, but it was my entire and only world. I was taken outside the hospital just once for a sandwich, and it was terrifying! There was this whole other world out there!

My PPO insurance was quite adequate, and it was soon established I had zero fault in the accident, so the other driver's insurance was completely liable, but the time was up.

I did not feel I was anywhere near ready to go home, and it was evident I was still unable to care for myself, which placed the burden of near-constant care on my family.

My family, like most people, have work, school, and other real commitments that cannot be simply put aside or postponed to care for me. I should've remained in the hospital until I was capable of getting up, walking safely from room to room, and preparing food to eat, *at the least.*

My bag was packed with my medical devices and I was dressed, waiting for my son to drive us home. I was terrified and trying to put on a brave face and act like I was happy because I knew it was what people expected of me, and I did not want them to worry. I tried to play the role of a guy getting released from prison, but I was terrified to face the real world.

I was not relieved when we pulled into my driveway. I had never seen this house before and felt overwhelmed with the desperate need to grasp all this so that these nice people, whom I just met twenty-eight days ago, would not be burdened by this stranger who I thought I was to them.

We entered the house "I" had lived in for the past fourteen years with my son and in which I had spent ten years having coffee, dinners, and watching movies with this girlfriend person, and it was a foreign place.

There was an oversized green sofa, wide-screen TV, and an aquarium protruding from the wall. There were leaves embedded in the wall, a DIY-crafted fireplace, and a sheet of perforated steel fastened to the ceiling like a suspended wave.

I had an eclectic style of décor, to say the least.

"How's it feel to be home, Dad?" my son asked as we sat on the sofa, facing the fish tank.

"I *know* this is my house and that's my TV and my fish tank and my kitchen over there and all that. I know it *intellectually.* But none of it *feels* familiar. I don't *feel* like I've ever been here before."

This feeling, or lack of it, persisted for months.

6.

HOME AGAIN, HOME AGAIN

> There's only one thing worse than suffering:
> *Suffering for no reason.*
> —Krishnanand

> There's No Place Like Home
> —Dorothy from *The Wizard of Oz*

My son gave me a tour of our home, and as I went from room to room, I asked questions. We all assumed it would jog my memory and things would start to look familiar.

It didn't.

"What's this stuff?" I asked, pointing to a collection of bags, gear, and equipment in the thing called a garage where this thing called "my car" resided.

My memory was deleted, but my brain had some stored knowledge. I couldn't *remember* the things he was about to explain, but I was remotely aware of what they were. I was like an infant in a grown man's body. The young man, *called my son*, was teaching me. The irony didn't elude even *my* impaired brain and thinking: the boy I taught to walk and speak was now teaching me.

My son answered, "That's our backpacking gear. You and I have backpacked all over the High Sierras. That over there is your scuba gear. You've been a scuba diver for over ten years and taught me too. We went to Cancun and dove underground tunnels of freshwater tunnels called cenotes and we also went diving in Cozumel a couple years ago."

Can-coz-cenote-what?! It was all Greek to me. I was remembering prior lives better than this one!

"You've been all over the world. That's your tennis gear. You're a four-oh tennis player—pretty good and competitive. You play a couple times a week and saw Roger Federer and Serena Williams play last year.

"These are some of your awards and newspaper interviews. You've been on TV and radio, and you write two editorials a month for a magazine here in LA. You're a member of the Opioid Recovery Task Force here in Santa Clarita Valley due to the epidemic. You were the keynote speaker at a national conference a few months ago, and these newspaper articles are about your workshops."

This did not make me happy.

It seemed this Scott guy had this wonderful life of adventure and was admired and loved, respected and fulfilled, and now this broken guy who *looked* like him was about to ruin it by not being able to fill his shoes or do *anything* he liked.

I wanted to die.

    Again.

Every day and night I wished I'd never woken up from my coma. I silently wished I had not survived: I'd gone from being an inspiration to a burden. I *silently* wished it because to express it out loud would be even more selfish, causing more fear and worry to these people who loved me. They didn't need to hear my sad droning, so, I tried smiling instead—*for them.*

I was unable to climb the stairs to my bedroom, so I lived on the sofa, unable to go beyond the kitchen and bathroom. When they went to work, I was alone with these tormented thoughts of just praying and weeping to expire and make it easier on everyone involved.

My own suffering was barely on my radar. I was truly *empathetic* to others' worry, fear, and grief about me, and this affected me greatly, but I was fairly immune to being concerned about my own welfare. I just didn't want to be a burden.

Apparently, one of the things I brought back with me from The Portal was an unnerving volume of *empathy*. I had always been *sympathetic* to others, which was a cornerstone to my career as a counselor, but I was always able to separate their suffering and my own condition. I cared *so deeply* for all who came to me for help, yet my objectivity was never impaired by being overwhelmed by empathy. This sucked!

This empathy thing was automatic, and it never shut off! Each and every person I encountered had *radiation*. People are startlingly oblivious to the radiation they emit, but it's there. I could sense their inner pain, their fears, their sorrows. I was plugged into this frequency of humanity's dirty little secret: we're all suffering.

We're plagued by nonstop desiring and a deep-seated awareness that we are not happy, have never been truly happy, and are exhausted from the sustained denial of knowing we never *will* be happy. The pursuit of worldly happiness is neurotic.

Everyone had these two shadows: one was the shadow being cast by their body from the sun to the Earth, the other was this spectral shadow of their true spirit. The first one was part of matter and it just existed, like a stone or a mountain. The second one was not matter; it was their true self, their soul, yearning to be free and blissful. And the material shadow eclipses the spirit shadow, so they don't even see it. It was so painful because it was *all* I could see!

My psychic-intuition radio receiver was picking up every goddam signal being broadcast, and the suffering of humanity was a massive sound blast of static! It was maddening because *all I wanted to do was help them*, to remove their suffering and reveal to them that all they suffered from were illusions, that they were mistaking *wanting* for *needing!* We're all caught in the illusion happiness can be extracted from the world when our souls are crying out and screaming from within saying, *"No! I'm not happy! Please, save me! STOP giving me* worldly *things when I need* spiritual *things! I'm starving!"* They were stuck between *both* realms: the material and the spiritual.

Because I am viewing all there is through a spiritual lens, worldly entertainment fails me now. But it seems imperative I learn to appreciate worldly things. Why? Because I live in the world! I can't relate, connect, or function in a world of matter when I can't appreciate the whole of it.

I was an avid tennis fan, player and spectator, and as I try to watch the US Open, I feel I am *forcing* myself to enjoy it while restraining the thought of how senseless it is, anything is, that's not directly related to spirit. I feel like a phantom.

I was able to perceive *truth* but unable to do anything about it. I felt the world's pains, overwhelmed with an altruistic desire to alleviate its suffering. I wanted to shake every one of them to wake them up! I wanted to tell them to *stop* seeking happiness in worldly things and start seeking it in spiritual things, to expose to them the whole truth and nothing but the truth, which is that *everything in existence is absolutely perfect and just the way it is supposed to be,* with one single exception: their *perception* of it.

What the Buddha realized when he first left the palace was unavoidably clear to me: *Life is suffering, and the cause of suffering is desiring.* But Buddha was an avatar, a divine spirit who appeared on the material plane to show us the way out. I was just some guy all fucked up in a hospital bed! I was in *no* position to help anyone! It's like I had seen, and still saw, beyond the veil of worldly illusions, *the samsara,* but could not communicate or express it. I could barely finish a sentence without forgetting the thought behind it!

***

I slept off and on through the night. Same with the day—off and on through slumbering consciousness. It was not because of my anxiety that my sleep was sporadic but because the sleep mechanisms in my brain were not functioning and neither were my feelings: my brain no longer had the ability to produce the endorphins and other neurochemicals to produce feelings of joy, although it seemed to have an endless supply of depressing ones!

I felt like an alien who had inhabited this man Scott's identity.

I could not feel happiness or excitement or love or pleasure. I couldn't feel pain either, not even when I sliced my finger open while trying to wash a knife and was unaware of the blood and the injury till Brandon saw it and alerted me.

It is ironic and paradoxical that when we are deprived of the ability to emote joy, we still have easy access to feeling *bad.* This makes me ponder a philosophical conundrum: If we lack the ability to produce *happy* feelings, yet we experience *bad* ones, does this mean our organic nature is to feel bad? We don't need the *addition* of bad chemicals to feel bad; those feelings seem to exist independently.

Yet we *do* need the good ones to feel positive. I can attest to this because while I had no access to *any* good feelings, whatsoever, I was overwhelmed with sorrow and sadness. I remember sitting on the edge of my bed, sobbing uncontrollably for no reason other than not having a shred of feeling good and not even being able to imagine what good should feel like.

It is reasonable to conclude that my given circumstances were certainly more than enough to produce complete despair, but I can testify this awareness is simply *not* where my despair came from. I did not have the ability to wonder about how happy I wish I was, or once was, or wanted to be. I did not have the room, space, or capacity to have an actual opinion about the state of my life. I wept because bad is *all* I felt. I felt *nothing* else. Not anger or fear or regret or injustice or pain or even sadness or sorrow.

And this empty black hole, this void of feeling, made living insensible. I did not *feel* bad: I *became* it.

I had fused and become one with the *absence* of my identity, my personality, the world, living things, existence . . . and this was not formed by thought. This despair was an entirely independent substance that was completely immune to thought.

Not sex, love, money, my son smiling, my girlfriend in rapture, or a wonderful child in bliss could have any effect on me. I was unreachable. I was drowning in an endless sea of despair: mine, yours, and the other eight billion people on the planet. I was saturated in empathy sorrow, isolated and alone with nothing but an awareness of it.

I am not trying to beat a proverbial dead horse and repeatedly make a point that cannot truly be made. I seem to have an endless supply of expressions to elaborate this, and each one is deficient. As much as I can imagine that you, my dear reader, are nearly in tears from reading this visceral account, it comes as close to the actual experience as me saying that childbirth is probably *painful and amazing* or that orgasm feels *really good times a hundred*. There are no metaphors or expressions that can elaborate on the actual magnitude of these events. What I have expressed to you is not even an infinitesimal fraction of what TBI/DAI truly feels like.

You're right to be upset and immersed in sympathy as you read my account to the point of thinking, *"F-this! I can't take a whole book of this—I'm out!"* and look for the nearest waste can or open window out of which to fling this book. You'd be somewhat of a sociopath if you *weren't* considering divorcing yourself from this text ASAP.

But if you trust me, *I will lead you to the other side.* There will be silver linings here, and even though those silver linings are wrapped around a dark and scary cloud, at least the dark cloud *has* a silver lining, which is at least better than a dark cloud *with no* silver lining.

Endure.

I gave you this buzzword some time ago and I'm refreshing it here. We do not know if we can make things better, but they can certainly be made worse. Learning to take one step becomes truthful evidence that we can take two.

As far as I've come, it always feels like it's just an inch. And every inch I've progressed feels like light years of distance from where I was before . . . last year . . . *yesterday*.

YOU are not alone.

I . . . am with you. And if I can do this, YOU can do this.

I . . . am not superman. I am an average man with an inability to quit. I have been inspired by others, and I do not hold this lamp to see my own way anymore, but to illuminate the path for others so they can find their way here too.

Lemme raise the mood an octave:

Here's a dose of the science behind the anomaly of feeling emotionless: Your brain does not actually have *"feel-bad"* chemicals. Depression, sorrow, anxiety, fear, and the myriad of bad and negative feelings we experience are not produced by neurochemicals. *Negative* emotions such as sadness or depression, are produced by either a *deficiency* of "good" chemicals, like dopamine and serotonin, or by the overproduction of them. Fear does not have its own neurochemical either; it is produced by an overabundance of the stimulant adrenaline. Adrenaline produces positive excitement in the right amount and paranoia and fear in the wrong amount. We rely on what is known as SDNEs[2] to have emotion: serotonin, dopamine, norepinephrine, and endorphins. My DAI brain was not producing any of these.

Serotonin and dopamine give you feelings of joy, intimacy, and reward, like the "ah-hah!" feeling you get when you learn something, and norepinephrine produces excitement and energy.

My SDNE reserves were a dry well.

I was mentally, emotionally, and physically depleted. I had no energy, no anxiety, no joy, no excitement, no interest, and no clue. I was sleepy nonstop and physically fatigued if I stood up or dared to take steps. God loves irony: There was absolutely nothing severely wrong with my *body*. My muscles were fine, my bones too. But my brain was not capable of giving my body the right instructions. Whatever neurochemicals I had lay dormant within the glands in which they resided. They were on vacation and wouldn't return to work without the direct marching orders from my impaired brain. My brain's owner's manual for these mechanisms had been deleted, so it had no idea how to transmit these orders to its staff.

My *diffuse axonal injury* had shut down (or off) my brain's ability to manufacture or transmit the right chemicals. I did not have access to joy. This is what clinical depression is: the inability to produce "happy" molecules within the brain. While it seems like an easy chemical fix with meds to supplement these missing neurons, the side effects of these drugs are proportionate. When a medication supplements "happy" chemicals, a person may have delusions of grandeur and be unable to function in the normal world because they are too high.

This is how cocaine, methamphetamine abusers, and manic people have delusions of grandeur. Too much hyper stuff! When a medication reduces or shuts off the release of adrenalines, the person becomes more stable, yes, but they cease to feel anything at all, making them feel like a ghost. This is why people with disorder issues resist their medications: because even though they are more cooperative and stable to *others*, they do not feel present within their own identity. These "side-effects" are why so many people, including Chris Cornell of Soundgarden, Chester Bennington of Linkin Park, and Robin Williams all committed suicide in

---

[2] SDNEs have a fun and thorough chapter in my Project Addiction book.

spite of their antidepressants. These meds cause a paradoxical effect—intensifying the very symptoms they are designed to abate.

Even though I could not remember my drug and pharmacology training (I was and am an expert in the field), my instincts knew to just say no to the drugs.

Okay . . . now where were we?

Oh, yeah . . . I was home from the hospital and was soon able to sleep in a bed. I was not able to shower or get up on my own more than once or twice a day. The first few weeks at home are as cloudy to me as my weeks in the hospital, and I am sure my mind has selected to forget, or deny, this period to prevent permanent psychological trauma. I recall a few things, but I do not know the order of most occurrences.

Within two days, I felt like I was at a place I sensed was my home. Within a week, I didn't know of it any other way: I was home. It was natural and basic. The entire first month I lay on the sofa and my girlfriend/partner watched movies and TV with me when she could. Neither she nor my son rarely left me. But I felt alone. Nonstop. Even when I was NOT alone, I felt entirely alone. Not euphemistically, metaphorically, or existentially. I felt entirely alone at all times, even when I sat alongside another person who loved me very much. I could not *connect* or sense another's presence or feelings. I was distant. Remote. *Not there.*

At this moment, as I type this, it chokes me up. . . .

After a while, I began making efforts to push myself beyond my most immediate surroundings. I walked into my garage and out to the driveway in front of my house. I didn't do anything once I was there, but I *did* it!

I was driven to a few doctor's, physical, and speech therapy appointments, but it quickly became apparent that the effort by everyone to get me to those appointments was unnecessary. The therapists were all having me do the same exercises with only the slightest modifications, so we all decided to replicate these exercises at home.

My son became my physical therapy coach, and my girlfriend took me to a local store to buy puzzle books similar to the ones at the therapist's. I was given colored pencils to draw, color, and connect the dots, and I was soon reading, even though I rarely understood what I read. I was satisfied just to read the words. I didn't feel like I was making *progress per se,* just relieved to feel something as basic as mild satisfaction for being able to *do* something. I had a tiny, subtle sense that reading was *home,* like reading was a missing piece that needed to come home to me.

***

Within a few weeks, my son had me doing simple movements like stepping side to side, forward and back, and hopping up and down on *both* feet. (One would have spelled disaster!) He sat across the room from me and bounced tennis balls to me, some of which I returned! Soon he had me going outside and walking up and down the sloped driveway and eventually drove me to the nearby school to walk the running track. He was tough, and I like to think he'd had a good coach since I had been his baseball coach from the age of four until he got into high school and became a varsity all-star player in his senior year. He pushed me and never allowed me to say, "I can't." Instead of launching me too far, too fast, he pushed me *just outside the boundaries* of what I was capable of, assertively testing and coaxing me to go a bit further. His approval means the world to me, and he smartly capitalized off this with the right blend of disappointment if I didn't try hard and acceptance whether I succeeded or not. I got *Bs* for effort and *Bs* for execution. Never an *A*, so I would always feel required to do a little more to satisfy him and make him proud. It was unconditional love with conditions, and it was straight out from my own patented parent playbook.

"You wanna try driving?" he asked me around week ten.

"You think I can? I don't know what to do. You'll have to show me."

"Yeah. We'll just go round the block. I'll drive so you can watch, and then you drive back."

15 year old Brandon's graduation day from fire-academy.

He drove to the carpool parking lot by the freeway entrance several blocks from our house, the exact parking lot where I had taught him to drive when he was fourteen. I was clueless. "Okay, the long, skinny peddle on the right makes it go and the short one on the left makes it stop. Easy-peasy. Okay? You ready?"

The I-5 freeway loomed three stories below if I was incapable of stopping before the fence. I eased to the edge and then reversed slowly to try again. Voilà.

"You wanna drive us home?" he asked.

I eased onto an actual street and turned right and drove the four blocks to my garage. We switched places, as he said parking was more of an advanced skill.

We went driving a few minutes every day. It was never comfortable, but I was capable and determined.

"How'd you like it?" he asked me on that first run.

"Pretty cool. It's the first thing since D-Day that felt familiar. I couldn't remember how to do it or ever having actually done it before, but it felt like something I *had* done before."

I wept that night in joy. It was the first time I'd felt anything was familiar to me. I didn't care what it was or how trivial or random it was. Having *anything* feel familiar made me suspect that "I" was still here somewhere.

Our identities are the sum total of all our personal events and experiences that have led us to this specific moment. Without our past experiences and the memory of them, our identities are lost. Deleted. Everything you are relies on who you were a year ago, a day ago, a moment ago. Familiarity is a blessed feeling we all take for granted.

I did not know my past that had made me who I was. I was a clean slate with no point of reference.

I would like to proclaim that once the first feeling of familiarity occurred while driving, the walls came down and my memory was restored, but this was not the case. However, driving resulted in TWO major breakthroughs: I experienced 1) *familiarity,* which led to 2) feeling *joyful.*

Somewhere within this living flesh was "me." I no longer felt I needed to invent him or *find him.* I now felt I needed to *uncover* him. I was in here somewhere.

I began taking initiative.

I performed my physical therapy exercises on my own when my son was not home and a second round when he was. I kept it a secret, so he thought my improvements were only from our once-a-day exercises! He was proud of me, and I lived for it.

I began walking up and down the stairs multiple times a day and tried to do tasks like open a can of food, make a sandwich, and take out the trash. *"Why not?"* became my mantra to everything. and I constantly asked myself, *"What's the worst that could happen?"* and if the answer was anything less than death or injury, I would try it. Fear was not an acceptable reason to avoid or postpone doing something. I *feared* everything. The one emotion my brain seemed to have a never-ending supply of was fear. I felt nervous and fearful nonstop. It was as constant to me as the color of my eyes.

I don't want to give the wrong impression. Those who watched these events unfold when they were happening or heard about them, as you are doing now, have proclaimed how brave and strong I was. I *never* felt brave, strong, or fearless. I was terrified of every step and new attempt before, during, and after doing it.

What made me keep trying *was* fear. I was *terrified* when I walked up the stairs or did the side-stepping routines in my entryway that my son *insisted* I do. I was afraid to get up and walk to the front door, and sure as hell afraid of getting into the damn car to drive, let alone getting out! Unfolding my confused and uncontrollable body from a car seat was dicey!

But I was even *more terrified* of staying the way I was.

I was not living a "*Just do it*" Nike commercial. I was in a perpetual state of fear and did not know how long I could maintain a will to live as I was, so something needed to change. I figured there was an expiration date to my tolerance and endurance of my condition, and when that date came, I had best improve myself or I was doomed. I didn't think I'd have to resort to suicide. I figured I'd hit the proverbial wall and just give up the will to live and stop breathing.

I knew I was unwilling to live my life in a state of disrepair. I was not brave; I was a coward, too sad and proud and unwilling to see the beauty in life if I couldn't function. No . . . *Stephen Hawking* was brave. People who persist and find ways of accepting their limitations are brave. I am an embarrassing coward, and I am not saying this in a poetic sense for inspiration. I am saying it literally. I was terrified everyday of remaining how I was and was willing to do anything and everything I needed to prevent it.

Fear made me go the extra mile.

Oddities

An odd phenomenon was occurring.

When I was unconscious and asleep in the world, I was present and aware on the *other side, within The Portal*. When my mind became dormant *here*, it became active *there*. My physical brain slept, which freed my mind from matter, and I teleported to the Other Side. It was like an ongoing classroom on the other side. The teachings were in full swing as I entered, and I was just joining in.

It had been going since I awoke from my coma, but I was only now becoming aware of it. Until then, each time I would wake in the world, my time "over there" would fade and evaporate, like a dream, and I would completely forget it.

Slowly, I became able to retain basic things: who Brandon was, where I lived, how to get to the store (and what you did there!). With this new retention ability, I was waking from body sleep with awareness and remembrance of the things I witnessed, learned, and that were revealed to me on the other side.

I was not only retaining what I experienced the night before but also beginning to recall the nine earth days I'd spent there while in my coma.

It was all making sense now: I had not felt present here since my resurrection because I was experiencing both dimensions at once: this world and the other one. When I was awake here, I was disconnected and confused because half my mind was still over there. But when I was asleep here, my mind was fully aware there. Here was challenging. There made sense.

The secrets and truths revealed while I was there were coming forth in my memory. New ones were ongoing.

There was a profound quality to these insights that distinguished them from those in a dream. I woke with clarity and certainty not present in a dream. And since my D-Day, I'd *not* had regular dreams! I not only don't recall any but had not once had the feeling that I even dreamt.

Instead, I woke with a subtle sadness, as it was easier, more peaceful, and sublime there, and I missed it. I felt awake the entire time, attentive while I was there and rested as though I'd slept for hours.

Was I delusional? Was this brain trauma? Had my TBI blown some electrical fuses?

I started to record notes when I awoke. Writing is a bit beyond me still, so I took my digital voice recorder to my bedside so I could record notes as they came to mind.

7.

THE DEEP END OF THE POOL (A Brief Reference)

> "Just wait a moment," said Tigger nervously . . .
> —*The Tao of Piglet* (Benjamin Hoff)

> One man gathers what another man spills.
> —Grateful Dead ("St. Stephen")

We're about to start swimming in the deep end of the pool. This brief pause will allow you to grab your floaties and take a deep breath.

Terms and Glossary

Each term and concept is defined, described, or explored within the text, but this list of terms will make it easy to reference many of the esoteric, foreign, and Sanskrit words I've used. These are not alphabetized because sometimes one term describes another. Enjoy!

Near-Death Experience (NDE): The phenomena of surviving a near-death event or traumatic circumstance that reveals evidence of an afterlife.

Traumatic Brain Injury / Diffuse Axonal Injury (TBI/DAI): This memoir is an NDE account caused by a TBI of the DAI kind. These terms are explored and defined within the text.

Enlightened/Self-Realized: Personalities who are "One" with spiritual consciousness. Enlightened typically refers to those who have transcended material consciousness and merged their mind with the formless, omnipresent, omniscient, cosmic mind of creation. They have become "One" with "everything." These include yogis and mystics who experience "objective" reality and remain immune to "subjective reality." They are in perfect peace of self-contentment and are desireless. They have attained complete "soul awareness," experiencing their divine soul without material interference. These include Gautam Buddha, Shankaracharya, and other Saints of the monistic, formless aspect of divinity. It is a path of "monism": Oneness. Once attained, it is eternal, removing you from the *Wheel of Life* (reincarnation). Upon physical death, the soul merges with Divinity and the mind is terminated. Suffering is terminated because there is no mind to perceive it. This is called *advait* (ah-dwa-eet) in Sanskrit, meaning *non-dualism*, which is synonymous with self-realization.

Spiritually-Realized/God Realized: These are Divine personalities who are One with a personal form of the Godhead. "Realized" souls are One with their soul (jivatma), the same as "self-realized" persons are as well as One with the supreme, divine soul of God (parmatma). They experience the self-contentment as the Enlightened personalities do, along with the bliss (anand) of their personal form of God (Vishnu, Jesus, Krishna, Shiva, etc.). Upon physical death, the soul merges with God and the mind is divinized and retained. Suffering is terminated, as the mind now perceives Divine Bliss. This is attainment of *divine-duality*, called *dvait* in Sanskrit, meaning *mono-dualism*. Also known as *theosis* within Western, orthodox religions.

Stupid Humans: Everyone else! An affectionate, humorous reference of the collective of humanity: anyone who is not Realized or Enlightened. That's nearly all eight billion of us, including me. We are desire machines, experiencing separation of our mind from our soul and the Godhead (total duality). Our minds are a part of the material phenomena (maya/samsara) and incapable of pure perception of the Godhead or our soul. The separation is an Eternal Condition (original sin).

Soul's Journey: The collection of experiences that pertain to a human's journey to attain Enlightenment/Realization. Typically, it occurs over many lifetimes of effort and progress.

Sanskrit: The oldest known language within the world, considered by many spiritualists and mystics to be an eternal language. Hebrew is suspected to be the same and/or a derivative of Sanskrit.

Aspirated (a): Most Sanskrit words do not end in *a*. The "aspirated *a*" adaptation is a side effect of the British colonialization of the subcontinent of India. Out of respect for origins, this text will typically allow the aspirated *a* parenthetically. (For example, it isn't yog(a), it's yog, not karm(a), but karm. However, these words are indeed hard to pronounce without adding the *"uh"* sound!)

Maya: The material phenomena: anything and everything that is not One with the Godhead or an extension/expression of the Godhead, in other words, the world, you, me, the universe, etc.

Samsar(a): The concept that the material phenomenon (maya) is an illusion and unreal. Sanskrit texts actually state that maya is absolutely real; it is only the *conscious perception* of it (good/bad/beautiful/painful/etc.) is the illusion.

Karm(a): The cosmic law of cause and effect. The Sanskrit texts are its origins, so we look to those to define what it is and how it is used.

Sanskars: The cosmic law of character, attitude, mood, preferences, and tendencies. Sanskars are similar to karmas, but whereas karm(a) governs events and circumstances, Sanakars govern our dispositions and attitudes. Waking up *on the right/wrong side of the bed* is an example of a good/bad sanskars. They are stored within our consciousness and come to the surface based on cosmic influences and events. An innate attraction to spirituality would be considered a spiritual-sanskar. A preference of vanilla ice cream and a disdain for Rocky Road could be considered a sanskar. Then again, liking ice cream with marshmallows is just bad taste!

Satsang: Means "divine association" in Sanskrit and refers to attending meditation practice and services within the community. You "go" to satsang like you "go" to church.

Sadhana: "Tools/resources" in Sanskrit. Sadhana refers tonyour spiritual practice, like meditation or prayer. You "go" to satsang, but you "do" your sadhana.

Darshan: Means "viewing" in Sanskrit, but in a spiritual context. You "see" your family and objects, you have *darshan* of a deity, temple, holy site, guru, and other sacred things.

Eastern and Western: It is traditional amongst scholars and enthusiasts to simplify thought and systems (spiritual/religious/medical/etc.) into Eastern and Western. Generally, Eastern includes Sanatan Dharm, Buddhism, Zen, I Ching, and others. Western ones typically refer to Abrahamic religions (Judaism, Christianity, Islam, and their many sects) and Hermetic mysticism (kabbalah, alchemy, ceremonial/ritual, etc.).

Dogma: An official set of beliefs within a system that is accepted by the members of a group without being questioned or doubted.

Religion: A system of thought and beliefs that center on worship, reverence, and dogmas. Religions focus on material living with spiritual intent and provide parameters to do so properly (ethics, morals, rules, guidelines, rituals . . .).

Mysticism: Systems primarily focused on personal experience over dogmas. Mystical systems provide knowledge and practices to progress to a goal of spiritual consciousness (Enlightenment/Realization). While most conventional thought considers mystical paths to be offshoots of religions, most mystics believe it to be the other way around: Mystical practice is the original source of a religion. Example: conventional thought is kabbalah is the mystical path within Judaism. Kabbalists see kabbalah as the source/essence of Judaism.

Yog(a): Literally means "union/join/unite" in Sanskrit. It is where the word "yoke" comes from and describes the harness that joins a plough to a beast of burden, implying it to be the tool that is used to join things together. Yog is the device to join the human mind and body with spirit. There are many paths of yog, and all teach a varying form of the same goal, which is to be *joined/united* with the Godhead.

Yog(a) paths—Hath(a), Ashtang(a), Kundalini, Bhakti, etc.: Hatha yog encompasses the area most are familiar with: the system of physical exercises. It is one of the eight branches within Ashtang(a) (Sanskrit for eight branches) revealed by the sage Patanjali. Each yog path is a tool used to attain union with the divine. Bhakti yog (Sanskrit for devotional surrender) is the core and overlying path of all of them. All other yog paths lead to bhakti; only bhakti stands on its own.

The Underground Stream: An ancient term within mystical cultures used to this day. The Underground Stream refers to the true, actual, and authentic set of origins, histories, and workings of humanity. This is the collective of unadulterated knowledge that mystics accept and is verifiable with research behind/beyond/before the conventional versions, which have been modified over the ages to serve religious and political agendas.

Occult: Defined conventionally as supernatural, mystical, magical beliefs. It is a word of Latin origin (*occultus*), meaning "secret, *hidden in plain view.*" The latter definition (hidden in plain view) has been systematically removed by organized religion founders to stigmatize the occult as "bad." The *in plain view* is a direct reference to The Underground Stream, declaring the truth is available if you know where/how to look for it.

Open and Closed Systems: Western religions are often labeled as "closed" systems, Eastern as "open." Closed refers to the dogma of a system of thought and practice that insists it is the *only* correct one, rejecting and disqualifying any that contradict or disagree with them. "Open" systems are more inclusive, with a *whatever works* perspective so long as it is authentic and true.

Torah/Bible: Out of respect to the original religion of the three main Abrahamic religions, this text will refer to their main scriptures accordingly: Torah (or Tanakh) is the Judaic term for the five books of Moses (the Pentateuch) along with the other thirty-four books. Muslims also typically refer to it this way. Christians refer to it as the "Old Testament" and/or the Bible.

Capitalization: Most holy names, references to God, Saints, as well their possessive pronouns (He/She) will be capitalized to differentiate Them and out of respect.

Author's note: This text does its best to honor, respect, and adhere to each faith's dogmatic parameters. The author apologizes for any errors and assures that any errors are unintentional and due to his own ignorance.

Why This Book Is So Long

As its author, I do not personally feel that I am the architect of this experience. I did not consciously volunteer for the events and circumstances portrayed. Fate, destiny, the will of God, chance, serendipity, astrology, and a host of mysterious factors are the true authors of this tale. It begins at my death event and concludes when it stabilized. While there is never truly an *"ending"* to someone's life, this set of events took nine years to complete itself.

It is long because it is four books in one:

1. **A personal memoir of a bizarre and phenomenal set of circumstances:** It is my attempt to triumph over tragedy.

2. **A guidebook of recovery through the trauma of injury.** While mine was/is a brain injury of the severest sort, I hope my story functions as a guide for others in recovery from traumas of other sorts as well, physical, emotional, psychological, and spiritual. Much is offered to provide game-changing, potentially lifesaving strategies others can use to recover from injuries and particularly TBI/DAI.

3. **A guide and resource through the NDE phenomenon.** Whether you are an expert in NDE or an enthusiast, this book also functions as a resource for understanding the phenomenon. The NDE culture and studies related to it are shared as well as my firsthand experience with it and my experience's own unique features.

4. <u>**A reference for spiritual, religious, and mystical systems.**</u> Long before his NDE event, I was a lifelong theologue, studying religion and practicing mysticism since my youth. I am a certified expert in many and proficient in most spiritual concepts and appreciate them all. I see life and my experiences through a spiritual lens rather than a material/worldly one. The supernatural quality of my lifetime has become rather undeniable, and my life's work has been to share spiritual perspectives on mundane affairs. The perspectives I share are authentic and verifiable. The references and concepts I use and share are true to their origins and sources. I make a tremendous effort to remain objective and true to all that is presented. If/when I offer a subjective opinion or theory on a spiritual concept, it is noted as such (I think . . . my own view is that . . . I suspect but can't confirm . . .).

Most text is presented as matter-of-fact to not disrupt the pace, mood, and context of the narrative with constant footnotes and long-winded definitions and resources to qualify them. I do not declare myself to be spiritually omniscient! I am just presenting what I know through experience and then verified with study, research, and application. I encourage all readers to doubt and confirm anything presented. Most things presented are easily confirmed online, and I hope to *earn* your confidence in what and how I present.

I am a creative-narrative nonfiction writer. This means that everything I write is truly nonfiction. It is not merely "based on" or "inspired by" true events. Nothing has been exaggerated. What I'm presenting is approximately three-fifths of the whole account *and it's still long!* (The other two-fifths were edited out of the narrative but are as equally important as what remains. Edits were necessary so as to not overwhelm you. Some of the anecdotes that were removed will appear in blog posts on the site for those who want more in certain sections.)

There will be contradictions: As a mortal, flawed, human person, I am confident and prideful in one chapter and humble and insecure in another. I have learned and follow the spiritual axiom of *"prideful in the world, humble in my heart."* The world is rather dog-eat-dog, and as a full-time resident of planet Earth, I have learned and earned my pride and confidence. I have paid dearly for all I have accomplished, and I've put my back into my labors of love with little to no help from other humans. This makes me proud and confident. I have also witnessed and become a part of undeniable miracles that humble me each and every day with inexpressible gratitude for the spiritual forces in my life. This humbles me. The paradox is this: In worldly terms, I'm an overachieving miracle man who never gives up *and is proud of it.* In spiritual terms, I am nothing: I am a flawed, stupid-human desire machine in awe each and every day at God's glory and obvious presence surrounding all of us.

I'm *proud* to serve Him, but I'm humbled by the slightest opportunity to do so, humbled as to why He would bother with me at all. I'm *proud* to know of Her and have direct association with Divinity. I'm *humbled* and mystified as to why I am blessed in this regard. I am no better, and in many ways much worse, than so many within humanity.

I want to try with every part of my spirit to be worthy of Her love. Yet the only thing I *truly* know is that I'm not and never can be. Yet She loves me anyway, completely, unconditionally, and selflessly. And She loves you the same way too.

***

Thank you for inviting me into your life and giving me your time. I hope my story entertains, illuminates, enlightens, mystifies, and satisfies you. It is my honor to be your host and share time with you.

Are you ready?

8.

DIALOGUE WITH THE OTHER SIDE

> In the dark night of the soul, bright flows the river of God.
> —Saint John of the Cross

> I'm not afraid of death because I don't believe in it. It's just getting out of one car, and into another.
> —John Lennon

Who am I?

Your worldly identity and personality are part of the material phenomena. Your consciousness is what makes your worldly identity. It is attached to your soul, but they are different. Individual identities are not relevant here within celestial realms. They are not Divine as your soul is. You are a Divine soul. All souls are divine.

Where am I?

You are in a dimension between the spiritual and the material. It is known by many names in many religions and spiritual philosophies: Akash, the Bardo, afterlife, purgatory. . . . Your physical body is made of dense matter. It was in a coma being kept alive with machinery. Your subtle-energy body was dormant: it is made of subtle energy, what you know as chakras. Both your physical and energy bodies are in the world of matter, which they are a part of. Your material bodies are in a hospital.

Your causal body is your mind and consciousness: it is even more subtle than your energy body. It is made up of your karmas, destinies, memories, thoughts, and true knowledge you have acquired and accepted over many lifetimes. Your mind of consciousness is less confined to the physical world. Your consciousness is now experiencing both realms: the realm of matter and the realm of spiritual energies.

Is this permanent? Perceiving both realms at once?

Your consciousness will take some time to fully connect and settle in with your physical and subtle body. Your physical and subtle-energy body will always remain in the realm of matter. Your body of consciousness can exist in both dimensions simultaneously. Your perceiving of this dimension will fade as your mind settles back into the physical. With work and practice, you can sustain awareness of this spiritual space for as long as you like.

Why did this happen to me?

Everything is in balance. These events occur to maintain balance in the Creation.

A Divine power that manages Creation is cause and effect, what you know as karma.

Everything that happens to you is a cause and effect. Every good event in your life is the effect of a good action you did in another life. And the events you feel are bad are effects of bad actions. The Spiritual Government does not actually recognize actions or events as having "good" or "bad" qualities. The cause and effects are simply proportionate and of similar character.

Spiritual Government?

Yes. All features of the Divine realm are merely extensions of the Divine Godpower. The material realm is managed and administered by Divine agents. We are all One with God, but simultaneously separate. Some call us angels, spirits, deities, gods or goddesses. We are the Godpower's loving servants.

Consequences from a previous life? Not this one?

Most karmas are not instant. Every deed you do in a life is recorded and stored here, in the Akashic Records. They fructify—manifest—over many lifetimes.

Not all at once?

No. They are spread over many lifetimes. Karma is the force, like gravity, that binds you to the material phenomena. There are far too many karmas to experience in one life: It takes a moment to take or save a life, but the punishment or reward takes longer to fulfill. You have infinite karmas collected over infinite lifetimes.

Your death tragedy was not a malicious act of the other driver who hit you; it was an accident. In another life, you inadvertently caused a similar tragedy to another living soul, so your event was similar to restore and maintain a cosmic balance. Please do not think of it as punishment. It is not a punishment any more than a good event, like winning an award of money, is a reward. Whatever you do is a cause, and whatever you experience is an effect.

This spiritual system of justice, balance, and order is merely a teaching tool. Now that you have the true knowledge of cause and effect, your free will is enhanced. You can have conscious awareness of your intentions and actions. With this understanding, you will be more conscious of your choices and put more effort into living righteously.

But if an action is merely an accident, why is there a consequence?

With more awareness and mindful living, most accidents are avoidable. The effect of an action is not determined purely on the action itself. It is influenced by the intent. Causing harm deliberately has a very strong effect, while causing harm accidentally, without harmful intent, receives a much milder effect.

You cannot know, nor have access to, the action you did that caused this. This knowledge is divine and not accessible to human souls. The law of karma is governed with God's love and is merciful. Accepting our fate with gratitude is divine. Try to accept your fate with gratitude. This is what karma is for: to grow.

Are there deeper reasons and meanings to these events beyond mere cause and effect?

God is pure Love and Grace. The order and arrangements of events are all designed to provide souls with spiritual opportunity. The more challenging the circumstances, the greater the opportunities there can be. Many souls receive Divine interventions. Few receive Divine involvement that is obvious and undeniable. You have friends in high places! Your circumstances are extraordinary! Someone very high in the spiritual hierarchy has gone to great lengths to provide you with such extraordinary dynamics.

But if we forget our prior lives and actions each time we are reborn, how can we learn from them and choose to live righteously?

It is God's Grace of mercy that allows you to forget the collection of karmas one accumulates over many lifetimes. A soul's material mind would be overwhelmed by them.

You do not consciously remember these lessons you are taught here within this celestial space, but these lessons and this knowledge remains within your subconscious and unconscious minds. Over time and with effort, they become more prevalent in your decision-making. Surely, you've met people who are just naturally good. Surely, you've met souls who are naturally bad. No one is naturally either good or bad. They have natural tendencies because they have cultivated these qualities over recent lifetimes. Over time, they learned through the rule of karma that they will always reap what they sow. Karma and the lessons we learn from experience are God's grace, God's heartfelt teachings to you, providing opportunity to live in righteousness but to always have free will to do so.

I have tried to be a decent man most of my life. My sins and failures seem ordinary and do not seem as severe as so many I see who are having good lives with wealth, health, and love. My death and the suffering I am to endure from this does not seem appropriate considering my efforts to live righteously. Why?

Karma—the law of cause and effect—is perfect and just and does not make mistakes. Your transgressions and sins in this current lifetime were when you were younger and are not uncommon or severe. You have indeed lived within righteousness for over twenty material years as an adult. The affects you are receiving in this life are not from actions you made in this life; they are from previous lives. All of your actions and intentions are stored in a karmic dimension, often referred to on Earth as the Akashic Records. The consequences and effects of your actions will fructify, bear fruit, in coming lives. Your death experience and the suffering you will endure from it are from actions you made in past lives. These consequences restore and maintain balance. Karma is a perfect system of balance.

But if I can't remember the actions I made to bring these consequences, how can I learn from them?

You're learning now, here from within this spiritual space. It is up to you to try to retain and remember the law of spiritual cause and effect you're learning here. This knowledge is already within your <u>unconscious</u> mind. With every effort you make to live righteously in your human life, this knowledge becomes more accessible to you. This is your conscience, the subtle feelings you get that tell you if something is right or *wrong—your intuition, your moral compass. Righteous choices become easier each time you choose them over wrong. Wrong choices will become easier each time you choose them as well. Choose wisely. Whichever you choose strengthens one and weakens the other. However you choose becomes your natural tendency. These are called sanskars. Karma regulates events and circumstances. Sanskars regulate attitudes and tendencies. Choose well; choose wisely. Righteousness is available to all who pursue it and have the will to live within it.*

You're saying there are many layers to these events. The surface is the universal laws of cause and effect. The deeper layers are about spiritual opportunity and progress. My situations are going to be nearly impossible to endure. It seems to be purification by fire. What if I cannot survive it? What if I lose my mind or lose my way?

We will never give you more than you can handle. But We will take you to the limits of your endurance if you allow Us to.

I do. Do what must be done to purify me and raise me to purer spiritual consciousness.

Granted. Try to remember you asked for this.

Why is my death experience so lonely and shadowy? I'm not experiencing white light, love, comfort from departed loved ones, or angels. I've heard many tales of these being features of death. Am I undeserving of them?

You are not being deprived of benevolence in your death experience. Your faith and confidence in the Divine are stable and mature, as is your certainty of life beyond death. The Spiritual Government provides comforting images and presences to those who need them to cope and adjust to the dying experience. God is merciful and allows reflections of what a soul understands love to be in an effort to comfort them. The presence of white light, departed loved ones, spirit animals, angels, or other personalities are extracted from a soul's spirit and mind. What they experience and witness are expressions and reflections of their own definitions of love and comfort. Do you require solace to accept what is happening to you and to know the Divine loves you unconditionally and limitlessly? Are you afraid? Do you feel alone?

No. I feel loved and protected. I feel your loving presence and need nothing more.

I am seeing images of my return to my body. I am seeing a Life Preview. I am seeing how difficult it is to be, as I will not remember whom I was or who I am. I am seeing tremendous loss as I will be disconnected from those I love and who have come to rely on me. I am scared, scared of not being close to them and everyone moving on from me. This extraordinary event is going to set me apart from them, and I see it will take seven years before my soul fully settles back within my body. What am I to do, and why will there be such loss?

The material time required is not for your soul to reintegrate with your body. The seven years of material dimension time are for your mind. Your mind is attached to your soul so it can carry on and progress with its experience and lessons. Your life's experiences and lessons always remain within your unconscious and remain with you, life after life. Your soul is divine, but your body and your mind are material. Your mind will need seven years or so to reintegrate to the material plane of living. As it does so, it will slowly forget this experience unless you put heartfelt effort into remembering and honoring it. If you do, your mind will remember; if you do not, your mind will forget. It is up to you. Free will is God's Special Grace. You will always be able to draw upon this experience for strength and to remember that a greater will is at work within your life. There is no meaningless suffering. God loves you and allows you to suffer to learn and come closer to the Divine.

I can only see vague visions of the future as I return to live again. I can see it is going to be hard and I will have significant loss and I am scared and do not want to go. I want to stay here, where it is safe and divine. Can I remain here?

This is not your time.

The large events you fear are destined to pass for your benefit, though you cannot accept that yet. Human souls cannot view the future in detail or else they may interfere with it. Destiny is a Divine responsibility, not a human one. You can have confidence that everything will unfold with Divine intervention as always. You can transcend hope and faith with confidence. Have not just faith or hope, but confidence that the Divine is with you with love and protection. God will never allow you to suffer needlessly.

How am I to cope? No one will understand me and may think me crazy when I share my experience and what I'm learning. They will think I imagined this. Am I imagining this?

Worldly people will always doubt spiritual things. It is unwise to convert or convince others of your spiritual perceptions.

I will be very lonely and may become bitter. I see myself struggling to accept this as God's Grace as I have human needs of love and acceptance and companionship, yet these insights and truths will make it nearly impossible to relate to others. What will I do?

God will provide. Have confidence, faith, and hope. God is your Divine parent and will never abandon you. You must strive to trust God to provide you not with what you want but with what you need—spiritually. Faith in God during your darkest hours is opportunity to love God. Try to align what you want with what God wants for you. When you want what God wants, you are on your way to spiritual enlightenment.

How shall I live? I will need to feed my body, live indoors to be safe, and be healthy to remain undistracted from bodily needs. To live in the world, I must work and interact with the material world.

The material world is at your disposal: You can use it to evolve with love, knowledge, and service to the Divine, or you can use it for idle entertainment. Because your mind and body are material, they are attracted to the world and drawn to it. Because your soul is divine, it is attracted and drawn to the Divine. Your body and mind are often in conflict with the soul: Your material mind has forgotten you are a divine soul and seeks happiness in the world, while your soul influences your mind to pursue happiness in Spirit. When you align your mind and body with your soul, you will live righteously and in peace.

When you live spiritually, your material concerns become small. Overcoming material suffering is not a "test" but an opportunity to experience Divine, unconditional, limitless love through free will.

***

As explained previously, this did not occur like an actual dialogue. There was no one there in any conventional understanding of it. A divine, intelligent, and loving personality was with me. What I experienced within The Portal was "uploaded" into my consciousness. It was stored within my mind and much of it was gradually retrieved/remembered over time.

I do not reject doubters or disbelievers. It is far too laborious to convince or persuade. All I can offer is what I perceived and came to know and how. Take it as you like. . . . Is this an account of actual events? Or was I having an existential delusion brought on by my severe brain trauma?

Personally, I don't care. Whether it was imagined or actual, it was what got me through it. My NDE went on with an intense magnitude for four years nonstop. It settled to a milder degree over years four through seven and stabilized over years eight and nine. My NDE is not an event of my past. It is an ongoing event, as I choose to remain mindful and interactive with the experience.

I came to refer to this spiritual-realm as The Portal: It was just a term I used one day and stayed with it. I came to refer to the contacts and communications within The Portal as Akashic Agents. These are my own terms. Call it what you will . . . angels, spirit guides, my imagination. . . .

My life leading up to my death event had been very spiritually productive.

***

My early and lifelong enthusiasm and pursuit of spirituality had been cultivated over many lifetimes and was bearing fruit as spiritual *sanskars*. My fascination with spirituality, theology, and religion had given me advantages.

It is taught in the Vedic scriptures that there are three types of karmas and sanskars:

1. Material
2. Neutral
3. Spiritual

Material Karmas: Actions and thoughts for material concerns—such as wealth, health, welfare, and love—are to satisfy our material comforts and desires. If material desires are pursued at the expense of others and cause harm, they result in negative consequences. If we fulfill our material needs and desires honorably, they cause positive karmas. These are *not* realized in the lifetime they are caused in. They are stored within the Akashic space and play out over future lifetimes.

Neutral Karmas: Actions and thoughts satisfying basic needs are neutral karmas. Eating breakfast, washing the car, going to work, and most basic functions do not cause effects.

Actions and thoughts that have spiritual intent are stored within the Akash for future effects *and are also realized instantly and over the span of our current life.* Once again, our ex-Beatle, John Lennon, was spot-on when he sang about *instant karma!*

Material and neutral actions and thoughts can be *converted* to spiritual ones with intention. Eating your breakfast or washing the car are plain ol', everyday material actions convertible to spiritual actions and thoughts with *intention.* Any action and thought you have can be *consciously* dedicated to spirit. If I think lovingly of God or any Divine association (Akashic agents, angels, Jesus, my Guru . . .) *while* I am preparing and eating my breakfast, this material, bodily action becomes a spiritual one. A sadhu (spiritual practitioner, i.e., yogi) eats her breakfast quietly with an inner dialogue: *I am eating my breakfast cereal to keep my body strong and healthy so I can serve God if I am called on to do so. If I am not distracted by hunger, I can focus on spiritual love when I pray and meditate.* In this way, material actions are converted to spiritual ones, creating spiritual karmas and sanskars—*events, opportunities, and attitudes.* Practice makes perfect!

And vice versa: If we have malicious thoughts during material and neutral actions, they can be converted to bad actions, and if our material actions are dedicated to material pleasures, they bind us to worldly ideas and thoughts.

My accident and miracle of recovery is a *karmic event.* My never-say-die attitude is an innate quality of my character, which is a *sanskar.* We are all a mixed bag of karmas and sanskars. No one is purely good nor bad, neither is anyone's life all punishment or reward. It may seem like it sometimes! But the actuality is we are all experiencing a mixed bag of good and bad karmas and sanskars.

My lifelong spiritual quests were blessed with authentic teachings and an innate ability to separate the right ones from the wrong ones, so I was rarely misled in my spiritual quests. All my spiritual pursuits were graduated: I was always progressing from basic spiritual arithmetic toward higher spiritual math. My spiritual journey had been progressive.

I was blessed with the ability to move on from a truth or philosophy once I was ready to accept the next higher teachings.

I am grateful I had the right understanding of karmic laws within the recesses of my mind. This latent acceptance gave me the endurance I would continue to need.

Accepting these hard times as karmic consequences of the universal law reduced potential self-loathing and God-loathing too. If I hadn't the correct understanding of these laws, would I have blamed God for my suffering instead of having spiritual accountability? I wanted to handle these hardships with as much grace as I could muster because I knew, in some way or another, I deserved them.

As dark and hard as it would be, throughout these trials of my soul I tried hard to be mindful of my God's loving willingness to cause me pain to give me opportunity to grow and progress within my Soul's Journey.

I am spiritually sorry my Divine Father had to resort to such drastic measures to help me grow but grateful He did. I felt His love in every ounce of pain.

Did causing me pain so that I could learn and progress cause Him pain? As a father, I had said many times, "This hurts me more than it hurts you," to my son, and it was sincere. I was willing to cause him pain to learn lifelong lessons. We all learn the hard way, but do we need to?

Much of the deepest pain I felt, and still do, is the shame of needing such hard experiences to progress toward God. The thought of my lessons hurting my Divine Parent more than it hurt me is intolerable.

I was indeed fascinated and very tempted at times to remain on paths I enjoyed and had great power with. In particular, my involvement with ceremonial magic, alchemy, Kabbalah, and Hermetic esotericism was very alluring. I was also in hot pursuit of re-experiencing my Kundalini awakening.

My 1992 Kundalini awakening had me certain it was the surest, most powerful, and potent way to become enlightened, and I was dedicating my life to it. It was such an abrupt and intense shift in consciousness that I naturally assumed it was my destined path of spiritual illumination.

This is not the time nor place to explore it in detail, but a full Kundalini experience is a mind-expanding phenomenon that is indescribable and absolute. The event is presented in my first memoir, *A Stone's Throw*.

My pursuit of spiritual enlightenment had been lifelong, relentless study, research, and arduous practice.

These circumstances have allowed for profound differences in my NDE experience. What I was exposed to and especially my retention of it was greatly influenced, and I personally feel, enhanced, by my direct association with True and eternal paths: I entered the *other side, The Portal,* at a rather stable and advanced stage of spiritual awareness and practice. This allowed me unusual access to mysteries and to eventually retain them.

Time-Released Spirituality

Much of what I gained and retained of my exposure and experience with The Portal was put on time release! My injured brain did not recall all of it until my brain injury stabilized. It took some time to gain access to what was uploaded during the NDE. Recalling and accessing insights gained from within The Portal has sort of trickled in over time and is now an ongoing feature. Many insights I received while in The Portal surface when they are ready and needed. I have a lot of *"Oh, yeah! I remember now"* moments of Portal uploads I was unable to access before.

There are several dimensions to reality. Western spirituality teaches of four: heaven, hell, matter, and purgatory. Buddhism and Sanatan Dharm (Hinduism) teach there are *hellish* abodes and *celestial* abodes, and then there's the one in between, which we're in right now: the material one, *samsara* or *maya* in Sanskrit.

Even our material world's science has theorized of eleven or more dimensions to our physical reality. We all experience just four of them: three spatial and one time. Quantum String and M theorists cannot offer any insight to the others beyond our perception because, well . . . *they are beyond our perception.* Perceived or not, these other dimensions are scientifically theorized to exist all around us, all the time.

In the Eastern traditions there are eight hells and eight heavens; each successively better/worse, with the rather neutral material plane in the middle.

In the above and below realms, you are there to receive your earned karmas: the consequences of your life's choices, thoughts, and actions. Being sinister and causing harm in a life can result in one of the hellish abodes. Being virtuous and religious can result in a celestial, or heavenly, abode. Once the debt or credit is settled, you return to the material plane. Only on the material plane do you *create and make* new karmas: the others are just for receiving.

In each abode, there is a guide, *a buddha,* if you will, who helps you make sense of what you're experiencing and tells you how to avoid returning to it. Not wanting to return to hellish purgatories is understandable. But why would you not want to return to a celestial heavenly abode?

In the heavenly abodes, there is no illness, it is paradisiacal, the inhabitants are virtuous and kind, and there are luxurious comforts. But it has two downsides: 1) It's temporary. When your karmic deposits run out, you must return to the realm of matter and pretty much start over because you depleted your karmic bank account to zero. 2) Even though it's luxurious and beautiful and paradisiacal, there are still human faults and defects because *desiring* still exists there. And desiring is the root of all evil, ills, and suffering, hence the first two of Buddha's Noble Truths: Life is suffering, and the cause of suffering is desiring.

There are only two results from desiring: greed or disappointment. If our desire is fulfilled, we want more or better almost immediately. If a desire is unfulfilled, we are disappointed. This wisdom is promulgated in nearly every spiritual philosophy.

The *buddhas* in these realms are like personal guardian angels as well as communal: They enlighten everyone with reminders that the ultimate goal is not heaven but perfect enlightenment /realization, which leads to no more incarnating in *any* of the realms of samsara. Even though buddhas exist for everyone, you have a very intimate and personal relationship with them too. Same as when a buddha, avatar, or guru is on Earth. I speak from true experience when I say that when my guru is in front of thousands of people, each one who is surrendered to Him feels like they're the only one.

The only point and purpose of the material realities with their multiple dimensions is to *get out of them.* The true purpose and meaning of life is to realize you want out of it and to attain eternal divinity.

"We are not human beings having a spiritual experience. We are spiritual beings having a human experience." —Teilhard de Chardin

Doorways

I'm not in a hellish realm below nor a celestial realm above; I'm mostly a ghost in the material one in between. I'm in The Portal, a.k.a. The Bardo, a.k.a.

Antarābhava in Sanskrit. Whom I interact with here is a formless buddha; an angel, sage, guru . . . these are Akashic Agents.

They are not God Himself, but they are One with God and are fused with Her mind, heart, and intellect. They are authorized agents of God and do not, *and cannot,* steer you wrong. They are *selectively* omniscient, meaning they can know anything at will, but don't unless it's relevant. God . . . knows *everything, all the time.* Akashic agents and celestial Buddhas know what they need to know and share what they need to with you.

They may take the form of Moses or Christ or Muhammad (pbuh[3]) or your dead and favorite Aunt Shirley or puppy, Toto. Their form, or lack thereof, is rather irrelevant and is just a matter of convenience: whatever makes sense to you so you feel safe and faithful in their presence.

Henceforward, I will refer to the source of light, truth, clarity, and knowledge I received directly from there as the *Akashic Agents.*

Why Akashic Agents?

No reason. My interaction with the presence on the other side was formless: no body or face, just character and personality that was gracious and loving. I had no desire nor need for a form there.

These Akashic Agents became the connecting force God took within my life to guide and protect me.

A Summary for Easy Reference:

1. The soul is Divine and not made of matter, but pure spirit. It is our essence.
2. The physical, subtle, and causal bodies are made of matter: physical, energy, and thought.
3. Cause and effect: cosmic justice and balance is sustained with karma and sanskars. Karma regulates events and sanskars regulate character.
4. Current life circumstances are destined by prior life karmas and sanskars.
5. Intent of an action is what causes an effect, not the actions themselves.

---

[3] Peace Be upon Him (pbuh): Islamic tradition requires this to be mentioned when the Profit's name is used.

6. Most memory is forgotten from life to life.

7. Living spiritually helps us remember the Truths we gain within The Portal.

8. Living spiritually helps us retain our spiritual progress life after life.

9. Death experience features are determined by someone's personal needs to help them adjust to the event: angels, loved ones who have passed on, white light, etc. are customized for each individual.

10. You are not alone and feel enveloped in perfect love that is personal and intimate.

11. Life-Review and Life-Preview are standard features for everyone, whether they remember them or not. These are used as teaching tools to encourage personal commitments to return and live more spiritually.

12. Confidence in the Divine is more powerful than faith or hope.

13. Returning is not a choice: When, where, and how a soul returns is destined. Souls are often given the impression of a choice to empower them.

14. God Herself is involved with every part of our lives, and Spiritual Administrators are always present.

15. Yearning for what you *need* spiritually is more valuable than what you *want* materially.

16. The material world is at our disposal to use as a resource to evolve spiritually. It is not for our entertainment. Our spiritual obligation is to pursue spiritual ambitions, not worldly ones. The worldly phenomena lure us, so it is important to resist its superficial charms and quest for spiritual ones.

17. My death experience was beyond standard due to two factors:
    a. My lifetime of spiritual study and practice
    b. My direct association with an avatar

18. There are seventeen main dimensions of the material phenomena
    a. Eight hellish
    b. Eight heavenly
    c. One worldly in between
       I got the impression that there are many subdivision dimensions too. The eight main hellish/heavenly dimensions may have several subdivisions.

19. The hell/heaven abodes are for receiving karmas for a duration of time before returning to the world. Only in the middle worldly dimension do we create new karmas. Desiring exists in all of them.

20. There are *buddhas/teachers* in each dimension that illuminate the truth and encourage us to move on and away from hell/heaven and to aspire for Divinity only.

21. Akashic Agents (guardian angels / spiritual admins) are present within The Portal. They take on any form that pleases you to assist you on your soul's journey.

22. Only the Divine realm is perfect and desireless.

23. The Divine abode is above, below, and omnipresent. Once attained it is eternal. It is the purpose and goal of existence.

9.

THE PORTAL

The world has three spatial and one time dimension. The fifth dimension is celestial, the seventh is Divine. The sixth is of Divine Love Consciousness which connects them.
—Swami Prakashanand Saraswati (The Sixth Dimension)

Absent in body, but present in spirit.
—Paul the Apostle

Can you picture what will be/So limitless and free
—The Doors ("The End")

This dimensional concept has been described in alarming detail in many ancient texts. Each and every religion has a version of a state of being in between life and death. Mystical paths do too. What's the difference between religion and a mystical path?

Religions focus on the worship of God by adhering to the laws and rules, i.e., *dogmas* of their belief systems. Mystical paths provide methods, practices, and formulas for attaining union with spiritual consciousness. Our global culture has divided these into two cultures: Eastern religions and paths and Western ones. Western ones are considered *closed* systems and generally refer to the three Abrahamic religions—Judaism, Christianity, and Islam. Eastern ones are considered *open* systems and include Buddhism, Zen, I-Ching, and Sanatan Dharm (Hinduism). Eastern mysticism includes the Buddha's 8-Fold path, Zen, I-Ching, and the many paths of yoga within Sanatan Dharm. *Open vs. closed* systems refer to their acceptance, tolerance, and inclusion of others; Western closed systems have a *my-way-or-the-highway* attitude with an emphasis on thou-shall and shalt-not rules. Eastern open systems have an *all-roads-lead-to-Rome* mentality with acceptance of any true and sincere path to spirituality. Western is exclusive, Eastern is inclusive.

The Eastern religions accept the process of reincarnation, so their system is far more complete than Western ones. Western religions that don't accept the reincarnation feature of a soul's ultimate journey to liberation from matter have reincarnation references too, it's just a little vague and rather elementary, so we'll deal with it first.

The Western concept of the in-between dimension is called *purgatory*. Any soul not qualified for heaven, but not evil enough to qualify for *eternal* hell, goes to purgatory: a *temporary* place where they are *purged* of their defects. Once they serve their time in purgatory, they then move on and up to heaven, so long as they let their evil ways go and have served their time like a man! There's no guarantee a soul in purgatory will go to heaven once their time is served: it's merely an *opportunity*. You got some work to do there, but it is looked upon as God's merciful grace that you're given a second chance to avoid *eternal* hell. If you waste your time and opportunity in purgatory and do not learn and come to terms with your sins, it's on to hell instead.

The Western religion's purgatory concept mirrors the Eastern ones, which came first. Actually, the majority of Western religious thought, dogmas, and philosophies were imported from the Eastern ones. So now we'll explore the Eastern concepts of The Portal.

I've already told you the name *The Portal* is my own. When I arrived back to Earth from the in-between state, I didn't know what to call it, so I just gave it a harmless and nondenominational name. Purgatory has an inaccurate stigma of being hellish and Bardo is a bit exotic for many Westerners, so I selected something convenient and personal.

The ancient Eastern names are *antarābhava* in Sanskrit or Sanatan Dharm (Hinduism), which becomes Bardo in Buddhism. Ancient civilizations in Mesopotamia and Egypt had nearly the exact concepts, as it had only just migrated from the East and had yet to be over-dogmatized by the organizing Western religions.

Antarābhava/Bardo is central to these ultra-thorough and precise spiritual philosophies. How to prepare and endure The Portal dimension in between life, death, and rebirth is vital. *The Tibetan Book of the Dead* and the *Egyptian Book of the Dead* are both instructional manuals. They teach the living how to prepare for dying. The massive library of Hindu scriptures is, in its own way, the same thing: Sanatan Dharm's Vedas, Upanishads, Shastras, and all the rest teach you how to live right and develop spiritually so you can progress toward the end game of liberation: *no more incarnation to the material world.*

These scripture-manuals provide very specific instructions to be applied when nearing death itself. Why? Because you're about out of time, so you better get it right! The way you live in *this* life determines the factors, features, consequences, and circumstances for the afterlife and/or next life/lives. It's like a karmic bank account: whatever you deposit into your account in *this* life is what you'll have to withdraw from in your *next or after* life. If your deposits are in a currency valuable and stable and you have a lot saved up, then your next life ATM withdrawals are of the most valuable currency from a stable economy. But if you deposit *bad* deeds into your karmic bank account, you'll have just a few Barundi Francs to withdraw from, and since a Barundi Franc is 0.00049 to USD, and even less to the Euro, it's going to be rough.

How you deal with The Portal plays a role too. We're not going to go into the *Books of the Dead* to study how to use your time in The Portal to have a safe transition back to Earthly matter: it's beautiful, valuable, and necessary. I have a full copy of the *Tibetan Book of the Dead* and others, so what I present here is verifiable. What I was uploaded, experienced, and witnessed within The Portal verified what these texts teach. You don't have to have an NDE to learn how the Transmigration of the Soul works! The knowledge of life, death, and the afterlife has always been available! But it can be hard and rare to study them.

I just want you to understand why and how The Portal works so you can get the themes and contexts of what's being presented in this man's experience within it and how it was, and is, constantly affecting my life.

To understand life, you have to understand death.

The Eastern systems teach there are eight stages of the Bardo; each stage exploring the death event and transmigration of the soul back to matter. The reason to study and practice what is prescribed is to avoid getting *caught* in one of the various stages of the transmigration process. The reason Tibetan Buddhists are confident they have just had a single Dalia Lama is because each one has followed the *Book of the Dead* process to reincarnate as Himself and be able to be found and identified in his next incarnation. There have been fourteen Dalai Lamas since the title role was established in 1390, but Tibetan Buddhists feel there's just been one Lama in fourteen bodies.

If a soul's mind experiences nothing but fear, grief, loss, and unacceptance of death during the transition in The Portal, they can get caught and not move on. These are the *ghost* realms and others. The entire point of a human life is to become *liberated* from the cycle of the ever-turning Wheel of Life and Death.

Our experience within The Portal is influenced and regulated by our life's work and preparation. Our life's work and preparation are regulated and influenced by our *prior* life's work and preparation. If you have spent several lifetimes working with and following very material, mundane concepts, you don't get much insight as you transition, and you certainly don't retain much. Lifetime(s) of spiritual thinking create proportionately revealing Portal experiences, and your retention and ability to understand them are proportionate as well.

The Portal is an intermediary dimension: It is not within the actual Divine realm, but neither is it purely material. But it is well above the dense dimension of physical matter and even above the psychic supernatural level of it too. Yet, it is *not* Divine either. You're not in *direct* contact with God Him/Herself; you're just closer, and the veils of material illusion are thin enough to allow *closer* contact. The angels, Akashic-Agents, etc. are in *direct* contact *with* God.

Within the Akashic space, your two main bodies (physical, subtle) are not present nor even relevant. Only your *causal* body lives on and experiences The Portal: your *karmas, sanskars,* and *manas (mind)*.

- Karmas: your destined events and circumstances
- Sanskars: your destined attitudes and moods
- Manas: your mind/consciousness

I can't tell you in perfect and absolute precision how this all works, but here are the basics: I'm a mortal man, not a Buddha, Christ, or Guru. There are four parts of the overall mind. In yogic/Sanskrit terms they are:

1. Manas—sensory awareness
2. Buddhi—intellect
3. Ahamkar—ego/identity of self
4. Citta—consciousness

Manas is the storage unit for our memories and what we directly perceive.

Buddhi makes sense of what is in Manas. This is your cognitive ability.

Ahamkar is your personal and individual sense of *self:* the ego, superego, and id in Freudian terms.

Citta is pure consciousness. That is not to say it is pure as in perfect. It is pure as in raw: it simply *is.* It is not burdened with memory, sense awareness, or ego. It is just actual awareness, often referred to in New Age speak as the *higher self,* in artist speak as *the creative tunnel,* in sports speak as *in the zone,* and invoked as *Zen-like.*

All four of them interplay with one another and rely on one another: none of them can function at their full capacity without the others, yet they also exist and function independently.

Within The Portal, my manas, buddhi, and ahamkara were dormant—like asleep.

I was just *citta*—pure, raw consciousness. It wasn't mine or individual. It was a part of the overall consciousness, like a single drop of consciousness in a gorgeous sea of consciousness. It was paradoxical, as I simultaneously had an individual existence but was also One with an overall consciousness.

It was a desireless state.

Now, *that's* ideal! No wanting or needing . . . ! Try it sometime! It's really peaceful! And because I was not influenced by desire, I had no need or use for will. I don't recall it being present at all!

I wasn't even curious. It wasn't like I just wanted to know things and therefore *knew* them. I was a small part, a tiny feature floating in the cosmos of thought, knowledge, and emotion. I was a *part* of knowledge and truth, not really separate exactly.

But I was *not* omniscient! While I was saturating in the Akashic regions of truth and knowledge, I was only uploaded with what I was qualified to receive. What was available to me were truths and knowledge I had either accumulated in several lifetimes and/or I was *qualified* to know.

This is a feature both the *Books of the Dead* and Vedas agree upon too: You perceive the overall *collection* of your *own* knowledge relevant to your current status. An individual who has invested years of life into spiritual practice and study is theoretically more likely to have more access to spiritual uploads than those who have not.

Part of the reason a Roger Federer and a Serena Williams are such tennis phenoms is because they have developed these skills over more than this life. Same with Mozart: a composer who's a prodigy by the age of seven is a carryover set of skills.

A spiritualist will do the same. The more time in a life dedicated to spiritual pursuits and progress, the more dividends it pays the next time around. Maybe Einstein was the reincarnation of Isaac Newton: very possible! Newton was a spiritual alchemist: the only reason he accepted the offer to be a professor at Cambridge was to fund his work as an alchemist. Einstein said science without religion is lame, religion without science is blind. He rejected the opportunity to work on The Bomb because he was philosophically a pacifist and became vegetarian as he got older too. They both clearly exemplify having access to way more genius than one life can account for!

Most get a bit of both, and it is percentage-proportionate: a man primarily dedicated to material ambitions and family and only marginally involved with spiritual concepts will reap the same. And vice-versa.

These tendencies are stored within the manas section of the mind and can be reignited once we follow our intuition to do so. It's rather mechanical.

The Akashic space, *The Portal,* doesn't really concern itself with material concepts, only spiritual ones. It is a spiritual dimension after all.

Whilst many NDE-ers report on gaining access to truth and powers previously unknown or which they'd even been interested in before their NDE, this is because they had spiritual/mystical carryovers from *recent* lifetimes. They were not prevalent enough to carry over consciously in their current lifetime but were recent enough to be latent and shocked awake by an NDE or some other revelatory life event.

***

My life prior to my NDE was entirely committed to spiritual knowledge and practice. I also had a healthy and stable material life I enjoyed very much. I just wasn't overly attached to it. I certainly was dedicated to material success: ambitious and hard- working to create material comfort, safety, and opportunity.

But I didn't take it for granted and always viewed my material assets as resources to fund and provide my spiritual progress. It takes money to make a pilgrimage to sacred spiritual sites in India and to have the time and energy to study and do spiritual path work. This takes a stable material life; *for me, anyway*. I'm just not evolved enough yet to live the life of a Sadhu monk in a cave without a bank account.

What I accessed and what I retained from The Portal was proportionate to my level and status. I've been a *spiritualist* for several lifetimes, but far from a perfect one, and in each I had either lost my way or at least detoured from the direct path's progress, but I had accumulated an extraordinary amount of spiritual knowledge and practical experience in past and current lives.

That's what *The Book(s) of the Dead* are all about: investing *this* life in spiritual knowledge *and practice* to reap what you sow in the next. The major reason my Kundalini event at twenty-five was so prodigious may have been because of prior life work with it. I seemed to have had an entire life of supernatural occurrences. Is this partly due to prior-life study and practice?

We've *all* done it: spent many lifetimes in a row pursuing spiritual truths and have accumulated enough progress to have a good starting point from which to progress in the next. And we've all lost our way, been detoured, or generally forsook our spirituality and deviated back to the material. We're all on varying points of the spiritual/material spectrum. We're all the Fool within the tarot deck, on his journey from matter to spirit. We each have an opportunity to accept spiritual initiation with The Magician of card number one and of spiritual downfall when we interact with number 16, The Tower. We go back and forth through the human condition until we get it right and arrive at the trump card, number 22, The World, which doesn't mean *matter*. The World card represents the end of the major arcana of the deck and is total liberation and illumination.

Wherever you are in your Fool's journey, go forward, never back. And eventually you will pass the Wheel, go directly past Death and be given the password from key number 20, Judgement, to get *the entire World in your hands*.

10.

DIE BANDIT

How long will this last, this delicious feeling of being alive, of having penetrated the veil which hides beauty and the wonders of celestial vistas?
—Sascha Shulgin[4]

Fairies wear boots and you gotta believe me.
—Black Sabbath ("Fairies Wear Boots")

Die-Bandit is an anagram of TBI-DAI-NDE, which seems all too appropriate. I definitely looked at my condition as a bandit: a robber or outlaw operating in an isolated or lawless area is the dictionary description for *bandit*. I've definitely been robbed by an outlaw within a lawless area: The Portal had rules and laws, but the earth plain is the Wild, Wild West for me. And I was a frail pioneer trying to migrate to a new life. Actually, I was trying to migrate to my *old* life. Actually, I was not trying to *reinvent* myself. I was a bit of a pathological overachiever before which I'm A-OK, fine with.

I was convinced there was a secret formula to restore me. Fuck doctors. I knew intellectually and intuitively the medical field is a profit-driven machine lacking vision. As mentioned, when I have a headache, ibuprofen is great: I was not applying voodoo or magic love beads to solve my issues. But having a severe set of conditions science currently admits is beyond them motivated me to look not just *outside* the box but well beyond it.

---

[4] Sascha Shulgin is the psychonaut pioneer who discovered/created the entheogen/empathogen MDA.

Absolutely anything and everything was on the table: surgery, therapy, electroshock. . . . I'd try *anything,* including psychotropics and psychedelics.

Bandit-Dad-Smiled

That's a much nicer anagram! That's an anagram of TBI-DAI-NDE *combined with* LSD and MDA: two drugs known to cause paradigm shifts, often for the better.

The last collection of events I was aware of before D-Day was when Janete and I sampled the empathogen MDA. My soon-to-be-released book on addictions included detailed descriptions of each and every drug out there as well as behaviors, like gambling, porn, food, and shopping. My "dope days" had been prolific, so there were a few drugs (very few) I didn't know about and hadn't tried (very, very few). MDA was one of them. I felt duty bound to sample it before writing about it.

MDA is the core molecule within MDMA, known as Ecstasy, a.k.a. Molly. But MDMA is impure due to noticeable amounts of methamphetamine—it's speedy because the second M in the title is the meth. MDA, sans the second M, is a pure and subtle empathogen with zero amphetamine tainting it. It's called an "empathogen" because that's what it causes: wonderful, encompassing, undiluted empathy.

I am a psychonaut—a pioneer of consciousness exploration. Psychonauts use various psychoactive drugs and plants to experience profound and altered states along with mystical experiences and practices like ceremonies, rituals, and meditation. Shamans are psychonauts. I have a whole chapter titled Psychonaut in the *Project Addiction* book too.

While I'm careful not to encourage or recommend psychedelics, empathogens, and entactogen drugs as beneficial, it is hard to miss the fact that in my work, I wholeheartedly support these as psychiatric tools. I admire Sascha Shulgin, the author and molecular scientist who has pioneered great work with empathogens as a therapeutic tool. I myself had been drug free for over a decade: this was not drug abuse; it was "experimental research."

When I went to Switzerland with my son, we walked the route Albert Hoffman took on the day he documented the first LSD-acid trip, now known as Bicycle

Day, because he rode home from the lab that day, trippin' balls on acid, on his bike. Including this within the book made the whole trip a tax write-off!

Because my death event took place just a week after the two weekends my partner and I took MDA on the beach and had a glorious time, I still had some leftover in my freezer at home.

I felt confident of two things in my desperate hours: 1) that Ayurvedics had the medical knowledge to reboot my brain. If it is even possible to restore my brain to pre-injury status, and 2) MDA, and possibly LSD, might be able to hit the reset button within my consciousness. Ayurvedics is the branch of Eastern medicine far more advanced than neuroscience and is holistic and homeopathic. My MDA research supported the conclusion it potentially had the right stuff to help me reconnect neurons severed due to Diffuse Axonal brain injury.

Authentic psychedelics do not actually *alter* your perceptions, they *enhance* them. The reason the psychedelic experience is so revered by visionary thinkers is because psychedelics allow us to witness more of *objective* reality rather than our own conditioned and convoluted *subjective* one. So long as you can handle it, which some can't.

The Portal, NDE, mystical, spiritual, and ecstatic states do the same thing: these heightened states of consciousness dissolve the personal ego and allow us to experience ourselves and the world around us with pure perspective. When you see yourself and the world *beyond and behind* the veils of illusions created by ego and human culture, you see and experience its raw beauty. I was having a "good trip" with The Portal experience but having a "bad trip" in the material world.

This doesn't mean everyone should drop acid or go get hit by a truck to induce heightened states of perspective. However, in my desperate condition, I'd perform my own parietal-lobe lobotomy if I thought it would work, anything to stop this madness, anything to show my loved ones I'd be all right, anything to abate the perpetual state of woozy-dizziness I felt each moment I was awake.

I read through my own MDA research notes from my *Project Addiction* manuscripts and the chapter on it in the book. I barely saw any downsides and the empathogenic-psychedelic state could remove the blurry, illusory view of the world I constantly perceived. Or . . . *it could make it worse*. I had nothing to lose and everything to gain, and I had a couple of hundred milligrams leftover in my freezer.

I wish I had a lot to report here, but it didn't yield much. An MDA trip is pure empathic love with fluid affection for humanity. It induces the way we could, and should, feel all the time toward ourselves and one another: total acceptance and affection. I was not short on these qualities as my ongoing exposure to The Portal had switched on empathy levels to very spiritual proportions, paradoxically making it way difficult to function. The LSD trip has this effect too, but it is rather intense and can be quite rough, as it systematically removes ego-driven perspectives. I had never had a bad LSD trip, but was not willing risk the intensity of it. MDA is quite gentle in its revelations.

I have taken over two-hundred trips on LSD in my lifetime. It is not a foreign territory to me. The psychedelic-peace-love-acceptance neural pathways had been so well traveled I knew my way around without needing the drug. I'm not saying I was in permanent flashback! I'm saying the layers of reality the psychedelic (and mystical-ecstatic) states reveal were now a regular part of my perceptions. So much so that the last time I had visited with LSD in my thirties, it barely affected me. I was *already* in an expanded state of perception. Psychotropics had benefited me greatly in life. Could they make a difference now? Could they have a neutralizing effect on my TBI?

Due to the psychedelic and mystical explorations and experiences of my life, I always had access to rather hidden-from-plain-view levels of reality. The core of the sixties counter-culture revolution began in the Haight-Ashbury District of San Francisco. The Grateful Dead were just a horde of trippers who played free concerts in the Panhandle of Golden Gate Park and Ken Kesey was a guy who made some money off a book, *One Flew Over the Cuckoo's Nest,* which drew people together for epic road trips on his psychedelic school bus called Further. If you were hip, cool, and genuine of spirit, you could get on the bus with the other Merry Pranksters. A person wanting to join in with the Merry Pranksters needed to be endorsed by an existing member who would verify if you were cool and stable enough to join by saying, *"Yeah . . . they're cool: they're on the bus."* Being *on the bus* meant you *got it:* you understood the psychedelic culture well beyond pop terms. You've tripped before, and it was beautiful. A lesser-known personality of the Merry Pranksters and the man who was truly the hub of the entire psychedelic revolution was a guy few know of today: Neal Cassady.

He was the actual person Jack Kerouac based Dean Moriarty, his main character from *On the Road* on. *On the Road* was the seminal book that gave birth to the Beat Generation, which spawned the sixties revolution. Neal was also a main player in Hunter S. Thompson's book, *Hell's Angels,* which launched his career before *Fear and Loathing in Las Vegas.* Neal wasn't just *on the bus,* Neal . . . *drove* the bus. He was the actual driver—loved and adored by all, and he didn't give two shits about anything but love and good times. *Neal was a trip.*

I'm *on the bus.* Brandon is *on the bus.* I have often been looked upon as a driver of the bus.

Psychedelic substances have profound interactions with our brain chemistry, and mine was severely damaged. That's what the *world* does: society, culture, desires, ego, self. . . . These are how we are conditioned to worldly perspectives and lose sight of mystical ones. True and experienced psychonauts and mystics use various ingredients and methods to press the reset button. The theory is our primordial state of awareness, ungarbled by material concerns, is the state of living within the proverbial state of The Garden (of Eden) which equal innocence. Spiritual work is designed to reinstate perception of The Garden and sometimes, psychedelics can be used as tools to give us a boost.

***

So I decided to try it. I did *not* have a bad MDA trip the night I took it. I was alone, my partner was at her home around the corner and was on standby in case I needed assistance, and Brandon was working the late shift. There were no downsides to the trip, but neither was there an upside.

It's a matter of *elevation:* The reason LSD no longer had much effect on me was my consciousness had evolved to exist within an elevated plain of awareness. Only the spiritual and/or mystical, which are natural and pure, could truly reach the elevations I typically lived in. LSD doesn't get you that high. Many spiritually advanced people are virtually unaffected by psychedelics and psychotropics. When Harvard Professor Richard Alpert brought LSD to a bona fide Guru in India (Neem Karoli Baba) and asked him, "What does this mean?" he was shocked at the Guru's reply. Alpert was seeking an answer to life's mysteries and what LSD's role was to expand consciousness. And Karoli Baba upended the vial containing several hundred micrograms of LSD into his mouth! Alpert thought the old man was going to freak the fuck out and need 911 stat! But instead, he said, "Siddhis? No siddhis!" which means, "Power? No power?" And he was totally unaffected by enough LSD to trip-out the Mad Hatter. As an Enlightened, God Realized master, the Guru's consciousness was already well beyond psychedelia. Alpert became Ramm Das, wrote the funky book, *Be Here Now*, with the Cookbook for a Spiritual Life chapters, and the rest is history.

Many rely on drugs for elevated states, which is not the actual intent or purpose of these tools. They are meant to provide a *gateway* to higher perceptions. Once their purpose is realized, you leave them behind and do it organically. Otherwise, you end up a dope fiend (and I should know!).

Unfortunately, my brain trauma was out of reach for a substance-induced state to remedy. The MDA did very little for me because of the severity of my trauma and the magnitude of my ongoing cross-dimensional perceptions of matter and spirit. Like psychedelics cannot reach spiritual elevations, this empathogen could not access the depth of my injuries. It didn't feel bad; it didn't feel good, which, in its own way, was *bad*. I can assure you it is simply impossible to not feel sublime and beautiful with MDA in your system. My dizzy-not-present/not-myself condition did not improve with the MDA; neither did it worsen. I certainly felt the effects of the drug, but it was totally eclipsed by my mental and neurological condition at the time. I spent several hours feeling the surrealness of the drug's effects but did not experience anything revelatory.

Sometimes, the sad and tragic news is the only answer to grasp is one you don't and can't accept: *it takes time.*

If . . . I was to get better, if it was even possible, which by all accounts it wasn't, it would take *time*. I could intellectually accept this logic, and I was, in a practical way, willing to wait it out. The problem wasn't about patience or acceptance. The problem was I did not think I could survive it.

If a genie were to come out of a bottle and tell me that in year nine of this experience I would be restored, I'd do the time, like a model prisoner assured of release. The fear and loathing, and the desperation, came not from an inability to wait it out. It came from feeling every moment that all I'd do is suffer without ever getting beyond it, like *Groundhog's Day* in hell.

I'd do my time and take my sentence like a man. But if it was not possible to get better, then I didn't want to try. I didn't want to torture myself even more with excruciating efforts if I was *not* going to get better, which was my daily experience. I needed an ROI (return on investment).

If there was no chance at ROI, I preferred to die and just go on to the next life. I didn't want to come back once I saw in my Life-Preview what was waiting. Actual death seemed a far better option than "Near-Death."

I'm trying everything: physical therapy, brain exercises, studying, supplements, prayer, begging, bargaining, and denial . . . and now psychotropics. And I'm as fucked up and disconnected to my material mind as ever. The logical truth was I had indeed been improving, but it was too slight in comparison to the damage for me to notice anything beyond being fucked up. My earlier comment of frontal lobotomy was no joke. I was on borrowed time, dreading what seemed inevitable: an asylum.

_11._

THE WAYBACK MACHINE

> The only thing constant is change.
> —Tao Te Ching

> The Edge . . . There is no honest way to explain it because the only people who really know where it is are the ones who have gone over.
> —Hunter S. Thompson (*Hell's Angels*)

While life is full of surprises and many unpredictable things, there is one set of things you can rely on: *change*.

Winter becomes spring, which becomes summer followed by fall, and this is totally predictable. Yet we are in a constant flux. The more things change, the more they stay the same[5], *and* the more things stay the same, the more things change.

The driving experience with Brandon was a huge triumph. I've always placed tremendous value on a car. When I was a poor kid on the streets, I was subject to whatever and wherever I could find shelter and food, whether I liked it or not. I was a slave to others' whims without any resources of my own. I ate what I was offered and could afford and slept where I was allowed. When I bought my first shitty car at eighteen, after two years of sleeping in busses and parks, I felt freedom. If I didn't like where I was, if I didn't trust whom I was with, if I felt confined or controlled by a circumstance . . . with a car, I could just leave. I prioritized a car over a home, and still do mostly. A home binds you to a single

---

[5] French writer Jean-Baptiste Alphonse Karr, 1849

place: chores, upkeep, maintenance, taxes, mortgage/rent ... but a car is mobility, freedom of motion, and liberation at will.

The milestone moment of driving had brought me my very first feelings of familiarity and joy. It was the first time I'd experienced hope. It was such a foreign emotion, unknown to me, but such an exhilarating feeling! Hope! I'd heard of it, and people were telling me to have it ad nauseum, but since I'd never experienced it before, it was an abstract and esoteric concept.

Housed within the same garage as my car was another machine: *my motorbike.*

It didn't haunt me or cause PTSD when I saw it. It was just a thing I would eventually figure out how to deal with.

I got it repaired at the dealership where I bought it, and its repair was minimal considering. It certainly fared better than I had. The owner of the dealership and his wife were astounded to hear my story. We had interacted many times over the five years I'd owned the bike that would end my life, and I knew them well. But at that point, I could not remember them.

But I remember the first time I saw the bike. It was 2008, and Janete and I were walking through a Target parking lot toward my car one night when I saw this odd but cool-looking motorbike parked near me. And just like that, it clicked: *I wanted one.*

MP3 500 motorbike: the "Wayback Machine".

I had never been a motorcycle rider, and I wanted to add this feature to my repertoire of life experience.

I did my research and followed my fate: This bike is a 500cc scooter from Italy. No clutch or gears, it is a twist-and-go scooter, with two wheels in the front and one in back. It is not a trike or a Spyder: the two wheels in the front of the bike are pretty small, and when you accelerate, they *unlock*. This means they are not steered on an axle like a car. They pivot, so you lean into your turns the same as a motorcycle. It's a brilliantly engineered motorbike that doesn't sell much in the US, but I saw one at every traffic light I stopped at in Italy, Switzerland, Germany, and most of Europe. They're badass!

I was joyful at my car-driving attempts, partly because of the quality time it gave me with this young man, Brandon, whom I was getting to know and who is cool to do things with. But in no way was I considering riding that bike *ever again*.

The event was destiny, but the details are variable. I know that even if I'd stayed in bed the morning of the 19th, my death event was fated, so I woulda been struck by lightning in my bed! We live within an omniverse with multiple dimensions running parallel to one another. We experience a single timeline, but there are many possibilities.

We live in an Eternal Present: We are confined to the *here and now*. We can recall the past and ponder the future but only in abstract. Each moment we experience has multiple timeline potentials. On my D-Day, I turned right instead of left on my motorbike and fulfilled this TBI-NDE timeline. The wheels of karmic destiny were put into motion the night I saw that bike in a Target parking lot in 2008. It became the proverbial vehicle for my date with Death.

***

I asked The Portal: "Is there a parallel universe somewhere where I turned *left* instead of right that day?"

My Akashic Agent answers: *"There are countless timeline potentials. There are dimensions of reality where you turn left that day and ones where you stayed in your office or even stayed home all day. But these timelines exist in a rather phantom sense: They are not hard timelines. They are nebulous and unformed, just as your turn-right one was before you actually did so. Once you commit to one over the others, it becomes solid within the material reality. The others fade away instantly."*

These destinies took shape the night I saw my first MP3-500 motorbike and wanted motorbike riding to be part of my life and identity.

But now, I decided to sell the bike.

It was barely banged up from the incident, was worth several thousand dollars, and I certainly didn't need it anymore. Only someone with severe brain injury would even consider keeping the bike with what I was going through!

To be responsible, I felt it was proper to make sure it functioned well before selling it to be sure I wasn't screwing someone over. So I took it on a test ride.

Keep in mind, this so-called *scooter* is 500cc with a top speed of 90 mph and weighs over five-hundred pounds. It is called a *touring* scooter because it is designed for freeway commuting and long-distance touring. It has storage space beneath the seat, and I'd had it equipped with a cargo container on the rear and saddlebags. This wasn't no kid's toy.

I needed to be sure it was repaired properly (hopefully better than I had been) before some potential buyer came and test-rode it. I donned all my gear—jacket, riding pants, shoes, helmet, and gloves—just to putt to the end of the cul-de-sac. And yes . . . I even put on my Museum of Death t-shirt. Go big or go home, right? Your time of death is predetermined, so why not dress for the occasion?

I was able to putt past three houses to the corner, but I was not capable of making a U-turn in a small space, so I rode around the corner till I found a wide enough space to U-turn. I made it back into the garage and parked: mission accomplished. But I felt something surge. . . .

A sensation of triumph. As I awkwardly rode that bike less than a hundred yards, I found myself repeating a mantra: *I'm still here.*

You didn't kill me, motherfucker. I'm still here. And I'm not tempting or laughing at Death by trying to live beyond dying. I'm not daring death by playing on the freeway. But neither am I going to live in a small box to prevent any risk: I am going to live. *I'm still here.*

As I watched my life unravel from the beautiful tapestry it had been to a mesh of chaotic patchwork, I began bike-riding on early Sunday mornings, when there was no traffic on the streets. I'd ride along country roads while the weekend warriors in suburban LA were just waking, giving me free and safe reign of the roads. And while I rode, *I thought.*

I pondered my life. My death. My love. My God. My future. My past.

The magical and never-ending events creating a string of pearls for my life to wear, the extraordinary triumphs and events creating a crown of thorns upon my brow.

Once upon a time, I was a king. A long time ago, I was a lord. Nothing had ever been easy or given to me without sincere effort, but all effort had yielded results: a career of helping others, a strong young son of virtue, and a sweet and humble lover who mesmerized me with her body and smile.

My MP3-500 became my wayback machine: my weekly rides at dawn were when I could be fresh in mind without interference to: *remember. . . .*

First . . . I remembered what it was like to remember. And on my bike rides, in my meditations, and in my dreams as I visited within The Portal, I began to see my life and learn as I began to gain the ability to remember. . . .

***

The MP3-500 bike became a symbol of the magic that *I'm still here.* The Museum of Death t-shirt sheared off me by paramedics also. I wanted to replace my shirt. As a statement: *I'm still here.*

The Museum of Death is a bizarre Hollywood attraction. There's a photo of a gory accident death scene on the counter where you buy your ticket. "Whoa, check that out," I said, pointing the photo out to Janete when we were buying tickets the year before.

 "Where was that taken?" I asked the clerk.

"We have that there to gauge people's reactions. Some people will freak a little just at that photo, so we don't allow them to enter. If they can't handle that photo, they will definitely not be able to handle what's inside. You can enter through that door when you're ready."

The museum is a gallery of sections dedicated to everything, from serial killers to mass-cult-suicides to Kevorkian's assisted suicide, replete with a replica of his

Thanatron machine. It is a twisted and authentic place. I bought the souvenir shirt with the odd, dismembered cartoon cat on the way out after the first visit.

Janete and I returned to the Hollywood attraction to replace my souvenir. But the clerk informed us they were out of that shirt and didn't sell it anymore. I was truly upset and shared my bizarre tale. "Hold on. Lemme go look around in the back . . ." and she came back with a replacement shirt and a manager.

Once the manager heard my story, she insisted I return and give a lecture. "Your story is truly fascinating. We have that small theater at the end of the tour where we host guest speakers."

I agreed but had to confess, "I'm honored, but I need a few months or so. I'm still learning to speak and walk. I've done a lot of public speaking in my career, but I'm not there yet."

"Well, come back when you can, and we'll set something up. The shirt is on the house."

Now I have two t-shirts: one shredded Museum of Death shirt and one brand-new. And yes . . . I put it on for my next Sunday ride, not to taunt death, but to wear it like a flag. *I'm still here.*

Sunday morning rides for quiet time. Vazquez Rocks, 30 minute ride from home.

To this day, my Sunday motorbike rides are meditations. I live in a complex suburb, but it is adjacent to rural desert country with mysterious rock formations along the Old Soledad Canyon Road. I bring a thermos of coffee and sit beneath the towering Vasquez Rocks. Sometimes my mood is gratitude. Sometimes it is contemplative. And I learn to remember. . .

_12._

HAPPY ACCIDENTS

> You were born together, and together you shall be forever more.
> —Khalil Gibran ("On Marriage")

> She doesn't know what happens when she's around.
> Think I'm in love
> —Beck ("Think I'm in Love")

On April 19, 2003, I fell in love.

A dent in my bumper,

A random fender bender of destiny . . .

    LOVE.

Life can go from dark to light in an instant too.

"Sonova-*Bitch!*" I exclaim out loud as my huge, Ford truck fender-benders with a green Ford Mustang. "This is *not* happening right now!"

Just great! I think. *What is this? Some spoiled college kid driving Daddy's Mustang? This is all I need!*

I'm sure the other driver is thinking the same thing, but I don't didn't care! I am late! I am under pressure. I have huge responsibilities this morning! A contractor had called me at 6.30 a.m. to talk about a job downtown. The appointment had been scheduled a week before, but he'd forgotten to invite me. And now I was late. This *cannot* be happening!

But it is. It is happening, and I'd better deal with it or it will cost more in collateral damage. If I don't get to this appointment on time, it may cost me a $34,000 contract. I've got to get ahead of LA morning traffic!

Coincidentally, *this* accident took place on the 19th of the month too. But it was in April 2002 when this life-changing accident occurred.

I am not a *late* person: I am always on a tight-ass schedule, not because I run late but because I never over-pad my schedule. I'm like a freakin' engineer when it comes to scheduling: I know how long things take, including and especially drive time. Los Angeles is number four on the list of cities with the worst traffic, but as a veteran Angeleno, I have it mastered: I know how long things take at different times of the day and on different days of the week, and I smartly calculate the unpredictable things to make them predictable, except for one thing: having an accident.

I haven't made it two blocks from my house yet! I better get this over with quickly and get back on the highway before the four-oh-five turns into a morning rush-hour parking lot.

Just great! What is this? Some spoiled, college kid driving Daddy's Mustang? This is all I need! The woman stepping out of the green Mustang convertible is wearing track clothes and a baseball cap. It's pretty doubtful she knows anything about rush-hour commuting.

We exchange basics: driver's license numbers, addresses, phone numbers, insurance data. . . In spite of my frustration, I remain calm and cordial:

"I'm sorry, but I'm on my way to a meeting. If we could please set this aside till this afternoon. It's just a fender bender, so it's not a crisis."

She's amenable. She's not emotional or insensible, and our addresses showed we live within a single block of each other. "Damn," she gasped, "I only left the house to get a coffee at the AM/PM station. Weird because I always go after my jog, but today I went before."

"Yeah. That *is* weird," I say, not really listening. I ain't got time for her existential musings. I nod, smile, tell her I'll be in touch, and drive off. My situation is sensitive: As the sole proprietor of a commercial contracting business, I have commercial risks when I am driving in a professional capacity.

Opportunistic people and insurance companies are cut from the same cloth as personal injury attorneys. Therefore, even though I know I'm at fault for having turned left in front of her, I can't say it. Gotta let the insurance adjusters handle it.

One very important thing to note: I had never been at fault in an accident in my life before that day.

It's a stressful day as I attend the job-walk with a general contractor who needs improvements made on a medical clinic. Next, I make my rounds to my other job sites to manage the crews and work: It's just another day ... but needing to dealing with insurance company bullshit adds a measure of high-octane anxiety. This makes me empathetic: The other driver also has to deal with the same shit and probably her angry father too. I can't admit fault, but I want to be a good human, so I call her when I arrive home.

She answers the phone, and I say, "Hey, I'm pretty stressed out from dealing with insurance, and I'm sure you are too. I just wanted to let you know that it'll all get worked out." I'm careful not to admit fault as I try to sound empathetic.

"Yes, I called it in too, and they'll handle it, but now I have to find a body shop and go get an estimate, and I don't really know how to handle these things." She emphasizes the timing again. "So weird ... I go to that AM/PM every day for coffee *after* my morning run and a shower. This is the only time I ever did my run and went straight for coffee."

"That *is* weird," I agree. "The meeting I was going to downtown was scheduled at the last minute too. Seems it was an unavoidable mishap. For what it's worth, I just wanted to say I know how unfortunate it is."

I can't even use the words *I'm sorry* because it implies liability, but I am sorry.

We chat for several minutes: turns out she's *not* some chippy-kid in Daddy's Mustang but a single mother of two. We even have a common bond: we're both single parents. She looked young when I first saw her because she was wearing jogging sweats and a floppy hat to shroud her pre-make-up, bare face and hair at 6:40 a.m.

- She is my age. Her birthday is just five months after mine.

- Her house number is identical to my own: 26117.
- Her house is directly behind me on the next street. My backyard overlooks her block and is in perfect alignment with her front door.

I feel awful: I know I'm at fault, and while I can't admit it, I will not stand in the way of the insurance adjuster's findings. Then she opens up to me. "That car and my house is all I got. I'm just getting on my feet after an ugly divorce and my kids struggling from it all."

I didn't care to hear about drama that had nothing to do with me, and I didn't get the sense that she was doing anything more than rambling. But my conscience nagged me overnight, so to put it at ease, I got clever: the next morning, I got up extra early and picked up two large coffees at the AM/PM and put them on her doorstep with a note: *"This oughta keep you off the road for a couple mornings. Enjoy!"*

Over the next several days, we have to interact, and it got me thinking:

For six months you've been miserable. You've had one failure of a relationship after another and have now vowed to never hurt another again and grow up.

I had cheated on every woman I'd ever been involved with except one and a half. The girl I lost my virginity to, my very first girlfriend whom I fell in love with, was one. The half was my ex-wife: I cheated on her too many times to count *before* we were married. But once I took marriage vows, I was uncharacteristically loyal until we separated, and our divorce was filed in 1994.

After several years of casual dating and a couple of relationships, I became involved with a woman for five years, but six months before this happy accident, we'd had a dark breakup. After that, I vowed to be good or be alone. Since I had zero experience at being good, it seemed a monastic life was the only alternative.

I ate my heart out for six months: I broke it off with the few women I saw to spare them any further heartache. I loathed myself after nearly three dozen lovers and over ten in-love girlfriends. I didn't just break some hearts: *I was good at it.* I shattered them. I am so romantic and passionate I was the man they all desired and dreamed of. My romancing with poetry and passions was always authentic. When I loved, I showed it. Authentic loving wasn't my defect. Authentically loving several partners at once was the defect.

And it was authentic: The reason I was always such a good liar was because *I believed my own bullshit.* I could easily pass a polygraph because when I said I love you and touched a woman with passion, it was sincere. I was never faking it and never felt I was lying to others. Then I woke up one morning and had a moment of spontaneous, objective clarity: I was a piece of shit.

I am not worthy of love and should not be permitted to be involved with *any* woman, especially the amazing ones I get involved with. The final heartbreak was too much. I shattered a mature, respectable, charming woman who did not deserve anything other than honesty and commitment.

Oh . . . she *never* knew I had other girlfriends; that wasn't it. I had a clean, don't-ask-don't-tell silent contract with anyone whom I dated. I never actually lied. They just knew not to ask. My unspoken creed was *don't ask questions you don't want the answers to.* If you would have asked me straight out, I'd have told you. It would be painful and would put an end to the gorgeous romance we had.

And I *always* planned on stopping. Just like drugs and donuts, each time I cheated was going to be the last.

I'm an addict: Narcotics were my drug of choice for years, and it was mostly behind me. But my sex and seduction addiction was vibrant and *in the house!* I didn't want to *fuck* every woman. I wanted to *seduce* every woman. But seduction leads to fucking. And that leads to romance and a relationship because I just can't say no. I wasn't a love-'em-and-leave-'em type, no. If we had fun, got along well, and had great sex, then *why in the world would I leave 'em?*

My addiction to sex/seduction made my prior IV dope addiction look like a bad habit in comparison. As a matter of fact, I was always willing to stay off dope to seduce and get with a girl. I now realize I had always just traded one drug for another. I had been out of control. My last two girlfriends (yes, simultaneous) deserved better, and when I had this moment of, *I'm-a-piece-of-shit* clarity, I did them a favor and ended it. For their own good. And they were both shattered. There were two other rather casual FWBs (friends with benefits) whom I stopped seeing too.

This episode of clarity went on for four months of lonely self-loathing to a degree eerily similar to the rock bottom I'd had with dope nearly ten years before. When I hit rock bottom with dope, I vowed to quit and have never used since, with the exception of a single relapse episode. It was that relapse episode that led to this ultimate rock bottom with sex and love.

It was actually the 9-11 event that triggered my rock-bottom addiction to sex and seduction. (Hang on, cuz this is a trip.) I had this FWB I would see weekly along with my other two. She was a bit of a drunk, but she was really sexy and successful, and it was not serious for me. We had a date on September 10, 2001, and as we chilled on her sofa with drinks, chatting, she was rambling on about something that concluded with, ". . . *cuz you know how* they *are* . . ." This "they" reference was a bigoted, racial comment. She said it so casually, with a comfortable assumption that because I was white, and we got naked together, I must share her prejudice. I knew I had to two options: I could say,

"WHAT . . . did you just say? WHAT THE FUCK?" and walk out.

Or, "Excuse me, but I don't appreciate your racial bias, and I don't think we should spend time together."

And then my pre-evening-sex penis came up with a third option:

Say nothing, get what you came here for, leave in the morning, and cease all contact with this racist.

I chose the third option, and when I woke in the morning and went on my way, I saw my phone had been blowing up since 6 a.m. My girlfriend, sister, and everyone I was close to had been calling and texting nonstop and were insane with worry when they couldn't reach me. The Twin Towers had just been attacked, the world was a different place, it was horrifying, and I was unreachable because I was compromising my values and betraying my girlfriend to get laid.

I had my phone off and was more absorbed in my own personal and trivial shame of being intimate with a racist than knowing what was happening when the world was terrorized.

This was my sex/seduction addiction rock-bottom catalyst as I saw what I was willing to compromise just to pursue it. It red-flagged the array of possibilities I was a warped man who was incapable of being available and present to loved ones—people I truly valued—just for pussy. This is when and why I took a personal vow to never act on this addiction again.[6]

***

Let's go back a bit more . . .

When I'd completed my first memoir, it triggered a massive relapse. I was no normal dope fiend. The drugs and people I had once been involved with were sinister. My method of writing is to truly relive my past, so it comes out visceral. I toured locations of my past to actually sit in the spaces and meditate to connect with the events I was writing about. The book won awards because you don't just *read A Stone's Throw*, you *experience* it.

I put myself on the line as I began to wrap up the book. I wanted to expose the *true and actual* experience of what dope, addiction, and withdrawal actually feels like. One reviewer has said that reading *A Stone's Throw* is the closest thing to doing the bizarre things told of without *actually* doing them. I've had a lot of tearful reactions to the book because of what it invokes.

This relapse went on for two months. As I had a second moment-of-clarity-event and quit using, it forced the other moment of clarity of my *actual* addiction. And it's not about drugs or even sex and seduction. I am addicted to experiences that take me beyond the ordinary.

I am so bored and restless with this bland world that I crave and require extraordinary experiences. Anything less and I feel like I'm sitting in a death row cell. And, just like heroin and my own drug-of-choice, methamphetamine, you build up a tolerance, which leads to needing more and more and higher volumes: snorting dope becomes smoking dope which becomes shooting dope. Too much of everything is just enough. Supernatural drugs and sex are the two most out-your-mind/out-of-your-body experiences you can have. Love and sex are as far beyond the parameters of standard human experience as you can get. They are ecstatic.

---

[6] 9-11 and my warped values put me in a spiral for months. One method of coping with the 9-11 horror and feeling useless to help in NY was I found a random spot in LA's Griffith Park (like NY's Central Park) and constructed a twin towers monument. A large group of Armenians were gathered for annual mourning of their genocide, and we bonded while I built this thing. It was featured in the *LA Times*: "Anonymous artist erects Twin Towers statue in park called *Never Forget*." I have a few photos but never acknowledged the art. It stayed in place for years and was covered in flowers, candles, and wreaths by visitors.

This rock-bottom realization convinced me I am not suitable to be involved with romance in any capacity. Yet, I couldn't live without it.

The inner voice posited: "*Your pursuit of women has been rooted in lust. You need to do the exact opposite. Don't think* seduction, *don't think* sex. *Why don't you try to have a normal fucking dating experience? This woman is nice, she lives around the corner, you're the same age, both single parents. So what if she's average and looks like a frumpy suburbanite. Maybe that's what you need! Grow up!*"

So I asked her out: "Hey, you're really nice, and we're both single parents. Would you like to go out?"

I had been on *two* conventional dates in my life; that's it. Dating for me has always been brought about by a kismet-type connection. Just twice have I met a girl, asked her out, picked her up, dropped her off, and said the goodnight kinda thing. Just twice. Way too boring and beneath me.

I've had first dates at Halloween festivals, renaissance fairs, and met many girlfriends at parties and through other social conventions, but never really did the "*Hi, how are you doing? Wanna go out sometime?*" protocol. So I decided to try it. Whatever I'd normally do, *do the opposite*. I asked her out because she was nice, not hot. I hoped I'd be able to look past her average looks and see her for who she was instead. For once, I wanted to try.

Well, that was pretty short-lived!

I pick her up for our date and she is *h-o-t, HOT!* This girl's got a body that is blinding it is so brilliant! I don't mean she kinda or just sorta exceeded my expectations, I mean she is *gorgeous and sexy with a dynamite body!*

Her morning jogging outfit and frumpy hat had obscured her virtues!

Our date is something very bland. I don't know what people do on dates! Go to the movies? To dinner? Good God, no! In our neighborhood is a community event at a rec center, and we agree to go together. It's dull. And so are we. Neither of us are enamored by the other, and there are no sparks or chemistry. Two hours later, I drop her off and we have a pleasant and unaffectionate goodbye, and I go around the corner to my house and decide to salvage the boring Saturday with a beer or two. Or three. Or four. . . .

I sit down with a cold one and decide to smoke. A few times a week, I drink beer with some tobacco; other than that, I don't smoke. As I sip and blow smoke rings, I am weirdly happy and cannot stop smiling.

What're you so happy about? I ask my inner mind.

"Because this is how it feels when you meet the woman you will spend the rest of your life with," is its bizarre and unreasonable reply.

Yeah. Right. She's not a bad person, and she's definitely hot enough to ask out again, but that was about the most lusterless date ever!

"Say what you want: you can't stop smiling, and it's because you were just reunited with your long-lost lover and you're home.*"*

I pay no attention to this crazy jive talk.

She and I get together again in a couple weeks, and I take her to Hollywood. To make it more adventurous, I suggest we take the newly opened subway. It was another okay date, *nothing special.* Nothing bad, but nothing special.

Because we lived so close to each other, she would occasionally just drop by: no call first, and there was no such thing as texting yet, so she would just come by. I normally loathe unannounced visitors, but she was spellbinding to me.

She is in very tight clothing, accentuating her flawless body, has a wild head of blond hair blended with auburn, and she wears glitter.

Yes, glitter. Little sprinkles of glitter all over her body, and each time she leaves, I have little shiny reminders of her visit left behind. I know a grown woman wearing glitter on a date is juvenile, but I absolutely *love* it!

Her hair, her face, her clothes, and very ample cleavage were *glittered*. I was impressed and flattered she tended to these details when she visited me. She would come in, we'd chat, make out a little, and then she'd abruptly leave. I was left with a rigid hard-on, high off the mutual seduction, and was so distracted when she would leave that I could not stop thinking about her.

I knew it was all very deliberate, and I admired her craft of it. And she was a *good girl:* This was not a girl you move fast with. And she made this gently clear.

"I don't have sex with a guy unless I know him very well. Just to let you know."

This was in the midst of make-out kissing: She would just pause and say stuff, and then we'd kiss again. A lot.

"At your pace, my dear. I'm enjoying this all as it is happening. I'm in no rush. This is courtship at its finest."

Our deep and long talks on my midafternoon sofa consisted mostly of me elaborating on the mysteries of life. She enjoyed the deep end of the pool and was not taken aback when I told her I had very little interest in small talk. She confessed to not being smart and barely able to read well, yet she was endlessly curious. It was a match made: She wanted a man who did not judge her for her limited intellectual capacity, and I liked sharing time with a woman who didn't even know what *pretentious* was, let alone how to be it.

I never asked her when we could consummate our attraction. One day, like any of the other dozens of afternoon chats we had, she pulled back from our locked lips and soft gropes and asked me, "Will you be my boyfriend?"

"Yes." And that was that. We didn't dissect or analyze the labels or dogmas of the label. We became boyfriend and girlfriend right then.

We met by accident on April 19th, and it was now June. My birthday approached. "Would you like to go on a road trip?" I asked.

"Yes, that would be fun. Let's do it." I noticed she never asked where or how or what; she simply said yes. If she liked an idea and was into it, she just said yes. Such a positive word and superior to *maybe, I dunno, no. . . .*

"Okay . . . let's get a map and open it and just close our eyes and drop a finger to pick our destination."

Coalinga.

As bad it was, we both laughed and agreed to let fate guide us. Coalinga has a hospital and a prison *and that's it.* It is the dry, hot, central desert-lands of California: there is absolutely no reason anyone would ever go there intentionally. We agreed we'd just drive there and see what came next, knowing we could go there and stay for three days or drive right through it, but it was our starting point.

We took her convertible up Interstate 5. We were happy and gorgeous. Once we got to the virtual ghost town of Coalinga, we diverted to the coast: a long cut across CA heartland of cows and agriculture to the 101, southwest to connect to the remote coast of Pacific Coast Highway. We went north along the Gold Coast. I got us a room near Ragged Point and mentally prepared for a sleepless night as I anticipated lying awake all night next to this sweet but forbidden fruit. No problem: I'd endure lying next to her allure without pursuit. It was the day before my birthday. And she gave me my birthday present early.

Our passions were sacred and pleasurable. Our bodies intertwined and bridged together.

She was fragile, having only dated two men since her divorce going on two years. She'd been with only a few partners in her life and had been married just after high school and was true to him for over a decade. I am her polar opposite: too many lovers and jaded by my own libido. But we had something sacred in common: we were both reinventing ourselves. I was now a different man, she, a different woman. And we knew nothing of each other's pasts, and our personal histories with each other were clean.

The next day we drove to Monterrey and Carmel, which epitomize romance. We toured and walked and held hands and laughed and I fed her oysters, which she'd never had, teaching her to slurp them and swallow without chewing. So much of everything for her was a first-time adventure, having lived an ordinary life. The only thing I enjoy more than first experiences is giving someone *their* first experiences. Since I have no innocence of my own, and never have, I celebrated giving new adventure to hers.

She admired me and enjoyed my plethora of insights, knowledge, and awareness of such a vast world and always having an answer and knowing where to go and how to get there. That second night, on my birthday, our passions bloomed in a seaside hotel in the middle of the afternoon.

With delicate fingers and firm tongue, she came from a prolonged arousal. I gave her all I had, my fingers and jaw cramping from the delivery of her pleasure. She would confess, breathlessly, that it was the single best orgasm she had ever had. I felt satisfied with such an honor.

Our drive home repeated the same system we had for driving up: We drove with an ultimate destination in mind, but the moment either of us became curious about an alternate highway or road, *we took it*. A few of them were dead ends we chuckled at, and a few others led to surprising destinations.

My favorite parts were when she would say to me: "Let's park and make out a little." Her absence of convention and social inhibition linked excellently with my wild-adventurism and practical sense. She would just say things on her mind, as she did not have the overdeveloped intellect that causes a convoluted filter. The drive home was music: nonstop rock and roll we both sang loud to, and I felt symphony within my heart.

We went back to daily life but were within a magical spell of our adorations: always together, especially when we were apart.

We lived in a spell 24/7. Sure, I went to work, and she went to her classes to become an aesthetician, and we tended to our children and worldly duties. But she would raid my room at night as I slept, snuggling her nude form into my bed, and we would play passionately as the sun came up. Then she'd leave and we'd go about our days.

Brandon was at his mother's nearby three nights a week, making my home our lover's sanctuary. Her children had no idea about me: we were each other's secret until one morning as she was slipping back into her G-string to return home before her kids got up for school, there was her green Mustang in my driveway with the horn blaring, her two teenage kids laughing in the front seats.

Turns out they'd been hip to mom's affair for some time and had terrific humor and were amused by it. This was a demonstration of what type of mother she was for them, and they accepted me right away. They'd all been through hell, having all gone to bed one night and had their lives upended when her husband's affair was revealed. Her kids were devastated by the breakdown of their idyllic family. Now they were thrilled Mom seemed whole again.

A random afternoon, I gazed deep into her speckled eyes as I thrusted atop of her and blurted softly with purpose, *"I love you."* It was not mentioned or discussed. Within a few months, being in love was a mutual understanding, and we saturated each other in an epic courtship.

***

"Oh, my God! That was *you?*" We lay in my bed, nude as usual, our afternoon pillow talk becoming revelatory.

"No way!" She howled as we both reeled from what we were discovering. More magic to our magical romance.

"Brandon and I were down at the school playing catch a couple times a week that summer! *That was you?*"

It had been casually mentioned her kids had gone K-6 at the elementary school around the corner, and I mentioned Brandon and I used to practice his batting, fielding, and pitching there. She suddenly remembered seeing us there.

"Greg, my ex, and I were volunteering to plant trees that day; I remember because of how you were with your son. I knew something was wrong in my marriage. It was the very next day I found out about his cheating."

"I'm not exaggerating, Janete. I was so lonely, and I saw you and the small group of volunteers planting trees and looked at you."

"I know! I remember you looking *right at me*. I was thinking, do I *know* this man?"

"I was gazing at you with envy: There you were, this beautiful girl, so petite and wonderful, and I was thinking, '*Look at that guy she's with. He takes her for granted. He doesn't appreciate her and doesn't give her love and magic like she deserves.*'"

"I swear I was thinking the same about you! I thought, '*There's a real sweet man and father and I wish I had a man like that.*'"

We both had seen each other in a fleeting moment, and it had been etched into our heads. But then there was more . . . one afternoon's post-coital pillow talk led me to reading her a chapter from my newly written memoir called *Peace, Pot, and Purple Microdot.* I tell her of this wild adventure I'd had at the 1983 US Festival.

And she chimed in, "Oh . . . my ex used to talk about that concert all the time. He used to bring it up and tell people of this crazy time he had and this guy he ended up with and they shuttled people to the front gates from the parking lot to get enough gas money to get home."

"That was me!" I exclaim.

Not only was one of the principle players in this heady chapter of my memoir the man who would become her ex-husband, but that weekend of events had actually been a catalyst for her marrying the guy in the first place!

She asks, "The other guy at the concert . . . was it Rick *Veloz?*"

"Yes! Rick was my best friend! He told me this guy, Greg, and he were best friends before he and I became partners in crime together. Greg, your ex—was our ride to the concert!"

She counters with, "Greg used to buy pot from you guys. At Rick's house." Our eyes went even wider, simultaneously exclaiming, "I *met you!*"

"Greg dragged me over there to score, and *you were there!*"

"I was always there."

Janete and I had crossed paths on several occasions since high school and never knew it. It was inarguably agreed fate had been bringing us together for a long time. We had been in the same room nearly a half-dozen times over the last fifteen years and never actually connected or even formally met. And now we're in love like no other love. Because of a happy accident.

"Your kids came over here when I first moved in!" I recall. This one should've been obvious, but neither we nor our kids ever remembered up to now.

"Yeah. You were the new guy who moved in, and they wanted to check you out because they saw you had a kid and wanted to see if you guys were cool or not."

Her kids had dropped in on me just after I had unpacked. They met Brandon and all played on the rope swing in my backyard tree, but we never got another visit. "Because you told them Brandon was at his mom's a lot, so they didn't bother you. You told them that they were welcome to come over anytime but asked to meet their folks, so we'd know where they were."

- We'd gone to the same high school, JFK, before I was expelled.
- We crossed paths later when her then-boyfriend bought pot off me and my best friend.
- Her ex had been best friends with my best friend *before* I was.

I didn't know this Greg guy other than he and my soon-to-be partner-in-crime buddy had a falling out, so I took his place. Losing his BFF to me was the catalyst for his proposal of marriage to her. Just before his proposal to her was this epic US Festival episode, each and every element playing a role to lead us together. Her ex and I had spent three days together having an adventure he would never forget. The *Peace, Pot, and Purple Microdot* memoir chapter is hilariously clever, with profound, psychedelic depths.

"It seems fate has been trying to get us together for a long time. Our paths have crossed many times over twenty years, and yet we never met. Here you are, living almost next door, and we still don't meet. Our fucking street numbers are identical! 26117 Abdale, 26117 Oakflat! You'd think we woulda at least been forced to interact by mistaken mail deliveries by now. I've been in this house three years, and we're right across from each other, yet we never met. We shop at the same grocery store, gas up at the same station . . ."

***

I was not quite as intuitive as I now am and would become just a few years after this pillow talk conversation. Otherwise, I would've seen the details of our *past lives* together as well. And the deliberate manner with which she and I had fashioned reuniting in this lifetime.

But even then, in the early days of this magical courtship, I saw behind the veils: the reason we had so many narrow misses before our accident day was because we spiritually wanted to wait.

"If we'd gotten together sooner, it would've ended," I offer. "We were both too immature and selfish to see the bigger picture. We waited until we got our growing-up shit out of the way. Finally, fate itself said *enough is enough!* Having crossed our paths so many times and we didn't get the message, the Fates intervened and said *fuck it* and made us collide. They didn't know what else to do to make us see our destinies."

For our first anniversary we have a grand plan: We are so far beyond making lifelong commitments. We are ***SOULMATES*** with italics, bold type, underlining, and capital letters. One of our early dates had been a strange and mystical walk along the Venetian canals in Long Beach. I had turned it into a lovely story to join the volumes of almost daily poems I wrote for us. During that walk, Janete had remembered a dream she just had, a dream of the two of us walking in an exotic country, me, with a brown bag or case as we wandered through streets like the canals we walked along now. So it was decided: we would have an adventure in Italy to make this dream a reality.

We were to enjoy our first anniversary as a couple in Florence, Italy. There, we would have a private ceremony to exchange vows, informal, just the two of us.

Our courtship was effulgent well into and beyond the first year. While most romances stabilize within a few months and even show signs of complacency within a year or so, our passions are as full and radiant in Italy as they were the first days we courted each other. She still wore glitter when we went out or just had romantic evenings in front of my fireplace, the glitter transferring to my own body, my bedding, and all around my home, making her presence ever-shiny.

Our twelve days in Italy were novel: We felt we lived inside exotic poetry. We strolled through street vendors on the Piazza Della Signora and barkers called to sell us cartoon caricatures, but my muse had a casual suggestion. This was her forte: she would say these random things that would spark my mind and roll into a beautiful idea, just like here, her random dream memory inspired me to activate this sojourn to Italia, and here we were.

"Instead of a caricature, what if we got a portrait?" Turns out this was not so random: she'd actually thought about this. And she knew that to plant a seed in my head would bring it to fruition, as I am a giver of life to ideas.

We chatted with a random street artist who was no street vendor but turned out to be a very skilled man. We agreed he would make a portrait for this wedding and anniversary epic. I secretly told him to meet me later that evening in private to discuss the piece. I met him alone in the courtyard of the Basilica of Santa Maria Novella. I spoke for thirty minutes, nonstop, about how we had met, how we had narrowly missed each other in our youth, the Long Beach canals that led us to this moment, and several other anecdotes.

I concluded my inspiring briefing by saying, "We went for an afternoon walk just before we came here. Being ever in love, we took a rest in the open lands of the hills and deserts around us where we often walk. As we cuddled, we got heated and made love beneath a desert tree. As we got lost in our adorations and pleasures, we became oblivious to our surroundings. The more aroused we became, the more we became surrounded. By the time our lovemaking pinnacled, there were a dozen wild birds and animals all around us, celebrating our devotion."

I left this artist and new friend this final set of images and thoughts as a testimony of the opportunity he had before him. "These miracles, like the birds and bees flocking to us in the desert that day, are common for us: we have one magical moment after another. Please incorporate that into your portrait of us."

I had no idea if I had made an impression on him. "One more thing. . . . I am a spiritual man with my head in the heavens all the time. I am her connection to cosmic things, up above the atmosphere. She keeps me connected to the Earth so I don't float away. I love her. She's my gravity."

He then accompanied me back to the pensione room where she waited, and he directed us in various poses to model for the portrait.

The next day, Janete and I crossed the Arno River of Florence. It was sleepy and quiet due to the midweek lack of tourists and the pretty rain drizzling. We entered a five-hundred-year-old cathedral, and it was empty. We stood at its altar and exchanged our own vows to each other, promising to love and be together through the rest of our lives.

The rings we placed on each other's' fingers were two-dollar souvenirs from the relic church's gift shop. We had no use for government license or permits or diamonds or gold. Our *true* wedding rings had been etched to our bodies already: each of us now bore a tattooed ring on the *right-hand* ring finger, signifying *spiritual* marriage over worldly: lemniscate-ouroboros—serpents eating their own tails representing infinity, the primordial Om symbol for peace and spirit in one loop of the serpent's tail, astrological signs in the other. Mine was the sign for Cancer, hers, the sign for Sagittarius, humble and true signs of our love for each other and the mystical forces we honor. We will wear them all our lives, never to be removed.

From here we drove to Vinci, Pisa, and the coast. Back to Florence to catch a train to Rome and tour the underground catacombs, the Vatican, and its art, and then a train to Venice, where we spent glorious days with chamber music and an otherworldly evening with an orchestra in full powdered wigs and costumes.

With no reservations or destination, much like the days we consummated, we rented a car in Bolzano and drove into the Alps of Austria, wandering and getting lost in the country. Just as prophesied by her dream, I carried a small brown backpack to secure our daily travel items. What she had envisioned had become an absolute truth.

***

Our portraitist agreed to have our art ready before we left for Venice, but it wasn't. He agreed he'd have it sent to us in Rome, but it wasn't ready. Like DaVinci with the *Mona Lisa*, this artist kept postponing, saying it wasn't quite complete. When we arrived back in Firenze with just a few remaining days before our departure, he said it was complete, but that the cost was nearly double, going from a few hundred to nearly a thousand euros. He assured me, "When you see it, you'll know why."

And I did.

It is flawless. It is perfect. It is a masterpiece. He used very rare and difficult sketching-stroke techniques. It was not just worth the extra fee: *it was priceless.*

If there is any *objet de art* that could be worthy of our romance and the magic it exuded and radiated to all who came within its circumference, this portrait is it.

We had it framed in custom rosewood with a moisture barrier and non-reflective Plexiglas.

And life went on: I was the captain, and she was the celestial stars above to navigate by.

***

While everyday life of work and children and regular circumstances bound around us and within us, we always maintained our magical bond. A bond that all could witness yet could not fathom. It was private. Our bond needed no other's validation or witnesses. We were regular people on the outside and had similar dramas as others, yet we also remained aloof and had a private sanctuary within each other. And we knew it.

Our life plan was poetic: We had secured an acre of land in the forests near the Northern California coastline. We'd each come into a few thousand dollars from bad investments being returned to profit and scratched out enough to buy this property and begin planning and permitting to build our retirement home in the woods by the beach: She is a spirit of the sea, and I am a spirit of trees, and this land satisfied us both.

***

Our favorite pastime is soul-searching conversations.

"There is a downside, Janete. As deep and beautiful as our love and bond is, if it ever ends, one of us will have to move. Being neighbors is providence now, giving us such easy access to each other without having to live together. But this neighborhood isn't big enough for both of us to live in if we ever break up. And we know who that will be: *me*. I'll be the one who has to move if we have a tragic ending. And the only type of ending we might have will be tragic. We can never pass each other by on the street casually. We've altered this geography."

She and I are Soulmates. I knew this psychically and spiritually after the first uneventful date that we had a bond of eons. I saw two paths for us in the first days of our coming together: In one universe, we separate. And the magnitude and majestic force that reunited us in this life would be matched to take us apart. Only a power as grand as our love could ever cause it to tear. In a parallel universe, we live as humble kings and queens till the end of day.

Destiny is predetermined. Or is it? Free will is fate's antidote. We are the captains of our destinies, but there are more things in heaven and Earth than are dreamt of in our philosophies. [7]

---

[7] *Hamlet*: William Shakespeare

_____ **13.**

HAPPY PILGRIMS

When you discover who it is you belong to, is when you discover who you are.

—Jagadguru Kripalu Maharaj

—Ludovico Einaudi ("Gravity")

Janete and I are two well-traveled pilgrims.

Janete's father was an Armenian immigrant who joined the US Army to gain his US citizenship. He was stationed in Ethiopia and Germany during her childhood. Before we met, she had toured Europe twice with her children.

I was less intercontinental before we met. I had been in a dozen states in the US, to Mexico, and to the Cayman Islands, but never overseas until our Italy trip when we traded vows. Before that, my frugal lifestyle only looked at intercontinental travel as a fantasy. Once the Italy trip broke my intercontinental hymen, I went all over the place.

Since I became a bhakti-yogi, I went to India annually, typically with stopovers in exotic places along the way, from the UK to Japan. Having to choose between tourist traveling or spiritual-pilgrim travel, I chose to apply my resources to spiritual sites.

Our stellar romance deserved nothing less than a ten-year anniversary sojourn as epic as our worldly one. That Italy trip for vows was on the one-year anniversary of the day we met. Now we were approaching our tenth, and I wanted to have memories we could draw from once we were grey and could say *"remember when . . ."* to each other.

This would be my fifth trip to the Land of God, as the ancient Egyptians once called it. I'm comfortable with Asian particulars and peculiarities and excited to be our tour guide. Her childhood in Africa primed her to Third World dynamics already too.

I laid out our itinerary over several fun collaborations over coffee and park walks and it was set: Our route would require stamina but would allow us to experience Asia's spiritual legends. We would travel over 1,200 miles in nine days and walk the soil of the *tirths*: significant holy sites of the subcontinent. We would travel all four *tirths* of Siddartha Gautam Buddha, our own Guru's ashrams, and many *leela* (divine plays) sites of Radha Krishn. It would be an epic journey to be sure.

***

We arrived in Delhi, taxied to a nice hotel near the airport, and, at sunrise, met with the travel agent I had secured. He gave us our proper papers, confirmed we had the right visas and other documents, and gave us a detailed, written set of schedules and contacts. It was ambitious and complicated, and it *all went like clockwork!*

Day 1:

After that morning café, a regular taxi took us back to Indira Ghandi Airport, where we took a ninety-minute commuter flight to the northeast side of the subcontinent. Sure enough, our next taxi/driver[8] was waiting and easy to find. We wasted no time, driving just three-quarters of an hour to Bodh Gaya. As we stood along the shores of Muchalinda Lake, my partner extracted my storehouse of information as I become our tour guide:

"That lonely statue of Siddartha in the center of the lake is canopied by the hood of a great serpent, Janete. After six weeks of fasting and meditation beneath the bodhi tree of legend, storms drove the soon-to-be-Enlightened master there, and

---

[8] Taxi in Asia and Mideast is a relative term. These are cars for hire; private men and women who make a living providing transport, usually by a flat fee determined before you get in the car. Its Uber without an app! Tripping through these regions is a trip!

the Snake King, Muchalinda, protected him by spreading his great hood over Gautama while he remained in samadhi."

While we strolled the grounds of the Buddha's transcendence and took a few photos of the 50-meter/160-foot-tall "Great Awakening" Mahabodhi Temple, I relied on notes I'd stored on my phone. "This edifice is one of the oldest brick temples in India, the original one was built over 2,300 years ago, and this one is still close to 2,000 years old."

Janete was distracted by the beautiful children who pleaded to have photos taken with us with our arms around them. She is a magnet to innocence, as children and animals are drawn to her wherever we go.

"Why are those men arguing?' Janete asked me. "There's a pair of men arguing over there, two more over there, and there's a whole bunch by the tree. They're all in orange, like sanyasis."

"This is more of a Tibetan tradition, but pretty common in all Buddhist *sangas*, the yoga community of monks. They are debating the philosophy. One monk makes a point that is then challenged by the other. It's not really about winning, losing, or even proving a point. These debates provoke deeper thought and inspection of the philosophy."

"I like it! One just sits while the other stands and speaks and claps his hands."

"That's the protocol. Hand-clapping emphasizes your point. After a few minutes, the other monk challenges these ideas and the points made. It forces both to ponder and be quick to navigate to Truths. Cool, huh?"

"Yeah, very cool, but *don't try it at home!*"

We wandered on . . . "Is that *it?* Is that the Bodhi Tree? It's huge! Wow, I can't believe I'm seeing this very thing we watched in the documentaries."

"This tree is grown from a branch of the original tree. I hear there's another one in Nepal or Tibet."

"I like how the sites here are the real ones. How did they keep track of the actual sites over such a long time?"

I explain: "Most were documented when they actually happened and preserved. Typically, Eastern spiritualists realized the significance of events as they were happening. Western ones end up being part fiction, but Eastern legends are pretty accurate. Most of what we'll see over these next nine days are for-sure, real-deal sites."

We circumambulated the massive tree, soaking in the sphere of the many *sangas*, camped out in large groups around the base of the tree's trunk, adorned with large ribbons.

We paused for a snack of *litti chokha,* the local sweet treats of dough balls, from a roadside stand.

"The man who was once a prince came here, Janete, because He'd had enough. He had spent several years among the holy ones, the *sadhus,* in the forests, mastering and surpassing even the teachers. He was capable of fasting for weeks, emaciating Himself to skin and bones, while staying in samadhi trance, a state of meditative consciousness, for days."

"The biography documentary we saw said He came here to give up, right?"

"Kind of, yes. He left the *sanga* out of frustration. His deep trances of samadhi only lasted while He was in meditation. But once his trance would be over, he was still aware of the subjective reality of needs and desires. He concluded those paths and practices could not liberate Him from *samsara,* or rebirth, permanently. He saw their limitations."

"Did He come here alone? Was there anyone here back then?"

"He came alone. He left his *sanga* brothers and said farewell to them, and they were distraught. I think a few asked to go with Him, but He refused them. The guru of the *sanga* gave Him blessings, telling young Gautam that there was nothing more he would gain from the paths He had mastered."

"He sat beneath it and refused to move, but how did He not starve if He sat there for forty-nine days and nights?"

"A yogi of his skill is able to extract *pran,* his life energy, right from the atmosphere."

"He just absorbed the life energy with His will?"

"Exactly."

"And He was hit with storms and demons trying to keep Him from Enlightenment. Didn't you say in that workshop you gave on Him this is like the *Jesus in the Wilderness*?"

"Yes, and Jesus' time in the wilderness was approximately forty days too and was the catalyst to begin His mission. Same with Mohammad (pbuh), who would spend months in long, meditation prayers in the cave before He became illuminated too. Our Maharaji too spent time in seclusion before giving *Satsang* to the people."

"There's gotta be a connection between the time of Enlightenment and reincarnation then, right?"

"Yep. The Vedas teach it takes forty-nine days to reincarnate and our sages and avatars replicate this to keep a theme that reveals to us that Spiritual Illumination is not easy and will take you to death's door. They metaphorically die and spend the forty days or so in seclusion before emerging reborn to begin their mission on the Earth."

She chuckled. "No pain, no gain, right? Enlightenment isn't for pussies! Isn't that what you say?"

"I do! *Ha-ha-ha!*"

"But if the Buddha was not *spiritual,* why was he attacked by, like, demon spirits trying to keep Him mortal?"

"Yeah, Buddhism is actually agnostic, just indifferent to God, not really taking a side or getting involved with that angle. That's one of the first contradictions that got *my* attention, yeah. It's more a philosophy, yet there are tons of spiritual references through His story too. Remember that Buddhists see Him as a mortal man who *became* Enlightened. Sanatan Dharmis' see Him as an avatar. That makes more sense to me, that He was dispatched to Earth to provide a path to Enlightenment when the anti-God sentiment of Monism was the only thing many would accept at that time.

"Buddhists fully acknowledge spiritual forces like those that interfered and those that assisted, like the Serpent King. But it teaches that even these attachments must ultimately be done away with. It's not a process of God Realization, it's a system for Self-Realization. Remember that God Realization is Oneness with God and Self-Realization is Oneness with you."

"So, in this way, He's a Guru. But I like it when avatars act like people. It makes us feel like if *they* can do it, I can do it. That's what I want: just peace. Oneness with Everything."

"Correct, Janete. Keep in mind, the Eightfold Path puts an end to suffering, solving the first Noble Truth, but it also puts an end to joy and happiness. Once you return to the Source, your mind is d-o-n-e, *done*. No suffering, no bliss either."

"Yeah, but no more reincarnating. Total Om Shanti!" she says, laughing.

"The mantra of Om Shanti is for perfect peace, yes. But our Maharaji describes it like a divine coma: you're done reincarnating, so suffering is over, but you have no awareness of this. Om Shanti, yes! But you remain ignorant to it. Personally, I want eternal bliss, not just peace. I been through too much shit during eternal existence. I want the brass ring! I want Maharaji, *forever!*"

***

After several hours of absorbing the site of the Bodhi Tree in Gaya, our designated driver took us over five hours of country roads to the Deer Park of Sarnath. We circumambulated the *stupa*, built so long ago on the actual site where the Buddha gave his first teachings.

"He walked, Janete. The five hours that we just drove, He walked. When He got here, several of the monk *sangees* saw Him and recognized, *on first sight,* that He was Enlightened. They immediately begged Him to share what He knew."

"Right here is where He gave the Four Noble Truths? Tell me again . . ." she asks in a subdued voice as we feel history surrounding us.

"One: life is suffering. Two: the cause of suffering is desiring. Three: to end suffering, you must end desiring. Four: *you can do this in this lifetime.*"

"Did He teach the Eightfold Path here too at the same time?"

"He did. Legend has it He went on for hours without break, and his *sanga* brothers were spellbound."

"I wish I'd seen that."

"Maybe you did. You've had a strong pull to the Buddha, and that can only be from *sanskars* you've earned. We're here because of you, Janete. We're going to my picks of bhakti-yog sites too, but I included these buddha sites in our trip for you. I'm so glad we get to see these sites and meditate on them together."

A short hop and a thirty-minute drive, and we are registering during sunset at a roadside inn outside the holy city of Varanasi.

Day 2:

"We got a full day, but let's start with coffee and jam on toast!" Our tray of morning treats is at our doorstep as requested, delivered by the humble hosts of the inn.

We took advantage of our sleeping routines of early to bed, early to rise. The January sun was still low in the sky as a new, local driver took over our transport well before others were on the roads. A local to the holy city of Varanasi was essential to cut down the time of searching the sites and getting us to a good boat to float the Ganges. We clasped hands wrapped with mala bead garlands as we sailed the surface of the holy Ganges. We said prayers while we threw flower petals into the water as an offering to the river avatar.

We were in awe at the funerals on the shore, burning bodies to send them to heaven by dispensing their loved one's ashes into the waters of the infamous Ganges River, held to be an avatar goddess of purification and forgiveness.

"This is where we get the baptism ritual from. It is believed here that the Ganges River can wash away your sins, so the funeral cremations on the shore are to ensure heaven for those departed."

"But this is toxic," she insists. "They're putting all these ashes into the river all day long. It's been going on for centuries. I don't like it. Let's get off this boat and walk the streets. This town doesn't feel right to me."

Her instincts were her own, but we synced. While I appreciated the holy city's significance, the town was a bit more focused on death for us to relax in. Animal sacrifices and nonstop cremations made death more present than life's pursuit of truths.

We spent the entire day in a city we both felt was reminiscent of the Vatican in Rome. There was an undeniable blend of commercialism with hopes of effortless salvation.

"Which building is the place where Maharaji was declared Jagadguru?" she asked.

She referred to our own Guru's 1955 titling of Jagadguru Tam: the Supreme Guru of all the Jagadgurus, after He spent days blowing the minds of the nation's religious scholars, reconciling all the main Hindu philosophies and revealing how they all actually spoke of One path: Bhakti Yog.

"Ha! I don't know. And it's probably surrounded by gift shops and souvenir stands outside too! Remember that?"

"Yes! You still have the magnet of the pope? I haven't seen it on your fridge."

We laugh together. "It's in a box somewhere," I say. "I was just being sarcastic, so having it out was just disrespectful. But if the pope police ever come-a-knockin' to burn me as a pagan, I'll show it like a backstage pass!"

Our local Varanasi tour guide took us to more shops than temples, but the day was salvaged when we sat with a rustic yogi on a village road for a few prayers and photos.

"We're doing this just right, Janete. In three weeks, this entire subcontinent is going to be like Woodstock. The Kumba Mela festivals begin next month."

She quipped, "It might've been fun though. Our tenth anniversary during Kumba Mela?"

"This year ain't just a Kumba Mela festival, Janete. It's *Maha* Kumba Mela, and you know what that means. Regular Kumba Mela happens every year, rotating between the four host cities. But every twelve is a *maha* mela, and this place is gonna be overrun with 120 *million* visitors. You think *Burning Man* has gotten a bit crazy and commercial? This place is gonna be insane!"

The day concluded with a quiet drive to my Guru's village of Mangarh. The nearer I got to Him, the more introverted I became, as He filled my mind with longing for Him. Janete recognized my devotional trance-like condition and gave me space and silence for the duration of the drive.

Days 3-5:

Satsang kirtan played on speakers to wake the *satsangees* up at 4.30 a.m. Maharaji had already had His morning walk as rag-tag devotees, not obligated to daywork, took seats in the *angan* hall for morning *darshan*. It ended quickly, and as tired as we were and unaccustomed to a morning with no coffee, we sifted into the prayer hall to soak up *aarti* too. After a basic meal of rice and dahl in the dining hall, we walk-toured the temple and grounds.

"Wow!" Janete took in the village in daylight, marveling at the solid, sandstone temple of Bhakti Mandir with stunning black onyx pillars. "This is an entire village!"

"Everything we need is provided here," I told her. "An ashram is a self-contained community. The basics of bed, food, and all the rest so devotees can just *do sadhana!*"

Kusum Sarovar, Govardhan, India.

She adjusted well to the bidet-style toilets of India but opted to postpone showering from the spigot and bucket system until our next set of destinations.

I reminded her, "We're spoiled Americans, Janete. Our very frugal room is not a dorm like the local visitors. Back in the day, sadhana programs were almost nonstop from sunrise to midnight and there was no talking! It was pure sadhana! I heard Maharaji eased up because people just couldn't handle the contrast of worldly life to pure sadhana so quickly. Those must have been amazing days, long before the temple and a large sadhana hall was even built."

We only had a few days there, and I was conscious about *sharing* Maharaji's dham-village rather than oversaturating her. I had spent many days in kirtan meditations on solo trips, so I knew the best times and ways to navigate. I wanted my love partner to get the best of our India travels with no religious pressures, to take it all in and come to her own conclusions.

I guided her through the property, and she shared what I had hoped to hear. "It's so cool that right outside our room is that family's farm, untouched from a time forgot, but just over the mud wall is this whole complex," she said. "Do the villagers like this big ashram being here in their backyards?"

"They love it. Maharaji has put this poor, sleeping village on the map. People here have jobs because of all the work, building the temples and the new bhavan-hall. Each and every villager here feels a special grace to be born to a village where a Divine Avatar has appeared. This village has gone from a dust town to a historical destination! Instead of praying for house visits from faraway doctors, Maharaji's state-of-the-art charitable hospital is *right there!* And it's all 100 percent free. Same with the schools! These people are not ignorant to the magnitude of His appearance, and they know full well the specialness of being born where such a Saint appeared."

We had a coffee-seva with Maharaji in his room, enjoying His darshan. In less than six months, I would be dead. This was the last time I would see my Master in person. He knew what was coming, but my ignorance of future events protected me so I could enjoy His presence and His divine *dham*. Our new driver sat outside, our bags in the trunk, ready to make the longest of our car drives: eight hours in a small car to Kushinigar, the Buddha's final resting place.

Day 6:

Other than a roadside lunch of lentils and dahl eaten on a straw bench, we spent the whole time in the car with nothing to do but rest, sleep, meditate, and talk of deep things.

"Now you see the major contrast: Buddhist meditation is to quiet and still the mind. Do you have any luck with that?" I asked her.

"Oh my God, no! I can't sit still and quiet for a few seconds before I'm thinking about my day, my bills, my job, my son . . ."

"Right, but with the bhakti path, you can get swept into the verses and melodies and be more focused. One's a *passive* meditation, Janete, and ours is an *active* meditation. Almost no one can do passive meditations and quiet the mind for more than a few minutes. Kirtan lets us *direct* our mind and give it spiritual things to meditate *on*. We tune in and turn on, not off! The mind is fickle. The Vedas teach that only the path of bhakti can be used to become Realized during this materialistic age of Kali Yug. Our minds aren't strong enough to be silent. In this way, the Buddha taught the same thing: He left the forests to sit beneath the Bodhi Tree to show that even when you can silence the mind during meditation, which few can do at all, you still gotta get up and be in the world, which undoes it all. Truth is, the Buddha path during kali is just not possible unless you go live in a cave. Even then, I'll be looking for a Starbuck's in the Himalayas!

"The Eightfold Path is all on *you*. Other than the instructions on how to live and meditate, it's all up to you, and you're on your own. The bhakti-path is also about detachment from worldly desires, but it teaches you to *convert* worldly desires to spiritual desires. Good luck *not* desiring! It's like breathing: it's automatic! But when we desire God and Guru, it activates their protection. Now, with God and Guru being involved, we're not on our own anymore. *They* take divine responsibility for our Soul's Journey. Guru's *teaching* is essential, but it's His Grace that does all the work for us. You're not on your own anymore."

***

Kushinigar was a somber site. Far to the north in a dry region of India, it was the very place Siddartha Gautam Buddha, the Enlightened One, left His body and this Earth.

Janete had a profound moment, her first past-life regression, as she remembered being present when the Master, The Buddha, ascended from the planet to return to Oneness with Creation.

She was almost in trance as she gazed on the Buddha's *Parinirvana Stupa*, the 6-meter, nearly twenty-foot-tall statue of the Buddha reclining on his right side, facing west, representing the Dying Buddha.

She rose from kneeling, walked outside, wandered in a silent daze around the *stupa*-mound where His ashes rested. I kept at a distance to allow this profound moment of hers to play out, having no clue what she experienced until she shared it with me the next morning over tea as it gently rained on our room's tiny tea-patio.

"This was the first time I ever felt aware of my soul," she confessed. "I knew I had been there. I remembered mourning Him, thinking I could not go on without Him. I thought I wanted you to take me to the Buddha sites just so I could have my own personal path and teacher like you do. Now, I know it was instinct. I was *here*. I swear I'm remembering it. I wasn't at the other places with Him, but I was near Him when He left His body."

"Janete, I watched you walk the circle of the steppe of His burial plot, Janete. You were in a trance. I could see you remembering and mourning as you unconsciously circumambulated the site the way a trained monk would."

"Strange . . ." she said. "I always thought I'd feel special or happy if I had a mystic-type vision. It feels sweet but is sad at the same time."

Day 7: Lumbini, Nepal

It was dark as we arrived at the border of Nepal, which is as far as our Indian driver could take us. Somewhere past the guard-gate was a Nepalese driver waiting to take over. It was late for us: after 9 p.m.; it was raining, and we had no bearings. The Nepalese border guards over-scrutinized us, the two worn-out, hungry pilgrims, making us worry we would be left here at the border with no contacts. My travel-agent brother-friend was inaccessible and had assured us our driver would be there on the other side and knew where to take us. The border guards finally let us walk through the turnstile, and, sure enough, even in the dark, we found our driver who would be by our sides for the next four days.

The inn with a reserved room had a clause that if we didn't check in by 10 p.m., the doors would be locked till morning. At 10:05, we pounded on a door and were given after-hours entry to a sweet and comfortable room. We quickly saw how hospitable Nepalese were as our hostess offered us bread, jam, and figs to fill our tummies before we dreamt the night away.

Lumbini is where Siddartha Gautam appeared, so we had gone somewhat in reverse: we began our journey where He became Enlightened, then to Deer-Park site of His first teaching, to where He ascended and left, and now finishing with His birth-appearance spot.

Our awe persisted as we gazed upon the stone encased in glass, marking the spot where he first appeared. Janete clearly saw the legendary footprints upon the stone, but I was blind to them. Her Buddha sanskars kicked in each time we were near the Enlightened One. Like Krishna, it is said He first appeared in an adult form and then changed to a baby to begin His Earthly mission. I suspect if Jesus was an avatar, He did the same thing in the manger, appearing initially in full form and then taking the form of a baby.

We toured the village's dozens of international temples, entering many to light candles or just see and sit a moment. We took in all fourteen of the international monasteries, each unique in loving architecture and expression. We sat with apples for lunch on the shore of a sarovar (pond). We had the entire scene to ourselves.

"That's what I want my name to be." Janete confided this personal fact as we gazed upon the clear surface of the water. January had deprived us of colorful flowers, but a single perfect violet lotus sat up amongst the lily pads as it reached for the sun from the depths of murky waters.

"*Violet Lotus.*"

"I think it's beautiful. You *know* how I feel! Violet-purple is the color of higher consciousness and spirituality because it is the light frequency of the seventh chakra. It is called s*ahasrara* the *thousand-petaled-lotus* because when your *sahasrara* opens, you feel your mind unfold just like the lotus flower. Your primordial Kundalini energy travels from the murky depths of your physical body to reach the celestial heights of heaven. Same as the lotus, this scraggly weed starts at the bottom of a muddy lake and reaches toward the sun until it finally surfaces and blossoms. It represents the Soul's Journey, from dense matter to celestial spirit. I think Violet Lotus is a good name for you. Sexy too!"

Day 8:

We lay on our backs, glowing from exotic, early morning orgasms and profound pillow talk.

We were in a tree fort twenty-five feet above the ground. Our several nights spent at the foot of Annapurna Mountain, on the shores of Lake Pokhara, were in an actual tree fort. It was luxurious, and the Nepalese décor of humble furniture, huge skylight, and windows in the walls and roof enclosed us atop a banyan tree. We climbed a ladder to gain entry and hoped to see the birds of prey our Aussie hosts had rescued and given sanctuary. We learned the hang-gliding opportunity to soar alongside the birds takes a whole half-day to experience, so we passed on it with some sweet regret. It was kind of amazing to have one of our biggest so-called problems be choosing between hang-gliding at the foot of the Himalayas and watching the sunrise over Annapurna. We opted for the sunrise of a glorious light ascending over the snow-capped peak as we watched it from a quiet perch on another mountain peak.

***

We spent a half-day touring the back roads and villages by car. More than 203km/126 miles of small, rough roads wound us deeper into Nepal to the foot of the Himalayas. We took our time, stopping here and there to kneel and pray at village temples and admire mountain views as we climbed elevations in the remote countryside.

My lover delved into my mind, searching for ethereal secrets.

"What's the difference between Buddha's Eightfold Path and the eight branches of yoga then?"

"Not much. They are nearly identical in theory. But remember I told you that Buddhism is agnostic; it is for those who are somewhat resistant to the God concept and draw to the *Self-Realization* aspect of liberation rather than the *God Realization* aspect. Many were rejecting the God paths during His time, so it is accepted by Dharmists that He appeared to restore some sense of spirituality to the landscape."

"So the only real difference is that one is for Oneness Enlightenment and the other is for God. But I thought the yoga path is also about Self-Realization and Enlightenment."

"True. But God is present, acknowledged, and accepted within yoga paths. Buddhists aren't, like, *against* God concepts; it's the path of *The Middle Way*. So they're not really *against* anything. That's part of what's so appealing and beautiful about it. It's the ultimate 'open system,' and being *The Middle Way* means to accept all there is with total detachment and indifference. The major difference between Buddha's Eightfold Path and Ashtang Yog's eight branches is the goal. Yog is guiding you to the actual *threshold* of God Realization where you can *choose:* Self- or God Realization. If you want Self-Realization, you get to Samadhi and cross over, like Gautam did. If you want God Realization, you get to Samadhi and then surrender it all to God-slash-Guru."

Our talks continued on the foothill trails circling Annapurna and had lunch with mountain villagers who knew no English. They assumed we Westerners must be a *somebody* instead of just two pilgrims trekking the back trails and enjoying the views and hospitality of mountain folk. We walked for leagues and hours along the back trails where there are no tourists or shops, just nature and natives.

We picnicked along the trails. . . .

"Few people in the West, and even here in the East, even know that the first lines in Patanjali's Yoga Darshan are a warning," I explained. "He says at the start,

'*I am going to reveal the path of yog to liberate your soul from materiality.*' Janete, I'm paraphrasing, but he says, '*each of the yog paths are so difficult to complete that very few, if any, will ever complete them*' and those who do will take many, many lifetimes to pull it off. They require undiluted commitment and abilities that can only be attained after other lives of effort—*sanskars*. Each path, such as *gyan* (right-knowledge), *karm* (right-action), *dharm* (right-truth), and *hatha* (right-body) and the others only improve and can perfect their particular areas, and pretty much all of them will be needed to complete a soul's journey. All except one: *bhakti yog*.

"Only *bhakti* includes the results of all the others within it and exceeds them all too. *Bhakti* yog path can be done by anyone. The only skill needed is the ability to think and feel! Then he says when you master and perfect all eight branches of yog, you will still need to complete your work with total surrender and devotion—*bhakti*."

"Didn't you say He tells you to just skip it and just do *bhakti*?"

"He doesn't *tell* you to do anything, but He certainly implies it by saying Ashtang will be the most difficult thing that can be done, almost no one pulls it off, *or . . .* you can just do bhakti. He just gives you an option. Then He doesn't explain it and just moves right into the eight branches of the Yog Darshan. His mission wasn't to teach bhakti yog. Like Shankaracharya and the Buddha, they taught the path of *advait:* that the world is an illusion that prevents us from seeing that we are *already* One with ultimate reality called *Brahman*. Buddha just left out the part that even though the world is an illusion, God is real. Brahman is the formless aspect of divine reality and has no virtues or traits: It just *is*.

"Keep in mind our Guru Kripalu revealed, with scriptural, historical proof, that Shankaracharya, as well as the other acharyas that taught the other paths, revealed that bhakti was the only true path too. They just veiled it to fulfill a different mission. Kripalu Maharaj came to *reconcile* them and put all the pieces back together. The parallels of the Buddha's teachings and the Yogi teachers are unmistakable."

Day 9:

Our conversations took a long pause as we took a single-engine plane over the Himalayas, witnessing the grand peak of Sagarmatha, now known as Everest, to the camping-gear-buying world. Sure enough, as should be expected, our travels were interrupted with sickness, as my Western biology has conflict with Asian bacteria. I was sick and tossing my cookies, so our day of shopping in Kathmandu was cut short as I grumbled in a hotel overlooking the city. For no charge, the front desk dispatched a doctor to my room who gave me gentle medications, and I was on my feet by morning, ready for the next snafu as the Nepalese airport struggled with my mis-stamped visa.

It seemed our late-night border crossing from India to Nepal on foot had caused the border patrol to stamp the wrong page in my passport, and it looked like it might cause an international incident. We needed to make our flight back to Delhi to stay on track for our trip's climax to Vrindaban and Barsana with a side trip to the Taj Mahal.

On each leg of our travels, we had been escorted and transported by different drivers to appease local laws and borders, and my wonderful new travel agent, whom I will ever consider a personal friend, had everything arranged and taken care of. We never needed to worry about anything. The drivers were smart, kind, efficient, and knew exactly where we were going. India is the origin of so many profound things, and Uber is merely another commercial adaptation of Asian driving services with an app.

We were getting worn out but felt strong enough to remain in high spirits for the last several days. We had traveled over 4,000 kilometers (2,500 miles) within the subcontinent in nine days, all but a thousand of it by car over crude roads. We had hiked and walked and boated to temples, stupas, and tirths, gaining the darshan of many of the most significant and sacred sites known to humanity. It would be impossible to ever determine which part, what day, what place was the highlight of our sojourn. It was all unforgettable. Every moment a life-altering, staggering, and affirming piece of our Souls' Journeys.

<u>Days 10, 11, and 12:</u>

We arrived late in Vrindaban and began to tour in the morning. Our trusty, reliable rickshaw driver transported us across the Yamuna River to a sublime sarovar—pond—said to be made of Shree Radha's tears as she wept in ma'an for her Krishn.

We spent hours doing sacred parikrama of circumambulating many Leela sites, and Janete had to tie her hair up to discourage the monkeys from tangling with her tresses. As we exited one of my favorite sites, *Seva Kunj*, she purchased a glorious poster painting of Black Krishna, his midnight form. To this day, it hangs adjacent to the framed photo I took of the Maharas Tree we saw an hour later.

"This tree is born of the original seeds of the original tree from five thousand years ago too, Janete. Krishna's great grandson Himself planted this tree on the exact site where Lord Krishna beckoned the gopis to the most divine love dance of eternity. The *seva-kunj* site we were at is where He and Radha left everyone behind to be alone together. The essence of Divine Love in two forms was right here. This is it! The gopis longed for Him and He returned here to this tree where it all began with Him playing His divine flute to them."

Janete chimed in, "I always like how the leelas are mostly about sweet and fun things. The Western paths are all war and fire and stuff."

And I offer, "Sanatan Dharm has its epic battles and almighty God stuff too. But here—in Vrindaban—is the Krishn of love, not the warrior. Me too. I like the intimate connection more than the almighty, power one."

The rooftop of solid marble temple, Prem Mandir. It was under construction during my first visits. The craftsman carving the temple out of solid marble slabs assumed I was an American contractor and gave me full access to closed areas. I got to see the giant slabs of marble in process of being carved into the legendary picture images adoring the entire temple.
Prem Mandir receives more daily visitors than the Taj Mahal nearby.

***

We decided to forgo the usual ashram accommodations for a traditional hotel to have the comfort of high beds and room service. It turned out it was needed: this time, it was Janete's turn to react to Asian foodstuffs. Her need to vomit caused us to have to pull over to the side of a road, and I became committed to a very large gratuity for our chivalrous driver, who cleaned the mess and never complained about his car being ruined.

She was out of clothes, as her bag was puked on as well, so we sink-washed the light and silky pajama pants she'd bought in Kathmandu.

We were not in sparkly moods as we toured the Taj Mahal, posing for pictures for the tour-guide's included photos, straight from *Slumdog Millionaire*. It was all good, as we agreed the big, gold house/palace was the anticlimax to a spiritual trip. We went because we felt we *should*. When we shared the Taj Mahal photo album souvenir with family, all we could recall was how Janete forced herself to postpone vomiting while her fever raged.

Finally, we ended in Barsana, the village, the home of my dear, sweet, supreme, divine love Herself, Radha Rani.

We had a second wind as we surrounded ourselves for kirtan and satsangs held in the informal rooms of the temple during the off-season.

"I wanted to I save this one for last because it's so special," I told Janete. "This is such a divine place, and we can have a long and mostly casual stroll across the top of Barsana Hill and see over a dozen leela sites and small temples within a few hours. It's a great and sweet way to bring our journey to a close."

I wanted to make a new and exclusive set of memories for our visit, so we began with something I've not seen or done on my own in the holy land of Braj. We started our day on the far side of the village in order to walk through the entire village of Barsana, where the gopis lived five thousand years ago, and walked up the sacred hill.

As we neared the foot trails ascending to the hilltop, we were surrounded by children, gleefully asking we Western tourists for money and candy. We shared what we had and told them farewell as we began to trek up the stone trail. But one boy followed behind us.

"This one's persistent!" I said, nudging Janete so she would turn to see the boy who wouldn't give up trying to extract a few more rupees and candies from the Americans.

"Just give him what you've got in your pocket," Janete said. "He's probably hungry. He deserves it. He's not giving up!"

My bleeding-heart girlfriend needed updating. "I can't," I told her. "I have enough left to pay the driver and get us some lunch. I don't want to do another currency exchange and don't need to come home with rupees I'll never use."

It began to rain as we walked the narrow path to the hilltop. Hot sun is my Achilles heel and rain is hers. She stayed mostly silent so as not to ruin what was left to see, but she was clearly miserable. She knew I loved the rain, and this was the first time I'd seen rain on an India trip! Her quest for spiritual conquest made her resilient like I'd never seen.

Janete walking top ridge of Barsana Hill as it rained.

We walked the hill for hours and got soaked to the bone. The only thing we had to eat in the daypack was a couple snack bags of Lay's masala chips: *Only in India,* as they say!

The end of the hill was the climax of the day trip I'd saved for the end. We entered the temple *Ma'an Mandir,* and I approached the pujari priest. After we greeted him with a customary bow of pranam, he put tilak marks on our foreheads as we kneeled at the altar.

"Can you tell me how to get to the cave?" I asked him.

The poojari seemed confused and suddenly his English dried up. I used hand motions to communicate, but it was no good. He directed me to a dark corner of the temple where some young ladies had gathered. I inquired again about the cave with no progress. Finally, an English-speaking woman emerged.

"What are you looking for?" she asked. "A cave? I'm not sure what you've heard, but there is no such place here."

I turned to my dear partner "I swear, Janete, I've been here twice! Madhukar took me down there the first time, and I found it on my own after that. It's just dark, and I'm lost! It's the same cave Swamiji[9] lived in before joining Maharaji!" referring to our swami teacher who introduced the bhakti to us.

"Excuse me," the woman helper asked, "did you say Kripalu Maharaj?"

"Yes, we're His devotees, and we came here from Rangeeli Mahal ashram down the road," I said while brandishing my mala-bead necklace, exclusive to our community.

"Right this way . . ." she said, and with the mere mention of His name, we were escorted to the dark stairwell leading to the subterranean cells of the temple. As our rescuer turned to leave, she revealed an identical mala, showing we were spiritual siblings of the same Guru-Father.

On the near-pitch-black wall of the room was a small alcove where a few mendicant-sadhus sat. "That alcove is the actual spot Radha went into ma'an. This entire temple exists over that," I whispered to Janete.

Janete had a Divine vision. "I see her. I see it! It's wonderful!"

Lucky girl. I didn't have her inner vision but am grateful she did. One of the sadhus latched onto her feet, pleading with her. I did my best to interpret his pleas with my limited Hindi.

"I think he's saying you are his daughter reincarnated. He's very upset and is pleading with you to remember him." It was eerie, and she comforted the distraught sadhu with a hug.

Back on the hilltop path, we started to return to the temple-ashram at the far end of the hill while it rained steadily.

"That was sooo strange!" Janete said. "Do you think he was crazy? Or psychic? He was *crying* over me! I felt so bad for him."

"He may be crazy, or he may be a saint," I said. "Maharaji is giving you things to remember, Janete. He exists to give us devotional material! I doubt, as strange

---

[9] Swamiji refers here to the swami who introduced me to my guru, Shree Kripalu Maharaj.

as that scene was, you will *ever* forget your visit below the ground to a cell of Ma'an Mandir!"

Within a minute of hiking, we saw the local boy appear again, following behind us, wordlessly begging for a donation.

He had been our companion for over three hours and had not received a thing in spite of Janete's regular protests.

Finally, we stumbled, exhausted, to the gate of the ashram. Inside the gate was a snack shack where we could get lunch. The boy could no longer follow us because the gate guards turned him away. He sat outside the fence, within view, never saying a word.

When my order was called, I went the counter to pick up our veggie sandwiches and chips. Not one. Not two. *But three.*

I took the third sandwich to the gate with extra bags of chips and candy bars. The little boy was all smiles and grateful. I mused over the fantasy he was not an ordinary boy, but the prankster, trickster, Krishna, Himself, keeping us company as we walked His consort's hill and her palace. When I sat down, Janete placed an adoring kiss on my cheek. When we turned to the fence, the boy . . . *was gone.*

He is nowhere to be seen on the open landscape, gone in a moment, like a time traveler.

Final Day

The trip was ending. In the morning we would take a car to the airport and reenter a material world that now seemed so foreign and senseless. Our drive to the airport was quiet, as neither of us wanted to spoil the profundity of all we'd experienced with earthbound words. There was sadness as we both realized family and friends would beg us for details of our adventure, and it would all remain indescribable.

I meditated and reviewed the trip in my head as we prepared to say farewell to the motherland of God's sages, masters, and gurus. On the long drive and flight back into samsara, Janete whispered in my ear, "It was all magical. I hope I never forget any of it. I think the most important part for you was your friend Uddhao.

He is so special! I'll never forget how you looked at him. I want you to write that story down. I think you need to save it."

"I've been taking notes the whole time, Janete. I may never describe what he said that day, but I will tell the story." And so it was: the small story she referred to is included later in this text.

***

Five months from this time, I would be killed, and a sublime life would be transformed into a monstrosity I could not comprehend. What would sustain me in the darkest hours was the collection of spiritual events, like this journey, stored within my subtle body and mind. Even though I would become unable to access them with my conscious mind, their subtle presence would be my sustenance.

_____ **14.**

GET TO WORK ON TIME (A Guide to Recovery Strategies)

> God helps those who help themselves.
> —Psalm 121

> Eyes wide open all the time
> Because you never know what you might see
> —King Crimson ("Eyes Wide Open")

It was time to get to work.

Miracles only happen when effort is applied. The Red Sea didn't part itself: Moses made it happen. Fish and bread didn't just appear outta thin air: Jesus created them to feed the multitude. The mountain didn't come to Mohammad; Mohammed went to the mountain. God helps those who help themselves.

I was convinced my brain and body were beyond repair, but I had nothing to lose but time. Without the ability to work, drive, play tennis, or do anything and everything I had once enjoyed, I had time. I had to choose to either *"get busy livin' or get busy dyin"*.[10]

I began extensive studying and research on TBI, DAI brain trauma. I needed to become an expert if I was to solve this puzzle.

---

[10] "Red"—Morgan Freeman (*Shawshank Redemption*)

I looked over my personal library at home, a unique collection of 150 or so rare and hard-to-find books I've handpicked and studied from throughout my life, each one researched extensively to determine then authenticity of their content.

My book collection satisfies my insatiable curiosity for physics, the mind, the body, and the spirit. It contains volumes on spirituality, religion, mysticism, genetics, anatomy, medicine—both Eastern and Western—history, literature, cosmology, physics, psychology, philosophy, foreign languages, and a cache of poetry and biographies of bands and legends like The Grateful Dead, Morrison, and Marley.

I began my research with my medical and anatomy materials, searching for answers on how to repair my impaired brain and mind. I was determined to hybridize Eastern and Western medical systems to create a treatment customized to my particular circumstances—my weight, size, age, constitution, and type of injuries. I knew my situation was anything but generic, so I was determined to discover the solution that would be perfect for me.

Conventional medicine has a one-size-fits-all mentality lacking customizing of processes, procedures, and treatments.

My memory was nowhere near restored, but I was aware enough to know I'd had a rather prodigious intellect before the damage to my grey matter, so my first obstacle was my impaired brain!

But my ability to study, follow complex ideas, understand, and retain what I learned now seemed beyond my capabilities. While I knew I had always had an advanced intellect since I was a child, reading by the age of four and always surpassing what institution education provided and excelling academically, I was only just remembering who I had been. I was used to being able to devour material and quickly become an expert in any field, but I had no experience being *unable* to read and understand complex ideas or retain concepts and frame them into new contexts. Failing intellectually was new to me! I didn't have a backup method for learning. I begin taking audio notes.

Repeating key texts out loud helped imprint them in my mind and make them more "real" and easier to retain. It's a memory trick, like the use of a mnemonic device (*thirty days hath September . . .*). I replay my previous night's audio notes each morning.

I can't retain or really understand anything. I'm merely *storing* stuff in my broken brain, trying to load stuff in, so it's there if/when I might ever be able to think again.

***

Studying brain injury material was daunting. Nearly all of the info on the subject related to *coping* and *surviving* brain trauma, not recovering from it!

It was not too complex to understand because it's pretty fundamental: brain tissue, cells, and neurons are responsible for absolutely everything you do but are too small and too numerous (billions!) to repair. In fact, it's impossible to *repair* the damage to brain cells and neurons; they need to relearn what they once did. But it was emotionally debilitating to read about my slim-to-none chances of recovery, and I needed extra time to recover emotionally from the study sessions. The more I tried to learn, the more depressed I became.

The main thing TBI info teaches is how to cope. But I already knew how to "cope." Coping is a matter of endurance, persisting in spite of your own perceptions and feelings of being doomed from the start. The depression, anxiety, hopelessness, fatigue, and absence of a will were not my fault and were symptoms of a defective brain. I constantly told myself my feelings were nothing more than products of brain injury, but it didn't make the *black-hole-desire-to-die* feel any less real.

Knowing your depression or despair is a clinical and chemical issue does not make it any less dark. I was *intellectually* determined to persist, but I had an *emotional* desire to die to end my confusion and suffering.

These are not exaggerations for dramatic effect. I was angry and felt rejected by God, sentenced to live impaired and defective. I wanted to die and was hurt my wish was not being granted. I felt God had no mercy.

I decided to enter into a private contract with myself. The terms were:

1. Do all you can within your limitations to improve yourself and recover from your trauma.
2. Do not set a timetable or milestones; improvement is improvement and quantity or quality is not relevant.
3. If you are improving—by any degree—keep working at it.

4. If you do not improve at all in eight months, *consider* suicide.

That may seem pretty dark, but I already wanted to die, so this bargain was at least *postponing* suicide for eight months. If no improvement took place at all within eight months of serious effort, then suicide seemed a logical option. But I built in a death- avoidance clause: These terms simply allowed me to *revisit and re-evaluate* the suicide option, *consider* it, not execute it.[11]

I learned (relearned?) the true differences between holistic and atomistic medicine, fields I had once been expert in.

Holistic methods treat a living thing as a whole, not just a set of symptoms. Atomistic methods treat the separate parts independently, and this seemed counterintuitive to me. My <u>whole</u> being was impaired and damaged, not just parts. And the parts of my system not technically damaged struggled to function because of the damaged operating system, i.e., my brain. So I decided to put more *emphasis* on the holistic approach. I was open to both and applied anything that made sense but leaned more toward holistic than atomistic. I'm not picky: I don't have the luxury of modality preferences: pills, magic beans, virgin sacrifice . . . sign me up to any and everything that works!

Next, I studied treatment concepts of allopathy and homeopathy. Allopathy is designed to treat symptoms with an opposite approach: You have *this,* so we give you *that.* Homeopathy is treating symptoms with "like-treats-like": You have *this,* so we give you small doses of the same *this* to build up an immunity, tolerance, or even assimilation of the thing causing the problem.

Allopathy and atomistic approaches are considered *Western.* Holistic and homeopathic are considered *Eastern* approaches.

I trusted my instincts and leaned far to the East, preferring herbs and exercises over chemical medicines. The Eastern approaches *synced* with me—they felt right. Intuition is not a psychic event but a symmetry of logic, reason, and feeling. Like a muscle, it can be developed and made more fit. Since I felt I existed in rather spiritual dimensions, my intuition felt like it was the only well-functioning resource!

---

[11] My suicidal ideation was persistent for six years. The text will expand on it as we go and explain how I endured and broke through.

I turned to a book in my personal library on Ayurvedics, the ancient system of medicine and treatments founded within Hinduism. Ayur means long life of wellness in Sanskrit and *Veda* (vedics) means science and knowledge. As I studied Ayurvedics, it made sense. The foundations of Ayurvedics are to create a lifestyle of living well to prevent illness and defects: "An ounce of prevention is worth a pound of cure" mentality.

The Ayurvedic approach is not to "stop" the defect or illness but to "restore" yourself to your natural state of wellness—to restore balance and optimum potential to the living system, a system once pure and perfect and accumulated defects along the way, and Ayurvedics infers a hitting of the reset button. Indeed, I wanted to be restored to how I had been before a truck hit me in the face, killing me.

Western medicine looks for shortcuts, trying to solve a problem symptomatically without much consideration of the long-range effects (*side effects may include . . . vomiting, headaches, weight gain, suicidal thoughts, and DEATH!*). As a behavioral health professional and drug addiction expert, I have seen, far more than most people, the irreversible damages these so-called side effects cause with such minimal upsides.

However, I'm not down for a witch-doctor treatment of colored beads and fragrant flowers either!

But Ayurvedics showed me natural options and how to apply them while Western medicine relieved my immediate issues so I could exercise and experiment. I needed both, not one or the other!

Of the several documents on my wall verifying I am a certified counselor, specialist, and legal practitioner, the two I'm most proud of are my certification as a Master Alchemist and membership to the International Alchemy Guild. Alchemy is the Western treatment of Ayurvedics.

Much is lost in translation from East to West, but the practical-medical branch of Alchemy also teaches how to produce medicines synchronized with nature's order. When, how, and where you blend a tincture, potion, or elixir is as vital as what ingredients you use.

My Portal-driven intuition was declaring loud and clear the answer to my recovery was in Ayurvedics. It was a bittersweet intuition though: It was sweet I was being directed to solutions, but bitter because I lacked the capacity to understand or apply these formulas. *Yet.* But I didn't know it was a *yet* situation. I was told and accepted that my limitations would be permanent.

***

Western medicines scare me. They are created in sterile laboratories, and both the manufacturing process and the manufacturers lack spirit and heart. I leaned more toward natural remedies, such as herbs and foods and exercises that were natural. A natural substance is more easily assimilated by the body, broken down, used, and then eliminated, whereas Western meds are hard to process and eliminate, clogging up the bio-system.

The hospital food provided good example: I was *so* bad I could barely touch it. Brandon assumed I was just being picky. I stashed a plastic-wrapped, packaged dinner roll into my go-home bag. I stashed it in a cupboard when I got home. *Four years later it had not changed.*

The dinner roll had not molded, rotted, or even staled to stiffness. It was as "fresh" as the day they had given it to me. I regret throwing it away. It was a great souvenir. That fist-sized ball of toxic preservatives being passed off as *food* summed up the entire medical experience to me. It was tangible evidence of what the medical empire truly thinks of you. Food you *pay extra for* in the downstairs cafeteria is quite good. But the food included in your stay is *shit!*

I chose herbs, supplements, and foods that would allow my body to do what it was naturally designed to do. I trusted my body would take care of itself if I gave it the right ingredients to work with. By reducing toxins and unnecessary foods and substances, my body wouldn't need to break those things down and eliminate them, creating a surplus of time and energy to apply to restoring itself.

Western allopathy carries a generic, one-size-fits-all mentality, unable to truly adapt to an individual's unique makeup, whereas holistic Ayurvedics totally *relies* on your particular chemistry and makeup. I have a *pitta-pitta* dosha. This means I have a doubly fiery constitution. Medicines and foods that aggravate my fiery nature are counterproductive, while substances and climates the cool me are wildly beneficial. To heal thyself, one must *know thyself.*

***

Post-hospital I had an Elephant Man skin condition! I'm exaggerating, but my face would become so affected I could not go out without scaring kids! Red blisters, discolorations, bizarre acne, and blisters. . . . I think the hospital drugs triggered a reaction that was untreatable. Now, with everything else to feel insecure over, I was turn-away ugly too!

I visited many dermatologists and specialists over the next several years and in year three had a tiny improvement from doxycycline. The only problem was that it turned my nose blue-purple!

I disregarded the doctor's dosage and tweaked to half a pill every other day. The result was a decent complexion (not great) with a less-blue nose!

In year five, I found an Ayurvedic practitioner. He gave me a $40 bottle of powder to mix in a glass of water twice a day. Voilà! I was normal in a month! Once or twice a month, I still drink this foul potion to maintain a normal complexion.

The same guy gave me another tonic that completely resolved my knee stiffness. I could not drive more than a half hour without excruciating pain in my knee, requiring me to pull over and walk it off. Ayurvedics works!

Resources and references are provided on the website.

The Benefits of Supplements

I searched for natural foods and supplements to accelerate my body's ability to eliminate toxins, heal, restore, and access its potential. Simple Athletics 101: hydrate and give the body food that's easy for it to process and digest. This is how top athletes have such tremendous abilities, physiques, and endurance. They don't allow their body to waste time and energy breaking down hard-to-digest foods.

I have been a strict vegetarian for over a decade. Vegetarian-based food (even the junk!) is like higher octane fuel for your car: it's easier and cleaner to burn and convert into energy!

Here is a list of the foods and supplements I have used to accelerate my recovery:

- Multivitamin high in C, E, and beta carotene, selenium, choline, melatonin, gingko biloba, and ashwagangda.
  - o Strengthens the whole body
  - o Detoxifies unwanted elements and toxins
- Selenium
  - o Aids breathing and blood circulation, cleansing the blood and lungs
- Choline
  - o Detoxes and improves brain and memory
- Melatonin
  - o Reduces anxiety endorphins, improves rest and sleep
- Ginko biloba
  - o Aids blood flow to brain, helps in brain healing
- Ashwaganda
  - o Improves body strength and resilience, reduces stress, and cleanses thinking and the blood

It is very important to buy vitamin products made from high-quality ingredients. Poor-quality vitamins are quickly broken down and eliminated before they can do the jobs they are designed to do effectively. Ever notice how you pee neon yellow when you're vitamin healthy? Bright yellow urine is the residual vitamin your body is eliminating. You want your vitamins to stick around and do their jobs and only time-released or organic supplements break down naturally so your body can extract and distribute them for use.

It is very important to take supplements with food! Supplements aren't magic beans! They *empower* and *enhance* your body's natural ability to perform to its potential. If you don't eat just before or with your supplements, they have nothing to interact and work with. This means they get peed out before they do their job!

- Eat right and take the right vitamins. I cannot put enough emphasis on how this system helped me become the medical miracle I am!
- Don't worry about the cost of these supplements. Yes, the good ones are gonna be pricey, but they will quadruple your money back in productivity, i.e., working for money! And they cost considerably less than the prescription meds[12] that do a fourth of the work and create more

---

[12] It would be great if our health insurance would cover vitamins, not just prescription meds!

work on the back end of life! All those Western meds have to be processed and detoxed eventually, but the organic supplements come in clean and leave clean!

These natural supplements all work in concert. Western meds need more meds to counterbalance them. When you take one med, you need another med to counteract the first one's side effects. Pretty soon, you're taking three meds for every one you're prescribed. You're borrowing from Peter to pay Paul again! You're earning $5 but spending $10!

The natural methods do not produce the quick, somewhat instantly observable results the Western ones do, but what do we know about shortcuts? Think junk food: cheap, easy, instant gratification—*long-term problems*. Think healthy food: not so glamorous, more expensive, and harder to prepare but is clean and good all around.

Think of this axiom I have patented: The quicker, easier, and more pleasurable something is, the more (proportionately) unhealthy for you—and vice versa. The harder something is to attain and acquire, the healthier and more rewarding it is for you!

No pain—no gain.[13] Reward is proportionate to sacrifice and effort!

---

[13] Jane Fonda might've been the origin of this catchphrase in the '80s!

15.

THE UNDERGROUND STREAM

As above, so below, as within, so without, as the universe, so the soul.

—Hermes Trismegistus

To feel inspired/To fathom the power/To witness the beauty
To bathe in the fountain/To swing on the spiral

—Tool ("Lateralus")

$$\varphi = \frac{1 + \sqrt{5}}{2} = 1.6180339887\ldots$$

—Fibonacci

Religious Rabbit Holes

When I was five, my tarot-reading, neighborhood-psychic mother took our little clan to various local churches so we could get a taste of religion. She was open-minded and allowed me and my two older siblings to make up our own minds if we liked it or not. I decided I liked the storefront Sunday Christian gathering in our little downtown of Prescott, Arizona. The stories about Jesus were pretty colorful, and at the end of the kid-friendly sermon, Kool-Aid and cookie communion was given. I was five: anybody who was giving away sugary punch and treats before lunch to a poor kid was my BFF.

My mom read tarot for extra dough and was a New-Ager before it was a household buzzword. In typical monkey-see, monkey-do fashion, I started looking deep into her five-inch-diameter crystal ball and talking about what I saw in it. Soon, some of her tarot clients were coming to see me. I don't know what Mom charged them for my scrying services, but I liked the attention, and the treats some of the ladies would give me were slightly better than the punch and cookies I got at the storefront church.

We lived on a country highway because we were poor: five of us in a three-bedroom house that was next to a cemetery with gravestones from the 1800s in our western town. Being haunted by ghosts was normal to me. Many small items around the house would vanish and reappear and images on walls and shadowy presences were just a part of my Saturday-morning cartoon time.

The hip 1970s Andrew Lloyd Weber opera *Jesus Christ Superstar* had just come out, and it was part of the regular music rotation in our house. I liked Jim Croce and Simon & Garfunkel too, but the *Superstar* album was more passionate and powerful to me.

When I first grasped the tragedy of the story, I had my first religious experience.

The news program *60 Minutes* was new too, and we watched it religiously on Sunday nights, so I was growing up with Safer and Wallace exposing crooked politicians and businessmen in a straight and direct manner. Much of what I gleaned from the news in the world was we are a race of charlatans, and at the core of most of the violence, hatred, and intolerance was religion. Weekly stories of sex scandals and war in the Middle East always had some religious rationalization.

By the time I was a preteen, I had concluded that religions were made up of opportunistic frauds and hypocrites. They all preached of love and heaven and then used it to justify hatred and intolerance toward anyone and everyone who didn't agree with their own set of dogmas. I didn't accept religion or spirituality whatsoever and saw it as an anathema to humanity, a bullshit way of yielding power and leverage by justifying whatever selfish, abhorrent hell someone wanted to promote by evoking God to justify it.

I began studying mysteries as a boy: I was fascinated with ghost stories and the supernatural and infatuated with Halloween stuff. Able to read by the age of four, I read two to three books at a time and still do. I wanted to get to the root, the core, the truth of this most influential and misunderstood source of controversy: God. By the time I was fourteen, I was a religious scholar.

My original intention in my youth to become a religious scholar was passive-aggressive. I studied it because I wanted to be able to debate religious hypocrites and beat them, publicly, at their own game. I would often bait local priests and pastors in theological discussion just to humiliate them and expose their ignorance. I was a hypocrite too: I pridefully enjoyed being a young boy humiliating adults in debate.

Intuitively, I knew not to use conventional resources. I read the Bible and others, but I studied different religions on my own with volumes of library books from all different perspectives. I studied history—*real history*—of the origins and evolutions of religions and spiritual philosophies. I studied their beliefs and practices to fathom their dogmas. These rabbit holes led me to an underground stream.

The Underground Stream is a term used within the esoteric and occult cultures and societies.

It is a euphemism for the Akashic Records. Akash means *space* in Sanskrit, and this celestial space refers to the dimension where Knowledge and Truth are stored. Most of the knowledge within the Akash is available here in the realm of the physical world too.

But did you know?

- That the Torah (Old Testament Bible) is an encoded formula for spiritual consciousness? Many Underground Stream sailors accept that the long list of names in the Torah (so-and-so begat so-and-so . . .) is not a genealogical list of the Jewish race but a mystical formula of instructions to attain spiritual power and consciousness.
- That the Kabbalah's Tree of Life, with its pictorial correspondence of the Tarot deck, alchemy's seven stages of The Philosopher's Stone,[14] Kundalini Yoga and Ashtanga Yoga's eight branches, which are identical to the Buddha's Eightfold Path, are all teaching the same thing in different terms.
- That Kriya Yog(a), the path popularized and brought to America in the '40s and '50s by Paramahansa Yogananda's Self-Realization Fellowship (SRF), is a path of Kundalini yog(a) blended with bhakti yog(a).

The true origins of religions and spiritual paths are available if you know where and how to look for them.

---

[14] Philosophers' stone is a euphemism for enlightenment as is Fountain of Youth, Xanadu, nirvana, El Dorado and the rest of the terms that refer to untold wealth and fortune. Not about material, all about spiritual!

Did you know?

- That the Latin word *occult* means hidden—*in plain view*.

The Underground Stream refers to the actual true history, origins, and machinations of humanity, particularly pertaining to religion and spirituality before they were altered and changed by organized religions and politically motivated historians. It has always been there but has gone underground to avoid zealous persecution of the truths.

- That the tarot is a pictorial version of Kabbalah's Tree of Life, developed so kabbalists could avoid persecution in the 1400s? The pictorial Tree of Life was also created so that illiterates could study and practice the path of Judaic mysticism.

Conventional history taught in schools taught me the basics about the Inquisition and the witch trials. But *Underground Stream* history reveals a holocaust-persecution of women by religious zealots deliberately invented and sustained by an organized religion for the single goal of monopolizing their religion by systematically erasing others from history.

- That the *papal bull,*[15] *ad extirpanda,* issued on May 15, 1252, by Pope Innocent IV is what kicked off the Spanish Inquisition. A genocide that lasted for two-hundred years and exterminated over 32,000 people. The message was clear: *Join us or else.* And don't just die—die horribly and torturously.

Now . . . the persecution of Jews and women and the plight of Native Americans and Black lives are politically correct, woke topics. But these and others have been a part of the Underground Stream all along.

When we Underground Stream sailors get together, we don't argue over the true identities of Moses or Jesus: We all know that their true names were Akhenaten and Yeshua. We don't debate over where Yeshua was for the mysterious eighteen

---

[15] Papal bull: an official decree of the Catholic pope that is authoritative. *ad extirpanda'* was the *papal bull* on Wednesday, May 15, 1252, by Pope Innocent IV that authorized the Spanish Inquisition.

years unaccounted for in the New Testament. True initiates know of this, and we chat casually about it.

The more I studied, the more I found: *Seek and ye shall find. Knock and it shall be opened to you (Mathew 7.7).* As I dug deep into the religious rabbit holes, I saw the beauty existing well below the surface. I found God down there, not the business-oriented, organized-religion God of zealots and snake-oil salesmen, but the God at the core of the Truth.

With deductive reasoning, I decided the Truth of God and spirituality would most likely be found at its source. What came first? Where did the God concept originate? I decided to work backward, tracing the trail of religious history to find its origin to authenticate it. If the God concept is genuine, then His source must be eternal and predate humanity. Deductive reasoning led me to conclude that if I could find the original source, the end of the rabbit hole, I'd find the Truth.

As I tunneled through ancient rabbit holes, I learned the true aspects of the Abrahamic scriptures and the fictionalized reinventions of them. Working backward:

Did you know?

- Mohammad (pbuh), a brilliant leader, frustrated with the primitive social and polytheistic themes of his time, created a wonderful religion to help people. He put a theologically monopolizing period on the end of it by declaring he was the final prophet, therefore making his updated version of Abrahamic religion the final authority.

He used the same business model the Christians had used when they pirated the monotheistic religion of Judaism.

- The founders of Christianity turned a Hebrew man who had spent eighteen years in India, mastering yoga to perform miracles and merging his consciousness with God Consciousness, into a savior.

They too monopolized religion, appropriating the spiritual-master Guru concept by stating Christ is not just *a* master, but *the one and only*. This had been pirated from the Judaic religion, which prophesized a savior. The difference is the Jew's savior is prophesized to save *them*: a race of people. The prophesized Son of David isn't for *humanity:* He's for the Jews.

Having dug all the way down the religious rabbit holes to the Underground Stream, I sailed along the shoreline and docked my boat at various ports of call and loaded my vessel with exotic power: Alchemy, Kabbalah/Tarot, Hermetic Magic, Pythagorean Numerology. . . .

These ports of mysticism focused on personal spiritual power and illumination. They were also ports of true religious history.

Did you know?

- That the Jews were the first monotheistic religion in the non-Asian world.

It started with the pharaoh Akhenaten's spiritual and religious revolution of a single-god religion, the Aten. This pharaoh did not force all of Egypt to follow his single-god religion. He built a new city for those who wanted a *promised land* in which to follow their own religion. The population was a blend of Egyptian and Hebrews. He called the city Akhetaten: *dwelling place of Aten*. Aten became Adonai, Elohim, and other derivatives in Hebrew.

This new religion and city were a threat to the priestly hierarchy of the Eighteenth Dynasty, so they pressured pharaoh's rival, Vizier-General Aye, to destroy the city. Pharaoh Akhenaten, his queen, Nefertiti, and thousands of Atenites were pursued by the wicked General Aye, so they made an *exodus* to escape.

Once the city was destroyed and Akhenaten was assassinated, mentioning his name was outlawed under penalty of death. His followers continued and went underground, using his nickname: *Mose*, which just means "son" in ancient Egyptian. Mose became Moses, and later, his son and heir, King Tut, was also assassinated so that the wicked Aye could take full power.

- That the prayer closing, "amen" means "so be it" is a derivative of Sanskrit's om, which represents the primordial sound of cosmic creation? Torah/Old Testament, Genesis, begins with, *in the beginning was the word*, yet never says what the word is. The word is "om" (pronounced aum—ahhh-ooo-mmm)

Deeper down the rabbit hole and along the Underground Stream, I learned the source of his monotheistic religion too. One hundred years earlier, the fifth pharaoh of Egypt's Eighteenth Dynasty was a trailblazing woman, not a man. She established trade with an unknown territory because Egyptians had a fetish for incense, and the best myrrh was in a land they referred to as *Punt (poont)*, which meant Land of God in Egyptian. Sacred incense and wood wasn't the only thing imported from Punt though. Egyptian religion was polytheistic, impersonal, and primal. Spiritual thought in the land of Punt was evolved, mature, and was of One god.

The region they visited was particular to a specific cult of Shiva. This was east-India. And that's where the trail went cold. With extensive and tireless searching, I'd come to the end of the rabbit-hole. I beached my spiritual kayak on the shores of the Underground Stream: I had arrived on the shore of spiritual and religious genesis.

The original source of humanity's spiritual concepts were all imported from a place called Bharata Varsh, now known as India, and from a singular, monotheistic, system aptly called, Sanatan Dharm: *The Eternal Truth.*

Did you know?

- That Sanatan Dharm (Hinduism) is a monotheistic religion? Contrary to popular misconception, Hinduism is not actually polytheistic. There are countless gods to pray to and worship, each with their own responsibilities: Brahma is the Creator, Vishnu the Preserver, Shiva the Destroyer, Indra is the god of rain and thunder, etc. But these are not actually separate gods. They are *expressions and expansions of the One True God.*

I look at many gods being but an extension of the One-God, kinda like Mr. Rogers. Mr. Rogers comes in the door at the start of the show in a coat, tie and dress shoes, like he's coming in from the office. Then he changes into a comfy cardigan and loafers to be more personal and friendly. They're both the same guy, but he's changing roles, from Mr. Rogers the tie-man to Mr. Rogers the puppet, story man.

The creator, preserver, destroyer, and other deities are His business attire. The One, loving, sweet Supreme God is as friendly and as comfortable as a cardigan and loafers. The God behind them all is not an almighty, stone-tablet etching, suit-and-tie wearing, cosmic-creator god of thunder and power. He/She *delegates* all those duties to the other gods that are mere extensions of and expressions of the One True God, who is gentle, pure, loving bliss.

- That many Hindus have become ignorant to the real name of their religion as Sanatan Dharm and that their religion is monotheistic. Most refer to themselves as Hindus too, forgetful this was a label invented by British subjugators.

My journey down the Underground Stream has been gorgeous. At four years old my religion was punch and cookies, by seven I was a disgruntled atheist, at nine I'd had my first religious experience.

By seventeen I was an LSD-psychonaut and a bit agnostically neutral while I studied witchcraft from my teens and into my twenties. I wanted to have influence with my destiny and with nature. I practiced it as a nature religion and used ritual and ceremony to create spells and potions of herbs like belladonna and flying ointments with the psychedelic potions of Deadly Nightshade. I took it seriously.

In my early twenties I enjoyed the psychic culture. Crystal ball scrying, tarot reading, energy-healing, crystals. . . .

At twenty-five I had an abrupt paradigm shift:

- I began to experience a spontaneous past-life regression. I did not even accept reincarnation at the time it began. It went on for months (and still happens).
- I had a mind-blowing, consciousness-expanding Kundalini event. My lover at the time was a Tantric-priestess, and she initiated the event through sexual yoga.

The Kundalini event was an intense psychic, psychological, and even physical event. I literally felt my own consciousness expanding in a physical sensation. It was awesome! And dangerous.*

This profound event initiated me to pursue Perfect, Spiritual Union and Transcendence through Kundalini Yoga. I wanted to become Enlightened, so I studied and practiced. I would fast for days at a time with multiple meditation sessions throughout each day, combined with intense yogic breathing techniques.

In my early thirties I combined my Kundalini methods with Western esotericism and became a third degree ceremonial magi, using kabbalah, tarot, astrology, and others to enhance and expand my spiritual body of energy and mind.

Did you know?

- That Sir Isaac Newton only took the position at Cambridge University to fund his alchemy work? Cambridge agreed, but only on the condition he kept his alchemy agenda and work secret, not public. He was trying to manifest the philosophers' stone. Gravity was an afterthought.

My spiritual search wound through the religions and saw their true cores were their mystical paths. Most think mystical paths are subdivisions of religions, but the opposite is true: Kabbalah didn't come from Judaism, Judaism came from Kabbalah. Yoga didn't come from Hinduism; Hinduism came from Yoga.

- That Kabbalah's Tree of Life is Hebrew yoga? Kundalini/tantra yoga to be exact.
- That the Star of David was imported and appropriated from Sanatan Dharm, representing Shatkona; the yantra-symbol of the male and female principles in union to manifest the *Mystic Child*. Kabbalah and Western esotericism use it to invoke/evoke the above and below (yin/yang).
- That Hebrew is a primordial language; each letter representing profound spiritual concepts, similar to classical Sanskrit.

Religions teach you how to worship God and live righteously to spiritually evolve: these are dogmas. *Mystical paths*, like yoga and kabbalah, teach you how to become One with spirit and actually *experience* God Consciousness. That is mine, and everyone's, singular goal of their existence, whether they realize it or not. To become One with God Consciousness.

***

By my fortieth birthday, I had a mystical curriculum vitae which included:

- Master Alchemist (2006—Flamel College)
  - Member of International Alchemy Guild
- Third Degree Ceremonial Magician (2005—Ordo Templi Orientis)
- Tantra/Kundalini yogi (with full-blown Kundalini event at 25—1992)
- Bhakti yogi (2005 to current)

- Master theologue and religious scholar (lifelong)
- Adept in all forms of Western and Eastern esotericism (Pythagorean numerology, Kabbalah, tarot, astrology, Taoism, I Ching, sacred geometry, and others)

These societies and modalities are dedicated to the various forms of mysticism to achieve spiritual illumination and enlightenment: *to transcend material consciousness and attain spiritual consciousness*. What may seem like separate methods and paths on the surface is a unified collection of paths empowering and enhancing one another.

And they all agree it can be, as Gautam Buddha said in His fourth Noble Truth, *done in this single lifetime*. But they also agree unanimously it typically takes *several* lifetimes.

The Underground Stream reveals each religion and path accepts the process of reincarnation as the Soul's Journey to Perfection. That each lifetime is continuum: the knowledge and experience gained and acquired is subtly retained for a progressive Soul's Journey.

These esoteric occult tunnel systems led to personal power of will and destiny. Yet, I always sensed more lay beyond them, that Western esotericism was far more advanced than their religious counterparts but was still in front of the veil I yearned to see beyond. These tunnel systems all came to dead ends, not connecting to the ultimate GodPower of Divine Love. They brought me to the threshold but did not have the actual password-mantra to enter the final Temple. The password was given when I began to associate with a contemporary master-Guru. I crossed the threshold into the inner chamber: India.

Now I am a bhakti-yogi, Sanatan Dharmist.

I am a Sanatan Dharmist because, at the end of the rabbit hole, I found the source of religion and spiritual thought, *and it was a logical, sensible, beautiful, useable, thorough system of truth and knowledge that addressed each and every area of the human condition, from health and wealth to family and God.*

It didn't rely on faith, magical thinking, or fantasy. While there are volumes of wonderful scriptures defying our practical sense of a scientific world, they are backed up with actual science too. Vedic Upanishadic texts describe the system of creation of the universe in alarming detail, including and even surpassing modern physics.

Did you know?

- That the swastika is a symbol representing our spiral galaxy? Sanskrit texts show a spiral galaxy, heliocentric system and describe black-hole singularities as the starting point of the universe before there were even magnifying glasses, let alone telescopes. Then some maniac pirated the swastika image, so it became the example of humanity's evils and gave it a stigma.

The themes and knowledge contained within Sanatan Dharm texts are so entire, complete, and understandable that they defy any allegation of being primitive or fantastic. These are texts so exact and sensible they don't just far exceed modern intellectual, philosophical, scientific, and psychological thought and reason, they *define them*.

- That the Kundalini path of yog(a) is for psychic attainments? It reveals the highest layers of the material phenomena, but does not, and cannot, reach the Divine phenomena. The Yog(a) Darshans, including the Kundalini Yog(a) Darshan, are very clear this path is merely a tool to use to launch toward God Realization. Its risks are profound as the inner experience is so intoxicating (and dangerous) that it can take the yogi *away* from the Divine realm rather than toward it.

Because of the origins of these paths advising it not to be used as the end-game path to attain God within your heart, I turned away from it and other paths such as ceremonial magick. In order to succeed at *any* spiritual path, exclusivity is required. A heart surgeon can't multitask!

I always suspected that if God were real and true, He wouldn't make us guess to understand Him. He would make knowing Him accessible and possible to anyone and everyone who longed to. Within Sanatan Dharm, I saw nothing less: The volumes of texts provide all there is to know in a sensible system to transcend material consciousness and attain divine consciousness, forever—*the end*.

In contrast, other religions are so allegorical and fantastic, no one can truly know what they're getting at. This causes a lot of arguments, which causes a lot of genocides.

I always suspected a true and loving God would not just give us one chance, with one savior to get it right, that a true, loving, divine parent would give His beloved children *infinite* chances and provide us with many, many saviors to come to Him. Sanatan Dharm revealed a sensible conclusion; that we are *eternal* souls and will carry on with *infinite* chances to join Him. He will send teachers and guides to us regularly to clear up our confusion, and when His stupid-human kids don't get it right, He'll try again, as any good parent will.

I mean . . . I *love* my son. I didn't sit him down at nine years old, explain all he needed to know about life, and then say, *"You're on your own now, kid."* When he has questions, I am there. When he needs guidance, I am there. When he seeks, I help him find. When he knocks, I open for him.

We all want one thing: to be happy. Permanently and perfectly, not partially or temporarily, but completely and constantly. The world is not made of this: It is flawed. Only God is made of this: He is perfect. She is bliss. The goal of our existence is to be permanently and perfectly happy, and this can only be attained by merging one's mind with God. We are all in search of God whether we know it or not because we are all in search of unlimited, perfect happiness, and only God is this. If there is such a thing as "God," then God is perfect bliss. The end.

Aboveground Stream

True spiritual knowledge and formula are accessible in both the Underground *and* Aboveground Streams. Spiritual scriptures and practices have been produced and revealed in the world since time immemorial. Over time, they often get convoluted and misinterpreted until they are mere shadows of what they were originally.

I mean . . . the King James version of the Bible is a far-cry from the original version in Hebrew and Aramaic.

Did you know?

- That the Knights Templar discovered original Jewish and Christian texts containing the real historical accounts of Christianity, which conflicted with Catholic accounts. The reason Pope Innocent II gave them unrestricted passage and immunity from taxes was to keep them quiet about what they had found.

Only about 60 percent of the entire scriptural texts exist in modern times. Things get lost in translation to say the least.

Then a sage/saint/guru/messiah—*Divine Personality*—descends upon this earth and straightens them out. This happens not just once in humanity's history, but often and as needed. Through these *avatars* we stupid-humans get the opportunity to associate with an illumined master and get the kinks and bugs worked out of our misinterpretations of scriptural knowledge.

Truth of God and spirit are *always* available within the Akashic dimensions and *frequently* made available in the world. Sometimes they're right in the open; sometimes they're hidden, but hidden in *plain view*. Truth is Eternal and Infinite.

Eternity is long. Infinite is a lot.

It is often said that life is short. And it is—*when it's good*! When life sucks, it is l-o-n-g, long! A good movie or roller coaster goes by really quick! But a bad movie or scary ride seems to stand still and takes soooo looong.

Eternity is long. The meaning of life is simple: *to live spiritually*. You better start getting it right cuz you're coming back for as looong as it takes! I don't know about you, but as great as roller coasters and human love and sex and good food and ice-cold lager beer is, I'm bored.

I've been comin' back here for eternity! There ain't nothing new to try! I would like to get it done and go to the *other side*. The Divine side, which is an ever-expanding, increasing, exponential bliss!

_____16.

DÉJÀ VU: Reincarnation 101

Birth is not the beginning of life—only of an individual awareness. Change into another state is not death—only the ending of this awareness.
—Hermes Trismegistus, <u>Corpus Hermeticum</u>

If I had ever been here before I would probably know just what to do. Don't you? Feels like I've been here before.
—Crosby, Stills, Nash & Young ("Déjà vu")

Shanti Devi was a young girl in India in the 1930s. Once reaching a cognitive age when she could communicate well, she was incessant about her need to *get back to her family*. Shanti insisted she did not belong with her birth family and begged them to return her to her real family, insisting she was the mother of a newborn and the wife to a man who lived near Delhi. Mahatma Ghandi and several other notable scholars heard about her case and got involved. She was able to describe her home, child, and husband and was taken there, if for no other reason than to shut her up once and for all. What they found was the girl's account of her home and family was spot-on and the now-widowed spouse from her prior incarnation explained his dearly departed wife regularly practiced specific yoga and meditation techniques to retain her identity in her next life. Apparently, it had worked!

I too, prior to my death experience in June 2013, had studied mystical and supernatural topics to near mastery. In many ways, I too was quite qualified and prepared for retaining and making sense of a death experience.

When my spirit reentered my body and I thought I was in London, it was because the lines between my lifetimes were as blurred as Shanti Devi's were. London is where I was in my very last lifetime.[16]

When I was first born in 1966, I was a *nuchal cord* baby: the umbilical cord was wrapped around my throat, and I was blue and not breathing. This was my first near-death experience. I cannot and do not recall any of that event. However, upon learning of the aftereffects of the NDE, it seems apparent I experienced one. Since infancy:

- I have had awareness of prior identity.
- I have had cognitive awareness.
- I've been intuitive (psychic).

I also had some unusual thoughts for a small child:

"Why do these people keep treating me like a child? Why do they keep calling me Scott?"

"Who <u>are</u> these people!? That's not my mom and dad! I don't know who my mom and dad are, but <u>they're</u> not them!"

Like Shanti Devi, I was convinced this was not my family and I was not a boy named Scott. But unlike Shanti Devi, I had no clue as to whom I had actually been prior. I felt lost and disoriented.

I was alarmed by my own thoughts, *"Whoa! You better keep your mouth shut about not being a kid or knowing who this Scott guy is or they're gonna lock you up. Wait a minute! How do I know they would lock me up and think I'm crazy? How do I know what 'crazy' even is? How do I know they lock up crazy people? I'm not even THREE years old!"*

The only thing more distressing than this confusing feeling of not belonging where I was or how I got there was being very aware of how odd it was to feel that way! The most alarming thing about my thoughts was how refined and complex they were.

---

[16] I have developed a pretty solid system for identifying a past identity. This will be experimented with soon and the results published to provide scientific verification of reincarnation: *inshallah!* (*Hebrew for if God allows*)

I behaved like a child and spoke as one but did not feel like a child. I felt I was a grown adult who had somehow done a *Freaky Friday* body switch with this Scott kid. Even though I had what seemed like well-formed adult thoughts, I was unable to communicate them. My body was that of a child and so was my ability to articulate. I felt like saying things like, "Pardon me, could you please tell me how to get home from here? I don't belong here. Unfortunately, I don't know precisely where I *do* belong or even who I am, quite frankly, but I know I do not belong *here*." But when I spoke, it came out more like this: "*Uhhh . . . 'scuse me, mista . . . I need to go home. Can you tell me where my mommy is cuz I need to go real bad!*" I thought and formed ideas as an adult, but my child-body brain and mouth said things as a three-year-old would. And I felt trapped.

Many people retain some awareness of their prior identity as they begin a new life. But it usually fades entirely within a few years and is forgotten and relegated to imagination. Reincarnation ain't a *belief,* yo. It's a fact.

Only Eastern spiritual paths explain reincarnation in detail. Western scriptures once did too, before they were edited by founders of religious organizations. (Yeah . . . did you know that Jesus was a vegetarian and that he spent time in Persia with Zoroastrians and in India with yogis? And did you know that his original teachings spoke of reincarnation? All part of the *Underground* Stream!)

In the Vedas, the functions of reincarnation and karma are detailed and are identical to what I "knew" within The Portal and have been sharing. The problem with the Vedas, the Torah (Old Testament Bible), and other divine texts is a human mind is not truly qualified to interpret them. *They are Divine concepts and require a Divine mind to interpret and make sense of. Whether large or small, the errors a human mind makes when interpreting Divine scriptures are enough to cause huge misunderstandings*. This is why I am not *interpreting* anything from scriptures or The Portal / Akashic space: I'm just copy and pasting so I don't get it wrong. Stupid-humans need a sage/saint/guru/master to learn the truths within the scriptures.

Mistaken interpretations are why our world's bloodiest conflicts and most grotesque intolerances are perpetrated by so-called *spiritual* people. It is a sad irony that the most violent acts throughout human history have been executed in the name of God, and this is in spite of each and every religion professing to believe in God's most sacred tenets of forgiveness, peace, and love.

The cartwheels these fanatics have to do to twist true spiritual concepts into rationalizing violence, hatred, and intolerance is staggering. You gotta try *real* freakin' hard to spin spiritual teachings to justify or even advocate causing suffering to other souls, which are also, by everyone's account, His children and therefore your brothers and sisters!

God doesn't give two cents of thought to what religion you come to Him through. He is simply waiting for you to let your damn guard down and come to Him with love and surrender so He can grace you!

This is the Soul's Journey: to have Union with the Godhead. To become divinized.

> What did the buddha ask from the cosmic hotdog vendor?
>
> *"Make me One with everything!" HaHaHa!*

Since the concepts of karma and reincarnation originate within the Sanskrit texts, it seems appropriate to look to them to understand them.

To summarize the concept of Infinite and Eternal Life as taught by the yogic texts:

- You have no beginning and no end. You have always existed and always will in one form or another. The first law of thermodynamics is that energy can neither be created nor destroyed. It can merely change form. Therefore, energy is eternal, and since your soul is a Divine energy, that makes you eternal!
- Animal, plant, or person, your energy has changed form countless times since eternity. This means your lives are infinite. Not *a lot,* not *many,* but absolutely infinite.
- Eternal and infinite are Divine concepts beyond our stupid-human conception.
- The force that binds us to the material phenomena life after life is known as *karma:* the law of cause and effect. Everything we do, say, and think is a *cause* destined to receive a proportionate *effect.* As long as we have effects to realize, we will continue to incarnate to experience them. We cause actions to attain happiness, which causes effects. Desiring happiness is an eternal condition, so we are perpetually bound to the material phenomena as we try to attain perfect happiness (a.k.a. original sin).

- The birthing experience eliminates the prior life memory as well as the in-between insights we gain while there.

- To transcend from the dross material phenomena you must become realized—i.e., enlightened—i.e., divinized (transformed from humanness to divinity).

- Being divinized makes you One with God. It does not *make* you God. It makes you immune to the consequences of karma, and you become all-knowing, all-loving, and all right!

- Once liberated/realized/enlightened/divinized, you will cease being a part of the *material* phenomena and exist in a purely spiritual context with no more material sheaths.

- Until you become realized, you will continue to incarnate within the material phenomena as you have since eternity.

Reincarnation 101

How it works:

Which came first—the chicken or the egg? Neither. This is a paradox called a *causality dilemma*. To explain the science and process of reincarnation, we'll begin with the chicken. In this case, *death*.

When your body dies, it begins to decay and decompose, and the life force departs from it. That sums up death. Not too complicated!

Before our death, the Spiritual Government has already arranged the majority of our next life's circumstances: family / country of birth, status, looks, health, etc. But since we were creating consequences up to the moment we died, finishing touches need to be added, and this is what is taking place on Earth while we are in The Portal. The Portal is a bit like a waiting room, where you wait for reassignment! (*Beetlejuice, Beetlejuice, Beetlejuice!*)

The Books of the Dead and Abrahamic religious scriptures both speak of the approximately forty to forty-nine days the soul remains without a body before it *moves on*.

The fetal body, location, date, time . . . all the mystical details the Spiritual Agencies use to manifest your specific circumstances are set! Your sun and moon sign, the vibrational frequency of your name, the astrology, numerology, and other frequencies have been tweaked and prepped and ready for your arrival! My resurrection on my actual birthday was an administrative protocol! It is an overwhelming and unfathomable amount of miraculous effort put in to synchronize your specific details with every other detail of an infinite cosmos and keep it in perfect balance. Big-Bang singularities with infinite subatomic particles unfolding in a universe are nothing compared to the Soul's Journey back into matter to take birth!

And then it's time to go!

Your spirit is *dispatched* to your new form, and if it is a human form, it travels through space and enters through the top of the skull:

- The soft spot on a baby's skull (the fontanelle) is where the skull bones don't ossify till the age of two. This anatomical feature is to provide an open entrance for the soul to enter the now-prepared body.

Our energy along with the mind energy gets condensed to squeeze into a material body again. You think *birthing* is a violent and traumatic experience? Ha! Try squeezing an eternal and primordial energy of spirit and consciousness into a little zygote! The birthing experience is too traumatic to retain anything afterward, causing our prior lifetime and awareness within the womb to be forgotten. Once we emerge into the loud, scary world, we're starting from scratch. The NDE is a gentler crossover, so many retain what they experience during the in-between state.

As suggested earlier, my retention of the NDE and Portal was largely due to prior consciousness work, while my practical memory was virtually deleted from both: the shock of soul reentry combined with DAI trauma.

The tremendous power and energy of spirit descends into matter and goes directly to the region of the heart.

Your physical body is constructed upon a framework of a subtle *energy-body*. Your subtle-body is a collection of energy *receivers,* called chakras in Sanskrit. Once your soul makes contact with the heart center, in a flash, your spirit divides into two currents; one travels up, the other travels down. The current splitting at the heart center enlivens the lower energy receivers: one in the solar plexus, one in the pelvic area, and one at the end of the tailbone—the coccyx. The current traveling up activates the energy receiver in the throat, which flows up and activates the one in the brow between the eyes, which then enlivens the crown center at the top of the skull.

Now *seven* energy centers making up the subtle-energy-body are enlivened.

The downward current comes to rest in the coccyx, and whatever residual energy remaining within it becomes dormant. The residual energy that goes dormant may be subtle and tiny, but its power is *massive*! The nuclei of atoms are tiny too, but their energy-power can provide energy to an entire city. Or destroy one!

The residual energy that comes to rest is powerful and potent and contains the seeds of energy that can ignite all the centers to their maximum potential. This dormant and residual power of the soul is called Kundalini in Sanskrit.

The upward current comes to rest just below the crown of the head in the pineal gland, deep within the brain (referred to as *the seat of the soul* by ancient Greeks). This is referred to as the *third eye* or *ajna chakra*. All chakras are now activated, and the physical form is now animated tissue: *IT'S ALIVE*! The soul-energy is at rest in the heart center with upward and downward currents flowing Above and Below.[17]

The soul's reentry to physical matter is so shocking the remaining memory and insights from prior life and The Portal are entirely compromised: bright lights, men in masks, bloody umbilical cords, noise, and chaos—that's what the world is to an emerging fetus!

This is no accident: it is a feature of the process since memory of prior life and The Portal is overwhelming and can cause insanity. Imagine you never slept: all your days were an ongoing, never-pausing stream of events. You'd go crazy! You need a rest, a pause, a respite to regroup and start fresh. If we retained all our lifetimes in ever-going consciousness, we'd lose it!

While a fetus develops within the womb, the spirit is housed within, and the mind is subtly active and aware. Within the womb, we contemplate the sum total of experience of prior life and The Portal, yet we are somewhat still as dormant as we were within The Portal: We now have a body, but, much like within The Portal, we cannot really move or interact with our space. But we're aware!

---

[17] As Above, So Below is a mystical axiom.

- Our energy-body is activated.
- Our physical body is forming within the womb.
- Our causal (mental) body is awake and coexisting in cosmic and physical space.

You may not remember it, but you were quite aware while in Mom's womb and becoming a bit anxious to get out of such a cramped space!

Finally, it is time to be released from the womb and enter the full physical realm: it's time to be born!

Our storehouse of knowledge and experience is no longer accessible to our conscious, material minds. We are forced to start over, with no recollection of how to talk, walk, or contemplate. Our *operating system* has been reset! Our internal hard drive has been wiped clean! There are always shadow-ghost traces of the original files, but they're buried deep and hard to retrieve!

When my mind+spirit reentered my physical form after my death-event, my hard drive was deleted. I experienced the reincarnation process as I returned from nine days within The Portal to my existing adult body and brain instead of into a new fetus.

Reincarnation 2.0

The system and process of reincarnation is as scientific as the birthing experience.

In the months leading to my son's birth in 1993, I studied the biological process of conception and birth. *What a miraculous series of events!* The myriad of minute details that must sync up *perfectly* to create life is astounding! Thousands of events, from microscopic to macroscopic, need to occur in perfect sequence and detail. The amount of these intricate details is so vast there are a million things that can go wrong and only a *single set of things that MUST ALL go right* for it to occur! Yet it happens nearly *400,000 times per day!*

This is even truer with reincarnation.

A countless set of dynamics all need to be arranged and each and every one must be synchronized with each and every other living thing in this entire world! Not just *this* world but the entire cosmos! Chaos theory reveals that when a butterfly flaps its wings in Peking, China, the disturbance of the air can cause a ripple effect that eventually influences weather patterns in Seattle, Washington. That makes sense. Everything is connected and interrelated. Therefore, on a cosmic-celestial level of reality, each and every life that begins (and ends) has a profound, ripple effect affecting and influencing every *other* life. Therefore, the Spiritual Government-Agencies-Administrators—*what have you*—must take the *entire* cosmos into consideration, determining when and where you'll be born and when and where the fates and destinies of your life will occur. Otherwise? It would truly be chaos!

There is a finite amount of matter in our solar system, on our planet, and within our bodies. It is impossible to know if one single atom being created or destroyed would cause the entire creation to unravel.

Energy can neither be created nor destroyed.

Therefore, it must be eternal.

Spirit is energy. It was neither created nor can it be destroyed.

Therefore, it must be eternal.

It can change form but will always exist and always has.

Born Again

Is it possible my nine-day coma and duration within The Portal was so that Akashic-Administrators could tweak and prepare for my reentry? Were they organizing, *and reorganizing,* my life's circumstances, modifying my karmas and sanskars to fit a new narrative and trajectory?

I suspect the Akashic Administrators had me reenter my physical body on my same birthday because I still needed to experience the astrological frequencies of a Cancer. If I woke from my coma within the same twelve-minute portion of a specific hour, I would have the same *ascending* sign too. It is your name and birthday providing your numerological correspondences too. Our fates and karmas are scheduled and maintained with cosmic formulas of astrology, numerology, and others. Reincarnating as myself required me to still live within many of the same cosmic frequencies and vibrations.

My NDE-Day wasn't just a life-changing event. It was a keystone domino causing a chain of actions and reactions that deconstructed my worldly life as I knew it. The ongoing deconstruction keeps forcing me to reconstruct from scratch. And any attempt I make to reestablish it as it was fails. It gets worse as I get better. It's uncanny.

What does it all mean? What am I being led to?

Is the thunderous hum I sensed within The Portal for nine days of coma the flute-playing Krishna, the deity of divine love? Is He my spiritual Pied Piper leading me to Him? Why is the divine presence ochre?

Some versions of the piper folk tale tell of the children being led away and into the sea, never to return. Another has them being led to a Shangri-la on a mountain where they lived out their days in peace and beauty.

Where am I going in this reincarnation within a reincarnation?

The similarity between my perceptions when I was born in 1966 and immediately after my death experience in 2013 was uncanny. Like a child, I was confused and disoriented, and struggled with dualistic awareness of current and past-life identities.

I tried to accept the medical, worldly theory: that I had lost this thing called a memory. But I felt I was a resident of this other place—The Portal—I had just left. I did not feel I was a citizen of Earth.

The most common aftereffect of an NDE is a loss of personal identity.

<u>Your identity is made up of the sum total of your prior experiences and events leading to this very present moment. With no past, you have no point of reference with which to identify.</u>

Once traveling to the "other side," your ego and sense of self evaporate. You are not this body or mind with this particular name and face; you are an eternal soul transcending time and material identity. When your citta (consciousness) leaves your body during an NDE and returns to the same body, you are experiencing a sort of *mini-reincarnation*. I died, went to a celestial dimension, and returned to the dimension of matter. Being aware of The Portal while living within matter causes severe disorientation. I was definitely confused due to the accident, but not the way doctors thought I was. The boundaries between conventional time and matter were all mashed up, so I perceived several at once. This happens with a full-blown Kundalini event too. Many people with TBI go insane, and so do a few NDErs and Kundalini experiencers. Does the near-death experience activate the Kundalini energy in some people, but not others?

As sublime and divine as it is to have a direct perception of your soul, it is challenging to have such awareness whilst living within matter.

Your *soul* is immune and virtually unfazed by your past because it remains separate from consciousness.

All memories of your infinite past lives are stored within deep layers of your consciousness. Sanskrit texts declare there are nine layers, and these are never destroyed. Even in the *prakriti* stage of the universe's total dissolution, our mind's layers with collected karmas, sanskars, and the rest go dormant but are never eliminated. This means there are countless past-life memories stored deep within the mind—they're all there! Past-life regression is when we access some of them. What we recall from past lives is relatable to current circumstances and people we currently know. We have karmic connections with them.

There are nine layers of consciousness. There are the conscious, subconscious, and unconscious, but there are multiple layers within those that are nearly inaccessible. The only way to safely access these layers of the mind, and the powers within them, is through rigorous yoga and mystical meditation techniques that usually require an advanced, enlightened teacher with mastery of those techniques. Most people who have the ability to past-life regress were taught by a master in a prior life, and those skills have been reactivated.

In other words, my passionate interests in mystical things at such a young age were carried over from past-life work: karmas and sanskars. I'm trying to make good spiritual karma-sanskar deposits in my spiritual bank account for next-life withdrawal.

That is, of course . . . if you believe such extraordinary things . . . maybe not. I'm just a guy with severe brain trauma, so what do I know?

_____ **17.**

ASTRAL TRAVEL

When a yogi astral-travels between realms, he cannot live a regular life due to
being present in two realms at once.
—Swami Prakashanand Saraswati (6th Dimension)

Embrace this moment, remember, we are eternal/All this pain is an illusion
—Tool ("Parabola")

Accident 2.0

My determination to deny my condition inspired me to take risks. Since I could
barely walk, I tried bicycling. Also, *very hard!* I had no balance and didn't know
how to ride a bike! The seat and posture hurt my lower back, so I stopped in a
few weeks. I never much liked bike riding anyway.

In the same spirit of denying my shattered status, I planned a weekend getaway
to the mountains for me and my partner. We had a cabin we liked to rent just
outside of Yosemite, and we decided to try getting away and doing something
normal.

I did the six-hour drive all right, and things went pretty well. I felt tremendous
healing within nature, since it helped remind me of who I am. I spent an hour
chopping wood on the outdoor deck for romantic fireplace-cuddling.

A few days after we returned, my lower-back pain from biking was now worse
from the wood chopping. I went to an acupressurist and a chiropractor dual
trained in holistic practices. I saw very modest results.

Then I became paralyzed.

I awoke in my bed and could not move. At all. It was terrifying. My phone was downstairs, and Janete wasn't due to come over for coffee that morning. I managed to roll off my bed and crawl on my belly to the head of the stairs. I managed to sit up and began to scooch down the steps, one at a time, on my butt.

"Janete, please call an ambulance. I can't move and am in a lot of pain." She was there in minutes.

You may not know this, but ambulances are not free. They are massively expensive taxi rides to the ER. I knew this, so she helped me scooch on the floor into the garage and into the passenger seat of my car.

I spent four days in a disturbing hospital room again. Talk about PTSD! I had already detoured well away from the hospital if I had errands to run in that part of town! Just driving by it would trigger a darkness like a hangover for hours. And I was already perpetually dark!

No one could figure out what was wrong with me. The chief of orthopedics spinal surgery was called in from vacation. He barely spoke to me, studied my MRI, and in a dramatic deadpan manner said to the nurse, "Clear my schedule and prep him for surgery."

Oh shit! There are the tears! I thought I was just going to jot down this incident, and I am apparently reliving this trauma as I write!

I spent the next fourteen hours hanging upside down, unconscious, while this spinal specialist removed the L4-L5 spinal segment and fused my spine together with four titanium bolts.

This spinal disc injury had gone undetected by the host of other doctors over my prior twenty-eight-day hospital stay. The spinal specialist got me into surgery stat because if it had been left untreated a few more hours, I would have lost the ability to walk forever.

I was so drugged out from the surgery I remained in a thick fog. My impaired brain could not deal with fourteen hours of IV- administered general anesthesia.

When they sent me home three days later, I was so confused I was once again incapable of knowing who I was. I could not move, laid on the sofa, and softly wept since I was obviously dying. I remember thinking all I had been through for the twenty-eight days in the hospital post-coma was *fucking pedestrian compared to this!*

I was immersed in a death paralysis. Not only was there no white light, but all was in dark shadow. I felt surrounded by a darkness of death agents. It was the polar opposite of being within The Portal.

Because I was so heavily sedated, I was unable to teleport to The Portal. I was alone. It was the darkest sense of fear I'll ever know. There are good and light angels of death, and there are dark ones too. I cannot offer an explanation as to why the dark ones were surrounding me that night.

My son, God bless him, left his bed to sleep next to me *on the floor.* He lay next to me all night. He knew I was terrified, and he knew I was on bizarre levels of drugs, and he knew it had to pass. As I drifted in and out of consciousness, he was there next to me merely to give me comfort. To this day, it remains one of the most gracious and generous and life-saving actions anyone has ever done for me. I am swept to deep tears of gratitude any time it comes to mind. He will never know his presence kept me on this Earth and rescued me from hell.

It took two weeks to clear away the drugged-out fog from surgery.

I had just learned to walk a few months ago. Now I had to do it all over again. After spinal fusion, it takes an absolute minimum of six weeks to become mobile and years before you regain full motion, if you ever do. No, no . . . this is far too much . . . I can't be expected to do what I just did and be thrust back into full crisis mode again. My first one isn't even remotely settled! My TBI/DAI didn't *happen* a few months ago as in *"the past."* That shit is in full crisis mode *now!* Now, on top of that, I've got this spinal-fusion-induced nightmare to deal with? Yeah . . . God loves me . . . *sure.*

The spinal column is far more than a means of upright support. The two main nerves within the spine connect directly to the brain stem: one is an ascending nerve carrying vital nerve communication to the brain center and the other is the descending nerve carrying the brain controls to the body.

The reason the surgeon rushed me into surgery was because my bulged disc between two vertebrae choked both of them. Within a few hours, they would've been damaged beyond repair. Between the damage to the spine, the nerves, and the disruption to the brain connection, all I had done previously was virtually deleted. My progress of several months was nullified.

And that's just the clinical medical diagnosis and prognosis. Remember, there is a whole other set of subtle-energy body complications. The energy channels aligning with the ascending and descending nerve channels along the spine are called Ida and Pingala in Sanskrit. The vital force of the underlying energy body—the chakras—resides within a lower center within the tailbone: *the coccyx*. This primal energy is the source of our vitality and consciousness. The ascending/descending spinal nerves and their subtle energy form, Id/Pingala, form a circuit to and from the pineal gland, energizing the body. This is what is known in Tantric yoga as Kundalini; the serpent power. In medical science it is known as CSF—*cerebral spinal fluid*. Both agree that CSF/Kundalini is absolutely essential to brain/mind function.

- Damage to the subtle-energy body will manifest as physical injury.
- Damage to the physical body will cause damage to the energy body.

Where this potent life-energy resides is in the coccyx, a small vestigial bone with three and a half tiny sections. The word Kundalini is Sanskrit and means *coiled up*, and the Tantric-yoga texts describe it as a serpent power residing at the base of the spine, coiled *three and a half times*. This means ancient texts, thousands of years old, have detailed the human anatomy long before microscopes ever existed.

The dawn of man was when man stood and walked upright. Walking upright created a direct flow of CSF/spiritual-energy flowing to and from the brain and mind. Intellectual and spiritual advancement is dependent on a vertical spine. This is why yoga meditations require sitting upright. A vertical spine is required to stimulate and activate the flow of vital, spiritual energy through the main seven centers and all the organs and light them up. As the CSF/Kundalini energy flows up and down, up and down, it becomes distilled, making it more active and potent. With proper methods and practice, the distilled energy reaches the final destination of the pineal gland, which is the physical location of the seventh chakra; *sahasrara—the thousand-petaled lotus*.

- The pineal gland was called the *Seat of the Soul* by ancient Greeks. It is where consciousness is located. The caduceus is the symbol of medicine and healing and is a direct image of the Kundalini power ascending up the spine to the pineal gland. Not kinda/sorta. The so-called *Wand of Asclepius* is the one and only ancient symbol of Tantric-Kundalini yoga representing the chakra-event of cosmic-conscious illumination. The event facilitates Christ-like healing powers too.

This event is the Kundalini event praised and sought after by yogis and mystics. Every mystical path known, from Kabbalah to alchemy, describe this event and yogic method to initiate illumined consciousness. As a man who experienced it full blown when I was twenty-five, I can assure you it is an unmistakable and unforgettable event permanently altering your consciousness. Many who are unprepared go insane from it. I came close. I am certain my Kundalini awakening event in my twenties played a *major* role in the intense magnitude of my NDE and my miraculous endurance of TBI-DAI.

This Kundalini event from my past played a major role in amplifying my mystical/spiritual abilities, capacities, and endurance. I've been living with an awareness of spiritual octaves long before, and Kundalini amplified it. Now an NDE was doing it again. As many Kundalini experiencers go insane, so do NDErs and certainly TBI'rs too.

It seems apparent many who have a TBI and/or an NDE are experiencing a Kundalini activation and are nowhere near prepared to deal with it or even know what's going on.

My Kundalini serpent power was charged and circuiting over the last twenty-plus years, and this spinal issue complicates it for years to come—in good ways *and* not so good ways. Too much Kundalini can drive you insane and cause you to lose your bearings. But too little for a yogi who is accustomed to its power and benefits can wear on you, like kryptonite.

Heavy Cross to Bear

Janete sobs heavily. "What do you want me to do? Please . . . just tell me, and I'll do it . . ." She has nearly collapsed on the floor of my master bedroom. "I just don't know!"

She is helpless to help me. My own sobs leak through my fingers and spread across my face as I cradle my head in my hands. "I don't know . . . ! I am so confused! I don't know what's happening!" The drool cascades out the corners of my mouth, and I cannot control it. I cannot explain what is wrong because I don't know. I cannot think. I cannot feel. I cannot reason, contemplate, decide. . . . I am not confused *about* anything: I am immersed, nonstop, in a sense of confusion and despair. My reply of "I don't know" is as literal as they come. I do *not* know what is happening to me, *ever!*

It is morning as I sit on the edge of my bed, head in hands, tears flowing convulsively. My brain/mind is ruptured. I cannot understand it or relate to it. I am dizzy every moment and more when I close my eyes to rest. It isn't just as though the world is *spinning* around, it is as if I can feel and see it turning on its axis all around me at its full 460 meters per second—or roughly 1,000 miles per hour. It is hurtling through space at 67,000 miles per hour on its orbit round the sun. I'm feeling its motion of 490,000 miles per hour through the Milky Way in the center of my brain. *And I can't take it.*

"I just need it to stop!" My brain trauma blends with an astral existence and never lets up. I am having a breakdown. She has never seen *pillar-of-strength Scott* have a breakdown before: I'd never had one. She wants to help. Her heart is in razor pain from the paralyzing helplessness: There is nothing she can do. If I knew what to do, I would tell her. Anyone. Everyone.

This is why there are mass shootings, bizarre cults of Scientology, and wacky conspiracists bent on some sinister mission only they perceive: severe brain trauma and near-death experiences will make you lose your shit. If I wasn't so previously stable and adept at mysteries, I would be throw-away-the-key insane right now. And I think I am.

I cannot take another moment of being dead. I cannot endure another instant of being damaged. My brain and mind do not work! I am terrified all the time and want it to stop any way it has to: my death, your death, global annihilation . . . whatever will put an end to this anguish.

And I do not have this luxury. Seeing her pain and helplessness is not helping. This amplified empathy from my conditions is as magnified to me as the expansion of the cosmos. In any moment, Janete is going to have a breakdown too.

"Do you want to go to a hospital?"

"No! They don't know shit! They can't help, and when they say it, I'm more freaked out! And then they'll medicate me, and I'm *not having a medical issue! I am having a spiritual crisis! I don't know who I am! I am confused!*"

How do you deal with that? As a qualified professional who has solved every crisis ever presented to me, I would reflect later on what I could've said and what she, or anyone, could've done: *nothing. Nada. Zilch.* This was indeed a hopeless situation with no remedy. I am fucked. FUBAR as the Marines call it: *Fucked-Up-Beyond-All-Recognition.*

While I remained in this state of crisis nonstop, 24/7, this was a rare moment of expressing it. After the first night at home after spinal fusion, I spent three nights at Janete's because I could not get up and move yet, and I needed constant care. After that, I was able to stumble up the stairs to sleep in my bedroom. I had a few events of soiling. I could not get up to the toilet at night. I would wake with the inability to operate my legs to walk the thirty feet to the toilet. My legs were fine but my brain could not operate them. Three times I whimpered in the dark to my partner who lay next to me on most nights now, and she told me to just go and then she would clean me, like an infant. Shame and humiliation reached levels I did not know I could travel to.

I was not too present during my death experience in June: I was within the safe calm of The Portal. This one, I was fully present and awake for. The NDE brought on by spinal fusion was terrifying because I was aware of it the whole time. I'm so convinced I am in a time of dying that I have summoned each loved one after another to say farewell.

I calmed down because I could not afford to let my breakdown cause Janete to have one, which is what was happening. Janete is not a person to go to in a crisis. Her ADD goes into overdrive when she is overwhelmed and causes her to totally shut down.

Everything about me as a living being was atrophying: I could not move, think, or feel at will. I was subjected to the slings and arrows hurled upon me by TBI-NDE. I didn't get a vote on what I felt or could think—it was all automatic.

I lay back in the bed in terror. I needed her to leave: I could not manage my terror *and* hers. I promised I would be fine, and she left the room and house *freaked out*.

I don't know what to do in this midnight moment but to lie back and breathe.

I wish for coma: coma was simple. I liked it on the *other side, The Portal*. I wasn't required to think, feel, or be concerned. I was just raw consciousness without desires. It was way better than *this side!* But alas, sleep rarely saves me either. Whether my conscious mind is asleep or awake, I remain aware. Traveling at light speed, like Han Solo's *Millennium Falcon*, through many portals to other lands and times. . . .

The intensity of despair over my condition triggers astral phenomena. Did you know that an NDE can be caused by severe distress? Yeah . . . you don't need to have your physical life threatened to activate an NDE. Pretty much any crisis completely overwhelming to your senses can cause one. It happens all the time. I truly suspect these mass shooting/flat-earth/conspiracists have not lost their shit due to what's scribed in their senseless manifestos. It is possible these violent perpetrators are having supernatural and existential crises they cannot deal with because of ignorance and bigotry, so they *snap*.

I mean . . . I'm a trained mystic with advanced spiritual knowledge and experience, and while I don't consider gunning down those who have nothing to do with any of my sufferings, I can easily conclude an animal-brained person—spiritually immature and psychologically limited—cannot possibly handle this. I'm a pacifist, so I may not want to kill, but I *definitely* want to die!

Pop culture mostly reports just on NDErs who have life-affirming episodes and a few scary ones that have happy endings (which I hope mine does, but the jury is still out on that). But there's gotta be hundreds, possibly thousands, who are having them with total breakdowns. Aquarian-Age optimists might assume that NDErs are chosen by the Akashic Agents based on qualifications. I can tell you that this is *not* the case. That's like saying all who are motivated to military service, policing, or politics are well-intended people. Fuck that! Obviously not. Some are, but some are violent fucks with power issues who are too stupid to make it in the private sector.

I have explained the features of a person's NDE experience are mostly provided based on their level of awareness. Unfortunately, some people can become overwhelmed by even the elementary levels of an NDE. That's true with many extreme situations. One out of twenty people I dropped acid with in my youth freaked out. I and my open-minded, intelligent clique of psychonauts had mind-expanding trips each and every time. But a few who took the exact same acid and dosage had bad trips. There's no pre-qualifying process to drop acid or to have an NDE. The Cosmic Government doesn't make mistakes, so all NDErs are somewhat *selected,* but part of that selection is to round out the bad too: mass shootings and stupid, shithead, easy-to-fix, societal problems are part of our planet's Collective Karmas: they need to happen because humanity is bent on learning the hard way. You know how many mass shootings have occurred in Australia since they began gun control laws in 1996?

None.

That's right: not less, not fewer, not a hard-to-calculate stat. Fucking *none.* They went from mass shootings all the time, just like the US, to *none*—over-fucking-night. Guns don't kill people; people kill people with guns. And some people shouldn't have guns. They got lots of guns in Aussie, yo. You just need to prove you're not a freak on wheels to get one.

In my NDE condition, I see the horror of humanity. The night before I wrote this chapter, a *World News* broadcast spent four minutes on the *second mass shooting that week* in the US and over *eight minutes* on the Johnny Depp/Amber Heard divorce trial. Just three minutes on Ukraine being molested by a Russian despot while no one does anything about it, and a total of six minutes on ads for new cars and prescription medications. I don't want to shoot anyone (except myself). But I am moved to tears out of wanting to help them. But I am as helpless to do so as my girlfriend is to help me during my breakdown. NDE is giving me cosmic clarity and TBI has removed my capacity to teach or share about it. *God loves irony!*

Lying down while crying tears of anguish, I travel through tunnels of dark and light: I witness many dimensions of the Celestial Realms. I get to glimpse them. . . .

"Am I going to one of these heavenly dimensions when I die again?"

Cosmic-Agents fill in the blanks for me: "You're seeing many of the options. Attaining Celestial heavenly abodes are available for those who live pure and righteous lives and dedicate to them."

"There are so many cosmic dimensions! I see that each one is pretty much tailored to your perception of God! Jesus is in one, Mohammad (pbuh) is in His own, The Buddha . . . angels, saints, white light . . ."

"Yes, the spiritual phenomena have no limitations. Whatever you feel is perfect is what you will experience in heavenly abodes. Some may want to reunite with pets, parents who have passed on, or their personal form of God, such as Jesus or the Buddha. All are One. Some may perceive paradise as a glorious city with utopian societies; some may experience them as quiet, peaceful gardens. God has no limitations."

"Cool. It's not one-size-fits-all! So anyone's version of spirit can have its own dimension?"

"The celestial realms are just for those spiritual founders who are legitimate. Each and every God Realized or Enlightened Master exists eternally within their own abode."

"What about the light? So many see light when they die and I've experienced light many times during states of spiritual meditations. And I was drawn by the lustrous ochre when my spirit left my body."

"The light is Divinity's radiance. It emanates from God's personal forms; it is the formless luminosity of God's grace. Above and beyond the light is the Divine form. God has countless forms; forms of Saints and Masters, forms of light and forms of knowledge and Grace itself is one of God's forms.

"Just as Divine light is God's radiance, so are the many forms of God's Grace an extension of the God Power as well. The source of them all is Divine Love. Above and beyond all the heavenly abodes is the Divine abode. This abode you cannot glimpse. Once you complete your Soul's Journey and surrender your mind, heart and soul, you can attain and become One with Divine Love Consciousness Herself."

I view the realms of hell too: each one as customized as the heavenly ones. The suffering I may experience in them is unique to my character: there are hells of fire and hells of ice; hells of physical pain and hells of emotional torment.

I continue to teleport beyond time and spatial regions, gathering the reviews of past lives over thousands of years. I see my many identities in many past lives:

- Ashayana: a Tantric initiatress who lived over 3,500 years ago

- Parennefer: a royal cupbearer to the pharaoh Akhenaten who witnessed a religious revolution
- Yusef of Arimathea: a witness to the Passion of the Christ over 2,000 years ago
- Gondamer: a squire to the founder of the Knights Templar, Hugues de Payens, whom the pope convinced to conceal the true story of Christ's missing eighteen years
- Amaia: a ceremonial priestess who performed the Drawing Down the Moon ritual at Stonehenge in the 1400s
- Brenden: a hermetic alchemist who pursued the philosophers' stone

A parade of past lives displayed my own relentless quest for spiritual illumination and perfection. There are many lives in between that are not explored, but they are of no consequence, average material lives of struggle and triumph that do not intersect with my spiritual journey.

I am stunned by the progresses I have made over multiple lifetimes and that I have witnessed the true histories of major spiritual and religious events.

I wonder, *Are these lives truly my own soul's reincarnations or am I just observing lives that reveal the true accounts of religious history to destroy the ignorance created by the fictionalized ones crafted by organized religions?*

"What's the difference?" Akashic-Agents can be rather curt. "Are we not all one soul? Whether these lives you're reviewing are your individual soul or another's, the events are true. You seek truth and have established a readiness to handle them. Ask and ye shall receive. . . ."

The Truth is revealed: there is ONE God.

One single, omnipresent, omniscient, omni-loving, omnipotent and beyond-time Creator. He is She; She is He. God has unlimited qualities, virtues, and forms, and appears in any way someone loves Her. Even a frog! All His forms are eternal and perfect! Whatever you think and love is what and who God can be and is!

I see in these life reviews that humanity has turned many spiritual paths into businesses of power, control, influence, and money. But at the core of each is the truth of how to attain God Consciousness. I am in awe of the historical figures that have shaped our planet's spiritual views and how much the religions and spiritual philosophies have in common. I am also unsettled about the plagiarizing of the original philosophies and paths by the founders of organized religion, how the glorious truths that spiritually *empower* people are stripped of their teachings of loving systems, time and time again, the stripped-down, quasi-fictionalized versions of religion *disempowering* instead, forcing exclusive reliance and allegiance with threats of eternal hells. No, sorry. The Godpower is not casting any soul to hell for *eternity*!

The boundaries between my past-life identities and current existence are blurry. This is why I am on the verge of a breakdown. The bad spell of this day does not pass like a brief fit, restoring me back to my regular, *albeit abnormal*, TBI-NDE state. I choke back the tears and beg for termination of life. But death comes not again.

Day to day my condition is unimproved, but my gratitude deepens: I am so grateful I was alone on my bike on D-Day. Occasionally, Brandon would be a passenger and Janete often rode on the rear seat to get coffee or just for a ride. I was on suicide's doorstep already: if anything had happened to one of them, I would condemn myself to suicide after suicide for many, many lifetimes.

I watch the cinema of Life-*Preview* as well.

Life-*Preview* is an NDE staple, provided so that we can see the potential results of how we choose to live. This is precisely why Dickens provided Scrooge with the Ghost of Christmas Future: so that he could learn to live more spiritually. Most NDErs recall the *life-passing-before-their-eyes* Life-Review phenomena, but few recall the Life-Preview part.

I view multiple timelines of my potential realities, timelines where I give up and don't fight for restoration, timelines where I become bitter and reject God, timelines where Janete and I separate, ones where we are old and dying together. I see timelines where I do *not* wake from a Stage 3 Glasgow coma for years, and the impact it has on others, only to wake to find that my loved ones have all moved on and my material goods have been sold at auction.

Each one has its benefits *and its pitfalls*.

There are timelines within timelines too: I see paths where Janete and I separate from losing our mate connection but reunite to an even more spiritual octave of love, ones where we remain apart, her losing sight of our magic, and ones where we remain together in spite of a lost connection.

In the world of living, these multiple timelines are too variegated to keep track of. But within The Portal, I am able to sift and select which ones provide progress to my spiritual quests over millennia. None are *hard* realities yet: all are soft. The various timelines get stored within my unconscious to provide subtle, intuitive *influence* of future choices.

Within the clarity of The Portal, I vow to sacrifice it all: I myself had asked for and was given permission to surrender my life and Will to a divine plan, which has led to these circumstances. I vow to stay the course and pray for and request the clarity and stamina to do the hard things when needed.

I must be some sort of self-hating masochist, cuz it's gonna get *real ugly!*

_____ **_18._**

SHAPPY ANNIVERSARY

> Why has God given me life only to send me such suffering now?
> —Job (40:2)

> You say you want to start something new/Baby I'm grieving
> —Cat Stevens ("Wild World")

> Shit+Happy = Shappy: a portmanteau of sad and happy
> —Urban Slang

It was June 19, 2014, one year to the day of my D-Day accident and nine days till my forty-eighth B-Day.

Lo and behold, this Thursday, the 19th of June in the year 2014 of the Gregorian calendar would indeed be quite different. Had I known it was the anniversary of my death day, I would've stayed in bed. By the end of this day, I would vow to hole up in caves on any and all future June 19ths.

The couple who had celebrated ten anniversaries on April 19ths was having morning café ritual. It was a day like any other over the last 365: I was inhabiting interstellar space as a walking dead, and she was sitting across from me over morning joe. We had nothing profound to discuss. It was just Thursday.

Just as a normal day 365 days ago turned into a supernatural event of shattering proportions, laying waste to all I knew of life and myself, so too would this June 19th let loose another wrecking ball to destroy what was left.

What can I say?

Hadn't I been through enough?

'Scuse me . . . wasn't I *still going* through enough?

My D-Day accident wasn't in my past yet in the slightest. There were not *good days* and *bad days*. Every day was as terrifying as the one before it, no more, but no less.

My partner and I are both oblivious to this D-Day anniversary, probably covering it with layers of denial, when we should be commemorating it as a triumph with a breakfast muffin with a candle in it. But that's not what occurred.

Coffee conversation:

Me: "Why are you concerned?"

She: "Because I don't know what to make of it."

One of my personal axioms is *don't ask questions you don't want the answers to.* If you want to be sure the Jenga tower doesn't collapse, skip your turn or don't play at all. Otherwise youse takes yer risks. . . .

"Why are you concerned?" I asked my romantic partner and love of my heart of ten-plus years.

"Because I don't know what to make of it. What if it's an STD?"

"How would that be? We've been exclusive for ten years now. Even a latent STD woulda showed up a long time ago. Yeah, why not? Go to the doctor and get checked."

Janete had disclosed she had some vaginal irritation and was asking me, rather suspiciously, if I had any symptoms. I told her no, none at all.

"Aren't *you* concerned?" she asked.

"Sure, I mean, certainly anything unusual should be taken seriously, but I also know the female body is a mysterious place. I'm out of my depth. If you're concerned if I did anything in our ten years together to be worried about, don't be. You've got nothing at all to worry about there. And I think you know this."

I spoke calmly because I wasn't worried about a little paranoid mistrust: It's common. I know my character speaks for itself. Janete could often get neurotic over minor things, being suggestible to cultural neurosis, but she also knew the man I was since we'd met over ten years earlier: honest and faithful.

Suddenly, there was an awkward pause. My dizziness and world-swirling brain trauma made it hard to focus as usual, but a SkyCam, outside-looking-in view just made me look like a guy who was having coffee with a girlfriend who was having a neurotic moment. But my Spidey-sense began to tingle. My automatic-pilot intuition was driving the boat, and it steered into my asking another Jenga question:

"Is there anything *you* know that I don't?"

The awkward pause was becoming heavy, like an elephant in the room.

"Is there something I don't know? Janete . . . never forget: *truth always comes to the surface.* I've taught you this and helped you see it in life. Is there anything you've not been open about?"

And then the tears came.

Gentle sobs. Quivering, frowned lips. Hands folded in lap, motionless except for subtle heaves of weeping.

I remained tactful, calm, mature. A flurry of thoughts too fast to even identify. I never knew anything but trust between us. *Distrust* was not even on my radar. I wouldn't recognize it even if it stared me in the face. I'd never experienced, nor even considered, mistrust between us. She was the essence of innocence to me.

While I am famous for being able to creatively and accurately recreate a scene, this event does not deserve to be detailed reality-show style. I refuse to glorify the tragic event of sincere love being threatened by a drama common to common people. What she confessed was common: *betrayal.*

How could this be? We were magic. We were special. Yeah, yeah . . . we all think this with our love. But the magic of the partnership I shared with you a few chapters back was authentic. And I was only scratching the surface. We've had nothing but extraordinary times. Not only were we exploring spiritual histories in Asia four months before my D-Day, but just two weeks before that, we were smiling and enjoying bizarre adventures in Newport Beach, when the beach city had a total blackout at the moment she hit the game-winning goal in our air hockey game while we were "rolling" on MDA! We reveled in a life whose routines were regularly interrupted by glorious experiences.

- Halloween celebrating in Chicago, Hollywood, Seattle . . .
- UFO sighting in Sedona and mystical meditations in the Painted Desert
- Backpacking in Yosemite, Tuolumne and California coasts
- Exciting tours of San Francisco (Our walk across the Golden Gate coincided with a jumper. As we strolled across the bridge and came across the crisis, Janete alerted the authorities I was a crisis counselor, and they asked me to talk her down. Sadly, she jumped just as I got into speaking range.)

Along with our frequent, surreal life experiences, we had a sensible life-plan:

Soon to become empty-nesters, we planned to build a home on the half acre of land in Boulder Creek, right next to Santa Cruz for the best of all worlds: beach life and mountain life combined. She and I spent a lot of good times in these woods along the sea planning a sweet life together to grow old in.

We weren't *having* a storybook romance: We *are* a storybook romance!

But truth always comes to the surface. . . .

I'm in the midst of dealing with a collection of insurmountable sufferings of the likes very few will ever know, even one of, let alone all of them, and they are coming all at once. And now I am being catapulted into one of the most severe trials and tribulations we experience as people: romantic heartbreak.

Can't I even catch my breath? It's a bit hard for me to catch my breath from the punctures in my lungs and the four titanium bolts just put in my spine, but can't I at least get a moment between tragedies to *gasp?*

We are both devastated: Janete is devastated by her transgression and causing me such pain. I am devastated because the only tether I had with the world was her and Brandon. Half of that was just eliminated over morning café on my death anniversary.

I try to do damage control as life must go on. Our daily duties of work can't go on hold due to marital crisis.

I'm calm. "Let's not go deep into this right now. Let's discuss this slowly and over time, not all at once."

She sniffles tears back in agreement.

Over the next many days, we agree on main points:

- We love each other and don't want to end.
- We prefer to take time to work it out.
- I am not strong enough yet to deal with this.
- She is sorry beyond belief.

Her error was not a malicious or a passive-aggressive attempt to punish me or a moment of weakness. It had happened years ago: 2009 or 2010. She confessed she was feeling insecure, paranoid, and jealous.

My career as a counselor was more successful than either of us could've predicted, and the attention and admiration I was getting made her envious and feel insignificant.

"But I never treated you as secondary! As busy as I was, you were *always* included and a part of my success. I shared *everything* with you."

"I know. I was jealous of all your accomplishments and felt worthless. I guess I just wanted to have an outrageous experience of my own since you have so many! I regretted it before it even happened; it meant nothing and I regretted it ever since and it had nothing to do with you at all! And I'm sooo sorry!"

"Well, it has something to do with me *now!* You victimized me the same way your ex had victimized you. How could you do what you knew was so unjust and wrong, especially with all the magic we've shared? You didn't just shit on me;

you shit on yourself. You have been good and virtuous your whole life. Why would you trade that for something so common and trivial?"

"I have no answer, Scott! It was completely wrong! I'm not excusing it. You were going to India and the US ashram a lot, and I wasn't included. You were giving workshops and the whole Goddam community was singing your praises: every Goddam woman in Los Angeles wanted to fuck you and be your wife! I got so paranoid; I just assumed you were fooling around with them. I didn't want to break us up, so I just thought I'd do it too and let you be. The moment I did, I knew I was wrong about all of it. I knew you never cheated. And now I ruined everything. We'll never be the same."

"Why the fuck did you tell me this? I did *not* need to know this *ever!* This was *your* cross to bear! Not mine! Now you've burdened *me* with your sin! I'm dealing with fucking brain trauma and don't know who the fuck I even am half the time. You can't imagine what I'm dealing with. And now this? You should've taken this to the grave!"

It also came to light that her transgression was during a brief time that I had a quasi-relapse with drugs. I'd had surgery on my shoulder from a tennis injury, and the evil doctors got me wrapped up on opiates. I managed it pretty well considering my addictive tendencies, but I was moderately involved with the drugs for nearly two months, which contributed to her act of infidelity.

All relationships go through some stagnation, which often leads to various types of transgressions. Usually in the seventh or eighth year is when couples experience doubts, which is when hers got the best of her and when this had played out.

"I was weak and stupid: The whole world is telling women we need to sow our wild oats and that men are all cheaters and that we're not being strong if we're not doing the very thing they say is so wrong. I fell into it. I fucked up. I'm sorry."

"Janete, the thing that honestly hurts me the most is that I love you and would do anything to protect you from harm. The pain your ex put you through made me want to kill him. Anyone that hurts you gives me rage! You hurt my best friend and lover, Janete. You hurt *you!* This has haunted you for a long time and will continue and I can't hurt the one that hurt you now! You hurt the woman I love and cherish! You hurt my best friend!"

We would never be the same: As with the fender bender that united us and the one that caused me to die, this wreck would transform things, and the damage was impossible to undo. You can change, you can grow, you can transcend, but you will never be the same from a before-and-after moment. You'll either be stronger or weaker, but you'll never be the same. Which will we be?

Stronger?

Weaker?

_____ *19.*

ISLE OF DENIAL

> Worrying is like a rocking chair.
> It gives you something to do but gets you nowhere.
> —Lao Tzu

> To conquer death, you only have to die.
> --Andrew Lloyd Weber (Jesus Christ Superstar)

Resurrection has made me mortal.

No . . . not *immortal:* Mortal. As in regular. Common. Average.

The drama I am experiencing with my partner is lamely common. The cheat-on-your-partner-to-find-yourself syndrome is so common its reality-show fodder. This situation is the one and only thing we've ever experienced that is common. I don't *do* common. I don't *do* average. It's way beneath me. Yet apparently, I had overestimated my partner *and myself,* as we are having a common drama that takes place in every tenth house on every suburban block in the pitiful world.

I can't separate the pains: My heart cannot decide which anguish to experience one moment to the next: Brain trauma? Bizarre NDE? Marital crisis?

It is all too much, and I'm dizzy and need to just slow this down. I plan on fulfilling my plans that were made well before death came a knockin'. I figure the safest thing to do is go into a *fake-it-till-you-make-it* mode: Try to act normal by doing normal things and maybe my spirit, my brain, and my mind will be fooled back to normalcy. I figured it couldn't hurt: act and do things that were normal is better than sitting in a dark room of an asylum.

Brandon just turned twenty-one, and I was determined to keep my plan to take him to Europe for this landmark birthday and give him his first experience abroad.

I had recovered from the critical phases of the spinal-fusion event and had been "authorized" to travel. His birthday is in May, but between paramedic school and fire-fighting academy, he couldn't get time off until July: a notoriously bad time to travel: families on summer vacay are annoying, costs are higher in summer, I hate hot temperatures, and *my lover of ten years just broke my heart.*

The trip was challenging for me, but Brandon would have a twenty-first birthday memory beyond the obligatory, bar trip with your friends. He did that too! But that was on his actual birthday, whereas our European trip was to be the grand finale of his twenty-first. We were in Dusseldorf, Germany, the night they won the World Cup, and Brandon had an unforgettable night celebrating with an entire nation! I could not go out into the chaos, so he went alone. Besides, as a newly turned twenty-one-year-old, partying off the hook on his first European vacay, celebrating a historic World Cup win, he didn't need his forty-something father hanging around! Especially one that needed looked out for like a child since I was prone to getting lost and confused.

We took the Eurail trains through Germany, Switzerland, France, and wrapped up in the UK. I made the right call: defying all odds to keep my personal promise to give my son a twenty-first he would never forget.

"Why are we getting off?" he asked me as we trained through southern Deutschland on our way to Berne, Switzerland.

"I gotta do something." I was deliberately vague to pique his interest. "We're just gonna get out here and take care of something. We'll catch the later train into Berne."

I asked him to wait outside with the bags as I walked into a shop in Strasbourg, deep within the Black Forest.

I came out of the shop. "Catch!" I called out while I fumbled a toss of keys to him. "You drive."

I had secured an Audi A8 so he could drive a high-performance machine along the Autobahn. We toured the Black Forest villages and the ruins of a twelfth-century castle before boarding the train to our B&B in Berne.

The Einstein Museum, four-hundred-year-old cathedrals, sky tram over to France, pints of beer in London pubs . . . I assume I had a very good time, in spite of barely being able to remember any of it. But I didn't do it for *me*. I did it for Brandon. I did it so that whether I was ever able to function again, he would have this wonderful memory I was part of.

Bosons and the Great Hadron Collider

I continued to keep all details about my personal scandal private. I had become enough of a freak show as it was. I was so ashamed with *victim guilt,* I continued to place my partner on a pedestal to others and allowed her to keep her dirty little secret a secret.

My uncle invited me to stay in an apartment he owned in Malaga, Spain. Everyone was very concerned about me, and this uncle suggested this as therapy for all I'd been going through, though he only knew of the medical issues. There should be travel packages: *accommodations for two in an exotic and oh-so-neutral setting to persist in a fantasy that what you once had and held dear for each other has a chance of surviving a totally unwarranted betrayal!*

Janete and I spent eight days in Spain with several days in France and Switzerland with train rides through the countryside. My personal highlight of the trip was a spontaneous trip to CERN; the home of the LHC: the Large Hadron Collider. To tour this international mecca of physics there is a six-month waiting list. I called them while in Geneva and took a shot: "You've got good timing," said the operator. "I just hung up with a couple cancelling their reservation. Can you make it here by 10 a.m.?" And I did. We could now add a Halloween in Spain to our trick or treat resume too. The cosmic energy governing serendipity was still alive and well, giving us opportunity to remember our Soulmateness.

Yet there was a steady, subtle, disconnect between us the entire trip. The magic we always knew was a dark magic now.

We returned from Spain, and it was like the exotic blessing of a vacation never happened. Our connection was cloaked in shame now. She was ashamed for committing a cardinal sin. *I was ashamed too.* It's called victim guilt.

Every betrayed partner feels they were cheated on because they are insufficient: not attractive enough, charming enough, funny, smart, blah, blah.

I was torn between wishing the guy she had cheated with had been a godly prince of a male specimen and a shabby homeless drifter. The former I could at least grasp: he was *better* than me. But the latter was comforting by being obvious it was not about *me* or what I lacked but about her own defect, which all cheating is. Infidelity is about the cheater's defects, not the victim's. I absolutely did not ask her for details and banned the topic from discussion. The past is where it belongs: in the past.

The person in question was irrelevant, but this haunts you as you try to block out imagining it. And I was already haunted. I was a hauntingly haunted, fucking ghost, haunting the world while being haunted by myself and a material world that was foggy, obscure, unclear, and phantom-like.

My meter was full. Icing on the cake? C'mon! As I asked myself what I would advise a client to do under these circumstances, it became oh-so apparent this had accumulated to a *beyond- tolerance* quantity.

My life since NDE-Day has become a perpetuating series of waiting for the other shoe to drop. Each day I wondered "what's next." Obviously, fate and God have decided to *destroy*, me and since I have let them down by living through death, they keep having to invent new traumas till I am institutionalized.

Clearly God hates me. But I'm an *Eastern* spiritualist, and we know God is all love and does not hate. Someone musta switched me in the ICU to the Western religious, burning-bush-condemning God ward. Cuz God's definitely fucking with me now!

20.

SECOND HOME SANCTUARY

> The work is always inside you.
> —Rumi

> In the end, it's about enriching the lives of those who
> will read your work, and enriching your own life, as well.
> It's about getting up, getting well, and getting over.
> —Stephen King *(On Writing)*

I was in darkness. The burden of it all was too surreal and massive to cope with. I retreated to my office, a home away from home, a bubble, a sanctuary. Writing allows me to escape. Books have always been my theme parks: When I read a good book, I am teleported from mundane, futile living to imagination. Now, as a writer myself, I am the actual engineer and composer of the theme parks. If I want to go on a scary ride, I write one. If I want to go on the tunnel of love ride, I compose it. Instead of dropping acid for the umpteenth time in my life, I write bizarre stories and philosophical explorations of mind and spirit. In the writing world, everything is the way you want it to be. If you don't like a character, what they say or what they do, you fucking change it. Paradoxically though, what I write takes on a life of its own. I'm just the conduit the ideas tell themselves through which need to be 100 percent true. My work is never *based on* or *inspired by* true events. I give the real deal, without exaggeration or embellishment. Truth is stranger than fiction, and my life is a fucking carnival ride without safety bars.

Writing in my office is *mine*. I play music that stirs up the emotional chunky stuff in the bottom of the stewpot, and I get lost in my craft. I'm a word sculptor, and I *love* the art and ability to craft emotions and thoughts that are evocative and invocative. I wanna make you feel shit. It's purging and cathartic: I export my pain, give it to you, and hopefully we both feel better. My current existence is wall-to-wall suffering and dying, but within the walls of my office space I live.

Beyond my office walls is a strange world where no one understands me or itself. When I drive the roads, go for coffee, stop by the store, or whatever trivial thing needs done, my safety-creative bubble gets burst. I found myself on a planet of confused people trapped within the illusion of matter, oblivious and ignorant to the beauty of their own spirit. Everywhere I went I felt all could see the scarlet letter of my partner's betrayal emblazoned upon my breast. I could not even manufacture the *illusion* of normalcy as I felt my NDE, brain trauma, and now heartbreak was on display to all who viewed me.

My office and work provided haven, as did my ongoing connection and presence within The Portal. I sought refuge within The Portal, needing strength and perspective, meditating with astral travel is like Shangri la.

The Akashic-Agents within The Portal have total acceptance of me. They never "*tell*" me what to do or not to do. They just tell me what can happen next if I choose to follow their suggestions. This was becoming a new mantra: *what's next*. "What's next" became the label I gave to directives and suggestions I received from Akashic Agents. I tried to look at all they advised as "what's next." It used to mean "when is the other shoe gonna drop"; now it's something more positive.

I was *told* it was time to leave. That's *what's next*. To break with my love relationship and endure the adjustment of all that was happening far away. Pack up, tidy up, and get out.

I felt the signs, intuitions, and circumstances were all adding up to an obvious conclusion to leave. Spirit guides don't literally "speak" to you in an audible voice. They communicate through inceptions of thought, which are supported by "signs" if you know how to see and read them. I've always been fairly bilingual, speaking human and "signs" pretty fluently.

The signs my time in SoCal needed to come to a close were adding up. I *hated* being there was one such sign! The collective consciousness of the nearly four million people in a region that has earned its reputation for material shallowness was making me ill. My NDE antennae received psychic signals nonstop, and I could not turn it off. The angst, suffering, shallowness, and dysfunction of an entire region was on my inner radar 24/7. I can see how TBI sufferers become delusional. They're not having delusions; they're just picking up the more obscure layers of reality, and I began to suspect Los Angeles would someday be the inevitable *ground zero* for the inexorable zombie apocalypse.

The other signs were: severe brain trauma, loss of memory, and the collection of unmanageable nerve defects combining with the first and only real relationship crisis my partner and I had ever encountered; I needed out.

Not a road trip or a vacay to Europe. O-U-T: *out*.

The home I owned and had lived in for fifteen years on a small and quiet cul-de-sac had become another sign to get out: four of the six homes in the cul-de-sac had been bought by families with noisy young children and pets. My child was a young man now. I didn't fit in family town suburbia any longer any more than I *fit* into a BBQ steakhouse as a vegetarian. Just not a good fit. I'd had a great time in suburbia, and it served its purpose well. When the fat lady sings and the curtain drops, it's time to leave the theatre.

I found myself daydreaming in my spare time about a new life in a peaceful place in the country. I spent most of my waking hours in my office with the pretty park outside my window, writing. It felt to me it was the *only* thing I could do well. In many ways it was all I ever wanted: writing whilst listening to sweet music from Ludovico Einaudi to Massive Attack while composing my own brand of symphonies in words. I was sad as a motherfucker all the time now.

In spite of my severe limitations, I managed to complete the book—a massive and complete guide to solving addictions with remarkably innovative methods. Unwilling to give up my sanctuary of creativity, I kept going: I wrote another book on starting a private practice and then did what I never knew when or if I would: I resurrected my first book and memoir.

Writing *A Stone's Throw* took over two years and nearly took my life. I'm something of a "method" writer, so I relived the story of my homeless, criminal days of being a dope-fiend in the '80s and '90s by visiting the actual places events occurred to capture their spirit. I wanted a fresh account of the horrifying experience of coming down from dope, so I did some. This triggered a pretty severe relapse with some very potent and mysterious drugs. It went on for nearly three months, and when I stopped, I pulled a Cat Stevens / Dave Chapelle: I secured it somewhere safe and walked away. I had three agents and two publishers offering me deals to finish it, but I couldn't risk completing it. Then I had another profound awakening and turning point, got cleaned up, and vowed to live right and, at the pinnacle of this episode, had a happy accident that brought me and my soulmate to each other's doors. Life went on and *A Stone's Throw* stayed locked away.

My connection to The Portal makes me feel immune to addiction and relapse now. Drugs aren't even on my radar. I am far too busy trying to survive each day. NDE-DAI-TBI had virtually deleted my memory and identity, so my addictive tendencies were gone too.

I felt I'd discovered the cure for drug addiction: get hit in the face by a truck, and if you survive it, you'll be a changed man.

Addiction, and any other pathology, are karmic things. Past-life drug abuse etches the *sanskars* of the affliction deep into your *ahankara:* sanskars are tendencies and ahankara is your "ego-self." These karmic debts had been mostly paid before NDE-Day, so the remaining residual sanskars of addiction got left in The Portal in old file drawers within the Akashic Records.

Not only did I prepare to release my first memoir, but I composed its final chapter. The original book ended with a profound rock-bottom revelation that made me decide to get clean from dope. But it did not include a supernatural event that caused it. I omitted the most powerful experience of my life in the first version. Why?

Because it is so outrageous and supernatural, I did not think any person alive would ever believe it or be able to process or understand it. I was afraid this would prevent it from being published in a commercial world, so I left it out. The memoir was reborn with a final chapter, Torsional Waves, and I thought it was one of the best pieces of writing I'd ever done.

It describes a mystical event that is rare: a full-blown Kundalini event activated by a Tantric priestess I was intimate with at the time. *A Stone's Throw* is about the synthesis of reckless youth redemption through spirit and spiritual forces far more than a tale of a youth gone wrong who straightens out.

Once all three books were written, edited, and designed, I set about producing their audio versions. A well-known music producer in Los Angeles was a client whose marriage I had saved, and he insisted on helping with audio production at no cost to me. I couldn't well manage the hour plus commute to his studios three times a week, so I set up a voice-over studio in my office. I may have been hiding from and denying my problems, but I was getting a lot of shit done in spite of my traumas!

People kept assuming I was "okay" because of all I was doing; meanwhile, I regularly confessed to my inner circle that each day was a terrifying event. I was telling my closest loved ones I was in constant distress, regardless of how it looked, but they all thought I was being metaphoric. I was exhibiting the classic male reaction to heartache and crisis: I became a workaholic.

With arduous study I learned the publishing business. I established my own small publishing company, formatted, designed, and released my books in print, eBook, and audio. I learned as I went and produced top-shelf product to be proud of. It was no small feat to execute executive level publishing as a nobody, novice: vendors, awards, international distributions ... publishing is a complicated business, and I was becoming an author and publisher the same as I'd become a successful contractor and counselor, learning from scratch.

I still had *no idea* who I was, *no idea* what I was doing, *clueless* as to how I would survive day to day, and *mystified* I was not hospitalized in a psych ward. I only felt good when in my office, totally isolated, with sweet music playing as I wrote for hours. All other times, I felt broken, scared, and nervous.

My ten-year relationship was shattered. What disturbed me most of all was I would never know how I would be handling this if I weren't brain injured. If I had never died and was brain-trauma-free, how would I be handling the end of everything? Was my mind being absent from my body *helping* me cope by unplugging me from it or was it hindering me? I could only wonder, as I had no points of reference for either: Being fucked up was all I knew now. Was my connection to spiritual and eternal things within The Portal helping me sever worldly attachments to accelerate spiritual progress? Or confusing my ability to tend to worldly things? Or both?

***

Janete and I continued our routines: The sense of gratitude between us for being magical people was only subtle now. I was in pain and sick and tired as shit of being unappreciated for my stamina. Yes . . . I deserved a medal on my one-year death anniversary, not a hammer to the heart and head.

We had many long walks in the woods and deep conversations. She had an expectation I was still this magic man who would demystify the mysterious and make it beautiful again. I knew she was lost. I knew she'd felt directionless for many years in spite of my efforts to assist her in creating and attaining goals and personal passions. I knew her regret over a single transgression years ago was sincere. So I kept my grieving private, trying to sustain my role as the man she could rely on for support and answers.

Wanted: Aspirations

We sat on a felled tree in the woods where we walked daily, speaking of deeper things:

"I get it, Janete. You don't feel *fulfilled*. You have a satisfying, happy, secure life that is drama-free, and you've had your heartaches in life, but you feel you've not really *accomplished* anything that so-called matters."

"I don't, no. I don't have anything I can look at with a sense of pride. I'm a good person and know I'm blessed, but I'm bored and need something more. I feel like I'm nothing. I wonder what I would be if things were different. I wonder all the time. Like, am I missing out on a life I can't see? Like I have no purpose."

"In a parallel universe there's another you and another me. In that parallel universe there's the 'me' that never did dope, never cheated or lied. . . There's another universe where you made different choices. We can never access that universe, Janete. We can't see if we are happier there or here. But with effort and risk, you can certainly change things here and explore the possibilities."

"I need to find myself. I don't know who I am without you, my dad, my mom . . . all the people I depend on. I need to find myself."

Even though it seemed the severity of my problems trumped hers, I tried to help her.

"Do you think it might help if we took some time off? A temporary separation? No dating or seeing other people; just thirty days of not seeing each other to sample being solo. To 'find yourself?'" That lasted about a week. She called and came by and confessed she loved me and was bored without me. Her smile was wide and sincere and gladdened my heart.

I had done some thinking too. I wasn't happier during our week of separation, but I looked at the logic of it all: the betrayal, the doubts, and the willingness to separate. Was all this her exit strategy? Trying to ease me into an ending? I knew "we" had died when I died, and if "we" were to live again, "we" would have to reinvent ourselves and be reborn. But I was in no condition to guide us through reinventing our loving partnership. If I were to save us, save her, I needed to be whole again. *Which didn't look even possible.*

This was the final "sign" that leaving was "what's next." I'm learning the Akashic agents will just keep piling shit on to make their point, so I figure I better get packin' before it gets worse. Oh my God! Can there possibly be a "worse?" Hell-to-the-yeah there can be! And I do not, not, not think I can survive the current crap, let alone a subatomic particle more!

I kept my decision to leave private. It became the only secret I would ever withhold from her. We were over, and in order to have a chance at living again, what we had been had to die: "*we*" needed to have a near-death experience. Be reincarnated, be reborn. Set it free and see if it comes back. A separation and poetic reunion aligns with our soulmate storybook romance. And I fully acknowledged this is no Hollywood movie. A happy ending is not guaranteed.

I was going to finish what I started with a swansong of support by helping her gain the healthy sense of true independence and self-reliance she longed for and needed. If it was going to end permanently, I wanted to end it gracefully and with no regrets. I wanted to know she would be fine without me by helping her find strength and inner power before I left.

She needed an accomplishment to be proud of. Many people feel their lives are unremarkable, and this leads to recklessness as they try to compensate in unhealthy ways like drugs and infidelity. She had been dependent on others her whole life and needed a personal achievement. So I put an idea into her head: *an inception.*

Before she knew it, I was helping her train and prepare to climb the highest peak in the continental US, Mount Whitney. Climbing Mount Whitney in a single day would be a personal achievement that had many layers of context for her. It had been a dream of her father's, who had died a year after my near-death experience. He did not get to realize his dream before he died, and she regretted not making that dream come true for him. And I felt that if we were to go our separate ways, the climb would empower her with the confidence she needed to do well without me.

She did it.

I did not imagine climbing this mountain would be the answer to all that she felt was missing, but it was a start. If I was to exit her life, I wanted to give her the parting gift of self-reliance, to show her she could do extraordinary things. I knew the small plaque I had made for her commemorating her achievement would remind her of her power. I hoped it would also remind her of my love once I left.

Many marriages go through temporary trial separations after such transgressions as my partner's. It can be an effective way to restore and renew. I had counseled many marriages through such things and was able to help them restore their commitments.

An Anvil on the Camel's Back

All the signs needed to exit were clear except one: how can I leave the one person who has been my only true-blue friend and whom I love more than my own breath?

Brandon was now twenty-one. Even the most stable individuals have to *come of age.* Brandon's youthful rebelliousness was mild compared to what I'd seen as a family counselor, but still too much for me as I was not running on full power.

Brandon would argue over things we agreed on! We could not connect as our roles had shifted. He needed his own independence more than a father figure.

So . . . my partner is going through midlife crisis bullshit *and* my son is going through the *I-hope-I-die-before-I-get-old* maturity crisis. And me? I *am* a fucking crisis! Everyone around me is losing their fucking minds, and I'm just thinking *at least you* have *your mind!* I don't even have one to lose! It's stuck in some ethereal dimension of space! Oh . . . I *know* where the fuck my mind *is*. I just can't access or use it in this material world!

My outer life is being reduced to ordinary quotidian. Only my inner life is still paranormal, but *not* of a brand I like!

Many people go through marriage crises. Many people buy and sell homes, lose a career, start new ones, transition from nesting to empty-nesting as parents. Many people experience disease, cancer, and injury. But very few do, nor can they, endure *all of them at once*.

21.

SHOPPING AT THE AKASHIC RECORDS STORE

> There are cosmic laws which govern the use and
> attainment of psychic powers.
> —Swami Prakashanand Saraswati (6th Dimension)

> Another dimension, new galaxy/Intergalactic, planetary
> —Beastie Boys ("Intergalactic")

There are many common features of NDE. While each NDE is as unique as the person who experiences it, they are like fingerprints: We all have fingers, but each fingerprint is exclusive.

What you bring back from the Portal Store of Akashic Records is up to you: who you are, how you're built, what your *level* is. . . . The more awareness and knowledge you have of true spirit and machinations of life and existence, the more you access and retain.

The term NDE, or *near-death experience,* was formalized in 1975 by Raymond Moody. The earliest recorded NDEs were in the 1700s, but the phenomenon has been known about for centuries. There is now a vast amount of research available on the subject, and the majority of it is useful and accurate.

It is widely perceived within the NDE research community that having an NDE *rewires* you. Your brain and nervous system get circuited differently while within The Portal, and many side effects carry over providing psychic ability and more advanced, spiritual perspectives. The brain neurology and branches of psychiatry that lack vision categorize NDE phenomena as *delusions*.

The "wiring" on the *other side* is different than the material plane. With different and fewer time and spatial dimension boundaries, the mind functions differently. This is how many NDErs come back with psychic, intuitive, and/or healing abilities.

While on the *other side,* you have the Life-Review and Preview giving you access to various features of your past and coming lives. Many don't retain these features of the dying experience, although some do.

An NDE's duration and the NDEr's open-mindedness seem to be significant factors in the profundity of an NDE as well as retention of the experience. Most NDEs are mere moments in duration and most NDErs have little to no prior spiritual training or passions, which can reduce the overall degree of the experience.

In 2018, I attended the national conference of IANDS—the International Association of Near-Death Studies. I had a conversation with one of the directors of the Seattle chapter, Greg Wilson.

"Your NDE is quite extraordinary, and your retention of it is remarkable. It seems this is due to your prior training and experience in spiritual and mystical fields." That was a watershed moment for me, which gave me much-needed perspective of the bizarre, supernatural quality of my so-called brain injury.

I knew *nothing* of NDE at that time. As a lifelong student of spiritual mysteries, I'm sure I'd heard of it, but it wasn't an area I had studied. I was relieved when I first learned about the NDE phenomena and the global culture of NDErs and enthusiasts. I wasn't so alone.

At the start of this crisis, I had no understanding of brain trauma nor the supernatural qualities of NDE. I was entirely alone in the experience.

I was not exposed to the NDE term and phenomena until four years after I was killed and how and when I was led to learn of it kismet which will be shared later. Like a twelve-step group, there was *support.* At the very least, it was comforting to know this rare phenomena was not exclusive to me. I was also quickly disappointed. I had most of the commonly reported features of the NDE, yet I had several that were not just unique but were not even in the wheelhouse of others. You'd think I'd be used to this dynamic: I began having rather supernatural occurrences since early childhood.

Though I was mostly ignorant to the NDE phenomena up to this point of our story, it is helpful if *you're not*. The only reason I can now author this account is because I have hindsight and knowledge of what happened. The context is important, so you get a sneak preview of NDE, The Portal, and other juicy stuff. If I told the tale in all present-tense, you'd be just as confused as I was as you read it, and it would be no fun at all. Well ... maybe not *as* confused: TBI-DAI/NDE was overwhelming my thinking and feeling apparatus. Hopefully, yours is fine. ...

There are some standard elements to the NDE that are universal, such as the Life-Review and Preview. We all get them. Most every NDEr reports on the Life-Review: your whole life passing before your eyes. The Preview one is universal too. The reason some don't report it is because they don't retain it.

Nearly every NDE I have been exposed to was profound, but mostly what you'd expect: a car accident, a fall, an illness, heart complications... Me?

I didn't just get a TBI: TBI is so common and in the news that it is only slightly more common than mass shootings in America lately. Mine was a DAI: the most severe form of TBI, which few ever recover from and even fewer are known to be able to come back via self-care.

And let's not forget the coma, right? No, no ... not just a coma, but a Stage 3. There are fifteen levels of Glasgow Coma Scale, the lower ones being more severe. While you could argue there are two levels worse than mine, Stages 1 and 2 are just reference points. Stage 3 is synonymous with death. Stage 4 has more hope, as it can be treated. For Stage 3 and below, EMTs shrug their shoulders and say a prayer: it's out of their hands.

My NDE just *had* to be unusual too. Go big or go home, right?

My NDE was not a brief OBE (out-of-body experience) as most are. The majority of NDEs are over within seconds, a few last minutes, and a couple are longer. The longer ones almost always involve coma or vegetative conditions, but those are pretty rare.

Here's the science, and I'm not going to separate conventional *science* from spiritual science. I'm going to elaborate on the *way things work*. These are not my *opinions*, conjectures, or my personal theories. What I am stating here is *fact*, which is supported by volumes of spiritual texts, direct knowledge uploaded within The Portal, *and* personal verification: *I saw, felt, and heard it.* You're welcome to the opinion I am TBI-delusional in spite of the fact that I appear rational, logical, stable, and well-adjusted. Maybe I *am* crazy. Crazy people always think they're okay, so I may be okay since I doubted my sanity regularly throughout this experience.

Let's jump right into the juicy stuff of what most NDErs bring home from it:

- Evidence of an afterlife
- Evidence of spiritual/cosmic dimensions of reality
- Academic abilities/knowledge previously unknown
- Psychic/intuitive abilities

The first two, evidence of afterlife and spiritual/cosmic dimensions of realty, are universal. It's not an NDE unless you retain some awareness of life extending beyond death. Many, many people die and are revived each and every day in the world. This does not get included within the NDE culture unless there is some *retention* of the experience. So everyone who has an official NDE reports having some version of events that made them undeniable. It has already been explained the reason some see Jesus, some see Buddha, and some see passed-on loved ones and pets is because the Akashic Agents provide perceptions one is familiar with. Unfortunately, this means the NDEr starts proselytizing that *their* version is now direct evidence their version of God is right, so therefore, everyone else's is wrong. As you may expect, this tendency is particularly strong with Christian-based NDErs and Western religious adherents.

I have been a guest on several NDE podcasts. One of the earlier ones, I had a terrific interview with a very nice woman. We connected, and she gave me respect and latitude to speak from the heart. I knew nothing about her before the interview; our only interaction was her emailed invite to be her guest. I was the first guest she had who wasn't a card-carrying Christian, so some of her YouTube followers gave her hell for it. Even though we never mentioned Christian views or religion, she caught a lot of flak for having this *Buddhist-hindu-hermetic-mystic* on her show. She and I got along well, and she confessed during the interview she had rarely felt so comfortable sharing and asking questions of someone as she had with me. See for yourself:

Youtube: Pegi Robinson—NDE TV, NDE TV Presents Krishnanand, Epic Journey Through Reincarnations https://www.youtube.com/watch?v=qXTpnT9VyVo.

This is how Western-Abrahamic religions are referred to as *closed systems.*

Getting confirmation of life after death via your NDE is universal: it's is what an NDE is. Then your *own mind converts* this message and evidence to concepts you are personally familiar with. The more closed-minded or religiously zealous you are, the more you will unconsciously convert pure divinity and spirit to particular religious brands.

Many NDErs don't have religious affiliations. The majority of them report the *white light,* angels, and passed-on loved ones. If they were raised in a Christian-based nation, like America or Latin American regions, they will typically convert their NDE ingredients to Christian too. Jews see Moses; Muslims see Mohammad (pbuh); Hindus see Vishnu. . . . You get my point.

The bottom line is this: *What you see, contact, and experience within The Portal is what you are* attached *to! It is your "field of attachment" that predicates your post-death experience.* Good news/bad news for you: If your attachment to your pet or family is very deep, you will indeed see them and reunite with them. This means you are 100 percent destined to return to the material phenomena and continue your dramas with them. Why is this potentially bad news? Because it is unwise to form such emotional attachments to pets, forcing you to reincarnate as one! I have had a string of lifetimes with my son (several I can recall and access), multiple with my sister, and oh-so-many with my partner, Janete. Our karmas are as intertwined as a DNA strand, and karma has a gravitational effect like a tractor beam, our spirits and lives draw each other together again and again. This is where you get the *soulmate* feeling and concept. It's legit!

However, from a purely spiritual point of view, this is *bad!* If you love God with the same devotion and attachment, then you move up and on toward Divinity! Let go; let God as they say!

The final two NDE features:

- Academic abilities/knowledge previously unknown
- Psychic/intuitive abilities

These are not universal to NDEs but are very common and vary in degree. NDErs who subscribe to Western spiritual paths opposing supernatural concepts, like Catholics, come back with merely visions of heaven and a presence of God and/or Jesus (which are indivisible). A few others return with some wider views, which can erode their existing religious tenets and cause spiritual crisis as what they experience conflicts with what they held to be true. An agnostic NDEr may convert to religion or embrace spiritual beliefs, and a New-Ager/spiritual/not-religious type may have their views considerably expanded.

Some return with new abilities:

- Intuition, extrasensory perception (ESP), clairaudience, clairvoyance . . . and some report having been endowed with healing abilities.

Sadly, I have found most of these reports to be irresponsible. A visit to the *other side* will certainly activate dormant centers within your energy body and causal/mind bodies, which carry-over, but like *any skill or ability*, you're not a freakin' master because of it!

People who've had *no* prior experience, exposure, or training in these skills are like toddlers with firearms. They run around shooting their mouths off about being psychic healers merely because they perceive a few things intuitively. They were never trained to use their psychic abilities properly, only know the basics, *like how to load and pull the trigger,* and don't seek proper training post-NDE either.

The same with most dime-store psychics. I became friends with an NDEr at the Seattle IANDS convention, and we stayed in touch. This woman had previously been an agnostic materialist. Her NDE *woke* her up and provided her with self-verified evidence of the supernatural, and she became quite sensitive to others. Empathy to an intuitive degree is ultra-common post-NDE. Without any prior exposure to the paranormal, she bypassed doing *any* research or studying about her newfound perceptions of empathy and psychic sensitivity. She went from housewife (her words, not mine) to *healer*.

She established a lucrative practice as an animal healer. Great. Helping souls in animal incarnations is gospel. But during a visit to my home, she displayed a subtle trance-like state and declared my cat was being threatened by another neighborhood cat that needed to be healed of its aggression, and many spirits were in my house that were quite threatening. I politely finished coffee with her, walked her to the door, and severed all contact with her. Someone needed healing in this space; *that* was certain. Many develop an unlisted phenomena from NDE too: FoS syndrome—*full of shit*. She came back from visiting the Akashic-Records Store with a complimentary gift bag of fundamental intuitions and never studied or trained to use them: like a toddler with a firearm!

Who am I to question or criticize another NDEr's perceptions? I'm a trained adept of mysticism and practitioner of spiritual paths, *that's who*.

I've dedicated my life to spiritual mysticism. By the time I had my NDE, I was an expert in many, proficient in most, and adept at several. I studied, learned, practiced, qualified, and initiated. I had a *sixth sense* since I was born, scrying in crystal balls when I was four. I never thought my intuition was anything otherworldly: I assumed it was normal. Maybe not *common* since most others seemed to miss what I thought was rather obvious. My psychic, tarot-reading mother always advised me to keep it on the DL.

Post-NDE, my abilities and intuitions were not *new*, but they certainly took on new qualities and features. A reliable intuition had always given me an edge, but mostly information that could help guide or assist someone to grow and mature. This enhanced my skill as a private counselor: I knew what people needed and where their spirit was trying to lead them. Many clients were *brought* to me for higher understanding and safe introduction to it. One woman came to see me to quit smoking. By the middle of the first session, her smoking habit was solved as she said, "I wasn't brought to you to quit smoking, was I?"

"No. You only *started* smoking just a month ago because your spirit was manifesting an excuse for you to reach out in a way you would not resist." We spent the next several years working together as I became her spiritual fitness trainer.

Psychic intuition is not to be used for contacting passed-on loved ones or locating lost items like your fucking cellphone. Responsible yogis and mystics never allude to such things or sell it as a service. They assist others to only help them grow spiritually.

But now . . . I was suffering from *conventional* psychic phenom like hearing other's thoughts and sensing rather trivial things!

I have zero use for conventional psychic ability! The ESP awareness the woman in front of me in the drive through is cheating on her husband who's embezzling from her business is useless information. My Akashic Records gift bag allowed me to see with perfect clarity when someone was full of shit! It gave me a reliable *full-of-shit* meter.

This is the age of deception and materialism, called Kali Yug in Sanskrit. Multiple times a day I swing from loathing to empathy for humanity. I loathe the oligarchy of advertising that portrays this false expectation that any agent/doctor/medicine/policy/service represented by some smart-looking person holding a tablet has the inside scoop on the app/site/service/subscription that puts your peace/joy/wealth/success/love/health just a fucking click away. And . . . anyone *not* using the product or service must be a shitty loser, so register *now!* I'm overwhelmed with empathy for a majority of people who either a) believe this crap or b) have accepted over-hyped lies as a new normal and have become immune and oblivious to its dangers.It took years for society to make a sensible rule to put health warning labels on cigarettes. We need the same thing for credit cards. They advertise life is just better with more access to things and stuff, but never mention the crushing debt and lifelong enslavement to financial institutions that want you to live your entire life in debt, debt, and more debt.

As my intuition is screaming for me to just go back to comatose for relief, I console myself with the fact that *everyone* perceives this stuff so I don't need to soapbox about it. But the economic argument doesn't support that. McDonald's and the Kardashians make millions not just in spite of being toxic, but *because* they are.

Most of the NDErs I meet were fine the day after too: no debilitating injuries or defects. They almost died, dusted themselves off, and began preaching about stuff they never knew anything about and didn't even accept or believe a week before. Suddenly, they feel qualified to save the world with spiritual light, yet they do not do a Goddam thing to polish, refine, or enhance these new perceptions by studying them.

I got two items in my Portal complimentary gift bag that were semi-useful:

1. My addictive tendencies were terminated.

I'd been clean from hard dope for over twenty-five years. My sobriety was stable enough to make me an innovator in the addiction recovery field. Yet, I was always aware my addictive tendencies were there, lurking in the background of my consciousness and waiting to pounce if given the opportunity. Whether it was the cosmic rewiring from the NDE or nerve rewiring from TBI-DAI, I woke from my coma as a *non-addict*.[18]

2. Desiring had been reduced to an inconsequential degree.

Pre-NDE/TBI, I was a normal man: I liked food, an occasional drink, sex, sports, entertainment, . . . etc. I craved water all the time and *loved* ice water. I loved popsicles and ice cream too. Post-NDE/TBI, I was indifferent to most things. I was never hungry or thirsty; was uninterested in conventional entertainments like sports, TV, and movies; and my desire for sex and intimacy leaned far more toward emotional connection than carnal pleasure.

Not bad swag from the Portal store, but these gifts did more to set me apart from others, as these are things we all can bond over, and now I didn't give a shit about them.

I got life-shattering losses and suffering, but no R.O.I.

I was in the hospital for a solid month, had to learn how to walk and talk again, stayed in a creepy-fog for over four years, and all I got at the bottom of the NDE Cracker Jack box was a decoder ring I already had two of. I was *already* intuitive and a healer *pre*-NDE. What a gyp.

Let's learn about subtle reality too!

My condition was paradoxical: Your *soul* is the battery pack for your body. It is the power that *enlivens* your physical form: no soul, no life; your body is just tissue. The nagging question became, *how was my body alive after death if my soul was within The Portal?*

Living things are made of:

1. A physical body
2. A subtle body
3. A causal body

---

[18] A term I innovated in *Project Addiction—the Complete Guide to Using, Abusing and recovering from Drugs and Behaviors.*

The *physical* body is plain and simple to understand: bones, blood, tissues, organs, etc. Your five senses (sight, taste, hearing, touch, smell) are the apparatus you sense the world with. Your brain is a part of this and is the physical apparatus that *senses* the world: physical senses take it in and the brain interprets it.

The *subtle* body is your body of *energy*. What are known as *chakras* make up the energy body. There are 114 of them, and seven are the *main* ones. They are connected by circuits of meridians. The subtle-energy body is the *frame* the material body is superimposed on.

The *causal* body is your body of mind and of cause (*manas* in Sanskrit): mind is consciousness and has three parts: your *ego-self* (*ahamkara* in Sanskrit), intellect (*buddhi* in Sanskrit), and perception (*citta* in Sanskrit). The causal body is the storehouse of your karmas and sanskars.

- Karmas are the actions and consequences regulating and governing our events and experiences.
- Sanskars regulate and govern your attitudes, character, tendencies, likes, dislikes, etc.

Karmas and sanskars are the *causal* elements regulating and governing your human experience: your events and attitudes respectively. My accident and miracle of recovery is a *karmic event*. My never-say-die attitude is an innate quality of my character, which is a *sanskar*.

My *physical* body was in a coma and being driven by machines while in the hospital. This means my *soul* was present: no soul, no life. My *subtle energy* body was also present. It was all fucked up from the damage too, but the energy body is the underlying foundation the physical body is built upon. Like our skeleton provides the frame for our skin and organs, the energy body provides the frame for the physical body. Both the physical and energy bodies were within the realm of matter in a hospital bed.

The *causal* body is only necessary if you're actually conscious and *causing*: actions or thoughts. Without actions or thoughts, you're not *causing* anything.

My physical body and subtle body were present in the material phenomena the entire time before and during my NDE.

My causal-body, my consciousness—i.e., mind—my *ahamkar, buddhi, and citta,* were not.

During my coma my mind was within The Portal as it was not needed to be in my unconscious body. Once awake from my coma, my mind was in both: the material and the celestial phenomena: The World and The Portal.

The physical and energy bodies cannot exist in two locations at once: They're far too dense. But the mind can. The mind is a subtler energy you can't measure. And mine was discombobulated. The intellect part couldn't do its job fully without synchronicity with the ego-self or perceptive-self. They all rely on one another. My causal body could not orient itself. My true identity is spirit, not body; yours is too. My mind had clear and sharp awareness of my causal being—lifetimes of citta, ahamkars, karmas, and sanskars. My intellect could not reconcile being a spiritual being in a material body. The confusion I am experiencing during peak NDE is due to vacillating between the two: my consciousness is not in one or the other. With one foot inside the doorway and one out, I'm not in or out of the room: I'm both.

This is why *bardo* means *in between.* It's not all spiritual nor material, it is both simultaneously. This does not translate in the physical realm.

Everything in the material realm is *spot-existent:* It exists in the here and now. Except the mind: It is not omnipresent, but it is less confined to the here and now. With your mind, you can remember the past and contemplate the future and transcend the *now.* You can imagine and virtually experience other places and experiences liberating you from pure *here.* You're still limited within material phenomena, but you're not confined exclusively to the physical part because the mind has some versatility.

The summary conclusion is mysterious but sensible: My soul left my body for just a few moments at the death event and then returned, activating my *subtle* body, which activated my *physical* body while my *causal* body of mind and spirit remained within The Portal during the coma and then existed in both places simultaneously for several years.

And it was a bitch.

22.

INDIGO CHILDREN AND SOULMATES

Being deeply loved by someone gives you strength, while loving someone deeply gives you courage.
—Lao Tzu (Tao Te Ching)

Coming out the other side/Step into the shadow/Forty-six and two are just ahead of me
—Tool ("46 & 2")

Indigo Children

The term Indigo Child came about in the '70s. It refers to children (who, of course, become adults) who have natural, innate spiritual tendencies, abilities, and understandings. The theory is there are several human beings who have evolved DNA and are naturally advanced. I prefer the term "*46 & 2*," as it refers to the idea that regular folk have just *44* and 2: 44 autosomes and 2 chromosomes, but gifted, advanced, next-wave-of-evolution humans—i.e., Indigo Children—have 46 and 2.

I'm not fond of trend labels. I'm not a fucking unicorn-transoid-polyamorous-hipster-whatcha-ma-call-it. One of the ways you can identify an Indigo Child/adult, if such a person exists, is they won't be cool with your labels: they're *very* resistant to trends and social norms, finding them beneath them. If this is true and Indigos are real, then I am a *card-carrying* Indigo. Label me and I'll leave the room muttering expletives under my breath. I'm not starting a hashtag movement as an intuitive, mystic, NDEr, Kundalini survivor, hard-core addiction recoveree, or any other of the miracle achievements I've been forced to endure in this life. I'm not proud of it, I'm not "special," I'm not "chosen," and I don't know where John Galt is either (LOLOL! But I think I saw him on a midnight flyer train!).

I have *never* felt like I'm a natural citizen of this planet. I was having deep doubts and existential musings when I was *three!* I've seen and been aware of multiple layers of reality my entire life and wondered how the hell I got here and where my space pod was so I could go home. I learned to adapt and blend in. Other than a wide plethora of perspectives and accumulated knowledge, I seem like anyone else.

- Parent
- Homeowner
- Entrepreneurial sole proprietor
- Partner, friend, brother, son . . .

The differences are in the asterisks. On paper, I'm just a single parent who coached pony baseball, but the asterisk notes reveal the details of not even knowing he wasn't my DNA child until he was three and how I battled to protect him and preserve my role in his life, setting Superior Court precedence that permanently modified family-law. How Brandon became a firefighter is as Indigo as anything else I'm involved with.

Yeah, on paper, I'm just a guy who started a couple businesses and had some success. But the manner and degree of the businesses have deep shades of Indigo. I did a one-eighty career shift and was the first and only one to provide private practice addiction counseling without holding a degree.

I'm not much of a conventional friend or family member either, which is also true of the Indigo. I've always been cool with them and close but have never felt like family members and I are truly connected. We're all good, but this is because I keep my deep perspectives mostly to myself because we just don't have it in common. My family is good, smart, normal folk. I'm the black sheep, living this existential, supernatural life.

My love life? I already went through how the latest affair came to be. While not all my romantic liaisons are of such magical caliber, the themes are unmistakable. How many guys do you know who lose their virginity to the first girl they meet, fall in love with, and make love their first time on a canopied bed with the light of a full moon streaming in through French doors that open onto a balcony on a breezy summer night, with chiffon curtains rustling the whole time? This *first-time* event was so beautiful it activated the *hopeless romantic* in me for life. Who does this?

Indigo Child? I dunno. What I *am* is a human soul trapped in the material phenomena who knows he doesn't wanna be. What I am is a soul in a man's body who sees more and knows more than most, and it is lonely. What I am is an expert in religion, theology, mysticism, and spirituality, and I'm pretty well read on physics, biology, DNA, cosmology, and many other branches of science. I'm an intellectual snob, insisting on films over blockbuster movies and each and every field of wisdom comes naturally to me. Math, I *suck* at, but Pythagorean numerology I do like Good Will Hunting. When I was failing second grade and was about to be held back, tests showed I was too advanced for second-grade curriculum and was failing because I was bored: bored, not slow.

I guess I'm an anorak* who loves Tantric-sex-yoga and did a whole lotta psychedelic exploration. If I'm able to be labeled, I'm an enigma, a paradox. It's rough and lonely.

> *anorak: strong interest, perhaps obsessive, in niche subjects that may be unacknowledged or not understood by the general public. See what I mean? *Who calls themselves an anorak?*

What I've *been* is a dope fiend, philanderer, criminal, thief, liar, cheater, loud-mouth, mean sonovabitch. And that's just in *this* lifetime!

I've also been a despot, a murderer, incestuous father, and coward in past lifetimes.

I am tired of paying for the sins of the father, sevenfold.

Whatever I did in other lives as someone else is not who I am today: I've changed. What I am now is a man trying to take his karmas with style and grace. I'm trying to take my punishments like a man and expose the truths to others so they can learn from my mistakes. You can learn from mine; it's way easier than learning from your own. Remember? There's only one thing worse than suffering: suffering for no reason. If others learn from our errors, we've not suffered for no reason.

<u>Soulmates</u>

Contrary to popular misunderstandings, you can have more than one Soulmate. I've had a couple in this lifetime.

Soulmates are romantic partners with whom you share several lifetimes of romantic involvement.

The almost instant, love at first sight, attraction we share with a soulmate is due to our higher consciousness remembering them and they us. Falling in love has the unique sensation of having known that person before *because we have*. The attachment we have with another binds us karmically, which destines our paths to cross again and evokes past feelings when we do.

A glorious feature of soulmate love is that it is far less *conditional* than usual. We are bonded more from prior connections and enduring struggles together than by personality. We bond over character, which runs far deeper than personality.

My sibling sister and I have been husband and wife, siblings, and even parent and child in prior lives. Brandon and I have shared teacher/student and apprentice/master rapport in recent lives.

Two of the grandest loves I've shared in this lifetime were with soulmates. My mystic partner and Kundalini-Tantric initiatress, dear friend, and lover in this life, Lia, and I have been lovers many times. We shared several lives focused on magic, mysticism, and spiritual practices. We speak a secret language: We rarely have to speak to understand each other, even over great distances and after long periods of not being in touch. When we speak and collaborate on mystical concepts, we speak in terms as adepts and scholars that few outside can understand. What may seem vague or obscure to others in our conversations are well understood between us privately. Kinda like inside jokes, but with an added octave of profundity!

How can you identify a soulmate?

One sign is how you meet.

The manner in which Janete and I met, how our lives had crossed paths multiple times before, how we fell in love and the depth and *brand* of the love we shared was hallmark soulmate stuff. It's not too common (or poetic) for soulmates to meet online or at Starbuck's—*but it happens too!*

The bizarre fashion and coming together my lover, Lia, and I shared is hallmark as well. Two years before we met, I had a haunting dream of her and that same night was forced to drive seventy miles to a friend's house in north LA. On the way, just an hour after the dream, my tire blew out, forcing me off the freeway at 3 a.m. to find an open garage to fix it. Where this occurred was less than a block away from where Lia lived at that moment, but we had yet to meet in this lifetime. Three years later, we would spend many long nights in our mystical practices with tarot, numerology, and sexual magic, all in her Long Beach apartment just two blocks from the twenty-four-hour service station that fixed my tire that night. She had dreamt of a mysterious stranger coming into her life too.

The way you can call out and identify the type of prior relationship you had with someone in your current life is a formula. I'm going rogue here: This is not a field I studied in the Sanskrit texts, nor in Western mysticism. I have sampled and witnessed enough of these dynamics throughout my life that I have developed a theory on past-life connections.

1.   Take a look at the *nature* of your current rapport with someone.

Romantic? Sibling? Boss? Teacher? Lover? Enemy? Rival? Don't look at the actual *label* of the relationship; the context and/or quality of the relationship is what matters, not the label. My sister and I get along far more like sexless husband and wife than we do brother and sister, a good indication we were spouses most recently. Brandon and I function as father and son, but far more as teacher-student. I never feel he *belongs* to me nor I to him. He has entered this life endowing me with the *opportunity* to teach and guide him. In this life, I am in the teacher-guide role; he is the student. That doesn't mean it is a repeat of the same. In *this* life I'm the teacher, but in our last life together, *he* was the teacher and I was the student. I'm paying it forward.

Many mothers and daughters struggle to get along. As a young girl matures, she often becomes far more defiant of her mother than her father and vice versa. It is very common for mothers and daughters to have been past-life rivals, and it has carried over. Same with sons and fathers and, of course, many siblings reincarnate, feel a soulmate connection because of being family once upon a time, mistake this for romantic love, and get married, typically resulting in a loveless asexual marriage. They become more like sibling-partners than husband and wife. My sister in this life refers to me as her *soul-brother*. We've always had a soul-to-soul connection and been aware of a relationship over several lifetimes in various contexts.

The hard ones are the ones we *don't want to see.*

Denial is pretty. Reality is ugly.

We've all been sinister, corrupt, wicked, violent . . . you name it. After several, thorough past-life regressions I had to confront the bad with the good. I've been rich, famous, kind, charitable. . . . I've also been a murderer of children, an abusive parent, and a sexual criminal. Bitter pills to swallow. Few who do the true work of past-life regression go toward these lifetimes. Most people settle on their lives in Atlantean times or remember they were Napolean Bonaparte. Sorry . . . a bit convenient. Unless you confront your own wickedness, you can't resolve these past karmic debts and get unbound from them.

It is time to divulge the past-life secret of my final Soulmate in this life.

Yes, obviously, Janete and I have several lives together that were magic and tragic to Shakespearean levels. But the one I didn't want to see, the one that has more influence over our karmic debts and obligations in *this* life is far too dark and shameful. Just after we had romantically intertwined in this life, I saw two potential timelines: harmony and catastrophe.

In the harmony one, we remain loving partners throughout our lives. In the catastrophic one, she hurts me like no one else possibly could. If your heart breaks over another, it is exactly *proportionate* to the quantity/quality/magnitude of your love and affection for them: The more you love someone, obviously, the more painful it can be if they hurt you.

We've all hurt each other. We've all helped each other. We have *infinite* karmas to fulfill. I hurt Janete in our last life together.

So let's get right to it. The last life Janete and I shared was father-daughter. Brace yourself, because this is going to be exactly the tabloid scandal you think it is. Her mother died at birth, so I took on the role of a single parent. I was a good and virtuous man: religious and ethical. I was in the English army. This was during the occupation of India. I requested reassignment from the UK to India because I was privately ashamed. My daughter and I had developed an incestuous relationship. The last life Janete and I shared together was our very last most recent one, and we were incestuous lovers.

There. I said it. Out loud. For the first time.

Even though she was complicit as she became post-pubescent, it was my responsibility to disallow our intimate connection. She was a child. I was an adult. We were close. We were all each other had after her mother had died. She loved me. I was lonely. She was as near to my departed wife as someone could come, and it triggered shameful urges that I eventually gave in to. No, I did not molest or abuse her in the conventional sense. She was complicit, and even initiating in many ways. It didn't matter: She was a child; I was her father, and that kinda thing fucks you up.

Out of guilt and shame and not trusting myself to be her father any longer, I requested reassignment to India and virtually abandoned her. She had developed deep, romantic feelings for me and saw me as her husband, not her father. This had gone on long enough for her to feel it was all right if it remained between us. Until I abandoned her.

I didn't just disappear: I told her I was going, and I told her why. I set her up with cousins to live with, and I went to India to serve. This was during the climactic peak of India's independence (1947), and as British troops left India, I went AWOL to remain in India. I sought spiritual truth as I struggled with my sins and shame and was introduced to bhakti-yog. I took a vow of *sanyas* (renunciation) and remained in Vrindaban, India, never contacting her again.

Then I was killed, and my daughter, who thought she was my lover, never heard from me nor ever even heard I had been killed. She lived her life convinced I had abandoned her and, as she matured, had to come to terms with the incestual relationship she and I had over which she had no closure.

This is surprisingly difficult to speak of and not because of the obvious shame from inappropriate behavior. It is difficult because past-life regression brings more than memories to the awareness of your consciousness. It brings the feelings. I loved her. I felt terrible for abandoning her. After that life, with Portal Life-

Review/Preview, I saw how I had hurt and confused her when I left. It haunted her for the rest of that lifetime.

This pain between us created powerful karmic obligations. It obligated us to want *closure*. When I died in this life, her spirit-conscious experienced PTSD from being abandoned by me again. Even though I came back from the dead, it was a bit too late. She had already shut down to protect from the pain of being abandoned again.

Our life in the 1400s ended tragically too and needed closure. We have a lot of baggage. It's designer brand stuff and quite gorgeous but still heavy baggage.

The context of our relationship in this current life has been similar: we *were not* related in any way, but she is like a child in many ways (she does not disagree with that), and I am a natural father-figure, leader, with a very avuncular quality to my character. I have existed in a serving, teaching, healing, mentoring, guiding role to nearly everyone I have been involved with, including people I meet in the most casual manners. It's what I am and what I do, and I stay in my lane and fulfill it best I can: I try to inspire, motivate and empower others. That is predominantly the context of all my relationships. And I don't mind: having a role in others' growth makes me feel important and useful.

Much of my endless, virtually unconditional service to those who seek my help is out of karmic obligation: nearly every client seeking my counsel and guidance in *this* life is someone I screwed over in a past life. My clients in this life help me pay my bills: both utility and karma. When I go well above the call of duty and help them when no one else can or will, I pay off a karmic debt and it is a *grand relief!* To pay back a karmic debt in a healthy, win-win fashion is highly recommended!

We share karmic debts with absolutely everyone we become involved with; some good, some bad, but each soul we interact with may be an opportunity to fulfill karmic destinies.

Modern-Life

I was the engineer of the adventures Janete and I shared, always wanting to keep things fresh and unique, and they always were. One of our grandest anniversaries was a two-day backpack in Yosemite with two nights of strawberries and champagne at the grand Yosemite lodge. She idolized Stevie Nicks in her youth, and when the band finally reunited, I got us tickets, and we went the first night the McVie's were back with the Mac. We had listened to Beck lounging nude and in love at my fireplace on many evenings. He was the soundtrack to so much of our courtship and we saw him in a small deco-theatre in Santa Barbara and toured Zen gardens the following day. Ludevico Einaudi at UCLA was the one she said was the most special musical event she'd ever heard. Even though I had also taken her to see Tool *twice*. The concerts, museums, gardens, forests, and parks we toured were carefully selected to be unique and private. Nothing was ordinary nor done in ordinary ways. A few concerts were post D-Day: Puscifer in Seattle, Beck at SB, and Ludevico at UCLA.

Part of my motivation to share these experiences with her was to broaden her horizons as a teacher and mentor—like a father figure.

Our final backpack trip was about a year after NDE-Day. It was my first attempt at reclaiming this sacred ritual of backpacking. As I crumbled on the side of a trail, too sad at my broken limitations and being a disappointment, she pep-talked me to keep trying. This five-foot-two, hundred-pound girl/best-friend, took the ten-pound bear-canister out of my pack and carried it in her arms so I could have enough balance enough to go on. Against all odds, with her motivation and help, I made it to my haven of Rancheria Falls and made us dinner over a fire in the wilderness, feeling I could go on. We're soulmates.

My life . . . has been one legendary event after another. She confessed many times, "My life before us was backyard BBQs and shopping. I was totally asleep spiritually and miserable. I just didn't know why. You woke me up."

"We've done this for each other in a dozen lives, Janete. This time it was my turn to wake you."

The magic of our legend spilled over for her, and we both reveled within it. It was no longer mine; it became ours again. I had plenty of magic to share.

Valentines of Blood and Roses

We all dream of love and deep romance. Even those who become jaded by a broken heart still pine and long for true love. I have counseled dozens and dozens of couples who had been betrayed, abused, neglected, or just lost the spark and magic of honoring a partner they once admired. In spite of this, everyone needs to believe true love exists in the world somewhere. *It does.*

Janete and I sustained *courtship* for over a decade: always keeping our romance fresh, alive, and dynamic. The majority of days of life must pass in mediocrity to survive and remain well: we all gotta work, tend to the chores and lusterless duties. I recognized these tar-pits, and we were determined to never get stuck in them. The actual glitter she wore went away, but we never stopped putting in the time and effort to be sexy, fun, alluring, and special to one another. We made conscious effort to live in perpetual courtship as much as possible and make romance in our lives together. The glitter of *stable*-love may not be as shiny but has a shine and sheen that is steady and runs deep. And my poetry may not have been composed daily as it had been once, but I still composed verses to her and to our lives and the mysteries which she was my muse of. The tenth-year anniversary we shared in Nepal and India was accompanied with a hardbound book of ten years of poetry to her. I personally printed, cut, and pasted the over one hundred poems inside the pages of the velvet-covered book. Each poem a testified expression of our shared magic.

Arno River, Florence, Italy

Yes: we had it all.

We are beautiful, creative, and enjoy a union of intimacy we all only fantasize of. It is strong and vibrant and spans many lifetimes.

We also live in a mundane world: bills, kids with issues, family dramas, occasional bickering over coffee, and good-ole argument-fights too! We're still human.

Our arrangement was one of individual enhancement:

"A good and healthy partnership is not about completing one another. It is about empowering one another's individuality. If we're each the best persons we can be, then we'll be great partners. My role is not to complete you, but to *enhance* you. And vice-versa. You push me to be more than what I am. I push you to become more of who you are. As we both learn, grow, and improve our character, we both benefit. Then it becomes perpetual: we keep doing it, neither of us ever settling on who we are but always accepting each other as what we are today and what we're becoming too."

We don't *complete* each other: we *inspire* each other.

It's real challenging to sustain magic in an unmagical world. Where the majority are shallow and selfish and unwilling to reciprocate and to *earn* reciprocation. She and I both always feel as though we have a secret everyone is trying to figure out and we're just living it.

But just as fate-destiny-karma intervened for us to meet in a fender-bender and take vows with each other, this same force of spiritual origins placed that MP3-500 motorbike in our path in a parking lot one night too.

Is it true? That all good things must come to an end?

That death is a part of life? And life only emerges from death?

Death and resurrection: one thing dies, another takes life. . .

23.

RETREAT

> Integrity is your destiny—it is the light that guides your way.
> —Plato

> Wherever you go, there you are.
> —The Adventures of Buckaroo Banzai Across the 8th Dimension
> (Earl Rauch)

Just imagine. . .

A voice over a tinny PA system arouses you from dreamless sleep. Her Chinese-Asian accent is unmistakable:

"Ladies and gentleman, the seat belt light is on. Please secure your safety belts for our descent. We will be landing in Wuhan in nineteen minutes."

Your seat belt is already secure. The fog-fugue of sleep is thick as you become slowly aware.

Wuhan, China? What?

You realize you have no idea how you are about to arrive in Wuhan, China. You have no idea how you're even on a plane. You went to bed last night, as usual: after a light snack, teeth brushed, and face washed . . . it's the last you recall. The announcement continues. . . .

"Please be sure to fill out the customs form and have your passport ready."

You look down at the entry-form placed in front of you while you slept. You do a quick search in a confusion: no passport wallet or anything you might need. Your panic is subtle as you assume this will all make sense once you've fully wakened.

A quick search in the seat-pocket and an open of the overhead reveals nothing but more questions:

Where am I? How did I get here? I don't remember getting on a plane. I don't have any business in China. What is going on?

You handle the little pen they placed with the customs form and realize as you look at the lines to enter info: *Name? I don't know my name. Passport number? Nationality? Departure city? I don't know any of this. How did I get here? China?*

But this is no dream. It is sharp reality, and there is no doubt as a feeling of emergency catapults you from sleep-brain to wake-brain. You see passengers fumbling with smartphones. You don't have one of those either. You have clothes on and nothing else. You know you're *you,* but don't know *who* you are.

The plane touches down. Taxis to a gate. People gather things and begin to exit the craft: citizens to the right, visitors to the left for customs. Panic is restrained by the surrealness of the situation. Panic yields denial-humor: *This can't be happening, so it* isn't *happening. Somehow, someway, I will soon understand how I'm imagining this.*

You don't know who you are. You don't know how you got here. You have no ID. You have no money or phone.

Go ahead: just take a real moment and imagine this scenario: waking on a plane landing in a very foreign country you've never been to without any papers, understanding, or even knowing your identity. As outrageous as it is, try to imagine how you would be forced to *feel.*

***

"Whoa, Krishnanand! That's intense! Is it like this every day?"

"For the first five months, yes, it was like that every day. It's paradoxical now: it's like I know and remember stuff, but it's never familiar."

I am explaining my condition to my curious friends. They are my spiritual family: a small band of people I have known for nearly ten years. We are spiritual brothers and sisters on the same path of spirituality. We see each other once, twice a week at our local meditation center in Los Angeles.

I have just delivered a tearful goodbye, surprising many of them who have been concerned about me for these many months.

"Do you have family there? Janete's going with you, right? What about Brandon?" They are reacting to the news of my decision to leave LA and move to the PNW: the Pacific Northwest, Washington State.

"No, I have to do this on my own. We need to separate for a while. I don't want my problems holding Brandon back. You guys know him: he's such a solid young man, and at twenty-one he is at such a critical stage of his independence. I can't burden him, so I'll go on my own and we'll visit. He's getting a place with a friend."

"Janete's not going with you?"

My sadhana family knows very well how close we are. We became devotees to this path together, yet I was far more dedicated. They only knew me and her together.

"No. You guys know I've always been a 'go-to' guy in all things: here and at home, if I am needed for anything I try to serve it. I need to recover from my accident, and to do it I can't take care of anyone else for a while."

No one knew one thing of our inner-drama. I suffered madly from victim-guilt at her indiscretion and was too personally embarrassed to speak of it. I also didn't want to gossip about her and influence others' perceptions of her.

Saying goodbye to my spiritual, ashram family was heartfelt and painful. The first attempt I made at restoring my life was to return to satsang. My first appearance to the meditation center after my hospital stay and two months of home-quarantine was awkward. I could only vaguely connect to these people and my spiritual path of sadhana. Our center-manager, a motherly figure to all of us, invited me to do the aarti: the waving of the candle in front of the altar to honor God and Guru during verses sung that honor them with joyful melody.

I stood at the altar and could not remember one thing: how and when to pranam (bow), which circular direction to wave the aarti candle tray, when to stop, and the fifteen minutes of song-verses I once knew by heart were entirely unknown to me. And I wept.

Facing the altar, with my back to the small congregation, I wept. Not because my devotee sister, Sarina, had to tell me how to light the candles and how to wave the tray or because I could barely stand upright without losing my balance, I was so dizzy. I wept because I was *here*.

I had somehow survived this terrible tragedy and was alive and standing at my spiritual altar with my spiritual family, honoring God and Guru. Nothing else mattered.

Sarina invited me to do the aarti most of the time now, and I wept discreetly throughout the song, overcome with gratitude of miracle: I'm still here. I am alive and I am back. Honoring and praising my God of love. *Beatified.*

For nearly ten years, this small group of brothers and sisters had been my spiritual peers and we were bonded. We had the same spiritual father in our guru. We have all dedicated our lives to the path of bhakti yog taught by Rasik saints of India over five-thousand years. We all share a single goal of spiritual enlightenment.

It has been a time of mourning. Our beloved Maharaji left this material planet nearly twelve months ago. His Grace and teachings were available to the world for over ninety years. I am both confused and grateful for his departure occurring during my trauma. How would I be mourning if I was more aware? I never felt He was gone though.

It never ever even occurred to me I wouldn't know these core members of my spiritual family the rest of my life. But I had to leave.

<u>Retreat</u>

Real-estate is all about location. A great house in a bad location has little worth, but a bad house in a great location has big value. Same with business: *what* your business is, is less important as to *where* your business is.

I want to remain in The Portal where it's safe. Where I forget about the world and my losses. But I am only allowed to visit there now as my body is alive within the realm of matter. So I decide to move.

I wanted to be away from all the constant reminders of my condition: the intersection of the accident just a few blocks from my office, the streets and avenues of my neighborhood, the stores, gas stations and every street light, road sign, tree, and rock on the ground was a brazen, stark reminder of who I *wasn't* and that my life was over. My body and brain had been damaged, my marriage shattered. It seems all I can do is watch it burn. I didn't belong there. I didn't belong anywhere, and every element of my hometown was a PTSD trigger.

As a rogue and restless spirit all my life, there wasn't one section of the sprawling Los Angeles region, known as SoCal, which I had not lived in or near and wasn't haunted by the ghost of Scott Spackey. For those not familiar with SoCal, we'll take a brief tour:

- Ventura County is to the north-coast
- Orange County is to the south
- Inland Empire is the desert region to the east
- SCV/Antelope Valley to the north, which is where I currently live
- Los Angeles proper and the SFV—San Fernando Valley—in the center

I have lived all over SoCal. Having moved there, against my will at thirteen, I had lived all over the region, worked in every county, and know LA/SoCal far better than it knows the back of its own hand. There was not a single area I could drive through without having an anecdote to share from my life in it. Since Janete and I had spent the last ten years as a couple, there were very few places, *very few indeed*, not haunted by a gorgeous romantic episode of our beauty together. The few places, *very few indeed*, in SoCal not haunted by the spectral presence of our soul-mate phantom presence were haunted by me, myself. I had an entire first memoir of life-experiences all over the region. And many of those, and many not in either category, were inhabited by the memory phantoms of father-and-son.

There wasn't a single place in SoCal that wasn't possessed by my life's phantoms. My condition of massive disrepair and loss was such I could not view a single memory with affectionate nostalgia. Even the satisfaction of having the ability to *remember* was marred. I didn't actually remember in the manner you would know of it: no connection or familiarity sensation. Just the facts, ma'am, just the facts: I was here, I was there, I did this, I saw that . . . like a bland newspaper article. Nostalgia was replaced with apathy. LA felt like a place I was last seen and my ghost was haunting it. There was no nostalgia. Just stark reminders of who I'd once been and was no longer.

PNW or Bust

I'd had a recurring dream in my late twenties soon after my son was born: in the dreams I searched for a street called Rainier but could never find it. This dream recurred dozens of times over just a few weeks. It was so intense and recurring I had actually found a few Rainier streets in the SoCal region and visited many of them. In the dream, I was supposed to go there: Rainier.

Nothing ever came of it, but I never forgot it, and it inspired me. In early 2000s Brandon and I vacayed in Washington State to see Mt Rainier. We had a fantastic trip: Mariners vs. Dodgers game in Seattle (Dodgers won!), Puget Sound ferry travel, visiting a high-school friend who had relocated to the PNW years before, and of course . . . a couple days at Mt Rainier.

Janete and I had visited Washington too: we had spent several days of her birthday touring the Puget Sound from Olympia to Port Angeles, taking a ferry over the border to Victoria and walking the famed Butchart Gardens with Christmas displays. The entire state is like a garden of forests and lakes!

Mt Rainier is iconic: it is a huge shape of the Cascade Mountain Range. It sits alone in a quite flat region of WA. Flatlands end in this abrupt, mammoth, lonely mountain so massive and such a contrast to the landscape it literally generates its own weather patterns. It is a magical place. It is believed Mt. Rainier is a goddess who has taken the form of a mountain, similar to Annapurna in the Himalayas being an avatar of Adishakti. Rainier was beckoning me again. The recurring dreams I had and the couple visits there were catalysts to relocate to the PNW.

I hated LA, always hated living in a Goddam desert, always loved forests and trees, and always assumed one day I'd end up retiring in the woods. This had been our mutual plan, Janete and I: to build a home on the Boulder Creek property and retire happily ever after.

As my life and dreams continued to unravel from TBI-NDE, I made alternate plans. Akashic Agents subtly directed me to leave LA and consider relocating to the Pacific Northwest.

The home I had found in Yelm, WA was a four-acre home that looked and felt like a 2,300 sq. ft. resort. And it was just a forty-five-minute drive to Mt. Rainier.

The manner of how I came to live there is worthy. It has the signature of the supernatural:

While I was confident I was being directly directed by Portal Agents to relocate, I still had to do it responsibly. The spirit world can tell you *what* needs done, but you still gotta figure out *how*. I did some research and decided to begin with a recon mission to the area.

"Where you goin', Dad?" asked Brandon as I passed by with a suitcase in hand.

"I'm flying to Seattle, renting a car, and driving to Mt. Rainier to find a place to live."

"Oh, ok. Cool. Be safe."

What may seem as father-son angst during stressful times was not. In spite of our recent tensions, we got along fine most the time and love and respect still were the foundation. This action was not out of line with my historical character: I was always a man who did what the fuck he needed to do and did so smartly and adventurously, so Brandon was not all surprised at my reply as to where I was going.

I had also been easing Janete into the new idea of relocation and the concept of a *trial separation*. I presented the idea that if we were ever able to reconnect and reunite, we had to literally start over. We could have a long-distance relationship for a while. "You'll be able to get away every month and have a romantic vacay. We won't be in each other's faces all the time with all these *complications*. When we get together it will be new. Fresh. Good times without the dark. Reinvent . . . put some distance between us and what has happened and build some good times that don't reek of tragedy."

We agreed it was somewhat inevitable: I was drowning in trauma and no one could help me. I had to save myself and get out of *the land of PTSD*.

I drove from Seattle airport toward a town outside Mt. Rainier national park called Yelm. I checked into a modest hotel in the country, watched the Dodger game on my laptop, and rested. Got up, had coffee, and as I walked back to my room, had an inner dialogue:

"What the fuck are you doing? You don't know one fucking thing about this place. You wouldn't even know where to *begin* to find places to live! You don't know a soul here, never been here and have no plan! The only research you did was if it had a vegetarian market in this town!" Which it did.

I had no come-back argument: I was in Yelm, WA, and had no idea how to even consider places to live. And I was staring at something while I inner-argued: a newspaper machine. The machine displayed a magazine inside a door that said *take one!* So I did. It was a *houses for rent and sale* magazine.

I relaxed in my hotel room in this beautiful country community and looked through it. Nothing extraordinary, so I made a list of a few places to drive by and see if they were worth inquiring about.

One was in the neighboring community, Rainier. A good sign. So I went to it. It was nice. I walked around, looked through windows and over the back fence. The Rainier community was not so good. The subdivision-town of Rainier is not at the mountain, but the house was fine. It wasn't like I'd found the Golden Ticket, but I was satisfied with the results of the first effort.

I drove by a few others in Yelm and Rainier and called it a day. Over a beer and the Dodger game, I felt inspired to scan the rental magazine a bit more. I wasn't finding anything and was suspecting I had misinterpreted The Portal's directive to come here. I was always sure The Portal was infallible; it was just my *interpretation skills* that could cause error. What the fuck did I know? I'm not bilingual: I don't speak Portal.

My last day and I'm feeling nonplussed. The trip looks like a goose egg. I like Yelm, love WA, but I didn't see one thing that motivated me to feel it's *what's next*.

I sat with a beer and the ball game feeling disappointed, licking my wounds with the solace of *at least I tried.* Out of boredom and subtle desperation, I scanned the rental magazine again.

Whathefuck?!

The listing for the nice house I looked at in Rainier was not the right house. It wasn't even for rent. I had misread the house number and was *one digit off*. The actual house for rent was at the *end* of the same block.

Well then. Since tomorrow's your last day and you gotta head to the airport by 9 a.m., you better get your ass up early and drive by to at least know you covered all you could. Don't go home empty handed. Don't be a pussy: get up early and drive by at least.

I arrived at the correct house about 7:30 a.m. in a quiet, sleeping, Saturday neighborhood. I parked at the curb and walked up the driveway property past the rather obviously displayed *for rent* sign. I peeped through windows and over the fence to the rear yard as a car pulled into the driveway and a woman got out, looking at me with justifiable suspicion.

"Pardon me!" I blurted. "I'm *not* a peeping-tom or stalker, I promise! I saw this house was for rent and was just driving by to see it."

"Oh! Great! It is, and I'm the rental agent! I'm meeting a prospective renter but not for twenty minutes if you wanna come in and take a look."

Akashic-Kismet.

She could see right away I was not into it: small house, kinda crappy.

"I can see this may not be right for you. I got another property that's not been listed yet; you might like better. But the current residents are there now. You can dive by, but you absolutely cannot disturb them. And it won't be available for two months."

Everything has been bupkis, but I'm desperate to salvage this trip and willing to squeeze it in just to gain favor with fate. My GPS takes me thirty minutes to a lonely country road with no outlet. It keeps saying, *you are here,* as I pass an empty field. We're clearly lost.

I U-turn and head out of the one-mile-long road with just five houses on it. A couple with a dog is at the road checking their mail. The homes are all a solid 100 yards set back from the road. They're estates more than homes. The couple look at me with tense suspicion as I drive slow, scanning each property like I'm scoping my next robbery. I use my last disclaimer again, "Pardon me! I'm not a stalker, I promise. An agent sent me over here to see a house for rent, and I seemed to have gotten lost."

"Oh, what's the address, maybe we can help you find it." Country folk are always so helpful.

"Yeah, it's 4344 Kinsman, but Kinsman ended at the cul-de-sac turn, and I didn't see it."

"Oh! That's *our house!*"

Akashic-kismet #2.

"It is!? I'm so sorry, the agent told me not to disturb you and that it wasn't even available for a couple months. I was just driving by to cover my bases."

"Yeah, it won't be, but do you wanna come up and see it? I mean, you're here now, so c'mon up!"

Does that qualify for kismet #3? The timing of their checking the mail and inviting me in? Ten-four it does!

It was perfect: four acres of grass, surrounded by forests, with Mt. Rainier filling the view from the south. Hardwood floors, built just a year ago, a firepit 50 yards off the back patio. It was a paradise. *I was home.*

I got home and told Brandon the story of three kismets, and he replied: *looks like you're moving to Washington.*

_____ **24.**

LA DESPEDIDA CIUDAD LOS ANGELES
(Farewell City of Angels)

> Even angels long to look into these things.
> —Peter the apostle (1:12)

> Motel money murder madness
> Mister mojo risin', mister mojo risin'
> —The Doors ("LA Woman")

Having been in direct contact with entities many would label as *angels*, I feel qualified to say Los Angeles's moniker as the City of Angels doesn't fit. LA is a glorious place that is arguably harmonious considering the melting-stew-pot of cultures, but it is not angelic. You are side by side, sardine-can style, with everyone: Caucasian, Mexican, Armenian, Iranian, Black, Salvadorean, transexual/transgender/gender-dysphoric, rainbow-unicorn-metro-hetero . . . Yet in spite of the cultural tensions, LA's communities and cultures are quite tolerant of each other. What choice do you have when you're all dependent on one another for something eventually?

Prejudice goes out the window when you need your car or home repaired, something moved or hauled away, or any number of services, from doctors to artists, that are ethnic providers, so Angelenos get along pretty well. Unless someone cuts you off on the four-oh-five: then it's *go time*.

Don't get me wrong: I love LA.

I'm an Angeleno through and through. It helps I have never had any preconceived dislikes of others. I don't have a prejudiced bone in my boring, un-ethnic, white-boy body. I love LA's diversity, the culture, the glorious variety of entertainment and food, the Dodgers, and the LaLa thing. But anyplace that is a city to millions is gonna wreak of toxicity. New York, Chicago, London . . . it ain't the *places* themselves. You put just *twenty* people in a ten-by-ten room and you're gonna have problems, and twelve or more of *any* twenty people gathered have issues: disorders, defects, problems, etc. Big cities aren't bad. It's a problem of *density*.

In spite of my need to distance myself from a toxic collective-conscience of millions condensed to a small region of real estate, I was gonna miss the place. I didn't just have a history with LA: my entire adult life had been spent there. It's what I knew. Yet . . . I figured since I barely knew who I was and could not actually connect to myself, let alone the city I'd been in for over thirty years, it seemed time for a change—to say the least. I was a stranger in a strange land, regardless of where I was. Life in a metropolis was too much for my fragile state.

I was running on sort of Portal-dimension autopilot: I was the person doing the thinking and decision making *on paper,* but even years later, I would look upon my moving as a task executed by the invasion of the body snatcher entities whom had taken possession of me. My arms and legs did things but "I" was just a passenger of the actions. It never seemed that "*I*" was even present, let alone being the director or performer. I was a ghost.

A common feature of the Near-Death Experience is to have a sense of foreboding. Your receiving antennae is a huge radar dish, collecting signals from all over the planet. Even the most stable can start to suspect apocalyptic predictions though. If your NDE has a conspiracy-theory type of side effect, living with nearly three million other people will enhance it.

Many NDErs thrust from material consciousness to spiritual awareness are intellectually unprepared for the rather obvious signs of the planet's decline and dive deep into cooky conspiracy theories. I suffered from the absolutely biggest NDE *and* TBI, so I was eligible for losing my shit in *flat-earth, JFK, Elvis and Mairlyn are still living, X-Files* fantasy bullshit.

My NDE radar had me tuned into spiritual octaves that put glaring lights on humanity's suffering. Everywhere I looked was pain and suffering: people in the stores, on the highway, jogging in the park. . . . I could *feel spiritual ignorance and denial* and their suffering. And their ignorance *to* their suffering. Ignorance is not used as a four-letter word here: it simply applies to a humanity largely unaware that most everyone is *spiritually suffering*, regardless of their material status.

That was the hardest one to perceive: a planet of souls wracked in denial of spirit and dedicating their lives to meaningless pursuits of fashion, food, and superficial entertainment. And this is not exclusive to Los Angeles; it is global. The world had no integrity, and it was a scorching awareness for me all the time in a location also known as *Tinsel Town*. I wasn't trapped in *contempt* for humanity; I was trapped in spirals of sympathy and empathy for the planet.

As a private-practice professional, I was quite adept at remaining emotionally detached from clients. I was passionate in my work and had an honest compassion for all who sought me out but had a natural capacity to remain objective. You could say I had tremendous *sympathy* but was not overwhelmed by *empathy*.

Any counselor who is overly empathetic cannot last. Any counselor who is deficiently *sympathetic* should get a different job. Please note the difference: *sympathy* is feeling bad *for* someone and wanting to help. *Empathy* is taking on their emotions as your own. Empaths cannot remain objective and administer life-saving methods in crisis. They *want* to be counselors, but should *not* be. NDE had raised my octaves of empathy to uncomfortable levels.

And my counseling career specialized in *severe* crisis.

Sure, I had clients that just came to lose weight, get motivation, and basically just self-improve: walks in the park for me. But 70 percent of my clients suffered from severe disorders, traumas, and addictions that were no walk in the park: they needed a sherpa to take them up K2.

When I started out it was all weight-loss and stop smoking stuff. When I woke up depressed every day after nine years of commercial contracting, I needed an abrupt shift. My personal crisis of career led me through a labyrinth of career considerations: construction consultant, management, planning. . . . Being in commercial construction since I began as a $5 an hour laborer at fifteen made sense to stay within the field.

But what I actually wanted was 180 degrees different: writer/author, presenter/lecturer, teacher/mentor. . . . Being an expert in mystical and spiritual modalities, I was qualified, certified, credentialed, and documented. I knew my shit.

It had been a dream (and even an assumption) I would someday devote my life to providing spiritual/mystical insights and growth to people: like a spiritual fitness-trainer.

Not a *master:* I'm not delusional nor spiritually narcissistic, and I sidestepped the temptation to start a cult for sex, power, and money when I was younger (but I seriously thought about it!). But having an honest career in spirituality that could support me was a tough nut to crack: as much as I wanted to follow my passions, I also wanted to feel safe, secure, have a nice car, decent home, provide for my son, and live well. I *grew up* poor as fuck. I didn't need the lessons of poverty to give me the virtue of humility. I'd not forgotten my quasi-homeless years and having nothing before. A life with money in this material-mad world is necessary.

As I studied others who were on the spiritual new-age lecture circuit, I saw a fairly common theme: most had some sort of credential that *legitimized* them to the world: PhD, BA, or MA degrees or some *alternative* credential like Life-Coach or Hypnotherapist.

I was, and still am, anti-big-school: colleges are overrated expenses that make debt, and unless you're entering a field where a degree is required, like medicine or engineering, skip it if you can. Majority of people smart enough to handle college curriculum are smart enough to get even better educations on their own. University systems are Emperor's-new-clothes smoke screens: they've got everyone brainwashed to believe it is an imperative *Golden Ticket* to succeed. Bullshit. An equal number of super-successful people on this globe have no formal education as ones who do. And the majority of degree-carrying graduates work hourly jobs to support a family. Going to college for a career reboot wasn't an option for me back then.

Benjamin Franklin never went to college and neither did Richard Branson. And a whole lot of breadline homeless people have degrees. Do *that* math!

The hypnotherapy credential intrigued me, so I looked into it and that's how my practice began: I attained an accredited, *clinical* certification in hypnotherapy. The clinical credential gave me skills and status for serious issues. I loved it. It was a powerful modality to practice. And I was damn good at it.

Soon, my clients asked me to assist them with much more. They trusted me and my skills, and soon I was a popular life coach within my SoCal suburb. When that wasn't generating enough revenue to quit construction entirely, I got certified as an addiction counselor. My little practice that began as part-time from a sublet office went to over $300K a year, ten-hour days, six days a week (four-plus hours on Sunday too) nearly overnight. I was saving lives, making money, and doing something I felt *great* about each and every day. I was being referred to behind my back as *the cavalry counselor:* the guy to call to save the day when nothing else has worked. This is what led to the corner office over the park, which I turned right instead of left out of that oh-so-fateful NDE day.

I loved my work, and as an objective professional, I had an invisible forcefield protecting me from over-empathy. Coexisting now in matter *and* The Portal had caused this forcefield to disintegrate. I could not shut it off, so empathy made me depressed!

If you heard most other's thoughts, you'd change the channel. Not because much of it is toxic but because most of what people concern their inner thoughts with is boring and meaningless, which saddens me. People's consciousness is mostly trivial static; their *conscious minds* seek trivial pleasures, but their inner spirits yearn for something meaningful. Staying within the confines of my private office or within my home reduced the collective-conscious static I received.

Breaking the News

Janete and I fly to WA so I can show her around where I'll be living and she'll be visiting during our marriage-salvation-separation. We huddle close on the flight at 33,000 feet up:

"I just need some time. I need to heal from our issues and see if removing myself from *all this* will help me restore. I'm asking for your support, Janete. I'm asking you to endure this episode of our epic. I've shouldered the weight of all our desires and ambitions since we've been together. I've asked little to nothing, and I'm not *asking* now: I'm telling you I *need* you to support me as I do what I need to do to try to come back from all this. My mind and spirit have not reestablished yet in my body."

"Ok. You're right. You've been through too much and it's not been fair and I am truly sorry for what I did and that I've not been able to help you."

It was agreed I would rent this home in Yelm, WA, and we would have weeklong visits every three to six weeks. I would sustain my home in LA, continue to pay the mortgage, close my office, and pursue my author career. Being a paid and successful author has bad odds: one in thousands? Millions?

"I never told you this, but when you decided to stop construction and become a hypnotherapist/counselor, I never thought you'd make it. I thought there was no way a guy without a degree could do what you've done. What you made was impossible. I don't know if you can make the writing thing happen or not, but if anyone can do it, you can. But first, you gotta deal with this injury. I want you to get well, Scott. I'm so sorry this is happening to you, and I can't do anything about it. What you've been going through is terrible, and I've only made it worse. And I'm sorry."

Another reason to depart: Janete felt terrible about her betrayal and inability to help me heal from brain and death issues. My pesky empathy made it hard to be around her. She felt terrible for not being able to help me, and I felt terrible for her feeling terrible about it!

"And our personal issues. And Brandon. And career . . . nothing feels safe anymore, Janete. And moving to a new state where I know nothing and no one is the insulation I need for a while. I gotta start over. *We* . . . gotta start over. I died. I'm not back yet and need to get back to being *here*."

"But the doctors tell you it can't get any better. Everything you learned says it's permanent. You've come a long way, but you say it's no better on the inside since day one."

"Whatta they know? I'm having a supernatural event way outta their league. This ain't medical. They also told you I'd never wake up. They also said I'd be a vegetable. All I can tell you, Janete, is that my leaving here and trying is *what's next*."

I had barely mentioned my relationship with The Portal to her and not at all to any others. I had made attempts to explain the phenomena and features, but the ineffability along with her somewhat illiterate condition *and* my reduced ability to articulate made it too daunting and made me sound crazy. The Portal, my Past-Life Reviews and Regressions, my clarity of paranormal realities . . . *the severity of my inner confusion and dysphoria* . . . were mostly private. I was not hording nor keeping secrets. I just could not explain things so others could understand. I was completely isolated in this experience.

***

The preparation to depart was complicated:

- I owned a home;
- I leased an office;
- Two cars, my motorbike; and
- Brandon, Janete, and a community, all of whom I served and did not want to abandon.

But my practice was barely alive: I'd gone from full days every day with a small waiting list to a few clients a week. My office was a $950-a-month writer's den now.

And I wasn't just moving down the block or across town. I was relocating 1,200 miles away to an entirely new region. I had to prep my home for sale, get out of my office lease, and pack a 1,900-square-foot home of stuff I and my son had lived with there for fifteen years.

I did *not* know if moving away would allow a reboot of my romantic and parenting relationship. I only knew for a fact, that if I stayed, it would *never* recover. It was approaching points-of-no-return, and we needed to stop the bleeding.

I was doing what The Portal agents advised me to do: it's *what's next*. Go to Mt. Rainier.

This decision was firm and clear from a *spiritual* perspective. I was in anxiety all the time in the *worldly* perspective. The actual practical thought of moving and leaving all I once knew behind was frightening. But I felt an inner peace and relief when I imagined it and worked at preparing for it. It was supported by a clear intuitive sense as well as plenty of so-called signs, which I really appreciated but didn't need.

Whatever God/Guru/Portal told me to do, I would do, with or without *signs*. But I kept getting them.

- First, the finding of the house. That was huge signage!
- I was let out of my office lease without fees.
- Able to cancel subscriptions and memberships (tennis club, cable TV, etc.).
- Subtle and not so-subtle needs and preferences were available in my new locale.

- Moving arrangements, packing, and prepping things kept lining up without interference. That *never* happens!
- It was a seller's market for selling my LA home.

Most of all was the feeling of clarity that was a unique and specific brand of The Portal's support. Whenever I thought of going to the PNW, I felt relieved, and whenever I doubted or considered staying, I would get a different set of signs: a neighbor would do something offensive, a local utility or client would misbehave. . . . Something would go wrong that was unique to SoCal, and something would go right in the moving process. The "I" of body and mind wanted to stay, the "I" of spirit and *citta* consciousness felt peace with the directive to leave.

But material "I" was terrified.

I was not ignorant to the objective view: I was a man with severe brain trauma, struggling to get by every day, experiencing several of the worst and most trying events in the human spectrum (heartache, breakup, loss of career, alienation . . .) who was adding kerosene to the stress-fire by relocating his entire life to a totally foreign place *alone*.

What the fuck was I thinking?

I wasn't just moving 1,200 miles north to where I hoped I'd enjoy the scenery and weather more. I wasn't just reacting to the rat-race in my late forties to live in the country. I was going to leave everything I had known for decades to live *alone* on four acres in remote country, nearly an hour away from the nearest grocery, while experiencing severe brain trauma.

If someone, like a client, asked me to advise them on this idea, I would've used my accredited, respected, credentialed status to have them put on a seventy-two-hour psyche hold. I was terrified, yet the clarity of what was *next* was crystal to me. But was I possibly experiencing DAI-TBI delusions? That was certainly the more credible theory! This is only something someone does if they are *cray-cray-crazy*.

Even in the pink of health, this sort of transition is barely surmountable. A move of this magnitude has huge challenges and risks even in healthy circumstances! Yes . . . I gave consideration my choices and decisions were statistical products of TBI. I said to Brandon, "I don't know if I'm going to end up alone in a trailer park with Howard Hughes crazy-fingernails or get better and find my fortune as an author of great work and make bank off my addiction work. I only know it's *what's next*."

A private doesn't ask his sergeant *why or what for:* a private follows orders. Akashic Agents are my generals: They never order me, but whatever they suggest is always what they are actually telling me is best. *I accept it as "what's next."*

It may seem my *support team* should've had an intervention and tried to stop me. And truth is, the human part of me was doing this as a plea for help. I was sad when no one—not my son, not my partner-wife, her kids, all of whom I had enriched the lives of over and over again—didn't say, *"Please, don't go."*

If Brandon or Janete said to me, *"Please, don't go. I love you and don't want you to be so far away. I need you near to me,"* I would've stayed. But they didn't.

They would both confess later this was because of my determined reputation. The guy that got clean off dope on his own, changed father's rights in Superior Court, started two successful businesses from dust and dirt, had saved lives as a counselor, and led many to higher truths was a man who was going to do what he wanted, and no one was going to stop him.

"But you didn't even try." I later wept. I was *so hurt* they were letting me go. I was like that little kid making threats of running away. The little boy who has put his teddy bear and a peanut butter and jelly sandwich into a kitbag over his shoulder while holding the door open, weepily declaring, "That's it. I'm really going now. Don't try to stop me . . ." obviously wanting Mom and Dad's validation in a "No, son! Please, don't go! We *love* you! We were wrong to make you eat your peas! We see that now! Please stay!" drama.

I had actually done this exact thing when I was four. My mom asked me if I got everything and reminded me to take a blanket because it would get cold at night. "Yeah, I got it. And my pillow too!" I sobbed. She didn't tell me not to go but offered me a last meal, implying it would be smart and mature to accept before a life of fending for myself. It was dark when I'd finished the mac and cheese, so she suggested I wait till morning to get a fresh start in the daylight. *She was smooth.*

The fact remained my inner-pain was compounded to an acute suffering by them not pleading for me to stay. It had been less than twenty-four months since my death, less than twelve since I had been in the hospital with severe complications. Less than six months since my partner broke my heart. Someone should've said, *Yeah, no. You're nowhere near healthy or stable enough to be on your own 1,200 miles away.*

We all wanted it to be in the past, but it was an eternal present and having me around was probably like a big bruising reminder of how different life had become and would never be the same. Somebody should've stopped me: told me they love me and please don't go. God that hurt, being deprived of that. I felt they'd be happy without me around, all broken: out of sight out of mind. So I was going to take one for the team.

Brandon was supportive: he was involved in my process enough to be sure I was being lucid and that it was what I truly wanted. And it's not a son or daughter's job to make demands or question a strong parent. A good son is supportive in crisis, not challenging. As weak and shattered as I was, it always *appeared* I was ok.

"It's near impossible to know, Brandon." He knew absolutely nothing specific of the dramas of my love-relationship, other than Janete and I were not ok as a couple. "It's *what's next*. I know that for the first time ever, you and I cannot communicate. You're in a phase of life that makes you need to live outside my shadow. And I've cast a long shadow. I cast a long shadow of innovational living to inspire and motivate you to find your own way. I think the best thing for *me* to do in *our* relationship is get out of the way. I represent a sense of security and protection you no longer need, and so long as it's there, you won't expand on your own entirely. You need space."

"Yeah . . . I get that. You've given me all I need, Dad. It's up to me to make it work and use it now. You've taught me what you can for now. I gotta move on. Just like baseball: you used to explain the most complicated things of life in baseball metaphors. You coached my little league and then my pony ball teams until I was in high school. Then it was handed over to high school coaches and up to me to make it work without you."

"And you went varsity all-star. Exactly. For now, my *coaching* you is *temporarily* over. My role ain't nowhere near over; I'll always be accessible to you, but you need your own space to make it your own. We'll always be father and son. But we need to start to transition to *individual* father and *independent* son."

Janete was similarly supportive: not cheering me on to leave, but not protesting nor doubting me. I had disclosed to her similar sentiment on that plane ride to show her where I planned to heal.

"I've done what I can. I've shown you the magic of life and love. I've taught you how it all works and empowered you to self-reliance. Now you can see what Mt.

Whitney was all about. These last days have been the epilogue to our life together these eleven years, which is just one set of chapters. We're not done. It's up to us to make these tragedies a triumphant footnote to our overall story. Assuming I heal from brain and relationship trauma, we have more to do. Having doubts and struggles with each other is natural and even needed. But we can *use* this to reach a higher octave of love and appreciation for each other. That which does not end us can make us stronger. It's up to us, Janete."

"I know. And you're right; it needs to be done." Her hand on my leg, eyes, and smile shining toward me, "For both of us. I still love you, Scott. I always will. You've done more for me than anyone ever has or ever will. I am who I am now because of what you've done."

"I'm just getting started."

That phrase was another personal axiom: I'd always felt, in every phase of my life, that I was just getting started. I *never* wanted to feel completion. I *always* wanted to feel the passion of beginning new goals.

***

The owners in Yelm agreed to let me visit the home to get some measurements so I could plan a move-in strategy. It wasn't actually necessary, but it worked to let me show the house to Janete. She loved the house, which made me warm. We went for a brief tour of the area. I wanted her to see I was fine and making smart choices and to see how beautiful WA is so she would look forward to visiting her long-distance boyfriend.

"Think of it like this: many people have affairs to fend off stagnation in their lives. Don't we all want to have a private, secret lover who we see without complications? Someone we don't need to see *every* day and hear their tired stories and vent ours? Let's have an affair: we'll be each other's lovers. Living our own lives in our own homes and meeting the obligations of life that suck and are complacent while having a lover 1,200 miles away to look forward to. And when we get together, we'll just keep it simple, raw, and fun. No working things out. Just dating long distance. We can be each other's sanctuaries. That's how we did it when it was fresh. Let's start anew and make it a romantic getaway."

We both enjoyed the idea, and her family accepted that if anyone could do this, the King and Queen of Unconventional could do it.

Moving Day

January 1, 2016. I figured moving in the dead of winter was best to acclimate in the harshest of times. Why not do the hard stuff when the weather's bad? That way, I'll be settled in by spring and be able to enjoy it all.

Brandon flew up with me to sleep on the two sofas I'd bought while we waited for the moving truck to arrive. He was elated and impressed: Washington is a gorgeous, giant land of forests, lakes, and waterways. He put his back into the work and helped me set up what the movers brought in. We both enjoyed the nostalgia: packing and unpacking the articles of our lives was emotional and revealing. The box of his Cub Scout awards of pinewood derby, archery, and others made me cry. The box where I stored our decade-plus of memorabilia from countless Dodger games and our own team jerseys, his as ballplayer and mine as coach, along with his trophies from T-ball to pony-ball, let us bond big. These stored memorabilia declared the end of a time: his youth was over, the past twenty-plus years was a gorgeous chapter coming to a close. The next chapter was yet to be wrote.

***

I co-resided at both. I'd spend two weeks in Yelm, WA, and one in LA. I was trying to transition slowly to ease us all into it. I also had a lot of work to do to prep my LA house for sale. All I'd left in LA was a few boxes of clothes, a bed, and a chair, so it would be mostly empty to repair, restore, and repaint the house for buyers.

I traveled back and forth with brain trauma and death experience confusion. I was often disoriented.

"Where am I?" I asked my son at 2 a.m. I could not fathom where I was, but I knew him and called as I woke confused.

"You're in Washington, Dad."

"I am? How'd I get here?"

Groggily, he consoled me, "You moved there. It's ok. You were very smart about it. You did your research, packed all your stuff, and I flew up with you to help you move in last month."

Unlike the Wuhan, China, simulation, I would reorient to the basics within a few minutes. I had woke in the middle of the night, in the dark, not knowing who I was or where I was. I didn't know where else I *could* or *should be* either. I could not access references of my identity, making it feel like when I'd first come back from within The Portal, waking from the coma. I now retained who Brandon, Janete, and most others were day-to-day though, so I would call Brandon sometimes for clarity.

"Yeah, don't worry. . . It's all cool. You like it there. You got a great place. Go back to sleep, and we'll talk when it's light out."

Sometimes I cried back to sleep, sometimes I laughed. Alone.

Every day was like a puzzle, like a scavenger hunt, where I needed to work with the basic materials around me to gain insight to who and where I was. I didn't let it bother me much. I'd be in the grocery store with zero recall as to why I was there. Sure . . . that can happen to anyone to some degree, but I would be walking down an aisle and not even remember *going there,* let alone what I needed. All the other shoppers in the store and cars on the roads were having very normal experiences: *boring!* Me? I was having an adventure, having to figure out where I was and why I was there. My life was filled with mystery.

I was also lonely and often confused. I felt abandoned and rejected by the two people I had been a pillar to. I felt the entire community I had served didn't give two shits I was gone: the traffic signals in LA still turned green to yellow to red on every corner, the garbage truck still came on Fridays, and Follow Your Heart Restaurant—*our place*—still served vegan dinner to couples on Saturday nights. It didn't seem to even notice I was gone.

But I'd been gone for over two years now, since June 19 of 2013.

As my partner and I had got in the car for the airport, I am mindful to acknowledge this momentous moment: I had lived in this home over fifteen years. Brandon was a child and has become a young man. Remnants of a dozen Halloween Haunts held in the garage for trick-or-treaters haunt the space. The wire hooks dot the eaves where dad and son climbed the roof to provide signal lights to Santa. The fireplace I installed without permits that my lover and I have shared countless poems by; our nudity of body and spirit making us vulnerable to one another. The annual Christmas Eve open-houses, the alchemy lab I used to turn grapes to intoxicating spirit and nearly blew up the house with my ambitious concoctions, the post-season

BBQs of ten years of coaching pony ball, the sessions of fatherly-advice given freely to my lover's two children, and the laughs we shared poking fun at each other as they marveled at my floor of clear plastic sheets the kids named "lake-floor," and the glasscrete sheets covering the walls for an eclectic place to hang out and be unusual. This exit is not the last time I will see the place as I will be coming back and forth to prepare it for sale, but it is an end of an era. I allow a few tears to fall upon the palm prints embedded in the concrete at the end of the driveway that says 10-31-98; the day we moved in.

The quantity and magnitude of the last twenty- months is an obscuring cloud. I've died, reborn, learned to talk, learned to walk (twice), learned love, and lost love.

I have a timeshare resort within The Portal and a house with walls in the world, and I have been in a spell trying to coexist in both.

My karmas and fates have been kicking my ass, and I keep getting up and trying. I no longer know if I'm nearing the finish line or . . .

Am I just getting started?

END OF ACT I

ACT II

EXILE TO THE GARDEN

THE MIDDLE WAY OF THE END

00.

ALIVE AND DEAD

> A mind completely attached to God attains God Realization.
> —Ved Vyas (Bhagwatam)

> Even atheists are seekers of God. To seek happiness
> is to seek God.
> —Kripalu Maharaj

I try to remain positive. I try to find and tap inspiration. Was I *not* meant to come back from death? Are these events causing renewable suffering trying to fix a glitch in The Matrix?

I can't figure it out anymore. I don't know where I begin and trauma ends. I don't want to fight anymore because all it seems to do is cause cosmic forces to come at me harder and stronger. I'm not strong. I was once, but I am no longer.

I was an overachieving, alpha-omega man capable of manifesting his destiny. Cosmic forces apparently had enough of my shit and decided to show me, once and for all, who's really in charge.

You win. I surrender.

All my fighting and determination were my way of surviving. I didn't mean anything by it. I never considered myself special or magical. I just tried to get by and be safe, not homeless, alone, or unhealthy. It wasn't pride. I overachieved because doing more is what always kept me even. I put forth a pound of effort for ounces of results. It worked, so I put in a ton of effort and got pounds of results. I didn't mean anything by it. It wasn't hubris; my arrogance was unintentional.

Ever since I was born in 1966, all I wanted was to get into a rocket ship and leave this world for a Xanadu. I was aware upon world-entry I didn't want to be here. I wanted to be in some dimension I couldn't locate or identify.

Being here beyond my control, I made the most of it. I tried to find the cool things, the haughty things, the things I perceived had meaning and depth. I never tried to be "*happy*." I had no interest in such shallow irrelevancies. I tried to live in pursuit of fulfillment instead.

Now I am neither: I have no happiness and can no longer achieve anything fulfilling.

I'm not moving to the Garden to live. I'm moving to die.

In peace. Solitude. Privately. I've let everyone down.

I died and am unable to return. Half of my mind and spirit exist in a different dimension altogether. The half that returned can't figure it out and it doesn't want to. Its best parts are just okay, and all lead to disappointment.

I desire spirit now. Nothing else. But I'm barred from that, too. Half my half-mad mind wants worldly desires, preventing me from living spiritually. The other half craves spiritual desires, prohibiting me from worldly ones. They are in conflict. They both insist it's either one or the other. And I am not wise enough, strong enough, smart enough to fool them into getting along.

In the Akashic space within The Portal, I understand everything clearly and am desireless. The moment I am back in the world of matter, I am unsure of my course and shrouded by desires. Within The Portal, I am at peace with total acceptance. In the mortal world, I am unsure and have needs. Inside The Portal, my only desire is to please my Swamini Goddess of Divine Love. I don't care if I remain here or return to matter. . . . I don't care, so long as it pleases Her. Within The Portal, I am spirit; in the world, I am matter that doesn't matter.

I am neither a full-time resident of the spirit realm nor the worldly realm. I'm a fugitive of both. When awake in the world, I behave as a human—I eat, shower, buy groceries, and sleep, albeit restlessly—but I am aware that I only partially exist. I feel whole when my mind is dormant to the world but active within The Portal.

The lines blur; I have trouble knowing if my actions are in my current life or a former one. The intermittent cinema of past lives overlaps with the drama of contemporary life. I often have to reorient and remind myself that the people I am interacting with—grocery clerk, mail carrier, friend, lover—are not who and how *I* see them from their ongoing lifetimes and identities. They are modern people living in the present moment. Some days, the supernatural features of my mind not yet integrated with my body are fascinating and fun. Most of the time, it's just confusing and distracting. I live a parallel, dualistic experience; I'm not confined to the typical features of time and space most recognize as rules of the quantum world. I'm neither here ... *nor there...*

My life of Spirit within the Akashic space is sublime, but in the world I have a long way to go before it gets better.

My time within The Portal becomes clearer each day.

When a mind begins approaching the Godhead, it hears the Harmony of the Spheres. The diaphanous light of God's loving form surrounds it. And perhaps if it has surrendered its will and love, it will go beyond the harmony of the spheres and the sapphire, auric light and see the face of God.

I want to see beyond the ochre-orange Light and be with the source of the flute playing the harmony of the spheres. I want to see Her face.

GUARDIAN ANGELS: A PLAYFUL SAINT

> As soon as a devotee is willing to go to the ends of the earth for Spiritual
> Enlightenment, his guru appears nearby.
> —Paramahansa Yogananda   (*Autobiography of a Yogi*)

> I was sleeping (in the stupor of spiritual ignorance) since eternity,
> but the Grace of a *rasik* Saint has awakened me.
> —Kripalu—Siddhant Madhuri (pad-sankirtan)

God is Unknowable.

All religions and spiritual philosophies agree on this.

God is ineffable and exists beyond our capacity of understanding *unless* He imparts His Grace. With His Grace, the yogi devotee can know, merge, and become one with God.

Occasionally, an avatar arrives not to establish a *new* covenant as the Christ did, but to *reestablish* the Eternal Covenant, which has always existed in every space of this multiverse.

The reasons the Godpower avatars are uncountable, but one of the most valuable for we stupid-humans, is so we can *directly associate with the Divine in a personal relationship*.

It's pretty impossible to *love* God when He appears as a burning bush or pillar of fire. Avatars—that is, Gurus—are God making Himself or Herself accessible in *personified* forms we can see, speak to, hear, and serve. My own personal Guru—the enlightened, divine personality, avatar whom I've followed since 2007—is in charge of my particular circumstances.

There have been many, including the Buddha and the Christ. Some are eternally divine but may appear as ordinary people. Once you begin associating with them, you may sense there's something extraordinary about them. True avatars conceal their divinity, but over time, it becomes revealed within your heart.

Some remain secluded to radiate Grace to regions of the planet, while others come forth, interact with humanity, and illuminate the paths to True Spirit.

I now know...

The saffron-ochre presence when I died was my personal teacher and guide, *Guru*. Orange robes, or *dhoti kurta*, are the traditional dress for spiritual personalities in India. Like the white collar for catholic priests and jerseys for athletes, it is so we can recognize them as such. I was too disabled to see His Divine eyes and face, and I think I lacked worthiness. But His boundless presence provided the love and comfort I felt.

No one else can save me. I don't want to be saved; I want to move on. Not only has Guru been present through these ordeals, He is the architect and the engineer. He's in charge, but I kept getting in the way of His work by trying to improve my life and restore it to what it had been before.

Jagadguru Shree Kripalu Maharaj. 1922-2013

Scott died. It's time to move on. Let the Architect and Engineer have free reign. Let go and let Guru.

What is a *guru?*

The word is a title meaning *he who chases away samsara* A True Guru is an Enlightened, *Realized* soul beyond material consciousness. I often use the term True Guru, with a capital T and capital G to differentiate between *regular* gurus and real-deal ones. Our world is full of frauds, fakes, and even those who are well-intended but lack the full qualifications to fulfill their title. Any teacher of spiritual path, knowledge, and practice deserves the title of guru, *but in lowercase.* I am using capitals to denote when I am referring to *regular* things and *genuine* things. Genuine referring to their transcended Enlightened state and status: They are ONE with Divinity.

I accept Yeshua the Christ, Gautam Buddha, and a few others as genuine, Realized masters.

Synonyms for a True Guru are *parush* (pah-roosh): *cosmic-being*; *mahaparush*: *great-cosmic-being* and *jivatman* (jeev-aht-mahn): *supreme soul. Swami* means *master or teacher*, yogi is a yoga practitioner, *maharaj* is a *great king* or *lord*, and *mahatma* is a *great soul.*

It is customary to add the suffix *-ji* (jee) for informal affection. An Indian child may refer to his father as papa*ji;* you may refer to your friend Bob as Bob*ji*. We use the *-ji* suffix to reverential titles, too: Swami*ji* is not just *a* swami but an informal and more affectionate term for a swami. Mahara*ji* is a more intimate, less formal address of *mahraj.*

 Cool... now that we got a little vocab out of the way, let's briefly discuss what true ones are and what They're *not* so you can easily grasp the contexts of these roles as our story moves along. This is important because I am suggesting that my Guru is the Engineer and Architect of my NDE and much more.

A True Guru is invested in your spiritual welfare and journey, and the Akashic Agents are your Guru's representatives that interact and facilitate. I have a Guru, *and so do you,* although you may not be aware of it, but you do have one. We all do. We all have a personal, divine associate personal to *us.* A Divine Personality, or Guru, is devoted to and protects many souls, but each of us has only one Guru. He or She watches over us in each and every lifetime we incarnate and in between, too. Our Guru is always ready and waiting to appear in our lives when we turn our hearts and minds to spiritual matters instead of worldly ones.

The way a Guru becomes *your* Guru is simple. It happens when you mindfully and heartfully accept them as your Guru and devote your spirit to Them. There is no formal ceremony or application process. I like this axiom very much: *your Guru is as close to you as you are now, and They are waiting, with open arms, to receive you. All you have to do is go to Them.*

A True Guru, or *maha*parush, is a Divinely Realized being. Their souls grace the Earth; their presence is not bound by material consciousness or desires because they have transcended them. Since they have no worldly desires, they are entirely free to impart wisdom, love, and grace selflessly and without cause. *If* they have any desire at all, it is only to Grace the souls with Love and Truth. They exist in a state of complete and total self-contentment, peace, and bliss. They are omniscient and omnipresent; they have access to *all* knowledge, *all* the time, and are not confined to the eternal present of the here and now. They are One with the Divine yet they appear and behave like mortal folks. They *conceal* Their divinity.

There are two classes of *Gurus: sadhana siddhi* saints and *nitya siddhi* saints. Sadhana siddhi saints were once like you and me; they were human, embodied souls with minds bound to karmas and material phenomena of maya or samsara. Through sadhana, or spiritual practice and surrender, they became enlightened and completed their Souls' Journeys to Divinity. Sadhana means *spiritual practice* like yoga, and siddhi means *enlightened or attained*. Therefore, sadhana siddhi saints have *attained enlightenment through sadhana*.

Nitya siddhis are souls that have *never* been under the veil of material phenomena; they are *Eternal Associates*. The word *nitya* means *eternal*.

Neither is superior to the other because, once you're divine, you're divine, and that's that: you're perfect. But most sadhana siddhi saints ascend to a divine abode when they leave this Earth and remain there in eternal bliss. Nitya siddhi saints regularly descend to the planet to teach, guide, and grace us wretched souls.

Here's a bold statement. Spiritual or religious sadhus accept The Buddha as a *nitya* siddhi who appeared and *behaved* like a *sadhana* siddhi to teach a path by example; he seemed to convey the message that *if I can do it, so can you, and here's how.* Yet, *Buddhists* view Him as a sadhana siddhi, a regular man who *became* Enlightened.

Many spiritualists suspect Jesus was a sadhana siddhi. He began as a man who was very spiritually evolved with many lifetimes of prior yoga work and attained Divine Realization in the life we know of. The organized, business-like church established He was not only a nitya siddhi but *the only* nitya siddhi.

The Western religious business model was to make their Guru the only one of all time and for eternity. This idea is called *appropriation!* They plagiarized the entire guru concept, tweaked His story with a crapload of fictional elements to fit a monopolistic religion, and completely omitted His eighteen years of sadhana in Iraq,

Persia, and India. Another story for another time... My next book will explore the Underground Stream's origins and practices of our world's religions and spiritual paths: *all of them! And the true stories are more beautiful than the fictional ones!*)

There is no way to truly convey the complete concepts of divine personalities or actual spiritual phenomena. Details always get lost in translation and misrepresented by people who have good intentions but are still material beings attempting to explain divine things. Two things are essential for Spiritual understanding: a God Realized teacher and a sincere student. Divine concepts such as mono-dualism are ineffable and often seem paradoxical when expressed in the world.

The term mono-dualism is completely contradictory. How can something—*anything*—be simultaneously joined *and* separate at the same time? Same with karma, fate and free will. They automatically contradict each other yet coexist. In the *worldly* realm, paradoxes can only exist in theory. But in the *spiritual* realm, they are Absolute. As stupid-humans, we can't relate.

"But, Krishnanand, doesn't that mean most of what you're saying here is wrong? By your own logic, as a material being who has not yet attained Enlightenment, you can't accurately convey Spiritual Truth."

Yes. *And no.* I am careful in my composition to convey to you *directly* what I have learned, gained, and received. I am not embellishing or adding my *own* spin to it. The only latitude I take is when giving material examples, analogies, and metaphors to clarify an idea with more accessible terms. I learned this technique from my Guru! As mentioned before, anytime I offer you *my own* perspective on spiritual matters, I qualify it as such: *I was not told this, but...* or, *my own theory on this is...* Yeah, I'm not going to bad karma hell for being irresponsible by misrepresenting spiritual knowledge. I hear that dimension of hell is pretty crowded, and I *hate* crowds!

The way we stupid-humans can identify a True Master/Guru is through scrutiny. Doubt is not a sin or transgression. A True Guru expects doubt and even encourages us to apply close examination when determining whether a guru or spiritual path is legit. In the beginning, *you better!* The forest of spirituality is dark and thick, so we gotta be careful not to get lost!

A True Buddha or Mahaparush must have specific qualifications as taught in the Sanskrit texts:

- Constant involvement with, and only concern for, spiritual affairs, not material ones
- Everything they teach concurs with and is verifiable by Eternal knowledge and text—Vedas, Upanishads, Shastras, and other authentic scriptures specific to a path's religion and origins
- They will always present teachings *along* with scriptural truth; it's never just their *personal* ideas
- They provide not just knowledge and theory but also practices and actions to fulfill the spiritual goal.
- They Grace; with trust, surrender, and association; you will *feel* and *know* Grace, slowly at first for most, then more so as you associate, practice their teachings, and surrender to them over time
- They give Grace: the inner results you experience (love, peace, bliss, certainty, etc.) are not produced by *you!* As I mentioned, recovering from my accident was a miracle; *I may have done the work, but God graced me with results.* A sadhu meditates and practices what they've learned, but the results they experience are bestowed upon them by their teacher's Grace

The first burning question becomes: What's Grace? How will I recognize it when it is given?

Unfortunately, the answer is the same as what we tell a young person who asks how they will know when they fall in love: *you'll know.* Those who have been in love before know this is a valid answer. Those who've not will feel cheated by that answer until they fall in love; then it's crystal clear, and they *"get it."* There is an undeniable quality to love that is ineffable yet irrefutable and universal. You know it when you get it.

It's the same with Grace. No sadhu can tell you *what* it's like, but you sure will know it when you get it.

Love for your favorite food is a type of love; Love for your pet is definitely love. But they are on different planetary octaves altogether. Romantic love has a unique quality separating it from all others. And parental love? Fuhgeddaboudit! It's not just unique in flavor, baby; it's an entirely different animal! It ain't about quantity and not quite about quality either, as in more/less, better/best. Every type of love is different, yet they're all from the same wellspring. Divine Grace experienced through God and Guru is unmistakable. But be careful what you wish for; once you taste its nectar, you can never live without it!

All Divine Personalities from the beginning of time have taught about the Soul's Journey and how to reach its destination. The Soul's Journey is to attain God Realization: to transcend material consciousness and become One with God. Think about it; Christianity, Hinduism, Buddhism, Islam, and others all teach the same goal of Eternal Union with God in their distinct ways. And each has a Guru: Jesus for Christians, Mohammad (pbuh) for Islam, Gobind Singh for Sikhs, and so on. There ain't a single True religion or path without a founder or Guru except Sanatan Dharm because it is Eternal and doesn't have an origin. The original Guru of Hinduism is the Supreme Lord Himself, who goes by many names.

I could compose volumes describing what a Guru is and is not. I'm doing my best to briefly give you some context as it relates to this memoir. If this account inspires and moves you to seek further, *seek and ye shall find;* long for your Master to appear in your life, and They will. They will lead you to Them in fun and serendipitous ways!

Now let's return to the Wayback machine and go back in time, before my death and afterlife.

The Serpent Rises

In 1992, I experienced a cataclysmic, mind- and life-altering Kundalini activation. This event is intensely documented in my first memoir and is its climactic closure. Whatever most of you think about Kundalini is *wrong*.

There are very few actual accounts of Kundalini and a shit-ton of people who have had some minor, and some major, psychic awakening events that they *think* was Kundalini. As with the mahaparush concept, this is neither the time nor place to *fully* explore and explain Kundalini activation. If you're not sure you had a Kundalini event, you didn't. If you read Gopi Krishna's biography, *Kundalini: The Evolutionary Energy in Man*, and you can fathom and fully relate to what he's talking about, you *might've* had a real-deal one.

It is a conscious-altering, expanding event few survive without going mad. It is far more than an internal sensation: my entire body was involved with the sensations and many were *oh-my-god painful*. You actually, physically *feel* your consciousness *expanding*. It is not a subjective metaphor: it is a wild sensation, feeling the fabric of your consciousness physically stretch and expand. It is accompanied with intense physical sensations throughout the body as the primordial energy courses through your 114 chakras and jangles awake the main seven, ringing a quasi-omniscience into your sahasrara chakra in your pineal gland. I could not feel the top of my head for months—like it just wasn't there!

Prior to this event, I was on dope. A lot of dope, almost all the time. My psychedelic and entheogen experimenting went awry, and I became embroiled in mere pleasure-seeking narcotics. I had been involved with the supernatural and occult for most of my life, as described in the Underground Stream chapter earlier. My first memoir, *A Stone's Throw*, explores much of my mystical-bent and occult involvement as it follows my descent from spiritual pursuit into hedonistic drugs, sex, and gangster-life and emerging from it with a spiritual renewal of higher octaves. The catalyst of my sobriety and new spiritual pursuits was this Kundalini event.

By the time my Tantric Initiatress gave me a supernatural blowjob activating my Kundalini, I was *into* mysticism but had yet to really, responsibly *practice* it. Once my crown chakra blew the top of my head off with Kundalini power, I went from passionately interested in mystical things to virtually obsessed. I didn't know what the fuck was even happening to me with this Kundalini thing until I searched randomly, leading me to the texts and knowledge as to what it was rewiring my entire brain, nervous system, and my thinking and feeling apparatus!

I now know me and my initiatress in *this* life had more than dabbled in it together in previous lives. This made my Kundalini force already quasi-active: a little nudge (four hours of Tantric-yog-sex!) put it in overdrive!

Is it possible my Kundalini event was a byproduct of psychedelic experimentation? That NDE is a delusional byproduct of TBI?

Nope.

Do I seem irrational, illogical, unscientific, fantasy-thinking, or that I subscribe to blind faith? As a professional working with mentally impaired clients, I can assure you many of them are prodigiously smart and sensible too. However, the difference is they aren't capable of writing books and building houses: most of them can't even support themselves. But hey! Take your pick! Categorize me as TBI-crazy or NDE-illuminated; whichever suits you!

During the time of my Kundalini Initiation, I was in the midst of a profound, complex, and spellbinding past-life-regression too. It went on for months. Throughout my mystical career, past-life regression has been an accessible feature:

if I wanted to astral-travel through space and time, I had been trained to do so and practiced it well enough that I could, with varying results, but always effective.

As my Kundalini settled down and the event began to stabilize a little, I applied myself to study and develop it. I was also a new father, finally off of dope, and trying to navigate through custody and establishing not only sobriety but a career so I could get out of apartment life and give my son a home to grow up in.

In my spare time, I kept pursuing and developing my Kundalini consciousness: meditating with Tantric techniques nearly every day, fasting, and using rituals and other formula to cleanse my mind and get raw with consciousness and body.

Wat Thai of LA

"Yes, yes! I know... it's so paradoxical!"

"Right?! The very progress you make is what cancels it out!"

"And that's the challenge of Nirvana." The Buddhist, temple-monk sighs. "It is within the paradox where we find the peace."

The Wat Thai Buddhist temple twenty minutes south of my suburban home is a grand palace: elaborate and traditionally ornamented. In the main meditation hall are several alcoves five feet above the ground where monks will meditate, giving visitors the opportunity to view them while they strive for samadhi—the state of *no mind*. I have visited the temple many times, but today I seek advice from a fellow meditator. This monk indulged my inquiry and sharing:

"I get into deep trance pretty regularly. Whether a candleflame or a yantra, I can get to the point of losing sense of time and space. The physical space between myself and the focal point evaporates, but as I feel my '*self*' dissolve, merging with the focal point, I get *excited!* And that blows it!"

"Yep, your '*ego*' dissolves, and then your awareness of your ego dissolving brings you back to ego-awareness. That's as far as I've ever gotten. But you say this is regular for you now, right?"

It is refreshing to speak in depth to an Eastern spiritualist who's Western, like me. His oriental origins are in his eyes, but his speech is accentless. "Few times a week. When I can pull it off, I fast for four, five days with meditation sessions every one to two hours. Those can get intense. But those are even more ecstatic. I'm not in samadhi-trance during many of those so much as immersive profundity. It feels good, but it's not no mind."

Then he said something that jangled my nerves.

"How? How do you do this? I am in meditation four to five hours at a time, several days a week. I have only felt the merging of my consciousness with a focal point a few times. I can't advise you; you're way ahead of me." His regret to me was sincere, and we both bonded over an epiphanic moment he voiced for the both of us. "It seems we're not doing anything wrong. We need to practice and try—*to not try*—to let go of expectations. To try—*to not try*—to detach from the results and let go of the bliss-joy to revel within indifference."

"I agree. We have both been taught that it is the final stage of transcendence; to let go of the bliss-joy of mind-*fulness* to come to rest at mind-*lessness*. It causes me to question if it is truly what I want to arrive at: *nothingness or everythingness*."

My Maharaji would enter my life soon after this and tell me: "Samadhi is like being submerged in water to escape a swarm of bees. While submerged, the stings of maya cannot harm you. Eventually, you have to come to the surface, and the bees are waiting." With the Grace of my boundless Guru whom I'd yet to meet that day, my choice would be clear: *everythingness*.

I researched Kundalini to college degree levels. I've done the same with TBI and NDE too: all I share on any subject is only after a lot of research so I don't misrepresent such sensitive areas of knowledge.

This led me to sampling occult societies as I desired to associate with others who sought illumination as I did. I explored many and got attracted to Thelema, Hermeticism, and Western esotericism. My involvement with mystical societies was fulfilling and enjoyable: I had a great time associating with intelligent, highly cerebral initiates, practicing ceremony, and studying the philosophy within the Ordo Templi Orientis, founded in 1895 by Aleister Crowley. I took three initiations and became quite adept at ritual magick and familiar with Order of the Golden Dawn, Enochian Magic, Blavatsky's Theosophy, and completed the aforementioned Master Alchemy course, and others. All of these mystical modalities served to enhance and fully activate the Kundalini power.

My outer life changed over these times: sobriety, parenthood, romantic commitment... These things folded well into my spiritual pursuits, certainly better than drugs, sexual escapades and a life of excess. *I was growing up: materially and spiritually.*

Those close to me knew my spiritual priorities very well and were welcome to participate if they wanted to, but I never pressured anyone to lean into them: I kept my spiritual life discreet, not secretive. Janete attended OTO meetings with me and we meditated together and she enjoyed learning the mysteries from me since she did not have the capacity for self-study of them. Brandon grew up around them but also was never forced beyond healthy encouraging.

After all this labor and sacrifice and mystical progress, I imagined how Siddartha Gautam felt before He became the Buddha: *frustrated.* Proficient and near mastering so many techniques, paths, and formula, I still remained bound by the material phenom—i.e., *suffering.* When Gautam, the *sadhu,* finally mastered all the yoga and sadhana techniques and realized He was still *stuck* in material consciousness, He went to Gaya, sat beneath the Boddhi tree, and refused to move until He achieved liberation from material suffering.

Well, I *couldn't* go sit underneath a freakin' tree for forty-nine days and nights to become Enlightened! I had a child! And a sexy, wonderful girlfriend! And my construction career at that time had thirty-plus employees!

In my despair, I lay in my bed one sunrise and wept aloud: "Goddammit! You come into my life—n*ow!* I can't live in this world without You present! I *need* You!" I wasn't praying or even begging God to enter my heart and mind, I *demanded* He do so! *Now*!

The surge and fire within my physical body and the spit and fervor spraying from my words and mouth were uncontainable! I had not an ounce or molecule left in my body as I demanded God enter my life: "In person! I am sick and tired of abstract concepts! I want and need to *feel* You! I need to *see* You! No fucking burning bush! No white fucking light! I want to *see and touch You! In person!"*

This went on for nearly an hour. Longing and needing to be connected with God's presence and power consumed me. There wasn't a molecule in my body not anguishing for Divine association. Eventually, I calmed down and got out of bed: lost and useless, moving like a worthless robot through the meaningless events of the day.

Lightning Strikes

A day or so later, while sitting in my office space at home, I whined about the same thing to the girl I loved. I diatribed over having *all* this knowledge and experience and training and how fucking useless it all was if I could not pull off the whole Enlightenment thing. I stubbornly sat under my own proverbial Boddhi tree, digging my heels in: I refused to move, try, or go forward with spiritual things without direct contact. I declared I would shove my entire alchemy lab in the fucking trash and set fire to my YHVH Hebrew yantras drawn upon the walls of my meditation room and destroy the magic circle in the center of its floor. *I was done.*

At the end of my tirade, I threw a magazine sitting on my desk across the room as emphasis. My very non-cerebral, quietly peaceful girlfriend calmy glanced at it while allowing me to rant uninterrupted. When I was out of breath, she picked up the magazine and commanded, "Here! Go to *this!* Stop bitching about it and go see how others are doing it and figure it out!"

This was in response to my final bitching that all my higher-learning was a waste and I should just start a cult: teach all this magical stuff as an adept, charge money, and bank off it. This was a moment of crisis in faith. Had my life of spiritual adeptship been a waste of time? Were the atheists right after all?

The thrown magazine had landed open to an ad: "*Divine Love Consciousness: come join us for a discourse on Divine Love Consciousness with live kirtan.*" And there was a day, time, and address with a photo of the presenter: some late-thirties woman in the orange robes of a Hindu monk.

Janete had this uncanny ability to say and suggest random things often panning out to something profound and beneficial: she was my muse. So we went that Thursday evening to what I assumed would be a group of wannabe mystics talking about the age of Aquarius and mercury being in retrograde ad nauseum.

Always giving the benefit of the doubt, I set aside my expectations and entered a casual office space with six or seven other people there and took a seat. I kept my mind and heart open, *just in case.*

Over the next *just forty minutes*, this woman in orange *blew my fucking mind!*

She opened by requesting, "Let's all close our eyes a moment." As we sat in silence behind closed eyes, she smoothly spoke a quite beautiful Sanskrit prayer, even if none of us had any idea what it meant. She invited us to open our eyes.

"Let's begin with a few minutes of *nam snakritan*. I'll be singing some of God's sacred and divine names, and you can all repeat it, like a call-and-response. If you prefer to remain silent, that's okay too. All this meditation requires is to listen to the names and imagine that God is close to you and God's love and grace is contained within the divine name."

She played a few notes on the portable organ, called a harmonium, and melodiously chanted, *Jai Shyama, Jai Shyama...* Her voice was simple and beautiful, and it was easy to get lost in it. Some repeated and sang back, some stayed silent, and I did a little both, wanting to honestly sample something before making up my mind in any way. It was a little awkward and a little pleasant.

She then spoke for about thirty-five minutes. As an adept who has consumed many of the most advanced mystical texts in volumes of materials, I am very familiar with how it all works and how complicated it is to explain. What she explained in just a half hour took the library of knowledge I had accumulated in my big head and simplified it down so a goddam child could understand it! She did this casually and easily! What has taken me decades to learn and understand, she presented in just a *portion* of her talk. Then she went beyond it, taking it all to a higher level I always suspected but had never accessed.

She deftly concluded her discourse, "Let's conclude with another few minutes of chanting and a moment of silence. We'll be singing Gopala Jai Jai. *Gopala* is one of God's names of His divine love form and Jai is kind of like a Sanskrit hallelujah." She played a sweet and simple melody and gave another call-and-response tune of a simple name of God, *Gopala Jai Jai*.

After a moment of silence, she bowed her head to folded prayer hands and thanked us for coming.

"Waddya think?" I whispered to Janete.

"I thought it was nice. Simple and sweet. I actually understood what she said." For Janete that was a glowing endorsement. Her ADD made most of what was taught inaccessible for her, which caused her pain and sorrow. "What did *you* think? Are you glad we came?"

"Oh. My. God! You have *no* idea! You know better than most how fucking complicated spiritual knowledge is! Egghead mystics go out of their way to keep it so cerebral they exclude anyone who isn't their intellectual peer. She did the complete opposite! What she just did in half an hour is what takes *hours and hours* to explain and understand!"

The woman monk-yogini, dressed in the simple orange robe of a sanyasi-renunciate, stood by the table displaying a few CDs and books for further knowledge. When there was a moment I addressed her, careful not to embarrass her with praise, "How'd you do that?"

"Do what?" She smiled with a sly chuckle.

"I've been studying mystical paths and methods for years and have read volumes of works. You just condensed all of them into a more correct and more useable set in just a half hour. How'd you do that? I'm impressed and a bit floored."

"Oh..." she replied innocently cool, "that's not *me* you're picking up on or learning from. That's my Guru."

"Ok... who's your guru? What do you mean?"

"I mean if you're feeling connection and anything profound by what we talked about or the kirtan, that's *His* knowledge and Grace reaching you. It's not me at all."

"I'd like to know more. Do any of these books here explain in more depth?" She suggested one or two of the five books on the table and recommended a CD teaching the basics and giving a guided meditation.

"What do you mean *your guru?* How do I find a guru?" I was very familiar with the concept after having read *Be Here Now* some months earlier, which permanently altered me. I did not yet know that when I'd read *Be Here Now*, it had activated that True spiritual longing moment I'd had leading to this very moment.

"You wanna meet him?" Again, she said these things to me with a wry smile and so casually, like saying in a sidebar *would you like the winning lotto numbers?*

"How would I meet Him?"

"He'll be in LA in a few weeks."

I thought if I was to ever meet an enlightened master, face-to-face, I would need to travel to Tibet and risk my life climbing Himalayan peaks. Here this very American, very un-ethnic, average-seeming white woman offered to introduce me to her spiritual Master. She was from Texas for 'f'-sakes!

I accept and get the details of place and locations and go home in a lustrous fog.

This group has weekly get-togethers called *satsang* on Wednesdays and Sundays to learn and practice this path. I start reading the plain and simple book with the cliché-looking, white-bearded, Indian Swami on the cover and listen to the CD with its guided meditation most nights at bedtime.

I had done something similar with Thelema and Alchemy: I fully immerse myself into a method or path to determine on a practical level if it has merit. I figure the only way to see if something is worthwhile or not is to truly try it. I have sampled many practices, and a few of them were legit but had only helped me progress a tiny bit further. Maybe if I kept adding them all up, the collection of *bit furthers* would add up to a final stage of expansion.

The satsangs were exotic and awkward being from India and me being a Westerner, but the book and CD blew my mind with the simplicity and trueness of what they revealed. This was not complicated equations of spiritual mathematics, not over-intellectualized, occult metaphors to decipher through initiations, but a sensible, practical, reasonable way to develop your mind and spirit. This *bhakti yoga* path wasn't relying on magic or ritual or even faith! It was all so fundamental, yet no one had ever expressed attaining God Consciousness with such simple practices and information.

I mean... I *love* kabbalah and have known for years that is a Western system for Kundalini yoga to attain mystical consciousness. But it is *complicated!* Personally, I love that! I like the challenge. But other than deepening my senses, it is very mysterious, and I wasn't exactly transcending and tripping the light fantastic!

Do What Thou Wilt

By the time I met the Swami, I had completed two of His smaller books and was deep into a third of His books. He was a simple and unassuming man. Being in His presence was calming and intense all at once.

About midway into His much larger, more thorough book on the whole philosophy, I sat one evening in the meeting space of my local Ordo Templi Orientis with several brother and sister initiates. We were planning and rehearsing a play and some ceremonies for an upcoming public presentation. I was well respected by the Order.

I had donated my time and labor to remodel their space and regularly gave classes on various mystical modalities. Janete and I had attended the three-day OTO conference in WA-DC just months ago. We were all exhausted from the meeting and the rehearsal, and I reclined in the dimly lit room with my back against a wall while seated on the floor as our Soror (sister) and center manager fine-pointed the meeting to break it up for the night.

And in my head was a voice. Actually, just a thought, but it wasn't mine, so it was perceived as a voice: *you don't need to come here anymore.*

I did not question or take a look around for the source or meaning. I simply said, "Okay." We all rose, said warm goodbyes to each other as usual, and I left, knowing I'd never be back. I knew it was this Guru I studied, *my personal guardian angel.*

I continued to read, study, and practice the Swami's material and attend their satsangs when it was convenient.

I felt I had come home.

Along with the two small books I'd purchased I got a CD: *An Introduction to Divine Love Consciousness.* It had a thirty-minute speech on the philosophy and a twenty-minute kirtan sung by Him in Sanskrit, which I didn't understand. The instructions said to listen to it daily while trying to imagine God being very close. I followed these instructions and went to bed each night listening to it. It was so subtle: the effect it had a sweet, clear sense of protection and love.

For the next several years, my Swamiji's literature was all I consumed, reading His books like they painted the Golden Gate Bridge—starting from one end to the other and beginning again from the start. His teachings were not His own: they were the teachings of His Divine Master and Guru and the elucidations of Shree Kripalu Maharaji's teachings of the Rasik path of Raganuga Bhakti Yog. Each time I read the massive treasure troves of Bhakti's dharmas, I gained something new, and this would go on for years.

As a writer, I still enjoy other works of literature, but I am endlessly satisfied with closing each bedtime reading session with books from a personal library of fun, exciting, mind-blowing, sweet explanations of the darshans. The personal library stashed within the closet of my meditation room, packed with volumes of Higher Truths. Each one would be entirely over my head if not for my Guruji's elaborations on Sanatan Dharm and His number-one disciple, my Swamiji's sharing the meaning.

I never turned *against* my OTO brothers and sisters, nor did I decide Thelema, Hermeticism, Alchemy, and all of my Western mystical practices and knowledge was *wrong* or in any way sinister. For me it was a progressive movement: organized, Western religions were like kindergarten, New-Age thinking was like middle-school. Western esotericism and occult are like university, undergraduate levels. And Eastern spiritual thought was graduate level, and this path taught by Rasik Saints as the highest form of yoga and Spiritual Realization is beyond Enlightenment and is *post*graduate.

The same became true for the Kundalini yog(a) path. As I devoured the Swami's books to learn all I could of Sanatan Dharm and bhakti yog(a), He revealed Sanskrit quotes confirming it would interfere with the ultimate attainment of God Realization. As profound and mind-expansive as my Kundalini experience and ongoing pathwork in it have been, I stepped away from it to dedicate all my effort to the Swami's teaching and this Guru's path. And the results became evident. Even if they hadn't, the truth is the truth; you know it when you see it, so Kundalini and other mystical modalities had become as useless to me as a bus stop when I have a paid-off and well-tuned automobile in the garage.

I love them all. I respect them all. I admire them all and have been adept at sailing the Underground Stream to discover the Truths of Western religions and esoteric formula and apply them. But as I have spent my lifetime sailing The Underground Stream to deeper, yet higher, waters, they all kept leading to an origin and essence.

Alchemy, Yoga, Buddha's Four Noble Truths, Kabbalah's Tree of Life with the ten sephiroth and twenty-two paths expressed in the Tarot... they all talked of the same thing just in different dialects. Now I find this living Guru, who's actually alive and on the planet, not some historical figure more myth and legend than history, who is proving God is simple to attain.

It would be some time before I connected the dots between the longing I had experienced and this gracious turn of events. That God is indeed actually something I can *attain:* face-to-face, in person, not abstract or conceptual like a burning bush or flash of lightning, but in a real and personified form. An intimate, loving, personal relationship in a tangible and personal experience.

Fuck light! Screw Angels! I don't want symbols, equations, or archetypes! I want to sit down and touch, talk to, and be with Absolute Love! No almighty, bearded, majestic, robe-wearing, commandment-shouting, fire-and-brimstone kind of King or Lord! I want us to be *friends!* I want us to be *lovers!*

And this is what the Bhakti path of yog is all about: a path of practices to clean your attitude, connect *intimately* to the Godpower, and realize you ain't never been worthy of Her, aren't now, and never will be, *yet she loves you completely and entirely anyway!* Bhakti yog was teaching me how to be God's lover and friend.

Yeah... *that's* what I'm talkin' about! *That's* what I want, and that's where I'm going. I don't care about heaven or paradise or kingdoms! I just want to be near and to love Her! The Bhakti yoga path within the religion called Sanatan Dharm— Eternal Truth, teaches a path of having a personal and intimate connection with God.

Surrender Thy Will

When you finally establish a relationship with a True Guru, they become your protector: not financially or physically; you can still go broke and get diseases, *so be smart and careful!* Your Guru is your *spiritual* protector: He/She will intervene in your life when necessary to give you access to the right knowledge and methods to develop spiritually and clean your shitty mind up. She/He will provide you with opportunities to serve Them and to commit your head and heart to your sadhana. They'll give you *access* and *opportunity:* it's up to you to follow it and do it!

What my Guru has been doing with and for me since I feebly surrendered my own stupid-human will and mind to Him is protecting my *spiritual* progress, even at the risk *and demolition* of my material progress!

God and Guru work together to eliminate your *material* attachments because attachments (i.e., desires, as the Buddha pointed out) interfere with an unobstructed, unalloyed connection with God. Material attachments are wide and include more than just things and money. Even our attachments to family and lovers are material, hence why one Guru, a guy named Jesus, said, "*Anyone who loves* their *father or mother more than me* is not worthy of *me; anyone who loves* their son or daughter *more than me* is not worthy of *me.*"

Sometimes these have friction: destroying my material attachments is good, but because I am so spiritually unevolved, too much can distract me from my sadhana as I cope with absolute suffering. I'm not spiritually mature enough yet to have total acceptance and appreciation of my material attachments being violently severed from me one after another! I *know* it's all for my own good and spiritual progress, but it hurts like *fuck* and I can't make myself *let go* of them. I'm just a stupid-human!

As my spiritual attachments grow and increase, they *displace* my material ones. I don't need to remove or detach from them most of the time. It's like a I have a glassful of material attachments, and as I pour spiritual attachments into the glass, the material ones just get displaced and pour out. My cup runneth over has taken on a meaning I hadn't considered.

God's got dozens of Catch-22s with all of us. You gotta surrender the very things you are the *most* attached to! Our specific attachments are unique to each: some love money, some love status, some love love! That's one of my biggies: I *love* being in love. I *love* loving my partner and my son. These worldly attachments can interfere with *unalloyed* love of spirit.

When I read *Be Here Now* by Ram Dass, I was thirty-five. I grew up with this funky, odd book around my house as a child. When my mom passed, it was given to me to keep. I came across it quite surreptitiously while in one of many spiritual funks: wanting more and feeling like I'd never find the light. I read a few pages, and it was fun and weird. My girlfriend and partner, Janete, was across the country visiting family, and when she came back she asked, "Oh my God... what the hell have you been up to? What is going on with you? I been gone just a week!"

I had thin blankets on the downstairs floor, no pillow for my head, no food in the house, and no music or TV had been on in days.

"I don't want to live for comfort anymore. I want to live in austerity. I don't want my life to be about worldly pleasure anymore. I want to study and learn the ways to God, find a Guru, and devote my life to enlightenment." This was all said with deadpan stoicism.

She assumed it was a passing phase (which it mostly was) and indulged my desire to not sleep in a cushy bed with pillows and luxury. *Be Here Now* had activated my Eastern spiritual sanskars-tendencies. It has done this for many Westerners. Same with *Autobiography of a Yogi* by Yogananda: these seminal books have push-started many Westerners on their Eastern spiritual quests. It must be in the 70-80 percentile of Americans who dedicate to a full-blown Eastern spiritual path were initiated after they read *Be Here Now* or Yogananda's *Autobiography of a Yogi*.

My association with both these books was in 2005. My longing activating my Guru's grace to seek and arrive at Him with that sanyasi monk's kirtan program was less than a year later.

They are always watching over you (and every one of us) and just waiting for a moment of time where we turn our attention to True spiritual longing and are exhausted and exasperated from our endless and meaningless pursuit of happiness within the material world. Only when we give up, let go, and surrender do we become vulnerable enough to let Her in: *suffer the little children unto me, for theirs is the Kingdom of Heaven.*

They are poised, ever-present, and ready to come in when we hit our material rock bottom and have even a fraction of clarity for just an instant and say, *Enough! The happiness in the world is not enough! I've had it all for many, many lifetimes, and it only comes to disappointment!*

That... is our first moment of True *surrender*.

Knock... *and it shall be opened to you.*

***

I'd like to share a brief list of historical Bhakti yog Saints and encourage you to look Them up. You never know what *your* Guru will use to kickstart your spiritual sanskars!

- **Ramakrishna Paramahamsa (1836–1886):** His devotees consider Him to be an avatar of Ram. An illiterate man who was a scriptural master. As He ailed from cancer in His final years a devotee asked Him, "Master? You are One with God! Why don't You just ask Him to relieve You of all this pain and suffering You are enduring." And the Master replied, "Why would I take My mind out of *loving* God for a single moment for something so trivial?" His disciple, Vivekananda, is known for bringing yog(a) to the West. In the final stages  of his own life, Vivekananda wrote of his regrets of not fully understanding his Guru's true message: that bhakti yog, surrender, and devotion are all that matters.

- **Anandamayi Ma (1896–1982):** She was in spiritual ecstasy nearly all the time. Illiterate and poor, She had zero desire for any worldly comforts.

- **St. John of the Cross (1542–1591):** I do not know if St. John of the Cross is an avatar or was God Realized. I only know that what this Catholic saint did in His lifetime and all He taught was in direct alignment with the bhakti yog path of simply surrendering to God with unalloyed love. If He wasn't God Realized already, He was on the cusp. I am constantly blown away how exact His teachings (and St. Francis's) are to Sanatan Dharm's bhakti yog path and philosophy. His "Dark Night of the Soul" is one of the most profound and useable texts to learn of loving surrender to the Godhead. He composed the poem and it's elucidation while in a tiny prison cell for nine months (yes, nine!).

- **Chaitanya Mahaprabhu: (1486–1534):** Absorbed in the highest state of  spiritual bliss (*mahabhao*), Lord Chaitanya is considered a direct avatar of the personification of Divine Love Herself, Radha Rani. When He left the planet at thirty-eight, He vanished in front of hundreds of people as He ran to the altar of Krishna at Jagganath Puri. His states of ecstasy are legendary. I have pilgrimed/parikrama'd to many of His stomping grounds in Orissa and Braj in India.

  - **St. Francis of Assisi (1181 or 1182–1226):** I do not know if St. Francis was actually God Realized and avatars are not accepted by Catholicism, but if He wasn't, He was close. As He lay dying in a ditch, beaten and left for dead by bandits, He became annoyed with the passing peasants who rescued Him because rescuing Him interrupted His absorption into Christ's remembrance.

- **Neem Karoli Baba (c.1900–1973):** Considered an avatar of Hanuman and the  Guru to American professor Richard Alpert. Alpert converted to bhakti yog and became Ram Dass and wrote *Be Here Now*, which became a catalyst for bhakti yog in the West. Neem Karoli Baba was, and is, revered as a Saint in northern India

  - **Jagadguru Kripalu (1922–2013):** Considered an avatar of Radha Herself and a second coming of Chaitanya. No one ever saw Him  study scriptures, yet when He lectured to the Kashi Vidvat Parishat organization of hundreds of the most esteemed religious scholars, His knowledge exceeded all of them. He reconciled all the contradictory Sanatan Dharm philosophies, establishing bhakti yog as the true path they all taught. He did this when He was just thirty-five. He accepted the title of Original Jagadguru, which only four Divine Personalities had been recognized with over five thousand years. He taught and gave his darshan nonstop for over ninety years. And He is my only love.

- **Mātā Amritānandamayī Devī (1953–current):** Nicknamed the *Hugging Saint*, Amma, as She is known (means mother), often receives visitors twenty-four hours nonstop as she embraces every person desiring her darshan (vision), unwilling to turn anyone away. It is reported she has hugged over 37 million people worldwide.

There may seem to be a lack of Saints from Western religions. Western religions do not accept avatars, and if Sanatan Dharm is correct, they only appear within the yoga paths, which are India based. It's not bias: Bhakti yog avatars appear in the land Bhakti calls home: India

_____ **26.**

CHOW-CHOW-BANG

> I am not a human-being having a spiritual experience. I am a spiritual being having a human experience.
>
> —Teilhard de Chardin

> He just likes to do his own thing/He's a little man in a cat's body
>
> —Jane's Addiction (Maceo)

There are over eight billion people on the planet presently, and each one of them is a soul having a human-incarnation.

There are an estimated one billion domesticated pet dogs and cats in the world, each one also a soul but in an *animal* incarnation.

Once we factor in wildlife and insects, we get to the uncountable numbers of life-forms: each individual one being a soul in a various lifeform. Now add plants too. Absolutely every *living* thing is a soul in material clothing.

There are countless universes within multiverses and countless Earth-planets too. Ours is relatively small: our galaxy, planet, and population of souls is on the small end of the spectrum of life-holding galaxies. There are Earth-planets in other galaxies in solar systems a thousand times bigger with suns dwarfing ours. There's no mention in Sanskrit tabloids regarding the ET, UFO, interstellar connections: They don't say we never make close encounters of the third kind, neither do they say we do. It's *spiritually* irrelevant.

The Akashic knowledge teaches every one of the countless souls on *this particular* Earth-planet has lived here together for eternity. Therefore, it stands to reason that, over an eternity, you've had relationships with all of them at one time or another.

All the souls in *this* planetary manifestation coexist together forever, same as all the souls from another universe spend an eternity together, and never shall they meet nor in death do they part. When and if someone has a past life regression memory of living in an Atlantean or other-planetary experience, it's still here: could be tens of trillions of years ago, more or less, but it's still *here*.

The Atlantis that Plato described in his works truly existed. Xanadu, Avalon, and the other so-called mythical utopias were right here, on this planet, in long before prehistoric times. There is new science supporting our planet Earth has gone through several cylces of being dormant and being active. This concurs with Vedic knowledge. The engineering of ancient structures from Egypt's pyramids to Indonesia's Gunang Padang and Stonehenge are not testaments to early civilizations but testaments to survivors of prior ones who attempted to reboot what they once had.

Yeah... I've had intense past-life regression experiences well before my NDE that certainly seemed interplanetary. Some lasted a day or two, some were quick visions, and one regression went on for several months. Many of my past-life regression travels have been self-induced, some induced by others, and many activated by circumstance, like NDE.

Just as our physical bodies live, die, and are reborn again, so does our universe, galaxy, and planet, Gaia. As Sanskrit texts offer, there is a *pralaya* phase of material phenomena and a *mahapralaya* phase. Pralaya means dormant and refers to the stage when our known universe proverbially dies and goes into a dormant state for a long, long... *long* time; kind of like *cosmic winter*. *Maha*-pralaya is when the *entire* material phenomena, the *multiverse,* goes dormant and ceases to exist in form for a time that is *not* time, because even time goes dormant in that phase of creation/manifestation.

- Did you know nearly every ancient civilization has a deluge/flood story like that of Noah's ark? From the Sumerians to the Aztecs, all have a nearly identical story of the end of humanity due to a deluge with the exception of a few survivors left to repopulate the planet. They also all have a legend of the arrival of a great teacher who comes by sea from some unknown land and gives them knowledge from architecture and agriculture to astrology and religion. Ancient Egypt's Osiris and the Mayan's Quetzalcoatl are just two of the dozens of identical legends of ancient lores.

During these dissolved phases of Creation, all the uncountable, infinite souls become formless and reside in a formless dimension, like The Portal. Sanskrit scriptures actually say they reside *within* God—like *absorbed* by Him. And when it's time (haha... during these phases there actually isn't *time*), He activates the process of creation and manifestation, unfolding the multiverse and activating the souls to take life again. It takes a bit more than six days of work and one of rest for the Creator God to manifest the Earth and heavens, but the magical, mystical seven is prime allegory.

On one hand, the Western religious view of Creation is accurate and cosmos; life and humanity indeed had a genesis of a starting point and will indeed have an apocalyptic ending too. But it happens all the time and has been happening and repeating forever. Not kinda, not sorta, not a lot, but countless times since eternity!

This does not conflict with the Eastern proposition existence is eternal; it has no beginning and no end. And quantum physics is right too; energy is forever too. It cannot be created nor destroyed; it just changes form, going from pure energy to light to matter and vice-versa.

As a mystic, I experience past-life regression regularly. All the time. I meet people, interact as mere passersby, or get acquainted professionally, platonically, or romantically and see their pasts, present, and even futures. It used to happen automatically in early NDE days, but now I've found the on/off switch and the volume control, so it needs *permission* to present to my consciousness. Sometimes it still happens spontaneously, and I see a view of how we knew each other in a past life and the karmic circumstances drawing us back together. The more time I spend with someone, the more clearly their own past lives and Soul's Journey details become viewable.

One woman I met for harmless bedroom fun on occasion was a bit blown away as I shared some prior life insights with her. She confessed to being in a loveless and sexless marriage, and her partner had encouraged her to have a boyfriend, which is where I came in. Our pillow talk was revelatory.

"You and your mate were siblings in the last life you met each other in. When you first met, you both misinterpreted the feelings of connection as romantic instead of familial."

This triggered a total paradigm shift for her, and she called me the next week.

"It all makes sense!" she exclaimed. "Now that I'm seeing that we are more siblings than partners, I'm not angry with him anymore!"

This past-life consideration liberated her from a wrong expectation she had held. My work was done, I guess, because I intuitively knew we'd never see each other again, and our several attempts to hook up after that never came about. She crossed the threshold to acceptance and indifference, and their grudges with each other dissolved. Her gain, my loss, haha! I don't know, nor did I bother to meditate on, how she and I knew each other before. It was just a fling; our karmas this time round were satisfied, and we moved on.

But sometimes... I recall when and/or how I knew someone, and it is fun. It's always a little painful, but sometimes pretty harmless. Painful because there is *always* some sort of tragedy we shared because humans are stupid, driven by desires, and exploitive of one another. Fun because some of the elements of a past-life intertangling can give some good laughs, *so long as we don't get caught up in the shitty things we did then*. A little humor and maturity allows us to reunite with a past lover, friend, or even an enemy and not have hang-ups on karmic debts.

That's Chow-Chow-Bang.

Chow-Chow-Bang is the name my current roommate goes by in this lifetime. At this moment, as I type this, he just got up from where he was sitting just a foot away, walked in front of me, between my eyes and the laptop screen, pivoted, turned, sat, and laid down. I'm now typing with far more typos and backspacing as I awkwardly bowleg my arms around his furry body to reach the keyboard. You guessed it: he's a cat.

I don't like to say *my* cat, any more than you see me type or say *my* son, *my* girlfriend... These are living souls, not my possessions. They do not belong to me nor me to them. We share time and space and have done so multiple times in various incarnations in various ways.

Brandon was once my mystic-mentor and guide; a teacher of sorts. I have past-life ties with the priest at my temple whom I have coffee with regularly, and we chat about Joe Rogan podcasts and argue over who's better, Dodgers or Yankees. He's from Brooklyn, so he says Yanks, even though I try to enlighten him with the trivia that Dodgers are originally Brooklynites. The ashram's temple priest and I have a past before Doubleday even *invented* baseball. I remember a past life when he and I were grifters, stabbing each other in the back; it was just business. He doesn't remember shit of past life, but I do!

Chow-Chow and I were once partners in crime too. In *this* life, we're friends: I protect him with a safe and comfortable life, and he gives me low-maintenance friendship. He has his own private entry/exit pet door to the house and comes and goes as he likes. He prefers to toilet outside, so I rarely have to clean a litter box, let alone even put litter in it. He gets a free pass on the vegetarian-food-only policy in the house because there's no karmic consequence for him to be an omnivore. Even with his revolving outdoors, there's only been a few occasions of him being a predator. And most of those little, headless rodent gifts he brought in were just in the first couple years of his domestication. He's had autonomy since just after we were introduced.

* * *

"Just *look* at him! If you don't wanna keep him, fine, but just meet him once!" Janete had pleaded with me in 2010, three years before I would be killed.

"No! I don't want to! I take my son to Cancun for a high-school graduation present, and instead of just dropping by to bring in the mail, you start feeding homeless animals, drawing them to my house! I don't want a cat! I don't even like them!"

I came home from Cancun and saw small dishes of pet food scattered around the perimeters of my house and knew my bleeding-heart girlfriend tried to Florence Nightingale the homeless pet population.

I was able to do things like go to Cancun with my son, India on my own, and long road trips with my girlfriend because I was free: F-R-E-E, *free!* I had no dependent pet at home confining me and didn't want one!

A client who couldn't pay her bill offered me seven days of use in her timeshare when I told her I wasn't going to abandon her and her family because she couldn't pay me. I had been counseling her, her three daughters, and her husband for months, and they relied on me: no way was I going to abandon them over lack of payment. Turned out, the reason they were upside down financially was because of being suckered into a timeshare deal. So she insisted I use it in lieu of payment. Win-win: Brandon and I had an unforgettable time diving freshwater cenotes and drift-diving Cozumel to honor his high-school diploma, and all it cost me was airfare.

I violently throw the food dishes into the trash to make a point like slamming a door:

I. Do. Not. *Want a pet*!

The next day, she had snuck the pet dishes back. Finally, I agreed to *see* this scruffy wretch of a cat to shut her up and give my final veto.

See... I had perpetuated this anti-pet persona since we had met. In spite of being the initiator of our vegan/vegetarian lifestyle, I had her convinced I didn't like animals. The truth is I love them. The reason I didn't want a pet was out of sympathy: I don't think you should take a pet unless you have the time and heart to care for and love them properly. I *am and was* capable of this; I just didn't want to. People that get pets and then lock them alone indoors and are never home are going to captor-pet-hell. I was gone a lot and didn't want to imprison a pet in lonely solitude as I worked nonstop and lived my travel adventures.

I kid you not; he's got a sixth sense. He is annoying the fuck out of me right now as it is so damn uncomfortable to reach *around* him as I type and he lounges nearly on top of my keyboard. But I won't shove him away. It is sweet he just wants to be near me. He doesn't need anything, doesn't complain, whine, make a mess, never gets sick, and is almost entirely self-reliant. Yet, he's cuddly, cozy, adorable, and adoring. Even though he is outdoors seventy percent of the time, roaming through forests, rolling in grassy meadows, he's completely clean: his fur is soft, unsoiled, and only one time did I ever have to get a flea solution. He's never had them and never gets bit, scratched, or bothered. I don't know how he does it. I have thought of fastening my GoPro camera to his head to see where he goes and what he does, but he's earned the independence and mystery. He's the perfect companion: never too much, but neither too little. Low maintenance but affectionately dependent. He gives me responsibility and purpose to take the sting out of a worthless world celebrating Wheel of Fortune and respects McDonald's for having a *"healthy options menu."*

Why am I acting like an annoying pet-person and taking up content space in a book about triumphing over tragedy about a cat?

1. He deserves it: he's been my only consistent, present friend and companion throughout this whole ordeal. He entered my life three years before it began and is resting his head on my typing arm as I type this to you.

2.   It gives an actual, experiential opportunity to explore high concepts about past life and the nature of the soul.

It's very likely you and your pet are bonded by a past life. Whatever we are emotionally attached to in our life and at our time of death creates a karmic bond. Like a tractor-beam, our lives intersect and draw each other in. Yes, yes ... of course... kids, parents, lovers, and even enemies are karmic destinies. Most pet owners feel a unique and personal connection transcending the limited time they've been associated. Past life!

Yes, sure, every pet and animal has endearing qualities, and each person in a relationship with one thinks *theirs* is more special and extraordinary than any other: *that's love.* We *all* think our love is The One, the grandest, most special, and unique to all others. We are all endowed with this natural capacity to feel our experience is exclusive and stands apart from all others. But this just ain't so, and if I have to ever hear a non-parent tell me ever again their pet is *like* their child, I'm going to euthanize them.

I am not *bragging* as I share the extraordinariness of my life experiences: the magnitude of their paranormal-ness, the gorgeousness of my love affair, the complexity of my medical triumphs... I share them because I am now aware how extraordinary they are. If you like average people doing average things, go watch reality TV. I read books, watch movies and films, and go hear professional musicians because I do *not* want ordinary. Otherwise, I'd marathon *Desperate Housewives* and just see live music at the local hometown tavern.

We're surrounded and saturated in common/average/normality *all the time.* I go on a rollercoaster because I want something different. I SCUBA'd those cenotes because I want risk. I want the abnormal, not-complacent. If I want reality-show content, I'll go to the fucking mall and people-watch. I offer you this memoir because the experience can be inspiring. Not me: *the experience.*

Chow-Chow is not ordinary or just cute.

He and I knew each other once when we were criminals. I'm sensing it is late '20s, prohibition, when we were buddies. We were grifters and conmen. Moonshiners?

Bank robbers? I can't access the details, but I know one of us killed the other. It was no big deal; whether it was me who shot and killed him or he shot and killed me is immaterial. We had some sort of deal going down, and one of us killed the other to take advantage and keep the spoils without sharing. There were no hard feelings about it, so we really have no actual karmic debt; the *killer* doesn't owe the *killee* a thing. We both would've done it to the other under reverse circumstances.

I'm guessing I shot him, and I agreed to be his caretaker in this life to make up for it, but I'm not sure. Maybe he shot and killed me and has come back as my companion to make up for it. Or... I killed him, and he's come to burden me with the worry and care for him as a passive-aggressive penance! It's all good.

He is a Manx. I only recently learned this by coincidence. When he recently went missing a couple days, I became sad and desperate to find him. I'm living on about an acre, and half of it is pretty wild and he still comes and goes as he likes. Brokenhearted because I figured the last time I saw him was the last time I'd see him, I drafted letters and drove to the other ranch properties in my neighborhood, put them in mailboxes, hoping someone mistakenly adopted him. I recalled Janete had him chipped; a small computer chip had been embedded into his ear so if anyone ever found him, he was in a data base and might be returned. As I looked them up online, they required I update the data and asked his breed: I had no clue. I googled cat breeds, and sure enough, there was his identical twin! He was hands down a Manx breed of cat. Had I known this and what a Manx was back in the day, I might've auctioned him off!

A Manx is a rare breed, which is very valuable, and he was clearly purebred. Even rarer, Manx breeds are tailless: their tails are not clipped; they are born without them. But Chow-Chow has a tail, making him even rarer. He could fetch a cool $500.

Bred on the Isle of Man in the early 1800s, they are rare and highly sought after, being known as skilled hunters and great companions. There are folk lore tales and mythic histories of them.

If you want to see one, *google Manx cat with tail*: Chow-Chow is identical to the grey/black ones. And I do mean identical.

There are only three things that have remained constant through this NDE: Brandon, my Guru, and Chow-Chow-Bang, the cat. My Guru doesn't count: He's divine. And He is *mine* because He is also your and every other souls' who wants, accepts, and surrenders to Him. That's what saviors do: they make you theirs if you make them yours. Everyone and everything else are temporary. Brandon and I have *many* lifetimes connecting us. Janete and I too. But my Maharaji and I have an *eternity* together: always had and always will have. He's *mine*. He belongs to many others, but He is *mine*.

And I am His. *Only His*. I don't belong to anyone or anything else. Everyone else is simply *on loan*.

Janete is gone. The guys I played tennis with are gone. The twenty to forty other girlfriends and lovers from my past are not around. Every couple months, there's a new front desk clerk at the tennis club I play at. Neighbors, mail-carriers, aunts and uncles, and even sons and daughters are never permanent. Few make it with you just *one* entire life, let alone several. Brandon is a permanent fixture in my heart: *now*.

But the first zero to twenty-six years of my life, he wasn't even the proverbial gleam in my eye. We've had many, many lives together, but our relationship is not eternal.

The only thing in my life which I interact with *daily* is my Guru and Chow-Chow-Bang the cat.

I dread and deny the inevitable day when my close, daily friend and pal, Chow-Chow-Bang, leaves me for that great gig in the sky. *That's* the real reason I never wanted a pet: to avoid the inevitable heartache of losing someone who exemplifies innocence, humility, and comfort. I like animals because I've never had innocence of my own. I was full of shit at birth. I get to at least be *near* innocence when they're around.

I took a while to firmly conclude hoping he goes before I do.

I often felt me dying first would be way easier. But then I thought of how much I'd freak out about who's gonna care for him if not me. We understand each other, and it would take too long to get well enough acquainted with him to let him be the free, well-rounded, spirit he is in this life. If I die with Chow-Chow on my mind, that binds us karmically, and I *don't want any* karmic bindings forcing me back to the world.

Chow-Chow reveals the depth of my attachment to loving worldly things regularly. Several times, he has disappeared. As a free spirit with his own entry/exit access to the big, outside world, he comes and goes as he pleases. But he is smart and usually within a visible circumference of the house. He occasionally breaks from his reliable routines and goes on some mysterious adventure which only he knows about, and I begin to mourn. By nightfall, I am *totally convinced* I won't see him again and doing all I can to come to terms with what I know to be true: that time of death is predetermined, he and I have a limited time together, his ultimate experience as a soul is not my responsibility, and *blah, blah, blah*—my shoes are on, flashlight in hand as I scour the forests calling his name, unable to focus on much else. Yes, Chow-Chow certainly has the capacity to bind me to the material phenomena if I am not careful with my loving attachment to him.

Let me repeat: whatever we are attached to in *this* life is what we will be bound to associate with in the *next* life. Take your pick: friends or enemies? Pets or God? Whatever you desire and are attached to in your mind and heart is what you're getting. Your final thoughts at death carry a *lot* of weight to where you go next!

My Maharaji has mentioned to a few devotees over the years some animals that become pets to devotees were once His devotees who lost their way and are now in animal incarnations.

The other day, he parked his furry butt at the doorway to the meditation satsang room and meowed until I opened the door so he could nap inside. I conceded but told him with a playful finger wag, "But not in the altar! You can nap in the big space!" and the two closet doors to the altar remained closed. I came back by in five minutes, and, lo and behold!, he had opened the altar doors and snoozed inside the altar to be with Radha Krishn and Maharaji! How he opened the freakin' door is a mystery! That's sanskars, baby! He wanted to be near God and Guru and made it happen!

God and Guru have been laying waste to each and every attachment I had, which may give me a clean slate to die with no attachments. It is Their Grace. But be careful what you wish for. I have had many heartfelt pleas to my Spiritual Master to do whatever He felt was necessary to help me become spiritually perfected and not return to the shabby, material phenom ever again, so if He is taking a wrecking ball to my life, it is because I asked for it! The way to God is most often a purification by fire process.

He totally wrecked Job's life in the Tanakh account, and when Job questioned Him, God set him straight! Mine is not to reason why but to do and die (Tennyson). I try not to ask what is God's plan, striving instead to accept the changes as gracefully as I can, which I fail at regularly. I suspect the trick is to align our material attachments to our spiritual ambitions.

All attachments are bad for spiritual progress, which is why Abraham followed God's order to sacrifice Isaac on Mount Moriah, which he tearfully proceeded to comply with. But can some material attachments and relationships align with our spiritual progress and not be sacrificed? Yes, yes, of course I am attached to Brandon! But he and I entered this life with an understanding it could be a last one, and he will never stand in my way of exiting samsara. I will have given him all I have, and I have shown, by example, the way out of samsara, and our karmic account will be balanced. And he has inspired me to be a good man and so has Janete. Before them, I was a criminal dope fiend, but lookit me now!

Chow-Chow and I don't owe each other anything. Unless I am struck by lightning, my nearly supernatural health should provide me with a long while after he leaves to get closure over missing him and have nothing but gratitude for his company. I have done what I can to provide him with spiritual association: he sees my Guru speak on video, listens to kirtan, and even joins me sometimes in my home satsang room during meditation. He's a cat training and preparing for his upcoming human life and developing spiritual sanskars. He's not a kitty having a spiritual experience; he's a spirit having a kitty experience.

I share this because I hope you will keep in mind that during the *entire* saga you are hearing in this tale, Chow-Chow is present in my life. All the dark and light, the miracles and the tribulations, he's in the background. He may not be mentioned in my tales of lonely woe and adventurous journeys, but he is. Keep that in mind. I'll try to mention him from time to time just to remind us all that even in the midst of fortunes and misfortunes, there are constants. That's God's grace through mercy.

One final thought: as an independent man, I chose not to have pets. This deprived Brandon from a childhood with one (except at his mom's) but allowed us to have a worry-free, more liberated lifestyle. For about ten years, I had a few tropical fish with very fun and creative names. I have a unique formula for naming animals.

Brandon was given a writing assignment when he was in fourth grade: write a story about wagon train families to show you understood the lessons on the time. He wrote this hilarious story of a family and the wagon train cook's name was Chow-Chow-Bang.

Around that time, Brandon and I started backpacking in the high sierras: ten-thousand feet up, backpacking for a week in the wilderness, and we gave each other nicknames to use just when we hiked as a secret and private kind of bond. I won't tell you mine, cuz it's lame, but his was Chow-Chow-Bang. As he got older, it was too childish to use, and when this wayward feline came into my circumference, he adopted the name, as I adopted him.

He also answers to Chow, Chow-Chow, Bang, and Bang-Bang, and even Pi, which is a derivative of Pie, short for Piewacket from the classic movie *Bell, Book, and Candle* with Kim Novak (yum) and James Stewart. Piewacket was overused as a pet name, so I spun it to refer to the mathematical equation. Besides, it fit better on the ID tag he wore when he was getting lost in the snow when we moved to Olympia, Washington.

When Chow-Chow-Bang is in his final days, I will comfort him and hold him close and make him comfortable near the alter in our home satsang room. I will surround him with images of Radha Krishn and our Maharaji and play Hari Ram, nam-sankirtan, nonstop while he passes. So he can cross over to his new life with a fresh set of devotee sanskars!

_____ **27.**

SANITARIUM

> In Xanadu did Kubla Khan/A stately pleasure-dome decree...
> For he on honey-dew hath fed,/And drunk the milk of Paradise.
> —Samuel Taylor Coleridge (*Vision in a Dream)*

> I had heard the whispered tales/Of immortality...
> Oh, I will dine on honey dew/And drink the milk of paradise
> —Rush ("Xanadu")

I'm alone in the Pacific Northwest. Have I come here to live? To recover? Or have I come here to die? Am I running *to* something or running *away?* If I am to die again, I want to do it alone; I don't want those I love to witness my powerlessness. If I am part of the 10% of TBI-DAI sufferers who survive but wind up in an institution within four years, I want my friends and family to remember me as I was before. And if I am to fade away, I choose to do it in a sanitarium instead of an asylum. What's the difference? An asylum is a *storage facility* for those who may be a harm to themselves or others. A sanitarium is a *recovery resort*.

As a behavioral specialist, I've seen how CEOs and PhDs collaborate for profit over wellness. In our warped, dysfunctional, medical-empire culture, some lunatic doctor can transform your asylum stay into an indefinite sentence. For every patient, the asylum profits from *treating* conditions but not *curing* them. Nurse Ratchet doesn't want you to fly *over* the cuckoo's nest; she wants you to stay indefinitely so she has job security.

Asylums have lockdowns and provide dorm living; *sanitariums have open doors and private rooms.* My chosen sanitarium is a 2,200-square-foot home built just three years ago. There are hardwood floors throughout, a state-of-the-art kitchen, a three-car garage, four bedrooms, and an office loft. It sits on four acres of meadow grass surrounded by lush forests and a country road perfect for daily strolls. I've never lived on a property with well water, septic, and propane tanks. It's charming and luxurious, just what I need. When I get up on a cool morning, I flip a switch, and the propane gas fireplace generates a natural fire with radiant heat. If I'm going to feel like a walking dead phantom every day, I may as well do it someplace quiet and pretty. Fifty yards from the large patio is a fire pit where I can chill on cool nights with my MP3 player and lager beer. Asylums are for crazies who are poor; sanitariums are for crazies who have a little money.

My material life was stable. I received a shitty settlement of $70,000 from the insurance company of the guy who hit me, and I had a little over $100,000 saved up from my counseling practice.

My first career as a commercial contractor began with nothing but dirt and sweat combined with years of labor experience and *chutzpah; yeah, my family tree is Hebrew, so I'm entitled to use a little Yiddish.*

I took my bank account balance from $350 to $325,000 in three years. But Los Angeles corruption slowly depleted my motivation to sustain the commercial construction company I had created, and it ended with just $15,000 in the bank. I was 34 when I set out to fulfill a new life calling, 180° from construction to a helping career as a counselor. My practice started with a thread and a prayer in 2006. What began as a little hypnotherapy hobby bloomed into a full-time private practice specializing in crisis counseling which was lucrative by the fourth year. With total commitment, I brought my annual income back up to $185,000. With more work than play, I had saved $100,000 over seven years, excluding the equity of my home.

My inner-circle people were against my taking the insurance settlement offer. A few attorneys said I had a good case against the helmet manufacturer and the hospital for missing a few things. They thought I should hold out for a larger return on the claim. But I needed this to be over. Every day was an actual nightmare; I could barely function and couldn't think clearly. I was in a state of mental paralysis from existing in two dimensions, so I took the settlement. If this was going to be part of my *past,* I didn't want years of legal proceedings reminding me of it, especially if my injuries were permanent. I was in perpetual PTSD already and desperate for closure.

The settlement and savings weren't enough to retire with. But I felt confident that my books would make me a deservedly well-paid author, or I would fulfill the prophecies of the doctors, specialists, and TBI stats and die or be institutionalized soon.

Either way, I felt the odds were 50/50 that my material needs would be okay. But most of the evidence, including how I felt every day, supported the latter conclusion that I was fucked. I was relocating to die somewhere alone so I wouldn't be a burden to loved ones nor feel humiliated at being so goddam broken and useless. I couldn't take it; I felt worthless, which left me in a state of constant sorrow. As a counseling professional, I have concluded that what's driving *everyone's* unhappiness is a feeling of sadness when you're not living a life you deem fulfilling and valuable.

I've always struggled with an acute awareness that this globe's population is ultra-materialistic, except for those on hourly one-million-milligram doses of denial pills. They go to church once a month and do yoga twice a week; many drive a car with a C⊙⊜x⊙st (coexist) sticker to convince themselves they're "spiritual." Once they upgrade from hybrid cars to full electric, they think the afterlife in heaven is guaranteed. But judge not lest ye be judged; I, too, make material comfort a priority. The only difference is that material comfort and safety lets me focus on sadhana instead of survival, but I still desire luxury, too. I'm as flawed as most.

My material goal is to market my invaluable work of three published books and have the last laugh over brain injury, a scary pursuit against all odds. I had no doubt pre-accident, *"version one-point-oh,"* Scott would be an influential success in the literary world. I had *the chops* as a writer, wrote about hot topics, and was a marketer's wet dream: moderately handsome, articulate, well-informed, and always right by never saying anything wrong.

But Scott *"two-point-oh"* struggles to coexist and doesn't even *like* hybrid cars. This current version is *not* articulate or confident. He is a good writer, but it seems my marketing potential makes me more like JD Salinger than Hemingway. As far as *writing* is concerned, I admire Salinger well above blow-hard Hemingway anyhow. On paper, I'm just a guy in a mid-life crisis, moving to the woods to write his novel.

Many men and women have what we call a *mid-life crisis*. We often associate this with promiscuity and infidelity. However, the truth is that this is the phase of life when many quit jobs, return to college, start new businesses, or make other abrupt *join-the-circus* changes. I anticipated the need for a career change early on. I knew that one day, with my restless nature, I would burn out on counseling. My books would be my retirement package, intended to provide a revenue stream to support my partner and me through our golden years.

The work was stellar. But could this brain-trauma'd man in the height of a supernatural, NDE-induced identity crisis tour to promote himself as an author? Survival through starting *any* career takes one thousand percent focus that cannot be delayed nor distracted by personal issues. I've got oodles of personal issues.

They say behind every great man is a great woman. I'm familiar: Janete had been my muse and motivation since we met. But she was currently an emotional tumor of pain. She wasn't standing by her man like Ms. Wynette had prescribed; she had become a jagged little pill, as Ms. Morissette described.

A major element of my self-exile to the Pacific Northwest was to focus on *me*, which I had never done, not even in my hedonistic youth. Even then, I had a conscience. No one was going to *"just do it"* for me. I had to write, design, publish, and market my product. I needed some peace to do it, which translated to establishing some distance between me and the fucking abject pain that every inch of Los Angeles, my house, and Janete represented to me now.

I've asked my love partner to be supportive, and she has agreed, comforting me with:

"I am so sorry for everything. I understand you need some space and time to get better and forgive me. We'll visit all the time, and this will be a fresh start for us. You've been there for me through so much stuff; I'd never be who I am today without you. My kids, too. I know what an influence you've been on all of us. It's time you take care of you now. I support you."

"That's what I need, Janete. I need to know you're by my side. I live to serve; it has fulfilled me for over ten years. I've focused on you and your kids, had the weight of being Brandon's only reliable and responsible parent, and built a career helping others. I want to keep doing it.

"But I've got to see if I can straighten out this brain trauma first. I've been hit from all sides nonstop. None of us were able to prepare or adjust for this. We all went to bed one night, and then I was killed. I've got to figure out how to balance the supernatural with the natural: The Portal with the World."

"You will. I know you will. My mom, sister, and kids all believe in you."

"But they don't know about our personal thing, right? They must think this is all because of my accident, that I've lost my mind and am leaving everyone behind."

"They're really worried, but no, they don't know how I hurt you."

"Good. It's too embarrassing for us both. I don't want them thinking badly of you. After what your ex's betrayal did to you and your kids, they will have a hard time accepting your role in my decision to leave."

"I can't tell them! Thank you. If my kids found out what I did, they'd never forgive me, especially with this coming up with what you're going through."

"We're a family, Janete. Our kids are close; yours accept me as the man in your life and have always been comfortable coming to me. You and I have always had a sacred privacy that they respect. Your whole family respects me and the special connection we have. What's happened between us is none of their business."

***

My new residence was like a resort. I was in a place I had only dreamt of; bucolic living and gorgeous nature surrounded me. Mount Rainier, the icon of the PNW and Washington State, watched down on me from the horizon behind the home. Rainier National Park was just barely an hour's drive away.

We're not talking about California national park driving, no. Los Angeles to Yosemite was a brutal commute, and nearby SoCal parks were ghetto by comparison. But Rainier has magic: I would often not see another vehicle in either direction on my many drives to this paradise. Rainier's spirit was healing me. My visits were gorgeous. I walked, drove, hiked, and even camped out... alone. I felt she was helping me heal. The native name is *Tahoma: Mother of Waters*. She is a sight and presence to behold. I could see her on clear days from the rear two acres of my property, dominating the horizon. She stands over 14,000 feet, up and over the surrounding flat terrains of prairies, so tall and independent she generates her own weather patterns. She is captivating. Wherever you are in the Puget Sound region of Washington, she demands every attention.

To this day and for the rest of my life, I will always know she sent for me; *she was my sanitarium.*

Unexpected tears flow as I write this memory. I need to share some of the less-than-dark aspects of my time in exile. I want to thank her: send a card, a gift, or some token of my appreciation. It's a fact that I wouldn't have made it without Rainier.

Hindus hold dear to the idea of *avatars:* demi-gods and goddesses that descend to earth to provide frequencies of spiritual vibrations. The Ganges River, Annapurna Mountain in the Himalayas, and other natural sites are notable avatars. I have no doubt that Tahoma, also known as Mount Rainier, is one. She beckoned me, and the Akashic Agents within The Portal directed me to her.

A few times a month, I would make the meditative drive to Rainier and hike two and a half miles round trip to Carter Falls. The scenery is so gorgeous it easily rivals my favorite adored sites and waterfalls of the times I spent in the High Sierra backcountry. I rarely saw another soul because I would go midweek while nine-to-fivers were trapped in offices and kids behind school desks. I had this entire landscape to myself. To this day, I am convinced this mountain, this goddess-avatar, graced me with the power to learn to walk steadily again. Each time I hiked her trails, I would improve. I felt her presence while snacking on Clif Bars on the bridge below the falls at her feet, and she was also with me as I slept at home, sixty miles away.

Washington State is like one big campout; it is a massive forest that immerses you in nature. I was always minutes from a lake, river, or woods… and because there are so many, they're never crowded.

I regularly went to Tumwater Falls. My first trip was a forty-minute drive from my country home. I had no bearings and was easily overwhelmed by directions. I stopped at a 7-Eleven and asked, "Hey, my GPS says I'm right at the entrance of Tumwater Falls Park. Can you tell me…?"

"Yeah, man. It's right behind us. Go out the driveway and make two lefts."

Sure as shit, in the middle of this little city area of Olympia, the capital of Washington, was this piece of absolute wilderness. A gorgeous wonder of nature, Tumwater Park is a salmon hatchery where you can see these fighting fish swim *up the falls*, not just *upstream*. It is fascinating to watch them fight the current and conquer these raging falls to spawn. A paved path provides a leisurely twenty-minute stroll through the stunning views within the park. Midweek, this place was all mine, except for a few park custodians and maybe a person or two. I will always cherish my visits to Tumwater Falls; each was a healing meditation.

Nisqually Wildlife Refuge was just ten minutes from Tumwater Falls. A wide wooden boardwalk leads me two miles *into and over* Puget Sound. When the tide is *in*, the mix of fresh river water flowing down from the Cascades and salty seawater from the Pacific making up Puget Sound is just inches beneath your feet as you walk the pier. The soaked ground is a foot below you when the tide is out. The Twin Barns Trail near the entrance to the dock is lined with wild berries. Visitors leave the sanctuary with pockets bulging full of them. But I rarely see other visitors in this paradise. Because I come out midweek, I have the entire sanctuary to myself, rarely seeing even another sanitarium patient.

But I was lonely. All I knew and loved was 1,200 miles from here. My nearest neighbor was over a hundred yards away, and there were only twelve residences along this one-mile-long, no-outlet road. Washingtonians are rather introverted, and I am as well. But I go many days here without any human interaction. The static of collective consciousness in LA was in the high *megahertz,* but here it was in the low *kilohertz.* This was a blessing and curse; no static from other human minds was an asset, but the lack of interference made my *own* mind's radio waves inescapable. It took extra effort to block out the shocking awareness that I was really dizzy and didn't feel I inhabited my body. I wasn't sure where I was—the earthly realm or The Portal realm. I would occasionally wake up and call Brandon to ask him where I was.

The dizziness I felt when I was awake was as constant as ever. From the moment I woke, I would feel dizzy and confused. It was constant. Nothing could distract me from it entirely, but being alone all the time made my awareness of it more pronounced. Every few minutes, no matter what I was doing, I felt the sensation of the earth, the cosmos, and my head swirling round and round.

As a child, you played on the merry-go-round. If you could find a big kid to push, you'd spin as fast as you could until you were about to puke. Then you'd lay bets on who would be the last one standing when you would get off and try to walk. It was funny as fuck to see each kid zigzag like a drunk till they would fall down. Now spin that kid around to the point of *horizontal* vertigo; wind her up and let her go!

That's how I felt when I was awake. Even with my eyes closed and lying down, I would be lost and disoriented.

This perpetual dizziness in the world is diluted by the stability I experience with my connection to The Portal. Still, it is mentally exhausting to reorient back and forth between the two so frequently. I didn't meditate on my condition or circumstances: I ignored them. I endured and tried to function. I tried to coexist with the terror and sorrow I felt. I didn't try to make it go away or interact with it *at all*. Looking back, I see my strategy was a zen one. The only way I could survive each day without madness was to *observe* it objectively. But sometimes, the *subjective* reality of being a victim of horrific tragedy washed over me like acid rain, freezing and scalding at once.

Other times, I would laugh at my situation. I would drive along a road with zero recall of where I was going; I didn't even remember getting in the car. I'd be within The Portal one moment and then reorient within the material plane, wondering what I was doing in a grocery store. During one episode of wakeful, astral travel within The Portal, my phone rang while I was driving. "Hey, Dad, I'll be landing in forty-five minutes." This call jolted me back to the earth plane, and I had no recollection of where I was going or why I was in the car. I laughed all the way to Seattle-Tacoma Airport and picked Brandon up on time, thank God!

Weekly rides on the Wayback Machine—my motorbike—grounded me well. The rides were a meditation and required a zen focus, allowing me to coexist within the world and The Portal simultaneously. Many sweet and profound realizations would surface on lonely rides through the quiet country roads.

My meditations were often tearful sessions of begging. Not to be healed from brain and heartache but to be of spiritual service. All I wanted to do, and still do, is help people out of material darkness and see spiritual light. I was in constant sorrow over humanity's need for spiritual love and my inability to do anything about it.

***

Taking mountain walks and mowing the two acres of grass I lived on were parts of my physical therapy. I drew a hopscotch diagram on the back patio and forced myself to use it daily for agility exercise. It was tragically challenging to do something that small children do for play.

I filled my days trying to work and build a life, too.

I set up a recording studio to make a video version of Project Addiction, the *everything guide* to solving addictions. That LA music producer had put the idea in my head, and I started by making a couple of videos of book chapters for marketing. It went well, so I just kept going, soon making one or two every day. I spent most of my time recording and editing. I wasn't even clear why I was doing it, but it felt productive and essential to produce a video book to go along with the print, electronic, and audiobooks. Why not? It seemed better than basket weaving. A few videos for marketing evolved into an entire video course for addiction treatment.

I joined a local Toastmasters to sample public speaking again. I had been a member in LA for years and had a collection of award ribbons from local meetings. Other members lauded me with praise. My stutters and foibles were glaring to me, but others didn't seem to notice. One member was impressed by my posture because I always stood so tall and strong. We laughed as I replied my stance was due to four titanium bolts in my spine, not because of discipline!

I became friendly with another Toastmasters member who is a professional editor. She invited me to speak to her writer's group and encouraged me to hold a writer's workshop. She even connected me to the Washington library system so I could ask them to start carrying my books. Going into a public library and pulling my books off the shelf was pretty landmark. Holding two of my books in my hand in a public library gave me tangible comfort I was *real*.

I worked feverishly, trying to arrange guest appearances on radio shows to promote my books. For every four hours I spent soliciting producers around the US and abroad, I would get an interview. That's good, by the way, and that's how it's done. When you don't have an agent or a publicist, you invest hours of relentless networking for twenty minutes of airtime.

I entered my books into book festivals in the US and abroad. I investigated them to determine which were legit and which were scams, and that was healthy brain-recovery therapy. There were fees to participate in these festivals, and thousands of other entrants used them to sell and market their books. But I won a first or second-place award in every festival I entered.

I still served a few clients as a counselor via Skype video calls. The work was hard for me, but I certainly didn't feel I was in a position to reject work. Invitations to speak at a few conventions also allowed Janete and me to honeymoon a little. When an organization would ask me to present, they'd offer me a little money and pay all my travel expenses. I would insist my "assistant" come along so Janete and I could have a working vacation and spend some quality time together.

The touring helped promote the Project Addiction book since I was not taking on new clients. I'd had enough of working in the trenches of behavioral suffering. I was barely present in the world, so it was toxic to come out of the spirit realm to deal with mundane affairs. A few clients pleaded with me to stay involved because they really needed my particular brand of help. Though my heart wasn't in it as it had once been, the quality of counsel I provided was as good as ever. I could not abandon them, but I needed recovery time after each session, like a lingering hangover that took several hours to cleanse. My empathy caused a desperate need to assist them, but helping people with material issues drained me.

Humanity's defects are due to a lack of *spirit*, not the things we manufacture in our minds and bodies, but because of our attachment to material concepts. I was living in a spirit world now, and most people were not interested in spiritual help and knowledge to transcend worldly suffering. They wanted to know how to make more money, get more validation, and live comfortably with banal entertainment. My focus was on how not to desire them in the first place. A few clients sought me out for spiritual mentorship, and these sessions were never tiring. I could speak endlessly regarding spiritual subjects.

I just wanted my clients to feel safe and to see that their suffering was because of the pursuit of happiness instead of fulfillment. But very few wanted to hear the back-from-the-dead guy wax on about finding spiritual fulfillment over worldly pleasure.

I was unwittingly having a Buddha crisis; I saw the pains of the world and wanted to reveal the dharmas to escape suffering from desiring. But I was just a walking dead guy who used to be *a somebody*. I could now articulate well enough to speak on noble truths and paths to *conscious* enlightenment, but few desired this over *economic* enlightenment.

I was lonely, brokenhearted, dizzy, and confused about my identity. Every day was like serving time. All I wanted to do was remain in unconsciousness. I *liked* The Portal. In The Portal, you're *on hold*. You're just aware and have total indifferent neutrality. Waking consciousness was a state of desire. When my body slept, I was unaware of being dizzy, lonely, futureless… and my mind soared to The Portal. When worldly life was calm, I was more aware of and within The Portal. Being surrounded by 70,000 square miles of nature was serving its role. The only things it couldn't drown out were the frequent sounds of my tears of loneliness and the fear I was more dead than alive.

Janete would visit for a week, and in many ways, we were strangers. It was awkward and uncomfortable; we now had very little in common. I did my best to make her visits special and memorable; however, she was more interested in reality show content than in our usual talks of life and spirit.

I sensed Janete's layers of mind and body were awake, but her spirit had gone to sleep. She seemed even less *present* than I did. When she left, I would weep nonstop for the forty-five-minute drive home from the airport. *I was so lonely,* not in body or mind, but in *heart.* There was *no* love. I missed her; I missed *us.* It did not feel like something *we* were going through, but something *I* was going through. Our inner connection seemed shrouded.

Brandon could not visit much. He was young, had a job, and was trying to make his way through a phase of life that required self-centeredness. When he came, we had a great time touring Mount Rainier and Tumwater Falls. This new life and house allowed us to bond and get along. Despite our current differences, neither of us ever let them interfere with the respect, love, and value we felt for each other. We timed one visit to coincide with when the Dodgers came to play against the Mariners (Dodgers won!). Good times!
Just like with Janete, when I dropped *him* at the airport, I wept all the way home. When the only two people I knew and loved came to visit and then left, it would beam hot, blazing stadium lights on my own solitude.

I never felt I was progressing in my recovery, nor did I think that I wasn't. My daily task was figuring out how to live with my permanent conditions: brain fog, dizziness, difficulty walking, and coexisting in the worldly and portal dimensions.

The third anniversary of my death came, and I didn't realize it till a week or two later. It didn't seem like a denial thing, either. I rarely knew what day it was, and frankly, the passage of time was irrelevant to me. After a lot of stressful work, from repairs to permits and inspections, I sold the house in LA, where I had raised my son. It was an emotional end to a significant era in my life: Little League parties, hanging Christmas lights on the roof for Santa, father-and-son handprints in the new driveway cement… time to let it go and move on. I netted a small profit from the sale of the house and used the money to extend my sanitarium stay.

Janete and I had discussed visiting each other every three to six weeks. She would come to Washington to explore new places and get away from the LA grind of a retail job, kids, and an irritating mom; then, I would come to LA and spend a week doing familiar things we had always enjoyed.

Even though I was sopped in foggy, parallel dimensions, I put up a good front. Photos and home videos show me as a regular guy, despite knowing I wasn't. I sent Janete a video of me strumming my guitar and singing happy birthday to her. It looked smooth, but I practiced for days for the one-minute performance. But we all have intuitions; we can tell when we're talking to someone whose mind isn't *all there*. I may have acted normal and done the same things with, for, and to Janete as before my spirit vacated my body, but her spirit could sense I wasn't really in the *world* anymore. She did not feel present to me, either. I was in realms of spirit, and she was in realms of matter. It was hard to talk about, so we didn't.

Janete's intuition is not sophisticated enough to know *why* something doesn't seem right or developed enough to have a theory of *what* is wrong. We shared a love of spirit over a dozen lifetimes, yet now our souls could not connect. We loved and cared for each other as stupid-humans do, but the supernatural spark had been extinguished. Half of it was gone—*my half*—which had always been the beast of burden of our love in *this* lifetime.

Janete's father's death came less than a year after my *near*-death. That, and the tumult her transgression had caused, was too much. She did not trust me. She thought she could rely on me forever as we had done over multiple lifetimes. Then I abandoned her: not to Washington, but in a Santa Clarita, California intersection. *I died.*

It was all too familiar; several of our past lives together had ended in Shakespearean tragedies. In the midst of love, one of us died, so her spirit went on lockdown to prevent harm, like a reincarnation PTSD effect. It wouldn't make itself available nor accessible to the pain again. When I came *out* of my coma, she went *into* one.

When I opened my eyes and woke from my coma, Janete's spirit said, *No más; I'm done. I can't take another loss.* Her spirit went into hibernation-escape mode, common in romance. When someone hurts us, we become emotionally unavailable.

The only way to avoid heartbreak is not to fall in love in the first place. She disconnected from me, "us," and spirit rather than risk more pain.

I'm trying to reassure her I won't abandon her again. But my spirit and mind haven't settled within my physical frame yet, and the jury's still out on the whole recovery thing. That's a hard sell.

Thanks for Stopping By

It is time to go.

Janete and I have shared a grand week of lovemaking and country walks, and now this visit is over. We're far from having all the water under the bridge, but we're trying to spend quality time together. I miss her, even when she's next to me. I miss our natural connection. She is asleep to spirit, and I'm comatose from the world,

I am as emotionally prepared as possible for the long, tearful drive home alone from the airport. I put Janete's bag in the car, and we swing the car doors shut as the garage door opens.

"Oh! Shit!" she exclaims. "I forgot my charger!" Before I can offer to fetch it, she opens her door and bounds into the house, returning a full minute later.

Her eyes bulge; she beckons me to follow her with a *shushing* finger over her lips as if to guard a secret. I take a breath to shout out, *C'mon, we gotta go!* But my instincts kick in, and I accept her invitation to go with her, leaving the car running.

I follow her back inside and look to the rear of the house, where she points. The western wall is almost all windows, with a large patio outside with a reclining lounger for sunbathing. And there, perched upon the top rail of the chair is... *a bald eagle.*

The bird does not move. The windows between us are only twenty feet away, and this magnificent bird is just inches beyond the glass.

I've seen pictures. I've seen them flying in the sky above. But nothing, *nothing ever in my life,* could ever compare to the majesty of this bird of prey sitting so close to us.

We are spellbound! She is *huge:* three feet tall, perched with her six feet of wings tucked tight to her sides.

Janete and I often receive signals and transmissions from the Akash, such as the dreams that became vows in Italy and wildlife celebrating our lovemaking beneath a desert tree. Totems, spirits that take on animal forms to convey messages, sought Janete out *all the time*. The bald eagle came to see her and give her a message, as animals have done her whole life. She spent several lives as animals, and animal spirits often came to help wake her up.

Janete had spent some of her childhood in Africa as the army brat daughter of an Armenian immigrant army private. One of her earliest memories was of a strange beast she had seen on the savannah. Not an elephant, not a rhino, and certainly more prehistoric than the present day. The fact that her mother also saw it convinced her it was not her imagination. This magical beast had come through a portal dimension to contact her and activate her affection for mysteries.

Throughout her life, she was surprised by wildlife in the most unusual and mystical ways. Many animals came to her to die, making her afraid of her own power until I helped her make sense of it. "They come to you because they are scared and dying, and they sense that you are compassionate and were one of them not long ago. They come to you, so they don't have to die alone. They want their last moments to be with someone who will love them and see them for what they are: *souls*."

Animals regularly came to Janete to jolt her awake spiritually. They relied on me to interpret their requests.

Janete often pleaded with me to help her understand the meanings of her animal visitations. "They're beckoning you to be an animal healer." Animals have flocked to her like Dr. Doolittle for years. She knew it was extraordinary and not by chance.

This butterfly landed on her breast inside a moving train in WA DC. It remained on her for the entire one-hour trip.

That eagle was reminding her of her past. Over 400 years earlier, Janete and I performed magic rituals at Stonehenge. It cost her life, and she spent many lives in animal forms, unable to return to human form for many lifetimes. I had felt responsible for not protecting her in the ritual gone wrong. She and I remained separated and pined for each other for hundreds of years as a result. Her spirit bonded with animals over these lifetimes, and a spirit animal collective tried to recruit her as an animal healer. They sometimes spoke to me in dreams, pressing me to wake her to her destiny.

Before she and I had met in this life, her existence had been quite ordinary. When we became close, her life began to reveal the magical layers. Mine was already activated before we met; our reunion in this life activated hers, too, doubling our mystical experiences. She always knew I was a *spiritual catalyst;* those who grow close to me begin to have profound awakenings.

Bald eagles mate for life. Even after they raise their young to adulthood, these raptors remain monogamous and loyal, like soulmates, till death. Only then do they separate. Another reason for this totem's visit was to reopen Janete's eyes to our magic and Soulmate commitment to one another.

Minutes later, we sat in the car with the engine still running and paused before rolling out to the Seattle airport, "That was a totem, Janete. She came to give you a message. You've had them all your life, and she came here to remind you."

"This totem has come to you to wake you up, Janete, to seek and follow your calling. Please..." Tears came forth as I pleaded with her. "Wake up. Do *not* let your spirit go back to sleep! They need you! *I*... need you! You have a calling, and this whole drama thrust upon us is a part of it. Let's not live in this world anymore! Let's live the magic we deserve to live! Wake up!"

She shed tears along with me and agreed to allow me to lead her back from the darkness of ignorance and worldly illusions. Through the tears, she pled with me to heal from my injuries and help her. "I know... I hate this! You and I always had magic, and now it's all gone! I feel trapped in the world and can't find my way back! I'm afraid! I want to come back! I hate the world! I need you to save me!"

"We're almost there, Janete. I'm coming back to my body as fast as I can. I came here to get well. Just wait for me. My spirit is merging with my body, and it won't be long! Don't go back to sleep! Stay awake with me! The tragedy of my death is a *pause*, not an ending!"

She promised to try to keep her spirit awake and let me rescue her. I reminded her, "You just don't remember, Janete. We promised we'd find each other again, and whoever was asleep, the other would wake them up to who they really are. It's *my* turn. *You* woke me last time. Let's do it right and live our destiny."

We held each other, and for the first time since D-Day, we could feel each other's timeless love and spirits together. It seemed our spiritual union had been awakened. I was so relieved to have her back, to have *us* back. Our hearts and minds were finally present in the same place and time.

Our heart chakras swelled with radiant love as we held each other like never before.

***

Within days of her going back home, it was like it had never happened. The next time we spoke, I could sense she was a mortal human again. Without me as a spiritual lantern, her rather agnostic family, the materialistic suburbs, and doing what it took to get by dimmed her spirit light. She fell back asleep to spirit and was part of the world again. I could not keep her awake full-time, and when we separated, she slumbered again. I see it happen to people all the time, and it shatters me, which is why I need to be in the garden of this sanitarium for now. Many people have spiritual awakenings, but few *remain* awake.

But as her spirit slumbers, I am still in this tunnel, lonely and estranged, my loved ones 1,200 miles away. I'm taking one for the team, remaining geographically distant to allow Brandon to make his own way with tough love, sink-or-swim, hands-off parenting. I'm giving Janete the time, space, and opportunity to see what life is like without me and hope she chooses us and our magic of her own free will. It has to be her conscious choice.

Our last separation before I came here took less than ten days before her arms were around me, happily saying she missed me and her life was meaningless without us together. This separation isn't as simple as shining a little light to contrast our lives apart from our lives together. This one is because I *truly* need to heal. This one is a test. Aphrodite, the goddess of love, wants a sacrifice. A virgin needs to be cast into the volcano. In the legend, Aphrodite's husband and lover, Hephaestus, goes to Olympus to see if his true love will stand with him. Will she stand by her man during his darkest hours, as he has done for her countless times?

I didn't know if I had come here to live or die. I soon learned it was neither; I came here to exile and do my sanitarium time. It was *"what's next."*

***

The Buddha said the best and worst day of someone's life is when they realize True Enlightenment is real and possible. It's the best because they finally know why they're here, why they've been lost, and what they've been searching for; it's the worst because they will never be at peace until they have attained it. He concluded this with a comforting notion; it is only a matter of time until they become enlightened because it becomes the only priority in their existence. Gurus and Masters appear to bring this best and worst day to people worldwide, not just in their native lands.

Spiritual awakening is a blessing and a curse. Sorry, but if you're happy in your spirituality, then you ain't spiritual yet. If you are *grateful* to be spiritually awake, you may be awake or at least waking up. If you feel gratitude mixed with a restless dislike and virtual contempt for all that isn't holy and sacred, *now...* you're spiritually waking up. The dark night of the soul ain't easy.

True spirituality isn't all peaceful, kumbaya, whole-grain, holistic-organic yoga class. Spirituality matures into an incapacity to derive deep, satisfying pleasure from *anything* in the world. *That...* is the dark night of the soul. Years ago, Janete was humbly vocal about this angst as she first began to see the worthlessness of material life. "You ruined me. I already had a hard time liking the world, but I didn't know why. Now, none of it can make me happy."

"I know... And I'm sorry. But it was your time. And *I* didn't do anything, Janete. You sought me out, and we connected. The Grace of God and a Guru have spiritually awakened you."

"I'll never be the same, will I?"

"No, you can never go back."

"As sad as it is, I'm thankful."

28.

PUGET SOUND PURGATORY

Counting the stars in the sky, I spend each day and night, crying with falling tears
—Kripalu (Virah Madhuri,kirtan of longing)

Just when everyday seemed to greet me with a smile
Sunspots have faded, now I'm doing time.
—Chris Cornell ("Fell on Black Days")

My sanitarium time completed. Just as I was released from the hospital into a scary world well before I thought I was ready, my time in the sanitarium ended too.

I spent six dark, lonely, trashy months in a one-bedroom apartment with a college kid across the hall and a tweaker meth-head upstairs. The college kid is chill. The tweaker upstairs is up all night building fucking birdhouses or some shit requiring power tools and hammers between 2 a.m. and dawn. Twice I wake to see her convict-boyfriend sitting in his pickup truck with the engine running, parked two feet from my bedroom window.

How did I get here?

Three months before my lease was up at the resort-like home, my intuition commanded me to call the property manager, who told me the owners would not be renewing the lease because they were coming home to live in the house. Had I not had the intuition to call and ask, I wouldn't have known till thirty days prior. Desperate and rushed, I bought a quarter acre of forest near the Puget Sound and paid cash for a pre-planned home to be built. A 1,500-square-foot home built from blueprints you select from a catalogue.

What was contracted to be turnkey ready in three months took six. The shit-man, corporate contractor, sales rep was full of grand optimism before I signed the contract, but before the ink was dry, didn't give two shits about keeping the customer satisfied. There were enough cover-their-ass loopholes in the contract, so there were no penalties when three months in an apartment turned into six (Hiline Homes: crooked, lying, opportunists doing mediocre work).

I micro-managed the entire project to keep it under *eight months*. To keep their two-man skeleton crew moving forward, I cleaned the site weekly, painted the house, inside and out, myself, and then built a wood deck at the front and back doors to pass final inspection. I had personally hired and supervised the site-leveling to prep the ground, helped dig the foundations with a fucking shovel, and managed all the building permits and inspections. None of which was my job: I did it because otherwise it wouldn't get done.

I'm dizzy, find it hard to have balance, but by first of June, I'm moved in. I keep doing things as if I'm well. My body is not technically broken, so I do what I would do if I were healthy. I just pad in more time: if building a deck for my first time is two weeks of labor, I slate it to take four. Any chore that is an hour of work, I allow two, and I get it done. My deck goes from a few steps to the front door to pass final inspection to a 5'x20', redwood, pressure-treated, water-sealed deck. Since I have no actual wood-carpentry experience, I frame the whole thing out of 20ga steel studs. My memory sucks, but my twenty-plus years as a metal stud framer and contractor has left me with good tradesmen *sanskars*. The solo-work was rather meditative actually.

Purgatory began when I moved into the apartment.

- My possessions were put into storage, which I could not access.
- I didn't see Janete or Brandon because the apartment is too small, and I was embarrassed.
- I couldn't go visit them and get out of purgatory-hell because I couldn't leave Chow-Chow-Bang.

My loneliness was a poison I drowned in. I was in this tiny, shitty apartment because I knew I wouldn't be happy anywhere that would allow a three-month lease, so I bit the bullet and got something basic and no frills. Just walls with a roof so Chow-Chow and I could be safe, and I was close enough to the building site to go often to keep it going.

I lived in Olympia, right next to Tumwater Falls Park, the capital building and historic district. It helped take the sting out, but I felt so isolated and alone and as though Janete moved on without me. I slowly came back to who I was, orienting to the world, and it sucked: as a *spiritual being*, I was fine. But as a *human being*, I was fucking depressed!

I dug deep: using all the rationale and denial I could muster to endure what I forced myself to believe were the final days of sanitarium-purgatory. My fantasy of being reunited with my love and a life that is whole was what sustained me: I *had to* believe better days were ahead. Things were looking up, futures looked promising, but the present was as dark as midnight.

To pass the time, I published my fourth book, *Road Games—Bizarre Stories, Curious Tales*. It is a collection of eight short stories and is my only fiction work (though it is blended with true accounts). I got it released and record the audio so it was available worldwide in print, eBook, and audio. Seven stories I invented in my twenties when I drove long-haul trucks across the country plus a bonus story I'd never considered publishing. *Skyline* is a sweet and ethereal romantic anecdote. A simple story of a couple walking and talking along the Venice Canals in Loing Beach. It is actually the real event inspiring our sojourn to Italy when Janete and I gave vows. The other seven stories are like Stephen King meets *Twilight Zone* on psilocybin: twisted, darkly funny, with creamy doses of gratuitous sex and supernatural weirdness.

The brain injury portion of my death-event subsided. I was rarely confused or misplaced and could do nearly everything I once did, from chores of labor to playing tennis. I'd never be the four-oh tennis player I was once, but I could get out and hit against a ball-machine on advanced levels.

Even though coexisting with Akashic Agents and space became much more manageable, my daily life was saturated in ethereal syrup. I truly felt, each and every day, I served a sentence. I got this eerie sense, like all the time, I was fading away, becoming more of a phantom to Janete and the material reality I once was a citizen of.

I'm not trying to shit on apartment life: we all gotta do what we gotta do at various stages of our lives. But I did this: I went from low-class rentals I grew up in to the streets to apartments in my twenties, and even after Brandon was born, his first three years, we were in studio or one-bedroom apartments. I worked my ass off to get out of apartment life to home living and lived in the comforts of an actual house for so long now, I'd conditioned to it. This shit was ghetto!

Technically, it's not so bad: a large complex with plenty of parking, a rec room with pool tables and a gym, and my unit is an end unit: other than the tweaker bitch upstairs, I didn't have an adjacent neighbor. I had a small patio butting up to a football-field-sized open lawn. It was relatively quiet and affordable.

Chow-Chow was virtually grounded: it was unsafe to let him roam freely in an apartment complex, so h was trapped inside this shoebox shithole. He'd gone from four acres of playground to 650 sq. ft. of confinement. My sorrow of confined and shitty apartment living was exacerbated by his: seeing him suffering by being confined and having no capacity to understand it *broke my fucking heart!*

I did some research and bought two things:

- A leash
- A GPS tracker collar

The GPS tracker collar synced to an app on my phone. It would alarm me if he went outside the predetermined zone I set to it, which was a 150-foot circumference of the apartment. When it went off, I could track him within a few feet, *usually*. It was not exact, and sometimes it just told me where he was within twenty to twenty-five feet. That ain't enough!

When it snowed, he got lost: he couldn't smell his way back because the snow didn't keep his scent. I tracked him, but he wouldn't come to me, and it seemed all was lost. It was barely 35 degrees out, and if I didn't get him in before the sun set in the next hour, he would definitely not make it through the night.

In his confusion, he barely recognized me, and I couldn't get close enough to give him my own scent. He sat beneath a tree, terrified. If I moved toward him, he would run away and get more lost, and within a few more feet, the GPS unit would lose the signal altogether. So I laid down. On my back. In jeans and a t-shirt. *In the snow.* I avoided eye contact to neutralize his fear and embarrassment. I outstretched my hand to him, and not making a sound other than humming the theme to the TV show, *The Courtship of Eddie's Father*: *"people, let me tell you 'bout my be-esst friend! He's my one boy, my cuddly toy, my ups, my downs, my pride and joy…"*

This was the song I'd sing to Brandon when he was an infant, falling asleep, and it meant the world to me. Sure enough, Chow-Chow the Bang-Bang, a.k.a. Pi, inched slowly toward my hand where he could smell a familiar scent, and I... *GRABBED HIM!*

Tragedy averted!

Another one, he had wandered up a hill and was almost outside the GPS coverage by the time I even got close. I found him. But I was on *one side* of the fence and he on the other. I don't know how he got there, and he was confused and lost. It was over 100 yards down the hill to go around the fencing *and 100 yards back up* before I'd get to him. By then, he'd be gone, gone, gone.

I lay down in the dirt, calling to him, friendly and cheerful so as not to alarm him to get him to follow me. I coaxed him all the way down the hill from opposite side of the fence and coaxed him to the front door. Mission accomplished. There were several of these, but locking him inside was not an option: I'd rather he *die* being free, on his own terms, than live forever as a prisoner.

Janete didn't like to talk on the phone or text or even Skype, so all human contact, which was familiar for me, was sparse. I found myself going to the mall, so dated it was from the '70s, just to be around humans. Janete reassured me I was doing the right thing.

"But I'm lonely, Janete. I miss you and feel like everyone is moving on without me."

"I'm lonely too." But she never said she missed me. I never heard or sensed longing from her. The brief contact we had was rushed as she was irritated by talking on a phone. Her mild discomforts were always paramount whilst mine were an inconvenience. "But you chose to move there. It was your choice to be alone. There's nothing anyone can do about it now." It felt callous. I know it was true, my choice and all, but I remembered it being more complicated. I remembered commitment and support.

I dug deeper than ever before to endure this stark isolation. I obeyed the spiritual orders as I interpreted them, pushed myself into a corner I couldn't get out of. I believed and fully accepted I was cosmically-directed to move to the PNW and faithfully followed this intuition, but I ran out of steam. And money. There was no doubt if I had a way out, if I wasn't $135K cash-in on a house in mid-construction, didn't have a living animal to be accountable to, and could fly to LA, I'd do it. Living in LA during house build was never an option for two reasons:

1. Janete's twenty-seven-year-old son lived with her: he was on drugs now, dysfunctional, loud, unemployed.
2. I had to visit the jobsite several times a week as per contract. Even if I wasn't bound by contract, I knew the only way that place was going to pass final inspection this century was with my hard work and pressuring

Grand Opening

Finally... grand opening. The house was done. I'd gone through the legal process to recover my losses by the multiple breaches of contract with the contractor, but they had all the power and a loophole-tight contract: fucking people over was just part of business for them. I had to micro-manage the entire project, reminding me of the corruption of contractors. I painted the entire inside alone, did all the laborer work, and constructed the front porch. It is beautiful. And I know I keep saying it, but it's such a prevalent and dominating element of each part of this part of the story, it bears repeating: *I am lonely.*

I was in the woods, didn't know a soul, and lived alone. Can I, or do I, need to say more? I moved in in June, somewhere around my birthday/death day. Janete's visit to my new home was planned, and I was anxious. We've not seen each other for eight months now. I yearn for her: our cyber-video-call sex-life is like watered down Kool-Aid.

Brain trauma often has a side effect of impotency. It was a struggle the first year or so, but within the first month of being home, I was secure in the knowledge erectile dysfunction wouldn't be an issue! But I'd been with one partner for over twelve years now, and we had always been in love, so while I contemplated affairs and other partners while in WA, I felt more strongly about our someday reunification being even more sacred if I remained true to only her. *I*... was capable of moving on from her infidelity, but she and I *both* knew she was not capable of that if it had been reversed.

This was clear from the start of our relationship and a major reason why I felt she was an ideal partner. I had been a notorious philanderer since I had been devirginized at fifteen. Janete had been the *only* partner I had ever been true to.

Because of the trauma of her ex's infidelity and her intrinsic virtue, I knew from day one she would never tolerate the slightest sexual scandal. *I liked this.*

I learned as I matured the reason I had cheated on every girl and woman I had ever been involved with was because I knew from my intuitive subconscious they would forgive me. To quote Chris Rock: men are only as faithful as their options.

I wanted, *no, needed,* to be with a woman who would absolutely not tolerate a single instance of impropriety. More of my other axiom that *God loves irony*. This woman who'd been chaste and virtuous all her life had had her one and only transgression against the only man who'd ever truly earned her fidelity.

Sure... I thought of dating and considered options during my exile and even fantasized of many. But options were not available much: long ago, during the early phase of monogamy with Janete, I had constructed a force-field. I radiated a repellent keeping seductive women who might want to seduce me off my radar. Just as I had constructed a *tractor-beam* in my youth that *drew* scandal *to* me, I radiated a frequency jamming frequencies emitted by wanton women. I had decided to wait until it was officially *over* before taking any alternative actions. And by *official*, I meant it had to be ended *by her*. Or by me in a declarative way long before I *did* anything.

We had both agreed her ex's infidelity that wrecked their marriage was partly her fault: she had become a demanding woman who doled out sex on her terms and never validated the guy. When she had told me she forced him to agree to *sit down* to urinate to prevent the notorious over-spill, in their shared home, which *he* paid for by working nonstop while she tended to kids and home, I tenderly gave her a reaction:

"You emasculated him and deprived him of his rightful male ego in spite of his servile care for you and your home and kids. When a pretty woman with a nice ass and big tits stroked his validation, he went to her. It didn't matter that *your* ass was finer and tighter: man cannot live by bread alone, and you made this guy feel small instead of valuable."

"You're right. He deserved more than I gave him, and I pretty much pushed him into it. She doted on him, like I once did, and she saw an opportunity and took it. It was my fault."

"I wouldn't say it's *your fault,* but you were certainly complicit, and the outcome was suburbanite-predictable. In spite of this, he had other options too: a good man would've said to you the arrangement between you two was unfair, he was unhappy and dissatisfied, and then negotiated a settlement: treat me better, or I'll find someone who will. He's a pussy: he kept his mouth shut when his wife told him he couldn't stand up to pee. He's muthafuckin' guilty as charged and takes *all* the blame for breaking a vowed contract. But you're complicit."

I had been clear from the start of my *terms* of our contracted love-arrangement. Telling her during our courtship, over candles and soft music while we basked in each other's post-coital nudity, gently and with love:

"I don't ask nor need much. I will do all the heavy lifting in this relationship. I'll work and finance our lives together. I'll do most the thinking and figuring and will always include you in every decision before it's made too. I will stay fit, smart, healthy, and true and will never be dull and always romantic. The *courtship* dynamic will never end from me.

"All I insist is that you appreciate it. I don't need praise or flattery. I need to see and feel that you love having me in your life and enjoy the magic we make: don't take anything for granted. That and stay hot. Like you are, or at least try. You become one of those women who let themselves go once they got a marriage license to protect their joint account, you get bossy instead of sweet, and God forbid, *get fat,* then I am outta here. I will *earn* you, each and every day for decades, and will never get lazy loving you. If you don't appreciate this for yourself and get fat, it's over for me. I know it's superficial, but I know my weaknesses."

She agreed, feeling it was the deal of the century: she never planned on letting herself go anyway, was naturally easygoing, and had no ambition to work or need self-reliance on material things. It was a deal, and the stellar magic became poetry. Until death do us part... It was never said aloud, but it was implied in a silent contract I would not die at forty-seven.

If we can reunite and begin again after all this and have just that one relatively minor infraction, we'll be golden.

I pick her up at the airport and break the ice: "It's pretty normal for us to feel awkward, so let's not judge that. It's been eight months since we've been in the same room, so let's let it be what it is. Like a new and fresh courtship, let's capitalize on the awkwardness and make it a part of the adventure."

I was excited to show her the new home: she'd seen the lot on her last visit eight months earlier and some of the new town.

She liked my home. She was impressed with how beautiful it was and how I'd already made spaces for her, not as a *guest,* but as a partner: mi casa, su casa. She had her own closet and her own sink in the master bath. I did not want her to feel the discomforts of being away from home. My house in LA had been the same: she always had her own closet, sink, and the rest. My house was where we spent most of our together time, so it was as much her home as mine.

I had a wonderful road trip planned to have an adventure. I was doing my very best to give us normalcy in our relationship.

29.
FIRSTS AND LASTS

> Everyone desires only spiritual bliss. Worldly happiness is just an illusion.
> —Kripalu (Sankhya Darshan)

> One last voice is calling you/And I guess it's time you go.
> —Grateful Dead ("Sugaree")

As a private counselor of several years, I worked with many troubled marriages and relationships. Naturally, most relationship troubles centered on someone's infidelity. It surprised me to discover more than half of those transgressions were by the woman and not the man. Society has programmed us to think men are prolific cheaters. Part of my m.o. to put a lifetime of philandering behind me was to install a girlfriend in my life who was hot! My unspoken, silent contract was that to even *consider* a sexual dalliance with anyone else, she would have to be more desirable than Janete. Beauty is in the eye of beholder: it is *subjective*. To me, she was physically perfect. I loved her form and her look—her eyes to her smile. I never met a woman I desired more than her, so why would I risk that?

Janete was physically flawless: firm, tight body, lean and petite, fit, and truly without blemish. I loved her from the start and knew right away she would *never* tolerate a single sexual transgression. That was m.o. #2: to be with a woman that would not tolerate cheating in any way, shape, or form. Her first (and only) husband had cheated on her, and it was the death of their marriage: it shattered her, but she told him it was over immediately as he begged forgiveness, citing a decade plus of marriage and two kids to support his pleas of remaining together. Bottom line was she knew she would *never* be able to forget and see him unblemished again. She floundered from his betrayal for several years: becoming a single parent who'd never really worked or supported herself before. I admired her bravery and dedication to virtue. I was the one that restored her to believing in commitment again. Motis Operandi #3 was *I loved her.*

I vowed before we met to never willingly participate in the suffering or pain of another person. I had cheated on every partner I'd ever been with through my life: fourteen long-term girlfriends and over twenty-eight sexual partners; do the math. Janete was my first partner I'd been faithful to. God loves irony! The one person I *don't* cheat on makes me the only person she does!

The second group of society's relationship troubles is *complacency*.

Couples together near, or over, ten years get bored. They've heard all their partner has to say: all their stories and perspectives and can easily predict every part of them, from where they want to go out to eat, to vacations, to work, children, community... Men cheaters are just cheaters: they don't need some psychological phase to inspire them to fuck another woman. Women cheaters construct elaborate rationalizations to betray vows. Women cheaters rarely get caught. Women cheaters often sought me out for help, which was admirable.

It wasn't just out of guilt. Their initiating counseling was part guilt but far more motivated by needing to resolve this turbulent phase of life seeing them compromise their beliefs. They had a conscience.

Men cheaters rarely initiated counseling unless they'd been caught and were trying to do damage control. A few came on their own, which also was admirable, but most male transgressors suffer from a horrible syndrome: *wanting what we can't have*. The irony was most of the men who cheat, cheat with women who are less than *half* the caliber of their actual wives!

I was always stumped to meet these couples where the guy was rather average cheating with a well-below-average consort while they had a pretty hot wife who was pretty sweet too!

However, many of these wives had become *asexual*, losing interest in sex and intimacy, depriving their men of fundamental needs while exploiting them as fathers and providers. We need a new *#MeToo* movement for men who are regularly exploited and shamed for thinking they deserve a sexual component with the partner they took vows with. As another comedian once said, *women are like hurricanes: it starts out with a whole lot of blowin', wet and loud, and then they take your house.*

I advised my son to beware of hot girls: they get a lot of attention which develops into entitlement in this sex- and glamour-driven society.

The women who sought me out as a counselor because they were having an affair and considering separation or divorce was due to the complacency complaint: *He bores me. He's not fun anymore. He's out of shape. He's not romantic. He doesn't give me attention. He's too quiet/talkative/opinionated/unopinionated...* Meanwhile, most of them are as guilty of these pseudo-sins as the one they're complaining about.

They take zero initiative to be interesting themselves, but readily blame their husband for the complacency.

They met when they were young, they each changed as they matured, and the most vital element of affection and connection had not been sustained by *either* partner: intimacy. Closeness. *Courtship.*

We fall in love with someone because when we meet them, we are drawn with chemistry, and this triggers a collection of inspired behaviors: gifts, flattery, sharing, looking good to impress them... We have this mentality of wanting to be on their mind as they are for us, so we put in the time and effort to keep them intrigued. We want to be a partner their friends and family are *envious* of. I strived to be a man every woman in Janete's life would envy her for, *including and especially my faithfulness.* We want to be a person that makes our lover think of us whenever they have a romantic desire. During courtship, we all earn it. We're on our *marks:* witty, charming, and exuding our sensuality, to whatever degree we may have of it. And over time, we get comfortable and don't keep it dynamic.

My success at relationship counseling was stellar: cheaters, liars, betrayers, and complacency of the dullest kind were all retrained to inject new life in a predictably hopeless cause: *if...* the two wanted to work it out and were willing to work on it and applied what I advised, they were restored. One such couple stood out:

The woman had sought me out. She had moved out to an apartment. I advised separate counseling sessions, not joint. The man was distraught: he loved her and was prepared to do anything to win her back.

"She had been telling me for five years. She was not a shrew when she was telling me she was unhappy, needed attention, needed love and romance. She didn't yell or be mean. One day she was standing at the door with a suitcase in her hand. She said '*I'm leaving.*' I was sitting on the couch, watching TV—as always. She reminded me she'd been trying to help me and our marriage by demanding we have a life beyond kids, work, house, and TV, and she was leaving. Suddenly it all came into focus: she had not only been telling me what she needed, which was all very reasonable, she had been telling me for two years that if it didn't change, she would leave. I just never heard it."

He was in tears. Uncontrollable tears. He truly loved her and knew she gave him every chance to just be her friend and lover, and his laziness and apathy had pushed her to keep her word: she left.

I reminded him about courtship. I played the Cyrano role to his Christian character coaching him how to court her. "Don't even consider getting her *back*. You do *not* want *back* what you had. You want something new. Fresh. Dynamic. Make her want you, *or someone else will*. You love her? Then go get her and win and earn her affection. Have a goddam good time with it!"

It wasn't easy, but he won her love the old-fashioned way: *courtship*.

The regular exposure to failing relationships made me so aware of how special and blessed Janete and I had it together. We rarely reminisced, focusing more on present and future, but we had grand history in our ten years.

"I will never forget when you pulled me out of depression darkness, Scott."

"I'm not sure what you're referring to, but whatever I did was nothing. I just love you."

"It was when you showed up at my door and said 'pack a bag, we're getting out of here.' And you took me to the desert where we spent three days in a dark hotel room and the springtime desert, and you watching over me gave me light. That was one of the purest acts of love I've ever known."

She kissed me on the cheek, so innocent and simple. "It's what we do, Janete. The day a hospital called to tell me my mom was dying, I was walking across Santa Monica Blvd with a sack of day-old Panera bread for the homeless in the park and bagels for my crew working in the high-rise on Wilshire. I was so literally shocked it froze me. Do you remember?"

"Yes, it was so sad. You showed up at my house and told me. I'd never seen you shocked and not knowing what to do before."

"And you didn't ask me any questions. You said 'let's go,' grabbed a change of clothes, and said 'go to her.' You didn't even pause. I couldn't think on my own. My mom was dying hundreds of miles away, and I was so helpless. We drove seven hours. You never once asked when we would go back, what could be done... You were just *by my side* the entire time."

"It's what we do." Her gentle fingers wrapped around mine. "You gave a eulogy at my dad's funeral just last year. I don't know how you did it. I'll never forget the one you gave your mom when we went to Ohio for hers. I'm so glad I got to meet her once before she died. And you sharing Ohio and your grandparents and whole family with me. It made me see why Ohio was so special to you. Hey...! The week before your mom died, didn't you campout on our Boulder Creek property?"

"Oh my god, yes!" Her shift to smiles of light changes our gear. "Yeah! I was going up to be by her during the surgery! I was such an asshole! I was sooo busy, I couldn't believe she demanded I drive to NorCal to sit in a room while she had surgery! I'm definitely going to hell for not being more supportive!"

"Isn't that when you watched Holy Mountain?"

"Oh shit! The OTO brothers found I'd never even heard of it and snuck me a DVD, and I watched it on my laptop the night I camped on our property as I drove to see her. It blew my fucking mind so bad, when I got back to the OTO lodge, Frater Robert and a few others just *looked* at me and could tell I'd seen it! They go, '*So ... you saw it, huh?*' And I exploded! FUCK YEAH, I SAW IT! Holy shit! You guys said it was cool, you didn't say it was the most landmark, mind-blowing, mystical account ever put on film! You *knew* this was going to be a before and after moment!"

Frater Robert confirmed, "That's how it's done, man! You can't prepare someone for Holy Mountain. You just gotta lead 'em to it and let it happen!"

I'd left my mom once she was out of ICU post-surgery. It had been a touch-and-go heart surgery for hours, but all seemed well when I drove back to my busy, sole-proprietor construction duties. Two days later, when Janete told me to "just go to her," her love and support for me became the most generous, selfless act I'd ever been given.

<u>Firsts</u>

From our happy accident meeting and our first time making love in a seaside hotel two days before my birthday, we had kept courtship vibrant for ten years. I moved to Washington with hope to begin a fresh and exciting, long distance courtship.

All that mattered was *intention* and *spirit*. This landmark and milestone of our newest dramas and challenges was vital. This was to be the beginning of the turning point: I'd built a home and was safe. Home was *essential* to her. I was stabilizing. My spirit was coming *home*. I had learned to run. Learning to run is not a metaphor.

I retrained my brain to work my body. The first time I tried to jog terrified me: I struggled to keep from face-planting every step. But I kept at it; she and Brandon inspired me without knowing of their role.

The iconic burger joint Brandon worked at had a softball team, and Brandon had told me he played on the team. Seeing him play on my last trip to LA thrilled me and brought back a fountain of memories. I had taught him how to throw a ball and been a pony-ball coach for years, and we had spent countless hours playing catch and at batting cages. Dozens of Dodger games we shared every year since he had been four. Some of the purest, sweetest memories of my life were like fields of dreams.

Lying in bed one morning, I grieved over this nostalgia. I wanted to play catch. I wanted to have that *field-of-dreams* moment when I saw him the next time. But I was all fucked up: I could walk now, but run? No way! Pivot side to side and sprint under a ball to catch it? Not a chance. I sat on my deck, weeping with my failure as a father that I couldn't ever give my son a game of catch again. I decided to try to jog just a few steps on my next walk.

Then the inner voice spoke up: "How 'bout now?"

"Waddya mean now? I already went on my walk today."

"So? Go on another. If it ain't gonna kill you, then what the fuck are you waiting for? Tomorrow may never come."

So I did. Each day I tried to jog a few steps on my walk. Within two weeks, I ran over a mile every day, *uphill and down!* Downhill was *scary* for me! Uphill took stamina, which I had a ton of. But downhill took *balance*, which I had *none!*

I was like a little kid looking for a *nice job!* ribbon for my monumental accomplishment. Janete ran marathons while I had played as a four-oh tennis player for years. It excited me to show her my beautiful jogging route through the golf-course near my new home.

I found a club to rent a tennis ball machine to tennis train; I worked hard. I'd been a four-oh tennis player before. To give you some context, your average club player is 3-0 and your top, pro tournament players are 6-0. My groundstrokes were still 4-0 capable, but my dizzy-brain, uncoordinated footwork was 2-0! It took a day to recover from one tennis session: not physically, but mentally. I could now recall what I had been capable of, and it depressed me to see my limitations. Tennis had been a major passion of mine.

And Lasts

Her visit was just before my birthdays: a week or so before the end of June. I had only been in the house a month but unpacked and settled in, the fresh paint on the new walls a lovely shade of *please approve of me.*

She would come for a week and return home before my death-and-rebirthday of the 19th and 28th, but we would have the spectrum: some quiet time at home, local travel to dine out, take walks, and a journey to Leavenworth, WA—an alpine village at the foot of the Cascades.

Leavenworth is a Bavarian German town so much more authentic than any tourist trap. Founded and still populated by genuine Bavarians, this town is famous for its annual Christmas holidays. My own family tree is not just German but Bavarian.

A three-and-a-half-hour drive over the Cascades provides a full-spectrum tour of Washington: we would see the Sounds and forests, the high mountains, and the east side of the Cascades. There are *two* Washington States: *west* of the Cascades and *east*.

Western WA is Puget Sound: green, fertile, forests; water, water, water; and grey, grey, grey... Highs in the summer rarely reach the high eighties; lows in winter are snowy freezes.

Eastern WA is polar opposite: dry, warm, and sunny, sunny, sunny. A climate Janete likes a lot. I wanted her to see PNW had options, which we could compromise on as we retired and settled down.

The drive to Leavenworth is amazing and we got along well. The complacency factor of being together over ten years is present though: we have far less tolerance for each other's quirks and particulars. The very things we find enamoring in a new partner; the way they laugh, eat, stuff they don't get... become the very things we are sick and tired of after ten years of daily exposure to them. Overall, I sense she is more *indulging* my adventurous ways rather than appreciating and enjoying them. Part of me suspects she really doesn't want to do much of *anything*. Just relax and stay home. Which I'd be okay with if it included connection, deep conversations, and emotional and physical intimacy. But it doesn't.

I've always been the driver. She's always been an enthusiastic passenger. I was alpha/omega male. She was gentle and unassertive. I'm filling my role, but she seems to be phoning hers in.

We walk-tour the Bavarian town and have a good time seeking out vegan options in a *bratwurst* community. We're booked into a nice chalet resort and are synchronized with turning in early. It is reminiscent of the portion of our wedding trip into the Alps of Austria. The view is nice, and we are close. Our arms and hands intertwine, and the variety of the day coming to a close is poetic as we are comforted with being together. The evening is light and easy. I've paced our time and trip: We made love on her second night of arrival rather than right away. This had allowed us to connect in mind and heart after eight months of separation and her to refresh from traveling with proper rest without intimacy pressure. The road trip was planned for day four and five, allowing us both to sexually, romantically recharge before arriving.

This would give my testosterone time to recharge for a few days for a romantic and powerful second round of delighting each other over our road trip.

This visit and trip is multi-purposed: my upcoming birthday, our twelfth anniversary in April, a new home, reuniting after eight months of separation... many reasons for its specialness. That night, our passions were full and bright. We performed our usual repertoire, but with vigor: after a decade of healthy, satisfying sex with each other, we *know* what the other likes. Our positions, order of sequence of tongues and fondlings, writhings and moanings... a symphony we both are maestros of. She cums long and loud. Her orgasm is never an easy conquest: it took skill, patience, and often caused cramps to my tongue and neck to bring it to volcanic voluptuousness. But I cannot be satisfied unless she is first. Her climax fuels my own: her arousal and the power of being the cause of it brings my own, ready climax to a brim of explosion.

We lie in repose, like only satisfied lovers can.

She rarely broke silence. But this night... "I've not had an orgasm in months." She had confessed masturbation was not enticing for her. "That was the second-best orgasm in my entire life." I already knew the first: our second time together in Monterey. I never forgot it either and was always so honored to have given her the *one* that she would always remember. I never became deliberate to relive it: our sexual life and history as a couple was natural and without hang-ups.

"I love you, Janete. You love me too. We have magic."

We ventured for coffee in the early, sleeping town and casually went on our way, the three-and-a-half-hours back over the Cascades to sleepy Shelton.

It seemed like old times: we got along great, had an adventure, made love, and argued over trivial things at the end of four hours of driving and being tired of it and not stopping for food.

We still had several days to spend and would allow it to be uneventful: dinner at home and walks along the Sound and the bucolic golf course next to Lake Limerick. A movie was in order, so we went to the cinema for a flick of romance and fantasy, *The Shape of Water.*

Midway through the film, I wept.

"Why are you crying? I don't get it. What's happening?" she whispered. Another staple of our relationship was Janete liked me to explain art and film to her. I never did this with condescension; always with patience. I cherished her innocence and her enthusiasm to know more. She was ashamed of her limitations, but not with me. We both found the contrast delightful: me a cerebral-intellectual adept, she a simple and open heart.

"I'll tell you later ..." was all I could muster at the time, and I assured her it had nothing to do with the movie, and they were tears of joy, not sadness.

We sat at a Chipotle for a post-movie meal before going home. "I was tearing up because I was having a profound realization. The scene in the movie was those two talking and making plans. But in the *background,* behind the guy's head, a TV was on. Because the film is set in 1962, the show that was on it was from the '60s, before you and I were even born."

"Okay..."

"And in a very random thought, my mind just kinda identified and categorized the show playing in the background. Nothing unusual: you see something insignificant that you recognize, and your subconscious mind makes split-second acknowledgment of it, and you forget all about it."

"Okay..."

Janete is used to my answers having dramatic build up. "I knew the TV show in the background of the scene was *Dobie Gillis.* But *that's* not why it affected me. I instantly knew it was Dobie Gillis, but in that instant, I realized *how* I knew it: When Brandon was an infant and toddler I lived alone in a studio apartment after leaving his mother to save myself and Brandon from a life of dysfunction. I had him every weekend, so I could never go out. He was only eight months old, so I was bound to this tiny apartment on Saturday nights. I was sad, lonely, and had no one to talk to. I had no one in my life. I had separated from everyone I knew because everyone I knew was a criminal dope-fiend, and I was getting clean. Brandon is all that mattered to me, so I stayed home with him, and he was usually asleep by 7. There was *nothing* on TV so I passed the time with *Nick at Night.* You remember that?"

"Yeah... back when Nickelodeon was still kinda new and just showed old shows."

"Exactly. They were still starting out and couldn't afford to show new shows, so they banked off the old shit to make a name. They used to show *Mary Tyler Moore, Bob Newhart* and they showed this *Dobie Gillis* show too. *I wasn't crying because of nostalgia,* Janete.

Janete... I was crying, not because I remembered *Dobie Gillis* even. I couldn't give two shits about some lame sitcom from the 60s."

Her hand went to her mouth, "Oh my god. That's right: you *remembered.*"

"Yes. I *remembered.* Not only that that was the shitty, stupid *Dobie Gillis* show, but because I *could actually remember* how *I knew it.* This is the first time I've had an actual memory of who I am and where I come from. I... was *me.* I have a past and I was *actually* remembering it!"

This is the moment I realized that one's identity is the sum total of their prior events and perceptions that have led up to this moment, *the Eternal Present.* That's what you are. That's what we all are. Our identities are the sum total of thoughts and experiences that have brought you to *this* moment. And this one... and this one... and so on...

"I was crying, because I *knew who I was*. I knew where I came from. Fuck *Dobie Gillis*! I have been able to *recognize* things for a while now. I often have been aware of knowing things and people, like recognizing an actor in a show. But until that moment in the movie theatre, I never could tap *how or where* I knew them. I *knew* I knew them, but have never been able to grasp or reach how or why. This is the first time I *remembered* why something was familiar."

I was in tears as I shared this. Smiling goofy with wet streaks down my cheeks, my partner not sure what to make or say of it, just sincerely saying, "I'm so happy for you. You've come such a long way. You deserve it."

***

I tried not to think of her departure, focusing my attention more on her company than her impending absence and the glaring hole I was about to endure when I returned to my empty house in the sticks *alone*.

I began getting itchy. I came here to die. And I was *improving*. I was already a 3X *medical* miracle, but was now becoming a miracle-miracle: surviving was #1, not being a vegetable #2, functioning on my own #3. I was since told by specialists that it wouldn't last: like Charlie from Flowers for Algernon, I was destined to remain as I was having hit the limit of restoration, and to expect a *decline*. I'm supposed to be getting worse, not better.

Doctors are stupid.

30.

NDE GOES INTERNATIONAL

> May yoga, the science of personal contact with the Divine,
> spread in time to all the world.
> —Yogananda Prahamansa

> I am not digging the ditch. The ditch is being dug.
> —Zen Koan

It is the cusp of autumn, always a mysterious time of year for me. Many of the most significant events and shifts in my life occur in utumn, particularly surrounding Halloween. The Kundalini event that catalyzed a major paradigm shift in my reality perception was on Halloween itself. Nearly every major relocation in my life was in the Fall: the first home I rented, the first home I bought, the recon mission to WA that went all-systems-go and the signing of the contract for the Shelton home I'd just built was in October. I doidn't know whether to look forward to them with champagne or just wear football padding for protection. Could I get an autumn/Halloween insurance policy?

I'd never heard of IANDS.

Hell, I couldn't recall ever hearing of Near-Death Experience. In spite of my lifelong immersion to the occult and supernatural, NDE was not a subject I knew much of. *Until one day...*

"Yeah, he's a writer, like you. You guys should probably meet." The agent of the homeowner's association in my community is encouraging me to network. "He's like you: really into the supernatural stuff. His house is up the road, he lives with his wife, and they were in an accident too."

Anytime someone says they're *like me* without even knowing me, even if they do, is a red flag to avoid. But my need to network, which I loathe, is prevalent. My books aren't gaining momentum, and my financial future has a daunting expiration date. Networking couldn't hurt.

We sit on a park bench, he, his wife, and me, on the shore of the lake. "You had an NDE."

"What? I'm not clear what you're referring to. I had a who/what?"

"A Near-Death Experience, you know..."

No... I didn't. We sat sipping coffee, getting acquainted, and it felt good: he and his wife were two people with some depth. I get along with people well and have high social skills but don't personally enjoy the tedium of conventional socializing. This was creative networking with another mystic.

"I'm not familiar. For all I know, I may have studied it to expert status, and it may be one of the many areas deleted from my memory, but I don't have anything in my library on it, and it seems like I would if I knew anything of it." My attempts to master medicine, neurology, and ayurvedics during my trauma has been thorough. Doctors were like hourly employees anxious to do the minimum and just clock out at the end of their shift. I always knew the only one who could truly help me was me. I turned over every stone and not once had been led to this NDE, Near-Death Experience, concept.

"NDE, the Near-Death Experience, is the documented phenomena of people who die and come back. Odd that you're not familiar with it." He said this without placation.

"What you've described from your accident and the bizarre loss of your identity, memory, and awareness of an Akashic space aligns exactly with NDE. I can recommend some reading if you want. Matter of fact, IANDS is having their national, annual convention right over in Seattle next month."

"IANDS?"

"The International Association of Near-Death Studies."

This was too uncanny to ignore: a global organization and culture of the NDE phenomena was having its annual convention in my backyard in just a few weeks? Obviously, the Fates were hard at work again: putting me on this Puget Sound picnic table with a stranger cluing me in to this IANDS thing.

I looked into it, and bingo, there's this whole entire global community centered around NDE, and IANDS is a respected leader in it. The ongoing and obvious presence of spiritual guides in my life is as robust as ever:

IANDS was founded in the '70s and has had dozens of annual conferences in various locations throughout the US. And the next one is in my backyard in a few weeks. Yesterday, I never heard of NDE and today learned of a national conference taking place just ninety minutes away. I began to suspect one of the reasons I was "called" here was to connect to this group and gain the knowledge and insights that might reverse my condition by teaching me how to cope properly. I have not had a single person to talk to about my bizarre, supernatural conditions. Not one. It's been like navigating a kayak through unknown waters without a GPS, waters like Niagara Falls!

Doctors talked medicine and procedures and advised mental health professionals for my struggle to acclimate post-brain trauma. Friends and family were at a total loss and had *no* idea how to advise or even converse on my conditions. The conventional world had only one category for me: *he's losing his mind from TBI.*

The evidence of this assertion was credible: anyone ever told me about a guy who suffered severe brain trauma and abandoned all that was potentially supportive to live like a recluse in the forests, I would only reply with: *They're not okay. They need medical and psychological help, stat!*

But the contrary evidence gave me hope I'm not TBI-delusional. *What* I'd done was pretty crackers: abandoned my home and family and relocated 1,200 miles away alone with no support. But *how* I'd done it argued my rationality: I managed my life smartly, built a home, and continued to counsel and do live events with great success, and I'd published four award-winning books. That's not evidence I'm a *crazy artist.* Self-producing and promoting is evidence of being a *stable professional.*

I was ready: my identity was not yet *stable* within my body/life yet, but it *was* present now. My memory of *who* I had been was greatly restored; details and gaps were still prevalent, but I knew who I was every day. I knew my past, which gave me an identity. My past was fragmented and littered with gaps, but I had one: and it was improving!

I was motivated and certainly longing for some purpose and hope: romantically, financially, psychologically. I had subtle awareness my ability to sustain reason and sanity had an expiration date, and I had to meet some sort of condition or requirement to renew the subscription to them. I'd been living in a perpetual point-of-no-return state. Something had to give before it was permanent.

The new fear emerging was if I actually recovered from this and came face-to-face with the gravity of my losses and traumas, I'd be back where I started to avert tragedy: I'd lose my fucking mind. If the TBI-NDE smoke cleared, and I clearly saw where I was and what I'd lost, I was gonna lose it.

Some of God's Grace is the paradox of feeling perpetually disconnected from reality due to TBI-NDE. Living in a foggy haze allowed me to be less connected to my condition. I was like a ghost, so the four years of events were more *surreal* than *real*. The surrealness of my deal was enough to keep me from swallowing an intentional bullet. That… and I didn't own a gun.

I was hopeful but cautious of this conference: I'd had it up to my *yin-yang* with New-Age wannabes and pseudo-spiritual people and institutions far from qualified. I vaguely remembered the Whole Life Times *"spiritual"* convention years ago in LA: presentations from astral travelers who brought messages from extra-terrestrials, revealing the *inside secrets* of the pyramids and selling aluminum-cone-hats to prevent alien-possession. *For just $89.95.*

My memory restoration reminded me the world was full of opportunistic hacks holding themselves up to be experts in fields they had no actual training in. This was *especially* true in the spiritual market. Anyone who'd had a few serendipitous coinky-dinks started YouTubing like they were a prophet from God in spite of never actually *practicing or studying* theology or mysticism. They think Kabbalah was a fad Madonna promoted in the '90s instead of a complete and ancient system for conscious illumination.

I bought a single day ticket for the three-day NDE convention and committed to intense investigation from morning's opening-bell to late evening. I was open to getting a room and staying more if it panned out well, but also prepared to two-hour commute home and save the money if it didn't. I was still easily overwhelmed and always needed an exit strategy if I felt *particularly* awkward or uncomfortable. Some days I was dizzier than others, and some days it was hard to keep my mind in the material dimension.

The conference was a blend: some good stuff, some bad stuff.

Eighty percent of the presenters were simple people who lacked true articulation. They were so changed by their own NDE they felt *called upon* to enlighten humanity on the life-after-death concept. They were like A-Typical *born-agains*: getting on their soapboxes to preach to the world and be saviors. No thanks. But the remaining 20 percent were articulate and provided not just their own story but collections of knowledge and insights from NDE research. A few of them weren't half-baked: *just a few*. But that was worth the commute and $50-entry fee! Besides, I didn't get out of the house much, so...

I read through and studied the conference schedule. It was instinctive to pick the more authentic ones and set up a personal itinerary for the day, a skill I had learned by attending many writer's conferences over ten years. And one in particular really stood out: PM Atwater.

She is an author and researcher of the NDE phenomena. I attended her 1 ¼ hour presentation and was impressed: she knew her shit. She was of the same caliber of presenter I had always tried to be true to: articulate, casual, informative, and able to back up every goddam thing she said. I attended some others after her, but really didn't need to; I was just passing the time for a paid ticket. I knew she was my resource.

The choice of her several books to buy was easy: *The Big Book of Near-Death Experiences* by PMH Atwater.

Not just some personal story that is self-indulgent grandstanding. Not just a dry reference study of academics by some MD or PhD. This was *the* encyclopedia of NDE. Similar to my own book on addiction, it gave the science, the process, the machinations, the stories, the theories, the facts, the histories... It is *thorough*. It was a place to start. I'm a hard-sell: I can attend an event and not spend a dime on merch. I got her book and had her sign it.

By the end of the day, I knew the lingo, the stats, and standards of the NDE: how it worked, what the smart theories had been over time, and if the info was objective. Not *subjective* like the wannabe hacks with no respect for truth or knowledge. I don't know her; I've no arrangement with her for endorsement. I'm just telling you most of all I needed to know of NDE was in this *Big Book of Near-Death Experiences*.

I wept in elation as I drove home with her *Big Book of NDEs* aside me on the passenger seat. My enthusiasm to devour its contents curbed till bedtime.

Finally... I'd get some outside perspective that is credible and mature.

The bells were going off: my choice to come to PNW for exile, my meeting this other writer in my forest neighborhood, his role of introducing me to NDE and the IANDS conference happening in my backyard so soon. K-I-S-M-E-T: *kismet.*

The lights were coming on; as I read this whole new field of knowledge and science, it exposed me to an undeniable fact: that guy I sat with on a park bench by the lake who said I had an NDE was right!

I'd had nearly every symptom and condition of the common NDEs documented over 60+ years. I am brazenly familiar with the less-than-common features too. I have an unprecedented and unique host of my own but are obvious effects and symptoms of this supernatural phenomena. It all fit together.

And then the messages became clear and came in flowing:

I had been getting *phone calls* from The Portal for four years since my personal D-Day occurred. "Phone calls" had been the term I gave to the *transmissions* I received from The Portal, usually around 4 a.m. These messages and info had a clarity and quality that was their signature and were nothing like my own private imaginings or thoughts: they were instructions—*orders, if you will*—and insights to existence picked up by my now highly receptive NDE antennae. My own, personal intuitions had small features of healthy doubts. But Akashic-Portal-provided intuitions always felt clear and doubtless. Mine were tarnished by subtle ego and desire. Portal intuitions didn't have any of that.

One of my NDE side effects was a *Gospel Meter:* Gospel meaning *good news*, which is divine in nature, not temporal. When I read, watch, or hear *anything*, I can intuitively tell if it is gospel or bullshit. It is reliably accurate.

This is far more intense and accurately revealing than normal *intuition.* Intuition is a blend of healthy vision and intellect. But it's yours: you *own* it. More highly developed segments of your brain and mind are extra-sensory; you perceive more because you have a bigger bandwidth. This ability wasn't provided nor endowed to me by The Portal. It is developed by lifetimes of work and effort in consciousness. I was born intuitive and developed it more throughout my life too.

The uncommon and unique features to my NDE are:

1. I have clear view of what is true and accurate (the BS-meter!).
2. I have clear vision of futures and destinies (bigger-picture perceptions).
3. I have accurate and nearly instant access to past lives.

The first one is what I call the Gospel Meter, and this one makes it very hard to refrain from being vocal about bullshit. I not only see and know what is bullshit-lies and exploitive exaggerations but can explain, in detail, why and how: most of it's just trivial and annoying as we are saturated in used-car-salesmen personalities and a culture of superficialities. A few are helpful as I avoid potential threats and dangers from swindlers before they even get started. Many NDErs (and mediums) have this capacity; however, in an unprepared mind, these can become paranoia.

The second one is troubling, and I do my best to follow them without overanalyzing. Having visions of future circumstances and destinies is tricky; parts of the future are predetermined while other parts are not. Hit in the face by a truck event? Predetermined. Moving to WA, going to coffee with the guy who led me to IANDS, advising Brandon to wise decisions, bypassing useless and potentially harmful medical advice? Not predestined. They are future *options*.

The third one, the vision of past lives, is quite unique and hard to block out and can be very distracting.

When I meet people, I instantly see who they are in this lifetime in context to who they have been in recent lifetimes. It is painful as I see not only who they *think* they are—i.e. material bodies with a past of a single lifetime—but who they *actually* are as a collection of multiple lives. I see them as a spirit, not a person. I see the waves and ripples of their recent lives, karmas, and what the possible outcomes are. I see where they *can* go and where they're *actually* going. Where they're *supposed* to go versus their current trajectory.

My own past-life regression has been like a movie. It is the *Reincarnation Cinema:* nonstop shows of prior lifetimes in Technicolor, HD, and 3D. I dream them, see them, watch them play out while I drive, work, cook, clean, and *big time* when I meditate.

When I'm meditating with kirtan musical chanting, they come in full force and just play out. I'm like Li'l Alex from *Clockwork Orange*, strapped into a theatre seat with hardware forcing my eyes open to watch, and I can't turn away.

Fortunately, I don't need to turn away: unlike *Clockwork Orange* viddy-videos, mine are usually enlightening and revealing. I am immersed in tears as I watch my current- and past-life episodes play out before me as I see, and know, the reasons why and what role they played in my evolution of spirit.

A director of the IANDS organization's Seattle chapter was rather stunned by my NDE account and side effects. And this guy had heard it *all!* He is the one who suggested to me the reason my NDE was so extraordinary and unique was due to my life's work, practice, and knowledge of mysticism and spirituality prior to my NDE. He was quite impressed with my spiritual and mystical *curriculum vitae*, and his theory of my prior practice as an alchemist, ceremonial magician, and Kundalini yogi within this very lifetime was these were connected to my NDE side effects as well as the quantity, quality, and my retention of what I experienced within The Portal. This made sense to me and was quite comforting.

He informed me very few NDErs retain the volume and details of their time *on the other side* as I did and suggested it was due to my spiritual expertise prior to my NDE.

Had my prior spiritual study and practice set me apart from other NDErs? I mean... other than that, we all had two legs and arms, brain tissues, and were nearly killed, but the mass majority of NDErs were *a-spiritual* prior to NDE. NDE was what woke them up spiritually. My coma had been clinical, but most others had been in *spiritual* comas before their NDE. NDE gives atheists and agnostics elementary proof of the afterlife. NDE expands your prior awareness by a few octaves. It can give an already practicing mystic-spiritualist prodigious insights.

I devoured Atwater's NDE text and began studying my own NDE in a broader light.

I attended several local chapter meetings of IANDS and connected with others in the community. I was thankful and grateful for being provided the missing-pieces to the NDE phenomena I knew nothing of. And most of all, *I was so relieved.*

I was learning I'm not crazy.

I had been experiencing most of the common features of NDE.

I learned what they meant and might imply. And then I learned how totally unique mine is, had been, and continues to be.

Now... if you're expecting this to be the break-through, watershed moment of realization removing all this tragedy and leaving only triumph, *just stop!* My time in PNW-purgatory-sanitarium was not yet over. I wasn't suddenly lost-and-found by discovering there was an actual name for my circumstance and a community of people to support me. Sure... it was comforting: *mildly*.

I still had no hope, no prospects, and no life: lonely, scared, spiritually solo, tragically sad with no direction. It seemed logical to me to complete my career as a behavioral expert: few to none know more on the matter than I, not a single program has the sincerity and originality so many addiction sufferers need. This book and my innovations saving lives was going to be my retirement package.

I soldiered on...

- Brandon visited me on The Sound. We kayaked, played golf... and it broke my heart when he left;
- I donned my gear and struggled, but pulled-off, a brief scuba dive in the icy waters of the Sound. I solo-travelled to Cayman Brac for a week of reef and wall-diving;
- I performed walking meditations in the Nisqually estuary and picked wild blackberries by the sack full on its wide boardwalk across the waters of the Puget Sound;
- I spent my days marketing my four books and reviewing my "death-journals"; the journals and poetry inspired by my death experience for the last four years;
- I spent lonely nights alone by a fire trying to block out the pain and loss of all I once felt was valuable;
- I worried for Janete; and
- I was so alone. So... so... so goddam alone. Every day. And there were zero indications or even a hint of it being less than lifelong.

I was invited to speak at a spiritual get-together and give a workshop on a mystical modality: a Spiritual Triangle System from the Middle Ages synthesizing Pythagorean Numerology, Astrology, and Tarot I had been using since my Kundalini event at twenty-five. With deep meditations and study, I expanded the system to include the sixty-four hexagrams of the I Ching and the twenty-two paths connecting the ten Sephiroth of Kabbalah's Tree of Life. They fit perfectly and brought this astounding system to a whole new octave.

The workshop demonstrated the natural relationship between these seemingly separate methods of divination, using my own chart and soul's analysis as a template example.

My personal reading sample was done for June 19th, 2013 which accurately predicted the cataclysmic shift in my life. I then shared a new chart with my resurrection day, the birthday I woke from my coma on nine days later, using my true, spiritual name Krishnanand.

Due to this reading and direction from the Akashic Space, I decided to go by Krishnanand full time now. It felt as if a ton of weight lifted from my spirit.

I realized the reason nothing worked and only got worse was because I tried to live as Scott instead of accepting my true identity as Krishnanand.

I respected being referred to as Scott from all those who knew me before D-Day and use Scott still to promote the books and appearances I made nationally to avoid confusion. But I began to introduce myself to new people as Krishnanand, and it felt like a breakthrough.

But Krishnanand is a young boy still learning from the turbulence of new life experience. Scott had been a successful and accomplished adult. I wasn't yet capable of letting him go.

And when a monkey reaches into a jar to get out a banana, he gets stuck: His fist around the banana is too large to retract from the jar's opening. It's only when he lets go of his object of desire he becomes free of what binds him.

My hand will remain stuck in the jar awhile yet. Each time I get smart and strong enough to let go of who I was, I get stupid again and stuff my open palm in the jar and hold on, with a death grip, to that fucking banana.

It's better to be hungry and free than hungry and stuck. Let go, let God, as they say...

Janete had been home for two months from our visit. I planned on visiting LA for Halloween so we could have our traditional tours of Halloween Haunts. Our anniversary/birthday/housewarming/reunion visit is still moist from our simultaneous orgasms when I get *The Call*.

AGONY IN THE GARDEN

O my mind! The world is futile. Why are you wasting time on worldly love instead of
pursuing Divine Love?
—Kripalu Maharaj—Siddhant Madhuri

I am a man of constant sorrow. I've seen trouble all my day...
—Soggy Bottom Boys (Folk Song)

If she's gone I can't go on ...
—"You've Got To Hide Your Love Away" (Beatles/Lennon)

I need to give up. I have sustained one blow after another. Most of the harshest and
most challenging things any human can go through in a lifetime have *all* happened to
me, condensed into four years, yet I'm still standing. Most people experience one,
maybe two, of these tragedies: lose a home or business, get cheated on by one they love,
endure injuries to their body... but *all* of them at once? Back-to-back?

Yeah. No. Fuck this. Fuck that, and fuck you, too.

Eighty percent of DAI injuries cause death or institutionalization within four years.
I've had ten times the expected complications, trudged forward, and I still get *more?*
I'm living the entire spectrum of human tragedy condensed into a back-to-back series
of events. I can't catch my breath between devastating losses. And that's not just
because my lungs were punctured and I've yet to breathe well.

No.

I quit.

Hamlet's a Wuss

I cannot access the direct memory of Janete telling me it was over.

I remember where I sat, some of the content, and quite a bit of the pain and self-loathing ensuing over the following weeks. But I can't seem to recall what she said and why. The best I can do is *paraphrase*.

It was a classic *'Dear John'* scenario. Janete is rather unremarkable regarding communication and emotion. She expressed to me, *via the phone*, she did not want to continue and told me not to call or contact her anymore. The call lasted less than ten minutes. There was no time for histrionics, argument, or protest: I handled it as gracefully as possible. My mind, brain, and heart were too paralyzed to draw the moment out. There was little to say, so I said little. I took it like a man, the best I could.

There had been no drama, fight, or disagreement. Two months after her visit, she called to break it off with me. She feebly explained she needed to *move on*. It had been four years since my death event, and she had satisfied some arbitrary *Seinfeldian* requirements of time before breaking up, and it was over. Sixty days ago, when she and I were visiting, not once had she mentioned *moving on*. Twelve years of partnership, and I do not even get a two-week notice. My world, *or what was left of it*, came crashing around me. I realized the true gospel: *her housewarming visit for my birthday was her premeditated farewell.*

My NDE side-effect of psychic intuition was in the red zone.

She felt she had done due diligence, had a mourning period, and now that I seemed to be getting better and was in my own home, it was safe to end things and *move on*. She had met the cultural and social protocols, granted me a final visit with a consolation fuck, and said no more.

I'm stunned. Shocked! For the first time in four years, I'm showing signs of true restoration. I'm going to be okay. And *now* you're ending it?

I could accept and even sanction ending it if I were doomed for life, sentencing you to indentured servitude to an invalid. But now? No fucking way. *Please don't...*

I had even *offered* to end it several times over the last four years. Back in the hospital days, I had told her from my heart that she was not obligated to stay by me. "You're still young, Janete. I don't want you to live a life of caregiving. You can move on. It will crush me, but my life is *over*. The specialists all agree I'll never recover. Go now while you can before I beg you not to leave me alone in this nightmare!"

I made this offer gently during the ensuing years. I would not obligate her to indentured servitude, and I told Brandon the same.

And it wasn't selfish. I wanted Janete and Brandon to be happy, which is why I had chosen to give up the ghost in the hospital and die for realsies. With me six feet under, they would heal and move on; but if I were alive-but-dead, they would never be free of obligation to me, even if it were self-imposed. I was willing to take the bullet and finish what the specter of Death had started.

The voice of God promptly pointed out that I could be an inspiration to them if I recovered. And I've been busting my ass ever since!

Goddam my NDE-mystical-psychic-supernatural-intuitive mind! Fucker! My deductive reasoning is now covered in a sticky goo of psychic awareness. As Janete tells me in a few sentences, and in less than two minutes, to move on, the truth meter of intuition is a siren, screaming out the hidden truth:

She had made up her mind *before* her visit.

Her visit was her farewell. She came because she needed to know I was *okay*. I had a home and was improving.

Her farewell visit was to absolve her of potential *guilt*.

"Are you seeing someone?"

"Yes. I started dating, *and I think you should, too.*"

"How am I supposed to date? Two months ago, you were here, and we made love. I'm *just now* beginning to orient back to the living. And now I have a shattered heart to mend? This man you're seeing, is it serious?"

"I like him very much. We're together. You'll find someone; I know you will."

Wow. Cool. Her endorsement casts away all the bizarre pain and suffering that has been a twenty-four seven experience for four years. *Snap—just like that!* She makes it sound like she's doing me a favor. The only thing worse than heart-breaking rejection is knowing your lover is with another. Yeah… try *not* to conjure those images when you're alone, alone, alone and trying to accept what you cannot change.

Janete had planned this visit to justify ending our relationship. Now she could put down in the log books that she had mourned for four years and remained a committed girlfriend by sticking around. This was also restitution for her earlier transgression, which caused me to go into exile to begin with.

She saw her last visit as a consolation prize. Something to absolve her from what she knew she would do: break us up. To balance the account.

No! It's so *not* even-steven!

I suffered a massive brain trauma. Ever since, I have dealt with identity confusion, existential crisis, and coping with being a medical miracle trying to survive each day. You told me you had once betrayed our vows and magical love in an immature act of selfishness *on the first anniversary of my death day!* You should've taken that bit of news to your *grave!* I *never* needed to know that mistake, *ever!*

My reaction to your crime was to train you to climb a mountain so you could feel *empowered and fulfilled.* I drove you there and sat in a shitty motel room for ten hours; I ate cold pizza in the desert and felt lonely, confused, and betrayed while you conquered an iconic mountain. And when you got to the bottom of that mountain, I was *there*, waiting with open arms to embrace you. And I brought *fresh* pizza because I knew you'd be starving. The next morning, you slept peacefully as I drove five hours back home. I even framed your hiking permit for Mount Whitney, showing the date and the time of eleven hours and nineteen minutes, to commemorate your achievement. *That's* support!

No!

You came to Washington to allow *me* to give *you* the second-best orgasm of your life after also giving you the first one. We'd be together for what *you* knew was the last time, but I had *no* idea. No, this did not balance the scales of justice!

You told me weepily that you would always cherish me for all that I'd done. You said you are the *whole* woman you are because of my support and guidance for over ten years. This is not okay! I already *knew* what I had done for you for over twelve years. My record of account includes helping you through clinical depression and providing parental guidance to your kids. I had dedicated my life to you and *far exceeded* what one person could do for another.

I supported you like a genie in a lamp. Anytime you rubbed it, I popped out and solved your problems: kids, money, Mom, how to support yourself, and self-discovery. And don't forget that lengthy list of adventures we shared over three continents!

You had *one* thing to endure for me: I was *killed*. Not my fault! Not about *you!* And instead of going the distance and finally seeing evidence I was triumphing over tragedy and praising me for climbing a *real fucking mountain* and embracing me with open arms as I had done for you during the dead center of my *real fucking tragedy,* you give me the '*I think we need to move on'* thing?

It has gotten to the point that I *dread* having a "good" day. I am smart and mature enough to enjoy and honor it, but I'm now *fucking programmed* to know it will be accompanied by a loss. Murphy's Law: the day you get a ten percent raise is when your property tax goes up *fifteen* percent! Yeah, a bonus at work is a godsend and *neutralizes* the expense, but it's hard not to feel shitty over not getting ahead instead. Ya follow?

Some may contradict: "C'mon, Scott... how can you say that? You survived a horrific accident. How 'bout finding the Yelm house and moving there? What about having some money and now even building a home? Aren't those *good?"*

No, mutherfucker, *they're not.* That's like saying I was *lucky*, and I told you once before 'lucky' is when you *almost* get hit in the face by a truck, not when you do but survive! Don't you *dare* minimize my constant suffering. It hasn't improved, nor even remained the same; *it has gotten worse and worse and worse!*

Nothing good has happened to me in over four years! Nada, zilch, zero. The few things that I could categorize as "good" were mediocre, only relevant to survival, and they were always, always, always quickly followed by even more tragedies.

Good is when you get a *twenty percent* raise, and your property tax goes *down* ten percent!

I've heard that God only gives you as much as you can handle. Then why am I being *punished* for being able to handle so much? By that logic, being strong and capable is a fucking curse. If I were lame, stupid, incompetent, and easily overwhelmed by the most trivial things, my biggest challenge would be choosing which shade of *autumn peach* to paint the fucking bathroom. It would not be *'here ya go; deal with death, spinal fusion, amnesia, inability to walk, love of your life cheating on you, abandoning you, and counting the days till you're out of money and have to live in a shelter.'*

My capacity for tragedy is being exploited while my now ex-girlfriend has all she had before she met me, money gifts I gave her from my settlement, *and a new boyfriend.* I shouldered all our stress because she was so easily overwhelmed. So, I am punished for withstanding more while she is rewarded for being incapable of handling anything? This feature in the world is possibly the only aspect that can test my faith; evil, shallow, self-serving assholes get tax breaks and low-interest loans while salt-of-the-earth folks stare down evictions. Karma's a bitch—and I don't mean 'bitch' as in challenging. She can be a real fucking cunt.

I had slaved tirelessly in every area of my life. I served my family, partner, and community; my mental, physical, and spiritual fitness was strong from hard work. Nothing had been easy or free since day one.

I went to bed one night with a beautifully simple, dedicated, and loving romantic partner, a wonderful son whom I adored, and a full and genuine spiritual life. I had earned respect and admiration thanks to a successful career dedicating my time, mind, and heart to the salvation and rescue of others. I was healthy, fit, attractive, and authentic in my personality and character. Then I awoke from a contented rest to discover God had taken a *wrecking ball* to my life.

Every brick and stick I picked up from the rubble and smoking debris to salvage and reuse to rebuild the shelter of my life have spontaneously combusted. I have nothing, and I am nothing. I am physical matter taking up space in the world. I wasn't supposed to come back, I am *not* supposed to be here, and this is the only logical conclusion why, no matter what I do, it all remains the same or gets worse.

Ya see... when you *actually die*, life goes on without you. The world keeps spinning around, and the people who loved and relied on you learn to fill the void where you once were. You become a memory. Even Einstein, while never forgotten and whose life work will forever benefit planet Earth's humanity, became mere *text*.

No one ceases to go on because you do. But a loving and merciful God removes you from the equation, so you have no awareness of life moving on as if you never existed. You don't actually *witness* it and have it rubbed like salted thorns into your wounds.

And this is what's happening to me. I take up space on Earth and breathe the air, but because of a glitch in The Matrix, I've been allowed to return when I wasn't supposed to. Everyone and everything is moving on as if I'm not here, and I'm forced to watch. I've been *the world's greatest Dad* and helped Brandon get his own place and save money; he's begun a life I am only peripherally involved with. I taught Janete how to live, laugh, and love, and she's reaping the harvest with another sharecropper.

I've accommodated her in every way. Now I'm leaving it all behind without even a trail of breadcrumbs, and soon there will be no evidence of me ever having been in Janete's life. If she takes our photos off her walls and out of her phone, trashes her commemorative Mount Whitney plaque, and lets some other guy's sloppy dick take my place, she will forget all about the magic and enchantment we shared that has no rival in the annals of love.

I'm such a dumbass. I felt terrible about leaving and gave her $3,500 from my settlement to numb the sting of having me, her provider of all things extracurricular, moving 1,200 miles to the north.

My so-called final act before departure wasn't a guilt trip for her betrayal or to make her struggle through an awkward breakup scenario. I moved to a whole different part of the country, so she could do it all by phone.

***

When the call disconnected, I was alone.

I was 1,200 miles away, and there was nothing I could do or say. What is the remedy for a broken heart? There isn't one, dummy: just time. You become an *ouroboros* of heartache. The circular infinity symbol of a viper devouring itself, the same image Janete and I tattooed on our ring fingers together.

Heartbreak is self-perpetuating. It feeds itself *with itself*. Every moment you endure suffering provides empty calories and bad carbs for it to become stronger. It doesn't just continue and remain the same; it expands, causing waves that crest and never ease up. Those waves move ever forward, *away* from the shoreline, deeper into the sea, only to be absorbed by an even bigger wave's crest. It's like a really good orgasm *in reverse*.

Each moment, you are convinced, without a doubt, you *cannot* handle any more, *and yet you do*. You can't escape it; you can't even sleep to get some relief. You're FUBAR: *fucked-up beyond all recognition*. And you know it. The End.

Let's get something crystal clear here:

I am *not* filled with angry sorrow over losing a girlfriend. It is the proverbial straw. In four years, I have been killed, tortured, lost, broken, shattered, lost my life, my mind, *and my spirit*—none of which are metaphorical, mind you—yet I have been a goddam champion through the whole thing. I don't just deserve a *consolation* prize or a fucking gift certificate. I deserve a *grand prize trophy* to reward my "A" for effort.

No one has reduced my pain or looked out for me beyond fundamentals. *No one* has confirmed I am real and not an illusion or that they are truly proud of me and will remain by me in these darkest hours.

They have moved on.

I just want someone to love. Someone to love me as well. Someone to be proud of me, someone who wants to know me, be with me, and let me care about them.

Everyone is moving on without me. Brandon is *supposed* to; he's my son, and he should carry on and honor his loving father by doing just that. I expect clients, family, and the guys I played tennis with to move on because they aren't much more than acquaintances.

But the woman I have given poetic magic and stellar romance to, taught the true *meaning* of life, and showed her how to live it? No, bitch. You don't fucking *move on* when the tough is finally getting going.

I did all I did, as everyone does, to secure and protect an investment. I gave you undying, unconditional love on one fucking condition: that we would saunter into the sunset and grow old together. Not *alone*, but together.

I've come a long way, but in Janete's mind, my potential to be a full breadwinner as before has been compromised beyond repair. She may believe that the life we shared and the future we had planned together died when I died, and despite stacking evidence to the contrary, I am not a viable partner. She is taking applications to fill the position of lover-provider. Her visit was my severance package. I've gone as far as I can, and it is not enough.

And I do not disagree; I am not getting any better. I don't feel any less dizzy from DAI-TBI, I still struggle to walk and talk, and even though I can vaguely see some of my memory through the fog, I'm still not quite *here* as I straddle between The Portal and the world. My physical and subtle body stands before you in the flesh—blood, bones, and chakras— but my *causal* body and mind remain in an obscure reality of The Portal. I am trapped in a land without borders, entombed in a space without time, bodiless and ethereal. Scott is no more.

It is time to make this a unanimous reality. If Scott doesn't really exist, then let's end him once and for all. I have taken the red pill: NDE and my other life experiences have removed the illusion of The Matrix. I also tried the blue pill to coexist within The Matrix veil of illusion, where my body is forced to exist. *Now let's try both.*

Is it possible? There's no heaven, no portal to God, no spirit or soul within us? Creation is just a cosmic coincidence. Am I merely having long-term DAI brain damage issues?

Why should I choose *between* the red pill and the blue pill? Hamlet's soliloquy plays like a mantra in my mind's shadows. To be or not to be...

Whether'tis nobler in the mind to suffer
The slings and arrows of outrageous fortune,
Or to take arms against a sea of troubles,
And by opposing end them? To die: to sleep;
No more; and by a sleep to say we end
The heart-ache and the thousand natural shocks
That flesh is heir to...

Legend has it I was once a dope fiend. Would a dope fiend take one *or* the other, the red *or* the blue pill?

I don't think so. He'd take both. To be or not to be...

To take *both* pills and cease to suffer the arrows of outrageous fortune and, by opposing, *end them.*

I've had enough.

I am at the end, starkly alone in this new house with no spirit, laughter, love, or friendship beneath its roof.

As the call disconnected, the 1,400 square feet of my brand-new home encased me like a coffin. Every room, alcove, and closet were virtually empty. Only my loneliness fills every inch of it. Washington state surrounds me, but even its 70,000 square miles are too small to contain my pain.

I have no one to call. I know no one here to see, to reach for, or to cry to...

The only two souls I know, my son and my Soulmate, are 1,200 miles, or 63,300 steps away. And my mind imagines that she is not alone. She is comforted by a man; she has a lover by her side in her home, supporting her in this hard act of breaking my heart, leaving me so entirely... alone.

I wipe the tears from my cheeks with my hand, for there is no one else to wipe them. I breathe deep to brace myself for the inescapable, ever-present loneliness about to descend upon me. It will be my only companion, never to leave my side, in sickness and in health, *till death do we part.*

There will be no task equal enough to distract from the loss. There is no exile large enough nor long enough to hide away from the crushing weight of nonstop ache of the soul that will set in and become a new nightmare in each moment of wakefulness. No pause, respite, or recess to hide within for any moment to be unaware of this newest and most severe tragedy. I have no shelter to hide under as not one area of my life has joy: my body, brain, and spirit have been denied light and given only darkness for four straight years. The only shelters I have to hibernate within are the structures of the existing horrors of injury-induced reductions.

My

Heart

Is

Broken.

The Akash is silent this night. I am submerged in material consciousness, suffocating in worldly pain, and cannot catch breath of spirit.

Both my spiritual master and swami teacher are no longer present upon this earth to speak with.

The spiritual path of detachment from all worldly things has taken its toll. I've surrendered everything now. I have nothing, and I am nothing.

I am alone. Alone is me. I have achieved Oneness with Loss.

I wander, like a zombie, over a block of hours, my reality settling in—crushing me. I retreat to my prayer room to seek union with God and my Spiritual Master, to wave off the specter of darkness filling me up. I sit on the floor, allowing a soft, slow song of kirtan to ease in. I know it matters not what I do: the lightless realization of my true condition will not be ignored. The tears come as I speak aloud to Her...

I do not ask for forgiveness. Murder is an unforgivable offense, and suicide is murder, so I do not ask for forgiveness.

I have failed. I cannot rationalize going on. The evidence of a life of ongoing agony is overwhelming. There has been no other theme more constant: my life, should it continue, will be more tragedy, and I will experience it alone, in a forest of exile. I do not see the logic in continuing. I will spend the rest of my days in loathing of myself and, eventually, loathing You. The weight has become too much. My bed has been made, and I must lie down in it.

I cannot lift a mountain above my head. I do not have the strength. I have done my best to endure and even triumph, but my best is not enough. You have not allowed it. I accept that the consequence of self-murder will be eons of lifetimes trapped in a dimension of Hell without spiritual opportunity. I know this. I am sorry for disappointing You. I'm sorry for not dying when I was supposed to. I am sorry for not salvaging my lover's spiritual growth. I'm sorry for not recovering faster and better. All I want is to please You. I have failed and cannot endure what You have graced me with. I am sorry I have misled You. Sorry I caused you to overestimate me. I have no value any longer.

Eyes filled with tears, my head bowed, I sank to the floor in a pain of sorrow...

In Your omniscience, how have You overestimated me to think I could endure more? How have I fooled You into thinking I'm as capable and strong as You seem to believe? Since You know everything I am, could ever be and have ever been over countless lives, how did You not know where my point of breaking lies? And why? Why have You brought me to this threshold of bottomless pain? Why did I live beyond death? Have I lived to suffer and now to die?

I've done my best to make You proud, not give up, and endure all You have thrust upon me. It has never been enough. I cannot triumph over these tragedies. My power is no match for

Yours. You had to know there would be a breaking point, and it has been delivered. I am defeated.

Tears stream from my sorrow, my head upon the floor, my body convulsing from shame and defeat...

You've created an orchestra of elaborate circumstances for me to grow, expand, and love You more. But I have no more love to give.

The love within me for God and Guru is a large mass pushing against the walls of my heart, too large to be contained and as boundless as I can imagine. Yet it is not enough. The chakra wheel of my heart is too small to contain the ever-overflowing love within me for You. There was no reason to be a jealous God; my love for my lover was just human. You are all I've loved.

On my hands and knees, fluids flow from my eyes and nose as I beg forgiveness...

All I want is to please You. All I want is to do as You ask of me. In my feeble way, I've tried to do as You've told me without question or consideration. But I'm a stupid-human; I can't know what You ask of me. I'm human; You're Divine. I've done my best to interpret what I think You are telling me to do. But I get it all wrong all the time.

Am I to save my Soulmate and finish a mission we had? Am I to go live in a hospital and stop trying to recover? Is this all to pound into my thick, stupid skull that I'm not supposed to try? That I'm supposed to give up? Surrender and succumb to what has happened and stop interfering with human pride and determination?

My words come through heaving breaths, muscles wrought, total destruction; I am a mass of sorrow and failure, alone in this space...

I accept the punishment of hell for taking my own life. I've no choice. I cannot endure more. Despite trauma and injury, my body stays resilient. In spite of wanting death, my living persists like a taunting. My broken shell of physical form may live on for years and years, yet I cannot live on in this ongoing, never-fucking-ending, pure, and ever-continuous anguish. I'm a failure; no one cares for me nor wants me despite all I've done and been. I'm just in the way. I shouldn't be here, interfering with how things are supposed to be. Somehow, I found a secret passage and defied Yamraj, the god of death. It is time I accept my fate and fulfill my obligation to Yamraj. I have not once prayed to You for material happiness, restoration or to burden You with worldly trivialities. I am not asking forgiveness for what I will now do.

Yes… I accept hell and accept that it will be infinitely worse than I can imagine. I've no choice. I've come to the end. I accept defeat. I am sorry. And that is all I am: sorry. Letting You down is my only regret.

I am so very, very sorry.

To commit such a sin, to murder myself. God… my dear Maharaji… I do not ask forgiveness.

I am unforgivable for what I will do. I love You. Only You. I cannot endure. I'm out.

END ACT II

ACT III

ALMOST HOME

THE MIDDLE OF THE BEGINNING

_000._

OUT OF EXILE

> As long as you are in exile, no one shall be king.
> —Prince Bharat (The Ramayan)
>
> Hang it up and see what tomorrow brings.
> —Grateful Dead (Truckin')

Your exile is over. Go home.

A message softly sings to me, its harmony gently radiating from within The Portal; it drifts amongst celestial spheres, tenderly arousing my quiescent consciousness in the dark hours of morning...

Your exile is over. Go home.

A salient signal... Phrases within Sanskrit texts which are very important are said three times. This message came to me on three consecutive nights as well.

Your exile is over. Go home.

For the first time, a message is broadcast from within The Portal with an emblem: a representation of a quality, an idea... a beautiful and strange star, unlike any yantra symbol or sacred geometry I've ever seen. Each night, it floats toward me, landing, fusing to my arm, and marking me. It rests lovingly, breathing with a pulse as it expands and contracts within itself.

I cannot fathom the meaning or power of this report of an order blended with its star sign.

I am to die. Akashic angels are silent on my decision, which I take as approval; I conclude I was never meant to return from death. But I sense the sincerity of my decision has activated this new message and mystical symbol. I cannot make the connection between them and am clueless about anything beyond my own pain. Each day, within moments of waking, my circumstances soak in, and I know I will marinate in them until I am fortunate enough to sleep again. Once awake, I have only thoughts of suffering again.

I now know that each day, all day, I will constantly be aware of my solitude, heartache, and failure. With original sin, my soul was cast from the gardens of heaven to live in the world of matter. I want death to be the end of my exile. Does "go home" mean returning to God's Divine Abode?

The fire that once resided within has become a low spark; I now lack vitality and am too exhausted even to consider the meaning of mysteries anymore. I am no longer a spiritual being having a human experience but a mortal man of flesh having a suffering experience. And it's senseless. My exile is over. Time to go home.

_____ _32._

__YOGMAYA__

> There are just two dimensions: the Divine realm and the mayic (material) world.
> —Kripalu (Prem Ras Siddhant)

> A mere touch of Whose yogmaya controls and manages the entire universe.
> —Kripalu Maharaj (Prem Madhuri)

All tragedy is Grace, not *tests*, but opportunities to spiritually advance.

In my foolish pride, I joke God must *really* love me more than most. *You only hurt the ones you love*, and if this is a true axiom, then She must love me *a lot!*

Suffering can be proportionate to growth: *that which does not kill you makes you stronger.* By this logic, that which actually *does* kill you must make you superman! But I add a caveat to Nietzsche's quote: that which does not kill you *might* make you stronger; it depends on how you handle it. Some crack under pressure, some thrive. I've always been an over-achiever-thriver when under pressure, but a man can only take so much.

As I agonized over the cause and purpose of my ongoing, relentless suffering and loss, I arrived at conclusions. The severing of my attachments has been very selective: Brandon and I are still strong; Chow-Chow is still my daily buddy; I still have my galaxy-blue, STI Subaru; and keep landing on my feet with house and home. My body stays strong in spite of TBI-DAI and spinal fusion, to the point I do not experience the slightest fever or basic cold for over fifteen years and counting. I've not gained an ounce of weight over fifteen years and counting too. Okay . . . I've not lost any either, but at fifty-plus, I'm pretty satisfied to stay fairly fit. I am attached to all these material things: son, pet, car, house, wellness, fitness. . . . But the few things I absolutely cherish and rely on have been shattered, and the loss of these few areas compromise my capacity for happiness of the others. But God doesn't just want some of your attachments: He wants your biggest ones! The ones you cherish! Why? Because those are the ones you'll dwell on during a death experience, forcing you back to maya!

1. Career: no matter how hard I try my career isn't taking flight.

Regardless of doing the impossible and executing the path of success of author-presenter near perfectly, my bank account stays the same; my virtual anonymity as an author and specialist-innovator persists.

- My work is top-drawer: websites, counseling, writing, marketing, promotion . . . are validated by awards, recognition, respect, and lauded by all who come in contact with it, yet *four* books, dozens of appearances, dedicated followers, and heartfelt fans isn't adding up to more.

I'm mystified how I can do everything right and get nearly no results. It is especially frustrating to see shallow, heartless people who barely sacrifice get rich and famous. How did Van Gogh die poor and unknown and the Kardashians make millions?

That's Yogmaya: the miracle-power of God. Yogmaya is Sanskrit: *yog* means *union*, and *maya* is the name of the *material-phenomena* (world-universe . . .). It is the name of the Godpower used to make the impossible possible.

Moses raised his staff to part the Red Sea and channeled God's miracle power. Yogmaya is the Godpower that flowed through his raised staff. Yogmaya is what put paramedics yards away from my hit-in-the-face incident and made me wake on my birthday. It's also the Godpower that made me turn right instead of left that morning, put on a Museum of Death t-shirt, and put the thought in my head of riding my bike to work that day. Sometimes yogmaya works *for* you, sometimes *not*.

Yogmaya does all this: the good and the bad. But God only ever has one, single intention for you: to draw out your spiritual sensibilities and lessen your material ones. It's all designed to bring you closer and to give you opportunity to not wander farther away. Yogmaya defies material logic. It's like quantum physics: Heisenberg's Uncertainty Principle makes no sense, but it's reliably true.

The only thing that makes sense is Yogmaya is running rampant in my life.

- My perfect, worldly, love is freakin' *immune* to logic, reason, and passion.
- My career life is blocked and impotent.

Janete is under a spell: she's completely lost sight of who I am, who she is, who *we* are, all that we made, did, planned, and bonded with. She has traded *down*; dating some average guy in the suburbs, watching reality TV, working a retail job, and living with her adult-dysfunctional son, in spite of her mate offering her a grand life of depth and purpose. She's even eating meat sgain. That may not sound major to you omnivores, but, over time, vegetarianism is more than just a dietary preference. It's sacred. I think this can only be due to yogmaya.

A grand example of yogmaya is given in the tenth canto of the Bhagavatam: baby Krishna, who is the all-powerful, blissful, loving avatar of God Himself who has descended as a child to Grace us with His innocence is caught by his adopted mother, Yashoda, eating dirt. Kids will be kids, right?! She gets upset, and Krishna knows He's about to get a whipping. When the all-powerful God agreed to descend as a boy who would change the world, he agreed to do so *without* omnipotence: He would appear and act like a regular boy, not as an all-powerful God. But sometimes he *slips*!

As mother Yashoda grabs a switch to spank Him, she checks His mouth to confirm his disobedient soil-eating. Baby Krishna let's yogmaya intervene: as she looks into His mouth, she sees the entire universe: infinite galaxies and eternal time are displayed in the tiny baby's mouth. Mother Yashoda is so overwhelmed he gets out of the whipping!

Now she has seen her little boy is not just some little boy! She just saw the proof her little Kanua-Krishna is all-mighty God!

The final act is when Yogmaya causes her to *forget the entire thing*! Within moments of witnessing uncountable galaxies in her baby's mouth, she figures she imagined it and within minutes forgets the entire thing.

Krishn uses Yogmaya in the Bhagavad Gita when he reveals His Godliness to Arjun, instantly showing him actual infinity, eternity, and all of creation: "Now I have become death, destroyer of worlds!" as Arjun begs Krishn to return to a human form as his dear friend.

That's yogmaya!

She can overwhelm your senses and reason, make you forget who you are, and also part the Red Sea. Yogmaya saved my life but is now sabotaging all attempts to restore it!

Avaranatmik(a), that feature of Yogmaya which makes the soul forget we are divine and think we're just human, has overcome Janete.

Just as Pharoah was unable to pursue the Israelites across the Red Sea, so am I being prevented from restoring any and all attachments not related to my Soul's Journey.

The mystery to solve was why is yogmaya fucking with them? My so-called material attachments made me feel safe and stable, which helped me pursue spiritual growth. Pain is a major distraction. So why, God? Why?

The Torah/Bible's Book of Job tells of when Job questions God, "Why have You made me Your target? Why have You given me life only to send me such suffering now?"

God sets him straight with a potent diatribe, listing the countless things He has done, such as Creation of the Heaven and Earth, without Job's permission or involvement, emphasizing Job is not qualified to question a damn thing and should just do as he is told out of respect, if for no other reason! And Job is humbled by the lesson.

So my first and primary conclusion as to why Yogmaya is wreaking nonstop havoc in my life for over four years is, *nunya:* it's none of my damn business! God has His reasons and mine is not to question why but to do or die!

As a prideful, stupid-human, I wonder if I have a bigger calling.

Was my *behavioral* counseling career preventing me from a stronger dedication of my *spiritual* career? Was worldly success obstructing my spiritual focus? Am I supposed to help propagate bhakti-yog rather than assist people's mental health? Am I supposed to shift to a more spiritual type of counseling instead?

Ok. No big deal. Fuck it. My career as a behavioral innovator was sweet, and I'm honored to save so many from destruction, but at the end of the day, it is a *worldly* service, not a *spiritual* one. Time to move on.

But what about yogmaya taking a wrecking ball to my love life?

My Guru Himself taught we shouldn't go to satsang hungry or tired: eat well, rest well, so you can actually focus during sadhana time. Now that I'm starving for love and companionship, and in my case, sexual intimacy, I can't focus on a damn thing but my loss and grief! I thought working at my career for material safety and comfort and tending to my romantic life for emotional safety and comfort were healthy, smart ways to sustain my *spiritual* life. Yet, in spite of my material losses and sufferings, the level of spiritual devotion during sadhana is deeper than ever. It's the entire *rest* of the time I struggle to see past my material pain!

What is being revealed to me is the true depth of my attachment to worldly love. The pain of its loss is certainly compromising my sadhana overall. This is another religiously universal concept. Torah/Bible again:

"For He is a jealous God who will not tolerate affection to any other. . . ." (Exodus 20.5), and the Jesus one I already quoted: "Anyone who loves his mother or father more than Me is not worthy of Me" (Mathew 10.34).

The Bhagavad Gita too:

"Only those who worship Me with *exclusive devotion* attain Me" (9.22).

My stupid-human *intellect* accepts this truth, but my stupid-human *emotion* remains attached to worldly happiness. Have I been justifying my worldly attachments as necessary to my spiritual stability?

My worldly attachments have to go.

They cannot serve my Soul's Journey. When you complete kindergarten, it's time to move on. Much fun as playtime and naptime was in K-class, you gotta move on to 1-6 and onto college someday. When you finish your meal, pay the check, and leave a tip because it's time leave the diner to bring home the doggie bag to Fido, it was good, but now it's over. They've filled their purpose. The fat lady is bellowing an aria.

In the spiritual context, all which I have lost are *disposable items*.

Akashic Agents set me right, not as blunt as God did with Job, but they reveal my erred thinking:

"You are given such rare opportunity. Your Guru hasn't *taken* anything from you. God has *given* you what is needed to complete your Soul's Journey.

"Your life was full. Like a glass with water to its very brim, there was no room for anything more to be added. God and Guru wanted to give you *more* Grace. To give you more spiritual growth, expansion, and opportunity. When your Guru *added* more Grace into your spiritual vessel, it *displaced* the waters already there. God didn't *take* anything, God *added* more, and as a result, your cup runneth over, and many of your material attachments, as quenching and hydrating as they were, got *displaced*. You didn't have any more room in your glass, and when you went to the *other side,* you came back with *more*.

"The two taking up the most volume in your head, heart, and life were your career of helping others and serving your partner. The fullness of these two took up so much room in your glass that when it overflowed with Grace, they were displaced more than any others. Because they were at the top.

"And here you are, trying to refill your glass with Kool-Aid, instead of drinking of the *amrit*-nectar you've been given. You're a fool."

Maybe not as *blunt* as with Job, but pretty hammering, just the same.

While I never see my helping-career as "*bad*," maybe it is time to help myself. Maybe the one that needs spiritually saved is *me*: "Physician heal thyself . . ." (Luke 4.23). If I die (again) tomorrow, I'll reincarnate back to the same Groundhog Day circumstances: pursuit of worldly love and trying to be some sort of mental health savior to the world.

"God and your Guru, who are One and the same, *and you know it,* have worked yogmaya miracles, not just to spiritually save and provide for you but to make their involvement undeniably evident so that you would have *no doubt* of their involvement. And if your so-called loving partner—who you saved, rescued, completed, and provided for in every material and spiritual way—could not see the outright miracles and *join* you instead of pursuing her own selfish and shortsighted needs, then her waters got poured out as God's waters got poured in."

"Wow. Don't hold back. Tell me what you *really* think!"

"What more do you need? You've been given a True Guru that is a *direct descension* of God's loving aspect: Rasik Saints are rare! To directly associate with one is rarer. To actually be capable of understanding their words and taking them to heart and become devoted to them is rare beyond imagination.

"You have been graced with prodigious intellect, intense passions, supernatural endurance, and capacity to learn and practice your path combined with a lifetime of cosmic events, one after the other, your entire life. Are you willing to trade all that for a girl who rejected you the moment it seemed you might be unable to provide her with comfort? Which temple do you pray at?"

"I thought I could have it all: I had true love in the world, admiration and respect, success, health, and status, *and* I was totally dedicated to my God and Guru. I thought I was doing it all right."

"You weren't doing anything *wrong*, Krishnanand, except trying to have it all. And this is why you've been given such opportunity through His direct intervention of Grace through Yogmaya. Don't waste it. Through many lifetimes, you have put yourself in this rare position. You've tried for *infinite* lifetimes to become God Realized and have failed in them all. You're being given opportunity to progress and even complete your Soul's Journey to Divinity.

"You can't see the forest through the trees; you don't know how close you are, nor how far you are, to the other side of the forest. But you can only run *in* halfway. Because then you're running out. Don't look behind to see how far you've come. Look forward to see how far you can go."

"I will do my best to commit my life to spiritual progress and not to material concerns. I don't care for heaven nor reward. God can love me or hate me, whichever She wants. I only want Her to be pleased with me."

I vow: To continue my Soul's Journey. To endure the slings and arrows of outrageous fortune, not by opposing nor ending them.

"I will do my best. I cannot stop desiring: love, comfort, validation. . . . I am a desire machine. But I can commit to not *acting* on them if they don't serve my Soul's Journey."

Remember: these weren't actual conversations. I'm a human, not "One" with the Godpower. I'm merely relating them to you as dialogue from my perceptions of the uploads, resulting in meditation/contemplations. They often seemed like direct contact, but more like inception/thought-transference.

_____ **_33._**

TO LIVE AND DIE IN LA

> Abandon the mind which is only thought.
> —Hath(a) Yog(a) Pradipika

> Standing on a hill in my mountain of dreams/Tellin' myself it's not as hard, hard, hard as it seems…
> —Led Zeppelin ("Going to California")

Autumn 2018—Year 5 After NDE-Day

My exile is over. Time to go home.

Where is home? What is this star? Where am I to go? I cannot carry on in a state of desiring any longer. Please… please… leave me be now… let me *go*. Let the exile from heaven to earth be over. During my life, I've lived in five states and have had more than twenty-five home addresses. I've also camped out on friends' sofas and park benches throughout my youth, so *where's home?* If it's where the heart is, then it's Los Angeles, where Brandon and my Soulmate currently reside.

I take this direction to return to SoCal from the *exile is over* message and fold it into my scheme of ending things. To reduce the hellish consequences of self-murder, I want to research Sanskrit texts and see if I can find a *loophole;* are there provisions for suicide? It will be time-consuming to look into this as well as settle my meager worldly affairs. It will take a few months to prepare and carry out self-execution.

Out of respect for God and Guru, I will still try to make a life of peace, happiness, safety, and health, *just in case.* I've entirely abandoned any hope of recovery from my cornucopia of disasters, and I'm well past giving a shit; I *never* liked the shallow, shitty, superficial world anyway. I approached every day of worldly life with a positive, wholehearted disposition and a *why not, might as well make the best of it* attitude. I have always been pretty optimistic for a cynic.

The plan is simple: remove Janete from my will and leave only Brandon and my Guru's charity organization to receive my insignificant property and assets. I'll arrange to dispose of my personal possessions and *my body* so I won't burden Brandon with the stress of taking care of it.

My initial Google-driven research of what the Vedas say about suicide is that it needs to meet the criteria of *Ahimsa*, which means *do no harm*. First, there must be irreversible suffering: a big check mark on that one! Second, suicide should not be violent and should not involve anyone else. And third, I don't want to put anyone out emotionally or financially.

I got it: I will put on my SCUBA gear, surface swim out into the Pacific Ocean from the shore to an area at least sixty feet deep, cut off my air supply, and drown peacefully. I can't think of any other way that is less violent and scary. And if I make all my arrangements ahead of time, no one will need to stress out over material things. Since it will look like an accident rather than suicide, Brandon will struggle less to get closure on the loss. I don't have anyone else in my life, and my family relations are rather peripheral anyway. I will make sure Chow-Chow is safe and secure.

It will take time to move, make final arrangements, and spend some quality time with Brandon before I go. And if life should go from dark to light again, I'll stay; I may as well be open to alternatives. A new Soulmate would be nice! I'm suicidal, not stupid: if my lover asks me back; if my material life with career begins to turn around; if my brain trauma and NDE fog lift so I can feel human; or if anything indicates I won't live forty-plus years in perpetual disasters, I'll stay.

In the meantime, *I'm done*: tired, fuel on 'E,' way past bedtime, emotionally bankrupt, the party's over... I'm ready to go now. I do not want to live, and not just because my life sucks, which it emphatically does. I don't see how any of it is worth it. I'm cool with life generally sucking because that's the nature of the world to a spiritualist: once spiritual Truth removes the veils of material ignorance—*samsara*—you see that you can never be happy in the world and exist only to become spiritually Enlightened and Realized. A troubled life is a real sadhana motivator for achieving Enlightenment—*Buddhahood*.

Removing the veils of ignorance, or seeing through *samsara,* rising above the "veil of illusion" as kabbalah's Tree of Life instructs, is considered God's Grace, too. Realizing only spiritual reality is worthwhile makes you dedicate your life to sadhana. You make a pact with the devil that you will endure the shitty material world simply as a means to an end; you'll live and do what you must while progressing on your Soul's Journey.

Human lifetimes are precious because only in human incarnations can you complete the Soul's Journey to spiritual perfection. It takes human consciousness to connect and do the sadhana work to pull it off. In animal lives, we receive karmas, but we don't create them. In animal incarnations, we run primarily on instinct as we move toward human incarnation again. Insect lives are pure instinct, without the ability to reason and ponder. It continues up the ladder: sea life, primates, and, I suspect, domesticated animals are souls in *human training.* By closely associating with people, Chow-Chow kitties (and meow-meow doggies!) are like internships; they learn through direct association how to be humans. The abused ones become human shitheads, so treat them right, or it's straight to pet hell for your next round! Sanskrit texts teach us we can only do sadhana in human life.

But there's a fine-print clause in the spiritual contract. Western religions barely even mention it; they promise that if you believe, you get to pass *go,* collect the $200, and go to heaven, the end. Eastern ones tell you that final transcendence to Divinity requires direct association with a Guru or Savior. The Vedic, Upanishad, Shastra, and Yog texts all say you need a Guru to complete the Soul's Journey.

Why?

Because stupid-humans cannot contact God *directly.* The Western religions explain this, too, but in veiled ways: Christian-based ones tell you straight up: no Jesus, no heaven. You gotta believe and accept Him as your one and only personal savior. This is in direct alignment with Sanksrit: you need to associate and surrender your mind, will, and heart to a Master—a Divine personality, who will then grace you with the final act of God Realization. Islam is less Guru or Master-focused, teaching that living a religious life with total surrender to Allah (God) will get you into heaven, but the formula for living the qualifying religious life is *only* in the teachings of Mohammad (pbuh) as the final prophet, so he fulfills the guru role. Judaism is similar as they await their prophesied messiah.

The fine print in the VedicYog spiritual guide states the Master must be two things: He must already be Enlightened and Realized since only one who *is* divine can impart divinity; he also must be alive and on the planet when you do your final surrender.

Well! That's it! I'm done! My Guru is indeed a Divine Personality, already Realized. Because He is a *real deal* Guru, *Mahaparush,* He spent over ninety years on this planet teaching and revealing the path and practice of loving surrender. I learned what to do and have been precise in doing my best to follow and surrender to Him. There's just one problem:

He's gone.

The Sanskrit texts teach us that it is imperative to surrender to your Master while you are both still alive. People are notorious procrastinators and should try to recognize the rare blessing of having a human incarnation, spiritual sanskars, and associating with an avatar when they can.

But my Guru ascended to His Divine Abode five months after my accident when I was in the throes of my death experience and suffering from a brain-damaged identity crisis. I barely knew which way was up, let alone where heaven was. My opportunity to have final surrender and grace by His direct association while still on Earth has expired. Let's face it; even if I hadn't been enduring TBI-DAI during His last days, I don't think I was quite *there* yet. I was a good devotee. I did seva and traveled to India to have His darshan as often as I could. I studied the path proficiently and did formal sadhana twice daily as directed, for weeks at a time at His ashram in the US and India. However, I was still a stupid-human desire machine attached to material happiness; I was far from complete and total *surrender,* which *all* religions require.

My death wish makes sense now. I have *no one* in my life and am alone every day with no prospects. My career seems determined to fail, and poverty will come in a matter of time. And my Guru is gone, so I can progress with sadhana but not reach perfection.

I counseled several suicides in my career. Those that are hysterical and emotional are not the ones to worry about. The calm and rational ones often have valid, not emotional, reasons to die. These suicides have a plan; they approach it like business, dotting the i's, crossing the t's, and crafting an exit strategy. I didn't *want* to die. I *wished* instead to emerge from this mountain of putrid ashes and live. It didn't have to be happy or even *good* living; I just needed pauses, intermissions, and occasional lower levels of total anguish. I'm honestly *trying* to lift the mountain above my head, but I can't. I'm about to pass out from exhaustion. And I had better take final actions while I'm still intellectually available.

***

Sisyphus is the king of Corinth in Greek mythology who cheats death *twice* by trickery. Zeus wants to put a stop to this dangerous precedence. When Sisyphus dies a *third* time, Zeus damns him to complete the task of pushing a boulder up a hill. Each time he nears the top, the boulder rolls down, causing him to begin again *for eternity.*

The message is that mere mortals should not mess with the natural order of things. I was killed; since I had somehow cheated death, I was cursed like Sisyphus to suffer for all my effort, with no reward.

I plan to follow the "orders" of ending my exile and going home to SoCal with these two agendas: to be *and* not to be. My primary objective is "not to be;" to self-die once I have made proper arrangements and settled my affairs. In the meantime, I'll see what I can do to make a life worth living. Instead of "what's next," it's all about "why not."

I secured airfare from Seattle to LA and began researching where and how I would live while I made death arrangements. The "exile is over" message came with that visual, too. I had no idea what it was, so I googled "symbols of stars" Within a few pages, I saw it; the many-pointed star symbol appearing in my 4 a.m. visits was a *hendecagram:* an eleven-pointed star.

It wanted to be *on* me. So, I got a henna tattoo to sample it for a while. Sure enough, after having it for three weeks, I knew it belonged and began to suspect why it was important; stars are sacred geometry used as banishing symbols. This many-pointed star on my forearm seemed to act like a black hole, a singularity that condenses matter to an infinite point and then releases it to some other dimension. Quantum physics calls packing matter into a black hole *spaghettification!* I hope my TBI-DAI gets uh-oh-spaghetti-oed!

Other than hell's consequences for suicide, there's really no point in being here anymore. Every day is a tragic reminder that I'm garbage and will suffer in loneliness without any purpose to others or humanity. I can't take twenty or thirty more years of this shit. No fucking way. I've endured more in these last five years than many have in a lifetime. I'm not saying it couldn't be worse because for someone, somewhere, it is.

I am saying my suffering is compounded by the abruptness of the shift and harshness of the contrast. Maybe I could handle my life being so bitter if it hadn't once been so sweet. Contrast is what they inject me with for an fMRI; I don't need it in every other shitty context of my life.

God's infallible irony: my emotional, worldly attachments, which possibly obstructed my Soul's Journey of complete surrender, have been forcibly removed, allowing me to focus on God Realization more exclusively; that's a blessing, right? But the pain of being brokenhearted and lonely while staring in the face of future poverty makes it pretty darn hard to meditate on spirituality. It's a bit of a *catch-22*; my material attachments are taken from me to clear the way for sadhana, yet their removal makes me dwell on them. How can I just *let it go?* That's a tall order for a stupid-human who's kinda-sorta AFU (all fucked-up).

I have one primary mission: to die. My two secondary missions are resurrecting my life with a faint hint of stability, extending at least a tiny bit beyond lonely suffering, and helping Brandon.

If I can accomplish the first of my secondary missions, I will inevitably postpone the death wish. Don't mistake this for *bargaining,* the third of seven stages of grief. I'm not making a deal with or threatening God or Akashic Agents to *help me or else.* I'm not *quitting.* I've come to the logical, sensible conclusion that I will do more harm to my Soul's Journey if I should live in continuous suffering for thirty more years of life than if I self-die. I'm not God-bargaining for a better life. I'm merely acknowledging that if life didn't horribly suck all the time, I'd be cool with sticking around.

The second one, helping Brandon, is a swan song kinda thing. His life was tragically rerouted because of my NDE, and his firefighter ambition was sidetracked. He was a volunteer fire cadet at a busy, reputable fire station in LA and was going to paramedic school when I was killed. Recently, he lost his apartment and his job. I had gone through a dozen jobs by the time I was twenty-one, but he had only had one since he graduated high school. How he lost it is cruel irony: he got that first job and lost it for the same reason.

When Brandon graduated high school, I gave him presents and told him, "You have two months to party and enjoy being free from academia; you earned it." He'd never been in one lick of trouble in school, was a varsity baseball player, and graduated with low Bs and high Cs despite moderate ADD. But despite being a very stable, easy-going kid, he was no momma's boy!

"You need to get a job within two months. If three weeks go by, and all you've done is apply at mall stores that sell skater shit, I will get your job for you. What do you think will happen if I bribe a Taco Bell manager $200 to hire a clean-cut, handsome, articulate high school graduate who's played ball since he was four and was a cub scout? My advice? Go to *In-N-Out Burger*. Fill out an app. Ask for the manager and hand it directly to him and smile. Then go back every *other* day, ask for him, and say, *Hello, I don't want you to forget about me.*"

"What? That's *gay!* I'm not doin' that!"

"You got two months. Then I bribe Taco Bell. Know this: *all jobs suck*. The fashion stores in the mall are all run by shitty managers, and your first many years in the workforce are gonna suck ass. In-N-Out is respectable and has a great reputation for being a good place to work; they hire crackerjack staff, which means they got good management."

He reluctantly did it, and the manager hired him on his third visit. The manager had a second agenda, too; Brandon was well-known as an all-star ball player in our burbs, and the guy wanted a ringer for his store's softball team. The irony?

A few months ago, Brandon had a collision with another player in the outfield, which badly dislocated his finger; it seemed his ambitions of firefighting were over before they began. He was a star employee for years and had been hired as a ringer, but softball has now put him on disability and potentially ruined his firefighter aspirations.

After my death and eventual relocation, Brandon lost his apartment because of shitty roommate issues—part of growing up— and moved back in with his mom, which any twenty-two-year-old would feel is a step back.

He loves her, and she's a decent mother, but her level of dysfunction is way high. She suffers from a borderline personality disorder, which was acute when Brandon was young. Though she has stabilized considerably, she still has bizarre episodes from this virtually untreatable and most severe disorder.

Brandon has lived primarily with me since his youth. We had joint custody, but he had always spent more time in my home than hers, and even before he turned eighteen, he opted to live full-time with me and part-time with her. Our paternity case set major precedence and changed fathers' and kids' rights in California. Paternity fraud has become a term, mainly because of my case. I fought tooth and nail, sleepless nights in law libraries as I fought *in pro per,* without a lawyer, for months and won a landmark victory.

I'd been his primary parent, sole material provider, cub scout leader, and baseball coach since he was five and had helped him become a cadet at one of the busiest fire stations in all of LA. His mother loved him and had joint custody, but it mostly complicated my efforts to provide a life for him.

He was, and is, the best thing this world ever did for me. I'd love and admire him even if he weren't my son, which, thanks to paternity fraud, he technically isn't!

As I return to SoCal, he is floundering from the relentless blows of life and feeling hopeless, thinking seriously about military service so he can be self-reliant. I'm supportive, but neither of us is the *platoon* type. We're not *against* military service, but as spiritual mystics who have *both* experimented wisely with mind-expanding tonics: he's *on the bus.* No, silly... we did *not* do our psychedelic experimentations together. I didn't even know about his till he was in his early twenties. Mine were documented publicly; I'm not a father who keeps secrets. He's known of my sullied, checkered past and his genetic origins all along.

I want to help him finish what we started and was rudely interrupted by my death: his progressions toward independence and self-reliance, to liberate him from his mother and mentor him. I'm not leaving until I give all I have to help him. It's what I do as a counselor for the community and what I did for Janete, too: *empower.*

I certainly had plenty of justified selfish, temporal reasons to return to SoCal: I wanted Janete and me back together. I wanted to be near my son. Who would categorize these as reckless? Anyone would feel this way. I might as well try before I die so this King Arthur would get his Guinevere.

The plan was: to find a place to live near enough to visit but far enough to respect boundaries; slowly and gradually expose ourselves to each other to reawaken her from the Mayic spell she was under that made her forget who she is; live happily ever after as we had always wanted. Then, if nothing improves, proceed to suicide as planned.

I *will* do all I can to try for life. Let this be known! I choose life over death, but not the one I've been having. I'll give it till I settle my worldly affairs, which should take three to four months.

I arrived in SoCal the week of Halloween for my recon mission. It was a sacred time for me because the most magical, mystical events of my life and all my major relocations always occurred in October. I will search for housing in South Orange County, a little over an hour south of where Janete lives and from my old house—not too far, but not too close. I spent my early twenties in that coastal region, and I was fond of it.

My henna tattoo of the hendecagram wore off, and my modest hotel room is within walking distance of three tattoo parlors. I scan each website and see if there's a kismet-type of connection. I want the artist applying it to have some spirit, if possible. I look through the gallery of their photos: huge, full-color, textured images of geishas, peacocks, fish... the usual. But on a barely revealed part of an arm sleeved in complex images was this obscure shape by the elbow: *an actual fucking hendecagram*. A few hours later, I was marked for life.

Janete and I spoke on the phone. Like a stalker, I called her work at Home Depot because she had me call-blocked. She was amenable and agreed we could meet *as friends*. It's hard for me to be caught in superficial conventions. Homey don't play that way. If and when *I* am in charge of events, I take them outside the box and make them creative and unique. For this go-around, *she* was the director, and we could expect nothing but cardboard-box suggestions. She suggested a movie and lunch. Far more than I thought I'd get, so it was a date.

We decided to meet in the carpool parking lot off the freeway by our neighborhood. "I'd honestly rather not go by my old house or the places we walked and lived together for many years, Janete."

"No, that's okay. Cody is home, and I'd rather no one know we're getting together. I don't need the questions. My entire family will know within an hour if my son sees us together."

She had stopped seeing the loser she had been dating. My heart skipped a beat, even though, with the same breath, she emphasized this get-together was just platonic. Yeah … *bullshit.* She knew how I felt and what my agenda was. We were now complicit. Let the dance of courtship begin: I was going to make *The Princess Bride* romance pale like an albino.

We have several '*our places*.' Follow Your Heart restaurant and the Arclight Cinemas are where we spent many date nights enjoying premium vegetarian food followed by a luxury movie. We talked about profound subjects.

"I'm never interested in *small talk,* Janete. You and I don't need to bore each other with work and family topics."

"No, that's never been our thing. I always liked how deep you are. Just try not to get too intense."

Strike one: she used to love my depth and intensity, and now I'm cock-blocked as she erects perimeters and boundaries. I share the story of the IANDS conference and what I've been learning about NDE.

"I'm not out of the woods yet, Janete. But I can see the tree line, and now, at least, the strangeness of the last several years has an explanation. Maybe I'll write about it; I don't know. I mostly want the whole thing behind me. I hope it becomes a distant memory instead of an ongoing event."

"I'm glad for you, Scott. You've been through a lot. I knew you'd be okay. You just needed to find your way out."

I introduced the NDE side effects topic, and she was intrigued by my extrasensory perception of past lives. She wanted to know more, and we spent most of that lunch on the outdoor patio of our fav place with my regaling her of her past identities.

"This is why you've always felt so lost. You have life-purpose missions you've never fulfilled, and the tragic ending we experienced lingers within your unconscious. Your love of animals and lack of empathy for people comes from this past life we shared centuries ago. We vowed to reunite and make right what we did wrong in that tragic ceremony at Stonehenge. Now, we're screwing it up. I blamed myself for the way you died back then. I pined for you for several lifetimes. Things are coming full circle in this life because this time, *I* died, and you pined for me these last four years. Let's end this karmic circle, Janete."

"It's over. It's been too long, and I've changed. The pain of all this changed me, and it took everything I had to get through it. I'm finally over it and accepted it. I can't go back and need my life to be simple. You're complicated, and I don't have the strength for that like you do."

"I'm getting stronger. We relied on my strength for this lifetime, and I'll carry the weight again. We've taken turns being the strong ones for centuries. This one is my turn."

"I need my own strength. I totally relied on you. It wasn't fair, and I have to do it alone now."

"I've never stolen your power or strength, Janete. I've done nothing but empower, support, and believe in you. I never *enabled* you."

"I know. You're the only one who's ever made me do it myself. And I'm so grateful. No one's ever done as much as you did for me. You didn't provide for me; you *taught* me how to provide for myself. But I can't go back."

I chose not to beat the point and suggested we drive over to the theater. "We don't need to figure it all out now. It's good to talk about these things. We both need closure."

But I had *no* intention of *closure*. I intended to continue. I placed my hand next to hers on the table, our tattooed wedding rings side by side.

She asked about the new tattoo, and her envy matched its rustic green ink. I explained the story behind it. I sensed her mind categorizing it as another indication of our independence from each other. I imagined someday she would also have a second tattoo, her long-desired lotus flower, both of us placing them on the same part of our wrists, just as our wedding ring tats were synchronized.

Trying on the new shoes of her being in charge, we saw a melodramatic movie. It was so simple and *heartfelt* that it was guaranteed a nomination: unoriginal, cliché to make moms cry. My inability to connect well to mundane dramas because of cosmic side effects during NDE made my mind wander to more significant things: *I wonder if they have a* vegan *hot dog at the concession?* I wasn't even hungry, just bored with the desperately predictable Hollywood blockbuster format relying on brand-name actors doing their first-ever drama performance. Carrey and Carell should stick to comedy and do us all favor.

My hand reached for hers, and she rejected it. I leaned in for a hug and kiss, and she pulled away. I respected the boundaries without argument or scene. I took it in stride with a few tears on the long drive back to Orange County, comforting myself with the Tortoise and the Hare analogy: slow and steady. Long game. Grace under pressure.

Overall, it was a success. We agreed to stay in touch. Janete would unblock me as a contact. I silently shouldered the insult of these things being presented to me as gifts. The ordinary had now eclipsed the extraordinary.

***

While I was there, I even went on a date. My vow of at least trying to improve living was sincere, even though I can't wait to see how karma's gonna fuck this up, too. Besides, Janete had told me she was seeing some loser. No, I didn't *know* him, and yes, anyone who isn't me is a *loser!* My backup date was just that: not a lack of Soulmate love for Janete, but certainly a lack of confidence in her ability to wake up no matter how hard I tried. There are a lot of people on earth who regularly deny spiritual destiny, so there's no guarantee.

I met the backup date online. If I was gonna relocate to SoCal, it was best to prepare. Real Estate is *all about* location, and I want to be close—but not too close—to my prior stomping grounds and be near a vegetarian and vegan market, too. This location research led me to a vegan dating site to see if I could get me some on my trip. This way, if I didn't find a place to live and couldn't reunite with the love of my life, at least I'd have had a good time and gotten a little confidence boost. The woman I met was vegan, pretty, and... *a Dodger fan!*

Hard to deny the providence! A vegan woman who lives in South Orange County who is not an Angels fan but a hardcore, diehard Dodgers fan? Sign me up! I liked her unique name, too: Delta. We had many good talks on the phone and texted regularly, and we were looking forward to meeting. The Dodgers were in the World Series that month so it was undeniable kismet! A Soulmate's a Soulmate: Janete, who's vegan but doesn't even like baseball, *or...* a new girl who's both.

The date went well. Then I directed my energy into finding a place to live, but nothing much materialized, and I felt lost. I stayed at a friend's house for a couple of days, deciding to make one final sweep through the *north* of LA to be thorough. I couldn't go home empty-handed; I had to dot the i's and cross the t's to have more to show for this mission than a mysterious tattoo and being unblocked from my ex.

It was bone-dry.

I had one day to look at places and couldn't get an agent to meet me. Real estate agents are usually *whores:* they will do *anything* to make a deal. Suddenly, I can't get a single one of these property-prostitutes to meet me and show me a few houses for rent. What the fuck?

I drove out to Ventura County's coastal area north of LA and decided to at least drive by some rental homes I found online since I couldn't get any tours. I stop for gas and ask the guy at the next pump, "Hey, I'm thinking of relocating here. Can you recommend a good area?" He gives me his real estate agent wife's number; *a damn good sign.* I go to her office, and she tells me, "I'm sorry, but there's no one here to show rentals, just sales. I've got other appointments, but if you're willing to work around my schedule, I can show you a couple *real quick."*

I expect "her schedule" to mean I'll need to wait till evening, sitting around with the proverbial thumb up the proverbial ass all day doing nothing. But I'm at her mercy, "What's '*your schedule*' mean exactly?"

"We have to go *right now.* We can't wait or postpone. If you're willing to come with me right this minute, with no delay, I can show you three."

How clever Portal Agents are!

"Deal. Let's roll."

Homes number one and two are dead ends: noisy streets next to elementary schools. I'll do what I gotta do to be near enough to date Janete but far enough to keep up the appearance that I didn't move back just for her. But I hope it doesn't mean being a neighbor to school bells and buses.

One last place…

The agent gives me an address, "I'll meet you there. Give me ten minutes to drop off a key to someone, and I'll be right behind you."

I figure it's my desperate rationalizing rose-colored glasses giving me this warm, everything-is-about-to-be-okay feeling. I pull up to a house that's $100 outside my monthly rental budget. It's a block from the beach. No kids. No schools.

I pull up to the address and park to wait for the agent. The phone rings. It's Janete.

I'm tempted to pass on the call until after I see the house in case my spidey sense of bad news is correct. And it is, as always. I *hate that*.

"I just want you to know... don't call or text me. I'm getting back with... *(loser)*. We're going to work things out. I don't want him to know we got together. It was wrong, and I don't want him to know about you."

Now she has a problem with misleading a boyfriend? Really? This fuckup she has barely known for a few months is where she's discovered loyal allegiance?

"Janete... this guy is *not* right. We don't just have a history, goddammit. We have a soul. This is an average guy who's trying to *control* you. You said it, and see it. Give us some time. Let the best man win."

"No... I don't want to mislead anyone. He made it very clear about loyalty."

"Fuck! Loyalty? Please! I agree: be fucking loyal. To something beautiful that never ended and got interrupted. Not to some band-aid of denial."

She insisted, wished me "luck," thanked me for "all I had done," and disconnected the call as the agent arrived.

I'm with a real estate agent and need to be a normal, smiling person with a pitch-black, blood-red cloud over me.

I'm in so much pain from the fucking whiplash of being accepted and rejected I can't breathe. My mouth is dry, and my world is ending, and I need to consider where I would put my office: upstairs or down?

I go into overdrive: *set all your personal shit aside, man. Do what you came here to do. Setbacks, man, setbacks. It doesn't mean shit! Focus!*

It meets my needs. "I'll take it." I don't feel triumphant. I am shattered and heartbroken. All over again. I am self-loathing with anger for being so stupid and childish after all I've been through.

But the house works; it is a dark silver lining, but it *is* a silver lining nevertheless. Out the back door is a narrow lane alongside a big green park. Less than a minute's stroll down the lane is a grand and beautiful beach. It is not your usual SoCal beach neighborhood: it is quiet, peaceful, clean, and discreet—the poster child for a *hidden gem*.

If I was even remotely familiar with what joy feels like, I'm sure I'd be feeling it, but instead, I'm feeling hollow and valueless. Like shit. Not even human shit.

I kill time doing a few solo drive-bys attempting to be thorough and stay productive to postpone the soul-crushing heartache that will assault me at sundown. I have to leave tomorrow for the long flight back to a dark, lonely home in Shelton, Washington. There will be no place to hide from the large, forested loneliness waiting to pounce and devour me.

I spend my last night on a friend's sofa near the Burbank airport. My mind wonders… wanders… and visions come cascading in… not from the Portal's Akashic Agents, but from a totem spirit; a consciousness of an animal collective: the Eagle totem and the beast Janete had seen in Africa are rattling my chains, not *asking* me to call her, but *demanding*. I argue with them, telling them it's beyond my control; she told me not to contact her, and I'm probably call-blocked anyway. They make it quite clear they will not leave me be until I try, so I phone her at 6 a.m.

"Are you certain of this decision, Janete?"

"No. I'm confused. I don't want you moving back here just for me. I cant take that pressure.

"I'm not. It is a major reason, Janete, but just one of several. It's time. You've got to accept that we have never operated from a purely material plane of thought. I had to leave. We had to endure this shift and now have to see it through. At the very least, we need closure. We can't end things the way they did. Don't forget the animals in the field, Janete. Don't forget Italy. Don't forget that we have been given a treasure of events that are not mere memories of good times. We have shared a past together that was magical. Fate knew these dark days would come. Can we appreciate the magic and tap our past to deliver us to the future? That is the challenge and the test. It's not about *nostalgia*, Janete. It's about gratitude and appreciation of the cosmic forces that were so creative and generous to us. Cosmic forces have gone to a lot of effort to give us evidence of destiny, from how we met to these dark times, too. By remaining open, without expectations, we honor them as they honor us."

"Okay... *I'll think it over.*"

I silently sigh in relief: 'No' means 'no.' When a woman says '*maybe,*' it means '*yes*' unless you screw it up. The doorway back into my life was ajar. I planned on driving a tank through it.

Missions accomplished.

I've got a hendecagram star inked on my arm, I've found an ideal home near the beach, and I am connected with Brandon, who's excited I'm coming back. I went on a nice date, and Janete is groggy but waking up. It is all encouraging, but the so close yet so far away sensation is painful. The closer we come to fulfilling a desire makes us sensitive to its potential for disappointment, and I can't take more teasing. My flight home is saturated in longing for a better life and for this surreal NDE to settle the fuck down and let me be.

I went to bed one night and literally woke up in The Portal, but as a corpse on earth. Before NDE-Day, I liked my life; it was virtuous, and its ending was too sudden. Couldn't I go to sleep again and wake up with it as it was?

Dorothy was a sage: *There's no place like home... there's no place like home...*

***

For you mystics out there...

The hendacagram, my eleven-pointed star tattoo, has continued to reveal more of itself. Just when I think I "get it" and understand the layers of mystical frequencies it radiates, it shows me more.

- *The number eleven is known as a Master number in Pythagorean Numerology. The "Life Purpose" number from my original birthdate is 56, which is distilled to an 11 (5+6=11)*
- *Meditating on it as a yantra, I eventually realized that this eleven-pointed star has 45 other points within it, bringing it to 56*
- *It is a Hermetic symbol, deeply connected to Kabbalah, representing the 11th Sephiroth on the Tree of Life, Thaumiel—Twins of God.*
  - *This is the "shadow side" of the Tree, the "Qliphoth."*

Traditional Kabbalists see the shadow side of The Tree as the chaotic side and the eleventh sephiroth, Thaumiel, as the back or shadow side of the first sephiroth, Kether. Kether is The Crown and represents the seventh chakra, Sahasrara. The Sahasrara chakra, fully open and activated through kundalini yog, represents unity with the Godpower—i.e., Oneness, cosmic illumination, and enlightenment.

Underground Stream sailors who submarine-dive into the Qliphoth see that side as far less sinister. They accept this eleventh sephiroth as the partner of Kether, not the dark shadow of it. Both schools take it to represent "duality." But traditionalists see duality as separateness from God. In contrast, Underground Stream mystics, such as myself, see it as "mono-duality" where the experiencer is ONE with the experienced yet remains separate to experience its bliss. The path of bhakti yog(a) is a path of mono-dualism.

Did you know…

- *The base of the Statue of Liberty is a hendecagram. The Space Shuttle's Solid Rocket Booster is an eleven-point star for proper thrust with slow burn. Cosmic, man, cosmic!*
- *Many mystics accept that the Pentagon headquarters are designed on Hermetic/Masonic formulae. The mathematics and geometry of the layout for Washington, DC, and the CIA are based on sacred geometry, including the rare hendecagram.*
- *Quantum physics has established there are eleven dimensions to reality. We all experience the three spatial and the one of time. There are seven others, curled up so tightly they cannot be perceived, even though they are all around us.*

I described the yantra image on this book's cover to its artist after a series of meditations. The face shown represents YOU, me, or any mystic seeking illumination. It also depicts Lord Shiv(a) and Lord Krishn with their sapphire, rain cloud complexions, each wearing a tilak—a focal point at the center of the forehead at the Ajna, or third eye chakra. The core of the tilak shown on the brow of the mystic is a hendacagram, an eleven-pointed star as it appeared to me in my vision. Meditations inspired me to direct the artist to add the green lotus petals to symbolize the Anahata, or heart chakra, with two extra petals for higher love octaves and the radiant glow and purple inner flower for higher consciousness.

The book cover and design and Within the Portal yantra were not even a gleam in my eye until this book was entirely written. Only during my cover design collaborations with the artist and the book's production manager did I realize the eleven-pointed star in my vision represented The Portal itself.

* * *

I returned to Washington after exhausting every option I could muster during my eight days in LA. The last place I saw was perfect. I began the stressful process of selling my Washington home and signed a lease for one on the beach in SoCal. Then the bottom dropped out.

The Portal *phone calls* are a bit cryptic, but always in my best interest. Worldly phone calls, not so much. "The owner won't accept a pet. She doesn't care that it's a cat. She won't make an exception. No, a larger deposit won't change her mind," the agent informed me.

The next call was from Janete, telling me it was over, *again*.

It all seemed a bust.

I had no place to move to and was back in the lonely woods of PNW alone. I have no access to SoCal now to seek living arrangements and no Soulmate to return for. My entire trip was a waste. Maybe my exile being over didn't mean to leave the PNW, but to leave this lifetime.

I was hanging by a thread. The loneliness of my exile was tolerable when I was all fucked-up with no actual identity and split between life in The Portal and life in the world. My spirit stabilizes in my material body, and the ratio reverses. It had been 20% in the world and 80% in The Portal; now it was 40% in the world and 60% in The Portal. I was becoming human, and it sucked.

Humans need love, attention, possessions, food, toilet, and sex. They need *happiness*, which we can never attain in the world beyond such fleeting 'temporariness.' And worldly pleasure is always accompanied by consequences: there are always bills to pay; nothing is free.

Janete had given me mixed signals; before I went to LA, getting back together was an absolute *never*. While I was there, it was converted to maybe, followed by never, followed by maybe, all within about thirty-six hours. My point is that I'm not deliberately omitting the *'Dear John'* phone call Janete made to tell me, *again*, that it was over. I can't remember it, and I can't tell if it's blocked by denial or NDE-TBI memory impairment. Even though the words were similar and the message the same—*you need to move on, we're through*—my intuition told me it was for reals this time.

I didn't suspect for a millisecond that this loser she had gotten involved with was true love or anything magical. I was sure we were supposed to reunite and spend our lives together, with an added depth due to what we're enduring. I also didn't think I was being forced to help her through another challenge and gently coax her back to the Truth. It felt *final*.

For reals.

The realization level of true *acceptance*. People have stigmatized this final stage of the seven stages of grief as something holy; once we arrive on the shores of *acceptance*, we experience a Zen-like peace. Nothing like this appears in behavioral journals. As a crisis counselor who has coached dozens of people through losses as common as heartache and as severe as child loss, I can assure you that *acceptance* is *not* a peaceful event.

Acceptance is merely that: acceptance. You now know what is fact and that it is beyond your control or influence. Denial is entirely removed; anger, depression, bargaining, and the others are no longer present, but you're certainly not *okay* with them. Ask any parent that has lost a child if acceptance made them feel okay or peaceful, and they will confess that they are damned to live in abject heart-agony forever and ever.

I was intuitive and insightful enough to sense and know that this breakup was for real, which is why I felt so tragically desperate.

God gave me poetry and magic; I worked my ass off for over a decade to honor and sustain that. For what? To kill me, remove my spirit, let it die, and then tease me with restoration just to annihilate it all? What was the point? What was the lesson here?

Well... that would be revealed in time. But not now. In my eternal present, I am brain-fucked, life-damaged, exiled like a hermit-hobo, living alone in the dark woods, and cursed like Sisyphus. I'm making valiant efforts to roll that fucking massive boulder up the hill, only for it to roll back down to start over. Sisyphus had it easy, though; my boulder is running me over on its way down, pancaking me like a goddam cartoon character! I'm not Darcy from Pride and Prejudice making an epic happy ending. I'm Wile E. Coyote.

I will spend fourteen months in SoCal before I realize I only got half the Akashic message right. My exile was over; that part I got right. However, *go home* wasn't referring to SoCal.

<u>**34.**</u>

<u>*KARM(a) AND KUNDALINI*</u>

Whatever is destined to happen, will happen, but a wise person can change his fate by
entering into Divine Love Consciousness.
—Swami Prakashanand Saraswati

As we drive up the California coast on Highway One, Brandon drives my STI to our
campsite in Big Sur. I'm on a mission: liberate Brandon from Mom's and give him the
opportunity to reboot his young life. We discuss karmic-branding along the coastal
drive:

"It's possible to know your *brand* of karmas, Brandon."

"I've never *won* anything in my life: no contests, lotteries, rewards, carnival games,
slot-machines, Vegas card games. . . It's not my *brand* of karmas, so I no longer even
play. I've never gotten anything for free, rarely had anyone buy me things, or even
assist me beyond one interest-free loan from my uncle of $2,500 dollars in a CD to start
my contracting business. Which I never touched and he got back with CD maturity
interest. That's one of my brands of karma: nothing won or free for me."

"I can see that, sure. But your construction career was successful and so was your
practice."

"Yes. The flip-side of that brand is nearly everything I ever slaved away at *on my own
and with no assistance* has yielded great results. A pound of labor results in an ounce of
results for me. That's my *brand*."

"Okay . . . not an ounce of labor for a pound of results but the opposite, right?"

"Exactly. Some people are opposite: some do nothing and make bank; some win
lotteries and bingo every time they play. I don't wanna jinx you, especially while you're
driving *my* car up Highway One, but you've *never* had a ticket. Yet you drive a WRX,
same as me, that *screams* I'm a hot-rod car driver, so pull me over: I go 5 mph over the

posted, and I get yanked to the side of the road. You go thirty over and got pulled over because CHP wanted to compliment you on your driving and car."

"No shit, that really happened. Is that why you ask me to drive when we road-trip? Cuz I got good cop-karma?" he chuckles as he downshifts.

"Yeah, it's cheaper: I get tickets; you don't!"

"You're saying that if you pay attention to the themes and patterns in your life's circumstances you can, like, *predict* your karma?"

"Yep. You know how I found the resort-like house in Washington? The way I was redirected from the paper ad to meeting the couple outside the house which led to moving there?"

"Yeah, that place was awesome."

"And then I got the Shelton property and built the house. And now look how I found and got the Oceanaire house I'm in now."

"Too freaky, man. Your new place is totally a beach-resort house. And didn't both the rental home in Washington and this one tell you 'no' because of Chow Chow?"

"The Washington rental yes, told me no. I wrote a letter with my trusty writing skills and persuaded them to accept him, even though the owner's allergic to cats, and he didn't want to fumigate after renters. This beach place on Oceanaire is four houses down from the one that told me no cats and rejected my application to rent."

"There's definitely a theme. Chow-Chow had a role in both places, and the way you found this ocean house is freaky too."

"Yeah, so maybe *I* don't have good house-rental karma, but maybe Chow-Chow does!" both of us laughing at the Chow-Chow charm.

To find the current beach-house rental, I had searched far and wide over three SoCal counties. I had given up and agreed to look at one last place with an agent I'd met at a gas pump. It was perfect, and I was ready to sign the lease, but when I'd gotten home to WA, the agent told me no cats, no exceptions. Twelve-hundred miles away, desperate to end my exile, I was shattered by romantic rejection and nowhere to move back to LA to win her back, help my son, and reboot my life.

In a desperate online search, I found a house four doors down that was soon to be for rent. As *"chance"* would have it, my sister was in the very same neighborhood that day, sunning on a beach she'd never heard of and never been to before that random morning. She agreed to look at the place and video call me so I could see it before signing a twelve-month lease, sight-unseen. My sister was in town just one last day before she flew back to her own house in Texas, and I was able to persuade the agent to give her the keycode to enter.

"You have to get this place! It is *so you!*" She knows I'm a bit exotic and eclectic, so I trusted her, signing a lease online the next day, having trust it would all work out.

 Our conversation pauses as we glide atop the iconic Rocky Creek Bridge and then continue exploring the machinations of karma. "What you're saying is that your brand of karma aligns well with places to live if you follow a formula that's particular to you. You gotta, like, go the extra mile, cuz nothing comes easy, but if you do, the results aren't just satisfying but really good."

"If I follow the formula, yes. But I can't bank on it. I don't do the diligence *expecting* it all to work out. Sometimes it doesn't. But if I *don't* go the extra mile, it's pretty damn sure nothing will manifest."

"Your brand of karma is all work gives you results, nothing comes easy, and it's pretty specific, like houses."

"A bit oversimplified, but lately, yes. My housing situation has been blessed. Even the shitty, horrible apartment time in Olympia was good in the sense it served the purpose I wanted: low cost to be safe while the house was built.

"My career has always been the same: ten pounds of effort for every pound of results. But I like it that way because I never take anything I've accomplished for granted. Blood, sweat and tears makes you value shit."

"You say your own brand is you never win or get free stuff. But your books won awards."

"Won is a very relative term there. I entered book festivals with thousands of other contestant entries. It wasn't a game of chance, like craps or poker. It was a competition of skill. I never won tennis matches for free, and I didn't win those awards for free. I earned them. They're not really awards, like free prizes. They're actually *recognition awards*. There's a difference."

The same had been for my fatherhood. I sacrificed it all to just be able to know him, never expecting anything more than knowing him at a distance but willing to sacrifice my entire life just to have even that. And now? Here we are, riding up Highway One to camp at Big Sur where I can offer him to live in the beach home and have his own room.

We break for lunch at Nepenthe and stroll onto the gift shop's outside deck overlooking Big Sur, soaking in the profound site of the Gold Coast below. The hundreds of windchimes honoring the space with mellifluous song provide a soundtrack as we exit the Underground Stream for terrestrial topics.

"If you want, Brandon, why don't you look for a part time job by me? If you get one, you can live part time by the beach in this grand house I'm renting and part time at your mom's so you can still be near your friends and stuff."

"Two of my best friends live in Ventura by you. I'm down. I'll think it over and see if there're any jobs by you."

We have a beer at the mountain lodge and the unplanned, unexpected opens up. I make some loose inferences to Janete and I being over. He stuns me with, "Honestly, Dad, I never really knew what you saw in her. You're this intellectual, spiritual guy, tuned into art and deep things. She's the total opposite: so basic and not smart at all."

"I never wanted to judge her on intellect. It's not her fault, and I evaluated her more on character than brain or mind. Why didn't you ever say how you felt about her?"

"It's your thing and you loved her, and if you were happy, it was cool. I never *disliked* her: she's cool and all. I just always thought you deserved someone more your level. I never said anything the same way you never actually *tell* me what to do. You always tell me your opinion and what *you* would do and let me figure it out. You influence me; you never tell me."

I kept my relationship areas private because these are not comfortable, appropriate areas to burden your children with. In this moment, I wanted him to know more. "There's a few things you didn't know that I kept private to not burden you with. The reason I went to the PNW was for the reasons I told you: to get better on my own and not be a burden. But there was also a private reason . . ." and in a sentence or two, I advised him of her transgression to our vows and how much it hurt and how the timing was more than I could bear.

"It was too much, even for superman: my brain trauma was beyond compare. I'm hovering between the world and stellar dimensions and get dealt the biggest blows to my material safety: my career was dissolving and the woman I loved and trusted betrayed me."

He was calm about some shallow girl hurting Dear Dad. "I figured something had gone wrong with you two. I didn't want to pry. It's your business. I'm sorry, Dad. For what it's worth, she was *never* worthy of you. Look at your life and what you've done. Now look at hers and what she's done: her son's a mess, her daughter is cool, but only because she raised herself, her sister's a shallow cunt, and her mom's just a suburb statistic."

"Haha . . . I can't argue any of that!"

"Aunt Christine feels the same way about her. We both know that Janete was never *on the bus*." His validation means the world to me. Not because he's *my son* but because he's a man of good character. He's *on the bus*.

***

Within a week of our return, he's full-time employed as a valet supervisor at the Embassy Suites on the beach, just five minutes' walk from my front door. He moves in full time, and I'm thrilled that for *once* something beyond housing karma is showing real promise!

"How the fuck did you land such a sweet job right around the corner?!"

"Simple: after a dozen dead-end applications to local bullshit places, I just walked up and told the valet guy I was looking for work. He said, 'Oh, you here for the valet supervisor position?' I said yes, got interviewed, and was hired. I start Saturday! I guess I got a good brand of good work-karma."

This new start has promise: a 2,000-square-foot home in a quiet neighborhood on a wide and gorgeous beach. The neighborhood's mostly million-dollar plus homes owned by retired professionals, making it not too kid-friendly: perfect! No screaming kiddies and soccer moms to annoy my peace! The beach is a hidden gem: flawless with easy access banked by a beautiful park with green grass with free yoga classes three times a week for just requested donations.

The yoga is to help restore my brain-body connection, damaged by TBI. Weekly rides on the MP3 500 motorbike let me enjoy the amazing views along PCH on Sunday mornings and nearby trail-hikes on Malibu coastal mountains give me quiet meditations on a peak overlooking the ocean. I'm depressed as fuck, but I'd rather be depressed here than alone 1,200 miles away from the one I love: *Brandon*.

I continue to work on promoting my books and rebooting my career, but since my death and rebirth, my karma brand has changed. It was still a brand of nothing is free and every success requires hard work, but no matter what I do in the behavioral field I am a reputable innovator in, it goes nowhere.

Book sales are small royalties, only a few of my video courses sell, and I sustain a few counseling clients. My current income just covers gas and groceries. The $3,200 rent and other living expenses are chipping my savings. But $3,200 rent for a 2,000-sqft beach house in SoCal is as much of a miracle as my death recovery! It costs $4k to rent just a 1,000-sqft condo in the burbs in SoCal.

I'm not seeing the writing on the wall: Janete and my clinical career are *dead-ends*. I keep going back to these dry wells expecting to pull up water. Finally, I begin to accept the career of my decade-plus of hard work and sacrifice was already over, without a severance check. *Scott* . . . was a behavioral professional who created Life-Mind counseling. *Scott* . . . died in 2013, and so did his practice. Only the ghosts remain, hanging around, thinking they're alive rather than accepting they are dead, dead, dead.

I review my own Spiritual Triangle reading for insights to my life: the one I did in WA to my true name and new birthday that revealed my worldly life was as dead as I had been. Scott didn't really come back; Krishnanand did. The sixteen-page reading, which is detailed and thorough, is not vague as it clearly directs me to let go of my worldly ambitions and that only spiritual ones will provide for me now.

But I'm in conflict: with my memory restored, I remember what it was like to live on the streets in my youth and grow up poor. I can't willingly volunteer for that now: my new normal has been material stability since I got off dope and became a parent and changed my mind, changed my life. Spiritualists live like monks: I'm not capable of living off the grid, tending a garden to live off the land. Too old, too damaged, too conditioned to morning coffee and central heat and air.

Back to square one: make my goldstar, author, counseling work provide a revenue stream allowing me to live comfortably enough to live spiritually. My author-counselor work is proud: it is real, it is authentic, it saves lives. It even nudges people, encourages people to look deeper into True happiness of spirituality. *Project Addiction* and my counseling work doesn't preach from a soapbox; it provides guidance out of worldly desiring. It offers, but does not preach, a spiritual way.

I persist on trying to have it all: material success and safety and love too. I've not come here to live, but to die. But I vowed to give it the good ole college try first. I'm keeping my word.

***

My new locale is just twenty minutes away from another Soulmate: Lia, my tantric, kundalini priestess, lives in the next town. We connect and have instantly deep connections and explore mysteries and I offer my sex to her, wanting my first time with another woman to be someone I respect and love. We develop a mature FWB connection: deep talks on mystical things with some sexual play. Her condition with cancer prevents us from much quality time though. She is a medical miracle too: but her treatments and symptoms limit her to a few hours of free time a week. My quiet surf home provides us sanctuary for many visits.

"Do you remember the one time you visited my house in SCV?"

"Oh . . . *the cats*. That one?"

"Yes . . . the UFO cats!"

In 2002, six months before I'd even met Janete, Lia's sixth sense had inspired her to a spontaneous visit the morning after I'd had a *very* strange night. I had just completed my first memoir and pulled a William Burroughs stunt: I sampled the bizarre, virtually unknown drug-without-a-name, which I call Crystal X, to give a first-hand account of it as it is vital to the memoir's climax.

So I tried passing my wakey-wakey dope night with my telescope one night. No, no . . . not to spy through neighbor's windows! I was actually stargazing!

And as it roamed around three or four in the morning in my oh-so-common suburb of sleeping families, I was outside chain-smoking and tweeking on my telescope. And three lights in the sky began to hover in odd circles above me in the not-too-distant western sky.

They would hover around in odd, curly-cue motions, stop, freeze a few moments, and hover some more. They were not unusual as far as lights go: no colors, flashing, or blinking . . . just plain white lights that moved around in this little space above.

As I focused the telescope on them, I saw nothing unusual close-up either: *just white lights*. No different than any of the stars in the cloudless sky. Because I was on dope, I assumed I was hallucinating and/or dramatizing over nothing. But they didn't go away: no hover around with a dramatic *whoosh!* And teleporting out of the galaxy in a blink, no slow, *or rapid,* ascension to Alpha Centauri, nothing special at all: just hovering around and pausing, hovering around and pausing. . . . This went on for easily twenty minutes or more. It was so uneventful, I actually wandered back in the house to make a sandwich, unworried if they'd be gone when I returned (and yes . . . even dope-fiends eat when strung out. I was a veteran drug user, so I maintained moderate normalcy: eat, toilet, shower . . . just no sleep!).

When I came back, they were waiting for me: and I do mean *waiting* for me. I got the clear intuitive sense they knew I was there and were watching me too, having fun with me. I sensed they were having a bit of playtime with an Earthling that wasn't going to freak out: I just took it in stride. I'd seen *a lot* of strange things in my bizarre life before then, and these weren't even my first interstellar travelers.

This playful interaction went on for well over an hour. I never saw how or if they encored the event with a lightning flash or zooming off to deep-space because I got bored and tired and decided to try to rest after not sleeping for three days. Lia and I had reconnected after several years of being out of touch, and she came to visit.

I told her this ET tale as she sat on my sofa facing the backyard I narrated about: I faced her, my back to the yard, as she faced me, able to see the land and skyscape I regaled about. Behind me was all glass, giving her full view of the rear yard and sky as my house was on a hill: my living room's rear wall was a twelve-foot-wide sliding-glass door. To be a good storyteller, I gestured to illustrate the positions and movements of my alien guests and gave my guest a fun and funny show of this story.

"As they hovered, Lia, in odd and random patterns, *not geometric or mathematical*—just random movements . . . they finally came to a rest and didn't move after about an hour or more. So I came in and lied down and merely thought, '*Wow, that was strange.*'"

"Tell me again what their formation was? The positions they were in when they stopped?" It seemed my mystic-sister-friend was about to propose a formula. . .

"It was just like this. . ." as I pointed one finger to 45 degrees, one at 60, and one at 90.

"Oh . . . you mean like that?" And she pointed out the sliding patio door, so I turned to look at her pointing.

"Whoamygawd . . ." as my jaw dropped. "Yes. *Exactly that pattern.*"

Three stray-cats had wandered into the yard as I narrated and sat themselves near each other in the exact placement as I had just described the night lights as being in. Three cats I'd never seen before in the home I'd lived in for three years and was quite familiar with any and all strays and non-strays of domestic animals in my neighborhood.

These three cats sat directly below the celestial space the UFOs had been in in the exact position of them.

Lia and I are so familiar with the unfamiliar, so frequently involved with the infrequent, and so accustomed to the uncustomary that there were rarely exclamations of *oh my god! Can you believe this!?* The *super*natural was quite natural to us. Yet, we never took this for granted or remained unimpressed with the blessings of witnessing them all the time.

"What is the message? What were they trying to tell me? I don't want to disrespect their efforts for conveying this to me by not understanding it."

And then she told me something that would stay with me all my life: "Don't try to fathom or interpret the mystery. You miss the point and what they're really giving by analyzing it. These fairy-types just came to remind you: *you are loved and not alone.*"

And just like that, like a Zen Master telling the Zen monk to stop looking at the master's *finger* but look at what it is actually *pointing to,* there was no need to explore, analyze, or talk of it. The fairy-lights and kitty-familiars were dispatched not to give Fibonacci Sequence or Stone-Henge logistics but to simply say *'hi.'*

"Haha . . . yes . . . I *do* remember that!" Lia's giggle has always been a charm.

Now that we're nearly neighbors, we get together often.She visits on the night of the Super-Blood-Wolf-Moon Eclipse. As mystics and astrologists, we agree to watch the rare event together on the beach, but when it gets chilly, we relocate to the second-story decking of the house. She assists me in a magic ceremony: my gestures and magic phrases to the cardinal directions during the eclipse to transmit a frequency of love, hope, and understanding along the lunar currents to all humanity. We lie together beneath a comforter, the sounds of the surf lulling us. . .

"Lia, if I'd shown up at your door that night and asked you to leave him and be with me for this lifetime, what would you have said?"

"I would've said yes."

"But you seemed so happy. The only reason I didn't ask was because I didn't want to be selfish and disrupt the life you'd made."

"You and I have been connected for many lifetimes. I've loved you in every one of them."

"And I too you. Lia, I was dead seton coming to get you that night. I had accepted our time had passed but never stopped thinking of you. We've had so many lifetimes that ended in tragedy. We've lost each other, hurt each other, held each other at death, became king and queen and master sorcerers. It would be nice to get one right."

"Haha . . . yes it would be nice to have one end in harmony instead of tragedy!"

We know we're coming full-circle in this lifetime. Her endorsement of my first memoir with permission to use her real name and photo in it was bonding. That story ended with the bizarre and supernatural Kundalini event she initiated with me and our tragic farewell to each other as we sacrificed our life together to fill greater roles beyond us.

At the climax of our Kundalini/past-life-regression soulmate connection when I was twenty-five and she was thirty-three, we were forced to make a choice:

The Akashic Agents were very present in my life at twenty-five too, appearing in the quasi-dream dimension then, saying, *"He's coming, and you can save him in this life as he has done for you."*

"Who's coming?" Back then I used to ask for explanations!

"Your teacher."

They did not mean Guru or Master teacher. It was clear within the telepathic message from Akashic Space it was referring to a previous mentor, guide, brother, or father in a recent life who had guided me. In this life, I was getting the opportunity to return the favor.

In the peak and midst of our love affair, I went to Lia and told her the news: my crazy, dysfunctional ex contacted me declaring she was pregnant with my child. My initial reply was, "*Do you want me to bring the hangar or do you have your own?*" This ex-girlfriend was just two months before Lia, and I wanted nothing to do with her violent, borderline personality.

But the Portal message had made it clear I should save him. Lia and I mutually decided, after deep meditations, this message to *save him* was paramount. Then I gave Lia the ex's fine-print condition I knew my ex would demand to not abort the child: marry her and have no other. Lia and I broke it off, sacrificing our many lifetimes' Soulmate love for a greater mission. We vowed to remain ever connected by heart.

After six months of marriage and a half dozen violent attacks, I left to try to raise Brandon outside of a dysfunctional marriage. When the smoke cleared and I was on my own again, I meditated on Lia and channeled how to find her.

"You never told me how you found me."

"To this day I still analyze my memory to be sure it's right, but as unbelievable as it is, the truth is the truth: I meditated on you and sought out where you were. I knew to get in the car and drive north and I would just know where to go. I drove toward Ojai, and my intuition told me where to exit and when to turn right and left and which door to knock on."

"You gotta be kidding me. I figured you had to talk to Ruth. No one else even knew where I was."

"How would I talk to Ruth? Not only did she not like me for leaving you, but I never had her number since I remodeled her bathroom in our first days together."

"So you just drove on intuition, parked, and knocked on my door?"

"Yes. I had remembered you once lived in Ojai and liked it but never knew anything else. That's why I went north. The rest was cosmic intuition. And I went there to propose to you like Hoffman in The Graduate: STOP: hello, hi, come away with me now."

"But you didn't. You didn't tell me to come away with you. Why not?"

"You invited me in, introduced me to your boyfriend, and all I wanted was for you to be happy. You were. And so was Roxanne. You and your daughter didn't need this upstart rocking the boat. So I concealed my true intent and left after our visit, glad you were safe and happy which is all I gave a shit about. I wanted to be with you too . . . but I wasn't going to compromise your happiness for it. Were you happy?"

"Yes, at the moment. But not for long. Yes . . . I would've left with you."

We lie together in comfortable silence, savoring the gentle sounds of ocean waves outside as our fingers intertwine and we float in a friendship of centuries.

Days later, we enjoy a stroll along the serpentine walking path on the beach. "Lia?"

"Yes, Krishnanand."

"Are you ready?"

Like abracadabra, this question has layers of danger and profundity for us. It was what she asked me the night she initiated me with kundalini and without even pausing to ask her, "Ready for what?" I just said, "Yes," and it was on.

"Can you jumpstart my kundalini again?"

"Don't you think it's already open and activated?"

"Yes, of course. And the death-event, time within the Portal, and brain trauma has booted it big time. But brain and spinal injury has damaged it too. It's not in the full-blown, lotus-blossom state: it's settled down. After years of pursuing it, I stepped away from it to follow the Rasik path of bhakti-yog. Psychic-supernatural powers can become so intense they are historically known for *interfering* with total, spiritual-Realization. But I'm desperate: my worldly life is shit to the point of painful distraction. My meditations are a fraction of what they were because I'm so miserable all the time. You know as well as I what a true Kundalini event is like: it's total, mind expansion. Undeniable and rewires your body, brain, and mind to mystical frequencies that you're immersed in them."

"But you know how dangerous it is. I'm not saying you were *lucky* before, but it was your prior life Kundalini work and your Guru's protection that kept you safe through it."

"I know: but I was a stupid kid then: alcohol, heavy dope . . ."

"I know! If I'd known you were doing what you did then, I'd *never* have initiated it with you. Of all the men I'd performed the technique on, you're the *only* one that got the whole effect. You are lucky, for lack of a better term."

"And if I could survive it as fucked up as I was then, I can make it a potent tool to elevate my bhakti yog work to completion now. Kundalini puts you on enlightenment's threshold, but I couldn't even *see* the door it presented then. Now I do.

"I experienced a conscious expanding event in spite of a toxic life. Now? I've been vegetarian and been doing beautiful sadhana taught by a Rasik Saint for over a decade. I had zero idea how to manage or use Kundalini then: I was just experiencing it. Now I know how to use it to reach the highest level."

"I don't know if I can do it, Krishnanand. I'm in crone phase of life now. I've got cancer. That Tantric blow-job, as you like to call it, is two to three hours of intense sexual technique and energy channeling."

"I understand, and there's no pressure, Lia. Your health and safety come first. If we can do it, I think we should document it with a series of video journals: the preparation with proper yoga, pranayama, diet, meditation. . . . Document this phenomena in real-time. I need a way out, Lia. I'm fucking drowning in loss over five years now, nonstop. I don't wanna live twenty more years and reincarnate because I'm too fucked up from material anguish."

In the end, as sympathetic as she was, her health prohibited her from doing it. "If you find another woman who will act as priestess, I can train her and show her how. Keep in mind, a major reason it worked on you and no others is because of our deep connection: we love each other and have for many lifetimes. That was a critical factor."

But alas, few to none in this materialistic age are anywhere near qualified to perform such a sacred act. My search for another priestess is a dead end. Yogmaya intervened once again. Few in the annals of mystical history are able to use the Kundalini force as a portal to Spiritual Enlightenment. It is a psychic-siddhi: a power that is a feature of the material realm, not the Divine. Siddhis are intoxicating and distracting from true surrender to the Godhead. I voluntarily walked away from it before without regret. Yet here I am, once again, trying to salvage what I once was instead of focusing on what I can become.

Will I ever learn?

_____ **35.**

LIFE'S A BEACH

> I am the Knowledge, the Knower of My knowledge, and I am Knowingness.
> —Krishn (Bhagavad Gita 15/15)

> I could put my arms around every girl I see/But they'd only remind me of you
> 'Cause nothing compares, nothing compares to you
> —Sinead O'Conner (Chris Cornell)

Writing is my gift: I can sell ice-cubes to Eskimos and Bic lighters to Satan if I write. My pen is far mightier than my sword. I will pull out all the stops and give it all to her: proof I am healthy and fine now, fitter and more handsome than ever before, charming and doing well materially by living in a wonderful house on the beach which she always hoped for. The lesser of these virtues is fitter and more handsome: they are truly way down her list of priorities. She took these attributes for granted when we were together, and she sincerely is not superficial in this category: she loved me because of who I was, not because I was also decent looking.

My pen being mightier than my sword, I went to work crafting a perfect script for a video-letter. Janete could never read a lengthy letter and was the true muse behind the reason I produced my books in audio and video: ADD people can't take in reading content; they need audio or video. A video letter will not only be a format she can follow but will be backed by my true personality: face, body-language, and voice inflections, all helpful to pierce a veil of denial and remind her. She had always appreciated the extra miles I went to communicate with her.

I set up my camera and light studio and told the love of my life who she is, who I am, who we were destined to be, and gave her the gospel.

A five-part video-letter addressing five topics:

1. Her Life-Purpose and Mission (13 minutes):
   a. Secrets (2 minutes)
2. Isibeau and Fatima (13 minutes)
3. The Truth (17 minutes)
4. The Ugly Truth (16 minutes)
5. Full Circle (27 minutes)

There is no greater, romantic sentiment ever expressed so beautifully in the history of man than what I portrayed in these letters. I defy any living being with a beating heart to watch these—*all of them*—and remain unmoved and unpersuaded Janete and I are destined to be side by side forever more.

I say to watch *all of them* because there is a total concept. This is *one* video-love-letter, not five. One letter with five parts:

1. Life-Purpose and Mission reveals for Janete her true gifts and capabilities to be a healer of animals. It explains the ongoing, frequent animal visitations throughout her life as a pleading from an animal-spirit collective. It details the path to become an animal healer and fill the gaping hole of feeling purposeless all her life. A path to fulfill a destiny and be self-sufficient.
   a. Secrets (2 minutes): The animal spirit she had seen in Africa in her childhood transmitted a very specific and private message for me to give to her. This was quite unexpected. I am not authorized to speak of it.
2. Isibeau and Fatima: Two of her past lives explained in detail how we had been involved and the tragedies that ended them. It tells of our involvement and why we had reunited in so many lives and what we could do with the one we were given in this modern age. It is an eerie and dramatic telling of verifiable historical events as I was able to accurately identify who we were in these lives: names, dates, and pictures from online searches.
3. The Truth (17 minutes): The Portal had revealed to me three potential futures for us as a couple: 1) How we would've ended bitterly if I'd not exiled to the PNW temporarily. 2) She remains spiritually asleep, and we never reconnect. Her animal healer life-purpose goes unfulfilled, and I continue my spiritual life but pine for her always, and we fail our combined destiny. 3) We reunite and live together on the coast offering our services; her as an animal healer, me as a spiritual one.

4. The Ugly Truth (16 minutes): a blend of higher-truths of spirit and calling out the sad, trivial, material dramas we were having and a strong, omega-male demand to cease it, and a plea to return to our profound destiny.

5. Full Circle: a full tour finale. Summarizing all the others and adding a video and photo collage of our ten years together. A tribute to our love, showing images of our vows together in a five hundred year old church on the Arno River in Florence, Italy, still photos of our trips from the Austrian Alps to UFO watching in Sedona, AZ, to our divinely graced tour through India and Nepal, as well as reminders that we have it all: not just the profound with exotic and spiritual pilgrimages but also vacationing with her family in Maui and our kids jumping off of waterfalls. Finally, closing with our opportunity to triumph over tragedy and the entire thing set to a soundtrack of her personal, favorite artist, Cat Stevens, and closing with "In My Life" by John Lennon and The Beatles.

Composing the video-letter is gut wrenching. My passions are on display. This is my final effort, not because I've nothing left to give but because I know for certain that if this does not and cannot wake and persuade her to reenter the temple of our union, nothing will.

Many sleep so deep within spiritual coma they cannot be aroused. If a Christ, Buddha or Kripalu can't wake people up, what can this stupid-human do?

I've done all I can.

I have committed my life to waking others to deeper layers of reality. I've intimately dedicated my passion of the profound to those I'm closest to, personally taking the duty to enlighten them, nurture them, and reveal higher ground to them. My serving Janete has been tireless. From Italy to Nepal, from pulling her out of clinical depression, and patiently teaching her The Way. *And she knows it.*

There's no more to be done.

The video-letters are edited and streamlined. They are shipped overnight with signature required so I know she gets them. I'm doing all I can to save the one I love and to restore our love. Then it is out of my hands.

There is no response.

I know she receives them but can never know if she watches them or if they are thrown in the trash. My mood is of the deepest blue. I'm out of bullets. It is up to her now to come round, wake up, see the light. She had last told me to not call or text her, so I have not. I've made it clear in the video-letter I will not persist. That I will respect her wish to be left to her own way. It feels *all* wrong and like a cardinal sin to abandon someone who gave me such trust, whom I promised I'd never leave, but there it is: she has made her decision and I am bound to it.

My final expression to her was that we will not continue another lifetime.

"We have been together in so many lives and experienced so much magic together and have been the best of lovers. I am dutybound to tell you that if we end this way, in this life, I will not see you again in another."

I remind her of the karmic dynamics binding us together life-after-life and vow to sever that in this one.

"My only objective is to become One with the Godhead; to achieve Union with my Divine Guru and Shree Radha, the perfect, female personification of Divine Love and Grace. I hoped we would assist each other in this life as we had done in past ones to progress in our Soul's Journey. But your rejection of me now is partly passive-aggressive: you know I don't want to reincarnate anymore, *ever*.

"I think you know I have a true chance at pulling this off in this life. You fear that I may reach Spiritual Realization, and if you don't, I'll abandon you again. But you have as much of opportunity to complete your Soul's Journey in this life too, maybe more; we just can't know.

"By rejecting me now, severing our perfect bond and reducing it to material dramas, your higher-consciousness knows my pining for you will bind us together again for next lives.

"No. No, Janete. I can't. I'm getting out. For good. You can either join me in this life's effort to get it done, or we can go our separate ways, but I will *not* allow our romantic karmas and need for closure bind me back to matter.

"I have suffered nonstop for five years, and it's still going on. I live and am well again: I'm not stuttering or confused any longer. This has all happened as an opportunity. You have a choice: come live a spiritual existence with me or remain spiritually asleep, back in the mundane world, without me. You can join me here—living in spiritual purpose, but I will *not* join you there in material living.

"Time is running out. Eventually, our karmas move on and take on new shades and hues that will not synthesize together any longer. I'm here. We can move forward together. But it has to be your choice."

***

The show must go on.

I have no contact with Janete, so I pine at a distance, trying to move on superficially. I date. Some good, some bad, mostly tragically hilarious.

Meeting women to date in a chaotic, busy world is an online affair now. The upside is you get access to a wider range of geography by reaching beyond your places of local errands and social hang-outs. The downside is it's tedious and distracting. But I need to move on, right? Janete has made it clear she is involved with another, and it seems my exile from her is not over, so I need to consider options. I prefer soulmate love that was destined, but a runner-up is better than a long and lonely life. Man cannot live on bread alone, and this man needs to get some trim!

The new clarity from my NDE brings light to this as I'd never seen it before. Janete never validated me. One of the benefits of having a lover in our lives is to feel valuable to someone we ourselves feel is valuable.

She was never validating or acknowledging of how hard I worked at being fit and trying to look good and give her an attractive partner to enjoy. The absence of any sort of physical validation had me convinced I was merely an average man. Being as dedicated to her and our partnership as I was made me also immune to the validation of others. It never even occurred to me women desired me and many clients had crushes on me. I only learned this post-NDE, and she was the one first putting light on it by telling me many women crushed on me.

Part of my determination to return to the love I know is to avoid the love I *don't know*. Janete and I had both agreed that at the very least, we could do no better than each other. We both got-off on exploring our own faults as a means to grow and improve as people and as partners:

"We've learned that the role *you* played in your ex's affair was that you never validated him, and when a pretty hot girl came around to gold-dig him, she did it by giving what you never did: compliments and validation. You deprive *me* of it too. I'm secure enough that I don't *require* it. But your reluctance to provide it says more about your own ego and fear and insecurity."

"You're right. I drove him to it. I really love you and know you're a great-looking guy. I take it for granted and compliments just don't come to my mind."

"I don't buy it; it's a subconscious attempt to maintain leverage: *you* feel insecure mentally and intellectually, so you deprive others of the validation *they* crave. It's actually a passive-aggressive strategy to feel safe and slightly superior."

God bless her: conversations of critiquing her were never arguments. We both encouraged and asked each other often of our mistakes.

"The upside of your depriving of validation is that it definitely makes me keep trying to get it. I keep being romantic, attentive, and work my ass off to stay fit and attractive and to be a good lover to you. It's classic: the way to get someone to *seek* validation is to deprive them of it, and they'll just try harder. It's one-oh-one Freudian. I enjoy being romantic and having the motivation to stay fit to please you. I know you could be with any guy on the planet, and I'm cool with working for your devotion to me. But I *am* a human male: it would be nice to get some affirmations. It's just human."

"I know and agree totally," she would reply gently and tenderly and promise to try more, which was sweet, but it barely changed for more than a week or so. Didn't matter. We're soulmates, partners, and I love her.

"You're the one missing out, Janete: I don't write you beautiful poetry, make sure you cum before me, and take care of you just for *you: I* . . . like it! *I* . . . get a kick out of romance and love and poetry and believing I am experiencing something magical. I'd rather live in my harmless delusion of storybook romance than to die in a dull world without fantasy. I am romantic with you because I *enjoy* it. Because you *let* me. It makes no difference if you do it back or even *get* what I'm doing. I definitely *want* you to appreciate it, but even if you don't, it'll never stop. I'm a romantic fool because I *like* it. You should try it sometime."

I existed in a bubble: my romantic relationship was healthy and stable *because I made it so.* My partner participated, but she was never the cause: we were both content with my being the cause and she being the effect. I saw relationship problems nonstop in my practice. My parenting and marriage benefited madly from my seeing the horrors of other families and preventing them in my own life.

Dating is far outside the bubble and is showing me no one on Earth is stable. I cannot involve myself with younger women due to the gap of life-experience: if they've never owned a home, been married, or had kids, the gap of common understanding is too huge. But the women I'm meeting who are more peer-like in mature experience are hefting *massive* baggage!

Online connections are a mosaic of dysfunction and surreal. The dating excursions I have are unnatural and truly unbelievable: unbelievable as in, if I told them to people, they'd automatically assume I was exaggerating or straight-up fictionalizing for comedic affect. I would never: truth is stranger than fiction, and cosmic-Akashic forces have always had a great time giving me bizarre circumstances at my own expense.

The protocol is simple: search online profiles, message, connect, text/call, meet.

I stood in front of a woman whom I'd arranged to meet at a local busy restaurant and didn't recognize her: she stood, in the flesh, not two feet in front of me, and I didn't recognize her from the photos she had on her profile and had texted to me: real-life her was easily twenty-three years older and thirty-five pounds heavier. I wasn't judging her for being notably less attractive, but was irritated at how stupid she either thought I was or how stupid she is: did she think I wasn't going to notice? This level of duplicity is a deal-breaker.

I shared several days of texts and a few long and wonderful phone calls with another before we decided the long, four-hour distance between us was worth meeting half way for us to get acquainted. We had a wonderful connection, and I looked forward to having a date with a woman of depth. She was nice, smart, had depth, and was moderately attractive. Ding-ding, we have a winner.

Same deal: *at least* thirty pounds heavier and *at least* twenty years older than profile photos. I tried to not be petty or superficial and enjoy our connection. It was a long-ass commute home, so I felt compelled to make the most of it with a *you-never-know* attitude. *Then she took off her wig.*

No, no . . . I'm *not* joking. She was also balding dramatically. She said she hoped to save up enough money soon for transplants from her job . . . *as an Uber driver.*

I love my life: I know at least someone's getting a good kick and a laugh out of it. Some Akashic Agents have a twisted sense of humor and must be bored and starting betting pools on the comedy here. I'm like Will Ferrel to the cosmic dimension: they can put me in one senseless, unreal, bizarre sketch after another, and I'll improv my way through it, laugh along, and come back for more. I wish *I* had a friend that took a joke so fucking well.

This last one gets sweetly stranger though: after spending hours in the tourist town and park of Solvang, a Danish town two hours north of LA, we sat in her car to chat before we parted ways. We're making out a bit, and I figure a little groping of my hard and neglected cock was the very least I deserved for being such a gracious gentleman. She insisted she never does this, but she cannot seem to resist, and . . . yay: I'm glad the seat reclines and I'm on the passenger side, so there's no steering wheel blocking her *headroom.* She may have been 3X the woman in real life vs her profile, but she made up for it with a long drink and a swallow. My long drive home was alright. Online dating was looking up; she was worth the commute.

In a few days, she blew up on the phone at me accusing me of being shallow for having issue with her new confession: she has herpes.

She is reassuring me that with awareness of protective methods, she can have a healthy sex-life with a partner who is sensitive to a few limitations. Here's the tally-card thus far:

- She's 62, not 52 as she had professed.
- She is 30 pounds overweight, which was undisclosed.
- She has no hair, which was also undisclosed.
- She has a lifetime contagion of a serious STD.

Yeah . . . *I'm* the bad guy in this scenario.

The most challenging thing about writing my first memoir was deciding how much of the truth I would share. In the early stages of its composition, I realized I wasn't being totally honest. I was trimming the fat on my own wickedness to make myself seem a heroic victim of circumstance rather than the narcissistic, hedonist I had truly been during my dope years. When I shifted from self-protection to visceral transparency, *I found my voice.*

Voice is essential to being a bonafide, literary *artiste.* It is an ineffable term in the author industry for your unmistakably, unique style that is exclusively *yours.* It is the coveted holy-grail of writers, and you either *have it* or *you don't.* You can't learn it or study it. Mine was inspired by Elizibeth Wurtzel and her first book, the memoir, *Prozac Nation*:

this girl was so raw and self-revealing. The protagonist heroin was a fucking cunt. She was *not* dressing up to make a good impression. She removed all the lipstick from the pig of her obnoxious and selfish persona. It was brave, and she put the truth of the events and the story well before her own ego. She inspired me to do no less, and as a result, *A Stone's Throw* went from a good story told well to a great story told powerfully evocative.

But when it was done, I realized, *Holy shit! This is* all *true and not even slightly exaggerated, which is why no one's gonna believe it!* Same with this memoir-tale; I am tempted to modify the true account by pruning it of its truths so it's not discarded as *Yeah, right: this has to be bullshit and fiction.* I assure you I am not only telling truths across the spectrum-board but not exaggerating one iota.

She was sixty-two, overweight, bald(ing), worked as an Uber driver, and judged *me* for having issue with her herpes simplex. Let's say I *am* making it up. . . Well, that makes me one of the greatest fiction writers of all time, because Tolkien couldn't come up with such fantasy content!

Unfortunately, my sex-drive is robust and healthy and is far more need than mere desire. I *desire* vegetarian food. I *need and require* food, period, or I'll die. I *desire* a comfortable and organized workspace. I *need* money to survive, which *requires* work. There's a difference, and if I go too long without food, money, or proper rest, I cannot function or focus to make them a reality. I must eat to work. I must work to eat. And I must have sex.

I'm not suggesting this is a universal feature of being human: many don't, and the need versus desire of it varies from human to human. Cool . . . you can be an omnivore, and I do not judge that. You can be *asexual*, and I'm rather envious at your indifference to a need that is an annoying distraction for me much of the time. But I need vegetarian food and sex to function at a high level. Two weeks going by without sex is like seven hours going by without food: it ain't gonna kill me, but the biological need for it progresses to total distraction of all others.

The line between need and want for love is blurry. We all need love. I have no doubt of that. But spiritual adeptship has illuminated the life experience that what we truly *need* is *spiritual love*, not *human* love. We're misinterpreting the soul's signal sent to the brain of needing love: your *divine soul* says *I need spiritual love,* but your *human brain* translates this to *I need human love; from my kids, spouse, peers, blah-blah-blah.*

Our brains are like foreign language translators. The mind uses the brain as its tool to express itself. Like your computer has a screen to display its contents, it translates the ones and zeros of binary language to words, images, etc. Much of what your soul says to your Mind and your Mind then says to your brain gets lost in translation. My soul is demanding *spiritual* love from the Divine. My mind/brain then misinterprets this to wanting *human* love within the world.

And all of your unhappiness and restlessness is due to this mistranslation as you seek happiness and love within *the world* instead of *the Divine*.

But knowing this is all *samsara*—illusion—doesn't make me immune to desire, does it? Nope! Even though I know they're material desires, I still want a girlfriend, an orgasm, and extra mustard on my vegan corn dog!

There are a few more rather run-of-the-mill dating experiences and a few hook-ups. Both become a hodge-podge of hit-or-miss tragedies and comedies. I give some serious thought to prostitution and/or erotic massage. But these do nothing for me: sex without emotion is like a heart with no pulse; I need connection or its virtual masturbation. Which is *very* unsatisfying; merely a tasteless snack to tide you over till dinner.

But then . . .I meet *her*.

Vegan. Spiritual. Beautiful. Super smart. Exotic. No kids, never married. . . . Akash is gonna have to get *pretty* creative to sabotage this one!

My Vegan Dating App is not paid, and the free version won't let me send a message to a woman who has sent me several messages. The free version doesn't even let me read her messages, but she's been sending a couple every day. My psychic-radar is ping-ping-pinging, and I have to meet her.

I buy $10 worth of *tokens* allowing me to give just three messages. Bingo!

She calls me right away, and we skype, and click, click, click: she's like my Lia: strangely psychic-intuitive. Dark hair, olive skin, and we are so comfortable and mature with each other: no fucking protocols or games.

We agree to meet right away, and I commute the not-too-bad one-hour to her condo in the valley. We hit it off, and the chemistry is ripe. Her Persian accent is exotically enticing. A nice lunch, a walk while chatting, some fiery kissing and groping, and we agree to put our passions on hold to not spoil by moving too fast. We have given full consent and are merely trying to postpone to not seem like animal-sluts. Cuz we wanna fuck!

Two mystic-intuitives, we easily connect to our past-life relationship without wonder. Like Lia and I, Violette and I barely have to speak to understand each other and never need to explain to each other what we mean or how we know things as we share equal but separate mediumship. We speak casually and comfortably of very advanced mystical subjects and our reincarnations. She's well read on spirituality, well beyond pop-topics. She knows who the fuck Madam Blavatsky and Gurdjieff are and has no confusion that Ekhart Tolle is more like mystic-candy of empty calories.

She comes to visit me on the beach and it is dangerously love-at-second-date already. We laugh, talk, fuck, walk, explore, and marvel at everything. As courting lovers can do, we rarely make it a few hours between sexual voracity. She is *really* sexual! She can't keep her hands off me, and it is so great and rare to be appreciated. My manor is to worship the female form of my lover, something few women know anything about in reverse. Violette is graceful and mature on the outside but makes no secret of her admiration of my fit and prime body.

Whereas so many women deny men any sort of validation, she rains on me with lustful adorations. She wants me naked and to hold, stroke, and suck my cock nonstop. As well as my chest, arms, legs, and the rest.

She's a bit overweight, but her ex-dancer body is delicious, and I believe her when she says she will soon be back to her 20 percent bodyfat, dancer body I see in the videos from her career as a professional dancer in Persia. Not *club* dancer: a music-video dancer for many of the top artists in Iran. The Violette in these videos just ten years earlier is FaF! Fine-as-Fuck!

Her current size works in my favor: a woman with a little weight is not quite as, how shall we say, *snug*. A petite woman is sweet-sexy but a snug-vagina for a man of above average length and girth is hard to bring to climax *first:* and I insist my lovers cum *first*. Once a man goes, he's done, so a man is obligated to serve his lover's orgasm first. Petite, tight women are hard to last for. Voluptuous, looser lovers are much easier to go long with. Part of the reason Violette enjoys me as a lover is because I can fuck her without climaxing for so long that I nearly pass out from exhaustion first. She thinks I'm a porn-star dynamo, when the truth is, she's just a bit wet and loose. I'm loving it, and we are both getting all we want. I want to discuss the Tantric-Kundalini potentials with her very soon.

This affair has legs: our past-life romances are providing wonderful contexts, and we're both so relieved to be with someone who *gets* the supernatural without explanation. We're spiritual peers, which neither of us get to ever have: we're always in the leader-healer-teacher role for others and left alone with our wide perceptions. Super-psychics are like circus freaks and zoo animals: people want to see us and watch us as oddities. They don't bother getting to know us. It's all about *tell me what I'm thinking right now* kinda shit, or worse, they try to bond with us: *Oh yeah . . . I sometimes just* know *stuff before it happens too! Do you know* (some pop-culture psychic fraud that is like the Dr. Oz of the supernatural media)? *Yeah . . . they're great. They're so in tune!* These people wouldn't last five minutes on LSD let alone having actual psychic intuition. We're enjoying the rare find of peer-connection with the bonus of nudity. Our vegan-vegetarian lifestyle is casual but sacred bonding too.

We are both already considering long-term, life-long togetherness and are grateful. But hey . . . we're still people, and I've learned some universal axioms in life: adults over forty-plus who've never had children have an underdeveloped maturity: they're selfish. Parenting catapults mindful people from self-centeredness to selflessness in an instant. I can recognize a *nonparent* within a few minutes of interaction, and this is 100 percent reliable. Other parents can too: we all can. Once you feel for and care for another living human being to the point that you're actually *happy* to clean runny-drippy-disgusting *shit* from them because they mean more to you than your own comfort, happiness, safety, or anything else in your known version of the world, you are changed.

True parenting brings you to a quanta of selflessness no other part of the Human Experience can bring. And it's instant: one moment you're a person and the next you're a parent. Parents are in an exclusive club nonparents cannot identify with on any level. And anyone who makes that affirmation of being *like* a parent because their dog (cat/hamster/fish/iguana . . .) is *like* their baby needs to shut the fuck up right now and forever. When fido dies, you burry him in the yard with a mock funeral, and after a customary mourning period *go get another one.*

When a child dies, your life is *over.* Forever. You will never have access to anything but inner-private sorrow for as long as you live and more.

Violette has never been married nor had children. On the surface, her being never married and no children is ideal! My single son is grown and independent and far more a roommate than a responsibility anymore. I crave a partner who isn't over-obligated to kids, parents, or lugging a ton of ex-spouse, carry-on baggage.

However, never-married and nonparent are two fairly reliable features of middle-aged self-centeredness. These life-experiences are classrooms of compromise and duty. She grew up in Persia-Iran and her father was an ambassador, which is a very privileged role. She went to college, grew up in regal homes, was beautiful, and became a star-dancer when she was in her twenties. She is sweet and generous: when I'm at her house she prepares food, serves me, and makes me as comfortable as a king: elements of her Mideast culture. I love it!

And I do the same when she visits my home: I treat her like a queenly guest. But when we go *out* . . . it is expected and unarguable that, because I am the man, I should, and shall, pay for everything. Whether this is lunch or dinner locally or whether we fly to Aruba: the moment we get beyond the threshold of her own front door, each and every expense will be mine. And as a Persian Princess from a life of status and wealth, her preferences are proportionate. Yet, cost is not to be even considered.

"In my country, that's just how it is: men enjoy treating their women like queens and pay for everything. It doesn't matter what she wants: she gets it."

"How long you been in America now? Never mind *culture*, Violette: we are spiritualists, you and I. We live by dharma; spiritual law, not man's laws. That's a very convenient and selfish approach to things. You have a great job, own your own home, have savings, and are quite comfortable. To keep balance and respectful equanimity in a relationship, both partners should participate in the expenses to some extent. I've been in relationships where I carried that duty, but that person made almost no money. And she still took me out occasionally, just to show her appreciation and keep me feeling validated. You're suggesting a set of rules and policies that are antiquated and impractical.

"I work as hard for my resources as you do. If you insist this arrangement is fair, then let's do it in reverse: I'll pay for everything we do *in* and *you* pay for going out. Out is *way* more expensive than in, baby. You want equal rights and equal pay but insist on *dating inequality*. It's sexist, and I suspect a woman of your evolution and experience knows this."

And . . . *that was about it.*

As evolved and mature as she was, her response was calm and intelligent, but we have hit an irreconcilable difference.

"I see your point, Krishnanand, but my culture is not American, and I don't usually date American men because they don't respect women this way." Her Persian accent was as sexy and musical as her dynamite body in the bedroom.

"You said yourself you've had no luck with Persian men because of archaic attitudes of women. You're contradicting yourself. This is a nation that has a horrible reputation of subjugating women!"

"It doesn't matter: I know what I want and what I deserve. I know what my value is and can't be with a man who doesn't respect this."

I've heard this mantra of *what I deserve and what my value is* several times since I've been dating. It holds no logic and becomes a catch-all for justifying lop-sided equations: a *fall-back* reply she can't support, like the word *"policy"*. A made-up term for rules whose origins and reasons are either long-forgotten or were never there. It's what the phone company or airline tells you when they're charging you *service fees:* "I'm sorry if I can't explain what a service fee is, sir; it's just . . . *policy.*"

I'm disappointed to say the least. Even though it had only been a couple months, our connection and equality were nothing to be taken for granted. Once again, I see evidence of the bizarre lengths my guardian-Akashic Agents will go to pound into my skull that I am going to be alone. I'm not good at *alone*.

I lick my wounds by rebounding—*er . . . I mean reconnecting*—to Delta, the vegan Dodger fan I'd met on my recon mission for moving here. We both endure the three hour commute between our homes and get together several times. On the surface, she's bridal material: vegan and a Dodger fan? Really beautiful and we get along famously. She's nine years my senior, but you'd never know it. Besides, it was disclosed on her profile, and she had her own hair, business, and no STDs.

We spent an entire day at the Self-Realization Fellowship in Malibu. All the years I lived in LA, I was so near to his center in Malibu and road-tripped many times to San Diego, yet had never followed through with a visit until this day. It is a marvelous sanctuary to meditate and study at.

"You seem down, Krishnanand. What's up?" she asks from her San Juan Capistrano home ninety miles from my Mandalay Shores home via cell.

"Nothing serious. Just bored with the tedium of life's struggles. Not much to look forward to day-to-day and I'm restless. I work, create, exercise . . . important routines, but still feeling very routine."

"Come with me: I'll be in Kauai competing in a volleyball tournament for two weeks. I've got a condo on the beach all to myself. It's all-inclusive, so all you need is airfare."

Sure. Why not? Too good to pass up: sexy woman, SCUBA opportunity, and a Hindu temple in the mountain forest to get my spirit on for just airfare and a few expenses? It's a good trip, and other than us getting banned from the buffet because of her militant-vegan vocal complaints, there's no deal breakers. Except one: how did we go to two Dodger games, spend several days and nights together, go to a concert, and have many great orgasms without ever broaching the spirituality subject?

It just never came up. Until I invited her to join me to visit the Hindu temple retreat on the mountain, and she went militant again. She wasn't just agnostic. She wasn't just atheist. She was anti-religion, anti-God, and anti-spirit. And if her vociferously loud complaining about animal rights in the buffet line were militant, then her diatribe— quite unsolicited, by the way—about spirituality and God were terroristic.

Well, we had our last moans and groans the morning before the flight home, and when the post-orgasm depletion of dopamine guilt wore off, I decided to bid her a friendly adieu once we were on the mainland. It is unkind to ghost a lover, so I gently told her a week later our differences were too large to ignore.

What am I learning from all this? What is the *spiritual message* contained within these human, worldly dramas?

1. That I have amazing stand-up comic material now!
2. That what the Buddhas, Gurus, sages, and masters all have told us is true: that each and every relationship within the world can never give you perfect happiness.

That dysfunction is a part of the fabric of humanity, and you can't get blood from a stone: human love is limited; only spiritual love is unlimited.

I was never at odds with this Truth: I accepted the limitations of worldly love and relationships and tried to make the best of them by giving more than I got and not being pissed off when people fell short of basic human kindness, consideration, and respect.

I'm not seeking nor expecting perfection. Just reasonable, mature reciprocation and mutual appreciation. Let's behave like loving adults, be reliable and consistent, and, most of all, be personally accountable. Let's have balance: hashtag-fair.

I had no doubt all human relationships were conditional. That with each and every one of them there are deal-breakers: abuse, lying, cheating, abhorrent selfishness . . . and I'm no different. My partner cheated on me and was insensitive to my tragic circumstances, so I left: to send a message. And it backfired.

We all want what we can't have. The stinky truth is Brandon was right: Janete and I were never really a match. Maybe I just loved what I *imagined* we were. I was okay with that too. It's not the soul in Janete clothing I love or desire, is it? It is the fantasy of true love and human harmony I romanticized. I fed it till it was strong, and when it decided to be my enemy instead of my friend, it was strong enough to kick my fuckin' ass. I want her because I can't have her. It's pathological.

What Brandon had pointed out about our chasm of differences was what my Guru had been teaching all along and what the Akashic Agents have made crystal clear during my death experience. I had developed an unhealthy worldly attachment. God and Guru cleaned house, removing my attachments to accelerate my spiritual progress.

Never do the sages, masters, and scripture texts say to *not* have partners and family. They simply state clearly these relationships should never be your primary attachment.

I will still date. I will still hook-up. I will still love and give respect and romance. I will still cum last, not first. I hope to find a partner to share space and time with again and to ward off the loneliness of being human. I will give wholeheartedly to a woman who appreciates this and gives in return. If . . .

If they can accept and respect my True lover is God.

Guess I better buckle down for the lonely life, cuz all evidence shows my request is a deal-breaker.

_____ **_36._**

BHAKTI-SHAKTI-PAT (And Disposable Items)

Bhakti yog reveals a safe and reliable path to Supreme Divinity who is the form of absolute peace and love.
—Swami Prakashanand Saraswati (The Sixth Dimension)

January 2019—Sixth Year of NDE-TBI-DAI

The three months I dated Violette were encouraging and gave me good reason to consider my "exit strategy" was not the right choice. She seemed to be all I could desire in a partner, in many ways the polar opposite of Soulmate, Janete.

Janete was petite at 98 pounds and 5'2"; Violette was voluptuous and 5'8". Janete was fair-skinned with blonde hair and grey-blue eyes; Violette was olive-skinned, a dark brunette, and smoky-eyed. Janete was intellectually challenged and never had more than a retail job in her life; Violette was a college-educated, cerebral woman with a successful career as a private school administrator. Janete wanted her spiritual name to be Violet-Lotus; Violette was Violet with an extra 'TE'. I've had a theme with lovers whose names have French suffixes: Brandon's mother was Yvette, two other in-love girlfriends were Yvette and Collette, then came Janete, and now Violette.

Violette and I seemed mature enough to have a romantic partnership without spiritual compromise. We had spoken at length many times about my chosen spiritual path and dedication to my Guru. Her reaction was a comforting surprise.

"I want to meet Him. I have felt His presence since we got together and I want to know Him. I think it's part of the reason we've been brought together."

She accompanied me to satsang at the LA satellite ashram and loved the experience. She asked to learn more and borrowed books from my sadhana library and watched some of His video discourses and a warmth developed between them.

"I'm going to His ashram for a few days soon, Violette. If you'd like, we can plan a visit together. I've not been there since well before my accident, so I need to go solo my first time back. But I would be thrilled to take you soon, if you'd like."

Her role perceptions of men and women were not total dealbreakers for me. If I could've afforded to provide the life of luxury she wanted, I probably would have; I just didn't. I was living on a budget and when we discussed these dynamics honestly, the light in her eye for me went to a dim spark. I wanted to continue as a couple, but she did not.

We were still together when I made my first visit to the US ashram since 2011. She enjoyed the photos I sent of the glorious grounds and temple and her enthusiasm excited me. We stayed in contact the entire time and felt she was a *virtual* visitor on the trip. I bought her a few books and an adorable LED light peacock from the gift shop. I was grateful; God seemed to be shining a light into my darkness and was determined to help me reconsider life over death.

***

My emotions were deep and textured as I flew out of LAX and went from beach life to the ashram. I was thrilled at the thought of entering my Guru's dham, established in 1990 by my Swamiji, His number one disciple. At the same time I was nervous, worrying that I may not experience the sweet thrill I had always known by being there.

My last visit to the US ashram had been two full years before NDE-Day. Would it be different now? Has it changed? Will its divine atmosphere still be pervasive without my Swamiji in residence? My dozens of visits there over the years had always coincided with His own visits. When Swamiji came from India to the US, He would tour the many satellite ashrams he'd established, like the one in LA. He'd spend a week or two at the 200-acre main ashram, too. I always went when He went.

This trip was planned as part of my "give it all I've got" commitment to restore life over self-murder. Soon after I bought the plane ticket and made the room reservation, I met Violette. Propitiousness is hard to deny; things seemed to be looking up. Violette was an *upgrade* in the love department and my sadhana struggles were smoothing out.

I was flooded with emotions during the 25-minute drive from the airport to the property. So many times I had made this drive and the familiarity of the highways, roadside stores, restaurants, ranch homes, and prairies brought a sweet nostalgia to my restored memory and identity. With every visit I made there over the years, I would be in tears of gratitude by the time I reached the front gate to the property—always open and inviting—as I came closer to my Swamiji's Graceful presence. And this visit was no different; while I felt the pain of His absence, a feeling of *coming home* compensated me and warmed me to my Soul.

I felt like a child. My enthusiasm and energy bristled from my very pores as I entered the gate, the parking lot, and the front office. I marched, tears falling from my eyes, through the beautiful doors into the *bhavan, or* sadhana prayer hall. The drapes in front of the alter were closed until evening, but I fell to my knees before it, grateful and blessed to be there. I enjoyed the anticipation of having darshan of the Radha Krishn deities within a few hours.

I wasted no time dropping my bag in the no-frills room above the dining hall, where I had spent many nights. Then I headed out to stroll the grounds.

All my fears of being unable to connect to the Divine space vanished. The few changes were insignificant; the main features were as they had ever been in my heart and mind.

Mor Kuti *mandal* in the forests of the US ashram.

Prem Sarovar, the gorgeous pond along the walking path behind the temple, remained unchanged. I stepped around peahens along the way to *Mor Kuti*. I paused to sit for a meditative moment at the smooth, round stone mandal covering the ground in the woods. It represents the sacred site in Vrindaban, India where Krishn took the form of a peacock to dance for Radha and cheer her up. Then I took a brisk stroll up to the top of *Barsana Hill* to take in the 200-acre view, its perch offering a direct view of the temple with its 60-foot-tall *shikr*, a tower of smooth granite, rising up before the lotus flower-shaped pools surrounding it. I was in heaven.

Radha Madhav Dham ashram.

I sat in my usual seat in the dining hall, adjacent to a wall with a large photo of Maharaji wearing a full flower garland. He kept me company while I dined on the vegetarian meal prepared by devotee brothers and sisters.

Evening satsang began and it took tremendous effort to contain myself, stifling tears while the prayer was chanted. We rose for *aarti* and the temple priest—the *poojari*—waved a finger beckoning me to join him at the altar to wave the candle. In all my years as a devotee here, I had never done aarti to the altar, and this *first-time* experience came as a surprise.

I sat in a chair off to the side of the large 1200-square-foot open floor; my age and injuries discouraged me from my old place upon the floor behind the kirtan singer and drummer. I became lost in the beautiful kirtan and was quickly immersed in beatitude. This side chair took the altar out of my view, but I could see the entire room. I gazed at the devotee brothers and sisters I'd not seen in years; we had been side by side for hours of meditations and discourses at our Swamiji's feet, and had worked together in the kitchen, the gardens, and my favorite volunteer work of all, the countless hours of physical *seva* in the forests.

Only a few devotees were strong and capable of hard labor, and I always loved putting my back into service for my Guruji, Swamiji, and the ashram community.

The path of bhakti yog is of kirtan and devotional meditation, but for me? *Service* is the most personally fulfilling part of sadhana. Nothing connects me more to God and Guru than working up a sweat. I do my best to meditate during chain-saw cutting, ditch-digging, tree-hauling and the glorious labor that leaves me scratched, bruised, and sore—each ache and scab a testament to feeling value in myself and love for Him.

I recall my sacred routines during my visits and am determined to revisit them. Immediately after morning satsang at 6.30 a.m., I would grab my coffee cup and fill it with the instant coffee and *insta-hot* water in the dining hall while kitchen sevaks prepared breakfast for the residents and guests. Rather than walk, I'd drive the hundred yards to the edge of a wooded area so my coffee would stay hot. This is a sacred ritual for me. It is personal and private and I am in near ecstasy at the opportunity to sit in my favorite spot of the entire 200 acres and think lovingly of my Swami and Guru while I sip my morning joe, pretending I am not alone, but in the company of my Masters.

My "spot" is a *ras mandal:* a circular clearing set back into the trees a bit, paved with beautiful stones. *Ras* is a particular style of Divine bliss and a *mandal* is a round, smooth stone with a subtle geometric texture. This one is about fifteen feet in circumference. It is quiet, set apart from many of the more popular walking trails, and I am especially fond of it. With my new memory abilities, I remember...

***

Years earlier, Swamiji had assigned me to clear a thicket of trees and thorn bushes in this spot. He wanted the ground cleared and leveled so this stone mandal could be constructed here.

The patch of trees and dirt within the ashram forest

At that time, the ashram was eagerly anticipating a two-month visit from Maharaji Himself. This would be His second stay at the US ashram. I had become a devotee just after Kripalu Maharaji's first visit, so I'd not yet had his darshan and was envious of the scores of ashram devotees who had.

There was a lot of work to do to get it ready. Swamiji would settle for nothing less than perfection for our Master's visit to His US dham.

Devotees came from all over to prepare, and I spent three to five days there every couple of weeks in an effort to help. This newest project would be a lot of work. Each day a few men would come to help, but they'd rarely make it back a second day in a row because they needed recovery time. We appreciated volunteers, but it was stressful to manage new guys every day. Some were not very labor-savvy and needed supervision to be safe and do the job right.

On the fourth day of work, a flood of spiritual doubts suddenly filled me. "What the fuck are you doing here?" my inner doubts argued. "You're a grown man with a professional career, a family, and a house with practical responsibilities. And here you are, digging in the dirt, brainwashed into some spiritual cult where you come sit like a child in a temple to meditate and find God. *What an idiot!* What're you? Six years old? What the fuck, man?! Grow up!"

I decided to finish my shift of work, then go to my ashram room, get on the phone, buy a plane ticket, and get back to the *real* world! Work, make money, have a good fucking time, be a nihilist! I felt I was having a moment of clarity, and saw that I had been duped and naïve.

At that time, I didn't recognize this as just a bad, spiritual sanskar that had spontaneously risen to the surface. I felt the illusion of this spiritual cult had been lifted, and I suddenly saw what a mythical fantasy spirituality is. It seemed *silly*.

Unannounced, Swamiji stopped by to check on the work and be sure it was going well.

He then did something truly unexpected (and it gets even more astonishing as we go). He asked me to tour some other sites He wanted to have excavated. I jumped on the back of His golf cart and He drove through the woods to show me several other sites. Meanwhile, I'm silently thinking, sure, I'll shovel-clear these sites... *if I ever come back!*

Swamiji was fun; the way He drove that cart through the woods, it was like riding in an off-road monster truck! He was really Red Bull about it, and His humor and personality were soft and gentle yet raucous. As He returned to the original site to drop me off, I did what was proper and pranamed, or bowed, to Him. And then He did something *really* startling:

He grabbed me! In a headlock!

As I bowed my head within His arm's reach, *he grabbed me in a headlock*, pulled me into Him, patted me on the head, and then let me go. It all happened so quickly that none of the other devotees even noticed it. I was slightly stunned, but a second later, I grabbed my shovel, and Swamiji scooted away on His cart. I didn't think much about it *at first*.

Over the next few hours, something changed.

I no longer wanted to leave. I didn't *ever* want to leave!

By dinnertime in the dining hall, *I was in a spell*!

I felt so beautiful inside my head and heart; everything in the entire world seemed absolutely *perfect!*

I felt perfect. *The ashram* was perfect. Everything I saw seemed *perfect:* the grounds outside, the dining hall, even *my metal dinner plate* was perfect. And the temple? The *bhavan-prayer hall* where I sat to enjoy that evening's satsang? GOD WAS EVERYWHERE: in the kirtan being sung, on the altar with the deities, and in the vast space within the hall. I could see Him in the altar pillars adorned with sculpted peacocks, in the intricate ceiling tiles, in the other devotees in the hall, all joined in kirtan-meditation, , and in the Sanskrit quotes lining the ceiling's soffits. Even the carpeting and the window and door handles had a lustrous glow. *Every molecule of every detail was precisely the way God had intended and was, and is, PERFECT!*

After satsang, I went to my quiet room to rest. I marveled at the floor, walls, bathroom—all built with such care and to meticulous standards. Perfect peace and understanding filled me to the degree that I did not need to comprehend *anything more* because I knew everything was flawless as it was. Everywhere I looked, I saw a manifestation of my Guru's Grace. It was like the entire world of matter was an extension of His own body; He was *everywhere, all the time!*

And I didn't sleep that night.

Not only could I not sleep, but I didn't *need to!*

I was not tired. I was immersed in love and longing for my Swamiji! I wanted to think only of Him, nonstop. I got up around 2 a.m., left my room, walked to the large pool of fountains and water outside the temple near His private room, and I just sat there.

I didn't need or want anything. It just felt good to be nearer to Him. I didn't want to bother Him or know if He loved or was thinking about me, too. Didn't know, didn't care! I am content just to love Him; I do not worry whether He loves me, either, because I *know* He does!

I felt His omnipresence and love surrounding me, and I immersed myself in thoughts of Him.

The following day, Swamiji had several speaking engagements in Dallas and Houston. Some of the devotees planned to attend and asked me if I wanted to go. Normally, I would reject the idea of a road trip with a bunch of people crammed into small cars for several hours, sleeping on floors at devotee houses. But I accepted the invite; I just wanted to be close to Him and didn't care about discomfort. I was in a deep, complete condition of love. It is all I felt in my body, and the only real thought I had was... *love*.

This love spell went on for *four days straight*. I didn't tell anyone. It was mine, and it was private. And I felt one hundred percent connected to Him! I felt as ONE with Him and His divine love. ONE!

Not only did I feel absolute love for Him, God, the ashram property, and other devotees, but also for the entire world and all of humanity. It was a sublime paradox. I was still aware of the flaws and defects of the physical world, of people's confusions, man-made disasters, and corruptions, but I was simultaneously certain that it was all okay. I saw beyond our expectations of what we *want* and think things *should* be and saw reality as it *truly* is: PERFECT.

Does a Spiritually-Realized Saint see a monodualistic sense of the material phenomena as perfectly flawed and flawed perfectly? A God-Realized Saint supposedly sees God *everywhere, all the time, and in everything*. I absolutely felt that everything, all the time, everywhere, *was just fine*. While I can't admit to being capable of actually seeing God in all of reality as a Saint might, I can *sense* His presence.

It may sound like a trivial awareness that everything is just *okay*, but imagine not having a shred of concern, worry, anxiousness, or fear. As stupid-humans, we have moments of this on a *great day* and can switch off the bad and see just the good. Yet, in layers of our *subconscious*, we know that problems still exist and life is imperfect. As happy as we are, we are subtly aware that we could be even more content. In this event, I could *not* be happier; *I had fused with happiness itself.*

The Rasik Saints teach about the monodualistic state of spiritual enlightenment: a perfect harmony with God's love and perfection *alongside* the pain of being separate from Her. The Buddhas see and empathically feel pain over humanity's suffering yet remain in perfect peace and bliss simultaneously. I was sampling this: the headlock my Swamiji put me in, and His pat on my head, had activated a profound contentment with the world, an endless love for God and Guru, and a longing to be with Them that was the sweet pain of honeyed separation.

Three days later, I quietly wept during the flight home, mourning separation from Him and not wanting to return to the uninspiring world. The love spell settled some but persisted softly. I bathed in it for days even after I got home, unable to answer Janete's welcome home inquiry of my trip, *"How was it?"* It was heavenly beyond words!

In Sanskrit, the transmission of spiritual energy from a guru is called *shakti-pat*. Over the years, I have pondered why Swamiji gave me this *shakti-pat* experience.

Was it because I was having doubts? Doubts of faith are called bad *sanskars*. They are consequences of past-life attitudes buried deep in layers of the unconscious which occasionally rise to the surface. Swamiji taught me, "When bad sanskars come, let them roll by. Try to ignore them until they pass. Do not try to battle with them; know that your Master is reducing them and they will pass if you try not to attach to them. When good sanskars come, take advantage by doing more sadhana and think of God and Guru during them."

I can never know why he graced me with His *bhakti-shakti-pat*. Nothing I could ever do in a thousand lifetimes would be worthy of the beauty he revealed to me.

I saw and felt a fraction of the Divine Love the Rasik Saints speak about: pure devotion of longing and perfect, selfless love. I know it was real and a mere fraction of what actual Divine Love is like. He gave me a glimpse, a Divine gift, *a tiny sample*.

It would remain with me in my darkest hours to come.

The *ras mandal* today: My personal "coffee spot" for quiet morning remembrance meditation

***

This latest trip to the ashram restored me. It had felt like *home*, as though I'd just been there and never really left during those eight years. Many of the residents knew about my tragedy. It felt so good to be *home;* I gathered many of them to a sitting room and explained where I'd been for all those years. They welcomed me, and many were tearfully moved by my tragic story. I shared with them so they would know I never meant to stay apart from them.

When I returned to my broken beach life, I felt slightly clearer. I know my spiritual ambition of God Realization is all that matters; I am being purified by fire. I know every part of my tragedy has occurred to assist me, and all my pain *is for my own good*.

I consider everything I've lost as just disposable items anyway: house in the burbs, counseling career, community admiration, tennis play, backpacking, parenting... *Soulmate.*

All of these relationships are physical and temporary. Most don't remain throughout a single lifetime, and we have no recollection of them in the next lifetime. These relationships with people and things are not eternal. They're disposable items and *just don't matter.*

Losing love is painful, but I console myself in the confidence that I tried to do everything right as a partner. For all the scandals I caused in my young love life, my behavior throughout this last ten years had no significant errors that I knew of. I had no regrets and must concede that Janete, too, is a *disposable item.* We gave each other everything we had to offer. My human heart will always miss her. But... she was never *on the bus.* Our roles for each other had been satisfied, so I am just as disposable to her as well.

I can mourn over all I lost, or I can be grateful for what I had, let it go, and move on to the ultimate goal of spiritual union. I had once begged and pleaded for God to manifest in person. And She did: in the form of my own God Realized, *nitya-siddhi* Saint, Kripalu Maharaj. A divine personality drew me to Him and revealed the path and practice to attain God Consciousness. He taught me how to end this eternal struggle of human consciousness and worldly desire.

But my Guru has ascended to His divine abode, no longer on this Earth, so I must survive here until He returns. I will make spiritual progress and substantial deposits into my spiritual bank account for the subsequent lives I'll have to endure till a Guru comes again to help me complete my Soul's Journey. And I don't like my chances: as the world detours deeper into materiality during this age of Kali and spirituality erodes, I'll need my loving Guru to hold onto and emphasize to me that my soul is divine and belongs to God.

As stupid-humans, we forget that the feature of *maya* called *avaranatmika* makes us forget we are actually spiritual beings having a human experience instead of vice versa. It took weeks for that shakti-pat bliss my Swamiji graced me with to settle down, *but it did.* I was not yet qualified to receive it permanently, and in that state of consciousness, I'd never be able to function in a material world. My kundalini event at twenty-five was such a mind-blowing, spirit-expanding, overwhelming experience it made it hard to relate and function, too. It took nearly a year to settle down to a more subtle phenomenon, *but it did*. It, too, has become a disposable item. I did not hesitate to discard it once I learned of its potential interference with my Guru's Grace. That which does not serve Guru, or God, is *a-dharm—non-truth*. Only that which serves God is true dharm.

Visits to my Kripalu's ashrams and the holy sites of India would put me into clouds of spiritual sweetness for weeks after I returned to worldly living. However, I could not sustain those warm, satisfying feelings once I had left, and this, too, is God's Grace. We could never function in the world in constant spiritual consciousness. Only a God Realized Saint has this capacity, and we often misunderstand them and believe them to be mad. When a True Saint demonstrates Divinity, they can be ostracized, persecuted, and even crucified.

It is critical to keep our sadhana steady and consistent. *"Think of me when you eat and drink."* That is Guru-Jesus' reminder to make our devotional remembrance as constant as possible, lest we slip back to materiality.

My brief visit to the US ashram reminds me that I am not a man of the world; I am on a journey. But once again, my view of reality blurs from the astigmatism of material desires. Violette and I ended shortly after, Delta and I were short-lived, Janete remains immune to my affection, my health is paradoxically robust and fragile, and my finances are still on borrowed time. The good things that occur are teasers that seem to bring me up just high enough to let me down for a more severe impact. My flawed, stupid-human material mind reverts to its original sin: perpetual desiring.

I am sad and lonely and facing several decades of being helpless while I watch my life deteriorate from a fucked-up death experience and brain injury.

It has been nine months. I've fulfilled my contract of allowing all that time of sincere effort to make a life beyond loneliness, sorrow, and loss. I feel I've earned an *A* for effort, yet my reality is a fat, red *F* with a GPA of 0.0.

I have put forth all my heart and soul to restore love. I've rescued my son from his decline, and he is on his feet again, not needing to worry if Dad is alright. I've dated with the best intentions and honest efforts to connect with a partner and give love while asking little in return. I feel confident I've done everything right, high aboveboard, to establish honest, premium work contributing to humanity at large. But I'm still at the starting line. It's time to get on with it.

This is a good place to die.

The wide dunes of sand along my comfortably rustic coastal home are meditative for watching sunsets. The vibrant Pacific Ocean is powerful, and below its waves is a gentle place, quiet and peaceful. Death by drowning is subtle. Other than a few moments of gasping for air, the brain goes cloudy. Once you submerge to ninety feet deep, you experience a depth psychosis: a mild state of confusion as your brain shuts down, trying to adjust to nitrogen release within the blood. It's comfortably numb.

My last death was unintentional. It's time to get it right.

Like Sisyphus, I fooled death and returned to the living. I am now doomed to push the boulder of my sorrows up a never-ending hill. Every step of progress I make is undone as the rock repeatedly rolls back over and on top of me. I will push no more.

37.

OUTGOING CALLS

> Celestial perception is experienced when a yogi enters the celestial realm through meditation.
> —Swami Prakashanand Saraswati (The 6th Dimension)

> Take this cup away from me for I don't want to taste its poison.
> —Jesus of Nazareth

You can't fire me, I quit.

I'm a walking paradox: noticeably damaged with dizzy-discoordination, making all physical activity challenging, yet I'm strong, capable, have no physical pain, and never even get a cold. I sleep well, go rope-climbing at a local gym, lift weights, run and walk twice a day, and do yoga two to four times a week. It's all awkward and taxing; none of it feels easy or natural, but it's all painless, and I feel the same all the time: bodily healthy, mentally stable, emotionally shitty.

I'm virtually an empty-nester and have no lover to share time with, and my Guru is no longer physically present on the Earth. I am in constant anguish, and it just seems that living is senseless.

In spite of all these catastrophes, my life-expectancy seems pretty long. I'm still physically strong with the constitution of superman and the bounce-back ability of rubberman. Even death doesn't kill me! There's no fucking way I can endure thirty to forty more years of deprivation and suffering. Maybe I *could*, but I'm not.

I accept I will go to hell. I accept it is a major sin. I still have no choice: I've done some research to find a *loophole* in the Eternal Truth to take my own life. I want to *lessen* the hellish consequence for self-death. Sure enough, it doesn't matter what crazy nonsense you Google, there's always something. The Vedas and Upanishads reveal a loophole, and I plead my case to the Akashic Court:

There are spiritual rules and laws permitting self-termination:

1. Suicide cannot cause long term sorrow to others.
2. Suicide cannot be violent or cause suffering to myself or another.
3. I must have an irreversible and intolerable condition.

One: My death will be seen as an accident, so Brandon will be fine over time, and it will not compromise perception of his father and mentor. I barely matter to anyone else. Two: my death-plan is clean with no mess and is not violent. And the third one? There is an overwhelming and undeniable body of evidence now this is not getting better, only worse. I think I qualify.

I am sick. I am tired. I am lonely. I am broken. I am useless. I am sorry.

The Portal Agents do not agree, but neither do they protest: the sense I get from them is if I truly feel I have come to a responsible and sensible conclusion, ok.

Hmmm . . . *that's weird.*

Portal is oddly silent in this matter. And I'm grateful. I take it to mean I am fulfilling all I can to be dharmic on this decision and will be doing this in the least transgressive way possible. Their odd silence on the request is like I've been put on hold with tech-support while they check with a manager.

After a few nights, they get back to me: *Call Katie.*

I have received many *incoming* calls from the Akash, and now it's telling me to make an *outgoing* call. So be it:

I accept and agree, but silently wonder: "Why would I call Katie? Her and I are friends and spiritual siblings, but we don't chat or call each other. It's natural to have a *reason* to call someone, and I don't have one. What will I say when she says, '*So* . . . what's up?'" after interrupting her at the multi-million-dollar company she is vice-president and co-owner of.

But I do it.

She and her husband, Peter, are part of the LA ashram community and I've known them for years; they're spiritual family to me

I dial and get her assistant who puts me on hold. As full as her schedule is, I expect to need an appointment for a call, but she gets on right away, and I say . . .

"Hey . . . Radhey, Radhey. . . . It's Krishnanand." Radhey, Radhey is the standard greeting we all have within our spiritual community, and I always use my true, spiritual name with my spiritual family, though they also know me as Scott.

"What's up?" she says, warmly confused at the unexpected call.

"I know it's unusual, but I felt like reaching out to you."

We small talk a few moments, which neither of us like to do, and she asks me how I'm doing and says, "You know . . . I was actually just thinking about you the other day. Do you know how far you've come, Krishnanand? Before you left for Washington, do you remember?"

"Not too clearly. It was a perpetual nightmare, and I was struggling every moment actually just to stand, walk, speak. . . ."

"Exactly. You were also this very quiet, shy guy. Nothing like you normally. Not saying better or worse, just saying it was so different than the man we all knew."

"That's because whenever I saw you, or anyone, it was always like the first time: you know, when you first meet someone, you're more formal and less casual because you don't know them, so it's protocol. I never felt insecure, just naturally humble. All our pride resides within our mind, and mine wasn't clocked in yet."

"Yes, I get that. It was sweet and gentle, it wasn't awkward, but it was like you weren't really here."

"I was only partially here and inhabiting my body."

"How do you feel now?"

"The same. Honestly, I may seem different on the outside, but it feels the same on the inside. I don't feel like my damage is any less, and it's not possible to get *used to it*. I'm far more spirit than body or mind. As grand as that sounds, it's very hard to be mostly spirit living in a physical world. It's pretty ghostlike. You don't get *used* to not being here, or anywhere else, either; you adjust.

"It's like walking into doors: in the beginning of this, my balance and coordination were so bad I would literally misjudge a doorway and walk into the jamb; my depth and distance perception is pretty skewed. The reason I don't run into door jambs now isn't because I'm better; I've just learned to compensate. My brain and eyes tell me the door opening is *here* and, and due to past experience, I know it's actually over *there*. I've just learned not to trust or rely on what my eyes tell my brain." I chuckle at this because: a) I think it's funny, and b) it's probably terrifying and I don't want to ruin anyone's day with sad shit.

Her curiosity leads to a few questions, and within a few moments, suddenly I am pouring it all out. I'm not emotional as I explain my circumstances, but explain as you do with anyone you're updating on your goings-on. "It just seems stupid to be so stubborn about making my life good again. My karma isn't allowing it. I *don't* think I was supposed to come back to life, and I'm just taking up space. I found a loophole in the Vedic-Yoga texts that make provisions for suicide, and I think it's time to just wrap things up and call it a day—or a life."

"Hold on . . . Krishnanand, I gotta call you right back. Can you give me a few minutes?" She was a busy executive, so I acquiesced.

"Yes, of course, And no worry, Katie. Call me if you can and if it's convenient. There's not much to talk about. I'm fine with everything. . . ." And I was truly oblivious I had just disclosed suicidal intentions like I was having my appendix removed on Friday.

She called back in a half-hour and I had totally forgotten she was calling, "Oh, hey! No . . . no problem . . . don't apologize. It's the middle of the work day, and I'm sorry I interrupted."

"Please just listen and don't argue with me: I'm going to send you to India. I know you've got some financial limitations right now, and I'm going to get you a roundtrip ticket to go to Mangarh. Please don't interrupt. . . ." as she heard me take a breath to speak. "Please don't refuse, and I have just one condition: promise me you will meet and speak with the DiDis in India before you take any actions on this idea of yours."

I promised. Three times. She insisted I make a pact with her that I merely *postpone* my decision until after going to India and speaking with three Saints: our Guru's daughters. It was reasonable, and I felt socially and dharmically obligated.

I've been candid about my struggles to many over these few years. No one did anything beyond listen, and even that was mostly gratuitous, social requirements. My brother and sister had shown intense concern, but beyond listen, could offer no solutions to improve my circumstances. It was out of their league.

I had shared with Janete many times I had lost my mind, was not in my body, was inhabiting another dimension, and was not *present*, but she could think of nothing other than to weep and sympathize for me. I was always *her* savior; she had never needed to be mine. It was out of her depth.

I never disclosed to Brandon the anguish I had been in nonstop. He's my son, I am his father, and I would never burden him with my problems. Other than casually and philosophically, my surreal drama has been ultra-private: no one could understand, and I could not possibly educate them enough to even grasp the edge of the NDE phenomena combined with a major brain injury.

This moment with my sister-friend, Katie, was the only person outside of my inner circle I had ever opened up to. Years ago, she had some personal issues to work through, and apparently, I had counseled her for several months. I was just serving a friend and spiritual sister, doing my job. Her husband, Peter, would tell me later she had always been grateful to me for how much it had helped her and that she cared very deeply for me. Seeing what I had been going through was tearing her up as she felt powerless to help.

I had never received assistance beyond infancy from my parents, community, or the world at large; I was always independent because I'd never had a choice. This was verifiably the first and single time in *both* of my current lives someone *did* something to help me beyond emotional support. I'm a rare bird; I seek actions and solutions, not support.

This is a true sister-friend. So few people are worthy of respect any longer, and I find my circle of people I'm willing to associate with smaller and smaller. I guess I'm a judgmental prick as I prefer not to associate with anyone or thing I may not respect.

As a spiritualist, it is part of my path to be cautious of who and what I associate with. I do not feel I have the right or authority to judge *anyone*. Whatever faults each of us has is unique to our current and past life circumstances. I strive to be accepting of others unless they're just downright shitty people; people who intentionally do themselves and others wrong are not healthy to associate with. Not because they're *bad*, but because I will opine and criticize them inwardly without wanting to, and that's not right. That's bad dharm. Rather than judge them, I simply don't get involved.

It's natural: our minds make conclusions and criticisms of others without us even trying to; it's automatic. Having negative, judgmental thoughts is not a sin; your human mind will manufacture them all on its own. Bad thoughts are only a sin when we *attach to* them and don't counterstrike them with good ones.

I once asked my swami-teacher, "How do I stop having critical opinions of others and the world? They just appear in my mind on their own, without my so-called permission."

"That's a natural product of material consciousness. It is only bad karma if you *follow* or *attach* to these thoughts. Do not try to *stop* negative thoughts. Think of something else that is good that takes your mind away from the bad thought. It is very difficult and can be exhausting to *stop* an unwanted thought. It is much easier to *replace* a bad thought with a good thought. You must not *attach* to negative thoughts."

Sage advice from an actual Sage. It took time and practice to make this more natural, and it has reduced my karmic-intake by volumes! Maybe in my next life, I won't even have automatic bad thoughts needing counterstrikes.

This gem of wisdom became a cornerstone of my addiction counseling as I trained clients: *Don't spend a ton of energy stopping trigger-thoughts of using. That's exactly what your addict-mind wants you to do is battle with it. When you fight it, you still become attached and feed into it. Do and think of other things instead.*

The bhakti-yog path discourages you from needless associations with things not aligned with your healthy, spiritual lifestyle. You can't totally prevent interacting with things you disagree with; there's too many, and to live in the world, you must take the bad with the good. Unless you go live in a cave, you better learn how to live in the Kali-Yug world without judging it all the time, because judging anyone or anything disrupts your spiritual devotion: Criticizing others increases pride. But *Bhakti-yog is a path of spiritual humility.*

Swamiji elucidated, "Until you are God Realized, you are not capable of seeing *only* the good in people without being distracted by the bad. To protect your sadhana, it is wise to have fewer associations in the world and try to be selective of those associations *without judging them.*"

This has become the core of my personal choices in dating and relationships too. I *prefer* to date a vegan-spiritualist, but I can't seem to find a good one and don't want to exclude the other dating candidates in the world with some sort of personal judgement. I *prefer* to eat dinner at an *all-vegan-vegetarian* restaurant too; it's just easier. I don't have to be cautious or concerned they truly understand what my dietary preferences are; I can just order anything on the menu., When possible, it's just better to stick to the associations aligning with your beliefs and reducing your judging of others. *I'm not anywhere near perfect!* Who am I to judge anyone for being an omnivore, agnostic, or atheist? In many past lives, I've been there too.

I don't go to dog parks either. I'm not *against* them; I just don't have a dog. I'm not against them or judging them; we just don't have anything in common. But I had amazing theological discussions with a Muslim Imam in London and even a Jehovah's Witness once!

Yog systems, particularly karm-yog and bhakti-yog, help reduce your karmas binding you to body and world rather than spirit. This is the *ahimsa* part of Buddhist philosophy: do no harm. Judging others and eating animals is a willful participation of causing harm and binds by karmas. I try to avoid both if I can. Humility is the absolute core of bhakti-yog. Judge not lest ye be judged.

I work hard to avoid judging myself too. Spiritual teaching has taught me to be self-critical to improve and be accountable, but not to a point of self-loathing. Self-loathing is a spiritual transgression: self-loathing is synonymous with disagreeing with God; like you're smarter than Him. If God loves you, who the hell are you to disagree with Him by self-loathing? I don't love myself: I love that God loves me.

I don't self-loathe for wanting to die and have this nightmare end. I don't feel I have any value any longer in the world and my constant sorrow severely compromises my spiritual pathwork. My suffering finds surreal ways to become exponentially worse, and there is no value. My suffering is just providing evidence of my personal axiom that the only thing worse than suffering is suffering for no reason. I'm not learning a goddam thing from it, and no one else is either. I'm either a burden or a ghost.

But all reports show that I will be required to bypass The Portal and go to a temporary hell-abode for an unknown amount of time if I self-terminate. A spiritual sister has now persuaded me to put a pin in all plans, and I am existing in a *virtual* Portal: I have promised to suspend all thoughts and intentions until I return.

I better pack: looks like I'm going to India.

_38._

GAME CHANGER

> I am there for you forever.
> —Kripalu Maharaj

I'm being spoiled. A *business-class* ticket is emailed to me with a memo from my satsang sister, Katie: *I don't want you flying coach with your injuries. You'll be more comfortable in business and better able to focus on your reasons for going.*

Nineteen hours of coach flying is brutal, and the jet-lag is like hitting a wall when it catches up with you. I'm relieved and hope business class is different enough to endure it intact. I can't imagine . . . I've never traveled outside of coach.

Suddenly I'm popular: another devotee sister I haven't spoken with in years calls me via WhatsApp. Marsha moved from the States to the ashram in India five years ago. She offers to assist with the arrangements for transport and lodging, which is customary within our community.

"Raju will meet you at the airport. Do you remember Raju?"

"He's the *satsangee*[19] *driver* right? Personal Uber for devotees?"

"Right. Same as it ever was: he'll take you to the Delhi ashram to eat and sleep a few hours and take you back to the airport for the early morning, one-hour flight to Lucknow. Another satsangee driver will pick you up in Lucknow for the three-hour drive to the Mangarh ashram. Can you handle nonstop air and car totaling around twenty-six hours?"

---

[19] Satsangee is a yog term for members of the spiritual community.

"I guess we're gonna find out. What's the worst that can happen? If it ain't gonna kill me again, I'll be there."

I'm familiar with the process as my memory is mostly restored now, and this will be my fifth trip to India, though in many ways, it's my first: my memory is restored *mostly*. But my memories still lack the quality of familiarity or personal connection. The majority of memories pre-TBI-NDE are still like newspaper clippings.

The satsangee on the phone is another sister I had counseled in the past, and we have a good bond too. I am embarrassed when she brings up my private contemplation of suicide. "Please try not to be embarrassed, Krishnanand. Katie knows how close you and I are, and she knows how much I've worried for you since I heard."

I'd had a strong reputation with all who knew me, from every department of my life, of being the advisor, counselor, and motivator, not a *charity case* wracked with sorrow. I was voted *least likely to commit suicide* by everyone my whole life. This wasn't because of a light-hearted, jovial disposition: I'd been a bit dark philosophically all my life, but I've been strong and driven.

The satsangee community knows the basics of what I've been through and have been supportive and concerned. I'm the *last* person anyone would've ever thought to need support or assistance. I had counseled many devotees within our community and helped many and had been honored to do so, each at the direct request of my Swami-teacher. I feel ashamed and uncomfortable to be the one in need now rather than the one helping others.

I try to not feel humiliated as it humbles me.

She does not judge and is too happy to help: both she and Katie reminding me of helping them and so many others. "So just shut up and let us help *you* now!"

"On one condition. . . ." I insist. "You can't prevent me from saying thank you or expressing gratitude. I *know* what you're doing is selfless and that appreciation can increase our pride, which is technically a *bad* thing for a bhakti-yog, but if you really want to help me, you'll allow me to express my gratitude *at least a little*." This was requested in full-flowing tears as I am so entirely overwhelmed at the love and concern being shared with me.

"Ok . . ." they had both agreed to my condition. "So long as *you* know *we* . . . are not doing *anything*. It is Maharaji's Grace that is intervening for you. We're just doing His service."

"Mutually agreed, yes and ok. But you are being the *agents* of his Grace. I am grateful to Him, first and foremost, but also to you for being willing and making it become tangible. Thank you."

***

In the midst of a logistics and trip detail conversation with my spirit sister in India, she drops a mushroom-cloud bomb on me.

"Huh? What're you saying? Say that again," she repeats, thinking I actually didn't hear her rather than was shocked by what she said.

"You know . . ." she says casually, "attaining God Realization through Maharaji's Grace in *this* lifetime."

"No. He's left the planet. The scriptures in all the philosophies teach that your guru must be *present* to grace you with final Realization. They don't have to be there in person but still have to be on the Earth."

"C'mon . . . you know that doesn't apply to Kripalu."

She is assuming my intellectual level and post-graduate status as a bhakti-yog means I know this hidden feature to our path, *which I don't!* As long as she's been on the path and as much of a hardcore devotee as she is, I think she's whack!

"That only applies to *normal* descensions! Silly! You know that. Maharaji is the direct descension of Radha Herself. It makes no difference if He's on the planet or not!"

"No . . . I do *not* know this. What are you saying right now? Where does it say in our volumes of literature by the actual Rasik saints of history or in the countless speeches given to us by Swamiji and Maharaji that we can attain final, ultimate, God Realization, Grace, *after* His descension is over here?"

Being less of a book scholar, she could not quote the chapter or verse, but assures me this is so and that memory-loss, brain trauma must've deleted this knowledge from my mind.

"Not a chance. *This* is not something I would've forgot."

"Look, if you don't believe me, Krishnanand, ask other devotees. This is pretty common knowledge. It's what we're all living for."

A yogi does *all* he can to complete the Soul's Journey in a current lifetime.

Your guru must be on the planet to give you final grace. I'd read it a hundred times. It helped define devotional life: against all odds, become worthy of total surrender and grace to a divine personality before you die, or in this case, before He does: I was born in 1966. He appeared in 1922. He ascended in 2013, when I was reeling from my DAI, just six months in. I'd missed my chance to complete my Soul's Journey in this lifetime.

The backup plan is to continue living a spiritual and virtuous life to continue making progress. Sadhana progress is never wasted because it carries over into the next life. Living a virtuous life builds good character karmas and sanskars which carryover, life after life. Having material resources, a mate companion, being a good parent, and a giving human-being were material investments to a spiritual goal: that's dharm. My passion for restoring my life was both: material/emotional stability lessens my suffering, which allows me to be a better sadhu-yogi.

I'm trying to salvage my life so I don't live my final years in bitterness. I'm trying to create enough good karmas by being good and make spiritual progress to secure good position for the lifetimes I'm going to have to wait for the next Guru opportunity.

My decision to die is because I have *no* reason to persist: my life sucks from every angle, and I can't complete my Soul's Journey in this lifetime because my Guru's descension has ended. I'm convinced I will soon become so bitter from suffering that my devotional sadhana will become negative. I think I'll do less damage to my progress by suicide than by living.

But if this is true, that I can complete my Soul's Journey in *this* lifetime, my suffering may not be purposeless.

Sure enough: I talk to a couple other long-term, well-educated, and genuine, *original gangster* devotees who confirm her prophesy. They pretty much laugh when I ask, assuming I'm just fucking with them by confessing I don't know this. I don't recall ever, once coming upon this vital secret while studying and practicing this yog path for over a decade. One that I speak with is my long-time brother and friend, Nikhilanand, who is one of the main *prachareks* (preachers) within the US mission.

How did I possibly miss such a vital secret?

"It's not actually a secret, Krishnanand," says Bhaiya Nikihilanand, "but it's not front-page knowledge either. Your casual devotee may not know this, but it is inferred in our scriptures. It's kind of like how Radha's name is never even mentioned in the scriptures. It is the Rasik saints that reveal Her as the Absolute Divine Love power. Some things are too high and sacred to be mentioned in words." He quotes scriptures in Sanskrit to make his point and interprets them: "An avatar is a divine descension, but an avatar-i is Shree Radha Krishn Herself. Our Maharaji is not merely an *avatar:* He is an avatar*i*, and the little 'i' on the suffix is paramount."

I didn't know that I could still become God Realized in this lifetime once my Guruji had ascended.

This changes everything!

Did God and Guru take the wrecking ball to my material life, using Yogmaya to brain-warp Janete into rejecting me in spite of our history, deep love, and her core character? Was I being *saved* from material success as a behavioral counselor and author to prevent me from developing more worldly attachments? Would these *worldly* attachments have ultimately obscured and reduced my spiritual progress?

It's the only thing that makes sense, *because none of this shit has made any sense!*

As I meditate on this truth being revealed, I receive clear vision from Akashic clarity: *Yes.*

"There was nothing *wrong* with the life you were living except the attachments were subtly strong enough to prevent you from full-surrender to the Godhead."

I'm not *happy* by any stretch of the imagination. But this news is profound and gives my Soul's Journey new purpose. Indeed . . . *I must live on!* My suffering is not for nothing!

I have absolute confidence and trust in my Guru for being the Architect of it all as it needed to be.

A story comes to mind: Five-hundred years ago a man came to history's greatest Rasik Saint, Lord Chaitanya Mahaprabhu while He sat beneath a large banyan tree: "My Lord," the man beseeched, "I am a common man and great sinner. I've never done anything worthwhile with my life. I only now see that becoming One with God is all that matters. I know you are omniscient, so I ask you: how long will it take this sinner to become God Realized?"

Mahaprabhu waved His arms above His head. "Do you see the leaves on this banyan tree?"

"Yes, Master, there are thousands of them."

"That is how many lifetimes it will take you to become God Realized." The man grinned from cheek to cheek, and he gushed with joy. "Did you not hear what I said? I just told you that it will take you thousands of lifetimes to become Spiritually-Enlightened. Why are you smiling?"

The man laughed heartily. "Because! The Lord Himself just told me I can make it! All is *not* lost! Someday, I can be with God!"

"Now . . . do you see how many *branches* are on this tree?" Chaitanya flourished upward again. "With that attitude, it will take you just *that many*."

The man became so overwhelmed with joy he could not contain himself and began laughing, dancing, and singing the Lord's name. He cared not if it was ten thousand or three hundred, he was overcome by the thought of ever being worthy.

Gaur Hari Chaitanya sweetly confirmed, "You can attain God Realization in *this very lifetime*."

Is there hope for me too? I became a devotee and servant of the Lord in 2005 in this lifetime. From the moment I accepted that God Realization was genuine and my Guru was the personification of it, I did not pause on the path and have tried to run as strong as I can to progress in this lifetime. But like the man beneath the banyan tree, I was distraught over my late start. I'd wasted my life and not found my Guru or His path until I was almost forty. I had to make up for lost time, immersing myself in spiritual practice. Nearly overnight, my life took new context.

I had been studying and practicing mysticism for years, but these paths could not bring me to ultimate God Realization. They lacked the direct Grace of a Divine Master. As a Hermetic mystic, I spent sixty to eighty hours a month in spiritual practice already. Once I became a devotee to Kripalu, it became exclusive to *Raganuga Bhakti*. Early on, all my material duties and actions were subtly converted to pathwork. I saw how each and every action in my life can serve my spiritual agenda if it is dedicated to it from the heart.

Instead of eating breakfast, I prepare and eat with a private, subtle awareness the only point of fortifying my body is to make it strong and well *to do sadhana*. Instead of working to pay a mortgage, I became aware a paid mortgage gives me the opportunity to have a safe place to live *and do sadhana*. Octaves were added to my personal relationships: going to a ballgame is fun, but is also a healthy antidote to life's stress, and less stress is *good for my sadhana*. Even pleasures of the body, from my tennis game to making love, become spiritual acts as they ease the pressures of life, reminding me how beautiful being a spiritual human can be. Affection with my loving partner and our sexual passions were elevated as they took on a higher meaning. I tried to view each and every act and action in my life as how they *served my sadhana*.

This was a relatively short hop: my past work with Tantric-sexual yoga had already taught me all of our worldly joys are the raw materials we can use for our spiritual gratitude. The goal is to be in God Consciousness *all the time*. And it had become so elementary to see the spiritual blessings in common, everyday occurrences.

Don't get me wrong: sometimes I'm just a stupid-human enjoying a walk-off homerun at a game, digging the point I scored from a killer backhand, or in raw, erotic pleasure as I lick, devour, and thrust a partner to mutual-orgasms. But before, after, and sometimes during, there are at least a few brain cells out of the billions rolling around in my grey-matter aware God is Great.

Spiritual awareness never diminishes worldly pleasures. Spiritual awareness enhances them. A good orgasm becomes a great orgasm! I learned the basics of this with Tantra yoga: to use your mind to direct and channel sexual, sensual energy into mystical energy. This is how the orgasm can become a religious experience!

Bhakti-yog takes the basics I learned in Tantra and others and elevates them to something simpler, purer, and sweeter: more spiritual. Spirit ain't all gentle and passive! It's intense and climactic! God is extreme! Intense! And also peace and bliss.

Can these six years of suffering be converted to sadhana? Absolutely everything happens for a reason. It is up to us to convert the reason to spiritual ones. I have hoped and begged to discover the spiritual connection to my suffering but have been too stupid to see beyond the suffering itself.

Clearly, the yogmaya power has been having a fucking field day with my existence. I am honored to provide Akashic-Administrators with such entertainments. Their jobs are probably pretty dull managing the karmas and destinies of nearly eight billion souls in human bodies. Very few lives are truly extraordinary: some, yes, quite a few maybe, but not a lot! Mine's like a fucking amusement park ride: *The Tunnel of Terror*, enter if you dare. But when it's all done, you had a good time.

Yogmaya has been taking a wrecking ball to my attachments. I've got to find the strength to be grateful for such divine intervention. I've been logically, academically grateful of my events, but only capable of episodic gratitude emotionally. Yoga Darshan and Upanishads all teach we should be grateful for suffering as it severs attachments. Maybe the Spiritual Administrators see I've got a real shot to become God Realized in this very lifetime. Maybe they're banking on my ability to endure these losses and complete my Soul's Journey. I just hope they've not overestimated me.

Yogmaya *had* to be involved with my missing this central and key part of God Realization in this life. My meditations have revealed a few possibilities as to why it was shrouded from me:

1. Maybe if I knew, I would have been lazy: if I wasn't pressed to fully surrender *now*, maybe I'd just spend too much time and energy enjoying my life.

But I hadn't been *phoning-in* my sadhana because of a good material life. My love-partner, parenting, and helping career played major roles in my ability to grow-up and actually *live* spiritually. The way each had come into my life was consistent with being provided by spiritual Grace: Janete and I meeting by literal accident, my parenting entering my life by paternity fraud, and my helping career being a one-eighty from my one prior. Was all this just to take them away? I think it's because I needed to grow up. Janete, Brandon, my helping career, and even vegetarianism made it possible for me to settle down from hedonism. These features of my life made me clean up my karmic-act!

2. Maybe if I'd known, I would've totally abandoned my worldly duties and obligations. That one's pretty likely. I'd thought about it seriously before and was actually talked *out of it* by two sanyasi monks!

As a newbie devotee in 2006, I seriously considered selling my home and leaving the world behind to live as a sadhu in India. I was advised to hold off and to consider there are many ways to serve your Guru's mission, and remaining in the world as a father, partner, and helping professional might be beneficial for many others and myself as well.

Nikhilanand advised on this too. "Maharaji tells us to not create *more* attachments. He doesn't teach us to abandon our family and responsibilities to remove existing ones!"

Was I capable of living ashram life, full-time? I don't drink tea and coffee is pretty bad and hard to come by in India!

Sure, the Buddha walked out on family and world to become enlightened and set the example, but I'm not the Buddha. If I'd neglected those who depended on me for selfish reasons, even spiritual ones, it might have backfired: guilt over it and abandoning the people I had encouraged being reliant on me.

All that's important is to work with what I got and to know my Maharaji is the engineer of this whole plan and to keep my hands and arms inside the car at all times until the ride is over.

***

I'm scared. Same as it had been with my visit to the US ashram, I'm nervous I may go to India and feel nothing. But my visit to the US ashram, as well as my return to local satsang, was all profound evidence my devotion was all intact.

Any Westerner's first time to Asia is overwhelming. It is like going to another planet. This cannot be exaggerated as it is so exotic and foreign your mind simply does not have the faculties to take it all in casually and recreationally. If you've done it, you know what I mean, and if you've not, there is nothing that can explain it. SCUBA diving ninety feet into the ocean with an air-tank strapped to your back into an underwater world of creatures and terrain you've never seen is *pedestrian* compared to a Westerner's first time to Asia!

I don't go to resort hotels in Delhi or to tourist sites like the Taj Mahal. I go so far off the beaten path many of my adventure sites in India are only known of by lifelong sadhus and in books very sacred to the bhakti-yog path. They're *not* on Trip-Advisor.com!

My TBI limitations make going to the mall an overstimulating affair, but I head to LAX with passport and visa to truck through TSA security and gate-terminals. There are people who cannot even handle the four-oh-five to LAX who *don't* have traumas, but I got to try. It is a huge struggle, and my injured brain is releasing chemicals of terror and anxiety, which are pretty convincing this is all beyond me. In spite of feeling terror, I persist: academically, I know it's brain trauma and can't be trusted. It ain't gonna kill me.

The gift of business class is a life-saver: I don't know what first-class is like, but holy shit! It *can't* be better than business! I have access to the airport lounge to relax comfortably with premium food, priority security clearance, and priority boarding. The most overwhelming parts are reduced by two-thirds. Once on the plane, the staff are not generically cordial as they are in coach; they are splendidly sweet and servile!

My seat is like a small, private bedroom: a good-sized TV monitor, shelves to store personals, spacious overhead, and my seat doesn't just recline: *it lies down.* Horizontal. There's no hustling or bustling as everyone has room to store luggage and get comfortable for the long-ass flight to Delhi. While coach travelers are being rushed to squeeze by one another and sit the fuck down and rush their meal selection in before take-off, I'm being served delicious champagne, strawberries, and cookies. I almost feel guilty: *almost.*

So *this* is how the other half lives? Complimentary cocktails, fresh appetizers, and warm face towels? God, I hope my memory works well enough to remember this because I do not want to forget it! And the food buffet in the airport lounge, preflight? Primo! This is quality vacation!

Hmmmm . . . what's that odd feeling I'm having? It's quite unfamiliar. Oh my gawd! *It's happiness!* For the first time in over seven years, I don't feel scared and sad! I am so grateful to feel this thing I heard of called happiness! And *my* happiness is a bazillion times better than these other passengers' happiness. Know why?

Because I'm supposed to be *dead*! I'm not just traveling in luxurious comfort like my neighbor across the aisle, which is a full *six feet* across, but have a bonus awareness I'm a walking-dead corpse, and it is the loving Grace of my Spiritual Master and a dear, devotee sister making this happen! The only thing better than flying business class to your Guru's ashram in India is going for *free!* The only thing better than going for free is going for free because somebody cares enough and loves you enough to pay for it! I'm going to embarrass myself if I don't put a blanket over my head to hide the sobbing tears of joy.

After twenty-plus hours of travel from driving PCH to LAX to a connecting flight in Tokyo, the voice comes over the PA:

"Ladies and gentlemen, please prepare for arrival as we have begun our descent and will be landing in Delhi shortly."

It's not a dream: the voiceover is in English, my passport and visa are right where I put them, my cell phone has WhatsApp hooked up, and . . . *I know who I am!* I'm not landing in Wuhan, China with no ID or knowledge of who I am or why I'm here. This isn't a weird, existential dream! I'm being offered gourmet coffee and a pen with the customs form to fill out.

I don't know if I can *handle* the foreignness of Asia-India or be capable of navigating from New Delhi to Lucknow to the ashram in the north, but I've made it this far, so I do as I always do: one foot and another until I either fall down or die. Make it up as I go and fake it to make it.

(After I wrote this chapter, I went to my private library of bhakti books and grabbed the first book I saw to search for an intro quote. The random page I flipped it open to had my Guru's image and that quote: "I am there for you forever.")

END OF ACT III

ACT IV
ANAND (BLISS)

39.

A VIDESHI IN KRIPALU'S COURT

Tipsy with Divine Love, I wander the lanes of Barsana saying, 'Radhey, Radhey!'

—Kripalu (Dham Madhuri)

In just six visits to India, I covered a *lot* of ground. I'm a restless spirit and do as much as I can. Each trip to India has yielded profound experiences that were magical and layered more evidence to my Soul's Journey.

What is the best thing to do in flight? Sleep. Even my reliable, holistic, and effective No-Jet-Lag supplement is no match for the wall of sleep you hit going to the other side of the world. It usually comes about twelve hours after arrival; you feel totally fine in an instant, and then you suddenly become narcoleptic. Remaining still for nineteen hours, even during a comfy and luxurious Biz Class flight, is challenging. Especially with brain issues! As I power down all devices and recline with a content tummy, I drift… sleep… dream… *remember…*

First Darshan

Weeks after the bhakti-shakti-pat experience in 2008, Maharaji arrived for His two-month visit to His US ashram. I ensured I was there the day He arrived and then flew back and forth from LA to the ashram to be present as much as possible. I'll always cherish the many glorious leelas (pastimes) we shared during the first darshans with Him. Brandon went with me for one week and Janete for another.

Oe day, I asked if I could do aarti to our Maharaji—the waving of the candle with a song of love for God and Guru. I could choose of dozens of opportunities for private darshans, and I selected this one because aarti is a significant ritual to honor one's Guru. It is private: I could spend a few minutes alone with Him and few devotee administrators.

"I may get nervous and forget the words!" I admitted to the assistant, who led me to His room.

"Oh, don't worry! Everyone gets a bit rattled, so I'll stay right there and sing it with you."

I stood to His right side with the candle and tray. The music began, and the lyrics came to my mind. I performed it seamlessly as Maharaji sat on His bed, surrounded by morning newspapers. I remained aware of the significance of making this memory while multi-tasking to remember the lyrics. It was a sacred moment, and I didn't want to flub it up!

As I sang this song of honor to Maharaji, He looked forward, not at me or even in my direction. He sipped His tea, completely ignoring me! He went about His business, glancing through the newspapers, books and other documents before Him.

My mind flurried. Was he testing me to see if I'd react? Get offended? Be bothered? I had made a $150 donation for this opportunity, and He didn't seem to acknowledge that I was just three feet from Him, singing glories to Him and God! I smiled broadly, accepting that He was not testing me or my humility; He was playing with me! Sure, I could react, annoyed that He was ignoring this crucial moment of my life and trivializing it. I could think poorly of myself for being so insignificant in the presence of this world-renowned spiritual icon. But I wasn't bothered.

I was thrilled! He was too humble to show appreciation and gave me a leela experience I would never forget! I loved Him for trusting me enough to toy with me, tempting me wonder about His Grace. Nuh-uh, no way, not a chance! Ha-ha! His playfulness made me feel so loved, and I was ecstatic! It didn't matter if He ignored me, left the room, or even told me to shut up because my singing was terrible. It was ALL good!

Asia or Bust

My first trip to India in 2009 almost came to a screeching halt when I arrived at the airport without a visa; I'd never been to a country requiring one, so I *didn't know*. I was packed, prepared, and dropped off at LAX, but I was denied boarding. I scrambled from Los Angeles to the embassy in San Francisco to get a temporary visa. Miraculously, I pulled it off and made it to India because I was far more concerned with showing God how hard I would work to please Him than any concern with actual results. I knew it was a test to see how far I'd go to make it. *How far would I go*? There was no limit to even consider. I'm prepared to swim there. Whatever it takes.

Namkaran: Name Change

On my second visit, I asked my Guru, Kripalu, to change my name to a spiritual one. It is miraculous that this common California boy had access to a world-renowned teacher of millions. One of the administrators advised me to show up outside His room at 8:00 the following morning. I waited, trying not to be nervous about being face-to-face with my Enlightened Master, one of just five original Jagadgurus in the last 5,000 years.

I was invited in and pranamed to Him. I sat on the floor while an assistant spoke to Him in Hindi about my request for a spiritual name. There was no ceremony or fanfare. He sat on the edge of His bed while I sat at His divine feet and received my name. When I left the room, a handful of devotees were waiting outside His bedroom door, excitedly asking, *"What'd He give you?! What's your new name?!"*

"Krishnanand," I replied. My head was swimming from being at the feet of a divine personality. I had appeared cool and collected the entire time, but inside, my heart had skipped beats knowing that I had been within arm's reach of a Divine Saint who changed my life daily.

When I announced my new name, there was a chorus of *"Ooooh! Ahhhh!"* followed by silence. When I asked about their stunned reaction to hearing my name, they replied, "Oh, my God! That's a beautiful name! Do you know what it means? It means *God's bliss!* And that's the name of His grandchild!"

I was too overwhelmed to process the occasion until hours later when I erupted in tears at my fortune in life.

Sadhu-Bhog

Each year, my Guru hosts a *sadhu-bhog (sah-doo boje)*, a day-long event attended by spiritual aspirants called *sadhus*. They live in the wilderness and dedicate their lives to attaining God Consciousness. They subsist in huts in the forests (called *bhajan kutis*) and beg for food and alms from local villagers, who are honored to donate to them. A *bhog* is a charitable event that provides food, clothes, and basic utensils like plates, cups, and water bottles for them, along with a few hundred rupees. Doctors also come to volunteer their time and medical services and to give basic medicines to the sadhus. During the bhog, there is a feast to honor the sadhus.

Hundreds of sadhus come to this annual event, and this year I am invited to attend, too. As a strong, able-bodied Westerner, I will assist with security to keep things orderly. The bhog will take place in the holy town of Vrindaban.

Sadhus enjoying the bhog at Prem Mandir temple grounds.

I've never been to Vrindaban before. It is the most sacred town to our tradition; it is where our beloved form of God, Radha Krishn, played as a child during their avatar descension over 5,000 years ago. I'm excited and honored to go!

After the four-hour drive from the ashram to Lucknow Airport and a one-hour flight back to Delhi, I secure a driver to take me to the ashram in Vrindaban, which takes another three hours. I'm exhausted from the first leg of travel over sleepless, bumpy roads. I get to the small ashram building on the edge of town after midnight. This is India countryside, not Manhattan; there ain't a damn thing open nor a soul in sight. There's a gate barring entry to the ashram, and I cannot enter. I see a three-legged dog yipping with three other handicapped, homeless pooches begging for food. My driver is about to leave me on the side of the dirt road to commute back to his family in Delhi. I may be sleeping with the dogs. After making some noise and calling the number I was given, an ashram woman comes outside and shows me to a room where I can spend the night.

It's February, so it's just 80 degrees outside instead of 95. I lie down on the bare mattress and conk out. I'm dead tired! I try to sleep but am kept awake by the incessant buzzing of mosquito wings at my ear. I can't stop them, and I'm getting eaten alive!

The mosquitos in Vrindaban are legendary. The Rasik Saints of the 1400s even mention them briefly in their accounts of beatitude! My only solution is to grab the blanket at the foot of the bed and wrap myself in it, burrito-style, so no flesh is exposed to these parasites! Now, I can't sleep because it is 85 degrees in here, and even though I've wrapped myself head-to-toe in swaddling clothes, I'm still getting devoured by mosquitos!

As the sun rises, I realize I am *toast!* With no sleep for two days, I'm about to be a man who *needs* security, not one who can provide it! I finally begin to drift off when the room door is thrust open. The devotee assigned to head the security has just arrived! I know the guy because he's an American devotee, too. His name is Madhukar, and we'll be sharing a room, so that's it; resting is over. There is no peace and quiet because Madhukar is well-rested and excited and has been running his mouth nonstop since he came in. I wander out of the room, trying to fathom a way not to commit homicide today from sleep deprivation.

I'm leaving; fuck this! I am miserable and having my second crisis of faith, the first being the day of Shaktipat from my Swamiji. I decide to call the airline and reschedule my departure from next week to today. There's no cell phone reception, so I go up to the rooftop, hoping to get a signal.

I wander to the roof and make the call. The airline tells me it'll cost over $500 to rearrange my flight. Fuck that!

The roof is private, and I appreciate the quiet to gather myself. I look over the town from my elevated perch. The view of this sacred holy town moves me, and water streams from my eyes!

I am well acquainted with the history of Vrindaban. The Goswami Saints that lived there, Lord Chaitanya's time there, and the dozens of leela sites of my personified form of Divine Love, Radha Krishn, are all before me! From this rooftop, I can see leagues of the hallowed city. I'm looking over a townscape of ancient temples and the Yamuna River.

And suddenly...

I'm not tired!

I don't mean I'm mind-over-matter, block-out fatigue from willful enthusiasm, second-wind awake. I mean, suddenly, I feel like I've had a nine-hour slumber and am sharp and fresh! My mosquito bites don't itch, I'm a little hungry, and I feel ready to *carpe diem*! I feel great! I suspect my renewed disposition is my Maharaji's Grace!

When I return, my new roommate breaks the news to me. "There's been a disaster at Maharaji's home ashram." He is referring to the one we just left.

"What happened?"

"Yesterday's bhog was for everyone, not just sadhus. We gave away food, money, medicine, and more. So many people showed up in need that it got out of hand and turned into a stampede, killing two people. Maharaji won't be coming here for this bhog because He needs to stay there."

We wander to find coffee and discuss what to do: Suddenly, we have two days to kill. We sit in a straw hut sipping still-boiling instant coffee, the only way Indians know how to serve it. Our casual talk takes a twist and becomes an intense conversation about the Kundalini experience. Very few know what the real-deal Kundalini thing is like, but the unique words we use indicate we both do. What are the odds that the guy I hang out with is one of the few who has had one?

We decide to make the most of the circumstances. Madhukar, my devotee-brother, suggests we pay a driver $5 to take us to the holy town of Barsana and do parikram there. Over the next five hours, we car tour and walk miles of paths to visit such holy sites. I am in rapture. I see the tiny hut where Sanatan Goswami lived when he wrote Chaitanya Charitamrita; he lived in that hut for years in solitude. I see the little spring of water Lord Krishn made when He struck His heel to the ground, *and I sip the water*. Finally, we walk the entire ridge of Barsana Hill, stopping at a dozen temples along the way. We finish at Maan Mandir, where my Swamiji lived in solitude for years before He ventured out to share the good news with the West. Madhukar leads me to a secret chamber in the temple very few know of and even fewer have an opportunity to access. We share a moment of silence in remembrance of God's divine act that took place in this very spot.

<u>Jagganath Temple, Puri</u>

February 2011

A few hours after arriving at Maharaji's ashram in north India, Mangarh, I settle in my room with a bath (bucket, spigot, and toilet) and clean up for satsang: the evening devotional kirtan chanting sessions. I'm disappointed that my Guru, Maharaji, doesn't make an appearance. I longed for a darshan with him after traveling across the world to see him. I hope He is feeling well; it is unlike Him not to join us in the prayer hall for evening satsang.

Bhakti Mandir temple, Manghar, India where Kripalu lives.

In the morning, I found out that He had gone. He flew to Bhubaneswar in Eastern India yesterday afternoon to host a five-day program for His devotees in the region.

WTF?!

My stay here is useless without His darshan! Being graced by His mere presence is worth thirty years of plane travel!

And now? Nothing!

A man with a thick Apu-like accent informs me, "You can go to Bhubaneswar to attend if you like. It is a free country, kind sir!" His sarcasm is polite, as Indians always are, but it's still noticeable.

"Please find me a driver."

"A driver will be here in fifteen minutes to take you to the airport."

I fly to Bhubaneswar to see my Guru. A taxi takes me to a hotel "for Westerners." Indians are well aware of Western culture and accept us, without judgment, as "spoiled" because we require running water in the showers and actual beds instead of floor mattresses. They call us *videshis (vid-desh-ees)*, a mild slang term for "spoiled white people." This hotel even has toilet paper beside the bidet-style toilet. Now dat's class!

As I check into the hotel, the desk clerk seems nervous and rather overwhelmed. He turns and whispers to other employees, and they point toward me. Something is up.

The clerk gives me the lowdown—room service details, Wi-Fi password, and check-out information—but somehow, he seems rattled by me.

The hotel staff behaves like little schoolgirls around me. The desk clerk, the valet... they can't seem to hold it together.

This behavior is typical in remote villages where they never see white people, so they assume you *must* be a movie star. But Bhubaneswar is a major metropolis and one of the most advanced, progressive cities in the subcontinent.

I am close enough to the satsang venue to walk from my hotel. My room overlooks the *bhavan (*hall*)* where my Guru will give darshan (divine vision) of His Divine Grace and hours of kirtan.

I am overjoyed!

My trip has turned into another unpredictable adventure. Maharaji is boundless. I just try to keep up.

There is no satsang during the day, so I have time to kill. I use Google to look at the logistics: I'm in the land of Navadwip, the town where Mahaprabhuji Chaitanya appeared and took birth. Nearby is the temple he lived near during the end of his appearance on Earth. He vanished from that same temple before dozens of people. It is a significant temple—one of the four major *tirths* in India.

The temple is as large as a city and is sacred in my tradition. The Jagganath Temple in Puri, to a Krishn devotee, is like the Mount of Olives to a Christian.

It's a three-hour commute through the dusty countryside, and I am in disbelief that I will take darshan of this dham. I arrive around 10 a.m. and take my place in a line of over seventy people waiting to enter. It takes me half an hour to reach the entrance. I am speechless and almost in tears; I cannot believe my sojourn has led me to a place I never considered visiting but always dreamt about.

The entrance is directly in front of me. A man with the classical Indian mustache of an official gazes at me. He is the gatekeeper. He casually shakes his head "no" and points to a sign: *"NO WHITES."*

It's the only sign in English for a hundred miles.

I tell him in my *chhota* (little) Hindi that he doesn't understand:

I'm no tourist.

I'm a qualified devotee.

I have traveled for four days to be here.

I wanna be the big-mouth American they expect and begin shouting, *"Yo, man! Do you know who you're dealing with? Do you know WHO my Guru is?"*

He dismisses me with a wave of his hand. I am a mere annoyance.

I quickly see that there is NO way he will make an exception.

I begin to do the videshi dance: "Lemme speak to a manager!"

There is no such thing.

"Lemme speak to your supervisor!"

No such person.

The man with the mustache is the first and last line of defense.

This is racist! You can't keep me out because I'm WHITE!

A local tells me it ain't about race. "White" just means tourist. They don't want tourists fouling up the place. It is preserved for the natives of Bharatvarsh (India). They don't wanna bunch of yoga-class-café-latte Westerners stinking up the place.

I get it.

I respect it.

I accept it.

I also begin to weep.

I'm standing only a few feet from entering the temple where my sacred Sadguru, Maharaj Kripalu, vanished into the divine abode during his appearance as Chaitanya Mahaprabhu five hundred years ago.

Providence has delivered me to this threshold, and *now I can't get in because of my skin color?!*

I am so sad and do not know what to do. I lower my head into my palms, and I weep.

No drama. No histrionics. Just tears.

Heartbroken tears. I long to have darshan (divine vision) of the altar Chaitanya ran to and vanished before. I am in *virah*, a state of intense spiritual longing. And then...

There's a tap on my shoulder.

"They cannot let you in. It is forbidden."

"Yeah, but..." I plead my case to this Hindu stranger.

"It's not racial. My name is Mahish. I am a priest, and I work within the temple. There's nothing we can do."

I ask him to show me to the office of security or management.

"This is not America. It will do no good to appeal!" he says with classic Indian cheer and sarcasm.

"Come with me," he continues. "Even as a priest, I cannot get you inside. But I can *show* you inside!

We cross the wide dirt road flanking the temple entrance. It's like a Western movie town: popup buildings on the opposite side of this temple city which I cannot escape.

The priest leads me into a four-story dilapidation, "This is a local temple library. We can see *inside* the temple from the roof!"

He gives some secret signs to the on-duty clerk, and we climb four flights to the roof.

LO AND BEHOLD, I AM GAZING DOWN INTO THE TEMPLE WITH A BIRDS-EYE VIEW!

Mahish, my new confidante and guide, gives me a virtual tour of the grounds, pointing out the enclaves and avenues within. "And that building, the open-roofed one to the right of the shikr, is where Mahaprabhuji vanished!"

As I gaze into the heart of the 800-year-old temple, I become absorbed in its prominence and sadhana.

Mahish escorts me on a parikrama around the temple walls. He points out the entrances, the posts, and the local temples surrounding it. We spend three hours on his bicycle-rickshaw, his thin frame peddling my big American body around the village of Puri surrounding Jagganath. Tirelessly, Mahish cycles me to the leela sites throughout the town where Lord Chaitanya gave satsang with his Goswami disciples. These are the very sites I had read of but only fantasized about ever visiting. I see the exact spot where Adi Shankaracharya, the first original Jagadguru, taught His disciples 1500 years ago.

Our tour concludes with the beach where Shri Chaitanya wept as he carried the lifeless body of His adored disciple, Hari Das, and set it free in the waves of the Bay of Bengal.

Mahish brings me back to the taxi lot, and we say our goodbyes. He asks for nothing, but I give him a modest gratuity for his efforts and thank him, from one sadhu devotee to another. He bids me well, and off I go.

I look back on this event and know that Mahish was a dasa (servant) of the Lord, dispatched to rescue me as my tears of longing evoked God's Grace.

That evening, I feel privileged. As a Westerner, I am seated in the satsang hall alongside my Sadguru, Kripalu Maharaj. I am the only Westerner (*videshi*) there. He makes small jokes at my expense in Hindi as I adore Him.

An Indian devotee chuckles and explains why Maharaji is ribbing me. "He says you are smiling at the actors performing on the stage, but you have NO idea what they are saying!" It's true, and now everyone nearby is chuckling, too. Being the butt of Maharaji's teasing is an honor, and I laugh with the other devotees.

Cricket Ain't Baseball

When I check out of the hotel, the clerks and staff act as unusual as before, like silly, love-struck teenagers.

"Excuse me, sir..." the clerk began in accented English, "I know this is terribly inappropriate, but may I please have your autograph?"

"Why?"

He looks ashamed, as if he's crossed a line. "I apologize. I shouldn't ask such a thing. Please forgive me!"

"No, wait a minute... *who do you think I am*? I'm just an American on holiday."

"Yes, sir. I apologize! It was rude of me to impose. But I am... we all are... such huge fans of yours. We may never get this chance again, so I must ask you to please let us take your photo and get an autograph. I am sooo solly, sir; please do not take offense!"

The other staff members gather around, waiting for my consent.

"No, please. I seriously don't know who you think I am."

They seem convinced I am a famous celebrity, trying to travel incognito to avoid fan mobbing, and they finally disclose who they think I am.

"We all know who you are, sir. You are Kevin Pietersen, good sir! We are honored by your visit! Please to allow to take photo and give autograph."

I stare at them blankly; I have no clue who Kevin-whoever is. When I return to my room for the last of my belongings, I ask Google who Kevin Pietersen is and find that he is an English cricket player and commentator now living in Australia.

The sport of cricket is as popular in India as the NFL is in the United States. I take a moment to read about this Australian cricket player they think is me.

YEAH, RIGHT!

I WISH I LOOKED LIKE THIS GUY!

I decide to do the right thing. I stroll back to the lobby and gather the staff.

"Okay, here's the deal. Each of you can take ONE photo with me, but NO autographs!"

Get a darshan, give a darshan!

Parikram Marg

As a modern pilgrim, I rely on guides and maps to make an itinerary. I want to absorb the ambiance and history of sacred places by squeezing in as much as possible. It can be stressful, and some may ask, "Isn't that counterproductive? How can you take it all in if you're rushing to keep a schedule?"

Sure, sure... but I think of my head as a storage disc, like an SD memory card. If I cram it full of stuff, I can review it and meditate on it later. I'd rather do too much than not enough. When I go to a sacred landmark, I take the time to think and meditate on it, but I do so with motion rather than sitting down. Most of the time, when we are at an event, we take in too much, too fast, to truly grasp the importance of it. Hindsight is 20/20, so looking back is often a far more effective way to remember.

The trip that was postponed because of the canceled sadhu bhog yielded something special. With extra time on our hands, Madhukar took me on a tour of an area that included two hidden-gem bookstores.

Getting authentic spiritual texts outside India is difficult, and finding English translations is even harder. They are few and far between; you must know where to look. Madhukar knew where to find them, and my carry-on bag quickly became a checked bag filled with powerfully amazing books not to be had on Amazon or in the West.

One of my favorite books is published by the ISKCON organization (International Society for Krishna Consciousness), commonly called the *Hari Krishnas*. The organization's roots go back hundreds of years and are aligned with the Rasik Bhakti path and traditions, as my own Guru is. Other than a handful of ISKCON's more cult-like adherents panhandling at airports, they're legit and have produced a third of my personal spiritual library. Madhukar encouraged me to read a book called *Sri Vraja Mandala Parikrama* to learn about the dozens of holy sites sacred to the Rasik lineage. This beautiful book is packed with color photos of the leela holy sites in India. It describes what and where they are and why they're revered by explaining what occurred in these spots over five millennia.

I bought the book and began to read through it to plan a tour of sites that intrigued me for my next trip. I skimmed through and put page markers on the ones that were 'must sees' for me. It was hard to be selective, so I marked them in four colors: red for *must see*, pink for *really wanna see*, orange for *if there's time*, and blue for *I hope to see that too!*

My skimming had turned into reading every word of this fantastic book, and by the time I had finished, there were multiple tabs on *every* page!

The book outlines a 30-day walking tour of holy sites, which is what *parikrama* means in Sanskrit. I wanted to do them *all!* I have read this tour book nearly a dozen times, cover to cover. I can imagine visiting all of the hundreds of places depicted.

I had to narrow down my choices. My India visits are typically only ten days long, and I intend to dedicate much of that time to my Guru's ashram.

I walk a lot and bonded with a rickshaw driver, Mahesh. To this day, he is my contact whenever I travel to India. Because of him, I can always cover a lot of ground each day, seeing a dozen or more sites from morning through evening. He's also the local who always reminds me to remove my sunglasses and to hold on to my daypack so the rhesus macaque monkeys can't jump on my shoulders and help themselves to whatever they can snatch from me.

One particular site intrigues me. It is a *sarovar* (pond) surrounded by an outdoor temple. A local *raja* (king) built it in the 1600s to honor a little play scene (*leela*) where Krishn and Radha share a few sweet and funny moments. I don't know why this place beckons me above others, but I will stop by if there is time on my way from Vrindaban to Barsana.

A Holy Sarovar

It is a sight to behold! Regal yet rustic, this open-air temple sits at the edge of a large pond. I am happy to be there and ask my driver to give me fifteen minutes to stroll around. I love water and want to sit beside the temple for a moment and meditate. I wander into a canopied rotunda with a Sistine Chapel-style painting inside. I am glad I took the time to enjoy this, but I still have one more stop before the long drive back to Delhi.

As I turn to leave, a thin man with a long, flowing, white beard enters. His English is quite broken, and I can understand only a third of what he says as he explains the images painted on the ceiling and walls. I suspect he isn't a homeless sadhu, which are plentiful in these wilderness temples. Maybe he is a caretaker of the site. I humor him as I look at my watch, waiting for a break in his oration to politely say, *pardon me, I gotta go!*

I'm a Westerner with a cell phone and a plane ticket. I've got important things to do!

He is so sweet and friendly, though, that I can't refuse to walk with him as he guides me on a tour, escorting me by holding my hand or elbow. Or perhaps he is using me to help him walk because he is old and somewhat frail.

We cross the platforms adorned by pillars aged by weather and moss to a small structure as ancient as everything else there, including my host. I look across the large pond and see my driver smoking and tapping his foot. I have to make a break soon...

"You'll have to pardon me. My driver is waiting..." Then I threw in a detail that would obligate him to excuse me. "I'm trying to stop by my Guru's ashram before I get to the airport in a few hours." By extolling the word 'guru,' I would go from a random tourist to a Hindu brother, and he'd have to pardon me.

"Oh... you have a *Goo-doo*!" he asks in classical, Asian-accented English, "Ah-cha! Ke nam hama Goo-doo?" I had spoken just enough Hindi with him to encourage him to try his luck. Lo and behold, I understand his inquiry! He is asking, *Who's your Guru? What's his name?*

With a bold voice, I reply, "Kripalu Maharaj."

Then he goes white and silent, his eyes growing big. "Your Guru is Kripalu? MY GURU IS KRIPALU!"

And just like that, we bond as brothers and spend the next hour together in his bhajan kuti, sharing wonderful stories of our Guruji that only he knew.

The old man tells me that when Kripalu was a boy, he spent some time as a mendicant, living in the forests of Vrindaban, years before He began His mission. My host isn't a random sadhu; he is the poojari, the priest and caretaker of this holy site. As it turns out, my Guruji—*our* Guruji—spent months here when my new friend was just a little boy. When our Guruji was a wandering mendicant, this poojari's family took Him in back in the 1940s. We laughed and wept at the amazing stories he told.

I brought him back to the car with me before I left. I gave him my prayer shawl from Maharaji's ashram, which I wore in the prayer hall during satsang, and a few other items of devotional merit. I also offered some money as a donation to the temple.

I had promised Janete that I would tell her about my friend, Uddhao. That promise is half-complete, as we would see him again soon...

The tenth canto is an important chapter in the Bhagavatam, the cornerstone of Sanatan Dharm scriptures. It concerns all of Lord Krishna's leela acts, including the pinnacle of our path in the Ras Leela. The eleventh canto, Uddhao Gita—*song of Uddhao*—ollows. In this chapter, Krishna asks the great sage and yogi, Uddhao, to go to Vrindaban/Barsana to settle the hearts of the devotees that long for him and love Him. "The gopis miss me so much they are in tremendous pain. You are a great yogi scholar. Please go to them and explain the truth of God's formless omnipresence." This was a trick; Krishn is a bit of a prankster!

Uddhoa is a famed yogi master who has attained spiritual union with the formless aspect of God, like a buddha. He tries to comfort the illiterate, simple maidens of Krishn's home village, Vrindaban, with the true knowledge that God is formless and omnipresent, so there is no reason to feel His absence. And then he gets schooled.

The gopi maidens' love for Krishn, the divine-love, personified form of God, is way beyond Uddhao's understanding of a formless God. In this canto, we learn the superiority of selfless love for the intimate, personified form of God over the impersonal, ethereal version of God. Uddhao's intellectual pride keeps him from accepting Krishna as the true Godhead. The illiterate gopi maidens reveal to him that he is an ignorant fool, too smart for his own good. Krishn sent him there not to educate the gopi maidens but to have them enlighten him!

The poojari who became my friend that day is named Uddhao.

I have remained in touch with Uddhao and visit him at this sarovar (sacred pond) every time I come to India. I wonder… Did my Guru, Maharaji, send me to this poojari because, like Uddhao, my pride disqualified me from Maharaji's full Grace? Krishn sent Uddhao to the gopis because he wasn't qualified for Krishn's direct Grace. I'm not qualified for Maharaji/Krishn's Grace, nor for that of the gopis. Did He send me to Uddhao, the poojari priest of Kasum Sarovar? I'm not worthy of this beautiful man's association, either. One of the greatest honors is to serve and associate with a devotee of the Lord. By helping those the Lord loves and who love the Lord, you are serving the Lord.

I visit him every time I am in India, and we fall into each other's arms with brotherly love. He is a simple, humble servant of the Lord, and I am blessed to have his darshan because our *Goo-doo* loves him so.

After NDE-Day, it seemed I'd never see my friend, Uddhao, again, and it was painful to me that I could not tell him how much I loved and missed him. I took a shot and reached out to the travel agent who'd made all the arrangements for Janete and me. I asked him if he could send my friend a message and a care package of medicine, food, and money to let him know I was thinking of him. Saurabh, the owner of Merry-Go-Travels, gathered the things for Uddhao and sent a driver to the remote site to deliver them with my message. Saurabh is a Radha Krishn devotee, too, and came through for me like only a brother would.

And I would see Uddhoa again, too…

With Uddhao at Kusum Sarovar: He put flower garlands around my neck and I put an ashram prayer shawl on him and a hat Maharaji had worn one day and I made a donation to get it for Uddhao.

Bhao and Mahabhao

I have experienced ecstasy many times as a spiritualist. The Kundalini event in 1992 went on for months, and sometimes meditations upon my Guru take my awareness of time and sense away entirely. In Sanskrit, spiritually ecstatic states are called *bhao* (bow). I know that any ecstasy I feel is a mere fraction of true spiritual bliss, yet it is beyond my mind and heart. The Kundalini yog ecstasy was profound, yet merely a ruddy reflection compared to the bhao given causelessly by my Kripalu Maharaj.

I have had the awe of seeing my beloved Guru enter into bhao on a few occasions. But a Rasik Saint's bhao is special and boundless, as He is the *personification* of Anand (Spiritual Bliss). The divine trance He enters is *Mahabhao*. I'd heard it described by the Goswamis of 500 years ago, but seeing it altered the projection of my life forevermore.

Parikram Pilgrim: Bhakti in Your Pocket

I am blessed to have had so many profound experiences in India. Each trip provided bizarre, magical adventures which were unplanned and unprecedented. I don't know why, and I do not think myself more worthy than any other soul on this planet. These occurrences left huge impressions on me. God is *everywhere!* Take one step toward Him, and He comes *running* five steps to you!

For example, with a five-hour layover in London, I exited the airport to the subway, called the tube, and got off at a random stop to walk the local avenues. I paused in a traffic circle, wondering why everyone was taking pictures. I asked someone, "What's everybody looking at?" "You really don't know where you are, mate? That's Abbey Road Studios, where the Beatles recorded!" Not spiritual enough? Maybe not, but the kismet frequency was ramping up!

I wandered on. As the sun began to set, I heard lovely chanting and followed it, mesmerized. It was the call to prayer and led me to a mosque. I entered and sat on the floor to meditate on God. Soon I was in tears as I realized each person in this temple has one grand thing in common: we all love and revere God. At that moment, someone tapped on my shoulder. It was the Imam; he asked me to come with him. I followed and sat across from him at a desk, thinking I had done something wrong. He wondered if this was my first visit there. We were quickly engaged in a deep, reverential conversation about loving God and enjoyed each other's company for nearly half an hour. God is omnipresent and nondenominational: temples in India, mosques in London.

The Vatican and many cathedrals in Italy took my breath away. The highlight of my visit was the Christian Catacombs outside Rome, where early Christians lived in underground dens to avoid persecution while staying true to their faith.

Then there were the epic travels shared within the Happy Pilgrims chapter.

Before committing exclusively to the bhakti path, I often went to an Art Deco building in downtown Los Angeles to hang out and have deep discussions and study sessions with

Theosophists. I also visited churches, temples, and cathedrals throughout LA to expose myself to various forms of worship and spiritual communities. I enjoyed hosting monthly study and discussion groups on mystical methods to spiritually network and share time with other seekers of the mysteries. Good times!

During my six trips to India, I toured dozens of sacred sites far off the beaten path, glorious places thousands of years old. Unlike Western religious sites, these historical locations and events are well-documented. While many are so old that they're no longer much more than patches of dirt with tiny crude temples, the awareness of their authenticity and history is mind-blowing!

With a five-day layover in London, I got adventurous and rented a car for a spontaneous trip to Stonehenge. I was the only person there and had the whole place to myself to meditate and ponder. I had significant past-life regression memories while I was there. It was an unreal experience!

Bhakti Mandir: The Temple of Divine Love

It's my last day.

I'm at a loss. I can't bear the thought of my reality. I arrived ten days ago and have been in satsang for four to six hours daily. Twice a day, our Maharaji joins us in the hall so we can enjoy satsang with Him present. It is mesmerizing! I get so lost in his darshan; I'm swept into the verses of the kirtan that live in His eyes.

His presence transforms the satsang hall from a sublime place to a divine one. Kirtan in the prayer hall is virtually nonstop from sunrise until nearly 10 p.m. My favorite time is mid-morning when only a handful of devotees are there. Only the hard-core devotees come when Maharaji's not there, and it radiates sincere love. The room is a bit packed during classical satsang hours when Maharaji is in the hall.

Maharaji sitting on his anghan during morning satsang. This is from my seat on the floor, just 20 feet away.

Satsang begins at 6:30 a.m. I take my place in the front row, seated on my air-padded mat when I hear the alarms.

The sound of shrill whistles and distant drums tell us our Guru, our beloved Maharaji, is en route from his anghan room to grace us with His divine presence and join us for morning satsang. Sometimes He sits and listens to our loving recitations. Other times, He may grab a microphone, create new verses for the pad-kirtans, and enliven them with his mood. He occasionally interrupts the kirtan and speaks philosophically to us. The natives of India in the room laugh and ooh-ahh at what he says in Hindi. I marvel at His casual, informal, always-giving personality. I might get lost by looking at his hands or fingers, spellbound by his smile, voice, and hair. Eventually, He rises and leaves in his motorized wheelchair to take His morning nap after being up with devotees since 3:00 a.m. As He exits the hall, many devotees run alongside Him, shouting out, "Jai Ho!" as the guards along His route blow whistles to announce, *"a Divine Saint is coming through!"* so that people can have the opportunity to see him pass by.

This last morning, my bag is packed, and I am ready for the three-hour drive to Lucknow Airport. From there, I will fly to Delhi and begin the long journey back to the United States. I have an hour before pickup and will spend my last moments in the hall with kirtan and *roop dhyan* meditation, remembering the loving forms of my Guru and of my God.

I sit on the floor, absorbed in my final hour of kirtan, and have a realization: *I blew it.*

I am so angry with myself that I can't contain it. This being my last morning, I should have asked for a brief, private visit to say goodbye to Him personally. It is customary for Westerners who travel so far to request to say farewell in person, and I forgot. *I totally blew it.*

This regret begins to consume me. *I love my Maharaji so much.* He is all I need and all I want to know. Seeing Him once is a miracle blessing, and I'm about to be separated from my loving Guru till I can return. And one never knows if this time is the last. Let's not just *carpe diem*; let's *carpe noctis,* too (seize the night) and go right for *carpe omnia*—seize it all! Any moment may be your last. The thought of wasting the opportunity to say farewell to Him, see His body before me, and transmit love from my heart before I leave, shatters me.

In a few moments, the kirtan I am immersed in becomes a distant harmony to me as my world shrinks, and the tears roll from my eyes and stream down my cheeks in regret.

I am so sorry... sorry that I am such a careless, worthless human, too stupid to truly realize the significance of all He teaches and miss the opportunity to be next to God. So sorry to be such a disappointment to Him. He teaches us and pounds into our heads that

God is *all* that matters. We should absorb every moment with Him into our minds, yet here I am, blowing my chance to be at His side. He gives Himself to us endlessly and selflessly, letting us see Him, speak to Him, and be near Him; to make us a tiny bit more enlightened today than we were yesterday. And I am so caught up in my meticulous travel details that I blow past the rare grace of having one last darshan of Him before I leave and return to the world.

And it's too late. My car will be here in fifteen minutes. I'll never make it to His room, ask to see Him, and be granted access when He is resting. My head sinks. I sing along with the kirtan, and the words are choked in my quiet, private sobs. Any other devotee might look at me and think I'm in bhao, a state of spiritual ecstasy, rather than shame for being such a stupid human to neglect such a divine opportunity.

What's that?

What's all that commotion?

Those are whistles blowing in the distance! Maharaji has left His room, and they are announcing it. Wait a second!

The whistles are singing in succession to His route, telling us He is coming *this* way, even though it's not time for His darshan in the hall. He was there hours ago and isn't expected again till evening, yet those whistles confirm that He is on his way!

The whistles announce He's passed the gate to the road. He has passed the turn to the temple, the office, the dining hall…

He's coming *this* way!

In an abrupt instant, my Guruji is at the entry to the prayer hall. I sit in the front row, pining for Him. This seat on the floor is where I sit every day, just inside the entryway. He arises from his wheelchair and saunters, with His unusual, characteristic gait, toward his anghan, the large bed where He reclines when in the hall. He lies back and relaxes, nodding his head to and fro with the kirtan melody and beat.

Devotees quickly crowd into the hall, desperate to see and impress our Divine Master by being in attendance at off-hours.

My tears go from regretting a missed opportunity to absolute joy. I consider that I might be delusional as I wonder, "Did He hear and feel my anguished longing and appear partly for me?" I don't know. I can never know. He says nothing; He just *IS*. His boundless presence is here now, and it is all I care about.

The Bhakti path, its Rasik Saint representatives, and my Maharaji put great emphasis on the significance of *longing*. Called *virah (veer-ah-ha)* in Sanskrit, the scriptures and saints teach that there is no higher form of love and devotion than longing. Your tearful, heartfelt, and sincere yearning for God and Guru evokes them in you. My Master has made it very clear that when you fully love and long for God and Guru, they become *your* devotee. They become the servants of their servants.

My yearning was true and without condition. I did not pray, request, or demand. I wept in longing, and He appeared.

Jai Ho!

Prem Mandir temple and ashram grounds, Vrindaban, India. Solid marbly, carved mostly by hand.

<u>**40.**</u>

<u>STRING OF PEARLS, CROWN OF THORNS</u>

> It is such a dham (abode) where Radha and Krishn always play.
>
> —Kripalu Maharaj (Rasiya Madhuri)

The ashram has changed. What was a village last I'd come is a small city now. My Guru's reputation had been worldwide before, but His limitless service to humanity has made Him globally legendary. His spiritual teachings are becoming a major religious revolution, and His charitable works worldwide would make the Red Cross blush. He is *my* Guru, but He is also Guru to millions of others. And it is good to be home.

I sit in the satsang area just outside his room, large enough for dozens of devotees to gather, where He used to give darshan every morning after His 4 a.m. walk. We now have morning satsang here at 4:30 a.m. to start the day, and I feel keenly aware of my here and now. I've uncovered a good reason for the NDE phenom: it intensifies your understanding of life's blessings. I was always aware of the micro miracles of life as well as the grand ones. But the idea that medical science predicted I'd be a bedridden vegetable but am instead an American pilgrim in western Asia fills my molecules with a sweet nectar.

Morning satsang ends, and people rise and filter out the door, but I remain seated. I've got nowhere to go but here. Breakfast will be in the dining hall in an hour, and this spoiled Westerner just wants café-coffee. I planned ahead and brought instant. All I need is hot water. My devotee-satsangee sister, Marsha, has agreed to provide hot water while we visit for the first time in years.

As I rise to leave the anghan, someone stops me. "Excuse me... are you Krishnanand from California?" asks one of the many volunteer satsangee administrators.

"Yes..."

"Don't leave yet. Bari Didi wants to speak with you. Please hold on."

I'm taken aback. The eldest daughter and the now-president of the charitable trust and mission knows my name, knows I'm here, and wants to speak with me!

I had met her on previous trips, knew of her reputation, and accepted her as a true Saint. Being in Her casual atmosphere was subtle but remarkable. Why would she want to speak with *me*? I don't matter and hadn't exactly announced my visit.

The volunteer brings an iPad tablet to me, and she is on Skype from the Delhi hospital, where she is a cancer patient. This is all happening so fast that I've not even considered what it means. She asks me how I feel and says she's glad to see me. It becomes clear that Katie didn't betray my secret only to Marsha but to this Divine Personality too.

"Yes, I'm doing better," I respond. "It's all very hard, and I don't want to be any trouble or concern, but I am doing everything I can to try to come out of this."

Bari Didi: she has such a fair complexion she was denied entry to Jagannath Puri too! The daughter of Kripalu!

We exchange a few sentences of conversation, and Her attention is comforting and wonderful. She is discreet with Her concerns, yet Her sincerity is intense. Interacting with a saintly personality is a bit mind-boggling: they're so *boundless* yet humble and accessible. Your emotional mind knows you're speaking with a *parush*, but your intellect tells you to just be yourself, for God's sake!

I walk from the anghan to Marsha's small ashram apartment for coffee and pause beneath a dark stairwell. I erupt in tears as I realize how profound my life experience and spiritual opportunity are: I am in India, having the direct darshan of a Rasik Saint who is concerned about me. I don't want to die now, *but I could* because living can't get more beautiful.

The complete and absolute sorrow I have endured nonstop for seven years is incomparable. In a few instances, the light from divine love and grace has eliminated the pitch-black darkness of tragedy.

How dare I?

How dare I ever need more? How dare I consider succumbing to the sorrow of matter instead of surrendering to the eternity of my divine parent?

A month ago, I could find no evidence of value in my life. And now, I am traveling the world in luxury, associating and conversing with a true avatar of the divine power of love. Just a few weeks ago, my life's purpose was to endure my current life and several others while hoping to deserve to meet my Guru in His *next* appearance. Now, I'm filled with the hope of an opportunity to meet Him again at the end of *this* lifetime.

My tragedies are unprecedented and off the charts. *But so are my triumphs*. I can't seem to be moderate in death or in life. It's either all or nothing. And at this moment, every shred and instance of suffering is so fucking worth it.

I would volunteer for it all again—*volunteer* for it, to be near and dear to *any* Saint. But I don't have just *any* Saint in my corner of the boxing ring, do I? I have *THE* Saint!

I spend four days in the ashram village. There is a sadness in the satsangee community. Maharaji ascended from here six years earlier, and now His eldest daughter is in the hospital with Her two sisters by her side around the clock. We are unspeakably grateful to have shared even a moment with Them, but their time is concluding here, and we already mourn Their loss.

I stick to my India travel routines: I travel to Vrindaban and Barsana to tour some of the sites sacred to our tradition. It is hard to do what was so easy before, but I just keep putting one foot in front of the other and try not to fall.

I visit my dear friend and devotee, Uddhao, at Kusum Sarovar. The last time I'd seen him was during the 2013 trip with Janete, months before NDE-Day, when I made that promise to write of our story with him.

I was distraught when I could not find him on the grounds. It was gently raining, and no one was in sight. As I returned to the car where Janete waited out of the rain, one lone visitor walked in my direction with his head bowed against the downpour. As we passed each other, he glanced up; it was Uddhao. Despite having met just a few times over many years, he recognized me instantly, grinned broadly, and we fell into each other's embrace. The three of us spent over an hour in his bhajan kuti hut.

He told us of his childhood when his family took in a wandering sadhu mendicant who would later become our Jagadguru, Kripalu Maharaji.

When Maharaji visited Uddhao's family in the 40s, He would suddenly appear from the woods adjacent to Kusum Sarovar. He would stay for days, sometimes weeks, and devour food offered to Him. It is said in The Bhagavatam that God and Guru relish anything offered to them with love, and this tall, thin, and youthful Kripalu would eat up enough food for five full-grown men in a single sitting. Whatever they brought to Him, He ate!

He would disappear for days, too, and Uddhao's family would mourn him, assuming tigers in the forest had accosted him. And one day, he didn't come back, and they lamented.

Twenty years later, a large tour bus arrived at Kusum Sarovar with dozens of spiritual devotees asking to have satsang on the beautiful landings over the pond of this sacred place. The young man-boy who had come to them from the wilderness years before was now a Jagadguru. He was considered the Jagadguru of *all* the Jagadgurus. He now came with happy devotees who had thought tigers ate him. They donated generously to the temple grounds and sang kirtan in unison.

As Uddhao finishes this story with his eyes aglow, I collapse at his feet, overcome with grace and gratitude. I recognize that I am in the presence of a Saint, tears gushing from my eyes. I reach out to touch and kiss his feet, but he withdraws them. This humble servant of the Lord removes His feet from my touch because he doesn't feel he is worthy of *me*.

Me. A worthless, material-minded man from the West. This is the depth of his humility. I cannot express how unworthy of him, or any True servant of the Lord and Kripalu, I am, yet he feels his feet would soil me. I have now kept my promise to share the leela we had with this devotee.

But during this latest visit, we found each other right away. This time I brought him special gifts from the ashrams, and we walked hand in hand across the road to his humble home. He introduced me to his eldest son, who introduced me to the cows in their garden. We then spent time alone in his small, private temple room, did aarti to Radha Krishn together, and he revealed to me a never-to-be-forgotten darshan he had with our Maharaji. It is one of the most profound and glorious things I've ever heard or ever will. Consistent with Maharaji's sweetness, it is simple yet magical. It is far too private and sacred to share publicly, but I draw from it occasionally to remind myself how blessed I am to have had the association with this dear devotee, Uddhao. I have documented this story and secured it away. I don't know if I will ever be qualified to share it with the world.

I bid my friend and brother goodbye and continue to my next parikrama stop.

Bhramar Geet (Song of the Honey Bee)

Years ago, my Swamiji revealed his particular fondness for chapter 47 in the tenth canto of the Bhagavatam. In this set of verses, a honey bee buzzes near a *gopi* (country maiden) who longs for Krishn. This is no ordinary longing, for she is in a state of *maan* (divine love anger). He explained the canto to a group of devotees gathered at His feet in the prayer hall early one morning.

"This maiden is no ordinary gopi." Swamiji's sly smile hints that something delightful is about to be explained. "This gopi is Radha Herself. Her very name is too holy even to mention in the Bhagavatam.

"Radha is sitting alone in the *vana* (forest), feeling the sweet irritation (*maan*) with Krishn. Only someone so close and beloved to Supreme God can have such feelings," Swamiji explains. "It is a *divine anger*, which adds a new charm to the *leela* (divine play). Radha is upset with Krishn because He has not returned from Mathura and has sent his emissary, Uddhao, instead. Only Radha can experience *maan*, and Krishn cannot live with Himself when she is in *maan*! He will do anything to please her and wants to return to Her good favor. So, he takes the form of a bee and buzzes to her, alone in the vana." Swamiji gives humble devotees the inner meaning, telling us that Shri Radha chastises the bee for being so thoughtless and insensitive. Her dialogue with the honey bee reveals the highest states of longing and love for God. Verses that seem cute and trivial to the untrained devotee have such profound meaning and depth it takes a Saint to explain their true essence.

I never forgot this tale and how Swamiji shared it with us. The leela site is included in my parikrama book, and I decided to go and see it. I walked the grounds, now barely a crude patch of dirt, in a remote area of the countryside. I met the poojari and reveled at standing where my Shri Radha had teased the honey bee over 5,000 years ago.

Adjacent to this site is where the renowned Uddhao parked his chariot 5,000 years ago. On this spot, the gopis enlightened him on the superiority of *personal, selfless, Divine Love* over samadhi consciousness.

My senses are so overwhelmed by the depth and meaning of my blessings I cannot react. I stroll the grounds, take it all in, and then return to the driver waiting for me. I look forward to hours and hours of sweet, blissed-out meditations from the memories of this parikrama moment. *Why me?* I always ask myself. *Why am I so blessed?* Thousands have done more *seva*, have Maharaji's close darshan, and have served in sadhana for years before I ever came along. Why me?

The answer I think I hear, floating upon the sound of a divine flute, is, "*What does it matter?*"

I spend my last night in the Barsana ashram, determined to walk the sacred hilltop of Barsana, as I have done so many times before.

It is an arduous, challenging hike through the holy village of Barsana and along the narrow trail winding up the hill to the temples at the top. I had saved this walk till the end of my *parikram* and had intended to set off after a leisurely coffee, kirtan, and breakfast, but something told me not to wait. I head out just after dawn and return before 8 a.m. with the whole day to kill rather than leave early and sit in the Delhi airport.

As I drink some coffee at a roadside hut with a thatched roof, I take out my cell phone and read my WhatsApp message: *The Didis will be in Delhi this afternoon.* I couldn't visit with them because of the medical procedures the eldest sister was enduring, but all three of them would be at the ashram center in Delhi in a few hours. The Delhi ashram is en route to the airport. Guru's Grace seems to be lining things up.

My driver is somewhere nearby. Many of them live so frugally that they sleep in their cars. It is considered disrespectful and insulting to offer them lodging or show any form of sympathy. I respect the Asian boundary and send a WhatsApp text for him to come *now*.

The Divine Sisters (Didis) are not receiving visitors, but it is a genuine opportunity simply to catch a glimpse of them. After all, I've come all this way, I walked the hill early, and it all seems propitious.

The trip to Delhi is nerve-wracking at best. If you ever want to have your own NDE, just travel through Asia! Don't drive yourself; you'll never survive it at all. Have a local driver take you where you want to go, and you will qualify for one or several NDEs! Everybody should do it at least once. By comparison, bungee jumping is for pussies! India driving is a unique adventure of near collisions with other cars, pedestrians, and even elephants. You can try to close your eyes and sleep through it, but the chaotic music of the Tata trucks' horns keeps you on high alert. I arrive in Delhi in one piece, thanks to the skills of my driver.

A handful of devotees in the Delhi ashram rejoice in the return of the ailing Saint. Nam Sankirtan reverberates through the large house as She takes her physical therapy stroll on the top level, where we can all see Her and enjoy Her darshan. My driver waits outside; I've got to rush to the airport very soon.

As I stand to go toward the exit, I feel a warm rush of gratitude that I was able to visit. Then someone calls my name: *"Hey, Krishnanand—Radhey, Radhey..."*

I pause, turn, and see a devotee I know from Los Angeles. "You can't leave," she tells me.

"Huh? What? I have to catch my flight. I'm already pushing my luck for time. Why? What's up?"

"Yeah... you can't leave. Choti Didi wants to see you."

Choti means 'youngest' in Hindi. Who the hell am I to prioritize catching a plane on time over following the request of a Divine Sister?

I wait in a doorway, and the youngest of the three sisters comes to me. She asks how I'm doing and what my plans are. I am surprised they know *who* I am, let alone that I am *there*. This stop was unannounced and spontaneous.

"I don't know my plans. I need satsang, Didi. The LA ashram is over an hour from where I live, so I can only go for formal satsang once a week. I don't have the focus to do it on my own as I should. I need satsang."

She suggests I consider moving to or near the US ashram, and I promise to do so. She can sense my mind, knows my heart, and does not need lengthy explanations. God is omniscient, knowing your thoughts and feelings at every moment. Saints are *selectively* all-knowing; they can sense what is in your mind and heart if they choose to look, but they don't do psychic stuff; it's well beneath them. I invite Her into my consciousness as we talk. She asks about my intention to die.

"I have accepted that my conditions may not improve, and my karmas are set in sorrow, but Katie's intervention through Maharaji's Grace and my being here have turned my attention. I am willing to suffer if that is my destiny. I've done my best to do so gracefully and with strength, but I'm out of energy. I will endure whatever God has planned for me."

She emphatically states that suicide is an unforgivable sin. That's it: the Vedic loophole for self-termination is officially closed! A true Saint has told me to my face that it will be considered a *namaparadh:* a direct transgression against your Guru which is unforgiven unless and until that specific Guru Himself/Herself forgives you *in person*. I will *not* do *anything* that offends my Guru! And it ain't about fear. He is personified love and grace! So it's more about never wanting to cause Him worry or disappointment.

"I will press on, Didi. Hell on Earth is not my choice, but I will adhere to your *agya*[20]. I will not harm myself, and I will look into relocating to the US ashram. Thank you, *Jai Shree Radhey*." And with a bow at the waist (*pranam*), I leave for the airport, my head swirling from so much divine intervention.

On the journey home, I decide to visit the US ashram and explore housing and living options to see what, if anything, develops.

My flight home was creatively engineered. I learned years ago to select a flight with a layover in a place I wanted to tour. With a few calls and some effort, you can change a four-hour layover to a four-*day* layover at no extra cost. Then I can fund my lodging and local transport to a place where I've never been. I had five days in London and visited Stonehenge on my last trip to India using this strategy. Next stop: Japan.

My four-hour layover from India to Los Angeles was in Tokyo. I rerouted the flight from Tokyo so I could depart from Kyoto instead and changed my five-*hour* connection to a five-*day* layover. The airline didn't give a damn where I flew from or when I departed as

---

[20] Agya is Sanskrit for a *direct order* from God/Guru.

long as it cost the same or less. If it made the trip more expensive, I just paid the difference. My Kyoto flight back to LA cost less, so they adjusted it with no problem.

I take the nuclear bullet train from Tokyo to Kyoto and can see almost the entire island out the train window. Mt. Fuji looks like a candy top on a cake. I spend four days walking the old capital of the island nation. In many ways, this may seem like a gratuitous account of events from a spoiled American—and it is, to an extent.

Travel to India is spiritual salvation, but this Kyoto detour is therapy. Some take antidepressants; I walk for hours in exotic cities.

I'm not trying to have fun. I can't because my brain damage still produces copious fear while being stingy on joy. Everything is scary, awkward, and hard, but so is doing *nothing*. I am in a state of fear and depressed uselessness, whether I am trying not to get lost in Japan or sitting on the sofa watching reruns of The Fresh Prince. Adventuring requires so much focus; it distracts me from the angst my brain is pouring from its broken synapses. No... I'm never having *fun*. Yes... I'm sad and scared all the time. So, why not do it in Japan? If I ever *do* get a life, I'll have something to enhance it. At the very least, it'll make a good story someday.

My fourth book, *Road Games—Bizarre Stories, Curious Tales,* is a collection of short fiction stories inspired by and based on my real-life adventures. Kyoto inspires a new tale, as my few days here have been both bizarre and curious. When you *plug into* the supernormal layers of life, they unfold in front of you. The quality of my life's events is similar to that of 'Neo' in 'The Matrix': I don't see the world through Matrix lenses but rather through magical, mystical ones. The bullets I dodge are just more proverbial.

I'm grateful, but I often wonder and even fantasize about normalcy. It looks so... *content*. And my bizarre circumstances are a double-edged sword: profound with triumph yet abounding in razor-slicing tragedy. My life is a string of pearls and a crown of thorns.

The Asia sojourn comes to a beautiful ending as my class of travel allows me delicious on-tap lagers in the Osaka business lounge. I text pictures of *Ain Soph,* the amazing vegan eatery I had discovered, to Brandon. Although it's a Japanese vegan restaurant, it has a Hebrew name from Kabbalah. It's a match made in heaven to a Zen/Kabbalist.

I arrive back in Los Angeles and home to the beach. I still *prefer* to be dead, no doubt. My life... *sucks ass.* My problems came with me to India and made it into my carry-on for the return flight, too. My loneliness and countdown to poverty are still here and ready to party. The grandeur of my residence, with its beach life and yog in the park, is stained by the daily reminder of how I haven't a soul to share it with. I often gaze weepily at the setting sun over the Pacific Ocean while sitting comfortably on a quiet dune. I am absorbed in the gorgeousness of it and saddened there is no one to enjoy it with me.

Intentional death is off the table. I now know that God- Realization within this lifetime is possible, but it seems well out of my reach. I am so unhappy that I can't see beyond the darkness. But I must press on. I must lay off the pursuits of love and career and concentrate on the pursuit of spirit.

The Didis made it clear that I would *not* be forgiven for self-execution, no matter how much I adhered to Vedic rules. It's time to keep my promise of looking into relocation.

It is time to dedicate this fucked-up, broken life to ashram life and full-time sadhana in the imagined hopes I can recover and function well enough to progress spiritually. My new fear is that I will fail at ashram life. I'm afraid that once immersed in a spiritual commune 24/7, I will discover my spirituality is not of the right stuff. I may find that I'm not the deep spiritualist I like to think I am but a superficial pseudo-spiritualist of the type I loathe.

It is a cruel paradox. I live in a vacation-paradise setting, and I am very happy on the outside. But *on the inside*, I live in a dark, shadowy place of isolation and friendlessness. God... karma... destiny... they all need to chill out with the irony. *I get it*. I don't need it hammered into me 24/7 that I am doomed to an existence of half-empty, not half-full. Life on the beach, *but alone-alone-alone;* life in a beautiful home, *but no income,* so I can never truly relax and enjoy. My son is home and becoming smartly independent from my loving effort. *But he is moving on,* as he should, which is an impending addition to my loneliness. He has his own life to live, and I never impose on or crowd him. We can have a beer and get along great, but at ages 24 and 52, we're not on the same social page.

I book a flight to the town of the US ashram. I reach out to a few people there and explain my intention to possibly relocate. One ashram sister is in real estate and will show me some rental options during my visit.

I feel like I've failed. I returned to California to restore my life and love and to help Brandon become more independent. The Brandon mission is accomplished. The other two are complete failures. I am ashamed and embarrassed about my secret of not moving to my spiritual home and sanctuary in the US to spend my life in sadhana, but because I have failed at being safe and whole in the world.

I had often thought that the US ashram could be a retirement destination for me, where I might spend my final years in complete sadhana to solidify my spiritual progress and secure after-life security. But I intended to have my life so stable and secure by then that I would arrive as an asset, not a liability. I feel ashamed that I am going because I have nowhere else to turn; no one else will have me. It feels disrespectful to begin ashram life out of desperation instead of heartfelt, spiritual love.

My love for the ashram, its community, and of course, my Swami teacher who founded it and my Guru Master who permeates it is unquestionable. But would I be stepping out of the world and retreating to ashram living if my career were healthy and I had a companion to share my life? I don't know.

I will go soon and explore the situation as I did with Washington and the Oxnard Shores beach house. I don't know if the mission to relocate will provide similar tell-tale signs, runway-lighting me to take off and land there as the previous two had done.

I've got a plane ticket to go. Is it *"What's next?"*

My exile is over, and it's time to *go home*, but did I come to the wrong address, wrong city, *wrong state*? Time to pack: Radha Madhav Dham ashram, here I come.

_____ **_41._**

OUT OF RETIREMENT

> "Keep your mind continuously attached to Me and do your duty."
> —Krishn (Bhagavad Gita)

It would be nice to retire from counseling with a swan song: a hard-core, hopeless case that only I can rescue and salvage. My specialized areas were anxiety, depression, and severe pathologies like OCD and borderline personality disorder. I had many swan song clients I would carry with me for life. I am warmed by the knowledge that they are functioning well because of our work together when MDs, PhDs, and MFTs failed them. The addicts I've helped are no easy, phone-it-in list of subjects. The parade of clients and families who prayed for me while I was in the hospital are glorious testimony to this. But it's all a blur. As grateful as they (and I) were for saving them, to be honest, *none of them were all that challenging*.

It was hard, rollercoaster work, to be sure. None were ever easy, but neither had any of them stumped me. *I always knew what to do next for them*. I developed a unique and custom formula to save each client. I often had to decide what to do in the next session, but I was never *stumped*. I never had a client that I thought I couldn't help. If a situation could be solved, I could solve it.

When am I *ever* going to learn to be careful what I wish for?

I.M. Hookup

"WAIT A MINUTE! I KNOW YOU!" This Facebook Instant Messenger typed all in caps to emphasize her eureka moment.

"How? How do you know me? I don't know anyone named Ariel. I'd remember that."

I occasionally get instant messages on Facebook, as men are regularly hit up by flirtatious women looking for an opportunity. Translation: scam. But as a single man, IM'ing to pass the time with flirting women is acceptable to an extent. Sure, I know they're likely a middle-aged, balding man in their mom's basement in some Midwest state, catfishing to see if they can sucker a guy into some cash with promises of sex and romance. But since I am wise to this stupid con, I'm okay with some sexting and fun photos.

But this Ariel girl and I have been IM'ing for a couple of weeks, and we've really bonded. She has not asked for anything or given any indication of doing so.

"You were my counselor!" she confesses. "I didn't recognize you by your photos because we only spoke by phone. I don't know you as Krishnanand; I know you as Scott!"

We were both suddenly intoxicated by the moment and switched to a phone call, talking for over an hour. She is on the East Coast (New York), and I'm on the West Coast (California), three time zones away.

She stops shrouding who she is, tells me her real name, and updates me on her progress, or lack thereof.

"I know I'm not clean, and it's because I didn't keep working with you. I swear I think of you every day! You're the only counselor who ever made any sense, and what you taught me has stayed with me this whole time."

While I was living in Washington, an associate contacted me; a woman who is a therapist, asking my advice on how to help a patient. "She's a heroin addict, and I need expert advice." She gave me some background on the case.

"You're way over your head with this," I told her. "This is a very serious, hard-core, IV, die-hard heroin addict who's smart and clever and will run roughshod over you. She and her addiction require a specialist. You want my advice? Put her family in touch with me directly."

"But I thought you weren't taking new clients."

"I'll make an exception. First of all, you're not just a professional peer; you're a devotee sister." (This is the same devotee-sister from the Guardian Angles chapter who hosted that first kirtan event I'd attended and introduced me to Kripalu.) "And second, she's not just a client. You said she's the daughter of one of the most respectable devotees and has been a resident at the US ashram for over twenty years. Put him in touch with me, and I'll see what I can do."

I did not know this father whose 30-year-old daughter was in crisis. He was desperate to save her and still recovering from losing his wife to cancer. He made it clear to me: "She won't speak to any of us and doesn't like or trust any professionals. Even if I *could* speak to her, I'd never convince her to speak with you. She *hates* counselors."

With my usual brand of innovative, never-even-been-in-a-box, customizing, I paved the way for him to have access to her and convince her to meet with me via Skype. In the meantime, I instructed him and the girl's brother, and other concerned family members to take the Project Addiction video course on their own. "I need you all to become addiction experts real fucking fast, and by taking the course as if you were an addict yourself, you will get as close you can, as fast as you can. Agreed? Those are my conditions to take this on."

They agreed and were grateful. I did not ask for full payment. I advised the father what my fee was and asked him to pay whatever he could afford, and told him we would never discuss it again.

This is the arrangement I had for years with devotees that needed help. My Swamiji had asked me to counsel many devotees over the years and instructed me to tell them my fee and let them pay what they could afford. Some paid my full fee, and many paid less, but they all made a sincere effort. This became the standard of my practice across the board: I never refused help to anyone, regardless of what they could pay. Although I never advertised free support, there was some gossip about it, and the community respected and admired me for it. I made a pretty good living for a high-school dropout. I particularly enjoyed making recovery affordable with inexpensive private sessions. It was a bit of a nose-thumbing to the recovery empire.

While I was in Washington, Ariel and I had just a few phone sessions together before she vanished into the underground drug culture again. Her father, a devotee brother I'd never met, completed the video course and book and was grateful. While I was unable to access and help his daughter, he had a real understanding of how addiction truly functions and was empowered to move on. "And," I reminded him, " if and when she resurfaces, you know not only what to do but what *not* to do. And how."

This seemingly random FB IM flirting with a stranger was none other than this daughter I had tried to help. And she was in need again, big time.

"This changes the context of our relationship now. We've been pretty hot and heavy with sexual innuendos, but as your counselor, it is unethical for me to consider you that way."

She disagreed. "But you're not my counselor anymore. What we've had these past few weeks is sweet, and it's the only light in my life. I don't need you as a counselor; I want you as a lover."

"As attractive as that is, and as much as I'm crushing on you now, you've just confessed to me you're in real trouble," I reminded her. Okay, since I am mostly retired from addiction work, you're technically not a current client. Since we haven't spoken in over two years, nothing ethically prevents me from having a so-called *dual relationship* with you. But as a man who cares about you and sees that the undeniable forces of fate have brought us back together, I have to try to help you before I try to fuck you!"

Ariel gives a good laugh, and we agree to remain in touch, and she will try to follow my advice. I'm relieved that this is not a possible bait-and-switch; she had not even alluded to needing help until realizing how she recognized me on FB. Even then, it took many conversations to drag it out of her. She was not looking for charitable rescue. She acted on an intuitive feeling, and now we were intertwined.

I'm somewhat used to the bizarre manner with which the Akashic Agents bring me to the ones I am destined to serve or be involved with, from Brandon to Lia, to Janete, to 70% of my other clients.

However, I also make it clear that, regardless of cosmic kismet, I'm not in a position to give free help anymore. The other condition of providing pro-bono or lower-cost assistance obliged the client to *apply* what I advised. If you get free or discounted service, you had better *use* it. If not, there are dozens of others asking me every day for help.

Mirabai (Ariel was her online alias) is the uncrackable nut. For once, I am truly stumped on how to rescue this woman.

- She is nearly 3,000 miles away
- She is being held captive by her heroin dealer
- Winter in New York is harsh, so continuing to refuse her dealer sex will put her on the icy street soon
- Her opioid dependence is up to 3.5 grams *a day*
- She has no money, and her cell service will cut off any day from long overdue payment

Any day now, her unpaid cell phone service will shut off, and there's no way to revive it. I am willing to assist her if it does not cost me money. I'll help her for free, but not at my expense because that can compromise objectivity! She's living in a scary apartment with her heroin dealer, who will soon demand sex and plans on prostituting her to others, too. Leaving is not an option. The record-breaking cold temperatures outside won't allow a withdrawing junkie to last two days. She has zero money for food, and her 3½ grams of use per day is *fucking excessive!*

Non-dope fiends can't understand the magnitude of this. That daily intake would be hard-core for a 200-pound Hell's Angel biker-type. Very few heroin addicts ever get that strung out, especially a 140-pound 5'4" *girl*! No fucking way! She may be exaggerating for dramatic effect, but there are telltale signs that indicate it must be true. She can't fool me; I lived in the dope culture too long, so I speak the language and know the score. I am successful at getting through to so many because they respect me for being real-deal like they are. There are subtle things we do and say that only an insider dope-fiend can pick up on. She's legit. If I can save this one, it's my parting of the Red Sea swan song case!

Mirabai isn't just a referred client: she *grew up* at the ashram. She was raised on the property since she was a child. She knew the philosophy, adored our Swami-teacher, and her father and mother were two of the founding devotees instrumental in its establishment. I've been a devotee since 2005, well-known and respected by the community; our meeting now, after all these years, can only be the work of *Yogmaya*!

We all agree on this: Mirabai, her father, and I are mystified as to how we've never interacted before.

The only way to save her is to get her away from the dealer, out of New York, and to California. But the logistics are impossible:

- I cannot break my policy of *paying* to help someone, but she doesn't have a dime
- She needs airfare to California and a ride to La Guardia Airport
- She needs food and water for the ten-hour trip across the US
- She needs meds to prevent such severe withdrawals, or she'll have seizures
- She has no identification to get through security
- She has four arrest warrants: three in Texas and one in New York

These are insurmountable. Raising Lazarus from the dead is easy peasy lemon squeezy compared to this.

I tell her I don't know how to pull it off, but I'll figure something out. "In the meantime, I need you to go to your clinic every day for your methadone. You and I both know you can't stop using: your intake is way too high to rely on just methadone. Heroin withdrawals will fuck you up bad, but methadone withdrawals will literally kill you; that shit's evil. Getting you off heroin will be a no-brainer for me. The methadone is going to be a bitch and will make you *pray* for heroin withdrawals again! I need you to titrate your dope intake down a *point* every three days; not *every day or every two*, but every three days, you shave off just a *point*. Will you do it?"

"Yes," she replied. She knows *I* know that a point is dope-speak for a tenth of a gram.

Next, I go through the legal protocols to confer with her counselor at the New York Methadone Clinic. He's on board to wean her down from the methadone as aggressively as possible, too.

My well-honed counselor instincts tell me she's ready. *Everyone* tells me they're done with the life and are ready to walk away, but 98% of them are full of shit. The other thing that has allowed me to succeed where others have failed is that I could bring addicts who were not ready to get clean to true commitment: *rock bottom*.

Mirabai was at rock bottom: scared, with no hope, and so good at using she could live the life into her sixties, just like her dealer-roommate. I told her if she didn't get out now, she would be one of the many lifelong junkies that settle on full acceptance. They will never get clean and don't even try. And there are a lot of them. She agreed that it was a final moment.

I have a master plan.

I scheduled a visit to the ashram to recon a residence so I can relocate. I need to get out of beach life, and I need access to my Guru's satsang. *I'm* desperate too. Maybe not like a junkie, but I'm also at rock bottom, spending far more time fantasizing about a Big Sleep than of restoration.

During my visit to the ashram, my mentality will be different. Instead of behaving as a visitor, I will imagine all I do as a resident to see how it feels. I will do satsang in the temple, walk the grounds, and interact with the residents through different lenses.

I ask to meet with Mirabai's dad during my visit. His partner/roommate is not too happy about his attempts to rescue his smack addict thief of a daughter and is keener on protecting him *from* her. He agrees to meet with me in secret and confidentially.

For the first two days of my spiritual retreat, I look at house rental options. I am thrilled to be in my Guru's US dham again, but the house hunting is disappointing. I'm convinced it is *what's next,* but the ten or more places I see are places I can only tolerate. The same mojo that secured me the Yelm and Oceanaire homes is not flowing. But I'll do what I have been advised to do because I'm not about to disrespect the grand gift of going to India and being told directly by a Saint to consider the option of moving.

On the third day, I meet with Mirabai's father and tell him all I know and that the only solution for her is to transport her from New York to my house in California. I've disclosed the somewhat passionate intentions between Mirabai and me, and he's not affected by the idea. I tell him about the hurdles in our way and that it comes down to finance, and that's the truth.

He can easily sense I am not looking for a handout or making promises I don't intend to keep. We have the same religion, the same spiritual path, and the same Divine Father Guru. He knows I'm legit.

He asks me to meet him discreetly after morning satsang and makes me take an oath never to tell a soul about our conversation. "This never happened," he says as he hands me an envelope with $3500 in it. "Do your best to save my daughter. And never mention this conversation or this envelope again[21]."

On my last day here, I lie in bed as my dorm room's overhead speakers softly broadcast the *aarti* ceremony beginning in the prayer hall. As I get dressed to head to the temple, my phone buzzes; it's Mirabai.

We talk a little, and I tell her nothing more than, "Get your things together. You'll be coming to California soon." She has no clue I am in contact with her father. I tell her that I simply used my status and reputation with the ashram community to raise funds to help another devotee. To this day, she does not know he was the one who broke his vow not to help her again because of too many broken promises in the past[22].

My devotee-sister real estate agent has one more round of rentals to show me before I leave tomorrow. More of the same: they're a bit far or crummy, but I'll bite the bullet, take the least horrible one, and be nearer to satsang. Living on the property itself is not a consideration. Many want to live there, and there is a probation period before being accepted as a full-time resident. Considering my decade-plus reputation as a bhakti-yog devotee, this bothers me. I would think they should allow a provision for me to bypass the regular newcomer protocol, but I respect it. I think it's best to live near and not on the property anyway. I may hate it. They may hate me. It is best to have a private retreat just in case.

But I know that any house more than twenty minutes away may be self-defeating. It's not too far, but how stressful will it be to make it to the dham twice a day with a twenty-minute commute? For a guy who's a bit broken, tired, and needs the spoils of comfort, it is sensible to predict that I will start off very disciplined; but within a few months, procrastination may become as regular as diligence. One last place to see...

And there's that feeling again: the same *welcome home* feeling I got when I accidentally stumbled upon the Yelm home, and the same *you're home* feeling when I found the beach house in California. As soon as we make a right turn onto the quiet country road leading to the house, I feel peaceful. When we pull into the driveway, I see an average, nonspectacular home with a half-acre lawn needing mowed. I feel... *safe.*

She escorts me in, and it's perfect! It is so close to the ashram I can hear the peacocks on the property cawing at each other. It is quiet and clean, and... *it has a fireplace.* There's half an acre out back, another half in front, and ¾ of an acre of private land sheltering me from intrusive neighbors. It is less than a three-minute drive, door to door, to the ashram. My exile may truly be over: *I'm home.*

---

[21] If this factoid is being shared, it is because he gave his consent to tell of it. I wouldn't break my word.
[22] Also sought her consent for this story so she knows from reading it here now

_____ **42.**

CURSE OF THE KITTY

> The goal of a soul is to receive the selfless Divine love of God.
> —Swami Prakashanand Saraswati (Towards the Love Divine)

> We're on a mission from God.
> —Elwood Blues (The Blues Brothers)

No cats? No problem.

I can be pretty high-strung. I stand in the center of the hardwood floor of the home I want to rent and become upset as I study the rental listing details. Rent amount? Check. Utilities and upkeep obligations? Check. Proof of income and prior rental references? Sure, no problem. I've got a PDF editor that can fictionalize bank statements, employment history, income proof, and references... On paper, I could qualify to rent Hearst Castle.

But wait a sec... what's this? *No pets.*

Here we go again! The *first* Oceanaire beach house had a no-pet policy, no exceptions, but it led me to the house nine doors closer to the beach. The home in Yelm, Washington, banned cats because the owner was allergic to them, but dogs were okay. I worked through that by sending a 'pen is mightier than the sword' letter pleading for an exception. I offered to pay a higher security deposit and insisted Chow Chow Bang was not a hair-shedding, litter box-shitting, smelly feline, and they accepted. Do I have to do that *again*?

How am I finding the only homes in the world with these bizarre requirements? This house is on an acre of land in the country! Who moves to an area like that without pets? No one!

My agent friend says, "No! All of the homes on my list allow cats. I did my homework. Gimme that!" As she rips the copy from my hands, she mumbles, "How'd *that* get in here?"

"Please...talk to them. Ask them to make an exception. No one moves to the country on an acre of land without a pet. At least this renter is a single guy with just a cat, not a family of messy kids and smelly dogs!"

Chow Chow bang busting a gut over his power of influence.

Sure enough, they recognize the benefit of a one-cat, childless, bachelor tenant, and a modified lease is en route. Chow Chow Bang is far more part of my solutions than part of my problems. He is a comforting friend, to say the least, and where I go, he goes. All's well that ends well.

Next, I share the news of my move with Brandon. He's happy for me and has been supportive since he first heard of my plan after the Japan-India trip.

"Don't worry, Dad, just go. I'll be fine. It will only be a month between moving out of here in March and my new roommates being available. It's no biggie. I'm just gonna live in my car."

"No, dude! I'll get a one-month extension."

"Dad, no! I work on the beach in a fucking resort, man! I can shower and even stay there for free or for a few bucks when a room is available. I can shack up with friends. I don't even mind crashing in my car a few times. I'm on the beach! It'll be good for me to rough it a little. I'm actually looking forward to it!"

As avid backpackers with portable cookware, tents, and sleeping bags that can withstand below-freezing temperatures, I know Brandon will be fine. He's right; a little struggle and a few nights on the streets helped make a man out of me when I was young. He is actually envious of my hard-luck youth and wants some tough-times stories of his own to tell someday.

Brandon was also more than okay with the idea of bringing in a temporary roommate from New York. "I'll convert my meditation room to a bedroom for her. You'll be working, so your life will barely be different. She's very cool and needs help."

Brandon knows very well I'm no pushover, opening my private life and space to people in trouble. My career as a counselor never interfered with our private lives or my parenting despite my savior-like dedication to clients. I had always been accessible to my clients in every way, but my personal space always had professionally ethical boundaries. I used my own personal life history as examples to teach them, which is a no-no in my profession. Counselors are never supposed to share personal details, but when you master the rules, you can break them. The cornerstone of succeeding with those in crisis was sharing a terabyte of relevant adventures and struggles I've had.

I rarely had a client say I could not understand their problems. The surreal set of difficulties in my life always provided first-person insights or at least reference points. The few real-life experiences I had no frame of reference for, such as childbirth and menstruation, were treated with total honesty; I had no analogies because I could not relate. What I could offer, though, were points that showed that I, as well as everyone, have gender, age, and social class experiences that may be unrelatable to others. But I *never* alluded to my own issues as being more severe or challenging than a woman's. If I did that, the Sisterhood of the Traveling Pants would seek me out like Frankenstein's Monster. I can agree that many female dynamics are more difficult to manage than those of a male.

We penis-wielding humans are a bit tired of being hypocritically judged, though. Women often consider us assholes if we can't be sensitive to their plights, but we are sometimes considered either weak or brutish for having our own. Do you think it's easy having a pineal gland that seeks power and sex nonstop? It's not a fucking choice, and I would bet that the mental and intellectual deficits we experience during raging testosterone are equal in magnitude to raging estrogen. Males and females may express hormonal insanity differently, but it's every bit as wicked. Women cry and men yell. But I have treated males who cry and females who are rageaholics. And there are very few lucky bitches and bastards that are immune to either.

I'm not bringing this wayward heroin addict into my home out of some hero complex. I am not comfortable with a treatment I would *never* condone—letting a client be an in-patient in my home. This is different. (That's what they all say, right?)

I am doing this for Mirabai because I feel it is a direct calling from my Guru, no other reason. I have an obligation to serve my spiritual family as we are all siblings of the same divine parent: our Guru, Kripalu Maharaj.

This has His fingerprints *all over* it!

- Random connection on Facebook? Yeah, it happens...
- An unusual spark between us? That happens, too, but as lonely and desperate as I've become, I haven't lost reason. We've all heard a story of a prison guard who risked career, family, home, and freedom to help an inmate escape because they were blinded by love. Yeah, bullshit. That's nothing more than two really unstable people.
- If Mirabai hadn't been a spiritual family member, I wouldn't give her the time of day. I do not know her or her father personally, but I'm aware that he isn't just a devotee on the same spiritual path. His historical closeness to our Swami teacher and our Guru is all the endorsement I need to go way beyond the call of duty.
- Every step of it gave me clear signs that I should keep moving forward.

The Riot Act

I had already told Mirabai, "You may think I am some do-gooder Samaritan. I assure you, *I'm not*. I'm a self-serving man with his own agendas, and I don't get involved with anything that doesn't contribute to them. I'm not a good father because I'm a good man; I'm a great father because I want Brandon to love, respect, and admire me. I wasn't a faithful and true partner to one woman because I'm chaste, but because I wanted her to love me and be with me *of her own free will*.

"I don't help you because I'm chivalric, Mirabai, but rather because I think there's a much bigger hand in this urging me to play a role in it. I don't know why other than you *must* be worth saving, or our Maharaji Guru wants to give your father some peace regarding his prodigal daughter. Or perhaps it's because I serve God and Guru, and I want *their* love and respect and am willing to earn it in any way they ask.

"I'm a selfish sonovabitch; if I wake up tomorrow and don't have this Quixotic feeling of rescuing you, I will simply walk away with no guilt. And some valuable FYI *for you*: if you make this difficult or turn into an exploiting cunt anywhere along the way, I will remove you like an ingrown hair.

"It is important that you understand the conditions of this intervention and one-time, one-patient recovery facility on the fucking beach in my private life. If you lapse, relapse, or fail to fulfill all the treatment exercises I prescribe, you will be homeless. There will be no warnings beyond this one.

"Make no mistake: if you get passage to sunny Southern California and think you'll get away with shit like you did in other rehab situations, you're wrong. Even one single lapse—you use *one point* of dope, even if it's smoked and not shot—there will be zero tolerance. So long as there's nothing here with your name and this address on it, like mail, I can have you removed within forty-eight hours by the sheriff.

"Here are my requirements:

- You will go to the clinic every day for your methadone dose and will titrate it down as I prescribe to get off it
- You will maintain your sleeping space and personal hygiene and not be a slob.
- You will apply right away for welfare and food benefits to contribute toward the expense of living here.
- You'll be polite and unintrusive as a guest in my home.
- You will drug screen twice a week. My onsite tests are high quality, so trust me, you can't cheat them or get away with using, *ever*. Not even one dram.

- You will do the Project Addiction video course as prescribed with no modifications. And you know what that takes: 20-40 minutes of video *every day*, and you'll complete the *take-away* assignments to show your efforts.

"Other than that, let's keep it casual. If I have to police or babysit you, you're out. I'll put your stuff outside and call the sheriff to remove you. I will advise him of your warrants, and he will be required to take you into custody. You know that, right?

"Your only job is *to get well*. Stay clean, eat, rest, detox. That's it. You're getting the opportunity of the century: a private BnB on the beach in California to get off dope. This is not some fucking dorm room at a halfway house run by Twelve-Step zealots or a facility run by PhDs with no real understanding of how this works. Follow my plan, and you will *learn* how to be clean. We'll wean you off the methadone as low as we can before you free-fall from the last milligrams. There will be a cache of vitamins and healthy ways to endure that brutal, final phase. You don't need to work or go to meetings. You'll use my spare car to go to and from the clinic, *and that's it!* I'm not getting my backup car impounded because you *pause* at a stop sign instead of stop. If you deviate from the five-mile to-and-from trip to the clinic even once, I will call the cops and report the car stolen, and you'll be in lockup by nightfall. And do you think the sheriff will provide methadone or give a single nutty shit about your withdrawals?

"I will bring you to California, get you off dope, and give you a chance to start over. You'll have two months because then I'm moving to the ashram. I've already signed the lease. What you do after that is up to you: stay here, go back to New York, or come with me for a couple of months to get on your feet and reunite with your dad.

"I won't yell or lecture. You know the rules, and if you break them, I will calmly tell you to leave. If you get ugly, *I'll* get ugly. Otherwise, this is your lottery prize, and you can thank our Guru for it. *His Grace* is intervening for you, just as He recently sent someone to intercede for me."

***

My instincts and intuitions tell me she is legit. I have a plethora of backup exit plans in place, and the sensible, practical part of me silently hopes she'll fuck up before she even arrives so that I will be excused from this seva mission. I could only imagine what Brandon thought when he heard my extravagant plans.

"I don't know, man, but if anyone can do it, you can. You went to Washington and built a fucking house and now gave me a place on the beach. You're definitely crazy, and none of what you do should fucking work, but it does."

"But I'm not *charmed*, am I?"

"Hell, no! You've had it *rough!* I know I don't say much, Dad, but you go through way more than anyone and keep fighting. It's true; your life is like weird magic."

"More like tragic-magic, right? I think that's what I'll call it now on my fucking dating app profiles. *My life is tragic-magic: a string of pearls and a crown of thorns.*"

We reviewed what to expect when Mirabai arrives. "When she gets here," I told Brandon, "she's gonna be detoxing very soon. She'll be closed up in her room and in no mood for interacting with anyone, so we'll barely notice her. If there are problems, I will handle them. You don't have to be concerned." I doubt he will be; Brandon is focused on getting his own life together and is rather indifferent to other circumstances.

***

The point of departure is looming. The funds are in place and plans have been staged. Mirabai and I talk and text daily as she tries to work with the detox clinic without her dealer-captor finding out.

I have engineered a rescue mission that would make SEAL Team Six proud. Our spiritual community is nationwide. There's a satellite ashram in New York, and I reach out to our preacher, Nikhilanand, who serves that area. He's only at the New York ashram a few times a year, but luckily, he's there when I call him. *That's tiny miracle #1.*

I address him as "brother" in Hindi and refer to my plan as a mission of *seva,* Hindi for *service,* which is central to our path. "Bhaiya, I need a seva favor, and I must be very discreet about it. You know Mirabai and her father, right?" He confirms he knows them very well, and I jump to the basics. "She needs to be on a plane this Friday, and her phone has died. I can't tell you who she's staying with in New York, and you don't wanna know. It's not dangerous, but you definitely want to be as low-key as you can. I need someone to go to her and give her the boarding pass."

I rattle out the address, asking if he's anywhere close by, assuming he'll tell me it's a big state and it's not near him. "Oh, yeah! That's just a few blocks from me!" We have a Hindu preacher dressed in orange robes from head to toe, with a beard like a Tolkien dwarf, and he is knocking on the door of an apartment in the Bronx where there are known heroin addicts. This should go real smooth!

Nobody answers the door, so he leaves a note for Mirabai at my request, a secret message that won't betray her departure details to her junkie pimp captor. It reads, "Got it! Call me. Urgent! Scott."

I knew I could rely on him, but there was one problem: "I can't take her to the airport that day. I'll be upstate before Friday." *Tiny obstacle #1.*

"Can you think of anyone else who might help in a delicate and sensitive seva?"

"Yeah! Rohit. You know him. He lives right in the same neighborhood." So, I call him.

"Listen, Rohit, we barely know each other, and you may not even remember me, but I have a seva mission to request of you." *Tiny miracle #2.*

I compel this other devotee to serve this rescue mission with no questions asked. He only knows that this stranger is the daughter of a respected devotee; he knows nothing of her condition or addiction. He agrees to bring her to the airport.

"You gotta pick her up at 6 a.m. to take her to the clinic on the way. It opens at 8 a.m. You gotta have here there by seven and wait so she can get her meds before the flight," I instructed him. "Then take her to La Guardia for the Southwest flight to LAX at 10:40. It's gonna be tight with the security shit because she has no ID. I need you to park and walk in with her. Try to problem-solve any issues that may arise." I keep waiting for this volunteer who knows me only by reputation to say, *Whoa, man! Hold on! 7 a.m. commute to a clinic and New York airport with no ID? What's next? You want the shirt off my back?*

And I did: "I need you to give her $20. I can't put her on a flight across the country with a four-hour layover in Chicago with no food or money. Too much can go wrong, and she doesn't have a dime, no kidding." I pause, and he's still on the line. *Medium miracles #3 through #9!*

Rohit doesn't interrupt, so I keep talking. "Please pack a lunch for her to take on the plane. It's gonna be 4 a.m. where I am on the West Coast, but my phone will be on, and I'll be standing by to advise. If her temporary library card is not enough of an ID to get her through security, give them the letter I'm going to send you."

After talking to airline administration, I drafted a letter stating that I could vouch for Mirabai with my status as a certified counselor. They added her to their database as an exception because she has no driver's license or passport. By this time, I know that God's Yogmaya is pulling strings again; there is no way in this fucking world anyone can get through a TSA checkpoint post-nine-eleven with a photo-less *temporary* library card for identification!

Even so, once they run her name for her boarding pass, her *multiple arrest warrants* will have her in custody quicker than she can say, *Bin Laden!*

Mirabai agrees she has nothing to lose. If she remains where she is, she'll be dead or in jail within a month. This is certain.

This New York devotee I had met only a few times agreed to these unrealistic requests. It was mystifying: I wouldn't have done it. No way. WTF? *Now we have a bag-o-miracles.*

Arrangements are set, but I can't reach Mirabai; she hasn't paid her phone bill, and the service has been shut off.

Finally, she calls me from her clinic counselor's phone. "You're booked on Southwest flight 578 out of La Guardia," I inform her. "Get yer shit together. You'll be tanning in sunny California by Saturday."

All will be lost if one detail is off by mere minutes. She understands the pickup time and knows to wait *outside* at 6 a.m. "This guy doesn't even know you—*or me*! He'll be there on Friday at six in the morning, so please make this shit easy on the guy!"

Departure Day

Bigger problem #2: No Mirabai!

I'm lying in bed, too agitated for deep sleep. Sure enough, the call comes: It's Rohit. "Dude! She's not here!"

"What do you mean?!"

"The pissed-off guy who answered the door says she left a half hour ago!"

"Drive to the clinic, please, and keep an eye out for pedestrians!"

Rohit drives and quickly spots her since she's the only pedestrian hauling two massive suitcases down the avenue at dawn.

He brings Mirabai to the clinic for her medication and the documents to show at the airport to clear her for the drugs she'll carry. Finally, after a harrowing morning of near-misses, they're *napping in the La Guardia parking lot with an hour to kill!*

Hooray, huzzah, om shanti, hallelujah!

I urge them to go into the terminal. "What're you waiting for?!" I shout into the phone at Rohit. "You gotta check her and her bags in with no ID and present that letter from the opioid clinic to allow her to carry those drugs! Go! Get in there!"

It took forty-five minutes for Mirabai to check in and get approval from the only manager on duty at 8 a.m. Finally, she waves goodbye to the devotee-chauffer she never knew before and goes through TSA. Meanwhile, I lie prone in my coastal bed, gnawing my nails down to the quick. Mirabai has no phone, so there will be no more communiqué till she arrives in Los Angeles. I can only confirm that her flight is on time. I won't know if she's on board or in custody till I go to pick her up.

My hour-plus commute to the airport is dreamlike as I bask in the ongoing evidence of spiritual involvement. I try not to be greedy, but the selection of wishes granted confounds me:

- Wish for reuniting with my lover? *Denied.*
- Wish for repair to my fucked-up nerves and brain? *Denied.*
- Career? Romance? Companionship? *Denied, denied, denied.*
- Save Brandon? *Approved.*
- Save some stranger addict from New York? *Approved.*

There seems to be a theme: helping myself gets me *bupkis, nada,* nowhere, but helping others is greenlit.

Before Mirabai got on the plane, I instructed her through Rohit's phone, "Get your luggage and just exit. I'll park and will be waiting outside your luggage terminal. And when I kiss you hello, just go along with it..."

She comes out, and we are face-to-face in the crowded pick-up zone. I go for my punchline, saying loud enough for bystanders to hear: "Hey, Sis! So glad you're here! Mom and Dad can't wait to see you!" I wrap my arms around her, both hands on her ass and my wet tongue giving her a sloppy kiss, causing an elder couple from Minnesota to gasp in shock at my incest joke.

I drive us home via the Pacific Coast Highway, enjoying the ocean view out the window and giving her the full Cali-welcome ride home. We both laugh and giggle off and on all the way home, never needing to say aloud how surreal this whole operation has been. We both know a divine hand has been at work. It doesn't need to be verbalized. The California coast has never shone so brightly.

***

Mirabai is funny, charming, and grateful. We set our romantic interests aside as she adjusts to a different time zone and withdraws from smack. Now she can only rely on methadone, which is not strong enough on its own to compensate for heroin. Thankfully, my collaboration with the New York clinic and the one near me was unexpectedly smooth. She is now a patient in their system and will get her detox dose first thing in the morning. Trust me, that is another miracle: the parting of the Red Tape.

It's nice to have a purpose again.

I can't seem to make a dent in the paralyzing coma that *samsara* has put Janete into, nor can I meet even one reasonably stable female. But I'm honored to be involved with something bigger than me and to be thought of for a seva project. My *spiritual* life has obvious trajectory. It's my *material* life that remains in asylum status.

But divine intervention has come my way in the form of a physical therapy clinic. A few months ago, I was riding my motorcycle along PCH. I stopped for gas, and as I rolled out of the station, I lost my balance on an uneven surface. The bike toppled over, and at over 500 pounds, I could not keep it from falling on its side. It pinned my left leg to the ground. Another driver rushed over and helped me stand the bike up. Other than the bruise on my leg, I seemed to be all right… until I noticed pain in my lower back.

I tried not to panic at the thought that I may have reinjured my spinal fusion surgery. Within a few days, I figured I'd rather be safe than sorry and went to the ER. I no longer had PPO insurance, but the state of California gave me medical coverage when I moved here. I didn't even ask for it. One day I received a form in the mail. I filled it out, mailed it back, and was approved for free medical insurance. I must've automatically qualified because my tax records showed zero income since 2014.

I think a tax audit in 2014 prompted the state to send that form. When summoned for the audit, I told the IRS rep I couldn't make it because I was unable to drive and could barely walk. I was certainly in no condition to understand tax questions; I was still doing grade-school reading exercises as part of my therapy.

Audits are no big deal. They're business-as-usual for sole proprietor business owners. Every few years, you are audited and paid a few hundred dollars on the deductibles you tried to get away with, which are caught by the system. My sudden loss of mobility and brain impairment truly moved the IRS adjuster. "My wife had a TBI three years ago, and it's been a real struggle." I heard his voice quiver as he shared. "Let me call you back and see what we can arrange, " he told me. He called back ten minutes later and told me not to worry about it because *it was all taken care of*. The IRS has not questioned or scrutinized me since then. I don't know what box he clicked, but I wonder if I have some sort of lifetime immunity from IRS audit. Cool: I'd rather be able to walk without dizziness than get tax exemptions, but I'll take what I get.

The ER nurse looked at me angrily when I told her I hadn't been to a doctor for over six years. They all said there was nothing they could do. I felt major PTSD symptoms just from *driving by* a hospital, let alone going *inside* one. I had to hold back tears as I sat in the waiting area for this ER visit because it evoked such horrors of my past ordeal. Denial is a wonderful thing. If it came in pill form, I'd have an ongoing scrip for it.

"You should've been having MRIs and fMRIs every three to four months!" the nurse scolded. "We need to check you out. Who let you go this long without care? Your injuries are some of the most severe for an outpatient."

They rifled me to the front of the ER line that day, and I had a complete checkup, fMRI for my brain, and x-rays on my back. I made an appointment to see a specialist and realized that free medical wasn't the garbage I believed it to be. I was getting care and attention I'd *never* received with my PPO and court-settled coverage from the driver who'd hit me.

Within a few weeks, I enrolled in a physical therapy clinic specializing in top-notch advanced sports recovery. The clinic provided ongoing support and care and booked me for follow-up procedures. Physical therapy was a game-changer. I had two sessions a week, and the staff told me they'd never seen anyone so aggressive in their efforts. I was just trying not to embarrass myself during my appointments. Within two months, I mastered the exercises and improved by a solid 70%.

It was still depressing because every session was a glaring reminder of my limitations, but I was beginning to feel more coordinated. I was still dizzy as fuck, and that never went away. But this therapy, combined with yog on the beach twice a week and a weekly visit to a climbing gym, certainly made a positive impact.

Brandon became a solo climber after watching *Free Solo,* a documentary profiling rock climber Alex Honnold. I once dreamed of rock climbing, and that thought inspired me to become a backpacker in the Sierras with Brandon in his youth. Our backpacking adventures led him to take it to the next level, pass me by, and claim his own sport. I watched him train at the climbing gym and was so jealous because I'd never be able to fulfill this dream of climbing with my son. I took what I could get and went to the climbing gym every Friday: for just $12, I'd get harnessed, and an on-staff *belayer* would feed my rope and advise me. Why every Friday? Because the Friday noon session had the least attendance. I had the belayer and the climbing wall all to myself. It was a helluva workout, and while I thought I sucked at it, it was fun and fulfilling. My self-critique was unfair, though. I did slightly better than average, and I had plenty to be proud of for being 50+ years old with a missing disc and brain trauma.

I advise *everyone* to *sample* everything that makes them feel sad because they think they can't do it. Try it. If you can do it at all, *try it some more.* Don't give a shit if you're not very good at it or don't have much fun. Indoor rock climbing wasn't *fun* for me; it was a bitch. I could scale that wall only three times in a 50-minute session. It wore me out, and my muscles worked so hard that I could barely grip the steering wheel driving home.

But after...

After an hour of yog in the park, which kicked my ass and made me dizzy to the point of stumbling... After fifty minutes on the climbing wall, making me too tired to take a beach walk in the evening... After twenty minutes of hitting a goddamn tennis ball against a wall and being grateful I didn't face-plant while I did it... After my weekly hikes up the Scenic Trail off the Pacific Coast Highway, where I soaked in the ocean view...

After...

I feel great. When it's over and done with, I can't go back and *undo* what I did. My somewhat pathetic efforts to be more capable than before are permanently etched in the annals of time. I don't feel just great. I feel *fulfilled*.

Every day is a challenge. I cannot stop the suffering or reverse my nerve damage to run across a tennis court and hit a backhand again. I'm fucked-up and seriously broken. But I'll be damned if death is gonna get a day off on my account. If that grim reaper blinks for a moment, I will dash out of reach. If karma eases its foot off my throat for a second, I'm going to jump up and sprint out.

These are the cards I've been dealt: no straights or flushes or even pairs or face cards. It helps to have a trick up your sleeve.

____ *43.*

TEXODUS

> Divine Love devotion is not anything apart from your goals of life,
> it is rather a *'way of life.'*
> —Swami Prakashanand Saraswati (Towards the Love Divine)

We've got less than two months.

My Oceanaire lease ends March 1st, and the new one starts the same day.

Mirabai makes Wonder Woman look like a wussie.

It normally takes years of titration to go from her dosage of methadone to zero. The clinic initially refused to follow my prescribed plan out of concern for Mirabai's well-being. We both sign waivers and accountability affidavits to appease them, and there's a betting pool to see how long she goes before begging for mercy and a higher dose. Her New York clinic counselor with the recognizable Brooklyn accent says it can't be done, but if anyone can do it, she can.

As a veteran dope fiend himself, he's been routinely flabbergasted at this rather small-framed young woman: he's never seen a female heroin addict survive her level of abuse *or* aggressive detoxing. I pump her full of high-quality, time-release vitamins and keep her properly hydrated. She follows my personally crafted diet with carefully balanced carbs, fats, proteins, and calories. I take her to the edge of what a body can handle and then some. She is suffering endlessly, but she has a sparkling disposition in spite of it and insists on shopping and preparing meals several times a week. Her cooking is gourmet to two bachelors. She doesn't make a mess in the house, and even though she resists my demands to take walks with me for circulation, she eventually gives in and does it.

Other than her obsession with true-crime documentary dramas on YouTube and cable channels, she's a delight to have around. We all get along well, and she is intelligent and respectful. She does not express her gratitude in words, but it is obvious.

It's nice to have a friend to joke and laugh with, and I'm pleasantly surprised I can get along so well with someone in her thirties. Our romantic and lustful intentions evaporated when she arrived, which I theorized for her:

"Swamiji and Maharaji have a bit of fun with me. They know I'll do anything they want of me, without question, but I may have difficulty interpreting their instructions, so they get my attention the failsafe way: romance and sex.

"They know that I'm mostly retired from helping others. The world can fuck off; it's either pay me or get lost when it comes to my superhero work nowadays. If you'd been a fat or ugly girl IM'ing me on Facebook, I wouldn't have even replied, let alone get involved. I need to get paid or laid, and then I'll bring all I have to the table. You and I started sexy and became very connected in heart. I wasn't blind to it being a matter of impulse that might not mean shit in the light of day. But once I signed on, I did it the only way I knew how: *all the way*.

"No doubt, that was part of the motivation; I wanted to fuck your naked ass and lie next to your nude body and have a sweet connection. But I knew that was a million to one in reality. I figured early on that Fate was dangling this pussy-carrot in front of me to get me busy. I'm okay with that and am happy to keep Akashic Agents entertained!

"We're not *lovers*, and we're not going to be. We have different paths to follow. But *you* needed rescuing, and *I* needed someone to rescue. I felt unloved and unappreciated, which I am! But Maharaji's evoking me out of retirement to save a devotee's daughter gives me purpose and helps distract me from how sad and lonely I am. I made that incest joke at the airport when I kissed you, but we were already more like siblings than lovers. We've both been through some rough times, and we needed a little fantasy to get this mission underway."

Mirabai agreed that there had been an attraction, and neither of us felt it was immoral or unethical to jump each other's bones. It isn't a big factor now. Maybe later. Maybe not.

We have our hands full. I have a 2100-square-foot house to pack and move 1400 miles away in less than sixty days. We have to get her detox stable enough to endure the drive to the airport, the flight to Austin, Texas, the drive to a new house, and then sleep on floors for several days until the movers come with my stuff.

She still has to decide whether to come with me, stay in Southern California, or return to New York. It's up to her, but I counsel her with my patented style. I never *tell* anyone *what* to do; I merely explore the most likely outcomes of the various choices one has. This way, they can decide on their own.

"You have just a few options. First, you could return to New York, where you have nothing and no one. I don't see this as much of a choice.

"If you stay in Southern California and get a job while you're still detoxing, you can get some cash together and find a room to rent. Not a bad option *if you can pull it off*. If you had three thousand dollars, I could even sell you the Saturn. SoCal with no car is not easy, and I can't and won't give it away. You need to find the job and the room quickly because we're almost out of time, and you've got another month of serious health issues. Even when you're done with methadone, you'll need two or three weeks to recover. You've been on serious dope for four years. Your body is shredded and needs time to rebound.

"Another option is to come with me; you'd be back in your hometown, and your ex-boyfriend will be out of jail there in a year. Your dad is also there, and you know the place. The downside is you left Texas for a reason, and you've worn out your welcome there. You got warrants and legal issues that could cause problems. On the other hand, you need to deal with these someday. Your reputable, respectable addiction counselor can testify about your addiction recovery in court, and with my endorsement, you can beat these out. The most you'll see is a month of jail time, but if you leave this alone, it's gonna bite you hard someday. And take it from an ex-criminal: it won't get you for years. It'll wait. It'll wait until you're happy, working, got a house, maybe a kid... *and then?* Bammo! You get picked up on some old warrant when you run through a stop sign taking your kids to school, and they watch Mommy being hauled away to jail. The sooner you deal with this, the better.

"If you wanna come with me, you can. I've gone well above the call of duty, but I'm not gonna set you adrift now that I've saved you from the shark-infested waters. You can have your own room, same as here, for a few months. It will give you a chance to get a job, reunite and make amends with your dad and brother, take care of the warrants, and go live your fucking life.

"Staying in SoCal is tempting; it's gorgeous here, but it's also expensive. It's a land of opportunity, but it's very competitive. There will be a dozen other candidates applying for every job and room to rent, and you got some very serious black marks on your current resume.

"I wish I had brighter news, but you and I are 'outta the frying pan and into the fire' people. You are honestly the only one who can even *dare* to claim hardship if I am in the same room."

Her eyes grew wide at my seal of approval as I endorsed her challenges. She knows that what I've been through is an entire *lifetime* of surreal challenges and blessings on an unprecedented level. At just 35, she was as near to my degree of struggles as I'd ever seen and nearly as strong. As I learned the unexaggerated details of her background, I was not only entertained but inspired. Many endure hard times, but I was cursed with a supernatural degree of them that makes all others boring by comparison. Mirabai is the real deal: hard-core dope fiend, graduate of the school of hard knocks, muthafuckin' survivor.

Growing up, I was involved with a sinister gang of notorious dope fiends and criminals, which I detailed in my first memoir. In my decade of counseling, I've rarely met anyone who came close to their level of offenses and drug abuse. I was so good at counseling because the never-ending stream of addicts I dealt with was child's play compared to what I'd seen and done. My clients respected the shit out of me because I didn't offer generic, college-degreed remedies. I presented the fucking truth, and they could not outsmart or outdo me. This little 5'4" woman was handling the fiercest withdrawals I'd ever seen with a smile on her face and a good attitude.

"But do as you will, my dear. I have to leave for the forthcoming chapter of my drama to see *"what's next."* I want the best for you and certainly hope my role in your journey will be long-lasting. But whether you stay clean or join a drug cartel, my mission is accomplished; I've taught and guided you and preserved your life, and you owe me *nothing*. You're better off now than before you met me. I'll always try to advise you and be a friend to you. But I can't support you materially. I can only support you emotionally, mentally, and spiritually, and even that has its limitations."

"I think I'll go with you. I know you've been unable to find a decent barber over the last seven years and three residences, so I'll come along till you find one."

Mirabai makes the best tacos in the world and gives me the best haircuts I've ever had in my entire life, hands down. She is multitalented but a little lost.

"I appreciate your concern for the barber industry."

"Well, it's my service to humanity. It's pretty obvious the next barber that gives you a bad haircut will trigger a mass shooting incident, so..."

"Hardy-har. Look, man! It ain't just another bad haircut for me. This back can only carry so many straws! You can hit me in the face with a truck and break my heart with lost love, but *for fucksakes, can't I at least get a decent haircut?!*"

***

I'm no longer running *from* something. Now I'm running *to* something: my Guru Master's dham.

I will move to this house in the country, go to satsang, immerse myself in sadhana, and do the only thing I like and am still good at: *write*.

Any time and energy I do not dedicate to sadhana will be spent writing. Awards don't pay bills. I will attempt to be a well-paid, solvent author; whether I pass or fail will be determined.

It's *"what's next."*

I'll move to the ashram with Mirabai, complete her rescue mission, and write my next book. This plan is crystal clear, yet *'write the next book'* is a bit nebulous. What will that book be?

Will it be a magnum opus work? The one I've always dreamed of composing? A single, comprehensive volume providing the true histories, meanings, and practices of this world's religions and spiritual philosophies? I'm familiar with them all and a master of several. Like Project Addiction: The Complete Guide to Using, Abusing, and Recovering From Addictions and Habits, I want to create a one-stop shop for all one needs to know about religion and spirituality. It will be a single master volume created so other spiritual aspirants don't have to read entire libraries of work like I had to do to understand them

Or will I document my TBI-NDE experience to help others maneuver through them safely?

I don't know yet.

I may have a big-headed ego, but I'm not keen on making it about 'me.' I never wanted *A Stone's Throw* to be about 'me' but rather about the remarkable events and triumphs of the human experience. I didn't even want to use my own name. I thought the mystery would be great marketing and would emphasize the theme that this could happen to anybody, even you. My book shepherd, a hired gun coaching me through the publishing process, persuaded me to use my name: "People will be buying *you and your experience.* When you tour to promote the book, a face and a name will be required." I crafted the entire 325-page book, cleverly and subtly, without revealing the anti-hero's name. I insisted it wasn't about *addiction per se.* It was about triumph over a wreckful youth.

My NDE story won't be about 'me,' either. I want to emphasize concepts and realities far beyond one man's identity. Besides, my losses are still too intense and ongoing to relive through my patented, evocative style.

***

I make as much peace as I can with the notion I'm abandoning Brandon and Janete. But Brandon's fine, and Janete has to live out her own karm. The gift of Grace recently revealed to me that I can attain Spiritual Transcendence in this lifetime. This adds context to the wreckage and extreme measures the spiritual forces have used to separate me from any potential distractions and attachments.

Mirabai and I plot the course. Very soon, her recovery condition is going to be incapacitating. Where we're going, she will not be able to continue a methadone treatment, so it needs to be done and over. Methadone is *far* more addictive than heroin and makes you more physically dependent, too. Heroin withdrawals will make you *wish* you were dead, but methadone withdrawals will literally *kill you*.

It takes *years* for addicts to wean down from methadone. It is a virtually useless treatment method that assures failure. It turns heroin addicts into methadone addicts. It was evil when it was discovered in the 1930s and a dead end when it was offered as a recovery tool in the 1960s. Mirabai doesn't have years; she has been using methadone for six months and was started at a high dose proportionate to her massive heroin intake. The clinic initially refused to cooperate with my aggressive titration plan, but after we signed the death waivers absolving them of all liability, they rethought it. It usually takes seven years to bring her dosage level down to where she is now after only two months. Now we are approaching the *free fall*.

'Free fall' is the term I've innovated to describe the point of a titration process where you can't go any lower. Anything lower throws you into withdrawals anyway, so further titration is not possible. This is where most methadone and benzo users get stuck: they *can't* titrate lower without causing the very thing they're trying to avoid: *sickness*. As an addiction treatment innovator, I'd much rather treat a 3.5-gram-a-day heroin user (which is very high) than a methadone or benzo dependency.

We have plotted it out: we will get her down to about ten milligrams a day, then she will skip a day here and there. The clinic will provide some capsules for our travel, so she doesn't go into convulsions on the plane. Once we arrive at the new house, it's free-fall time.

Mirabai will sequester in her room, where she can rest and endure the suffering any way she can. There ain't shit anyone can do for you during free-fall detox. All you can do is *endure*.

While she's going through the final detox, I'll be making house: moving in, unpacking, setting up...

The movers will pick everything up on one day, and we will fly out the day after. It'll be a long haul: five or six hours managing movers to protect my things and get it done right, followed by dinner from a can, then an overnight stay in a cheap hotel near LAX to rest up for our morning flight.

The Subaru has been picked up, and the Saturn will be our ride from the beach to LAX. Auto transport will pick it up at the hotel, and the shuttle will take us to the terminal. If one detail goes wrong, the entire plan will unravel.

Oh... and then there's the cat. Chow Chow is in his carrier and none too happy about it. The hotel does not allow pets, so we have to sneak him *into* the room, *out* of the room, and *onto* the shuttle the next day with no one knowing.

So far, so good. The movers wrap up by noonish, and we can head downtown: me, my angry cat, and a woman in the early stages of withdrawals violent enough to kill a horse.

After packing and loading the cars and a truck, we spend the final hours cleaning the rental home to secure the return of my $3200 deposit. I did my best to repair the two-foot-square hole I bashed in the outside wall to put in a kitty- door months before. I don't know how they'll miss the damage, but I did what I had to do; Chow Chow was *not* going to be a prisoner because there was no place for a pet door.

I say a tearless goodbye to Brandon by stifling my emotions so as not to embarrass him. I take a brief walk in the park and along the beach to soak up my last view of this paradise I leave behind in hopes of greener pastures. And we drive out. Brandon will camp out in his car next to the resort hotel where he works and where he once valet-parked Neil Young's very expensive Beamer.

Mirabai is virtually worthless as she's just trying to hang on with cramps and inner turmoil wreaking havoc on her. She's doing her best with withdrawal fever, so I try to carry the burdens solo.

"I'll go check us in and get two keys. Then I'll come to get you and give you one and tell you the room number. We'll walk in together. You walk about ten feet behind me with Chow Chow's carrier with a towel over it. I will distract the front desk as you go by and get to the room!"

Great. But there's one problem: "You mean I'm paying full rate, even though your elevator's down, and you're putting me on the *ninth* floor?"

"I'm sorry, sir. There are no other rooms available, and the elevators will be down overnight."

"Then how can you justify charging me the same rate? Never mind... I need to get some rest." I choose not to belabor the point. I am breaking enough rules to be told to leave as it is.

I explain the situation to Mirabai. We are both too fascinated by the creativity of Murphy's Law to do anything other than laugh at our perfect storm.

As I distract the clerk, Mirabai briskly walks past with a suitcase on wheels and a tote covered by a towel that could meow if it was so inclined. She reaches the stairs, and I join her. "Are you well enough to walk up nine flights? I'll take your bag. Think you can hike up with eight pounds of feline?"

And she does it. Fuck! Nine floors are a workout for *me,* and I'm not purging four years of heroin and methadone! We step inside the fleabag room, the quality of which can only be found next to a major metropolis airport. "Lie down. Just put Chow's carrier on the bed with you so he can see and smell you. That'll comfort him. I'll go down and get our bags out of the Saturn."

The Saturn will be picked up here at the hotel soon, so our overstuffed luggage, weighing within ounces of the maximum allowed for check and carry-on bags, has to come up with us. And they are loaded: two deflated air mattresses, sleeping bags, pillows, and a few changes of clothes, as well as two bags of dollar store groceries. Upon arrival, we'll have no car and an empty house, so we packed as many survival and comfort items as we could fit in our baggage. *And a Chow Chow kitty.* The cars will show up in a few days and are truly loaded: groceries, clothes, fold-out chairs, and a table so we can live like homo sapiens while we wait the week or so for the moving truck.

"We're white trash!" I declare. Laughter is the best medicine.

We are ideal. This is totally appropriate for junkies living in hotels. It has an odd nostalgia and causes my tweeker days to resurface in my mind: dope fiends, shabby hotels, mini-market food supplies, and praying you don't get caught by management.

We're champions: three of the most resilient beings on the planet in one room. We get through the night without too much incident except my loathing of the world each time I climb the 135 steps from the lobby to the ninth floor. The two big, heavy bags I dragged up must go back down at 6 a.m., too.

We get along pretty well, *considering.* No one is in a good fucking mood. Mirabai is just trying to endure: she feels guilty for not contributing and being bitchy because she is suffering beyond repair. There's nothing we can do for each other; we're each in our own private hell. Chow Chow Bang, too; he looks around the room and returns to his carrier voluntarily.

Somehow, I sleep. Mirabai doesn't, but she doesn't disturb me. I was smart enough to get two beds. The only thing worse than the hell of detox is the insomnia from it. All a withdrawing dope fiend wants to do is sleep because you're truly exhausted. But withdrawals cause insomnia, so you're awake through every agonizing minute. An added bonus to your suffering is knowing you did this to yourself.

<u>Wakey-wakey, eggs and bakey!</u>

With a little coffee and second-wind motivation, I haul our stuff down for departure. The shuttle driver is cool and says nothing of us having a cat, which is clearly a breach. We shuffle like zombies through check-in and TSA security. All is in order because Mirabai now has a California ID and a printed boarding pass.

We avoid talking about the obvious: we're both miserable and cannot possibly fathom why we thought this was a good idea. It all looks black, and neither of us is trying to do anything but tolerate it. We have two hours before departure, four hours of flight, baggage claim, and we have arranged a ride to the new house. We expect to be there around 6 p.m. It's a 36-hour endeavor: pack-load-travel.

Even though many things have gone wrong, like broken elevators, the main things have aligned: the door key is where it's supposed to be, the power is on, and we're all doing okay in various ways.

None of us, from Krishnanand to Chow Chow to Mirabai, feel optimistic about our triumph and arrival. We're just relieved it's complete.

44.

BLISSED OUT: SADHANA PURGE

एअक 'क्रिपलुहिं' बच्यो जगत महँ, निश्छल शैल सामान

Eak 'Kripaluhin' bachyo jagat mahan, nishchal shail saman

(All of the universe is moved to thrill by the sound of the flute. Except one: Krishn himself—the source of the ecstasy.)

—Kripalu (Murali Madhuri kirtan)

Guru's selfless servitude disables powerful maya so it cannot harm the devotee.

—Kripalu Maharaj (Sadguru Madhuri)

It is 6:30 in the morning, the day after our arrival. I enter the prayer hall of the ashram.

The sadhana prayer hall is expansive, with over 5,000 square feet of floor space. The open ceiling area, filled with intricate custom-molded tiles, allows soft light into the room from over twenty feet above. The high ceiling soffits house lighted panels with quotes from the Bhagavad Gita and Bhagavatam, revealing the simplicity of loving God to attain Divine Love Consciousness.

I enter the room where I have spent countless hours in meditation over past years. We devotees sat at the feet of Swamiji like children huddled around a storyteller as he taught Sanatan Dharm to us. I head straight to the altar, fall to my knees, and bow my head to the floor in pranam to the gorgeous deities upon the altar: life-size marble figures of Radha Krishn, She in Her traditional blue and He in His saffron yellow. They smile out at us from a setting of colorful flowers and trees as a smaller effigy of Saint Chaitanya gazes from the background. I rise with my hands folded in prayer and step back to take in the whole view.

The altar: closed during darshan, it is inappropriate to take photos when open. Photo pictured is from ashram website.

Two ornate pillars frame the sides of the altar. They stand fifteen feet high and are bridged by an elaborate header carved with sweeping paisley that cannot be described in English.

These plaster cast pillars are handmade from a unique method of molding called "shilpy", exclusive to artisans in India and hand painted.

It is a space of love.

Once upon a time, in the years before I had died and been resurrected, I would sit on a floor cushion in front of the altar, getting lost in its glorious details as I listened to sweet flowing kirtans composed by my own Guru. My older, less-supple body, with titanium bolts in my spine, takes a chair off to the side. This location suits me well. From here, next to a floor-to-ceiling window, I can CinemaScope the entire prayer hall before me and appreciate the few satsangees—my spiritual brothers and sisters—settled on the light blue carpeted prayer floor, ready to begin their day with ablutions of sadhana. Sitting off to the side with plenty of personal space, I gaze out the window to my right and see the *goprum*—the tower housing the altar. Over sixty feet tall, it stands like a sentinel overlooking the surrounding countryside. From my window seat, I admire its granite surface, so smooth and perfect. I study its base, adorned with *shilpy* molded figurines of elephants and mandalas. I crane my neck as my eyes follow leisurely along the length of the *goprum* to its tip-top. Every square inch is so intimately designed and constructed by its founder, my Swamiji, out of His loving devotion to Radha Krishn and our Guru, Kripalu Maharaj. Two hundred acres of stones, forests, free-wandering peacocks, dorms, dining hall, ponds, trails, creeks, laundry rooms, parking lots... they all breathe an expression of His love and Grace. Yes, I said peacocks.

Above: *My seat apart from the main floor adjacent to the window gazes at the shilpy elephants and mandals around its base. It is divine!*
Left: *The "shikr" tower housing the altar within*

Peacocks are indigenous to our motherland of India and often appear in the *leelas* of Radha Krishn playing in Barsana and Vrindaban 5,000 years ago. The ashram is home to well over twenty of them, and they roam as they like, often posing for pictures with their spectacular tail feathers spread as they dance. Yes... they dance!

Courtship: The peacock is dancing for the peahen on the veranda at the prayer hall entrance.

I feel so comfortable and at home in the prayer hall...

A young devotee plays a few notes on her harmonium, and a man taps a tabla drum as they synchronize and tune up. After a brief pause, a sweet melody with a soft, steady beat begins. As she gently sings, I become absorbed in the music. I meditate on the beautiful verses describing God's names, forms, virtues, and actions through His avatars and saints. I get lost in the verses composed by our loving Kripalu Maharaj and am aware of the blessing that I am not dead, in pain, confined to a bed, or in a madhouse.

Somehow, I have survived this saga. *Somehow*... I have arrived. A tear forms and spills down my cheek.

I am enchanted by the kirtan singer's verses, sung with a loving heart. It's like I never left. I know what I must do in the temple: *roop dhyan*, to purify my mind with loving remembrance of the Divine Love form and virtues of God and my Divine Guru. As with most meditations, the mind will try to wander...

My mind meanders through rooms of thoughts within a deep Atlantean sea of contemplations. I let it go; rather than coaxing it back to a disciplined meditation, I surrender to it. Its wanderings are not aimless; they follow a spiritual beckoning. God, Guru, or Akashic Agents lead my mind where they want it to go. I let them lead me to whatever I am to think, feel, and see. It's just my mind, and they can have it... *forever.*

I lose all sense of time and place as I am taken deeper into my soul. Memories of events, days, nights, regions, and episodes of the last six years begin rising to the surface. *And I cannot stop them.*

I am not in charge. My mind is now tethered to an unseen force that has snatched it and is transporting it wherever it wishes.

The last six years have been a blur, and I've had no way to measure or retain them. My mind's ability to grasp my memories has been impaired for so long that it is now a new normal. I don't know any other type of brain function but *mal*-function. The Portal experience, the brain traumas, the tragedies, the triumphs... One by one, they float into my cognition as a mosaic of events with no specific order. "I" am not remembering them; they are just emerging on their own.

Every scene of the last six years begins to span before me. So much of what I have endured from D-Day to the present moment has become like "lost years," suppressed by my loving, spiritual guardians for my own protection. My Life Review *within The Portal* was of past lifetimes over thousands of years, but the one I now experience is from NDE-Day, six years ago, to the present moment. They all flow together into a continuum of awareness.

Here in the hall, surrounded by kirtan in a *safe place,* the collage of memories I was unconscious of rises from the depth of my body and spirit to be released. They uncoil from the spine of my awareness, kundalini-like, ascend to the surface of the third eye of my perception, and roll out to be witnessed; many memories over regions of space and geography, from suburbia Los Angeles to country-living Washington, to coastal LA, to here and now. But the assortment of memories in this wakeful dream of Life Preview is of smaller things, little instances of thoughts and feelings that led to profound realizations and conclusions.

There are so many, both painful and beautiful at once. I try to be discreet so I won't draw attention to my quiet tears; I bow my head so no one can see the subtle body tremors from my gentle sobs.

They just don't stop.

I am seeing the Life Review, which is NDE standard, but instead of my whole life's events flashing before me in an instant, they are only of these lost years and are cinematic again:

I see forgotten scenes: the hospital nurse finding me in the stairwell, trying to climb the steps on my own, too impatient and scared of being hospitalized forever to wait for my afternoon physical assistance.

I'm seeing the phase just after D-Day when I spent entire days in my serene office writing books, surrounded by the vibrant sound of music and the loneliness of its safety. I relive the struggles of training myself to walk again with lonely, scary walks in the park next door and up the quiet, private hilltop. Catching breath through punctured lungs, unable to escape thinking about how the one and only person I needed to believe in me turned away in my darkest hours. Sitting in that office, I was paralyzed by grief and so impaired that I lacked the ability to imagine a better life.

Until this moment, these were totally unknown to me—repressed and stored within the Akashic Records, now being released for me to see.

Layer by layer, they rise up... thoughts stored in my cells, blood, bone marrow, and muscle fibers, emitting fragrantly from my pores. *I hate and love them.*

I *hate* them because I am reliving the true account of what I've been going through daily for six years. I'm seeing my pain *the entire* time as I'd never seen it. I *love* them because they reveal the direct *kripa—Grace—*my God and Guru have provided through it all. Most of what I've shared with you to this point has been in hindsight. I could not have told this story before now because I did not have access to the suppressed realities. I was unaware of these instances while they were happening to me. Only when I came here, meditating in the prayer hall and at home, did it all become known to me.

For six years, I had been using all my strength to endure every moment without really knowing where I was yesterday or any day. I was giving my absolute best just to remain alive and return to sanity, as I was perpetually unsure whether or not I was sane. Here, in my Guru's dham, *I am safe.* Within the sanctuary womb of His ashram temple, I can finally witness those years safely. The bliss of ignorance that has shielded me from those six years of anguish is evaporating. They continue flowing from the muladhara, or root chakra, at the base of my spine, to my ajna, third eye, so that I can see them safely. My protective sheaths of denial are disintegrating, and I am being cleansed of the horrors I've known:

The thoughts, feelings, and realizations that arose during my strolls along the trail of Mt. Rainier's Carter Falls, trying to make sense of my tragedies; the country drives to Tumwater Falls, and the lonely walks around the gardens, trying to make peace with the unavoidable death of Janete's affection for me; the jogs through the Lake Limerick golf course, with its sweeping views of the lake, determined to be worthy of Janete's love by being whole again; and being physically able to have a game of catch with Brandon someday.

Like a toppling chain of dominoes, these memories evoke a scene of Brandon and me in the park by the beach home, the vast sea in the background. Just a week ago, my dream of playing catch finally came true! He thrust the ball like a missile into my leather-gloved hand. How hard it was to catch that ball! But it took more effort to stuff away my tears of overwhelming gratitude to keep it light and fun. My happiness made the Pacific Ocean look small by comparison…

Flashback further to my friendly Washington neighbor in the woods, inviting me for sunrise kayaking. The serene, beautiful lakes with broad skies provided room enough for my paradox of sorrow, fear, and gratitude: sorrow for all I'd lost and was still losing, fear of the ongoing suffering, but thankful to be alive, aware, and immersed in a paradise of forests rather than the sterility of hospitals.

I walk beneath glorious amber-hued leaves along the tree-lined streets after a Saturday IANDS meeting. I savor the crisp, sunny day as I take in the charm of the picturesque 1920s homes. I feel blessed by the autumn air and simultaneously heartbroken, wishing the stroll was hand in hand with my lover, who no longer loves me.

I embrace the beautiful memories and let the bitter ones slip-slide away.

Satsang is purging me…

Each day's painful, cathartic purging of the past begins within minutes of meditation and stops when satsang ends. By the time I reach my car and drive to the main exit, I do not feel dark; *I feel cleansed.* After each satsang, I feel elated during the single-mile trip from the prayer hall to the house. *I am lighter.* The weight of these tragedies lifts from my shoulders. They surface from the depths of my spirit mind and are released *one by one.* The Spiritual Administrators are taking a bristly, wiry scrub brush and removing the cancer of my tragedy, cell by cell. For the rest of the day, I go about my business of unpacking, making house, and managing my affairs. When I return to the prayer hall for evening satsang, it begins again.

My mind is surrendered and seized. What I think and feel, and the selection of memories being purged, just happens. I am not involved beyond being the witness…

I pray silently. "My dear Maharaji, I hope these painful memories never stop. I would rather be in pain *with* you than be without pain separated *from* you." This realization causes more tears because I am so grateful for the ability to appreciate the gift of such devotion.

His nearness to me in each past drama I now witness is apparent. I'd felt so alone every day for six years, and I now see He did not just remain *close* to me during my crisis; He *cradled* me.

I was in His folded arms *the entire time*.

He was not merely present; His direct Grace put my ego-mind *on hold* for the duration. My brain-damaged identity loss was God's way of protecting me. As painful as it has been, I only experienced a fraction of it. God's Grace has been my shield.

Each night as I drift off to sleep, I have a dialogue with the Akash...

"You needed me out of the way, didn't you? You put me into a dormant state within The Portal so I would not interfere with you cleaning house of my life. By removing my *ahankar,* or ego, you had free reign without my attempts to *help.* I would've made it harder, so You removed me, put me in a virtual sleep, gave me respite within The Portal while you took a wrecking ball to the life which could no longer serve my Soul's Journey."

The reply was simple: *Yes.*

"There was only so much time to get it done, wasn't there? Shattering Janete and me, abolishing my career of *worldly* service and life in Los Angeles... my spirit was trickling back to my body and picking up momentum. It was all done in the nick of time."

"Your soulmate love was difficult to dismantle. Your will, determination, rich histories of past lives, and the depth of your love for one another required time to take apart. You both needed to see the truths of yourselves and one another."

"Will I ever know why it had to end?"

"The truth always comes to the surface, Krishnanand. You will learn the truth if and when you are willing. The two of you made pacts in several lives to reunite, binding to each other with karma out of love. But the human relationship is never eternal. Only God is your true, eternal friend and lover. All others are as fleeting as the cosmos themselves: here now, gone tomorrow, back again to leave and return, leave and return... But God and Guru are One and only. They are *constant.*"

I return to the prayer hall every morning and evening, and the power that purges my mind from traumas possesses me. The magic of the kirtan, the aura of the hall, and the presence of Maharaji in daily video discourses take control of my senses. Layer upon layer is revealed to me a*nd removed.* Each day is a healing event; I feel lighter and less burdened by my traumas. Lost memories arise, surface, and get swept away by a divine broom. They are washed away by episodes of tears that pour from me for ten, fifteen, or twenty minutes at a time.

The tapestry of occurrences is selective but not chosen by me. I am merely along for the ride through them as they surface:

The complex flow of contemplations as I meditated while walking along Oxnard Shores beach, mesmerized by the paradox of my curses and blessings... god, I was lonely and shattered! The beauty of a home on the beach, sharply contrasted by inner pain...

Yog classes in the park and private talks between my wonderful teacher and me; physical therapy in town; and lonely strolls within the wealthy beach neighborhood homes. I pondered the mystery of how I could ever be happy without the woman I loved and the prestige of material success.

I could not retain these tiny happenings daily, but I am seeing them now. Even during constant suffering, I never gave up. I tried to live beyond trauma and limitations despite repeatedly being kicked when I was down. Now I can remember more than the grand times of visiting the laser and art gallery at Samskara Wisdome with Brandon in Los Angeles a few months ago, father and son sharing an admiration of profound, mystical art. What stands out now is the sweet and simple two-hour walk through the city's backstreet graffiti art and the vegan counter where we lunched and chatted about music and the sublimity of everyday blessings: the *quality* time we shared.

This Life Review shows the ceremony performed with Lia, my cosmic BFF and tantric priestess during the Super Blood Wolf Moon Eclipse just months ago, which I easily remember. Then it jumps to the jokes we shared while waiting in line for a Halloween haunt, reminiscing over this life's adventures and those of past lives, too. In the midst of inner trauma and sorrow, I was making magical memories with actual magic. Fuck my tragedies! The blessings are *to die for!*

Life Review skips forward...

I relive the meditative motorbike rides along the Pacific Coast Highway. I remember the gratitude I felt, not only *despite* all the suffering but also *for* all the suffering. What a feeling it was, riding alive and free on my Wayback Machine motorbike, surrounded by stunning views of the ocean, open road, and mountains all at once. As full of sorrow as I was, my love for God and Guru and my awareness of life's beauty never fully stopped. Although shattered, I was *always* mindful of God's blessings and beauty.

The events that have led me to this metaphysical space of prayer and perspective are not the ones documented by tickets, fares, or photos. I am in this present space of purging and healing because of the chain of thoughts and perspectives I had *between them*.

The revelations that reframed who I was to become have been far more significant than the events that inspired them. Loss and tragedy were just raw materials that caused shifts in consciousness. Moments of inner revelations themselves had all been safely stored within the Akashic Records for safekeeping, suppressed until *now*. The thoughts and emotions I experienced during them now provide *the context, the concept, and the theme* that holds the real lessons within the saga. Six lost years of events came forward as a string of pearls and a crown of thorns...

And they just don't stop.

I am in the prayer hall twice a day: 6:30 a.m. and 7:30 p.m., totaling nearly three hours of meditation and contemplation. Each session brings tidal waves of catharsis.

The big events, like heartbreak and injuries, are the mere granules within a loaf, being revealed for the empty calories they actually are. Sprinkles of causes expand like yeast into effects. But the nourishment of this saga is *not* in the obvious carbohydrates of losing a soulmate, spinal fusion surgery, or a nuclear train ride through Japan.

True nourishment comes from small affairs, private thoughts, and endurance. I don't have a collection of traumatic occurrences to feel bitter over; instead, I have a treasury of raw materials for spiritual gratitude. All this pain, my collection of memories, and a battery of hundreds... *no, thousands...* of epiphanies and realizations are the proteins being used to assemble the real message:

You are loved.

You have *never* been alone; we have *always* been with you. We are *proud* of you. You took it like a man!

The Akashic Agents, the *dasa* servants of my Master, are telling me they are *proud* of me. *Proud?*

I often wonder if anyone could have endured everything better than I did. *But I don't think so.* With honest and objective clarity, I am fairly convinced that few people, maybe not even one, could have withstood *all* this and not become institutionalized. But I always felt I was a lousy devotee, failing to be joyful of the circumstances provided to me and lamenting my losses instead of appreciating them.

"You brought me to the total edge. How did you know I would make it?" I ask the Agents.

"We didn't. But you handled everything we rained upon you, so we brought more. We didn't intend to make you suffer but wanted to give you the opportunity. With each trial, you progressed. With each loss and challenge that you surpassed, you advanced. You always followed the support we provided and came through."

"But I almost *didn't* make it; my death wish was sincere. I was going to do it. Then all you did to help me evolve, and how you made me stronger by that which didn't kill me, would have been for naught."

"It was close, and we suspected we'd crossed the line. When you wept and cried out that we had overestimated you, we were forced to scramble. We answer to a higher authority, too, you know. If we pushed you too far and could not reel you back, and if you went through with the self-death act, resulting in a timeless damnation for you, we would be joining you in hell for it. Your Master's Yogmaya disabled your lover's acceptance of you and influenced your devotee-sister's heart to help you get to India. We communicated directly to you to call her, and when you did, you narrowly escaped severe tragedy.

"Your Maharaji loves you. He loves *all* His children, and if you had followed through with suicide, He would also hold *us* accountable, not just you."

I am realizing the duality of my survival and endurance: I… didn't do shit! All I did was survive and keep breathing. I didn't go mad because my Guru took over and protected me. The only thing I can take credit for is that I didn't give up; I kept coming back and trying one more time.

I can feel the suppressed memories being wrenched from their hiding places within me, flushed up to my awareness, each one a visual scene displayed… Brandon and I are going for a final lunch together at the vegan sushi counter near the beach house. I am confused and still putting forth great effort to avoid embarrassing us both as I try to walk without running into doors or tripping over curbs as we walk from the car to the order counter. I was so happy he was there, and we were reunited, although he had no thoughts beyond his delicious lunch and no idea that I was crying happy tears inside because he, of all souls, was the one given to me to father.

Brandon, now a young man, whole and alive and unaware of futures, strong, true, and of noble character; and me, being allowed to have a role as his teacher in this lifetime. I also see the past life we shared where he taught me. This is our continuum of sweet karmas together.

I see the absurdity of my sorrow for the loss of things I once thought were vital; for senseless worry over worldly trivialities, and my ineptitude to embrace what truly matters. To live for loving God and Guru is all that matters, regardless of what we're dealt.

I am unstuck in time. My life of six years is passing before my eyes, revealing that the order of events is less important than the continuum of them. Past lives, recent events, the eternal present, obscure futures… each a separate tile in a mosaic of an Eternal Truth.

Blissful Sanskars

The surfacing and purging of what I'd not remembered take place over several months. Some satsang sessions are the usual beautiful kirtan with bhakti meditation. I become absorbed in kirtans describing God's virtues. I marvel at my Guru Kripalu's transcendental melodies and His love of composing thousands of kirtans for our different moods. Like any stupid-human, sometimes I am distracted by concerns such as groceries, chores, and other trivialities, which disrupt my ability to focus spiritually. But most days, these deep, purging wanderings of Life Review rush forward, neither with expectation nor anticipation. I never know what satsang will bring.

I am teleported through these scenes. Guru is scraping them from the walls of my intestines, watery brain cells, and muscle fibers with his kirtans. Whether I am in the prayer hall, my satsang room at the house, or laboring with chainsaws and shovels to clear trails in the ashram's forests, the blissful purging goes on. All the events of these lost years have led me to this eternal present, here and now, each moment side by side with my Guru's love and canopied by His shelter.

When the last scenes purge, will it be over? I am becoming dependent on them because they allow such a personal connection between my Master and my heart; I beg them never to end. When they unfold before me, and I am in tears of pain from their astounding qualities, I beg them to stop but simultaneously pray to remain in them. As they roll through, I am afraid I will never stop weeping as I see what I have truly endured and have been protected from knowing.

Had I known these as they happened, as I am knowing them now, I would have committed suicide in an *instant*. I would've drugged myself to madness. I thought I had gone to the Pacific Northwest to die properly, but I was not permitted. I served my exile as best I could and eventually broke down, going toward self-murder.

I did all a man could do to find salvation, seek alternatives, and try to rebuild, and when _re_-building failed, I sincerely tried to accept my losses and build anew. That failed, too. Nothing worked, and life only got darker and grimmer. But I never gave up, did I? If this is what it takes to make my Master smile, bring it on!

I see how I tried to prioritize Akashic direction over personal desires and the favor this caused. I am blessed to have an intuitive link to Akashic Agents' guidance. The connection is reliable and consistent. Visions, messages, and inceptions are provided without request, which I would never do. And within the prayer hall, in the satsang space established by my loving Swamiji teacher, I feel the connection bypass Akashic Agents; it's as though my Swamiji and my Maharaji are speaking to me *directly*. Are they? I'm a stupid-human, unfit for direct association. But within the hall, the communication has a bolder, more emphatic quality. It has a *personality* that transcends the celestial, Akash. Personality I recognize: *Divine personality*, those of my Swamiji teacher and my Mahaparush Guru.

I know now that the ochre presence within The Portal was Him, my Maharaji, in His traditional orange dhoti, the robe of a master. The thunderous hum and harmony of the spheres was the Divine flute of Lord Khanaiya Kirshn. The body of God is the Divine dimension; it is the Absolute, omnipresent form of God—a body of bliss. As you travel through The Portal and approach the Divine realm, you can sense, smell, subtly taste and begin to hear God's music of bliss and see the radiance of Divine light. But beyond The Portal, past the harmony, fragrance, and light is His Divine Love form: *Radha Krishn*. The entire Divine dimension is made up of Their forms, personified in my Guru's form: They are He, He is They, They are not separate, but One.

When you finally qualify to attain Divinity, you bypass The Portal altogether to the Divine Abode. It is beyond The Portal, beyond celestial heaven, and above paradise. The Portal is not a *through* road to the Divine dimension but a waystation for returning to the material one of maya. From within The Portal, you can *glimpse* the Divine space, *sense* it, and *hear* it, but you cannot *see* it. Only with God's kripa—His Grace—can you have darshan of the Divine abode of Them. To see It is the final, eternal destination of God Realization. The meaning of my eternal existence is not to be within The Portal but to go beyond The Portal—to the Divine realm. The only *kripa* for me is from *Kripalu*.

***

A bhakti yogi strives to attain depths of devotional meditation that humble them to tears of gratitude for God and Guru. Conventional, dry, "passive" meditations to be of "no mind" are methods of frustration. The kirtan, the stories of Saints, avatars, the songs of humbleness, knowledge of the path, and other content given to us by the Rasiks through history, are the *material* we use to stimulate feelings of humility, gratitude, and devotion in our attempt to think of God and Guru. These are "active" meditations that are simpler and sweeter than the passive "nothingness" meditations on "light" and abstract spirit. The Rasik Saints of history know we are feeble-minded and easily distracted, so they have provided volumes of material to appeal to our various moods and personalities. Joyful kirtans, playful kirtans, and the ones my own consciousness becomes lost in, kirtans of longing. The longing for Divine Love Consciousness is the only one I can truly relate to: I long to be One with Divine Love Consciousness.

I've got six years of personal sadhana material. Now, when my mind wanders during meditation, as all minds do, it teleports through these "lost years," humbling me to tears of gratitude for God and Guru. He's given me a personal shortcut to spiritual ecstasy—a detour to *bhao*.

Some memories that surface are bigger and have more tumor mass; these take several rides to make it out of the tunnel. But I am always fully aware that I have nothing to fear: He brought me here to give me a safe place to resurrect my pains and allow them to exit. He brought me here for this blissful, purging Life Review.

Every event displayed visually is distilled and filtered down into the hendecagram tattooed on my forearm. I was instructed to get this tattoo because it acts like a black hole singularity: six years of traumas travel to the center of it, becoming more and more condensed as the black hole's gravity squeezes them all together and releases them to a separate dimension where nothing is, ever was, and ever will be. It is my own personal Portal.

The pain of the beauty, the beauty of pain.

The Rasik Saints speak eloquently of the paradoxical quality of spiritual ecstasy being *bittersweet*. It is bitter because longing for direct contact and vision of your God and Guru is painful when you cannot endure a single moment of separation from Them. And it's sweet because the longing actually *is* direct contact, and the union is blissful. This concept of bittersweet had always been an abstract metaphor to me. *Until now.*

The highest state of *bhao* is a *sweet longing*. A bhakt yogi *longs* to meet and have *sweet* union with God. I am sometimes utterly captivated by a longing so immersive that it overpowers me.

I had always longed for union with my personal Divine Love form of God, personified within my Guru, but it was somewhat *theoretical*. My longing for Him now is paralyzing to my senses. The pain of longing is immeasurable, yet I *never want it to stop*.

The Saints also tell us that one's pain of longing is *exactly equal* to one's love: the more you love something, the more painful it is to be separated from it. Why? Because the measure of sting in my longing for them is through to my core! I should celebrate because I have proof my love for God and Guru must be immense.

The Rasik kirtans tease about being careful what you wish for because once you taste Divine Love Consciousness, you will be a slave to its longing forever. Your need to be near and embraced by God will consume you. They caution a devotee never to make eye contact with Nandakumar, Krishn because once you do, you will desire nothing else forevermore. It will be the best and worst day of your life, realizing Divine Love Consciousness is actual. They are telling the truth.

Divine Love Consciousness is painful.

It is also so glorious and beautiful you want nothing else and will give your life to it. You no longer see any significance or value in anything but serving and loving God: period, *the end*.

Divine Love *hurts blissfully!*

The kirtan verse at the start of this chapter is significant. Krishn's flute represents his intimate loving form. When He leaves Vrindaban and moves to Mathura to fulfill the 'almighty' acts of his descension, He leaves the flute behind. This means that His most loving aspect remains ever present in Vrindaban— always accessible to those who love the lord selflessly. It is this flute which He beckons the divine maidens, the gopis, to the most sacred and glorious event of His divine appearance—the maharas—the dance of divine ecstasy. Only those who love the lord selflessly can hear His divine flute when He plays it. And Radha, the female personification of Divine Love Herself, who is His Soul, is the one who gives Him permission to do so

45.

NOT LIVING ON BREAD ALONE

> Be humble in your heart. But prideful in the world.
>
> —Swami Prakashanand Saraswati

> We are eternal, and the body is temporary.
>
> Make the senses a servant of the soul, not the other way around.
>
> —Shree Kripalu Maharaj

But I *do* have to function. The Buddha and the Saints lived as mendicants: they had no need or desire for material comfort or safety because they were always immersed in spiritual bliss. When St. Francis lay dying in a ditch after being beaten within an inch of his life by two robbers, *he didn't care!* His mind wandered to God, as it always did, and he sang with joy! When a passerby rescued him, he was initially angry at the man for disturbing his absorption in remembrance of God. Now *that's* true love and devotion!

I'm not that advanced. I live indoors and need to pay bills. Otherwise, my weak, material-enslaved mind will never be *present* at satsang, neither in the temple nor in my private meditation room at the house. If I don't shower, eat, exercise, kiss a girl, or have a beer... then I am *a bear!* I don't need any of these things in excess. But with no morning coffee, my only *roop dhyan* remembrance is of my whole bean, almond mocha cup of joe. If I don't do the morning BM, I'll be backed up by noon. If I don't get laid once a week, I get edgy. Two weeks without, and I'm grouchy. Three weeks? Climbing walls like an evil spiderman! A month? I don't know, and let's hope we never find out!

Is it possible to manage your material desires and personal needs in a responsible way that does not interfere with your sadhana? I cannot terminate my "needs," but can I co-exist with them spiritually? Is it possible to have a healthy, responsible romance that doesn't interfere with sadhana? Can I have my cake and eat it, too?

***

It's all adding up. The mosaic of my experiences forms a crystal-clear image, each tile adding a piece to this mysterious puzzle. I can no longer deny what is obvious.

Yogmaya took a wrecking ball to my earthly life's attachments, which were potentially threatening to my Soul's Journey.

Akashic Agents advise, "Your love partner was very nearly as you knew her—gentle, sweet, simple—and her transgression to you was insignificant. Why do you think it was revealed on the one-year anniversary of your death experience? It was something that had occurred several years earlier. Why was it concealed until *that* particular day?"

"You knew it would trigger a separation," I offered. "If I had found out *before* my death, she and I would've moved beyond it *together*. It took The Portal co-existence and the cacophony of multiple tragedies to make me take time on my own and go into exile to cope with the brain injury."

"Even *that* took a full year and a half before you separated from her."

The NDE gave me psychic clarity that removed the veils shrouding my attachments and brought truths to the surface.

I always gave others the benefit of the doubt, never wanting to be judgmental. But Janete secretly resented my Guru and spiritual path because it came *first*, putting her *second*. Willful interaction with things negative to our path is called *kusang*—bad association. *Satsang* is *spiritual association,* and *kusang* is *worldly associations* that are not just indifferent to your path but against it.

"Your level of self-surrender to God and Guru is strong," continued the Akashic Agents. "And there is no doubt they are your absolute priority. But your dominant thoughts of wife, children, pets, or even hobbies during the last moments of life will determine where your soul and mind go next. They create the karmic bindings between you. Only if your final thoughts, and the majority of those throughout your life, are devoted to God *exclusively,* will you attain Him upon death instead of worldly incarnations."

"Yes, I know that most people cannot control or contain their thoughts when confronted with death. Our thoughts automatically go to our attachments. You're saying that even though my spiritual surrender was very high, it wasn't high enough. She and I were so intertwined, and she was so dependent on me spiritually that my mind would most likely be *mixed* in my final moments: God and Guru *and* Janete."

"Yes. But spiritual government would not interfere with your loyal and sincere attachments—they're *your* business. But you prayed passionately for Divine Intervention to release you from all that interfered with your satsang."

"But Janete never interfered with my spiritual ambitions. She was supportive and respectful of my path and commitment. I went to the ashrams many times without her. She was always invited but declined. And six months before my death, we traveled together. I took her to Buddhist sites because she was attracted to Buddhism."

"She just wasn't as attracted to it as you had hoped. You both tried, but her conclusions were not spiritual. Lines were being drawn in the sand."

Indeed, I had done the math and learned her one and only infidelity must have been while I was in India on pilgrimage.

"Janete would never *put her foot down* with you, certainly not over something so valuable to you. No one would; you don't compromise your true values for others. You repeatedly proved this, especially when you left her for the trial separation."

"No, she was always more subtle. I cared for and nearly enabled her because she always projected this *deer-in-the-headlights* quality. I'm far too quixotic to resist that from a beautiful woman I adore."

Janete was the poster child for *damseling:* people, particularly women, who project an innocent need for help to provoke others, usually men, to intervene and assist them. I am the poster child for *rescuer's syndrome,* a man's way of affirming their masculine value. I don't wanna just swerve to avoid hitting the deer in my headlights; I'd rather rescue it from all harm.

I did my best to empower instead of enable, and she did her best to learn *how* to catch a fish rather than being given one, but we both were guilty of being lazy at times and giving in to these conditioned roles.

The problem was that during NDE and after, I wanted both to stop because, for once, I could not rescue; I needed *to be* rescued. Janete's exit strategy was largely due to *not* wanting to be my protector and having no need for a man who couldn't be a hero for her. Like any worldly couple, we had our dysfunctions.

"What would you have done if she had slowly and subtly insisted *she* came first over satsang? What would you do if she had slowly and subtly revealed negative thoughts and feelings about your personal form of God and Guru?"

"I'd like to think I'd try to help her see her error and bring her to reason. There's nothing but insurmountable evidence of Maharaji's saintliness. Our path just makes sense. She *got* that. She never disagreed with the philosophy or practice."

"What if it didn't work? What if her acceptance of *the path* was sincere, but she still rejected God and your Guru?"

"Oohhh... no, no. Nay, nay... There is no path without God and Guru! If I knew this, I would have to make a choice, and I would choose God and Guru over her."

"Are you sure?"

"I guess it's my nature to try to be accepting of others so long as it doesn't interfere with my own agendas. It's possible if she were private about it, I'd let it go. But that's still a transgression, especially if I *know* someone is against it all."

"Remember, you stopped seeing that vegan Dodger girl the moment you found out she wasn't just an atheist but *anti-spiritual*. Why? She had no influence over you, nor would she have interfered with your sadhana. But you didn't want to associate *intimately* with someone who was anti-God. You were protecting your spiritual karma, right?"

"Yes. Otherwise, I didn't give a damn. Her militant veganism aside, she was cool. Her other stuff wasn't a deal breaker. I guess it was inevitable that Janete and I would end. Eventually, as I always say, *the truth always comes to the surface*. If I'd known she wasn't just indifferent to my spiritual path but actually *against* it, it would have to end."

"When is the best time for bad things to happen? If you knew you were going to have four very *bad* days and three very *good* days in a week, how would you want them?"

"I would always take the bad all at once to get it over with and then have something to look forward to."

"Careful what you wish for..."

***

I suspect, but cannot know, that decades of impending bad karmas were condensed into a chain of events all linked together. Instead of our relationship ending with years of slow erosion after my TBI accident, our romantic partnership catapulted to the *deal-breaker* zone during the pinnacle of brain trauma. Too much, all at once.

Pre-NDE, there were subtle suggestions that Janete was more *tolerant* of my spiritual ambitions than part of them. Post-NDE, it seemed quite clear that she wanted a material life, not a spiritual one.

"Instead of a death event followed years later by career endings and the end of my relationship, they occurred one after the other in quick succession. It's possible that I may have stayed with Janete even after discovering her *kusang* qualities. After going through so much and having all that time together, I might've settled for the first time in my life. What turned her satsang into kusang? And why are you revealing this to me now, not before?"

"Partly what turned her away from Guru was knowing in her heart she'd never be first with you, always second. She is not spiritually mature enough to accept the guru concept and see Him as such. There is too much evidence in this world of charlatans and frauds, and most Westerners think that any spiritual teacher must be a con. She never mentioned it to you out of respect and to protect herself; she relied on you, and you provided for her. And she loved you. *To a limit.*"

"I had a shit-ton of bad karma coming in this life, and you have condensed it into a short time. That's partly because I asked for it."

"Yes... *ask, and ye shall receive.* You asked for the removal of *all* obstacles to your spiritual progress. Don't you remember?"

"I do. I really gotta stop that."

"Your will is *very* strong. Your depth and sincerity are intense. When you cry out to God, you do it with a magnitude and amplitude that is hard to ignore."

"I've been *yelping* pretty audibly for six years now, and my life has been *shit!*"

"C'mon! That's not fair!"

"No, I know. You've been by my side this entire time, especially when I was unaware and incapable of perceiving You. Is there a way to activate spiritual interventions that are not so damn painful?"

"You can cry and ask for help, but you cannot choose *how* God helps."

"But God and Guru seem involved with my material affairs, not just the spiritual ones."

"God will intervene in what seems like *worldly* affairs if they can assist you in spiritual ones. Your hedonist lifestyle in your thirties exempted you from Guru's direct association. Being a father brought you halfway to virtue. Settling down with Janete made you grow up."

"But you're not suggesting this woman was *used* to serve my spiritual progress and then discarded once I got what I needed, are you?"

"No. Your collective karmas brought you two together; you know that. We hoped from within The Portal that you would build a healthy *material* life together and support each other in your *spiritual* life. That's what all relationships are truly for. Wasn't that *your* intention, too?"

"Yes, of course. But I do see that Janete has changed. I was blind to it before my time in The Portal. She often thanked me for the blessing and the curse of removing her veils of illusion and waking her spirit up. However, as I became conscious during NDE, my own veils of denial were destroyed. How did I not notice her becoming more material and less spiritual just before my death?"

"We see what we want to see. That's what *samsara* is. The material manifestation itself is not the illusion of samsara; how we *perceive* it is the illusion. You wanted to see Janete as an angel-virgin, totally devoted to you, *so you did.* She helped preserve that by being good and concealing her truths. She had turned away from the spiritual and was on a course for the material. One of the things your Portal time did was remove your ego-self enough for you to see your own objective reality. We can reveal these secret truths now that you've moved on. You earned it. You needed to make choices based on subjective decisions. As you teach your clients and students, to take ownership of their decisions and actions, they must perceive them as their own. We couldn't tell you these things. You had to realize them for yourself."

"I've always been pretty good and better than most at recognizing objective reality over subjective samsara. Guess I had *my* blind spots, too."

"No one has tried to undermine the soul-spirit you know as Janete. We did all we could to help her, too. She followed your Maharaji; you showed her the way and motivated her. She is no less loved than you, and when she is ready to come toward Divine Love Consciousness, We will all be waiting for her."

"She was with me at my last darshan with Him in India. We toured the Buddha tirths, and she had Maharaji's darshan, too. Four months later, I was killed, which was the beginning of the end. Are these events related? Did He sense something in us that caused such an abrupt intervention? I mean... I know that karm regulates my death and the other big things. But with so much at once, I can only assume that my karmas were rearranged to fit a new agenda."

"That's above your pay grade. I'll tell you that *if* your personal Mahaparush *wants* to rearrange your karmas, *He can.* However, Sanskrit scriptures never acknowledge this."

"Those same books of knowledge also include many parables and lessons that show they can and do. No matter... I don't need to know. My life, body, and soul are His to do with as He wants. Scriptures also talk prolifically about Saintly personalities concealing their identities and involvement to make Themselves seem like regular people. You gotta be pretty blind and stupid to deny divine intervention in *my* case. My medical file alone is as strong an argument for Yogmaya miracles as the Plagues of Egypt."

"Yet, despite the overwhelming evidence, you met doctors and people every day who said it was all mere coincidence. Even her."

"You got me there. No... I can't personally invest my life in those who cannot see the evidence of God and truth surrounding them. Looks like I'm going to be pretty lonely, huh? I don't mind having a lover who's not spiritual or vegetarian, but only casually. I've got enough karmas to separate from; I don't need theirs, too. I'm sorry I failed with Janete. I tried every day to help her stay awake and in the Light."

"Maybe you tried too hard. But losing her way spiritually had *nothing* to do with you. It may have been too much in the sense that for every 1% you gave her for *her* sadhana, it prevented you from applying 2% to your own. No one *removed* your lover from you, nor you from her. All that was removed were the veils of perception so you could each decide if you actually fit. She has karmas of her own to endure that have nothing to do with you. You can't see the whole picture nor what will become of her."

I received the message that my *exile was over,* ending my Puget Sound sanitarium stay because Yogmaya had completed its business. Once I was no longer an option for Janete to return to, I was set free from the Pacific Northwest exile. Even then, our connection almost defied the Yogmaya influence. She was also torn about reuniting with me but knowing I would not abandon my spiritual pursuits, she chose to reject me.

"Is she left to the mercy of the world now? Without a spiritual lover? Did I get custody of our Guru when we divorced? Did the spiritual court give us a choice of which parent to take custody over us, and she chose the world, and I chose Maharaji? Did I fail her?"

"You didn't fail your lover, Krishnanand. Her Soul's Journey is not your responsibility— you're not a Guru or savior. You've been given an opportunity as a result of your efforts and surrender. You've been brought here to a holy dham for a singular purpose: *sadhana.* So do it. With all your heart and breath, do your sadhana."

It is painful to know she will arrive within The Portal after her time of death. She will see in her Life Review what she could've had and that association with a True Guru and path is rare.

***

I'm easily immersed in satsang in the hall, but distractions *do* persist. At my rented home, just a stone's throw away, Chow Chow Bang has to adjust to yet another house and environment, and a dear new friend is struggling through massive detox withdrawals. Bad movers are dragging ass to bring my material belongings.

The moving truck shows up five days later. There's a ton of broken shit due to manhandling items that were not padded, protected, or packed properly by these hacks, but my stuff is finally here.

Moving sucks. The movers I used from California to Washington were flawless. This led me to assume that's how the industry standard was. *Wrong!* The company I hired for the move back to California was a nightmare. As funny and surreal as it was moving to the California beach house, I decided against posting a review online; live and let live, but consumers beware!

I want this to be over. Just bring in my shit and get the hell out of here. After many hours of debate and legal dealings, they compensated me $300 back from the estimated $850 they caused in damages. Finally, I am moved in.

I am not in a position yet to determine if this is where I will spend my remaining years of life, but it is where I belong for a while, and I am tired of packing and unpacking.

Upon arrival, I'm blissed out. The gorgeous and peaceful ashram is next door, the weather is sweet, and within a few days, Chow Chow is coming and going through his own door, relishing the half-acre back lawn and the surrounding woods. Every time he goes out, I wonder if it's the last time I'll see him, but, as in Washington, I'd rather he lives a short life he wants than a long life he hates. It has to be his choice. We've all gotta own our karmas, fates, and destinies. He roams the forests and always makes it back for his naptime.

Mirabai is a champion. She does not obligate me to anything; within a few days, she is getting up here and there and trying to contribute some. I have lived alone for over twenty-five years, so the thought of a roommate is not on my approval list. But I tell her in honesty, "If... I was ever going to have a roommate, you'd be it." She wipes away a tear at my confession. We both joke sarcastically so much that sometimes it is impossible to tell if it's real or not. Other than Brandon, I've not shared a house with anyone. Brandon was easy because he's my son, so tolerance is high. Also, he's always been the most low-maintenance person I've ever known; Mirabai is in second place.

I'm settled in. I'm a bit of an overachiever, so everything is unpacked and put away within a few days, to the point it's as if I've lived here for a couple of years. It was the same in the other places. I'm more at peace and focused on things I actually give a shit about if my stuff's not in a box.

We arrive at this new place on March 3rd. The COVID-19 pandemic begins on March 20th.

In California, Brandon loses his job because valets are all laid off due to quarantines. I count my lucky stars that I am settled in just two weeks before the COVID shit hits the fan. Otherwise, I'd be trapped in California. The ashram is quarantined quickly, and I cannot enter the property. My heart breaks.

I can hear the peacocks on the property as I sit on my front patio with my morning coffee. I am so close, yet so far away. I am powerlessly confined. If it weren't for ashram access, I'd never live in Texas.

***

Life's a pendulum, and things look bleak again. Mirabai is getting well, but jobs are hard to come by due to a pandemic because some oriental omnivores caught a contagious virus by eating bats or some such shit. Brandon is back at his mom's, and it seems all I did to liberate him from parental dependence is for naught. I appeal by email for a quarantine exception to attend satsang, but I am denied. Within a few weeks, though, off-site residents can now participate in satsang again.

Mirabai and I have *the talk;* she can use the Saturn to find a job. If she makes payments, she can have it for cheaper than what I would sell it for. She loves the car, and it was always part of the plan. I don't need it anymore.

She and her father on the ashram property have mended fences and are reunited, and he helps her, too: a little money for basics like a phone and personal needs. I see a glimmer in his eye I'd not detected before. It's a light only another father could recognize: his daughter is safe and nearby. He had lost his wife years earlier, and his prodigal daughter has returned after he had accepted she was dead from OD long ago. I feel honored to have brought peace to his pain.

This... brings me joy. To have the privilege of helping good people. Her father was instrumental in establishing the ashram in 1990 and sustaining it all these years. It is a blessing I cannot express. m's servants is a top opportunity!

It has been my privilege to have counseled many devotees over the years. Mirabai is my swan song; no situation has been more challenging, successful, or rewarding. To finish my addiction counseling career with a devotee-daughter is too much.

***

Within the first nine months of arriving, things finally feel normal.

Mirabai is employed and has reunited with the man she had separated from three years before. She's on her way; she takes the Saturn, makes her payments, and comes over occasionally to barber my hair. A twenty-minute haircut takes three hours because we talk nonstop about things that don't even matter much.

Brandon is on unemployment and supplements his income with the COVID stimulus. He moved well south of where we lived into an apartment near another beach with two friends. He's in no hurry to find a job.

"Yeah... I know; as your father, I'm supposed to bitch about unemployment and stimulus money and encourage you to get a job, but take your time. The world is shit; you're gonna work your life away once it starts again. You have been a student, ball player, and employee all your life, so take a few minutes before it gets going again."

"That's how I'm thinking, yeah. I'll look hard for a job soon, and I won't pass up an opportunity that comes my way. But the world's in chaos right now, and I'm chilling a little."

The pendulum swings back to life being stable, and it's all good: I'm safe, Brandon's safe. I'm living spiritually and experiencing higher spiritual awareness than I have in years. I'm walking fine, running some, and doing a lot of hard-labor volunteer work on the ashram property. I enjoy this physical work very much because it makes me feel useful and close to God. Several days a week, I spend hours working in the beautiful forests. The labor is often solo, so I meditate on God and Guru the entire time.

My speech and articulation are improving, and I'm becoming less dizzy every day. All the hard work and imperceptible progress I've made are becoming evident. *I'm actually getting well.*

I'm back on dating websites accepting applications, but only for casual hookups because I'm married: to ashram-sadhana. I am not looking for love or a girlfriend for a while, maybe never. I don't want anything to distract me from my sadhana. Unfortunately, my need for sexual release and contact is enough of a distraction, so the dating-hookup sites are the best of evils: no strings, no commitments, and no need to lie, mislead, or play games. But my human mind and heart long for romance and connection. I'm doing my best to detach from thoughts of a serious relationship.

One young woman lives two hours away, and we agree on a business arrangement: she will be my sexual lover in exchange for my teaching her about spirit and mysticism. She also asks me to tutor her to get better grades on her college exams. She's hot, sexy, half my age, doting, and appreciative. We have a winner!

Despite her refusal to accept any financial support, I sneak cash into the to-go bag I prepare for her when she leaves: leftovers from the dinner I made, snacks for the trip home, and a few bucks for gas. I won't allow visits to cost this college kid money she doesn't have.

During one of her weekend visits, we tour the ashram. She is enamored by the spiritual property, and what I teach her about the path and the female personification of Divine Love, Radha Rani.

After her spiritual training, we spend the evening discussing kabbalah and alchemy. I do a full Within The Portal reading for her to gain mystical insights. After several rounds of healthy fucking and orgasms, she heads out to commute home. I am very satisfied and content with my circumstances, thinking, *Shit! If I hadn't been hit in the face with a truck, I would never be able to have this sweet young woman's nudity in my bed! I'd be tormented by the unrequited love of a woman I always cared for but who never validated me. It's a good day!* I look at the positive side of things for once.

As I enjoy the lingering fragrance of her perfume and our sweaty bodies on my sheets, *the phone rings*.

Right then, just a few hours after this young lover has gone, the phone is ringing; *it's Janete*.

I let it go. *For now*.

46.

FULL CIRCLE

> Like a wave and the water, there is only a difference in name and form: God and Guru are One and the Same.
>
> —Kripalu Maharaj (Siddhant Madhuri)

> Seeking happiness in the world is like licking your elbow.
>
> —Shree Maharaji (Kripalu)

She leaves no message; no text follows. That's expected: she was never a texter nor a voicemail-leaver. And I figure it must have taken *all* she never knew she had to dial my number in the first place.

I need to take this in. Let it settle. Go about my day and set it aside.

I chill out, go to satsang, and then to bed. I don't obsess, but I'm certainly curious: what did she want? She *knows* I'll see she called. Not leaving a message is a power play, forcing *me* to call her back. Will I?

I don't know yet, but I do know my intuition, and the Akashic Portal Agents will soon reveal the answer to me. This long-awaited event becomes a complete distraction, rupturing my sadhana.

Am I to return to Janete and finish what we started? Had I abandoned her, or had she abandoned me? Or were we both caught up in a drama of fate, equally at fault for the sad and whimpering ending to a dynamic series of adventures? She was the Soulmate of Scott, but is she the Soulmate of Krishnanand? How much of Scott is here now? Is this a test for me to let go of the past, which can no longer serve my ultimate goal of Spiritual Realization? Is this another opportunity for me to resist worldly desires for higher spiritual grounds? Or is this a chance for two Soulmates to enhance each other's spiritual journeys?

I have worked *so* hard and been through *so* much to accept that loss and heal from it. The agents and engineers of my destinies have gone to a lot of trouble to end things between us: *a whole lot.* What they have engineered and interfered with relies on the mysterious Yogmaya to separate us, and I don't want to betray that.

But what a sweet and poetic ending it would be if we were to reunite after all this, renew our love, and do the ride-off-into-the-sunset thing. Our beginnings were legendary, our story unparalleled. Or was it all in my fucking head? Yes, it was undoubtedly magical, but I have since realized that the magic was *me:* I wrote the poetry, orchestrated our Italy vows, and provided the doorways to higher truths... *my* spirit was the fire. But I found my spark in her. I didn't do it alone; *she was my muse.*

I do the math and make a decision. She had called as I was basking in the glow and marinating in the sensual juices of a lover. I have to consider the timing. We all wonder if that expected call from the ex will ever come, and we script a dozen different reactions based on our mood at the time: "No! Too late! You'll never hurt me again!" Or "Yes, yes... of course I still love you! I knew you'd call someday, and I was just waiting. I'll be right there!" And the less exciting but more considerable, "I don't know... we'll have to start slow and see how it goes."

Then again, maybe it was a misdial. Ha! Not a chance, man! She had blocked me a long time ago, and this was no fucking mistake! Maybe it was just a call to give me some news: someone we knew died or...? No. We both know each other too well. I taught her early on that when it is over, it's over; you have entirely separate lives. I truly don't give a shit about her family. We spent most of our time together and didn't mingle much with others. So, I imagine what the conversation might be like and run it through my head like an audition:

Me: "I see you called, Janete. Obviously, I'm curious why you'd call after all this time."

Her: "I just wanted to know how you're doing." I know she is not an articulate conversationalist. Our roles are pre-assigned; the burden of dialogue will be on me.

"No, let's not be conventional. It never fit, and it won't now. You knew when you called it was a big deal. You gave it a *lot* of thought before you acted on it. I can only imagine the lengthy and complex process of your decision to call. So, please... tell me, what's on your mind?"

I know I will *want* to hear, *I'm sorry; please take me back.* But that is unlikely. History shows she will *damsel* this thing, forcing *me* to take the initiative. It would be a deliberate power play for her to make me *work* for her inner secrets and views and deprive me of validation.

The Akashic Agents revealed secrets to me that were not restricted to lies and agendas. With death, I now had the clarity to break many spells I had cast upon myself.

Yesterday I was having mad-crazy sex with a howler of a lover, half my age and gorgeous. She made me fully aware that there certainly was an upside to being single again! Today? I'm turbo driven to a state of confusion. Should I resist a romantic commitment I've pined over for seven long years or consider reunion with worldly love? Which is best for my Soul's Journey? What will be the end result? Is romantic involvement a spiritual blessing or a curse? Over half of all marriages end in separation or divorce. *Fifty percent—yo!* That's staggering!

Let's face it; marriage ain't natural. Take two human beings who can never be alike and are constantly changing and reinventing themselves, put them in a 1900-square-foot house, add a kryptonite amount of stress from children and survival needs, and you're under nuclear threat. The stats on married couples being happy are so polarized they're unreliable. eHarmony, the online dating website, says 64%, while others report below 17%.

Partnerships are good. Family is good. But since today's average adult will have 2.5 careers in their lifetime, you can *expect* that by the time your kids graduate high school, you're gonna need a fresh start. You just ain't the same person anymore, and neither is your spouse. We gotta move on.

I call this the *when-harry-met-sally* opportunity; Harry has the long-awaited confrontation with the ex who broke his heart during a chance meeting at a bookstore. We fantasize that when the moment comes, we'll be dressed to the nines, looking great, walking along with a perfect lover, and making our exes green with envy to give us that closure. But Harry's situation is far more common; he looks like shit and is having a bad day, and his *ex* is with a new lover and looks great! Good luck bouncing back from that!

I'm convinced this was timed to give me an edge. The call didn't come during a sexual dry spell or after seeing one of those pain-in-the-ass Facebook Memories, flashing up sweet and loving photos that have become bitter reminders of loss! *Fuck FB!* This call came during a harmless episode of carnal fun with a sexy friend with benefits. My circumstances could not get better than this!

The inner-dialogue committee meets on the decision:

"Sure, you no longer have romantic love in your life, but you've had a grand variety of lovers to play with! Let's not forget that just a month ago, you had *two* guests over *at once*. And as nervous as you were about performing, *you were a stud!* In the man-mind, satisfying two women at the same time is a landmark event! Sure, you're lonely, and many of your latest lovers have required *compensation*. But how expensive was Janete? She had *no* money, and you spent *thousands* every year assisting her and providing *everything* from morning coffees to car purchases, from date night dinners to European vacations! How's that not reparation for companionship and sex?"

"Okay... but she was there every day, not just for a few hours. She was my girlfriend: a built-in date and companion."

"Sure. What'd that get ya? How stand-by-your-man was she when you were in your darkest hours, unable to treat for dinner? You took her to fucking Nepal, man! You toured the holiest sites in India to treat her to an incredible experience of deep spirituality! Sixteen months later, she told you she might need "to see other people." Does that sound like an equitable return on your investment?"

The bottom line was that Janete had shown her true colors. She had rejected me and all the magic I'd given her for a fucking plumber.

But my life is *finally* showing signs of restoration:

- I don't feel dizzy all the time anymore
- I can walk, work, and hike again
- I know who the fuck I am day to day
- I've had dozens of lovers in the last two years, and it's been *fun!*
- I have relocated to my spiritual home!

This last one hits home! I cannot deny my Guru's involvement in my protection. I cannot undo what He has worked so hard to undo! I cannot undermine what the demolition crew has done to my worldly attachments!

I do not trust myself to speak to Janete. I may become hypnotized; she may reject me or somehow reignite the pain I worked so hard to heal from. She may not answer, may tell me she is getting married, dying of cancer... there are countless possibilities, and none of them would be simple for me. The last time I contacted her, I sent a well-crafted, from-the-heart, sincere video letter because she would not speak with or see me. I need to send another.

I made a two-minute and eighteen-second video letter, casual and unscripted. I felt good and positive enough to ride this wave in. I just had my hair cut two days earlier, my skin was clear, and I looked fit and tan.

"I see that you called. I don't know why and realize it could be a misdial, but I want to address it. It has taken a lot for me to accept our breakup. I'm in a new place with a new life, and I ask you not to contact me. There's no reason for us to stay in touch. What was once very hard for me to accept has come full circle. I am very grateful to you for ending things and to Maharaji for His involvement in helping me determine that I couldn't restore us. As good as it all was, I need to be on my own to reach my spiritual goal. I don't wish you ill, nor do I wish you the best. Your life is not a concern for me any longer. I have arrived on the shores of indifference."

I posted it privately on my YouTube channel so only she could see it. I unblocked her number and sent the link via a text message that said, "Please open." Then I reblocked her number, knowing that wouldn't prevent it from showing in the call log. I checked back a couple of days later and saw she had watched it three times. Then I deleted it.

During our early courtship, Janete felt that her bitterness regarding her husband's betrayal of her and their children would never end. "Someday," I told her, "you will arrive on the shores of indifference about it."

Eighteen months later, she announced, "I've arrived at indifference with my ex. It has so much to do with you. Let's celebrate with vegan cake!"

I am pleased and surprised at how indifferent I feel. I am not confused, disappointed, or regretful, nor am I satisfied or pleased with the closure. I am grateful I could create and send that video letter quickly and respectably. And I knew I had firmly closed the door. There was no ambiguity in my message, which means I didn't leave the door ajar to encourage re-entry nor to exit myself. I didn't *slam* the door, either; I just closed it.

I know that if Janete had *ever* pursued me or had even asked me *not to leave* in the first place, I would reunite with her. If she becomes pursuant, I will take it as a gesture of love. If she persists, I will see it as poetry. If she makes even the slightest effort to fight for me, I will rejoin and care for her again: our journey will continue. But I know this will not happen because love has no pride, and pride has no love. Her feminine vanity prevents her from being bold enough to be a pursuer.

I feel satisfied I had reasonably demonstrated true love's humility with grace as a sacrifice and a life lesson. If she indicates that her admiration for me is genuine and worth being humble for, I will romance her again.

But I know this will not occur. There is a locker room full of forensic evidence to the contrary. I have *conditions* for *unconditional* love! I don't want to partner with an omnivore, agnostic, or atheist. Nor would I like someone unwilling to be humble for romance, either. I want more, deserve more, and with all I've been given now, I will not compromise these virtues for selfishness, neither hers nor mine. Yet, I do indeed miss her; I miss 'us.' I miss love, often painfully. Is it possible to have a romance in my life that doesn't become a compromising attachment? A partner with mutual sharing and support without after-life obligations and karmic commitments? I'm hopelessly romantic, so I persist in this belief.

Our connection is still present. After so many lifetimes as lovers and friends, I can still feel when she's thinking of me, and she often floats through my thoughts, too. The memories used to be nonstop, then daily, and now are only occasional. Thoughts of her are merely passing, not pondering. When I pick up the frequency of her transmitting thoughts to me, I can brush them aside. They linger when she persists, but I can disconnect from them within a few minutes. And I do not use my will to transmit them over space and distance. Maybe I can't *stop* worldly thoughts and desires, but I don't *act* on them.

I confess that the most significant reason for postponing this book's composition was to avoid reliving and potentially reawakening this loss. There's no doubt that I have accepted and moved on after Janete's decision, but have I truly healed? Will I ever? I feel tremendous guilt over not staying true to a destiny we are maybe supposed to share.

But my decision to not want love again is twofold:

- There is no need to experience romantic love again
- I don't want to compromise my sadhana for worldly relationships

As far as my appetite for love is concerned, *I'm full*. Quit while you're ahead. I don't want another child because Brandon has fulfilled that experience. I don't see myself getting another pet when Chow Chow moves on because it's not the idea of a pet I love; it's *him*. I will never experience the magic we all seek and few to none find. What Janete and I had cannot be any better; anything less disrespects it. I don't need a new guru, either. I have one, and He is the best!

Yes, Krishnanand, you might debate, *but your Guru is eternal and never leaves you. Romantic love is temporary, so you can replace it with a fresh one.*

That's always been my defect: too much of everything is just enough! As a drug addict, I always sought the better dope and the better high. But once you inject 60 cc of Crystal X intravenously, you have to admit and acknowledge it isn't going to get any better! And if you try, you're *just going to be disappointed*. Heroin is sooooo good that all any addict ever tries to do is recreate the first time they used it. They're not even trying to get a *better* hit or high; they're just trying to match the first time, *and you can't*.

God's love of irony? As much as I am convinced my sweet student-consort who delighted me the night before Janete's missed call was propitious, our affair ended. She and I met once more, but the two-hour distance and our 30-year age gap made it hard to sustain. Her refusal to accept money was a rare salve of comfort; what she wanted from me was spiritual, not material. I never considered her anything more than an *arrangement*, but I am grateful she was the one I shared this time with. She and I provided for each other at the right time and place, and once done, we became disposable items for each other. Maybe it was Yogmaya who brought her sweet, easygoing presence to me for what would've been a vulnerable episode.

Conventional dating remains a real freak show. One companion had a breakdown in my living room on our first date, and another screamed and ran out of my house in the middle of intercourse because she was ashamed of betraying the husband I didn't know she had! Two others became temporary stalkers. Dating is like the surprise toy in a box of Cracker Jack. You don't know which shitty treat of dysfunction you'll find, but you're guaranteed to get one. Sometimes you get lucky; there's a mistake on the assembly line, and you get *two!*

On the oh-so-rare occasion I meet someone who seems mature and stable, Yogmaya sabotages it with surgical precision. I fully understand that my Akashic Agents are always on the clock, protecting me from all worldly relationship attachments. But do they know that I can't stop trying?

I think karm, akash, and I have a wonderful, codependent relationship of proper dysfunction. They enjoy the challenge of interrupting my romantic exploits, and I get off on seeing them coming up with new ways to do it! They haven't caused me any pain with their sabotage. They are irritating, yes, but painful? Not really. I don't just give them a freshly racked set of pins to knock down; I leave them a *seven-ten split* to make them work for it!

On the dating circuit, I'm a fucking winner! Author, healthy, fit, single, stable, charming, good lover, blah, blah... I am *exactly* what all their profiles claim they're seeking. And I think I'm an exciting alternative to what they usually get to pick from: fat, balding, desperate men or moderately attractive narcissists who send dick pics! The Akashic Agents gotta be on their toes and on-call to sabotage *this* guy. But they toss the bowling ball with a physics-defying curving twist and knock down that seven-ten split every time!

Will I stop and admit defeat?

Nah. Why? It's become like a harmless hobby now! It's *ahimsa* dating, so no one ever gets hurt! I never lie, and I don't mislead or misrepresent; I'm a gentleman, cordial, polite, pleasant, and gracefully take no for an answer. I'm not spiteful or demanding, so my karm's good. I'm doing no harm whatsoever! And one out of every ten or so leads to two lonely people dripping in sweaty climax a few times. It's all good!

Eventually, I hit a wall, though. Hookups are unsatisfying because they lack intimacy. But conventional dating is a minefield of dysfunction. While it's possible to get to the other side without losing a limb, it takes a lot of careful, time-consuming navigation. It uses time, thought, and focus that can be applied to a simpler life, *though a lonely one.*

I miss intimacy. Quality time. Romance. Sensual play. And I especially miss seduction. *Being* seduced is great, too, but the slow, gradual, sweet strategies of charming a lover to desire you for your mind even more than your body is intoxicating!

It gives me pleasure similar to that of writing. The art of writing and seduction both require thought, strategy, and creativity and can produce win-win results. They help pass the time in fun, healthy ways in an otherwise dense and bland material existence.

But I can only write six to seven hours per day before I am so spent that my creativity becomes flaccid. I'm left with eight to ten hours to fill with meaningless ways to pass the time until I am recharged and my testosterone is refilled; then, I can write fresh again. I use this time for exercise, chores, and of course, sadhana. But as a stupid-human, I have a limited capacity for these, too. I can only exercise for an hour or so, then another hour of cardio on a tennis court. I hate chores and would live in nonstop sadhana if I could. But that's not realistic, either. I can only do *formal* sadhana, at the temple or in my meditation room, for an hour or three a day. Then what?

We tend to occupy our leisure time with TV or movies, but if you don't think those are weak, materialistic activities, you wouldn't be reading this book! Those who are spiritually inclined look at the entertainment of the physical world merely as a way to pass the time; We check out for a while to rest up for *real*-life stuff that actually matters: mysteries and God!

All I want to do is sadhana and write. But my limitations as a stupid-human push me to find quality ways to busy myself that are not spiritually counterproductive.

As tepid as worldly entertainments are, adventures come a-knockin'. I fulfilled a lifelong promise to Brandon in 2018 when I took him to see the Dodgers play in the World Series for the first time! I flew from Washington to Los Angeles, and the trip was therapeutic for me during that dark time in my life.

Moving ahead to 2020, our favorite team makes it to the championship once again, but I'm now 1,200 miles away, and money is tight. The COVID epidemic has Los Angeles in quarantine, so they will play at a neutral ballpark. Where? It may not be the work of Yogmaya, but out of fifty states to choose from, the World Series will take place in Dallas, Texas, a three-hour drive from where I now live! Brandon and I agree this must be fate. We're lucky enough to find affordable tickets, so he flies out to meet me, and off we go. A one-run win for the Dodgers makes the day even more special!

Months later, I got a return on a ten-year-old investment. I used this found money to break up my loneliness and invite Brandon to SCUBA dive with me in Turks Caicos for a week.

While I don't misinterpret these worldly entertainments as being Grace, they do take the sting out of the dark nights of the soul.

I took a road trip to New Orleans with a wonderful woman who financed the whole thing: I could get used to the sugar momma-sugar baby lifestyle! All I had to do was drive her luxurious rental car, plan the itinerary, and make reservations. We stayed in a rented apartment overlooking the city, had fine food delivered, toured the COVID-empty streets, and had Big Easy orgasms galore. She even bought me *two* T-shirts: one from the voodoo museum we toured and the other from the *Museum of Death!* Now I have three: the torn one I died in, the one Hollywood replaced, and one from the only other Museum of Death in the world!

Despite these glorious interruptions, my sadhana and writing remain dedicated. I have begun writing a fantastic novel based on past life regressions I witnessed within The Portal. I continue to have full regression experiences of *dozens* of lifetimes and identities. When I meditate, I can easily access the Akashic file records of many lifetimes at will for myself and others.

I can sit with another person and easily access their past life records and discuss it with them. I could, but *I don't* because it's an abuse of the ability and an invasion of privacy to access someone's past identities and Soul's journey without permission. But if they give me permission and request insights that may help them make spiritual progress, Akashic Agents give me the green light to look and share what I see.

But I premier my own Soul's lifetimes regularly now. I often wake in the middle of dream visions of past lives and see them within my consciousness during meditations. It can be annoying when I'm trying to study or meditate, and Akashic transmissions interrupt me to review past lives or receive insights and directives for *"what's next."*

My connection to The Portal is as vibrant and reliable as ever. I sometimes receive two or three transmissions a week, followed by radio silence. When they come, they are strong, with the hallmark persistence that has become their brand. I will put the cart before the horse and share these final two of this epic memoir account. The last one is less significant to spiritual travels, and I want to put it out here before closing with the final act and bigger-picture stuff.

In June of 2022, I had a complete draft of this book ready for editing. It had undergone several rewrites and self-edits and was ready for the final, professional editing stage. I got a small bottle of twelve-year-old scotch, had a nice fire crackling outside, and enjoyed the milestone of achievement. I began this book intending to write a 250-page account of a medical miracle and some minor sharing of my NDE; when I finished this epic volume, no publisher would ever consider it because it's the size of two Harry Potter books combined. To celebrate its completion, I took a brief trip to LA to see my 85-year-old father and my two siblings for a long-overdue reunion; the four of us had not been in the same room together for over ten years.

The visit was sweet but uneventful, so I drove the half hour to my prior beach house. I walked the lonely beach path nearby and hiked up the Scenic Trail I used to meditate on; as I looked out over the Pacific Ocean, I honored some dark nostalgia. I stayed at my sister's house for several days, and with too much time on my hands, it crossed my mind to contact Janete.

I put a pin in it, assuming it was a natural urge since I was just thirty-five minutes away from my old 'hood. The odd thing was the *quality*. This impulse to text her didn't feel powerful, risky, or even meaningful like it usually did; it felt harmless. That is why I didn't trust it! I chose not to act on it and marveled at this unprecedented feeling that connecting with Janete would be trivial when it clearly wouldn't be. I flew home, back to ashram life, yet the feeling—subtle, not nagging, and also unusual—still hovered over me.

To make a long story short (Ha-ha! Yeah, right!), I recorded a ten-minute, light, easygoing video letter to her and then texted her. "Hi, Janete. Surprise! It's Scott; it's Krishnanand."

She replied the next day. "Hi; hope you and Brandon are doing well…" and a few other basic niceties.

"I was going to send you a video letter. Would that be alright?'

"Sure. Is everything okay?"

"Totally fine, yes. Just sharing."

"I'm really sorry for the pain I caused you, Scott. You are a wonderful man and I'm grateful for all you did for me."

I sent the video letter and chatted about a few everyday, innocuous things. I told her of my recent trip to Santa Cruz, where she and I had spent so much time. "Yeah, the property we had is still there, and the town of Boulder Creek hasn't changed at all. It's a bit spooky being there with so many great memories and how sad things ended between us." I shared some photos of Brandon, now a full-time firefighter, driving me for coffee in the fire engine he worked with. I sent a quick hello from Chow Chow Bang as he purred in my lap on camera. We exchanged a few other texts, and that was it.

Soon the clarity of her texts converged with my Akashic-enhanced intuition: Part of our deconstruction by Yogmaya had been to spare me.

The Akashic agents had mentioned, "She has her own karmas to live out that has nothing to do with you." She texted that she had had some form of breakdown. I did not know the details and did not ask. But it had occurred to me several times over the years that maybe I was being spared a partner who would become unstable. There sure was a lot of evidence of this along the way, and it seems to have come about. Yes, I feel bad for her, and yes, I would've stayed by her side in crisis if we had remained together. But I cannot lie and say I am not grateful to be spared. I dodged a bullet if you will. I am not obligated to spend my life intimately connected with an unstable person.

I connect with Akashic Agents in meditation. "She was having a breakdown the entire time our relationship was ending, wasn't she?"

"As told before, Krishnanand, she has her own karma to live that has little to do with you. Her mental state was always delicate; your death and that of her father eight months later, then breaking up with you was more than her mind could handle. She's in a fragile condition, and there's nothing more you can do."

Akashic Agents saw the writing on the wall, chose the lesser of evils, and rescued me from a bad marriage. I've honestly had it up to my ajna chakra with confused, dysfunctional people. I've retired and have clocked out from counseling, permanently. I do assist a few with counseling, but it is now a hybrid with spiritual mentoring: I help train people for spiritual fitness, and some behavioral stuff gets addressed along the way, but I'm no longer available as a clinical case worker or behavioral savior. I would never have abandoned Janete, but her impairment would absolutely, definitely, surely, certainly, without a doubt, compromise my sadhana enough to prevent God Realization in this lifetime. I've been given a second life by dying and several opportunities to live a life of sadhana, and I'm taking it!

Her texts went silent, and I texted a final message a week later. "I'd rather not stay in touch. We've absolutely nothing between us but memories." And I am truly indifferent now. I cannot locate or even recall where the pain and injustices I once felt are. The framed portrait of our Italy vows no longer haunts me. Rather than avoid thinking about what I should do with the masterpiece, I've decided to remove it from its custom-made mahogany frame with its nonglare plexiglass and send it to her or throw it away. It is a disposable item, after all. I am excited to use the exquisite frame to house my one and only favorite photo of my loving Kripalu. It is the same image of Him I have had on my home altar since 2005. Waste not, *want not*.

The second Akashic transmission came much earlier and was the incentive to write this book. This intuitive Akashic directive wasn't *what's next*. It has become *what's now*.

_____47.

PROPHECY: LIFE AFTER

The past is bygone, the future uncertain. Make the most of this present moment
for Spiritual Realization.

—Swami Prakashanand Saraswati

Without love in a dream it will never come true.

—Grateful Dead (Help On The Way)

Live a life to die for.

—Krishnanand

I stand upon the Giza Plateau, taking the vision of the three great pyramids, Khufu,
Khafre, and Menkaure, through my eyes and into my mind.

I did not expect to be here, drinking in 4,500 years of ancient history, my palm full
of sand, drizzling back upon the earth as it sifts through my fingers.

I have spent an hour in this majestic place. First, I sat in silent meditation, undisturbed by tourists, upon a granite stone at the base of the 481-foot-tall icon of Khufu, now called Cheops. Then I circled the three grand pyramids and walked along the smaller pyramids built for the pharaoh's queens. Following that, I realized a dream I never imagined I'd achieve: gazing upon the 15-ton, ten-foot-tall granite tablet, the Dream Stele, lying between the paws of the Great Sphinx. Thutmose IV placed it there. The text carved into it recounts the orders he received in a vision to unbury the Sphinx to fulfill his prophecy of becoming Pharaoh of the Two Lands.

As a dozen or so tourists stalk the front lines of the pyramids, I find my way to the quiet, road-less-traveled backsides; I have them to myself in tranquil surroundings. They are *so* grand! Today, the Giza pyramids wear the **tawny tones** of the surrounding Libyan Desert. I imagine, *and I remember*, how they once shone brilliantly, clad all in white limestone that reflected the power of the sun from their flawless and smooth surfaces.

I meditate, channel... *and connect...* to my life here 3,400 years ago. My ancient grandfather served that same prophesied pharaoh as his royal cupbearer, heiring me the same role to serve Thutmose's grandson, who would one day become the religious revolutionary, Akhenaten.

I feel the bygone time of legendary dramas that brought an end to Egypt's Eighteenth Dynasty. The gentleness of the pharaoh lord whom I served and his warrior queen, Nefertiti, who brought monotheism to the consciousness of the known world before religious powers destroyed them. I miss them and the artwork showing their adoration for each other, the people they served, and one loving God. These tender rebels are not entombed within the Valley of the Kings. They are not remembered here on the Giza Plateau except by me: a wandering pilgrim questing for truth, standing upon a dune, my spectral presence taking in the view of antiquity. *I remember them.*

Akhenaten and Nefertiti: the only royals that ever had art made of them holding hands, hugging their children and *kissing!*

There is an additional, vital "hidden in plain view" secret in this image. To be revealed in *next book!*

I remember serving them daily and witnessing their selfless desire to share a higher truth of a one-god religion, offering a simpler, purer way to connect to a single source. History was deliberately altered to make it seem like they had forced others into their religion. But now I remember *then*, when my masters, Akhenaten and Nefertiti, created a *promised land* for spiritual aspirants who were through with primitive, multi-god religions driven by money-mad priests.

This final stop upon the Giza Plateau was merely an afterthought. I'd not planned to follow the beaten path of tourists. My itinerary only included sites important to my personal journey and research. I have no past-life recall of being directly involved with the pyramids. I've come to walk the lost city, Akhetaten, partially undug. Its true history is misunderstood and has been altered to erase it from history and add it to fictional biblical narratives.

In seven days, I have traveled nearly a thousand miles. I've sipped Egyptian coffee at roadside huts, drunk Sakhara lager alongside the Red Sea, and snacked from many mini-marts to keep moving forward rather than lose time in fine dining.

I will fly home in the morning. My stalwart driver, who has been my side-by-side companion and destination engineer, suggests I take in the graveyards in Old Cairo's Coptic churches and end with the Great Pyramids upon the Plateau. These sites are en route back to New Cairo, where I will spend my final night before the flight.

I honestly expected to be only mildly impressed. I'd seen pictures my whole life, and I typically avoid the pop-destinations. But as I stand upon a high dune overlooking all three pyramids and the Sphinx, I am overwhelmed once again. The tears of gratitude run deep. I am thankful for the magic and mysteries, and I honor the sequence of events that have shaped this lifetime.

I was supposed to be dead. Bedridden. A vegetable. Crippled, dependent, immobile... and here I am, in the Two Lands, with water still in my ear from SCUBA diving in the Red Sea a day ago, my phone full of photos of the Lost City of Akhetaten—the true source of Western religions.

Akhetaten and the sites of the actual exodus had been my only beeline stops. It is why I came. My dear devotee-friend-sister had funded another journey to India, but the COVID pandemic lockdown in India changed my plans at the last minute. The ticket was not refundable, so I diverted my course to Egypt to research the book I had been writing.

It has been a surreal, bizarre adventure. My driver, whom I'd spontaneously hired the morning after I arrived in Cairo, leaked that I was an American author. Local police were so impressed they provided an armed escort to usher me from region to region. I'm a nobody, but in Western Asia, they assume I'm a somebody. My crafty driver intentionally exaggerates my status to gain access to closed areas of the 3,400-year-old dig site.

The site's minister of tourism accompanied me to the capital of the ancient city. This government officer of antiquities was impressed and supportive of my project to restore the true story of the misunderstood, misaligned Pharaoh Akhenaten. I could see his passion for the project in his eyes. We bonded like brothers as we sat in the brilliant sunlight, hand in hand in prayer and meditation, between the pillars where the Great Temple to the Aten once stood.

I was no longer disappointed about my India trip's detour to the Two Lands. *I was meant to be here.*

I had always dreamed of writing about Akhenaten and Nefertiti and the religious revolution they inspired. My work on the story involved deep meditations to channel the archives of time and weeks of study to augment the years of collected knowledge of their factual history. My connection within The Portal revealed profound details with visions of those ancient times. The details were consistent with the unknown occult origins of Western spirituality—*hidden in plain view*. These images inspired me to sail far along the Underground Stream to the Two Lands and verify what I saw in meditative visions. The story went from a hybrid of fiction and nonfiction to radical insights into true history, now verified and soon to be revealed for the first time.

My presence upon the Giza Plateau and my sojourns into the Amarna region have invoked intense past life regression. I am not merely witnessing the history surrounding me but reliving it. I remember the beauty of my pharaoh and queen, Akhenaten and Nefertiti, during my life as their cupbearer and scribe. I warmly recall their love for one another, the people they served, and their devotion to a single God of light. And my clear memory of their persecution and forced exodus from their promised land makes me shudder. They once appointed me to document their saga so a future civilization would someday learn the truth and wake up to purer spirit. I will make good on that duty. I will tell their story as they always intended it to be; I'll put light on true history and bring it to the surface of the Underground Stream.

On my last night in New Cairo, I relax with a dish of molokhiya and rice. I gaze down from the hotel's dining lounge to the street below, sipping Egyptian lager and reflecting on the entire journey. How did I get here?

***

My dear, generous friend funded another India trip because I was working on several ashram projects and needed counsel and guidance from our Guru's daughters. They now manage the mission's charitable trust, which has constructed three state-of-the-art hospitals in the poorest regions of India. These hospitals provide their services free of charge and save innumerable lives. This same trust offers full education to thousands of poor girls with no opportunities. It also gifts food, money, clothes, medicine, and countless other resources to the poorest of Indians. It never misses a chance to donate when hurricanes ravage Jamaica and earthquake demolition causes homelessness in South America.

My own seva service project is nothing so grand. I am involved with property grounds work at the ashram, preservation and restoration of the temple, and bringing awareness of the path of bhakti yog to more Americans. I agreed to travel to India to seek support from the sisters who had advised me to become an *ashwavasi*—a resident at the US ashram.

***

My sadhana purging has settled down. Now that my years of exile, purgatory, and exodus experiences have been brought to the front of my consciousness and purged, my satsang time is less fiery. I often connect to ecstatic levels during satsang, but they are more of the devotional brand. I miss the intense closeness during cathartic purges, yet I am relieved to be free of the trials that have been purged. My Guru has dismantled many structures of sorrow that remained standing within my inner temple, allowing me to focus on creative work and the many seva service projects at the ashram property.

In the time I have been a resident at the US ashram, I have realized that I am a minority at satsang. Day-to-day, there are ten to twenty satsangees, mostly residents and of Indian origin. White faces are two out of five. But during festivals and sadhana intensives, the prayer hall fills to over a hundred visitors, and the videshi white faces become just three of *a hundred*. I am disappointed we don't do more to reach out to Western spiritual seekers here in the homeland of our divine ashram.

Daily satsang   *Sadhana Intensive*

From time to time, all of Kripalu's devotees wonder where their lives would be if they'd never found Him and the bhakti path taught by the Rasik saints. *We'd be lost*! The Western devotees often have a unique depth of devotion and gratitude for our Guru and our path. While most Indians are grateful to have been born into a family that gave them natural access to the path, Westerners feel a special grace was granted to them to have found the path within the forest of Christian culture. Western devotees are not likely to take the path for granted. We feel we were rescued from organized religious dogmas of the West and given the rare opportunity to become bhakti yogis. Our temple ashram's founder, our Shree Swamiji, brought Kripalu's teachings and the bhakti path from New Zealand to California and New York to give Westerners seeking true, Spiritual Realization the opportunity to do so. Many who had been bhakti yogis in past lives were in the West now, and Swamiji was on a mission to make it available to them.

I passionately express my feelings about the US mission's primary focus on Indians in America. "There are Americans who are fed up with organized religion's hypocrisies. They are lost, as we once were, and almost no effort is being made to offer them this path and a True Guru since our Swamiji has left. So many Americans are yearning for more than local yog studios. Westerners are being neglected, and it is *wrong*. This US ashram was established to provide the bhakti path to everyone. It is not just for Indians who are already familiar with the guru concept."

Our temple pracharek-preacher and my friend of over a decade agrees. "Touring and lecturing to Indian families and communities is easier. You're right; we are guilty of reaching for the low-hanging fruit."

"But you're Canadian. You know more than most that Westerners need more attention, and the US preachers and ashrams need to reach out to them. As a white man wearing the orange robe of a sanyasi yogi, you can connect more easily with Westerners. They look at you and think, *'If he can do it, I can do it.'* Everyone deserves a chance, Nikhilanand." A white woman in orange introduced me to the path well before my D-Day. Over the years, I facilitated and arranged many preacher discourses and meditations at local LA yoga studios, recreation centers, and my own office. After D-Day, I was incapable of that seva work. The only other LA devotee doing it retired and became a full-time ashram resident. The propagation of the path to Westerners had virtually stopped in the US. My meditations within The Portal moved me to empathy as I felt a collective conscience's spiritual pain and longing in the US for Eastern, open, yog paths. I hoped to motivate other pracherek-preachers in the US, like Nikhilanand, to do more Western outreach. "Many of Maharaji's past-life devotees are being neglected, and they need the option of finding this path."

One of the virtues of *open-system, Eastern* spiritual paths is that they don't *convert* anyone. Our mission is to offer knowledge and bhakti practice without pressure and invites people to learn more and sample. Bhaiya-brother, Nikhilanand, and other US Mission administrators agreed with me but did nothing to change it. I had privately conspired with a few American devotees to seek support and endorsement from the mission's three presidents and planned the trip to India to try. When COVID put India on full quarantine, I redirected to Egypt for another seva project: the book I was writing, tentatively titled Life-After-Life; the story of Akhenaten was a feature of that work. The other message and directive I recently received from within The Portal was to postpone that book to write this memoir of my Near-Death Experience.

I'd been working on Life-After-Life for four months. It is an ambitious work: a collection of short stories, each one exploring the true history and origins of this planet's religions and spiritual paths. Each story is told as a creative narrative of a soul's many lifetimes, witnessing the genesis of spiritual thoughts and how and why they are practiced. Rather than a dry, academic textbook of facts and accounts exposing the fascinating truths of spirituality, each story is told as a tale, synthesizing fiction with nonfiction. It is a one-stop shop of Underground Stream history and knowledge, told in a creative and exciting voice.

Twenty-eight stories explore the wonderful truths from Tantric yog over 5,000 years ago to what the Templars had discovered over a thousand years ago and was suppressed to preserve a religious institution. One life in particular was personally significant to me. I had suspected and come close to remembering this past life during my mystical career, but it has continued to become ever clearer since NDE-Day.

The thought that came into focus clarified my leanings and fascination with ancient Egypt, which I'd had since I was a boy. The more I meditated and researched what my astral journeying revealed, the more I felt drawn to tour the Two Lands and walk the grounds of Akhenaten's lost city.

Visiting places where I had once been physically present over 3,400 years ago opened floodgates of memories and sanskars from ages ago. I made direct connection with my identity as a mere servant of the court. I lived during a religious revolution that would alter history to the present day yet still remain obscured in shadows. I hope to brush away these shadows, reveal and bring to light this religious rebellion, and explain why it was altered for an organized religious agenda. That tourism minister I meditated with passionately encouraged me to bring this site and the story to the collective consciousness of humanity, too. Many mystic spiritualists look forward to a day when the Underground Stream's account of what took place in Egyypt's Amarna 3,400 years ago and its significance in the misdirection of this world's religions is exposed.

Walking the grounds where I'd once stood evoked memories and connected me to insights I'd not had access to by meditation alone. I gained a clear view of who I'd been then, what I had witnessed, and how it felt when these tragedies occurred in Amarna. I am confident I gazed upon my own tomb as I descended into the subterranean burial chambers of the king and queen's servants. If I was who I think I was, I stared right into my own eyes upon a 3,400-year-old cartouche. This was not planned, either. My previous life in this drama of old was nothing but a reasonable suspicion. It always seemed logical that sanskars drove an innate attraction to learn about Amarna and Akhetaten, but I had never had an actual regression memory of a life there. Not until now, when I descended into a burial chamber for royal servants and came face-to-face with *myself*. The regression instantly threw me back in time as I realized so much of the story I thought I was inventing was from memories. It was an eerie moment that answered so many questions.

Over the following days and weeks, it became apparent why I had been so fascinated by this period of history. As I created this semi-fictional narrative about it, it took on a life of its own like no other story I had ever written. It was writing itself and inspired specific research that led me to conclusions no other scholar of the period has yet drawn. And they were alarmingly obvious, having been *hidden in plain view* for over three millennia. I started to realize my semi-fictional account—the sections of the story not known by historians that I thought I was making up—were not fiction; I was *remembering* them!

My head was full as I flew home. I squeezed in every drop of opportunity by using a three-hour layover in Paris to taxi to the Eiffel Tower for café beneath its iron legs. I converted the three-hour layover in New York to a 16-hour layover which afforded three walking tours covering the streets and avenues from Lower Manhattan's Greenwich Village to Midtown's Empire State and Flatiron Buildings. These mundane activities provided for long walking meditations to allow my mind to sift and sort the details of my Egyptian experience. Once home from my intercontinental travels, I rested so I would be ready to get back to work on Life-After-Life with new insights and wonderful flavors of narrative acquired by walking Egypt's ancient grounds. I was a bit surprised when Akashic Agents told me *"what's next:"*

Postpone all other work and focus exclusively on your Near-Death Experience memoir.

Mystical Modalities

In the twelfth century, a band of anonymous mystics blended three mystical modalities together: Pythagorean Numerology, Tarot, and Astrology. It became known as the Divine Triangle, named for the three modalities it used within a blueprint map of the Pythagorean Theorem's right triangle. The system synthesizes so well that each modality amplifies the accuracy and details of the others. I began using this system in my twenties.

The logo and templates for
Within the Portal insights.

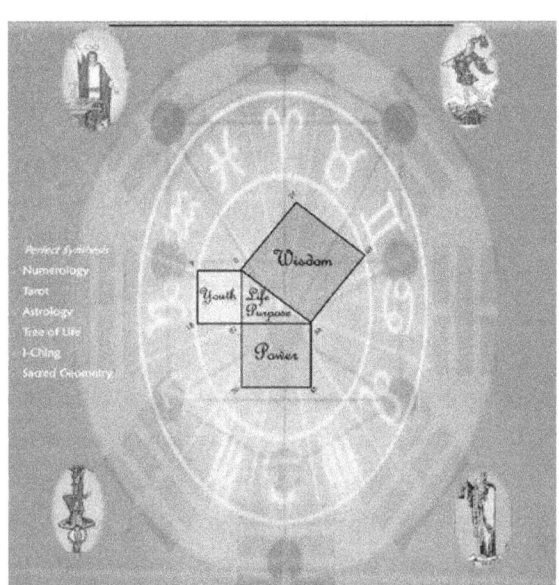

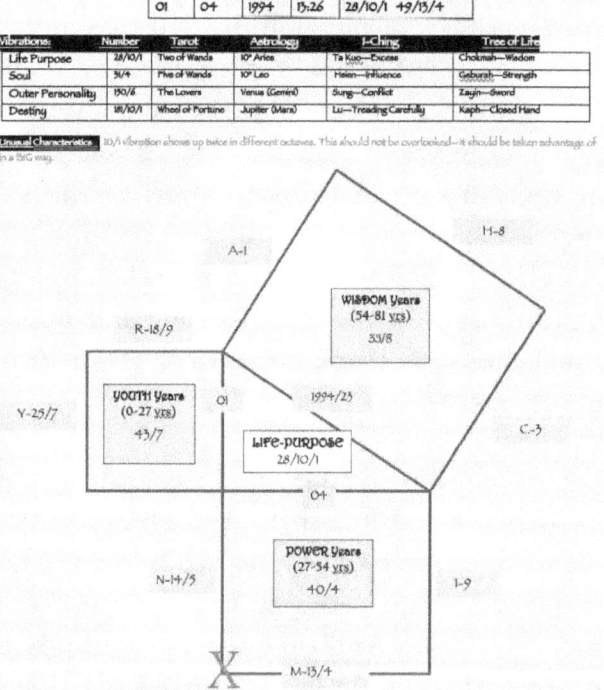

I was never interested in mere psychic predictions, i.e., *divination*. Whatever mystical tools reveal about my worldly affairs of love and fortune is only relevant to how they factor into my Soul's Journey. If you hoped this chapter's title, Prophecy, was referring to some Edgar Cayce-type predictions, you'll be disappointed. If you thought this book would celebrate some conspiracists who think Nostradamus was nothing more than a third-rate prognosticator, using so many vague predictions that he was bound to roll a seven at least a couple of times, you came a long way for nada. As I told you before, using psychic skills for entertainment or material predictions is irresponsible and a transgression. The only proper use of both mundane *and mystical* knowledge is for the Soul's Journey. The only true *dharm is spiritual dharm.*

I've already explained how I rejoined I Ching and Kabbalah's Tree of Life to the Divine Triangle system. They all enhance each other and provide levels of insight they cannot do individually. I modified the name to Mystical Triangle because I am uncomfortable using the term 'divine' for it. I also wanted to mind copyright laws for the book called Divine Triangle and have since named them Within The Portal insights. I am not *psychic,* and it may be the Indigo child in me that hates labels, but I never see mystical readings or modalities as anything magical. They are like meteorological forecasts: if you're trained in the science, you'll see what patterns are coming and how to prepare and take advantage of them. I see myself more as a *mystical meteorologist* than a medium. I'm like a mysticism *interpreter:* I speak mystical languages and translate them into spoken English.

As always, once the Akash directed me to abort the Life-After-Life project and complete the NDE memoir account, I did so without question. Even though I'd spent six to ten hours a day for the last six months composing Life-After-Life, it was to become *"what's next,"* and the NDE memoir you're reading now was to become *"what's now."*

While I didn't question their instructions, I asked Akashic Agents if it was alright to consult the Mystical modalities to see *how* I should proceed with the project. They granted my request, and I did a thorough insight into my personal process over the coming year, so I could be more aware and on the lookout for the right opportunities and timings lest I may miss them on my own. *And what a reading it was!*

Any doubts that I may have submerged under layers of *citta* were allayed! I naturally suspected that I would have many moments of serious doubt in myself and how to proceed with this project; materially anxious *sanskars* would surface from time to time, potentially paralyzing my forward progress. And indeed, it has occurred too many times to count as I produced this ambitious work. I have often thought, "Am I fucking crazy?" as this book evolved from a 200-page memoir to this mammoth guide of spiritual awakening and bizarre tale. I'm just a stupid-human, so doubts often come in the form of insecurities. "Who the fuck are *you* to teach anyone anything about spiritual awakening? What kind of egomaniac are you that you think anyone gives two shits about your dying, suffering, surviving heartbreak, relocating like a mad gypsy along the west coast, and taking up residence at an ashram?"

And then, I review the reading to know how to proceed. I pray for guidance during prayer hall meditation and quiet contemplations over morning coffee. Am I making the right call? What if I've misunderstood the message? Soon, I feel the collective of Akashic Agents, who work for my Divine Mahaparush, saying, *"Shaddup! Quit your whining and get to work! This ain't about 'you!' Do what you're told!"* They remind me that, as a stupid-human, I am not the architect or engineer of this epic. Like I was to that ancient pharaoh 3,400 years ago, I am merely the scribe, here to document the events. Mine is not to reason why but to do... *and die.* Ha-ha, mine might be in reverse order, though: mine is to *die and do* and not to reason why!

My Spiritual Insight reading revealed to me the life of this project. I know I am only the scribe, but I am honored, blessed, and oh-so grateful to have a role in something so sweet, fun, profound, and which may illuminate many things for many people.

I was barely home from touring the Two Lands of Egypt when this new Akashic directive came in. In April of 2022, cosmic intuition spoke loud and clear to me before sunrise on three consecutive mornings:

Postpone all other work and focus exclusively on your Near-Death Experience memoir.

I love how cosmic intuition is so adroit and brusque. It says much in few words, and there is never ambiguity. This message came with a vision, too: nothing as vague or symbolic as the hendecagram tattoo like before. This was much more cinematic, like a video flashback of the future.

I saw my life in a new place: buying a home, economically stable. The vision was of a not-too-distant future but far enough ahead in time that it was obscured. But it revealed that this project would provide me with the material stability needed to spend my remaining years enjoying a life of sadhana. All that is required to fulfill this destiny is the work.

Ya see... Destiny is not destined; it takes work. Many laypeople think that whatever will be will be, regardless of your interference or efforts. This is true with the *big karmic events* like birth and death, but we still have free will and need to put forth the effort to fulfill our fate. Once we set a course, we must design a plan of action to complete it. Many people miss their destiny because they neglect the work to bring it to manifestation. As earlier told, Akashic Agents often make it clear to me *what's next*, but it is up to me to figure out how, which the triangle insight does.

I don't need insight to do my *spiritual* pathwork. God and Guru have given all of us everything we need spiritually. It is up to us to put it to good use. Anxieties and insecurities often interfere with our spiritual efforts. Material safety and stability need to be established; otherwise, I am subtly, *but often not too subtly*, distracted during meditation sadhana. I'm only a stupid-human.

Using the Within The Portal mystical system, I did a reading to determine my course of action, and the reading *blew my mind*.

I did the calculations to peer into this new prophecy to gain awareness of the best way to proceed and avoid error. I broke it down into two areas:

1. My temporary year: the prophecy of insights over a 12-month period, birthday to birthday: June 28, 2022, through June 28, 2023. Keep in mind, I have two June 28 B-days now: Scott was born in 1966, and Krishnanand's birthday is June 28, 2013, where this tale began.
2. My temporary triannual: I've broken down the overall year into three separate four-month blocks for details.

With these insights, I could get a mystical view of how to proceed for the best possible outcome. I don't want to submit my book manuscript to a potential agent or publisher when Mercury is in retrograde and Saturn is in Taurus! If I can, I will prepare, plan, and wait until the cosmic elements are in my favor. I want the wind at my back, not in my face. These comprehensive readings not only tell you when and how to proceed but also when and how *not* to! They help you to expect the best and prepare for the worst. I accept this project as a hybrid of sadhana and worldly work: writing is my worldly career, but writing of spiritual concepts that may benefit others is intended as seva service. Most every minute spent in its labor is a working sadhana that fulfills my heart and spirit as I attempt to tell this story that I am not the *actual* author of—just the scribe.

The overall reading is eight pages of text, and I have posted it on the WithinThePortal.com website for your entertainment and verification of its truthfulness and accuracy. In summary, it has assured me of two things:

1. I will get assistance for its manifestation. This came in the first four-month period, June 28 to October 28, 2022.

I took this to mean an agent, manager or publisher, and editors. Sure enough, within a few weeks of receiving this insight, a young man I had never met entered into my life, and I into his, in unmistakable Portal-style, and we have been collaborators ever since. This project now has an agent/manager. Several other incidences within this four-month block have come to fruition as well. The second four-month block, October 28, 2022, to February 28, 2023, remained consistently encouraging.

2. I will produce some work and efforts that have the potential to illuminate truth and light to many, *so long as I am mindful of maintaining sincere integrity.*

The book was completed after months of nonstop work and combining the several chapters I'd written over the years. I was not stable or strong enough to finish it; during those years, I was just trying to endure it all but not document it. This time block also has several other forecasts that have all been manifesting as told. Remember, it ain't magic; these prophecies are coming true because I adhere to the Akashic Agents' advice on how to proceed. The agent/manager is a spiritualist, too, whom I did not seek out. He was a stranger who approached me at the ashram one day, asking me for spiritual counsel and a reading. During our conversation, I briefly summarized what I was working on, and he asked to be involved. His role is to help it reach many seekers and to discipline its integrity. Finally, as I polish this final chapter, it goes back and forth with professional editors to polish and complete it to what you're experiencing.

3. You will begin to realize significant rewards. It is important to keep in mind these rewards are manifestations of the hard work you have done over long periods of time.

Yep, pretty obvious this refers to an entire lifetime of mystical study and work and an episode of near-death and akashic connections; it's been almost ten years since it began. My *TBI* is done; it has stabilized. Yeah, it has left me with a few coordination and balance issues, but it's over. The *NDE* has been an ongoing event since it began and will never stop. It started as a spooky version of itself with my mind and *citta* being in two dimensions at once, causing a great deal of confusion; it has now transformed and has settled down to a glorious awareness of spirit and mind I never fully had before. I'm confident the inference about results from years of hard effort also refers to the storehouse of experience as an award-winning author and self-publisher over this great length of time.

And the last four-month block? Well… it prophesies, and I quote the mystical texts here, "as ye sow, so shall ye reap." Without the slightest ambiguity, it continues, "If you've been planning a business venture, this is the time to build the foundations and a phase that will put your finances in the black." This corresponds with the tarot's Key 8—Strength, suggesting I use the kundalini force to manifest spiritual concepts to the realm of matter. This phase of time syncs with astrology's Saturn and Leo frequencies of raising truth and knowledge up to visible light. The I Ching and Kabbalah correspondences are encouraging, too, but with not-so-subtle reminders—more like straight-up *warnings*—that staying true with integrity is required for success. The Kabbalah part comes in strong with an added reference to kundalini, which is useful and comforting as well. For you mystical gangsters, I'll just say that the Kabbalah correspondence is the Hebrew letter *Teth,* which means *serpent.* It links the Tree of Life's two outer pillars, *Severity and Mercy,* by crossing the center pillar of balance, *Mildness.* But I cannot report on the accuracy of this portion because it hasn't happened yet! As I write and complete this book and it is being polished in final editing, I am two months out from the start of the last phase of this prophecy.

The overall and full projection is thus:

- This book will be a material success and provide me with the needed resources to restore material security in my life. Being on borrowed time economically since NDE-Day, this is super comforting!
- This book will provide authentic knowledge and insights to many spiritual seekers, nudging many along in a better, more authentic direction.
- Much of my anxiety about survival issues will be removed, improving sadhana.
- The work itself is sadhana, as it requires spiritual focus and intent.
- I will relocate and establish a center for sadhana for myself and others.
- I must remain steadfast, sincere, and dedicated to truth for these karmas to be realized.

As mentioned, I don't need insight into my spiritual pathwork. God and Guru provide everything I need to complete my Soul's Journey. My anxieties and insecurities interfere with my spiritual effort; material safety and stability need to be established. This comprehensive insight into the destiny of this project and my personal process is certainly encouraging, and it gives me peace and surety in my many moments of doubt. While some justifiably see me as a big-headed know-it-all, the truth is that I am as wracked with fear of failure and insecurity as any other stupid-human. This Within The Portal reading shows me there may be light at the end of this dark, going-on-nine-year-long tunnel.

Will it come true?

Is the mystical meteorological data correct?

The complete Within The Portal insight and regular video journals to document this book's progress have been created and uploaded to a YouTube channel. They are time and date-stamped to avoid any suspicion they are made *after* things occur. We will see whether all this has been a legit cosmic set of circumstances or just a collection of TBI delusions.

Let's find out together. This book is complete; you're in the final chapter. I've documented my Soul's Journey through this nine-year TBI-NDE event. I've shared with you how it began; we are now in the present. The ending of this account is contained in the prophecy provided. And *you're* a part of it.

Without you, it won't be fulfilled. The prophecy of this project is that it will be materially successful, which relies on your purchase of it and the peripherals involved, such as classes, workshops, and perhaps readings for those seeking spiritual fitness training. The prophecy says it will assist those in spiritual awakening, which will result from you reading, enjoying, and gaining higher spiritual ground.

Whether you read this memoir and guide a day after it was published or years later, the time and date-stamped reading and the video journals of this project's progress were posted online to provide ongoing evidence of what I have documented here. You've come on this journey with me, and I invite you to its destination. Visit the virtual-akashic dimension—*the website*—and see how the prophecy is progressing. I will update the website regularly to document this journey in real time. One of two things will happen:

1. The projections and insights will not manifest or will be so vague they'll fall into a 1-800-psychic-reading-crap category. That will indicate I was, and am, TBI-DAI delusional, and all I've endured and shared with you is just a silly story.
2. It will come to be, and we will have well-documented accounts that spirit and life beyond death are not fantasy but undeniable and verifiable.

Was this author's work published, and was he paid enough to relocate and establish a sadhana center where he and others can practice spiritual training? Are many people benefitting from this book and other elements of the work involved?

If I can manifest the destiny of a spiritual center, I invite you to come and visit. If realized, there will be regular classes, workshops, and sadhana meditation sessions providing learning and training to develop and evolve spiritually on a variety of paths. These workshops and classes will explore the differences as well as the similarities they all share:

- Alchemy: the seven stages of practical and spiritual alchemy and how it is a Hermetic presentation of spiritual yog

- Numerology, astrology, tarot, I Ching, and other mystical systems will be taught, and their connections will be revealed
- Yog: all eight branches will be taught and instructed with particular emphasis on the bhakti path
- Saints, mystics, and martyrs: exploring the lives and teachings of history's spiritual teachers and sages
- We will present lectures and discussions, guided meditations, or watch a film and enjoy the art of spiritual connections within humanity and nature. We will celebrate and explore a variety of mystical, spiritual processes and systems. There are many spiritual centers worldwide, but few attempt to take you *beyond* the health, psychic, and peace realm of maya and heaven/celestial illumination. I hope to continue offering access—a portal if you will—to transcend these higher elevations to pursue the Divine realm, which is their source.

By including this prophecy, I do *not* intend to give evidence of psychic fortunetelling. I mean to show that, like predicting solar eclipses or the weather, it is a feature of the material phenomena—*maya!* It is a tool that can occasionally be useful to make progress in your Soul's Journey to Divinity.

I'm going to work so very hard to fulfill this prophecy. As I once said from a hospital bed, "I do not know if it is humanly possible ever to walk again. But if I can take *one* step, I can take two. I do not know how far I can go, *but I will find out.*"

I've stood upright since then and learned to walk, and I am trying to walk—nay, *run!*—as strong as I can to the finish line of my Soul's Journey. The path I walk upon is the bhakti path. Why? To attain bhakti. What will I do if and when I attain bhakti? I will do *bhakti.* You *do* bhakti to *become* bhakti...

No, this story... this book... is *not* over. It may end in the present with the *prophecy* of its future, but the final draft is not merely some cliffhanger without a conclusion.

This is the present time: April, 2023. I am caught up and have been telling you a story of past events; their details are complete because they are hindsight. I have to wrap this book up: complete the editing, create the cover design, and establish distribution around the world. It has life, and now it needs to walk. How do I tell you the ending *if it hasn't happened yet?*

We live in an eternal present.

We can time travel by reflecting upon the past; we can learn from it, and it can help define who and what we are in the world. We can contemplate and prepare for a future, yet it will always remain uncertain.

We sleep each night to break up the monotony of life's trials; we rest, heal, and prepare for a new day. We're born, we die, and we're born again, each death giving us a fresh start on a new life.

But reincarnation becomes like Groundhog Day at the DMV. Some days I feel like I'm at the back of the line, just waiting my turn. On other days I feel like I'm '*next*,' which is encouraging. Then there are times when I feel like I trudged through a long wait in line only to find out I forgot some silly paper, and I have to come back the next day and start over. One day, when they call me to the agent's window, I'll have all I need, and the Agent at The Portal will authorize me to move on, out, and UP. I'll get out of the line of reincarnation and complete my Soul's Journey.

Having multiple past-life recall is exhausting. It's an ongoing stream of existences that vary in context and texture but are still of the same fabric; you realize there are no new patterns to weave, no new costumes to try on.

I've not stopped preferring death over life. But before you roll your eyes at what you think will be another suicide-whining episode, my death wish is *not* standard. I'm *not* depressed or feeling hopeless or angry. There was always joy beneath it all because I was ever tethered to God and Guru.

My first cognizant thought as I emerged from the birth canal with my umbilical cord choking me was, *Put me back! Let me choke, motherfucker!* I looked at the world with its stupid bright lights and thought, *Is this it? Is this all you got?* It struck me as a dull and lusterless place, and I had no desire to be here.

My death wish is *existential;* I don't want to be *here*. I want permanent bliss—*anand*. Reincarnation is merely proof I didn't complete my Soul's Journey. I want to leave this material world and join God and Guru within the Divine abode, not within The Portal

I am no longer just *aware* of having so many past lives, I remember their identities, struggles, and missed opportunities—*countless times*—, and there is nothing new to get. I've literally and factually *been there, done that* with *everything*. And so have you. Reincarnation is relentless. It never fucking stops and the very best parts of the world aren't that great.

Love? You bet. Sign me up. I fucking perfected love. I will go toe-to-toe with any romantic notion and fantasy you have and *prove* to you I had it and gave it. And the result? Heartache proportionate to the passion. Even when they end great, they still end. Romantic love is no substitute for spiritual love.

Money? Please, let's not waste our time on this root of all evil. It can't buy you love, but it is *required* to buy happiness. You live in a material world, and if you are not safe or financially comfortable, you want out right this minute! And every cent of economic comfort comes with a dollar of stress.

Family? A fairly random collection of other stupid-humans who share your DNA. It doesn't make them, or you, good people. I like my son because he's cool, not because we share a gene pool. Hell, he and I *don't* share DNA. I don't care and never did, and neither does he. My mom and dad? Brother and sister? My two foster siblings? Aunts, uncles, and extended relatives? All good. Pretty fair people overall, with far more good qualities than bad. But if we weren't biologically related, would I select them in a first-round draft pick to be my fam? Good, but we can *all* do and be better.

Nature? Hiking and backpacking vistas and diving ocean depths give me endless satisfaction. But we moved from the cave to the track home for a reason; nature is a nice place to visit, but you can't *live* there. Maybe soon, though; I hear Wal-Mart is opening *two* stores in the heart of the rainforest!

This is the nature of the world: it is a nice place to visit, but *no one* wants to *live* here. Except the spiritually naïve. Any person with even the most remote self-awareness has realized that we are not *human* beings having a *spiritual* experience. We are *spiritual* beings having a *human* experience. Once spiritually awake, we know we will *never* be happy in the world. Human, worldly happiness is temporary and limited *at its best*. This isn't "negative" thinking or pessimism—it is *spiritual awakening*. We eventually begin to crave, desire, yearn, and long to end our quest for worldly happiness and love; that is when we begin *the dark night of the soul*. Only when we experience that dark night will we begin to see the light of *spiritual happiness*—the smoldering ochre of Her radiance and go towards Divine Love.

I don't actually want to *die*. I just don't want to *live*. And there's no alternative. *Or is there?* To live in the world is to die in the world. But to transcend living in the world is not to die. Immortality isn't about reincarnation, then returning from a death experience for eternity. Immortality is about *never reincarnating again:* to live, permanently and forever, in the dimension of Divinity.

Permanent exile to Xanadu. Paradise. Heaven. Golok.

The Buddha's Fourth Noble Truth about attaining enlightenment and ending eternal reincarnation to the realm of matter is that *you can do it in this lifetime*. My Guru Kripalu taught me the same thing and has pressed me *never* to give up or slow down. He unveiled the fact that I have spent countless lives seeking material happiness, which has always ended in one of two things: *greed or disappointment*.

A desire for happiness, when fulfilled, results in wanting more, but when unfulfilled, it results in sorrow. That's it. There's no third possibility. Same with existence: there's God, the world, and the soul. There is no fourth existence, so choose wisely.

***

I have lived.

I have died.

I have resurrected.

I have loved, lost, survived, and triumphed over tragedy. *And so have you.* I've been selfish and nearsighted of my own sorrows while mindless to others'. I have served my lovers, communities, friends, and family. And so have you. I have been humble, and I have been proud. I will dedicate my life to Spiritual Realization with sadhana and service with charitable donations, counseling, writing, physical labor, and however I can.

It's time. As I approach the final decades, years, months, and days of this one of infinite lifetimes... I want to serve one final purpose: *my soul*. Have all these events conspired to bring me to the threshold of Spiritual Realization? Has every loss, tragedy, and triumph brought me near the completion of my Soul's Journey?

But I want to do something new, something I've never done. I've experienced the entire human condition within this very lifetime. Life, love, family, health, illness, wealth, poverty, loss, *death...*

What I've yet to do is just live peacefully and meditatively, make progress, and acquire material stability only to support a spiritual life. I need to avoid fear, pressure, and restless ambitions. I want to live in quiet longing for *anand: bliss.* I want to become spiritually perfected, God Realized, and I want to do it *in this very lifetime.*

If I can make this prophecy come about, I will retire *from the world.* I will work to share spiritual thoughts and opportunities and serve a spiritual mission till I can work no more. But I no longer want it to be about money, safety, or security. *I'm tired.* It's been a long day; it's been a full life.

I am weary from eternal life.

I don't want to move anymore. I want to make the next home my last and live modestly but safely. To do my sadhana and share it with others with no pressure or profit. I don't know where I am on my Soul's Journey, but I must be close. We all are. Spiritual Realization of soulful beatitude can take many, many lifetimes. But it can also happen in an instant, and when it finally does, it is eternal. Instead of many desires, I have just one: I want sadhana. All I truly need is to desire sadhana: to just do my thing. *In the beginning, you do your sadhana. In the end, sadhana is all you do.*

I don't think it is possible to have a grander and more gracious opportunity to complete my Soul's Journey than right here, right now.

In this very lifetime.

Not one Life-After.

THE END OF THE BEGINNING

Within The Portal (outside-in):

◊ **White light radiance**

◊ **12 Lotus petals for *anahata* heart chakra**

◊ **Ochre ring of protection (Guru)**

◊ **Violet radiance for higher conscience, *sahasrara* chakra**

◊ **Ochre star banishing perimeter**

◊ **Violet hendecagram as saw in vision**

◊ **Ouroboros—serpent swallowing its own tail, "infinity & eternality" image**

◊ **Radiant light from Within**

◊ **Center: "bindi", focal point**

www.WithinThePortal.com

- Prophecy updates
- Portal Blueprint readings and insights
- Spiritual fitness training and mentoring
- Current events with Krishnanand

For bhakti yog materials and instructions: www.JKP.org (Jagadguru Kripalu Parishat)

US ashram, programs and materials www.RadhamadhavDham.org